AN IRISH WORKING CLASS

Explorations in Political Economy and Hegemony, 1800–1950

ANTHROPOLOGICAL HORIZONS

Editor: Michael Lambek, University of Toronto

This series, begun in 1991, focuses on theoretically informed ethnographic works addressing issues of mind and body, knowledge and power, equality and inequality, the individual and the collective. Interdisciplinary in its perspective, the series makes a unique contribution in several other academic disciplines: women's studies, history, philosophy, psychology, political science, and sociology. See page 567 for a list of books in the series.

An Irish Working Class

Explorations in Political Economy and Hegemony, 1800–1950

Marilyn Silverman

UNIVERSITY OF TORONTO PRESS
Toronto Buffalo London

© University of Toronto Press Incorporated 2001
Toronto Buffalo London
Printed in Canada

ISBN 0-8020-3531-0

Printed on acid-free paper

National Library of Canada Cataloguing in Publication Data

Silverman, Marilyn, 1945–
    An Irish working class : explorations in political economy and
    hegemony, 1800–1950

    Includes bibliographical references and index.
    ISBN 0-8020-3531-0

    1. Working class – Ireland – Thomastown (Kilkenny) – History –
    19th century.   2. Working class – Ireland – Thomastown (Kilkenny) –
    History – 20th century.   I. Title.

    HD8400.3.Z8T42 2001   305.5'62'094189   C00-933248-0

This book has been published with the help of a grant from the Humanities
and Social Sciences Federation of Canada, using funds provided by the Social
Sciences and Humanities Research Council of Canada.

The University of Toronto Press acknowledges the financial assistance to its
publishing program of the Canada Council for the Arts and the Ontario Arts
Council.

University of Toronto Press acknowledges the financial support for its publishing activities of the Government of Canada through the Book Publishing
Industry Development Program (BPIDP).

For Philip

Contents

Maps, Tables, and Figures

Figures

Preface

My colleague, Philip H. Gulliver, and I began field and archival research in the small town and rural hinterland of Thomastown, County Kilkenny, Republic of Ireland, during our sabbaticals in 1980–1. Over the years since then, we have paid numerous visits to the locality, staying usually for a few months during the summers of every second or third year. In fact, as I was completing this manuscript during 1998–9, we were again spending a sabbatical in the town – continuing to research, think, and watch.

This book, then, is one of the results of my long-term relationship with the people who live in, or are somehow connected to, this particular locality – in both the present and the past. For although a good deal of my research over the past two decades was pursued through the typical anthropological techniques of participant observation, my central commitment so far has been to historical anthropology – to acquiring and analysing data from a wide variety of archival sources and from innumerable conversations with local people concerning the past.

In my continuing effort to learn about Thomastown and its people and, most important, to locate them both in time and in anthropological theory, I have written this volume about one segment of the population who were known locally as 'labouring people.' Since at least 1800, and almost certainly earlier, these were the men, women, and sometimes children who, without access to land or capital, were employed as unskilled or semi-skilled workers in local mills, tanneries, landed estates, farms, shops, and public works. Sometimes, in colloquial usage, they referred to themselves and were described by others as 'the working class.' Always, however, they formed the majority of the population in the town and hinterland. Then, as the nineteenth century progressed, skilled tradesmen in the locality became included as part of this category.

Of course, labourers (and artisans) were not an isolated segment of society; nor can they ever be represented as such. Instead, their very existence was premised on the presence of those who had the capital with which to hire them. Such employers, themselves resident in the locality and tied into their own dispersed networks of kin, capital, and commerce, were invariably implicated in relationships with labourers through which they both influenced and/or coerced them at various times and in particular contexts. Necessarily, then, due recognition of such people and of the hegemonic process form an integral part of this account. So, too, do the processes of state formation and colonialism which were impelled and manifested through local agency. It is out of such empirical and theoretical strands that the present narrative is created.

My starting date is roughly 1800, because that is the time when archival records begin to offer sufficient information on local labourers. Records improved in the course of the nineteenth century, and by the first decades of the twentieth century people's personal memories and assessments of past times could be set alongside and against the information from the archives. This book, then, is rooted in both field and archival work. It is an analytical and historical ethnography of labourers: their experiences, ongoing social, economic, and political lives, and the reproduction of their understandings, common sense, and ideologies. It is intended to complement my earlier book, *Merchants and Shopkeepers: A Historical Anthropology of an Irish Market Town* (1995), and the numerous essays which also focus on Thomastown and which are detailed in the bibliography.

Over all these years that the Thomastown research project has been extant, it has been supported at various times by grants from the Social Sciences and Humanities Research Council of Canada (SSHRC), the Wenner-Gren Foundation for Anthropological Research, New York, and the Faculty of Arts, York University, Toronto. In addition, small grants as well as considerable practical assistance have been given by the Kilkenny County Council and the Thomastown Development Association. Throughout, I have also been most fortunate in receiving unstinted help and support from several local historians who provided me access to records which they had collected and which in some cases were from sources that are no longer available. They, and others whose interests were kindled by this project, pursued in their own ways some of the enquiries that emanated from my own work, and so together we created what were, in effect, joint enterprises. Many elderly labourers also have given me many hours of their time to tell me their stories and to comment in detail on the information which I extracted from the records. Finally, it is essential to acknowledge, yet again, my gratitude to the many local people who, since 1980, have been willing to give me oral and written information and to discuss with me, usually at great length, both the past and the present.

The Thomastown that Gulliver and I have experienced during the past seven years or so – during the era of the so-called Celtic Tiger – has seemed very different from what we had encountered earlier. Indeed, Thomastown people often now comment on the fact that 'it's different times now' and how 'it's getting so you wouldn't recognize the place.' The changes that both we and they are seeing are sited in the built environment, education and morality, consumption, technology, travel, women's roles, the labour market, and so on. In the context of this seemingly 'modernizing' and 'Europeanizing' Ireland, a younger generation knows little about the labouring pasts of its parents and grandparents. Thus, as Gulliver and I currently research contemporary political economy, I have felt especially compelled to narrate this labouring version of Thomastown's past – so that some understanding of it will not be lost, so that the experiences of earlier generations can be known and celebrated, and so that those workers from the past, who have invariably been left out of the history books and dominant historical narratives, will not be left behind. This book is therefore dedicated to Thomastown's labouring people – past, present, and future.

Marilyn Silverman
Toronto
September 2000

PART I

Encountering Labour in Field, Archives, and Theory

1. Political Economy, Class, and Locality

'About the time when late Autumn merges into Winter, Industry's capacity for labour's absorption exhibits a restrictive tendency ... For, by now, the farmer has reaped ... the road-worker has entered upon his slack period, the fisherman mends his nets against the coming season, and on the ebb-tide of temporary depression many a craft is adventuring. Until the ... State sets the pulse of plenty throbbing afresh, I know of no more effective method for the augmentation of existing resources than the pursuit of the rabbit.'

– TUSA, alias Paddy Doolan, casual labourer and poet, Kilkenny *Journal,* 11 June 1938

In the summer of 1980, my colleague Philip Gulliver and I began long-term field and archival research in 'Thomastown' – a southeastern Irish town of about 1,300 people and a rural hinterland containing another 1,400.[1] From the moment of our earliest encounters there, we were struck by the ways in which so many people in both town and country explicitly talked about themselves or others as 'labourers.' We were impressed by records from the past, such as the one by TUSA above, which used similar language. We also were often touched by the content of stories which people told. An example was when an elderly grandson of a long-deceased retailer described the ways in which so-called shopkeepers saw themselves and kept to themselves: 'A young chap, the son of labouring people, was working as a porter for my grandmother. One day, she took a quiet moment to explain to the lad the facts of life. In Thomastown, she said, there were gentlemen like the Major, farmers like the Doyles, and shopkeepers like herself. "And those are the classes in Thomastown," she said, ending rather perfunctorily.

"But please, ma'am," said the young lad, "what class would I be then?" And from the way she looked at him you could tell that he belonged to no class at all.'

In the Thomastown area, the fact of class and, also, the numerical preponderance of so-called labouring people kept leaping out from the archives and from our interactions in the field. Indeed, we were every day reminded of the centrality and pervasiveness of class hierarchy more generally: in how people spoke, dressed, and lived; in their expectations, education, and values; and in their sentiments and stories. We began to ask why. As we did so, we came to believe that Thomastown's labouring people should be sited in historical ethnography as part of the history of capitalism and colonialism and as part of an Irish working class which was invariably implicated in an evolving state, market, and division of labour after the turn of the nineteenth century. We therefore decided that it was important to excavate the history of working peoples' awareness, experience, and consciousness in Thomastown; to find and write about their intellectuals, organizations, and collective actions; and to explore how all these formed part of the materiality of their working lives, their cultural codes, and their social world.

By the Turn of the Nineteenth Century: River, Locale, and Class

The town of Thomastown, located thirty miles inland on the navigable River Nore, was founded in around 1200, as part of the Norman conquest of Ireland, by Thomas Fitz Anthony, seneschal of Leinster. Located upriver from the the key Norman ports of Waterford and New Ross on the southern Irish coast, the settlement functioned from early on as a trading depot for the distribution of English manufactured goods inland and for the collection of locally produced, export commodities (corn, cattle and hides, fish, cloth, metals, and foodstuffs). In addition, Thomastown was at the head of navigation on the Nore and thus became the trans-shipment point for Kilkenny city, the largest inland town in medieval Ireland, located twelve miles to the north on the same River Nore.[2] From its inception, then, the town was a node in a network of inland and international trade, part of world markets and the international mercantile system.

As an extension of this role, the town also was a centre for small-scale manufacturing, artisanal activity, and, by the late eighteenth century, retailing. In 1788 the *Lucas Directory* described the town's commercial sector. Its trade was illustrated by its three boat owners, three corn mer-

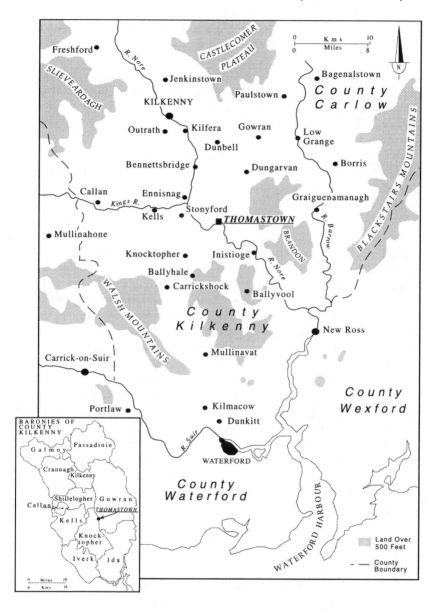

Map 1: Kilkenny Baronies and Regional Context of Thomastown

chants, two spirit merchants, and a general merchant. Its manufacturing
and artisanal activities were represented by three flour mills, a grist mill,
a tannery, three malting houses, a skinner's shop, and a soap-boiling
enterprise. Its retail function was exemplified by five drapers, three gro-
cers, two chandlers, two vintners, an apothecary, an earthenware dealer,
a liquor dealer, and an innkeeper. In 1802, according to a contemporary observer, the town had 350 houses, an increase from 300 in 1793,
and 'its trade is increasing.'[3]

This expansion in the late eighteeenth century was related to an economic boom occurring in Ireland generally. The boom was character-
ized by extensive capital formation, investment in public works (for
example, canals), the construction of new factories (especially flour
mills), town growth, an expansion of banking, and a growth in trade
financed by an expanding money supply.[4] In Thomastown, the boom
indeed saw a massive expansion of milling capacity and of alcohol production. This was associated with an increase in property speculation in
and around the town and, as part of this, with the construction and leas-
ing of 'cabbins' for an expanding labouring population. At the time,
too, outsiders brought capital into Thomastown while the expansion
itself provided investment opportunities, in housing and retailing, for
local capital. Yet an intrinsic part of this economic and entrepreneurial
expansion was the fact that the town's commercial sector was not particularly diversified. The millers and tanners were heavily in debt and the
malting houses and distilleries were to have only short lifespans. Indeed,
by the end of the second decade of the nineteenth century, it had
become clear to townspeople that industry was volatile and fragile, and
that shopkeeping and artisanal activities were the more secure and risk-
free ways for local people to build and maintain enterprises in the
medium term.[5]

What all this meant, of course, was that the locality was highly differentiated and that this had been so for a long time. In 1693 a list of the
freemen of the town included gentlemen, clergy, merchants, an innkeeper, boatmen, masons, skinners, carpenters, tailors, 'broagers,' 'cott-
ners,' weavers, cordwainers, corders, smiths, yeomen, and a labourer.[6]
By the late eighteenth century, such differentiation had been reproduced. What had accompanied it, however, was an increase in the
number and proportion of labourers. This was heralded by agrarian protests in the late 1760s in the southeastern Irish countryside as labour-
intensive tillage was abandoned in favour of pasturage in response to
increased overseas demand for beef and dairy products. As agricultural

rents increased in tandem, landlords and graziers were also induced to enclose commonages used by the increasingly hard-pressed smallholders and landless labourers. As well, both the smallholders, who grew corn and potatoes, and the labourers, who tilled potatoes on small, rented plots, were left the burden of paying tithes to the established Protestant church.[7] The number of landless, wrought by agrarian dislocations, invariably increased.

Against this background, it became 'possible to talk of the calculated paternalistic style of the gentry *as a whole.*' That is, there had evolved 'some reciprocity in the relations between rich and poor; an inhibition upon the use of force against indiscipline and disturbance; a caution (on the part of the rich) against taking measures which would alienate the poor too far, and ... a sense that there were tangible advantages to be gained by soliciting the favor of the rich. There is some mutuality of relationship here which is difficult not to analyze at the level of class relationship.'[8]

Indeed, in Thomastown, since at least the early nineteenth century and certainly until the late 1980s, this mutuality was incorporated within an emic,[9] culturally defined notion of 'class.' That is, local people – and those outsiders concerned with local people – categorized themselves and others into generally accepted occupational categories: as 'landlords,' 'farmers,' 'shopkeepers,' 'tradesmen' (that is, artisans, craftsmen), and 'labourers.' The term class was commonly used to refer to these categories in newspaper and government reports, as well as in everyday speech, and, taken together, the categories formed an all-pervasive socio-cultural map. What made this map particularly potent was that it also fixed these categories into a hierarchical order, or *status-class* system, which expressed the separation of some and the unity of others: in access to the means of production, the labour process, lifestyle, social relations, and expectation. The map, with its categories and hierarchy, formed a shared and essential part of the everyday language of all people, guiding interaction in the locality and linking people into wide-ranging networks. It constituted and reflected real constraints and possibilities which structured the potential and actual experiences of people as well as their perceptions of their material condition and possibilities. In Thomastown, and elsewhere in Ireland and Britain, the status-class hierarchy underlay people's experiences, forming the bedrock of their common sense, their individual consciousness, and their personal and collective perceptions.

This status-class map, however, only partly corresponded to an objective delineation of *class* as based on access to the means of production and whether labour was exploited. The status categories of labourer and landed proprietor were the only clear ones in these respects. Farmers, in contrast, had a changing relation to the land. They were tenants until the late nineteenth and early twentieth centuries; afterwards, they became owners. They also had varied relations to labour. Some hired workers (seasonally and/or permanently); others used only family labour. Retailers, too, were tenants until the late twentieth century and only some hired labour. Artisans in their turn might be waged, domestic commodity producers or capitalists.

There were in Thomastown, therefore, 'different languages of class.'[10] The above-mentioned essay by TUSA used not only status-class categories ('farmers,' 'crafts') but also class ones ('labour'; 'industry'). This does not mean, as Stedman-Jones concluded, that 'class is a discursive rather than ontological reality.' Rather, it means that different world views operated simultaneously; and that to write the history of Thomastown's workers requires an understanding of the continuing interplay between the two systems of categorization and of the ways in which the indeterminacies and redundancies created by their juxtaposition articulated with the needs, interests, and agency of individuals and groups.[11] Indeed, other categories were also relevant for TUSA – categories that denoted subsidiary occupations ('fishermen,' 'road worker') or political-legal positionings (rabbit poacher) which were appropriate in varying contexts at particular times. Such residual categories added to local complexity, capturing and creating additional identities based on economic activity and leisure, neighbourhood and network, patron and politics, association and family, state and bureaucracy. In so doing, these identities articulated with the status-class and class systems, entwining into ever-developing, everyday 'common sense' over the *longue durée*. From the perspective of the individual, it meant a complex consciousness, a *metissage* or braiding which points to 'multiple ancestry in language and culture as well as numerous voices within one speaker.' Importantly, this 'multiplicity of inheritance appears in constantly changing combinations,' rather than in 'hyphenated antitheses,'[12] clear oppositions, or fixed combinations.

Interpreting Locality

Anthropologists are known for their 'community studies' and such studies are often taken as the key feature and aim of the discipline.[13] To many outsiders, then, anthropologists are taken to be the experts on the esoteric minutiae of small marginal places. A premise of this book is that it is possible, and necessary, to focus on the local level without doing a community study.

In this view, the general locality called Thomastown is simply an unbounded context through which empirical and theoretical issues in anthropology and history can be explored. The logic is twofold. On the one hand, since the Cromwellian invasion in 1649 and even before, it would be misleading to describe any part of the Thomastown area as a 'community' – whether socially, culturally, or economically. It has never been a singular or bounded place. On the other hand, to explore trajectories, such as the criminalization of custom, the growth of labouring consciousness, and so on, requires detailed local research. This is because such processes have a complexity that only a local-based perspective can uncover and because all agents reside in localities and the nature of their local worlds invariably impinges on the trajectory of socio-economic and cultural processes. From all these perspectives, then, it is essential that an anthropologist study not a locality *per se* but the key processes that were manifested there and that have implications for our more general and theoretical understandings. It is out of that viewpoint that this volume derives. Phrased most generally, this book is not a community study nor is it the study of a particular locality. Instead, it uses a *local-level focus* to build general interpretations of both the past and the present.[14]

Exploring the Labouring Experience

What general interpretations, however, are of concern here? Succinctly, there are three: to suggest how anthropologists can study political economy and the culture of class; to construct an analytical ethnography of a segment of the European working class; and to portray the world of Ireland's labouring people. Each of these issues has its own antecedents, is associated with a particular paradigm, and is informed by focal concepts. It is to these that I now turn.

Anthropology and the Political-Economic Sphere

Between 1940 and the late 1970s, political anthropology was a vibrant subfield within socio-cultural anthropology. It then disappeared from the research and writing agenda, having reached a theoretical dead end and been supplanted by other foci. One of these foci was the Marxist approach which privileged the economic sphere and marginalized politics through its emphases on economic differentiation, class formation, and gender relations as these were rooted in the material bases of social life and/or in the local implications of a world capitalist system. Political anthropology also was displaced by a new emphasis on culture. This led either to a Geertzian world of static meanings and symbols which were virtually unconnected to the political sphere or, alternatively, to a Foucaultian world in which power was taken as so pervasive that neither it nor the political domain needed to be explored. As a result, what Lasswell described in 1950 as 'who gets what, when and how' became either an economic problem or a cultural fait accompli, divorced from the machinations of political leaders and the agency of political groups.

Yet political anthropology had yielded some valuable insights. Out of the structural-functional paradigm after 1940 had come an understanding of political structure – the nature of formal groups through which political and jural *authority* might be actualized and of the symbolic bases underlying the *legitimacy* of political regimes and offices. By the 1960s, a transactional paradigm allowed a different slant: the patterning of individual interests, choices and strategies which underlay the formation of political groups. Typologies of such *political groups* and *quasi-groups* (for example, parties, factions, coalitions, action-sets) proliferated, as did analyses of so-called *local-level politics*, actualized by inter-group competitions, alliances, and conflict and by the agency of entrepreneurial *leaders*.

Clearly, each of these two paradigms had theoretical limitations, omissions, and errors, all of which were amply demonstrated and discussed.[15] It was the general conclusion that these approaches were irrelevant in a world of global capitalism, universal exploitation, and class conflict. All this submerged the subfield. In the process, however, ideas that might have been useful during the Marxist turn in the 1980s were lost. For example, at a seminar I attended in 1988, the issue was raised as to how we might analyse empirical situations in which class consciousness and class action were absent. A young anthropologist, immersed in the dominant Marxist paradigm of the time, announced: 'What we need is a typology of political groups'!

I suggest, therefore, that there may some use in bringing forward elements of the political-anthropological past into the (post) Marxist present. For the story of Thomastown's labourers – as fishers, road workers or artisans – requires a broad perspective. This is because class struggle and consciousness formed only a part of their past, and to look

at those aspects alone is to focus invariably on the failure of their consciousness and of their struggle and to relegate them to a footnote in
anthropology and history where the political frontline is peopled by
those who are actively resisting domination and/or engaged in overt
class conflict. Thus, to understand their story requires not only that we
move beyond the economic sphere into politics but also that we incorporate notions of local-level politics: of political strategies and groups,
leadership and legitimacy, and the meanings, sentiments, and beliefs
associated with them. From this broadened view, the history of Thomastown's labourers becomes theoretically and empirically relevant to the
cross-cultural intent of anthropology, to social history, and to Irish
historiography.

Political Anthropology in the Present: The Concept of Hegemony

A way in which this can be done is related to the recent resurgence of
the political sphere as an independent object of anthropological interest largely through the stimulus of Antonio Gramsci's writings. These
have provided a Marxist respectability to the study of the political
domain and, also, a means by which anthropological Marxists might
respond to, and take part in, the recent cultural and reflexive turn in
anthropology. Gramsci, in short, through his concept of hegemony, has
provided a way out of economism and into cultural politics and political
culture.

Gramsci believed in the relative autonomy of politics. This was not to
deny a link with the economy. It was simply that the connection involved
a 'long and complex chain of mediations' which shifted through time.
Moreover, for Gramsci, a class interpretation of history did not focus
solely on the struggle between the oppressor and the oppressed. It also
required a study of the 'process by which a given ruling class successfully
avoided such confrontation by gaining popular consent for its domination.' Class politics were therefore about *hegemony* – about 'the process
of gaining legitimate consent within civil society as against holding it
together by a monopoly on the means of violence.'[16]

From the perspective of political anthropology, such a definition was
not unfamiliar. Anthropologists had long been concerned with the legitimacy of norms, the operation of consensus, and the structure of
authority. Yet Gramsci's notion of hegemonic consent was far more
nuanced than what had appeared earlier in political anthropology.[17]
Such nuance came from the class-based conceptualizations that underpinned his thought and from numerous interrelated concepts which he

explored. For example, Gramsci believed that the particular state of play between consent and coercion at any point in time was a matter for empirical investigation because the character of the linkage, and hence of the *state*, varied. Indeed, there were 'no linear models in the cultural role of the state.' Thus, from the eighteenth to the twentiety centuries, political change was not simply 'a pattern of state encroachment on civil society or popular culture [but,] rather, ... a series of qualitative transformations in state-culture relations'[18] which had crucial implications for that usual object of anthropological analysis – the society and culture of subaltern classes.

In part, variability came about because 'the line between dominant and subordinate cultures is a permeable membrane, not an impenetrable barrier.'[19] Indeed, for Gramsci, so-called *common sense*, that is, 'the philosophy of the multitude' or 'the ideology or world view of ordinary people,' developed through historical increments accumulated from the past, and these increments included the 'ideology of the class in power.' This was the result of the so-called *material structure of ideology* – that is, of institutions such as schools, media, press, and so on, whose task it was to influence common sense. Importantly, this prevented common people from acquiring a critical capacity.[20] As a result, the 'man in the mass' had

> two theoretical consciousnesses (or one *contradictory consciousness*): one which is implicit in his activity and which ... unites him with all his fellow-workers in the practical transformation of the real world; and one, superficially explicit or verbal, which he has inherited from the past and uncritically absorbed ... This verbal conception holds together a specific social group, it influences moral conduct and the direction of will, with varying effects but often powerfully enough to produce a situation in which the contradictory state of consciousness does not permit any action, any decision or any choice, and produces a condition of moral and political passivity.[21]

Moreover, 'subordinate groups could identify with the dominant culture – often for sound reasons – even as they sought to challenge it.'[22] However, common sense could be transcended when the worker or 'peasant reconstitutes the world through *collective action*. With this ... he comes to terms with his own position in the class structure.' This understanding is *class consciousness*. It was, however, only a first step. Self-autonomy and then historical self-consciousness had to follow. This movement from common sense to full proletarian understanding was mediated by a political education which came from an 'intellectual/moral bloc of workers' and their *organic intellectuals.* For 'all society is a school' and 'every relation of hegemony is an educational relation.' Thus, the 'legitimation process occurs in multiple contexts as does the development of alternative political outlooks.' As a result, 'genuine political education depends both on the "elaboration" of intellectuals tied to the working class to provide it with "organic leadership," and on the creation of institutional settings in which workers can raise themselves to a "philosophical" (as opposed to a mere "commonsense") view of the world.'[23]

From this short summary of Gramsci's thinking, it is clear that he was concerned to link culture and ideology, and consent and challenge, to objective institutional contexts, to individual actions, activities and social relations, and, importantly, to changes through time. In fact, it has recently become an anthropological truism that hegemony is a process.[24] For Gramsci, however, hegemony was always part of broader political process which encompassed *coercion* (via political society) as well as consent (via civil society). Importantly, too, Gramsci's work was not simply a meditation on the process of gaining consent. It was also a revolutionary agenda for destroying it, largely through the successful operation of class-based political alliances or so-called *historical blocs.*

All this suggests that, when anthropologists study hegemonic processes, they must focus on politics and political dynamics, broadly defined – as material needs, economic interests, agents, groups, and alliances – as well as on meanings and beliefs. Thus, in the context of the current cultural bias within anthropology today, I am arguing that anthropologists must address more than the extent and form of consent within subaltern classes and more than disembodied cultural forms and discourses.[25] I am therefore addressing the fact that the 'concept of hegemony needs fleshing out ... How exactly does hegemony function as a set of concrete linkages between the political and cultural spheres'?[26] These are the issues that can be explored through an historical ethnography of Thomastown's labourers.

Political Anthropology in the Present: The Influence of British Social History
The influence of E.P. Thompson and Eric Hobsbawm has been far less apparent in recent political anthropology than has the work of Gramsci. However, much can be of use, especially Thompson's notion of 'class experience,' Hobsbawm's ideas on 'working class culture,' and the work of subsequent social historians in exploring their ideas.

For Thompson, a class was 'defined by its consciousness and that consciousness is an outcome of experience ... No consciousness no class.'[27] However, so-called *class experience* mediated between, on the one hand, the economic base of society and, on the other, *class consciousness*. 'Class experience is determined by productive relations' while 'class consciousness is the way these experiences are handled in cultural terms, embodied in traditions ... and institutional forms.'[28] According to Thompson, therefore, 'class eventuates as men and women live their productive relations and as they experience their determinate situations within the ensemble of social relations and with their inherited culture and expectations, and as they handle these experiences in cultural ways.'[29] In this formulation was an effort to escape from the economic determinism in much of Marxist theory and to bridge the gap between the economic base of society and its political superstructure. That bridge was the experience of class.

Thompson, however, has been criticized for failing to specify the extent to which state repression, and other exterior forces, constituted the unity of the working class during key historical moments. It has been argued, for example, that the political sphere made the working class – that experiences in production were not key but, rather, it was political conjunctures involving old and new traditions as well as state repression. Thompson, in short, has been accused of too much economic determinism.[30] It has been argued, too, that the imprecision and historical specificity of the term 'working class consciousness' were not resolved by Thompson's formulations and that he ignored the 'disunity and sectionalism,' the 'particularistic loyalties,' and the 'widely differing experiences of everyday life' which also typified working-class history.[31] Such criticisms have also been made of Hobsbawm's work on the character of *working-class culture* under capitalism, particularly in Britain after 1880. He argued strongly for the idea of a single, shared culture at least by that time: one of shared meanings, experiences, and, most important, consciousness. For Hobsbawm, the culture was based on a sense of the separateness of manual labour (associated with segregation by residence, expectation, and lifestyle), a moral code of cooperation and mutual aid, and a readiness to fight for just treatment. For Hobsbawm, too, working-class consciousness required *formal organization* because 'the organisation itself is the carrier of class ideology. Without it, working class consciousness would be little more than a complex of informal habits and practices.' Organizations, in other words, like Gramsci's institutions, mediated working-class culture/experience and working-class consciousness.[32]

The debate on political versus economic determinism, the need to look more closely at consciousness and at the organizational dimension, and the issue of cultural homogeneity led other historians to develop the notion of 'experience' more precisely. Thompsons's notion of experience, they said, covered too great a 'range of subjective responses' in numerous contexts, both public and private. It also 'carrie[d] too heavy an explanatory load.'[33] Thus, the idea of working-*class awareness* was suggested: that working-class people perceived themselves clearly as working class, with a sense of belonging and shared distinctiveness but, and this is important, without any necessary sense of political activism on behalf of that class, that is, without class consciousness. The central notions of this awareness, at least in the 1930s, were respectability and deference. Absent was a clear 'image of the overall structure of society.' Working class-ness was simply 'a life sentence.'[34]

This notion of awareness has in turn permitted class to be tied to organization. That is, 'class sentiment' or 'world view' could exist as an 'unfocussed sense of grievance,' but if it was to lead to action 'it had to be linked to symbols and programs organised by specific individuals and organisations.' In other words, the 'ideological link' between sentiment and partisan political loyalty came, not from analysis, but from participation. This participation was not spontaneous, however, but was the result of mobilization by *activists* operating within a 'particular structure of political power.' In this view, 'culture is different from ideology': 'Cultures are vast internally contradictory arrays of memories, symbols, ideas and practices susceptible to a range of ideological interpretations. Working-class cultures contain tendencies both for fragmentation and solidarity. Working-class culture is a set of contingencies and possibilities. Which possibility develops will depend on the historical context and the actions of actors within the context.'[35]

This issue of 'which possibility' has led to other research avenues. Thompson was criticized for ignoring the role of *language* and meaning in shaping class experience[36] and for failing to specify where determination ended and *agency* began.[37] Recent works have therefore paid more attention to language, ideology, and meanings. In direct response, however, other historians continue to insist that context and agency are the keys.[38] In this latter view is embodied a refusal to dismiss *social relations* and the *material bases* of working-class life and culture on the grounds that 'language and politics' must still be rooted in 'their material determinations.' Yet these historians have tempered the notion of class consciousness to 'eschew an "absolute" view of class and to be concerned

instead, with context, experience and actually existing worker consciousness complete with its contradictions and ambiguities.'[39] Part of
this is the recognition that working-class culture has to be understood in
terms of the '*middle class* efforts to transform – by means of a whole bat-
tery of cultural institutions and practices – the character structures of
workers and to channel them.'[40] All such viewpoints can, of course, be
explored among Thomastown workers. In turn, the history of Thomastown's labourers can contribute to our understandings of class awareness, experience, and consciousness, and to the roles of agency and
organization in their construction.

The Working Class in Irish History
British social historians have tried to move away from studying 'traditional working class culture' and the 'rise of Labour'[41] towards more
nuanced understandings of class consciousness and meaning while continuing to analyse material and social relations in the production of culture among working people. The same cannot be said of Irish labour
historians who, like an earlier generation of British historians concerned with the British Labour Party and the failure of labour to gain
ascendancy in Britain, have remained focused on biographies of labour
leaders, the history of formal labour organizations (for example, the
Labour Party, trade unions) and, in the Irish context, the ideological
and practical consequences of the tension between nationalism and
socialism in political history.[42] Irish labour can also sometimes be found
as a chapter, or a footnote, to help explain the so-called great political
events of the nineteenth and twentieth centuries. Most often, however,
such references have assumed that labour outside Dublin and Belfast
was solely agricultural and usually ephemeral.[43]

This has meant that the social history and historical anthropology of
the labouring class in Ireland are strikingly undeveloped and that the
voices of workers in numerous localities, from both the past and the
present, are silent.[44] This raises several questions which this study
attempts to address. How can macro-historical viewpoints, depictions
of great leaders, and the study of national organizations be made to
articulate with more micro or local-level experiences? How can more
anthropological and social historical ways of constructing labour be
accomplished?

Constructing a Labouring Narrative: Conceptual and Textual Strategies

Together, the key ideas of class, *metissage*, local-level politics, hegemony, and experience comprise a broad canvas for representing Thomas-town's labouring past while the various concepts that are highlighted above clearly overlap and can themselves be woven into a single vocabu-lary for narrating the story of Thomastown's labourers after 1800. But, how should this narrative be constructed?

One possible strategy is to act like an historian and to privilege the temporal dimension, providing thereby a chronological or phase description through which the story of labouring people can be con-structed as a series of key events, dates, or time periods. Another way is to privilege the spatial dimension and to describe the various societal levels (for example, local, regional, national) and their relationships. Or a series of theoretical issues or conceptual categories can be made to form the chapter headings, with chronology and socio-spatial levels slotted in. Finally, it is possible to privilege thick description and allow the richest data to constitute the story.

In constructing the present volume, each strategy seemed to offer both advantages and drawbacks. Each also seemed destined to skew the text in particular directions. The use of chronology as the skeleton could obscure conceptual complexity whereas the spatial strategy might obscure theoretical issues. A focus on theoretical issues would, in turn, limit emic perspectives while, conversely, using only the voices of local people might parochialize and diminish their experiences. Finally, a focus on the richest data would ignore the implications of the silences in historical and contemporary records.

In the absence, then, of any overriding advantage or imperative, it seemed best to take an eclectic approach: to combine strategies in terms of what might work best given my theoretical and empirical aims, the nature of the data, and my moral viewpoints. The story, therefore, is nar-rated by all these strategies at different points. The volume is thus made up of five parts. In Part I, this theoretical introduction (chapter 1) is fol-lowed by an empirical and conceptual introduction to labour at the turn of the nineteenth century (chapter 2). There then follow three parts which are defined, generally, in chronological terms: 1816–84 (Part II); the last two decades of the nineteenth century (Part III); and 1901–50 (Part IV). I have used these periods for various reasons. The nature of the available data changes in some instances whereas, in others, empiri-cal differences in the political economy and consciousness – the results of slow and numerous accretions over the previous decades – appear to coalesce. Such points seem also to provide natural opportunities for halting the narrative and summarizing trends in structure, process, and agency. None of these periods, of course, is discrete or bounded.

Indeed, the ways in which they are linked and the processes of reproduction from 1800 through to 1950 constitute key foci of this volume.

Within each of Parts II through IV, I organize the chapters thematically. I do this because of the nature of the data but, more important, because of the ways in which Thomastown labourers in the 1980s saw their pasts. I also do it because it allows me to highlight key conceptual issues which emerge in particular temporal contexts in relation to my concerns with class, *metissage*, local-level politics, hegemony, and experience. Thus, in various ways and through various topics, these empirical chapters explore the interrelated nature of cultural codes, agency, labour processes, the state, and formal organizations. The implications of this textual strategy, these topics, and my wider theoretical concerns comprise the Conclusions (Part V).

2. Relations of Class and Thomastown's 'Lower Orders' in 1800

'Acts [of charity] must convince the lower orders that their distresses are not un-heeded by those of their fellow citizens to whom providence has been more liberal.'
— Kilkenny *Moderator*, 27 January 1820

When E.P. Thompson suggested that historians could analyse the reciprocity and restraint which typified relations between rich and poor in Britain after 1760 as 'class relationships,'[1] he was not suggesting that paternalism and its obverse, deference, were fixed. Rather, he meant that such relations were continually being altered and renegotiated such that, at any particular moment, the ideas, beliefs, and practices associated with them comprised the kind of ideology that Gramsci had labelled 'common sense.' In the Thomastown area in 1800, an essential component of common sense was class difference, and this infused the world views of people in all stations.

It was illustrated by the annual shows held by the Thomastown Farming Society. Organized by locally resident gentlemen to encourage agricultural improvements and, by implication, the value of their tenanted lands, the society awarded prizes for achievements in certain categories. It is these categories that display how labour was structured and differentiated by the landed class at the time and how a 'good labourer' was defined (Case 2.1).

Case 2.1: Defining Labourers in 1805

At the 1805 meeting, several prizes were clearly intended for 'farmers': for the 'best managed farm not exceeding 30 acres,' for the 'cleanest and neatest farmyard,' and so on. The prizes were a plough and harrow. For others who had no need of ploughs, the prizes were two guineas. They were awarded, first, to 'the cottager not holding more than 5 acres of ground who has his house and garden in the best order; the inside plastered and the outside whitewashed.' Second, there were two guineas for the 'labourer ... [who had] lived the greatest number of years, not less than five, in the same service and behaved during that time with honesty, sobriety and industry.' Third, two guineas were awarded to the 'out-labourer who worked the greatest number of days with his employer' during the year. Finally, a prize was given to the 'best ploughman ... with a pair of horses' and to the one 'with a pair of oxen of his own.'[2]

The Thomastown Farming Society was clearly of the view that rural labourers were distinguishable from farmers and that the former were internally differentiated.[3] Part-time labourers with a bit ground ('cottagers') contrasted with full-time 'farm servants' who lived on their employer's farm either in 'tied cabins' with gardens if married ('cottiers') or in the hayloft if single (servants). These were in turn distinguished from the casual ('out labourer') and the skilled worker ('ploughman'). From among these were individuals whom local gentlemen wished to separate out, acknowledge publicly, and reward materially. They were the 'honest, sober and industrious' labourers who had established relatively long-term and, thus, conflict-free relations with their employers.

Similar distinctions and expectations at the time were applied to non-agricultural and, often, urban-based, labour. Here, contemporary sources distinguished explicitly between 'tradesmen' and 'labourers.' The former were skilled artisans – 'journeymen in different branches of trade' and their apprentices. Indeed, they were usually not included as part of the so-called labouring class because their skills commanded wages that were far higher than those of labourers and because they wielded some control over their conditions of work. In larger corporate boroughs such as Kilkenny city, artisans in each trade negotiated with corporation officers both a fair wage and the right to limit the number of local tradesmen.[4] Their main obligation, in turn, was that they not combine to change their negotiated working conditions. The result, at the turn of the nineteenth century, was that artisans earned a daily wage of about 2s.2d.[5] This contrasted vividly with the 9d. per day earned by 'common labourers.' Moreover, the labourer's wage depended on his having work in the first instance, which was often not the case. Thus, contemporary sources always distinguished labourers in 'constant employment' from casual or 'day labourers.'[6]

The lines by which the gentry divided labouring people were therefore drawn according to relative skills, employment status (permanent or casual), duration of current employment, and personal attributes (honesty, sobriety, industry, and docility). However, material conditions of the time, typified by underemployment and low wages, also generated another commonly used category – the 'labouring poor' or, simply, 'the poor.' In Kilkenny city, for example, the poverty of workers, exacerbated by urban living, was striking to observers at the time. Even 'in the cheapest times,' it was said, 'they can struggle for existence unaided as they are by the little helps they meet with in the country: and in fact we find them, on such wretched diet ... clothed with rags, and famished with cold in their comfortless habitations: nor can they, though sober, frugal and labourious ... provide against infirmity, and old age, any other resource than beggary, or dependance, than the precarious relief of charity.' Estimates of living costs for a household of five, as compared with wages, confirmed this portrait of struggle. After basic food, minimal fuel, rent, and clothing were paid for, only the equivalent of 12 days' wages (10s.) remained for other necessities (tea, salt, candles), luxuries (alcohol), and emergencies (illness, accident). It was hardly surprising to contemporaries, then, that 'in cheapest times, they ... struggle for existence.'[7]

In rural areas, too, a similar struggle took place, caused again by the fact 'that plenty of hands can be procured' and, thus, by the exploitation of labourers as both consumers and workers. In a parish near Thomastown in 1802, a cottier arrangement, and hence constant work, cost the labourer, apart from a wage far lower than his urban counterpart, an additional 30–50s. rent for a tied cabin which was 'generally wretched.' That amount of money represented about 40 days of his paid labour per year. Moreover, the subsistence garden that he was allotted, for oats, potatoes, a hog, and poultry, was 'often the worst in the farm' and for this he paid a rent 'of about double what the farmer may do to the landlord.' On the other hand, if the labourer was not 'accommodated with housing,' that is, if he were a 'common labourer,' the daily wage was higher: 10d. and 'diet' (a midday meal) if he worked for a farmer. If he worked for a gentleman, no food was provided. Such a casual labourer also had to rent a cabin. If it had a garden, he was charged 30 to 50s. per acre. A cabin without ground could be had for 21 to 42s. a year.[8] In other words, the common labourer's wage was higher than the cottier's although the costs of his housing and garden were the same. However, the cottier had constant work, the common labourer did not. Given high unemployment, rural workers preferred cottier status – despite low wages, poor housing, high rents, and poor-quality gardens.

Underlying all this was a belief among farmers and gentry, as well as among workers, that wage levels had to be set by the availability of labour at any particular time. This meant that, when there was 'a hurry in farming business' (that is, harvest time), wages might rise, for a very brief time, to a shilling or 16d. a day. Often, however, even such temporary rises were precluded by the glut of procurable workers. In other words, wages were directly dependent on the market and employers were absolved from any responsibility to ensure subsistence levels. In addition, it was commonly believed at the time that the costs that labourers had to incur for housing, gardens, and food should form a ceiling for wages, not a floor. This was associated with the view that those who had capital and land had a right to cheap labour. Said an observer in 1802: 'Cottagers, or labourers, should ... not have so much land as to take up too much of their time, and render them otherwise than useful to their employer.'[9]

The overall effect was to create labouring lives that were lived at bare subsistence – lives that were, according to observers, 'wretched in the extreme.' The same observers, however, tended to locate the causes of such poverty, not in low wages or even the labour market, but in other factors. For example, the 'want of every kind of manufacture in which children of an early age might be usefully and profitably employed, occasions much of the poverty.' So, too, did high prices. On a large estate in south County Kilkenny, an observer remarked that a rise in the price of turf occasioned by a shortage of coal 'amounted to what was considered as a serious grievance, and was justly complained of by the poor.' The administrators of the estate in fact interceded to lower the price. Another observer mused that 'in good policy the articles of necessity ought to be kept at as low a price as possible' because high prices severely affected labourers, especially the poor.[10] In all this, no one suggested that wage rates be raised.

In any case, poverty was thought to be caused by the labourers themselves. An observer who suggested a complex crop rotation for improving gardens added that it would be difficult to enact because 'the poor people will naturally object to any system from laziness or ignorance.' At the same time, 'they should be bound down ... to follow' such plans because then the 'employer would have the constant use of his labourer, except for about twenty days in the year at the utmost, and the pleasure of seeing an industrious poor family striving under him, and their land (instead of being racked, as is usual in a few crops) improving by every crop.'[11]

In an ideal world, then, the employer would have access to constant labour even in busy seasons, the labour would be cheap, the labourer would be intelligent, well-off, and content, the prices of necessities would be low, the land would be improved, and the benevolent employer could assume the credit for this utopian state of affairs. However, it was equally clear to observers at the time that this scenario was not working out. Not only was there poverty among workers, but, more important, labour productivity and the labour process were adversely affected: 'For themselves, the labouring poor can make great exertions; but for others, or when not closely overlooked, they work in a manner most languid and indolent; their mode of living, perhaps, totally on vegetable food, produces a general debility, which must have powerful motives to overcome it; their habits disincline them for any species of task work, though they might gain double by it; and their labour, though nominally cheap, is in fact dear from the tedious and slovenly manner it is performed.'[12]

At the turn of the nineteenth century, too, these conditions were seen as worsening. Why? Because 'the increase in the price of labour does not bear a due proportion to the price of provisions. The latter has in many instances doubled in the last twenty years. During the same period, the average wage of day labour has risen from 6d. to 8d.' Fortunately, however, 'the food of the poor, potatoes' had not risen because they were 'chiefly affected by seasons, and fall to the old value again, in favourable years.'[13]

Political Agitation: Coercion and Consent

With the declining ability of artisans' guilds to dominate trade during the eighteenth century, and 'as manufactures grew and the gap between master and journeyman widened,' journeymen began to 'rely increasingly on combination for their protection.'[14] In 1801 in Kilkenny city, for example, 'journeymen taylors' combined to limit incoming 'strange journeymen' and to raise wages from 10 to 12s. per week.[15] In 1802 masons who were building a new jail combined for higher wages. At the assizes, they were 'severely punished' and had their 'names published in order to caution the County against employing Persons guilty of so great an offence.'[16]

These actions in fact reflected more general labour unrest among urban workers in the last decade of the eighteenth century. Fears wrought by the French Revolution, the dissemination of radical ideas, and the growth of reform societies such as the United Irishmen 'brought increasingly harsh measures to deal with combinations and associations in Ireland as well as in England. But they could not banish economic distress.'[17] Coercive measures were therefore augmented by efforts at social engineering and education. Problems in the woollen industry in several larger cities, for example, caused 'by what was considered to be the turbulent actions of the workers and their tendency to combine for higher wages,' led several Kilkenny entrepreneurs to establish a woollen factory which would 'avoid these troubles by employing only country people and by training them from childhood in the path they should tread.' This Owenite-type institution was located a few miles from Thomastown in the hamlet of Ennisnag. It hired young apprentices (aged fourteen) for a seven-year period, segregated boys from girls, made school and church attendance compulsory, deducted contributions out of wages for a pension and illness fund, and insisted on uniform dress and a point-and-reward system for skill, punctuality, and good conduct. In 1819 the factory was described in a Kilkenny theatrical production as a place where the 'hours beguile and man, poor labouring man, is taught to smile.'[18]

The Nature of Relief: Paternalism, Deference, and Dearth

In the common sense of employers at the time, the social and economic problems of labour could not be resolved by raising wages. Nor could rural-subsistence grounds be enlarged because 'the union of the two occupations of labourer and farmer, is injurious; for neither ... can be performed well.'[19] Instead, the solution was to 'relieve distress' through charitable works. But who would be relieved? The answer seemed clear: those who deserved to be. The 'deserving poor' were the infirm, elderly, sick, and physically disabled. They also were those who needed help during times of temporary dearth caused by rising prices, inclement weather, and potato failure. Like those rewarded by the Thomastown Farming Society, the deserving poor were honest, sober, and industrious labourers but had fallen on hard times through no fault of their own.

But how were they to be relieved? According to an observer at the time, monasteries and religious institutions had been 'intended as establishments for the poor.' After their abolition in the mid-sixteenth century, the poor came 'to depend on casual assistance, and private charity.'[20] Thus, at the turn of the nineteenth century, County Kilkenny had both charitable societies, funded by bequests or subscriptions, and ad hoc efforts of charitable relief.

Permanent societies or funds were not numerous. In 1802 there were fifteen for the county as a whole. One, in Kilkenny city, collected annual subscriptions to supply 'bed-ridden tradesmen and labourers, and their widows, if bed-ridden, with a small allowance, barely sufficient to keep them from perishing.' Another educated the 'children of the poor' in 'subscription charity schools' with 'the *most deserving* ... apprenticed to different trades.' As well, almshouses in the towns of Gowran, Inistioge, and Kilkenny relieved a total of forty-four resident poor. There also were a few permanent bequests for daily relief. Two provided bread, one to the amount of £7.10s. annually, while a third provided £32 a year simply 'for charitable purposes.'[21]

Far more common and important than permanent societies were the ad hoc collections in times of more than normal distress. Reports of the situation in Kilkenny city between 1799 and 1801 (Case 2.2) show the ubiquity of ad hoc relief at the time and the main form that it took: making provisions available at lower than market prices. The case also highlights the material and moral role of the gentry as benefactors and their public presence. Clearly, subsistence crises were not unexpected. Yet, if they continued too long or recurred too soon, funding problems could result, leading to a new crisis to which the gentry would respond.

Case 2.2: The Subsistence Crisis in Kilkenny City, 1799–1801
In 1799, 'the extraordinary price of fuel had placed it beyond the reach of the poor.' A volunteer committee was set up to collect money from 'citizens' in order to sell coal to the poor 'on reasonable terms.' Soon after, a soup house was set up, 'but the increasing distress of the poor' required yet another subscription which, this time, was used to buy 100 tons of oatmeal which was sold at a reduced price. In 1800 another collection had the aim of continuing the 'soup establishment until it became unnecessary.' The following year, however, a public meeting had to be called to consider 'the state of the poor and to adopt some effectual means of providing for their wants.' Apparently, high provision prices and 'very inadequate subscription' monies made it difficult for the committee to carry out 'this object.'

The committee pointed out that 'it was incumbent on the public to come forward with contributions' given that 'several persons are daily expiring from actual want of food.' The committee had spent over £2,100 on food but had taken in only £329. The gentry quickly responded. Within a few days, £600 was raised. The senior county aristocrat, the Earl of Ormonde, had given £100; other 'gentlemen' had given the rest.[22]

At around the same time, however, there is evidence of a growing recognition that ad hoc relief was only a partial solution and that it would be useful to broaden the frames through which the gentry provided aid. This outlook was manifested when the above-mentioned volunteer committee in Kilkenny city set up 'a permanent fund for the relief of the *sick* poor' and, out of this, built and funded a fever hospital and medical dispensary. Two earls, Ormond and Desart, headed the committee to plan the enterprise.[23] The same outlook was reflected in a new association, formed in 1801 under the auspices of Ormond and the Protestant bishop. Its members aimed 'to inform themselves of the real circumstances ... of the poor ... in order to apply the most effectual means for ameliorating their condition, which appear to be, the encouragement of industry, sobriety and cleanliness.' Prizes were to be given half-yearly 'to such of the lower orders ... as shall keep their persons and habitations in the best state of cleanliness, and exhibit the best examples of industry, sobriety and honesty.' The city was divided into districts and an inspector assigned to each. The inspector was to have dunghills removed and was to ensure that houses were whitewashed and pigs were not kept in dwellings.[24] Presumably, too, he was to select those individuals who should be awarded prizes.

This funding of formal institutions and the formalization of private funding, alongside research into the living conditions of working people and efforts to 'encourage' better habits, signalled that those who subscribed money were not simply claiming the right to define who should be relieved. Through their charitable works and monies, by 1800 they also were claiming the right to enter the world of the poor and to influence and educate the people whom they found there. Given that relief could be given only to the deserving poor, the poor had to be taught to be deserving.

In this respect, tradesmen were far better off than labourers – at least in the larger urban centres. In Kilkenny city in 1802, artisans had two charitable associations. The Charitable Society, founded in 1710 for bedridden tailors, had expanded to include all local tradesmen and their wives, 'without any distinction of religion.' It was funded by admission fees (5s.5d. for a 'city member' and £1.2.9 for a 'country' one) and by a quarterly subscription (2s.2d.). Society members met weekly to distribute £5 worth of relief to 'about forty objects.' The Benevolent Society, formed in 1785, was 'for relieving bed-ridden objects which did not come within the description of those relieved by the Charitable Society.' Its admission fee was only 1s.1d. and it too distributed relief via weekly meetings. Funds for both societies were augmented by 'charity sermons,' 'occasional assemblies,' and contributions from the gentry.[25]

Tradesmen everywhere were also helped by legislation. A Charitable Loan fund had been established in 1792 by the Irish Parliament to lend 'small sums to indigent tradespeople, interest free.' From then until 1800, over £5,400 was lent to 2,208 tradespeople in the county.[26] In smaller centres, however, 'friendly societies' for both artisans and workers operated only intermittently. In Thomastown, the one funded in the 1790s 'for supporting sick members, and for burials and masses' floundered in 1798.[27]

Thus, for ordinary labourers at the turn of the nineteenth century, most of whom lived in or near poverty and with virtually no voluntary organizations of their own, the only way to alleviate dearth was what was offered by the gentry: ad hoc relief during subsistence crises and institutionalization for disease. Access to these required workers to defer to the idea, in practice and perhaps in belief, that people from other classes could explore, evaluate, and alter a worker's values and lifestyle. In other words, a political economy organized by capital, and thus containing a great deal of surplus 'free' labour, created both the poverty of labourers and the public charity and ameliorative outlooks of the better-off classes. Paternalism and deference hinged on each other and both, in turn, depended on the presence of dearth. Together, they reflected the reciprocity, hierarchy, and exploitation that underlay both material conditions and common sense at the time.

Thomastown's 'Lower Orders': Artisans, Labourers, and Fishers

The voices of artisans and labourers in the Thomastown area are virtually mute at the turn of the nineteenth century. Yet something of their material conditions and experiences can be gleaned from occasional newspaper accounts, the *Lucas Directory*, memorials of deeds, personal conveyances, and parish birth registers. These suggest that the numbers of artisans in each trade in a small urban centre precluded the kind of collective experiences that typified the trades in larger centres such as Kilkenny city. Thomastown's smaller scale, as well as its greater dependence on its rural hinterland, also meant that different relations obtained between and among artisans and labourers.

Thomastown's Artisans: Class Positionings

From all available sources, we know of sixty-two artisans who lived in the Thomastown area between the 1770s and 1831. Although we cannot know how this number approximates the actual total, these sixty-two do illustrate the kinds of trades that were extant, their relative proportions, and something of the nature of local society.

The most visible non-agricultural tradesmen were shoemakers (numbering fifteen of the sixty-two), masons (eight), carpenters (eight) and smiths (five).[28] They comprised 50 per cent of the known artisans. When bakers (four), tailors (three), and saddlers (three) are factored in, almost 75 per cent of the artisans are accounted for. The remainder included two each of sawyers, weavers, tanners, butchers, glaziers, millwrights, and drivers, along with one nailer and a brazier. What all this highlights is the small number in any one trade and the fact that the overall number of trades found in Thomastown was small. Such conditions likely precluded the kind of combination and ideology found in Kilkenny city among those who shared a particular trade. Moreover, the domestic nature of Thomastown's trades, that is, the absence of artisans who produced luxury commodities (for example, hatters, cabinetmakers, silversmiths), suggests two further features. First, the local economy, although having an urban-based artisanal component, was not highly diversified. Second, the town's tradesmen mainly produced goods and provided services for local consumers rather than for the extensive trade networks in which the town was enmeshed.

The particular role that the town's artisans played in local society is to some extent visible from the memorials of deeds which recorded the mortgaging or conveyancing (lease, sale, bequest) of property. From the founding of the Deeds Registry in the early eighteenth century to 1831, members of Thomastown's lower orders were hardly visible as compared with those from other classes. Yet artisans did appear as both witnesses (Table 2.1) and agents (Table 2.2). With only two exceptions (Table 2.1), labourers, in contrast, were virtually invisible.

What is striking about the artisan witnesses is the extent to which they provided links between and among individuals from different status-

Table 2.1: Artisans as witnesses to legal conveyances, 1771–1831

Year	Artisan Witness	Conveyed	From/to	Other witness
1771*	weaver+	2 acres	merchant/*carpenter*	mill owner
1772	shoemaker	56 acres	landlord/farmer	[parish clerk/Inistioge]
1773	weaver+	5 acres	landlord+/shopkeeper+	miller
1773	weaver+	house & yard	landlord+/shopkeeper+	miller
1778	weaver+	house mortgages	spinster/clergyman	[not local]
1786*	gardener	£344 mortgage	merchant/*gardener*	*blacksmith*
1804	tailor	5 acres	boat owner/his son	schoolmaster
1812*	shoemaker	house lease	landlord/*glazier*	attorney
1815	mason	8 acres	mill owner/shopkeeper	schoolmaster
1816	shoemaker	small piece of ground	farmer/tannery owner	clothier
1816*	carman	2 urban plots	*mason*/landlord	[attorney, Waterford]
1816	gardener	house, Market St	shopkeeper/publican	schoolmaster
1816	car driver	£50 mortgage	miller/clergyman	clerk, Kilkenny city
1821	labourer (toll collector)	2 houses	*blacksmith*+/mill owner	farmer
1824	labourer	2 acres & 20 small houses	*blacksmith*+/sons-in-law	[farmer, Bennettsbridge]
1825	land steward	town houses & mill	landlord/her children	her son
1831	1. dealer *cum* shoemaker 2. baker	farm (52 acres & stock)	farmer/his daughter	publican

N.B. All people were locals, unless bracketed [ ]. Those italicized are also artisans.
+ Indicates that the artisan or property appears elsewhere in the Table.
* Indicates that this conveyance also appears in Table 2.2

Sources: Deed memorial nos. 285-478-189553; 292-81-18938; 310-312-206628; 310-313-206629;
344-474-n.g.; 383-398-254095; 580-218-395284; 685-405-471; 701-114-48640; 702-291-481388;
739-265-503600; 828-24-55760; 869-439-579439; 877-143-582143; and family papers, Thomastown.

classes. They not only witnessed transactions that involved other artisans as conveyors or recipients (five of the twenty-nine individuals whose status is known) but, far more frequently, they witnessed transactions involving non-artisans: landlords (seven), capitalists (four), merchants and shopkeepers (seven), farmers (four), and clergymen (two). In fact, only one of the fifteen transactions involved the conveyancing of property *within* the artisanal status-class itself. Moreover, of these fourteen inter-class conveyances, ten transmitted property between people who were themselves from different status-classes (for example, a merchant conveyed two acres to a carpenter; a landlord conveyed a house and yard to a retailer). It thus appears that artisans provided links among people from different stations in local society.

At the same time, these conveyances witnessed by artisans usually involved only petty properties: houses, plots of ground, and a few acres. (Only five of the fifteen memorials involved substantial property – two farms, a mill, and two mortgages for £50 and £344 respectively.) This concern with petty properties was also apparent when artisans were active agents as conveyors or recipients (Table 2.2). Here, the main commodity was again housing or house plots. In these transactions, too, artisans were mainly the recipients rather than the conveyors while the properties themselves tended to come from those of other status-classes (eight of eleven conveyances). This inter-class bias was also apparent from the fact that artisans often brought in those from other classes to witness their own transactions; from the nature of artisans' involvement in mortgages (a shoemaker and a millwright conveyed plots as security for their debts to suppliers and a gardener lent £344 to a local merchant); and from the two cases in which masons sold plots, in one case to a local landlord who was buying up labourers' housing at the time.

Table 2.2, like Table 2.1, thus points to the importance of petty-property transactions for artisans and to the active involvement of artisans in inter-class exchanges. Overall, Thomastown's artisans seemingly provided links between and among people of other classes and status-classes while being unlikely to develop organic relations within their own trade, or even among the trades more generally, both because of their small numbers and because of the local and domestic orientation of their production. However, as potential mediators between classes, as atomized among themselves in different trades and even classes, and as agents in, or as witnesses to, the conveyancing of petty properties, they were ideally situated, as individuals, to learn about the virtues that the gentry wished to inculcate among the lower orders.

Table 2.2: Artisans as conveyors/receivers of property, 1753–1831

Year	Artisan	Property conveyed	From or	To	Witness(es)
1753	mason	unspecified acreage	farmer cum middleman	–	3 farmers
1770	mason+	house+	landlord	–	n.g. [not given]
1771*	carpenter	2 acres	merchant	–	mill owner; weaver
1780	shoemaker+	small plot+	landlord	–	n.g.
1785	victualler	annuity	–	his wife	n.g.
1786	mason+	house+	–	n.g.	2 'gentleman'
1786*	gardener	£344 mortgage	–	merchant	gardener; blacksmith
1787	mason	house	n.g.	–	n.g.
1791	shoemaker+	mortgage of a small plot+	–	leather seller, Dublin	[all Dublin]
1793	millwright+	plot+	landlord	–	n.g.
1795	sawyer	house	landlord	–	farmer
1795	glazier+	house+	landlord	–	n.g
1795	car driver	8 acres	landlord	–	n.g
1801	millwright+	mortgage to a plot+	merchant, Dublin	–	[all Dublin]
1803	chandler, tanner	house	landlord	–	n.g
1812*	glazier+	house+	–	sons	attorney; shoemaker
1816*	mason	2 plots of ground	–	landlord	carman; attorney [Waterford]
1816	mason	house & cabin	blacksmith**	–	n.g.

N.B.: All people were locals, unless otherwise indicated.

+ Indicates that the artisan or property appears elsewhere in the Table.

* Indicates that this conveyance also appears in Table 2.1.

** The Table excludes the numerous conveyances generated by the activities of the blacksmith Martin Kelly, who also was a housing middleman. Two of his conveyances are listed in Table 2.1. His career and transactions are discussed below.

Sources: Deed memorial nos. 160-410; 292-81-189538; 315-386-213236; 377-100-250526; 383-398-254095; 438-240-282566; 481-292-317035; 483-550-317039; 630-191-433135; 702-291-481328; 852-62-569562; 869-439-579439; and family papers, Thomastown.

Table 2.3: Number of baptisms after 1798 in town and country

	1798–1808	1818–1828*	1829–1839
TOTAL:	1,765	1,921 (+156) +8.8%	1,951 (+30) +1.6%
Locale:			
Rural townlands	982	1,080 (+98) +9.1%	1,037 (−43) [−4.1%]
Peri-urban townlands**	142	151 (+9) +6.3%	146 (−5) [−3.4%]
Town streets	641	690 (+49) +7.6%	768 (+78) +11.3%

*Parochial records for the 1809–1817 period were incomplete and did not list addresses. This period has therefore been omitted.
**Peri-urban townlands are adjacent to the townland/borough of Thomastown. In many cases, they were extensions of the town.

Thomastown's labourers: the demographics

These lower orders had been rapidly increasing, according to Tighe's observations in 1802. He noted that Thomastown town had about 350 houses, an increase of fifty since 1792. In 1800, too, the population of the three 'civil parishes,' which included Thomastown town and vicinity, numbered 3,986. This was more than three times the 1,144 people enumerated seventy years before in 1731.[29]

Of particular interest, however, is that this growth contained rural-urban variations. The population of the most rural civil parish had increased by 75 per cent (from 373 people in 1731 to 665 in 1800). In contrast, in the civil parish adjacent to the urban area, numbers had increased by 270 per cent (from 274 people in 1731 to 1,014 in 1800); and in the parish that included the town, numbers had grown by 364 per cent (from 497 people in 1731 to 2,307 in 1800). Clearly, the town was most burdened by population growth before 1800. As to what happened after, this is visible from the parish baptism records which began in 1798 (Table 2.3).[30]

The totals for all 'townlands'[31] in Thomastown Catholic parish show that the high rate of population growth during the eighteenth century began to moderate during the first two decades of the nineteenth. Then, after 1828, the numbers and per cent of increase declined dramatically. Yet, throughout, rural-urban differences persisted. Until 1828, the increase in the number of baptisms in rural townlands (9.1 per cent) was greater than in the town streets (7.6 per cent). Afterwards, the number of rural births declined dramatically. This same pattern typified the peri-urban townlands, although the increase during

1818–28 (6.3 per cent) had not been as great nor had the decrease afterwards (3.4 per cent). However, in the town itself, where the narrow streets and labourers' cabins were to be found, the baptism rate continued to rise until at least 1839. In other words, the urban population continued to grow after 1828 while the rural population apparently stabilized.

This was not, however, because conjugal pairs moved from the countryside to the town. Of the 2,000 couples who married or baptized children in the rural or peri-urban townlands after 1798, only 170 also baptized a child while giving an urban address. Indeed, 50 of these 170 units baptized their older children in the town and then moved into the countryside while 23 conjugal units oscillated between town and country. Thus, only 97 of the 170 (or of 2,000 conjugal pairs), or less than 5 per cent of the total, married or baptized their oldest children in rural areas and later came into the town. This suggests that two processes were at work. First, the increasing population in one generation produced more children in the next. Second, it was unmarried labourers who left the countryside for the town. They then married in town and swelled its baptism rate after 1808. In fact, the more dramatic population increase in the town during the 1731–1800 period suggests that this was occurring prior to 1800.

This particular kind of rural-urban migration and the greater population growth in the town was largely about labouring lives. For the records do not suggest any increase in the number of resident retailers, professionals, or landlords. Thus, at the turn of the nineteenth century, the majority of people in Thomastown town were most likely labourers and/or artisans. Where did they work? In addition to casual or day work for farmers, non-agricultural work could be found in gentlemen's houses, the lime kilns near the town, small manufacturing establishments (corn and flour mills, breweries, and malt houses), or artisanal shops. There also was work 'on the roads.' In 1801, in the baronies of Gowran and Knocktopher (Map 1) which contained both the urban area and most of the rural townlands of Thomastown, £1,447 was spent on road works. This sum comprised almost a third of the total (£4,623) spent in the county as a whole, outside Kilkenny city.[32] In Thomastown town and vicinity, too, numerous labourers worked for boat owners who moved goods along the river from New Ross and Waterford and for locally resident 'carmen' who trans-shipped the goods which were unloaded at the town's quays, bound for, or coming from, Kilkenny city. The boat trade was labour intensive: river barges were pulled along the tow path by labourers, not horses. This suggests, of course, that labour commanded a low price in Thomastown. An observer in 1815 also noted that the 'men employed to tow are described as being rebellious and of disorderly conduct.'[33] Clearly, the town's burgeoning labouring class was fertile ground for the concerns of the gentry. Such labourers were also available for fishing.

The Salmon Fishers of the Inland River Nore

The River Nore was not only a highway for trade and a source of motive power for mills. It also provided salmon, trout, and eels both for local consumption and for sale. Salmon especially had long been highly valued, as were those inland stretches of the river which were amenable for building fishing weirs and/or which had deep pools that yielded particularly good catches. Such 'fisheries' had long comprised property which was carefully and explicitly conveyed.[34] In turn, such ownership had created conflict: fixed weirs and nets interfered with navigation. In 1537, for example, the County Kilkenny grand jury, which included two Thomastown merchants, complained of the large number of fishing weirs which stretched from bank to bank.[35] Three centuries later, this issue had not abated. However, in 1800, although fisheries and fishing weirs could be owned and conveyed, the right to fish in the River Nore was a public right, a common right. Said Tighe in 1802: 'The fishing of these rivers is free by custom to the inhabitants of the shores.' Tighe also saw 'country people' as the main fishers, using snap nets and cots.[36]

In tidal waters downriver from Thomastown, and in the Waterford estuary, salmon had been a commodity in both regional and export markets since at least the seventeenth century.[37] In 1800, for example, not only were salmon from these waters marketed locally, in New Ross and Waterford, but 'jolters' travelled from Kilkenny city to New Ross to buy salmon for 3d. a pound and then returned to Kilkenny city to retail it for four.[38] That the Kilkenny jolters bypassed such inland fishing areas as Thomastown and Bennettsbridge, only ten and six miles from the city respectively, and instead travelled thirty miles to the coast, suggests the unimportance of these towns in the regional salmon trade at the time. Indeed, Tighe used the term 'country people' to describe those who fished – not 'fishermen' or 'cotmen.' Moreover, during an 1834 inquiry into 'the condition of the poorer classes,' gentlemen were asked how labourers in their localities were 'maintained when out of employment.' Those from the Inistioge area, where the Nore becomes tidal eight miles downriver from Thomastown, noted that many fished 'in season.'[39] Three years earlier, in the household/census returns for Inistioge village, however, only four of the 134 households contained a 'fisherman.' In one of these, the other adult male was a mason. Of the three gentlemen respondents in the Thomastown area in the 1834 inquiry, none mentioned fishing.

All this suggests that salmon fishing on the inland, non-tidal portions of the River Nore did not provide households with full-time work; nor were there distinctively fisher households whose members did nothing but fish. Instead, in inland locales such as Thomastown, Bennettsbridge, and even Inistioge, salmon fishing was a means, and likely an important one, by which labourers and artisans supplemented either their own diets and, perhaps by selling a few fish locally, their wages. This highly localized character, as compared with the seeming 'rentability' and commercialization of the fisheries in the Thomastown area in earlier centuries, was probably related to Tighe's observation that the quantity of salmon in the Nore had decreased significantly over the previous forty years. This, he noted, was because of the large number of 'injurious' fishing weirs; the building of new flour mills in whose dams the young fry collected, to be caught and used as pig-food;[40] and the taking of fish 'out of season, at illegal times and in illegal ways' despite 'numerous acts of parliament' which were seldom enforced. For example, the closed season on all Irish rivers was legislated in 1758 as being between 12 August and 1 February. Yet the 'time is extended on the Nore, as it is said by custom, to the twenty-ninth of September ... but cots go out to fish beyond that time, or whenever they please.'[41]

More generally, acts of Parliament that constrained salmon fishing had been rapidly increasing in number and scope over the previous four decades, precisely the same period that Tighe had designated as one of decline. These laws not only defined the closed season but also outlawed particular technologies, regulated the workings and structures of fishing and mill weirs, and forbade the killing of young salmon fry or the catching of them in mill races.[42] Yet, 'in spite of these laws, little is done to prevent the fishery from rapidly declining,'[43] as people from all classes exercised their public right to fish. 'Country people' used cots and nets, gentlemen angled with rod and line for sport, landed proprietors attached fixed nets and weirs to their properties, and millers and their workers used the mill weirs to trap salmon.

Then, in 1807, a new type of fixed net ('Scotch net') was introduced by landowners in the tidal waters downriver from Thomastown, in the

Waterford estuary. According to Patrick Magee, an activist giving evidence in 1849 about what had occurred forty years before, this new and more efficient technology caused an expansion of the export trade which, in turn, induced landowners to set up more nets. As a result, economic and moral relations in the estuary fishery were disrupted. Before 1807, although some landlords had weirs, and although the fishers believed these weirs to be illegal in public waters, they tolerated them so long as the fish was for home consumption and so long as the landlord hired a labourer to work the weir. However, within a few years after 1807, landlords began to lease their weirs to tenants, for the profit of both through the export market. According to Magee, these weirs 'became so destructive that by the year 1830 our salmon fishery was reduced from about 500 to 20 nets.'

The impact of the new technology was also felt on the non-tidal, inland Nore. In Thomastown, for example, there was a growing sense that the inland salmon fisheries were declining as a result of the fixed nets downriver. Several meetings of gentlemen in Kilkenny city, along with their efforts to form associations 'to protect the fisheries,' show that the landed class was increasingly concerned to protect both their sport and the harvest of their weirs. Equally, however, the absence of any sustained news about these associations suggests that these efforts to stop the perceived decline were short-lived.[44] Yet the fact that so many people of different classes had interests in the inland salmon fisheries meant that the relations of class and deference which permeated local society would invariably impinge on what was soon to be seen as a major crisis.

Dyadic Relations of Class, Patronage, and Deference

Because of the glut in the labour market, the education of workers to be compliant and deferential could be pursued by anyone who purchased labour power (landlords, capitalists, farmers). It could also be pursued by those who contributed to charitable relief. However, the two groups only partly overlapped: not all employers were equally dedicated to good works and not all who dispensed paternal largesse were employers of labour. Yet, in general terms, people of different classes did gradually develop different norms and styles in relation to charity, a feature exemplified early on by the failure of the general citizenry of Kilkenny city to relieve the 1799–1801 subsistence crisis (Case 2.2). Indeed, at the turn of the nineteenth century, it was the titled and/or landed – the so-called

Protestant 'nobility and gentry' – who were crucial.[45] Then, as the nineteenth century progressed, local capitalists slowly added themselves to, and were accepted into, the category of gentry/gentleman and took upon themselves the burden of education though paternalism. What became particularly relevant for Thomastown's labouring people in this process were the highly visible differences that came to exist between landlords and capitalists on the one hand and farmers on the other in terms of their attitude towards charity. Whereas the former became defined as gentlemen in part because they adopted a paternalistic style, farmers were to become notorious for their charitable restraint. In this was reflected, of course, a distinction between those who owned the means of production (land, factories) and those who had access but not ownership (tenant farmers). These, in turn, contrasted with those who had neither access nor ownership and who had only their labour power (workers) and/or their skills (artisans). Such vested and opposed material interests, involving four main status categories and reflected in the presence or absence of paternal relationships, yielded three dyadic relationships which were experienced directly by labour: landlord-labourer/artisan; manufacturer-labourer/artisan; and tenant farmer-labourer/artisan.

The boundaries around each of the four status categories and, hence, the dyads were fairly rigid. Not only was the upward movement of individuals into higher levels of the hierarchy uncommon but such mobility usually did little to change the emic perception of the status-class of the person involved. Thus, landlords, on occasion, did invest in industry while manufacturers sometimes purchased tenanted lands. Moreover, only the very occasional labourer managed to learn a trade – the costs of apprenticeship and the patrilineal bias of training being severe constraints. Farmers, in their turn, did not become landlords nor did tradesmen become farmers. Here, the constraints on the accumulation of capital and knowledge were too great.

In Thomastown, too, were those who occupied contradictory class locations. These included smallholding tenant farmers who sold their labour and artisans who employed journeymen or apprentices. These were often flexible locations, however. The labouring smallholder and the capitalist artisan were frequently stages in the developmental cycle of households or short-term responses to external conditions such as price and wage levels. Yet sometimes these contradictory locations were associated with cumulative change. The size of what constituted a viable smallholding increased during the century, thus 'proletarizing' more and more smallholders. Or, on the odd occasion, an artisanal enterprise became a manufactory.

Local society at the turn of the nineteenth century, and later, also had its professionals, mainly Protestant but also Catholic: clergy, solicitors, doctors, and, in later years, resident magistrates, constabulary officers, and so on. It also had so-called shopkeepers, both large and small, who functioned in the realm of circulation rather than production. Although not dependent on the exploitation of labour, and although aloof from charitable ideas during most of the nineteenth century, both professionals and retailers slowly developed, in their turn, particular styles in relation to paternalism, deference, and dearth. The professionals by mid-century, and the largest retailers by the end of the century, came to emulate the cultural codes of gentlemen and to accept the view that a corollary of wealth, influence, and prestige was charity. Cultural capital and political capital became connected: good works yielded local influence and locally influential people carried out good works. At the same time, the vast majority of Thomastown's retailers, as small-scale purveyors of commodities to consumers, as kin and affines (in-laws) of farmers and as mainly Catholic, remained, like tenant farmers, firmly marginalized from the growing concern with the condition and behaviour of the labouring poor.

All this meant, of course, that the relative number and kind of people who became concerned with the behaviour and attitudes of labouring people gradually increased as the century progressed. Yet, at the same time, demographic, economic, and political changes took place. The nature of agency thus altered in tandem, as did the structure of reciprocity, hierarchy, and exploitation, leading to new definitions and common-sense understandings of dearth, paternalism, and deference. This complex interplay of the ideological and the material, as it fed continuously into, and on, changing relations among the class-based dyads, comprised the hegemonic process.

PART II

Labouring Experience in the Nineteenth Century

At a dinner held by the Friends of Civil and Religious Liberty, guests included Daniel O'Connell, John Power, Joseph Greene and Henry Amyas Bushe. After a toast to his health, John Power responded: 'I am ... a most warm advocate of the British connexion, and I am a Protestant from conviction, but a Protestant I hope without bigotry.'

Kilkenny *Moderator,* 3 December 1828

In 1800 the Irish Parliament voted both to abolish itself and to accept union with Great Britain. Thereafter, the few propertied men who held the vote in Ireland elected members directly to the British Parliament. Thereafter, too, the presence of the colonial state was increasingly embodied in the office of the lord lieutenant, appointed by the British prime minister and supported by a bureaucracy in Dublin which gradually grew as the state extended its jurisdiction into and over more and more areas of everyday life during the nineteenth century.

The 1800 Act of Union had been opposed by one faction of the Irish landed class and supported by another. The above-mentioned Henry Amyas Bushe, from Thomastown, was part of a family and faction renowned for its opposition. His mother was the sister of the nationalist parliamentarian Henry Grattan, and his cousin, Charles Kendal Bushe, MP and Thomastown landlord, was known by many local people in the 1980s as 'the incorruptible Irishman' because of his refusal to be bribed into voting for the union.[1] Such division among the landed class continued well into the nineteenth century, buttressed and cross-cut by other rifts which emanated out of political-economic and social interests that appeared or disappeared through time. These oppositions included, *inter alia,* Brunswickers and Orangemen versus Liberals,[2] Tories versus Whigs, resident landlords versus non-residents; the titled versus the squirearchy, the wealthy versus the not-so wealthy, fishing-weir owners versus gentlemen anglers, and, occasionally, Protestants versus Catholics. Such divisions, of course, were intrinsic aspects of the hegemonic process during the nineteenth century. They point more generally to the fact that any exploration of hegemony and colonialism requires some understanding of the competing ideologies and activities among those who comprised the dominant class(es) and wielded varying influences over government bureaucracy and the coercive apparatus of the state.

Indeed, in 1800, it did not appear to many such people that Ireland had in fact been militarily pacified. Organized insurrection in 1798 and continuing agrarian outrages had provided in part the rationale for the union. However, insurrection again occurred in 1803 and outrages continued. Efforts in the late eighteenth and early nineteenth centuries by locally recruited militia and yeomanry, organized by some of the resident landlords who also served as magistrates, failed to quell the violence. The Peace Preservation Act of 1814, which established a police force to be paid for out of local funds, also failed, in large measure because of the desultory response from the landlord-magistrates. In 1822, however, with increasing outbursts of violence, both an Insurrection Act and a Constabulary Act were passed.[3] The latter established a permanent police force paid for in large part out of central funds. By 1823, it had a force of 4,500 men which supplemented the 20,000 troops stationed in Ireland.[4] For the next one hundred years, the British state continued to confront sporadic outbreaks of violence. Most were confined to particular parts of the country and, until 1920, all were quelled fairly quickly by a combination of coercive and ameliorative measures.[5]

For along with coercion came other material structures which, both intentionally and unintentionally, educated those in both the dominant and subaltern classes. Created usually through parliamentary legislation, these structures were responses either to protests or to the successful intervention of interest groups, to notions of good government, to the failure of earlier policies, and/or to perceived practical necessities. For example, the removal of some of the penal laws on Catholics (1793, 1795) and Catholic Emancipation (1829) occurred, *inter alia*, because of the organized but peaceful protests led by Daniel O'Connell, MP, because some Protestant legislators opposed bigotry, and because some agents saw the potential for stability in the creation of an unfettered, Catholic bourgeoisie. The Petty Sessions Act (1827) and the Poor Law (1838), for example, were put in place in part because the older ways of dealing with crime and poverty either had failed to alleviate the problem or had fallen into disrepute. The National Schools Act (1839) was, at least in part, an effort to create multi-denominational schools for the improvement of Catholic-Protestant relations.[6]

Such laws and material structures were often, of course, moderated or changed by administrative regulations which supplemented the legislation. Most importantly, however, their actualization was affected by the actions and interests of agents who were authorized to administer them and this, in turn, usually occurred in interaction with the agency of the governed – their common sense, organizations, actions, and counter-ideologies. The material structure of ideology, in other words, was invariably manifested through local practices and meanings even as it contributed to their formulations. In this way, the historical ethnography of Thomastown's labouring people becomes an integral part of the narrative about the formation of the British state in the nineteenth century. In Part II, I explore these themes through the workings of the economy, politics, and the law.

3. Realizing the Working Class: Political Economy and Culture

'Farming distress is great; ... shopkeepers and tradesmen ... share ... in the general calamity ... [Among] labouring manufacturers ... 2000 individuals have applied for relief.'

– Kilkenny *Moderator,* 23 January, 16 May 1816

'Emigration ... through Waterford continues to an extent unprecedented.'

– *Irish Independent,* 12 May 1827

'[A coroner's inquest] on the body of Margaret Burke who died ... by ... coming in contact with a ... threshing machine while at work for Mr Franks of Jerpoint Hill ... exonerated Mr Franks and his employees. Dr Sterling stated that death resulted from mortification of a fearfully broken limb.'

– Kilkenny *Moderator,* 2 December 1874

The end of the Napoleonic Wars in 1815 brought extensive economic depression to county Kilkenny, as elsewhere in Europe. Local witnesses appearing before a parliamentary inquiry in 1834 described the political economy of the previous few decades. They pointed out how the export market for agricultural commodities had expanded dramatically as, equally vividly, local living standards fell. Thomastown's labourers and artisans were entrapped in a dual process of impoverishment and differentiation, exploited as both workers and consumers. Subsistence crises invariably ensued, reproducing both the relationship among paternalism, deference, and dearth and dominant attitudes about workers and the labouring poor. People of all classes began to emigrate. A trickle became a flood after successive potato crops failed between 1845 and 1848. As part of this demographic revolution, the town's urban functions slowly altered, living standards began to rise, and, alongside these trends, marriage practices reinvigorated the status-class bound- aries that divided, connected, and united local people. The common- sense idea of who and what a labourer was changed in tandem. By 1884 it was realized that a worker was no longer a landless peasant but a wage labourer. All these experiences, in their turn, became entangled with views from the past and with how workers saw themselves, thus forming essential parts of the process of state formation in both its coercive and its hegemonic aspects.

The 'General Condition of the Poorer Classes ... since the Peace in 1815'

According to the evidence given by a group of local witnesses to the 1834 inquiry,[1] the condition of the poorer classes had clearly and visibly deteriorated since 1815. As grain prices declined and wool prices rose, and as rents to landlords were increased, farmers had been turning from labour-intensive tillage regimes to livestock (cattle, sheep). Land- lords also had begun to reorganize their estates by amalgamating farms so as to receive higher rents from fewer tenants who, in turn, were expected to apply modern techniques. From the landlords' view, fewer and larger grazier tenants, given current commodity prices, were more profitable than small tillage farms. As a result, high unemployment among the landless and newly landless ensued. One witness estimated that, whereas tillage land gave employment to twenty labourers for every 100 acres, pasture furnished employment for only one herdsman. This situation was exacerbated by an increasing number of labourers who, 'for want of provision for old age and infirmity, are induced to marry early.' Their high fertility was seen as adding to a growing, underem- ployed population. Estimates by witnesses as to what proportion of labourers in the Thomastown area had constant (full-time) work ranged from a low of 30 to a high of 50 per cent. With such a superabundance of labour and declining demand, wages had been falling since about 1820. Witnesses said that they were now half what they had been a decade before.

Witnesses also saw that local conditions were exacerbating the grow- ing poverty. A main source of the town's wealth since the thirteen cen- tury had been its role as head of navigation on the River Nore. By the late 1820s, the river had silted and local landlords, capitalists, and professionals had been unable to obtain state funding to remedy it. In any case, competition from the nearby River Barrow and Grand Canal had marginalized the Nore, as had the eclipse of the southeastern ports (Waterford, New Ross) by Dublin and Cork.[2] By the 1830s, too, the town had been deindustrialized. The years after 1770 had seen numerous, local manufactories emerge: rape-seed milling, lime quarries and kilns, starching, chandling, brewing, tanning, malting, and flour milling. By the mid-1820s, as a result of changing markets, the post-1815 depression, and the growth of other urban centres, only a tannery, several grist mills, and two modernized flour mills remained.[3]

In such a context, witnesses in 1834, like observers in 1802,[4] carefully distinguished the 'permanently employed' from the 'occasional' or casual workers who were 'most numerous in and near country towns.' The former included cottiers, farm servants, gentlemen's labourers, and millworkers. Casual labourers, in contrast, worked 'on the roads' when possible and during harvests. They ensured their survival by growing potatoes on 'conacre' ground rented from farmers.[5] The two were also distinguished by income, diet, housing, place of residence, and morals.

Witnesses estimated that, given Sundays and holidays, a labourer worked a maximum of 260 days a year. Wages averaged 6d. a day (the same as in 1802). The full-time labourer would therefore earn £6.10d. a year. Depending on where he lived, he might also earn between 15s. and £2 by fattening a pig or two for sale. In contrast, the cottier's income would be about £9 per year (£6.10.0 in wages, 10s. from his wife's earnings, and £2 from fattening pigs). The annual income of the casual labourer's household, however, was only about £7. This assumed that he had 180 days of work in the year (£5.5.0), that his wife and children earned £1 ('having more leisure and better opportunities to earn more than the family of the cottier'), and that, without a garden, he could not keep 'as many pigs nor on as good terms as the cottier' and thus would clear only 15s.[6]

Given such low incomes, potatoes had become 'the only food of a great part of the labourers. The cottier, and above all the chance labourer, hardly taste anything better than potatoes and milk.' Indeed, many occasional labourers 'ate their potatoes dry' while constant labourers and cottiers had milk and the occasional herring. The cottier might also buy weekly provisions, spending 5d. on soap, 3d. on tobacco (or 6d. if his wife smoked), and 6d. for milk, salt, and occasional herrings. He also would buy three ha'penny candles. Generally speaking, said witnesses, potato cultivation had 'increased considerably' because farmers as well as labourers were poorer and had 'to live more on potatoes, instead of the meal and other produce which they consumed formerly.' This was exacerbated by population increase 'and because more pigs are kept and more cattle stall fed (in great part on potatoes) than formerly.' In other words, the livestock market flourished as living standards fell. The local pig population also was thriving: there were 'very few cabins without one or two pigs' either in town or country. By the late 1830s, wandering pigs had become a public nuisance.[7]

Labourers were also differentiated by their housing, which, in turn, was related to where they lived. Casual workers tended to inhabit the town's outskirts whereas cottiers lived in rural areas. In the countryside, cabins usually had two rooms and averaged twenty to twenty-four feet in length and thirteen feet in breadth. In or near the town, a labourer's cabin usually had only one room and did not exceed fifteen feet in length (by thirteen feet in width). Often it was occupied by more than one family. The town also contained two-storey buildings, but those that housed labourers were usually let as lodgings to several families. The rent for cabins also depended on location as well as on the amount of land attached. If a farmer allowed a labourer to build a typical two-room cabin on a bit of ground, it would cost the labourer £4 for materials plus his own labour. The farmer would then charge a rent made up of his own rental cost plus £1 a year. If a labourer built his own cabin in the town, he would pay 1s. per foot as ground rent. However, rent for a built cabin without garden cost £2 in the town and £1 in the countryside. Witnesses added that the most squalid housing was often set at exorbitant rents by 'speculators who are for the most part shopkeepers in the town.'

All cabin walls were made of stone and mortar, roofs were straw, and floors were mud. In the Thomastown area, both chimneys and flues were reported to be far more frequent than in other areas and 'very few cabins were unprovided with some contrivance for the admission of light.' However, 'only the cottages of gentlemen's labourers [had] moveable sashes.' In the country, too, all cabins had pigsties attached whereas 'want of space' in town 'compelled [most] poor people to do without them, and to admit their pigs to the shelter of their only room.' Finally, 'privies were unknown [and] not only to the labouring class.'

As to morals and habits, the parish priest noted that labourers who lived in the countryside were 'best conducted, having less opportunity and less temptation to do wrong.' Clearly, the thirty licensed pubs in

Thomastown town and vicinity were seen as culpable here. At the same time, labourers 'were anxious to stand well' with both shopkeepers and farmers. The former sometimes extended credit for shop goods (although at 'exorbitant interest rates') whereas the latter controlled access to conacre. Overall, employer-worker relations were described as good. For labourers 'were very slow to quarrel with their employer,' said a large farmer, and 'I find that they have a great deal of forbearance and were not at all prone to vexatious litigation.' However, contention between farmers and labourers did emerge over the tally of days worked and/or when a farmer refused to pay the wages. In both cases, after 1828, the labourer might appeal to the petty sessions. Here, the magistrates/landlords often did not force the farmer to pay immediately if he was in distress and if he did not give 'vexatious opposition to the labourer's claim.' In turn, the same magistrates were slow to impose fines on labouring people for trespass. Much depended on the damage they did; and when the culprit was poor, the magistrates diminished the fine as far as discretionary power permitted.

In fact, the presence of resident landlords was positively regarded by the witnesses for other reasons. The 'number of labourers whom a person of wealth employs about his demesne withdraws so many from the usual competition for work, that the want of employment is much less felt in his neighbourhood.' Moreover, it was only on gentlemen's demesnes that the wives and daughters of labourers might be employed. For farmers hired women only casually during harvest and took on unmarried girls only as farms servants. The latter lived in the farmhouse and 'as soon as they get married, they are thrown completely on their own resources.'

Since the 1815 peace, then, labourers had been caught in, and were part of, a wide-ranging process of impoverishment. Low commodity prices and an expanding export market encouraged the consolidation of farms and the displacement of labour-intensive tillage. This was accompanied by local de-industrialization. A glut of labour ensued, exacerbated by a growing population and the eviction of smallholders who joined the ranks of the landless. Thomastown's labourers thus experienced falling wages and severe competition for work. They also encountered high rents for poor housing and for conacre ground. Their diet deteriorated even as they fattened more pigs for sale. Thus, the markets for labour, agricultural commodities, and consumables conjoined to create wage levels and consumption costs that left virtually no opportunity for accumulation or extrication. Indeed, it had reached the point whereby, 'even during harvest, wages do not rise ... all that the labourers gain by that season is that those who earn nothing at other periods of the year are then engaged; but there is no want of extra hands, and therefore no extra wages.' As to how causal workers survived when unemployed, witnesses were vague. Labourers were seen to manage either by the 'benevolence of the public' and/or their neighbours, or on what they had earned when working. Overall, labouring households were being dramatically exploited through the processes of production (low wages) and consumption (housing, conacre rents, shop goods).

Labourers experienced this exploitation not only in material ways. They also encountered it through the knowledge that those in other status-classes claimed to have of them. Although these perceptions ranged from disdain and/or disinterest on the one hand to concern and paternalism on the other, all witnesses saw the labourer as wasteful, impetuous, and ignorant of his/her condition. How witnesses differed was in whether they located the causes in the intrinsic nature of labourers or in the conditions in which workers were entrapped (Case 3.1).

Case 3.1: Three Voices from 1834

Robert Cantwell and Thomas O'Keefe, large-scale Catholic farmers with long-term leases: 'If the labourer had employment, or any fixed means of obtaining a livelihood, he would not become reckless, as at present.'

Sydenham Davis, landlord: 'Labourers have no knowledge of spending the time usefully.'

William O'Connor, retailer and activist in the O'Connell repeal movement:'I am quite convinced that many of the labourers get married under the idea that they cannot make their condition worse than it is. I have reasoned with some poor people who were about to take wives, and I could hardly persuade them that they were doing what would be likely to add to their poverty; more than one has replied to me, "At any rate, if it comes to the worst, the wife can take to begging."'

The two labourers at the 1834 inquiry, David Ryan and John Brophy, spoke hardly at all. One of Ryan's minor asides, in showing the powerlessness of labour, perhaps explains why they said little: either they were overwhelmed by the company or found it pointless to intercede. A labourer's cabin, said Ryan, was 'kept in repair either by the landlord or tenant according to agreement. Sometimes the landlord undertakes it, but puts it off so long that the cottier strives to do it himself, although he knows he will never get any allowance for it.' No one at the inquiry, however, was concerned to address this lack of tactical leverage. Indeed, a comment by local solicitor James McEnnery suggests that neither he nor the others understood labourers at all. However, the fault for this lay with workers because, according to McEnnery, labourers 'are ... very unwilling to discover their real circumstances, and look with suspicion on any one who seeks to inquire into them.' Yet the fact that the local magistrates were becoming concerned with public health and such nuisances as pigs on the road, and also the fact that Parliament was concerning itself with the poorer classes, suggest that such inquiries were to continue.

The Quality of Charitable Relief, 1840

According to Thomastown's Catholic curate in 1834, the population of the town had fallen by 300 since the 1831 census. Nevertheless, 'there is as much want of employment here as anywhere else.' Moreover, because the supply of potatoes, 'the principal food of the labouring classes,' is entirely dependent on the produce of one year and, because of its bulkiness, almost of one place, 'if the crop fails in any one year, distress is inevitable to the extent of the failure.'[8] Six years later, such a failure occurred in the vicinity of Kilkenny city, exacerbated by the collapse of the textile industry. The response, as reported in the Kilkenny *Journal*, a Catholic and populist newspaper, showed clearly that paternalism and deference had been reproduced through time (Case 3.2).

Case 3.2: The Subsistence Crisis of 1840 in Kilkenny City
At first, in January 1840, the labouring poor seemed to be facing their annual winter hardship and, in typical fashion, the editor noted that it was 'gratifying to see the resident ... gentry of the county ... coming forward with ... true benevolence.' Blankets and flannel were donated and, because both were 'of home manufacture, the donors have conferred a twofold benefit in the way of charity and employment.' A week later, a Poor Fund Committee in the city reported that it had £58 in its coffers and would spend £20 to buy potatoes to be retailed 'at prime cost' to the poor, with the remainder for purchasing coal and straw 'to be dispensed in small quantities at half price.' As a result, said the editor, 'many are thereby saved from perishing of cold and damp.' However, he continued, there still were 'hundreds of families so poor that they cannot avail themselves of even the

*benefits of charitable distribution ... Hear this ye wealthy and great who draw
your incomes from this impoverished city and country and who ... never bestowed
a thought upon either, but upon occasions of your rent becoming due ... [Such]
heartless men [did] not even ... answer letters praying for aid, respectfully
addressed to them by gentlemen as respectable and certainly more humane than
themselves.' A few days later, perhaps in response, notices were published of donations from various 'excellent' gentlemen who 'recognise the just principle that
property has its duties as well as its rights.'*

    *Two months later, the crisis had not abated. At another meeting, donations
were received and discussion ensued on what provisions to buy. The editor
deplored the 'distress ... amongst the labouring classes owing principally to the
high price and dearth of provisions ... whilst ships are freighted with our produce
to feed the stranger ... What is to be done with those miserable beings who cannot
afford to purchase at any price, the smallest quantity of food? ... In this class we
... include ... discharged workmen who without any fault of their masters or their
own are ... in a most deplorable state of destitution.' A month later, as well as its
provisions shop, the committee began to give out free food. Such 'gratuitous relief'
was given only 'upon the most rigorous application.'*

    *By the end of August, the 'condition of the poor, as the season advanced'
became 'more supportable.' Still, 'able-bodied men may be every day seen loitering
about ... scarcely covered by a threadbare garment and their faces exhibiting all
the appearances of want. Our pseudo philanthropists will prescribe emigration as
a remedy.' But this 'avoid[s] a lesser evil to plunge into a greater one – from a
land of temporal wants to a country of spiritual destitution. Such is the state of
our poor.'*[9]

According to the *Journal*'s editor, the crisis came out of the dependence
of labourers on the potato, the decline of industry, the export of agricultural commodities, and the demands of some landlords for their rents.
Yet 'benevolent, resident gentry' had donated locally produced blankets
and funds to buy provisions. They contrasted starkly with 'heartless and
wealthy' landlords who donated nothing. Interestingly, farmers and
retailers were entirely omitted from this model. In their turn, labourers
as recipients had to purchase provisions, albeit at pre-crisis prices. 'Gratuitous relief' was given only as the crisis persisted and if individuals could
prove need and show that they were not responsible for their condition.
In this common-sense world-view, the idea of private property was
unquestioned although its ownership was seen as conferring definite
obligations. The presence of labourers and 'poor people' was equally

unavoidable: as the propertyless converse of the propertied and as the recipients of their charity. What the moral outrage of the *Journal*'s editor addressed, therefore, was that such labouring and/or poor people could not be adequately fed in times of unwarranted unemployment or crop failure. That there were those who were so vulnerable at all was to be deplored and alleviated but not altered. Indeed, the idea that an individual might emigrate from the dearth and crises was condemned as jeopardizing his/her spiritual needs as a Catholic.

Space and Class: Thomastown Town and Country in the Early 1840s

In 1845 forty-one retailers, about twenty-four notables (capitalists and professionals), and one or two farmers lived in the town, which, in 1841, had a population of 2,335. This meant that artisans and labourers formed the majority of the population. According to the 1841 census, they were concentrated outside agriculture. Of the 507 households enumerated according to whether they were in 'agricultural pursuits' (as farmers, cottiers, or labourers), in 'manufacturing and trade,' or in 'other pursuits' (as owners, workers, self-employed), half the townspeople (49.1 per cent) said they were in manufacturing/trade and 18.1 per cent were in other pursuits. This large, non-agricultural, labouring population was differentiated by living standard and residential location.

Thomastown Town
The town itself had long been divided by the River Nore. On the northern side, in the sixteen acres that comprised the townland[10] of Thomastown, was a core of four short streets (Logan, Low, Market, and Pipe). Most buildings here had two storeys but a few, backing on the river along Low Street, had three.[11] In 1845 all but five of the town's retail shops were located in these four core streets. Each retailing family lived above its shop while, behind the buildings, was a patchwork of outhouses, storehouses, bake houses, cow and pig sheds, yards, and tiny gardens. The main commercial street was Market Street (19 metres wide by 107 metres long). In 1845 it contained eight private residences; eleven retail establishments (five pub-groceries, two groceries, a hardware shop, two draperies, and one general shop), and the shops of six artisan-vendors (a baker, a butcher, a carpenter, two bootmakers, and a saddler). Market Street also was the locale for weekly, open-air pig and poultry markets.

Extending from the southeast corner of the core, and to the roads

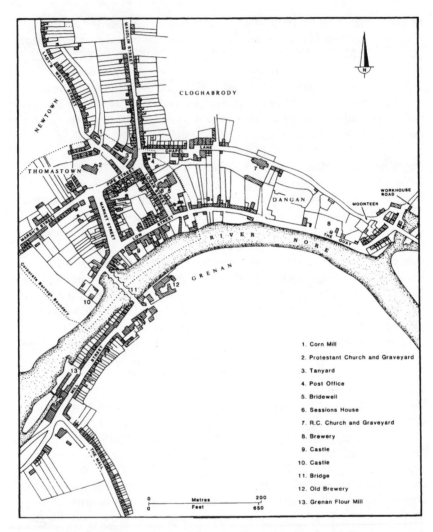

Map 2: The town of Thomastown, c. 1850

that led to New Ross and Graigue, was the Quay. There, river barges once had tied up near warehouses. In 1845 the Quay had a pub and a grocery. At the southwest corner, and across the bridge over the Nore, lay Mill Street, leading to the Waterford road. In that street was Grennan Mills and, off a side road, the Island Mill – the two recently modernized flour mills. Mill Street, and particularly the Mall leading off from it, was lined with houses occupied by workers. Also on Mill Street were three pub-groceries and the workshops of a blacksmith, a saddler, and a tailor. Other streets leading out of the core to the west and north (Marsh's, Ladywell, Maudlin, and Chapel Lane/Moonteen) contained the small houses of labourers but no retail shops. Some of the labourers worked in the tannery, located on Ladywell.

Clearly the core streets comprised the commercial centre. On the roads leading to it were industrial properties and, associated with these, residential space for labourers. The implications of this can be seen from the first property valuation carried out in the Thomastown area in 1845.[12] It shows how the organization of space in the town reflected the class structure. Table 3.1 gives a schematic diagram of the town, beginning with its four commercial streets ('core') and then the streets leading out from them. The general value of houses on those streets are inserted. The four core streets had the best housing, the secondary streets directly connected to them had housing that was of less value, and the houses on third-order streets continued this decline.

What features typified houses of different value? For town tenements, the 1845 valuators kept notes or 'House Books' in which they described, in more detail than did their published valuation, the nature of tenements. Houses for which the rent was less than £4, and/or which were valued at less than £3, had only a single descriptive remark in the 'House Books': 'one house exempt.' In the argot of the period, these would be 'cabbins.' They were of too low quality to have any value for tax or rating purposes. Into this category fell two-thirds of the houses in the town (Table 3.2). Insofar as this can be used as an index of standard of living, it suggests the pervasiveness of poverty among the majority of people at the time, that is, of labourers.

The extensiveness of the poverty, and of poor labourers, meant that the valuators left no descriptions of any of the houses in Ladywell Lane, most of the houses in Marsh's Street, Chapel Lane, Mall, and so on. However, for those living in the better houses, usually artisans, some notion of relative living standards can be gleaned (Table 3.3). Edward Murphy, a bootmaker in Market Street, had a house valued at £4.5.0. It was described as 'an old house with roof uneven and expensive to keep staunched.' It had 'but little yard and no entrance except through house. Has a lease [and] ... pays £5 a year rent for this and next house.' In that next house lived Patrick Connors, carpenter. The house, valued at £3, was 'old, roof uneven, expensive to keep staunched; has but a very small yard with entrance through the house. Yearly rent £4, has no

Table 3.1: Location and rentable value of town housing

Town Core Street	Second-order Street (& townland)**	Third-order Street (& townland)	Fourth-order Street (& townland)
Market Street (£5+)*			
Logan Street (£3+)	Maudlin (Newtown) (£1+)	Maudlin Street (Cloghabrody) (–£1)	
		Chapel Lane (Cloghabrody) (–£1)	Moonteen (Dangan) (–£1)
Pipe Street (£3+)	Marsh's (Thomastown) (–£1)		
	Ladywell (Thomastown) (£3+)	Ladywell Street (Newtown) (£1)	
		Ladywell Lane (Thomastown) (–£1)	
Low Street (£3+)	Low (Cloghabrody) (£2+)	The Quay (Dangan) (–£1)	
[bridge]	Mill Street (Grennan) (£2+)	The Mall (Grennan) (–£1)	

Source: Griffith's Valuation, County Kilkenny, 1849.

*Valuators assigned a rentable value to each house. The valuation that I have assigned to each street was done according to the fact that 65 per cent of the occupied houses in those streets was of the value indicated. The cut-off of 65 per cent was selected simply because it is a clear majority and reflects the dominant character of the street.

**Second- and third-order town streets were often extensions of an earlier-order street as these continued beyond the boundaries of Thomastown townland. They were in the townlands of Cloghabrody, Newtown, Grennan, and Dangan.

Table 3.2: Property valuations and the nature of town housing

	House Value:					
	1s.–19s	£1–£1.19.0	£2–£2.19.0	£3–£3.19.0	£4–£4.19.0	£5+
No. of Town Houses: (*n* = 365)	98 26.8%	103 28.2%	42 11.5%	38 10.4%	19 5.2%	65 17.8%
		243 (66.6%)				

lease.' A larger house than both was the one lived in by Matthew Kenny, a painter, on Pipe Street. The house was valued at £3.15.0 and it, too, was 'an old house not in good repair. Has no yard. Pays £6 a year which is considered high.' Just up from Kenny was a mason, Nicholas Davis, on Ladywell, in a house valued at £3.10.0. It, too, was 'old and roof sunk and not in good repair. Has no rear yard. Rent £3 a year without a lease.' Across the river, in Mill Street, lived sawyer Patrick Dawson in a house valued at £2.10.0. It 'was rather old and roof not in good repair and very poorly fit inside.' It had only a 'very confined yard with no entrance except through house.' In contrast was the house of Daniel Delaney, tailor, also on Mill Street. Delaney's house and outbuildings were valued at £7.10.0. The 'house [was] pretty well built and in good repair. Office also in good order. A small yard with entrance through dwelling. Occupant built the concerns himself.'

Generally, the sizes of these houses corresponded to the descriptions that had been given to the commissioners at the 1834 parliamentary inquiry. A cottier's cabin in 1834, with between 260 and 312 square feet,[13] more or less corresponded to a town artisan's cabin a decade later. However, a town labourer's cabin, at 165 square feet, must have been wretched indeed.

At the other extreme were houses occupied by the most prominent people in the town's commercial life, such as tannery owner Ryan, millowner Bull, and merchant Nugent. Ryan's house on Logan Street was described as 'substantially built and furnished inside and in good repair.' Bull's house on Mill Street, unusual as a single-storey dwelling, was 'neat ... well-built and furnished inside and in good repair.' Nugent's house, at the very end of Mill Street, was 'a gentleman's residence in a nice situation but rather too close to the town. House substantially built and furnished inside.'[14]

What emerges is a portrait of a highly differentiated town, with its

Table 3.3: Square footage of selected town houses, 1845

Occupier Artisans:	Street	Occupation	Square feet [Dimensions]	Immediate lessor
P. Connor	Market	carpenter	312 [12 × 26 × 18]	Edward Murphy, bootmaker
M.Kenny	Pipe	painter	342 [16.6 × 20.6 × 17]	Richard Sullivan, merchant*
E. Murphy	Market	bootmaker	380 [14.6 × 26 × 18]	James Geraghty, landlord*
P. Dawson	Mill	sawyer	408 [17 × 24 × 17]	Anthony Nugent, merchant
N. Davis	Ladywell	mason	475 [21.6 × 22 × 17]	Elisabeth Ryan, currier
D. Delaney	Mill	tailor	543 [23 × 23.6 × 21.6]	Anthony Nugent, merchant
Notables:***				
Ryan	Logan	tanner	888 [37 × 24 × 26]	Earl of Carrick, landlord
Bull	Mill	flour miller	1,092 [42 × 26 × 12]	James Ball, banker*
Nugent	Mill	merchant	1,504 [47.6 × 31.6 × 26]	William H. Greene, landlord*

*The lessor was not resident in the locality.

***Notables' include professionals and capitalists.

Sources: Griffith's Valuation (1849) and House Books (1845).

everyday class and status-class categories manifested in housing and in the allocation of inhabited space. However, it also is important to recognize that differentiation had led to gradations within classes and status-classes. Examples can be taken from among the above-mentioned artisans whose entrepreneurial abilities in acquiring and improving property varied considerably. Tailor Delaney's impressive concern, which he built himself, contrasted starkly with sawyer Dawsons's poor furnishings and ill-repaired roof. In the case of bootmaker Murphy, such difference was the result of intra-class exploitation as Murphy managed to pay virtually all of his own rent simply by sub-letting a second house to carpenter Connors.

Indeed, rents were often higher than the rateable value assigned to the houses.[15] This fact and, more generally, who the lessors were, had been of some concern to the parliamentary commissioners in 1834. It was noted at that time that conditions were not everywhere the same. In the town of Inistioge, for example, there were no 'filthy and miserable lanes which branch in every direction' as in the town of Graigue. In the latter place, these lanes were lined with cabins inhabited by occasional labourers who paid 'exorbitant rents to speculators who are for the most part shopkeepers in the town.'[16] Thomastown witnesses, too, generally assumed that retailers were the main lessors, reaping high rents for squalid housing. Said landlord Sydenham Davis: 'It is in towns that we hear most frequently of the canting of labourers' goods. There the landlords of cabins, being generally shopkeepers, cannot make use of the labour which the [rural] tenant may be very willing to give in payment of his debt.'[17]

Such assumption about Thomastown's retailers was in part true, at least by the 1845 valuation (Table 3.4). However, retailers by no means comprised the majority of lessors or let the majority of houses and town tenements. Instead, it was labourers themselves who, after landed proprietors, were numerically the most active in the urban property market. Indeed, if artisans are included, then labourers and artisans together made up more than half the town's lessors in 1845. Admittedly, these lessors controlled only slightly more than a quarter of the town tenements. Yet, though the number of tenements rented out by each labourer/artisan was relatively small and although such property-letting workers were only a minority, they were exploiting others of their ilk through the housing market. Moreover, most of the tenements let by labourers and artisans (70.9 per cent) were located in those town streets that had the poorest housing. The tenants of labourers and artisans

Table 3.4: Lessors of town tenements/houses in Thomastown*

	Number of lessors	No. of tenements let	Average no. let	% of total
Labourers	34	92	2.7	20.1
Artisans	13	35	2.7	7.7
Shopkeepers	17	53	3.1	11.6
'Notables'**	10	90	9.9	19.7
Landed proprietors	6	167	27.8	36.5
Farmers	3	20	6.7	4.4
Total:	83	457		100.0%

*Tenements included gardens, offices, yards, building ground and, occasionally, ruins as well as houses.
**Notables included manufacturers and professionals.

were thus most likely to be other labourers, and probably the poorest ones.

All this meant that patterns of exploitation, as actualized through access to housing, gardens, yards, and outbuildings (the latter crucial for pig rearing), created structural divisions among labouring people and artisans at the same time that it reinforced the fact that access to such properties were, in the main, controlled by those of superior status-classes. What was the situation outside the town – in the so-called peri-urban townlands and in the countryside?

The Peri-Urban Area and the Countryside
The five peri-urban townlands of Dangan, Cloghabrody, Grenan, Jerpoint West, and Newtown had long been linked to the urban economy. They abutted the townland of Thomastown and, indeed, some town streets continued unmarked and uninterrupted out of the town and into these peri-urban townlands. These peri-urban areas also contained industrial sites and land. The former provided jobs for some of the labouring class; the latter provided farm land but also, importantly, opportunities for middlemen to sub-let house sites and/or cabins to labourers and to rent 'town fields' to wealthier town residents who wished to pasture a horse or a cow or two nearby. Because of the ways in which these townlands were linked to both the urban space and the town economy, the nature of differentiation within them reflects something of urban life and can be compared with rural townlands at the time (Table 3.5 and Map 3).

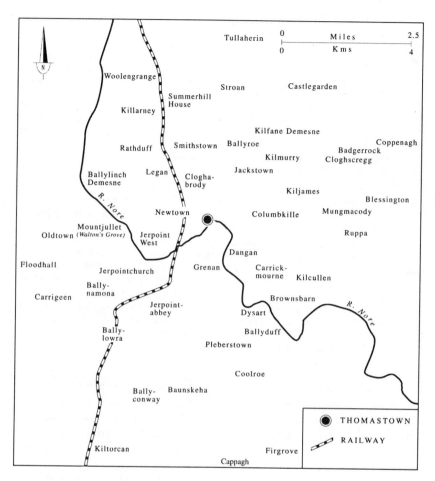

Map 3: The locality of Thomastown

From Table 3.5, we again see the numerical preponderance of labouring people in the urban economy: in peri-urban townlands, more than
half the people inhabited either a house (47.7 per cent) or a house with
just a garden (4.7 per cent). They depended on selling their labour. In
contrast, in the rural townlands that comprise the contemporary Catholic parish of Thomastown, only a third of the occupiers were landless.
However, in both peri-urban and rural townlands, another third of the
population were smallholders, and they were becoming increasingly

Table 3.5: Property-holding in peri-urban and rural townlands: Thomastown parish, 1845

Type of holder/occupier:	Rural townlands:		Peri-Urban townlands:*		Emic category
House only	23.6%	[129]	47.7%	[51]	Labourer
−1 acre	8.0	[44]	4.7	[5]	Cottier
.1–5.9 valued acres**	23.2	[127]	22.4	[24]	Smallholder
6-9.9 valued acres	7.9	[43]	8.4	[9]	Smallholder
10–19.9 valued acres	16.3	[89]	6.5	[7]	Farmer
20+ valued acres	21.0	[115]	10.3	[11]	Farmer
Total:	100.0% [547]		100.0% [107]		

*Occupiers who lived on named town streets that extended into these townlands are excluded here. They are included in Tables 3.2 and 3.4.
**Townlands vary according to the quality of land and the resulting value of agricultural output. Absolute sizes of holdings are therefore a poor way to compare sizes of farms across townlands. Such variation was recognized in 1845 through a money value that Griffith's valuators assigned to all holdings in all townlands. For example, the land in Badgerock townland was valued at £0.15 per acre; in Newtown it was valued at £0.96. Six acres of Badgerock were equivalent, therefore, to one acre in Newtown. 'Valued acreage' is the number of acres held by an individual multiplied by the value per acre which was assigned to the townland in 1845. The use of 'valued acres' makes all holdings, everywhere in the parish, comparable to each other.

impoverished as a result of the market (low commodity prices, high rents) and landlords' efforts to rationalize their estates. The extent of poverty in both locales, apparent from the low rateable value of most of the buildings (Table 3.6), is therefore unsurprising. Four-fifths of the housing in the countryside and peri-urban townlands was valued under £3. This was worse than in the town.

Who were the lessors? Over 260 holdings were sub-let by middlemen in thirty-nine rural and five peri-urban townlands. Over 60 per cent of these sub-let holdings were houses without ground or houses with a garden (that is, less than an acre of land). In the peri-urban townlands, only twenty-four tenements were sub-let, all by urban-dwellers.[18] Of these, a mason and a labourer rented out one and two houses respectively. The remaining lessors were retailers, capitalists, and professionals. Clearly, labourers and artisans had been constrained in extending their petty-property speculations into the peri-urban areas. The same was true in rural townlands where only ten intermediate lessors themselves held less

Table 3.6: Valuations of buildings,* 1845

| | Number of buildings in: | | | | |
Building value	Rural townlands			Peri-urban townlands	
1s.–19s.	191	40.3% ⎫		62	47.7% ⎫
£1–£1.19.0	124	26.2 ⎬ 77.9%		32	24.6 ⎬ 80.0%
£2–£2.19.0	54	11.4 ⎭		10	7.7 ⎭
£3–£3.19.0	40	8.4		5	3.9
£4–£4.19.0	21	4.4		3	2.3
£5 +	44	9.3		18	13.8
Total:	474	100.0%		133	100.0%

*Houses were not separately valued in 1845. Rather, the total value of all buildings (sheds, offices, etc.) on each tenement was given. This did not create a problem in assessing town housing (Table 3.2) because outbuildings were small and relatively few in number. In rural areas, however, outbuildings were more common. But because their quality and number increased with the size of the farm, at the smallholding level of the hierarchy, with few and small outbuildings, the total value given would have closely reflected the quality of the house itself

than two 'valued acres' of land. These ten were therefore either landless labourers or labourers with 'a bit of ground.' However, seven of these ten let housing in a single townland (Jerpoint Abbey), thus suggesting that their activities were part of a particular landlord's management strategy. In contrast, the remainder of sub-lessors in rural townlands, over 90 per cent, were farmers and smallholders. In fact, they were mainly farmers: over 80 per cent held more than ten 'valued acres.'

Thus, the urban pattern of intra-(status)class exploitation, whereby labourers and artisans sub-let property to others of their kind, was hardly an option in peri-urban and rural townlands. Moreover, apart from a small proportion of smallholders, some of whom let housing to labourers, stark lines separated the landed (farmers) from the landless (labourers); and it was the former who very clearly controlled the housing of the latter in the countryside.

The Condition of Labouring People after 1815

By the mid-1840s, the relation between space and class in the town was clear; so, too, was the numerical predominance of non-farm labourers in the town and local economy. The allocation of space, the structure of property holding, and the value of housing in both rural and urban areas also illustrated that both differentiation and impoverishment formed part of the economic depression which followed the 1815 peace and which was brought about by both local and international conditions. Thomastown people of all classes saw or experienced the intensifying poverty and had varying explanations for it. Yet the pattern of house-letting in 1845 also suggested that at least some artisans and labourers were distinguishable in terms of individual entrepreneurial ability even though outside observers were more inclined to see labourers as feckless and as contributing to their own poverty through a lack of education, suspiciousness, and reckless early marriage. Thus, when a major subsistence crisis struck the Kilkenny city area in 1840, the long-held view of the labourer as a natural malingerer structured the nature of relief. This same relief effort showed, too, that the relation of dearth, deference, and paternalism had been reproduced since at least the turn of century and that farmers and retailers remained uninvolved. What had since emerged, however, was a public and vitriolic critique from the Catholic bourgeousie of those who, while extracting profit from their properties, failed in their local paternal obligations. Equally excoriated were those who would weaken the Catholic faith by offering emigration as a solution to the economic situation. Yet massive emigration did ensue after 1845. Its effect on living standards, on class formation and boundaries, and on common sense was profound.

The Demographic Revolution and Changing Consumption Patterns

The population of Thomastown Catholic parish in 1861 was 59 per cent of what it was in 1841. By 1881, it was 46 per cent. The population of the town, in 1871, was half of what it had been in 1841.[19] Over that same period, the same census data show that living standards rose.

Consumption
Household size declined: in the town, the average number of people per house decreased from 5.5 in 1841 to 4.8 in 1881. Housing, too, gradually improved in a process by which the worst housing was most rapidly abandoned. Thus, between 1841 and 1861, 48 per cent of third- and fourth-class housing in the town disappeared and 56 per cent in the

rural area.[20] By 1861, over two-thirds of town housing was of first- and second-class quality, as was 40 per cent of rural housing.[21] Alongside this change was the fact that house servants formed an increasing proportion of the urban population: from 4 per cent in 1841 to 6 per cent by 1861. Literacy also increased. In 1837, eighty children were attending schools funded by the Earl of Carrick and the Protestant rector while three private schools in the town had another 230 children.[22] Thus, 57 per cent of people over the age of five were literate, according to the 1841 census. In that year, the new National School for both girls and boys was two years old. By 1851, the illiteracy rate was down to 39 per cent and, by 1881, to 29 per cent. Increased literacy typified both rural and urban locales and was particularly dramatic among women. Their illiteracy rates were halved in the 40 years after 1841, thus closing the gap between men and women.

Over this same period, the number of people per retail shop declined. In 1846 the parish had 181 people per town shop; in 1884 it had 93 people. In 1846, twenty shops sold groceries; in 1884 there were twenty-five. People were clearly buying more of what they consumed, and they had more cash to do so in part because wages were rising. Between the early 1820s and 1845, 6d. per day was what most farm labourers could expect, or about 3s. a week, *if* working full-time for a six-day week. As emigration began to cause a labour shortage, wages began to climb. By 1870, the *weekly* wage for a farm labourer in county Kilkenny was 5s.7d.[23] By 1880, on the farm attached to Grennan Mills, workers were being paid 9s.2d. per week and, by 1886, 11s. For workers in the mill itself, a weekly wage of 7s.6d. in 1873 had also become 11s. by 1886. For artisans in the mill, wages reached 28s. by 1886.[24]

Equally important was that local market prices remained remarkably stable (Table 3.7). In the case of potatoes, major price increases occurred during the 1846–9 famine but, by the end of 1849, prices had come down to about a penny a stone higher than pre-famine levels. Prices over the next decades rose only moderately, going up, at most, about three pence while fluctuating in particular years according to season and local productivity. In the autumn of 1865, the price was lower than more than a decade earlier. In May 1876 the price was the same as in 1853. Only between 1877 and 1880, a time of depression and hardship, did potato prices surpass 1846–9 levels. By that time, however, wages had risen considerably. Then, in the autumn of 1881, prices fell to previous levels and stayed there.

Table 3.7: Potato, flour, and pig prices, 1842–82

| | Potatoes* (per stone) | | Flour* ('thirds') | | Pig prices*** | | |
	May	November	May	November	Piglets (pair)	Stores (each) June/July	Fat Pigs (cwt.)
1842	4d.	3d.	22s.6d.	19s.	–	–	–
1852	5d.	5d.	22s.	20s.	–	[not given]	–
1853	6d.	–			–	–	–
1862	6d.–8½d.	5d.–6½d.	25s.	22s.6d.	–	–	–
1865	8d.–10d.	3½d.–5d.	20s.–23s.	20s.–24s.	26s.–45s.	45s.–63s.	55s.–56s.
1872	7d.–8d.	8d–9d.	26s.–28s.	27s.–29s.	–	–	65s.
1876	6d.	–					
1878	[record levels]**	–	28s.–30s.	24s.6d.	28s.–36s.	44s.–48s.	–
1882	[1845 levels]**	–	30s	24s.–26s.	24s.–40s.	45s.–58s.	90s.–120s.
1884	[pre-1845 levels]**	–	24s.–26s.	20s.–22s.	–	–	–

*Kilkenny Market prices, as reported in the Kilkenny *Moderator* and Kilkenny *Journal.* The type of potato was the 'champion,' which was neither the coarsest nor cheapest at the time. 'Thirds' was the cheapest, fourth-grade flour.

**Prices after 1876 were given per barrel, but the number of stones per barrel of potatoes is not known. The price per barrel in 1882 was 6s.6d.–7s.3d. (in May) and 9s.6d.–10s. (in November). This was virtually the same as the 1845 price when prices also were given per barrel (6s.6d.–7s. in both May and November). The 1882 prices were not an aberration. They were, for example, higher than the prices in 1883 (November) and in 1884 and 1885.

***Thomastown Market Prices were reported in the Kilkenny *Moderator* and *Journal.*

The long-term stability of local potato prices, and rising wages, allowed working people a more diversified diet. Flour and bread became increasingly accessible, especially as the price of flour rose only slightly through time and then, in the 1880s, began to fall. As the use of potatoes for human consumption declined, more were available for feeding pigs. In Thomastown market, certainly after 1865 when pig prices were occasionally reported, the cost of piglets declined while prices for fattened pigs almost doubled. More workers reared more pigs as a result. In 1852 the Thomastown area had 381 pig holders who held less than an acre of land.[25] More than two decades later, in 1874, after the population had declined by almost half, 307 landless households reared pigs.[26]

Relief and Poverty: Belief and Practice

More cash, increased retail purchases, and diversified consumption were accompanied after 1860 by growing access to emergency help from the local, public purse during times of distress. In 1850 Thomastown town became the seat of a 'union' under the 1838 Poor Law. A work-house and fever hospital were built. The premise of the legislators at the time was that all able-bodied adults should work. If they could not or, worse, would not, they could receive public assistance only by divesting themselves of all possessions, however meagre, and by entering the workhouse. The underlying common sense was familiar: to provide the able-bodied with unfettered aid encouraged idleness and malingering, the conditions to which workers were prone. The workhouse was the state's solution for both poverty and the inclinations of the poor. A coercive, regimented life in the house ensued: uniform clothing, poor food, unpaid compulsory work, gender separation, punishment for rule infractions, an in-house school which segregated workhouse children, and no egress.

Through such coercive practice, and in association with rising living standards, moral stigma slowly came to accrue to poverty – a stigma unalleviated by the notion, common earlier among local gentlemen, that one could be poor but 'deserving.' Even among labourers, as the idea of an accidental and blameless poverty persisted, stigma and shame came to accrue to those who were workhouse inmates and, thus, 'paupers.' That no one but the most destitute or desperate would enter the workhouse proved the point. Thus, the numbers admitted remained relatively stable through time. During 1854, for example, 262 people were admitted; in 1864, 363; and in 1874, 278. The majority were elderly and infirm, widows and children, and the sick. Most left after a short stay; some remained.[27]

The workhouse was funded by local rates on property which were paid by landlords, capitalists, tenant-farmers, and, occasionally, retailers. The rates were set, and the workhouse administered, by a Board of Guardians which was partly elected and partly appointed from among local ratepayers. That the board's affairs were overseen by a Local Government Board in Dublin introduced, as well, bureaucratic agency into the provision of relief and into the education of both the poor and those who were their guardians. However, as ratepayers, board members were mainly concerned with how their actions would affect their rates. Workhouse conditions invariably reflected the resulting parsimony.[28] So, too, did the amount of 'outdoor relief.' Made up of a few pence to get families through the weeks when temporary illness or particularly harsh conditions meant that the breadwinner could not work, only 396 people received outdoor relief in 1853 and only 253 in 1854. However, after 1861, numbers began to escalate dramatically: over 2,000 (including children) in 1867, more than 4,000 in 1874, and over 5,000 in 1885. In March 1853 the guardians distributed £1.19.5 in outdoor relief. This was the costliest month of that year. Three decades later, in 1884, the lowest monthly pay-out was £17.18s. Why did this increase occur? As living standards rose after 1850, so, too, did ideas about what was an acceptable level of poverty as well as an acceptable standard of living. To provide the poor and indigent with this higher level increasingly cost more even as prices stayed relatively stable.[29] It was soon clear to guardians that giving the able-bodied a few pennies was far cheaper than housing and feeding them and their families in the workhouse.

The Local Economy

These demographic, lifestyle, and cognitive changes after 1845 reflected a slow shift in the wider economy as it articulated with local life. According to the 1841 census, almost 33 per cent of the town's population was engaged in 'agricultural pursuits.' By 1861, it was 8 per cent. This meant that urban-based, casual farm labourers were emigrating and that those casuals who stayed were more likely, by 1861, to work in the industrial and service sectors. Signs of this change had been noted by witnesses at the 1834 inquiry. A decade later, their views proved prescient. In 1847, according to the first agricultural census, labour-intensive tillage land still formed 84 per cent of the land in use in the Thomastown area. It dropped to 38 per cent in 1851 and to 34 per cent in 1854. This replacing of tillage land with pasture diminished the need for labour. The situation was made worse in Thomastown because farmers turned to dry cattle and sheep for export rather than to labour-intensive dairying.[30]

Thus, the export of both people and livestock expanded rapidly after 1841, aided by the Waterford-Kilkenny Railway which connected to the Dublin-Limerick line. Funded largely by English capital, the line from Kilkenny reached Thomastown in 1848.[31] After it opened to Waterford in 1854, cattle bought at Thomastown's fair could be sold in London the next day. This also meant that imported consumer goods could be brought more cheaply to the town's shops. Particularly important was fuel. Because the locality had virtually no turf bogs, turf and coal were expensive. As a result, said landlord Davis in 1834, 'a fire is seldom to be seen in a labourer's house, except at meal times, for ... boiling his potatoes. They are driven to all kinds of shifts to get fuel ... They collect brambles and furze, and underwood ... Strange to say, trees are very seldom cut or stripped of their branches by the poor for fuel ... In summer the children ... gather cow-dung and horse-dung, which they dry and burn.' The town's apothecary added that the 'insufficiency of fuel contributes to the early decline of the labourer's health and strength. The dampness, and much of the aspect of misery in their houses, are attributable to the want of fire; and a proof is ... the great number of old persons who are partially disabled by rheumatism.' Father Cody added that 'in visiting the sick poor,' he found them to 'suffer greatly from want of fire.' Thus, 'when charitable subscriptions are made during a severe winter, it has been found necessary to lay out more in the purchase of coals than food.'[32]

Higher wages, more cash, and better transport alleviated the fuel shortage and improved the health of workers. Even in 1834, it was recognized that poor living standards affected their productivity. Farmer Cantwell observed that, 'in summer, when potatoes are scarce and dear, if I hire a man for an odd day's work, I find that he is by no means equal to the cottier who has been always living with me.' The only reason for this is 'that the one has his bellyful every day, while the other, when out of employment, had not ... more than one, or at most two, scanty meals in 24 hours.' A land agent added that 'the improvement about a labourer who has obtained permanent employment is very evident. The first thing he does is to get a good stock of clothing for himself and family.' Most importantly, 'employment also ... render[s] him more peaceable and moral; in fact, he knows that if he were not well conducted, he would not be retained.'[33] In other words, higher living standards and better health were seen to improve the labourer. They also heightened the expectations that employers had of his productivity, demeanour, and behaviour.

Thus, the demographic, lifestyle, and cognitive changes, as well as the expansion of the town's retailing sector and its new administrative and transport functions, articulated with a changed agricultural regime to alter the occupations of local people. Farming still provided indirect employment – for artisans (blacksmiths, masons, carpenters) and for retailers who not only sold agricultural inputs but also depended on the custom of farming households for non-agricultural necessities. Yet it was, and had been for a long time, working people who were the majority in both town and country. In the 1901 census, over 13 per cent of those who gave their occupation were artisans. Almost 52 per cent were labourers and, of these, 58 per cent were non-agricultural.[34] For them, it was the town's industrial and service sectors that were central.

In 1845, along with the two modern, export-oriented flour mills (Grennan Mills, the Island Mill), the town's industrial sector contained three smaller flour mills (Little Mill, Dangan Mill, and Jerpoint Mill) and a small tannery. In 1873, when Dangan Mill was turned into a woollen mill, it reflected conditions in the flour milling industry generally. For the same imported flour that lowered the price of flour for labourers as consumers was cutting into the viability of the Irish mills for which many of them worked. In 1880 the Island Mill and Little Mill, having been run as a single enterprise, were bankrupt – victims of an aging owner, a lack of capital with which to invest in new technology (steel rollers to replace stone grinders), and competition from other mills, particularly those in the major Irish ports, near to the imports of durum wheat. Grennan Mills continued. Between 1873 and 1886, an average of twenty-nine workers were employed. The tannery, too, did well at this time. Its ledgers show that its sales expanded after 1860, at first to buyers in New Ross and Waterford and then, by 1870, to buyers well beyond the locality. Thereafter, local sales were few and small as orders went to Belfast, Cork, and Sligo.[35]

Marriage, Kinship, and Locality, 1855–84:
The Boundaries of Status-Class

The changes after 1841 conjoined both to reproduce and to sharpen

Table 3.8: Status-class and marital endogamy, 1855–69*

Occupation of Bride's Father	Occupation of the Groom's Father					
	Farmer	Shopkeeper	Artisan	Labourer	Gentleman	Professional
Farmer	72% (47)	(2)	(6)	(9)	–	–
Shopkeeper	(5)	0% (–)	–	–	–	(1)
Artisan	(4)	(2)	30% (6)	(8)	–	–
Labourer	(7)	–	(8)	70% (40)	–	–
Gentleman	(1)	–	–	–	100% (4)	(1)
Professional	(1)	–	–	–	–	0% (–)
Total (n = 152):	(65)	(4)	(20)	(57)	(4)	(2)

*The figures include all the marriages of people resident in Thomastown parish for whom parochial data were available.

the social and cultural boundaries around status-classes and to intensify thereby an essential experience of being working class: how people defined themselves and how they were differentiated from others. One example was in the improved housing. Of the 459 households enumerated in the 1901 census in the District Electoral Divisions (DEDs) of Thomastown and Jerpoint Church,[36] 72 per cent of labourers and 69 per cent of farm workers lived in houses with three rooms or less. Only 30 per cent of farmers did so and only 12 per cent of retailers. Another example, constructed from parochial- and civil-registry materials, shows how the experience of marriage and kinship increasingly became the experience of status-class.

The earliest year for which occupation or *status* was given in these registers was 1855. By then, status-class endogamy was well-established among gentry, farmers, and labourers (Table 3.8). Artisans, however, were more exogamous, as were retailers and professionals.

These early patterns can be compared with those wrought by the 191 marriages which took place in the two decades after 1869 – between 1870 and 1889. In this latter period, people continued to marry within their status-class, but they did so in greater proportions. Eighty-three per cent of men whose fathers were farmers married within their status-class, as did 74 per cent of men whose fathers were labourers and 37 per cent of men whose fathers were artisans. Retailer endogamy was at 17 per cent. Clearly, the practice of status-class endogamy intensified as the century progressed. Boundaries and the experience of class intensified alongside. Ironically, therefore, a practice common to people of all status-classes served precisely to divide them from each other.

Table 3.9: Marriage, status-class, and locality, 1865–74

	The Thomastown person's marriage partner came from:			
	1st order field (same DED):*	2nd order field:**	3rd–4th order field: ***	Another Kilkenny rural district:+
Farmers (n = 46)++	21.7%	30.4%	34.8%	13.1%
Artisans (n = 43)	58.1%	25.6%	14.0%	2.3%
Labourers (n = 83)	55.5%	30.1%	8.4%	6.0%

*DEDs are administrative units. They have never had socio-political, economic or cultural significance. They are used, in this context, for ease of geographical identification.
**Those DEDs adjacent to the DED of the parish person.
***The third-order field was defined as those DEDs immediately adjacent to the second-order field, and so on.
+The Table omits marriages that occurred outside the county and abroad. However, a few parish residents did marry spouses from beyond the county.
++Only endogamous marriages were counted for farmers and labourers. For artisans, with low endogamy rates, exogamous unions were included to augment the number of cases.

Important here is what happened to artisans. Their relatively low endogamy rates likely reflected both their small numbers in the locality and their anomalous class positioning as waged workers, domestic commodity producers, or capitalists. However, artisans' marriages with those from the shopkeeping and farming status-classes declined radically through time. Between 1855 and 1869, 30 per cent of artisanal spouses, both men and women, married shopkeepers or farmers. Between 1870 and 1889, only 19 per cent (11 out of 58) did so. Whom did they marry instead? They married each other: an increase from 30 per cent during 1855–69 to 37 per cent during 1870–89. More dramatically, they increasingly married labourers: 43 per cent of men whose fathers were artisans married labourers' daughters during the 1870–89 period. In other words, the boundaries around artisans were becoming more impermeable even as artisans were also downwardly mobile. In turn, retailers and farmers were increasingly segregated from artisans.

These social boundaries had a spatial dimension, a feature seen in the locales from which marriage partners were drawn (Table 3.9). The kinship and affinal networks of Thomastown's labourers were the most localized while artisanal nets were more restricted than those of farm-

Table 3.10: Ages at marriage among farmers, labourers, and artisans, 1860–89

		1860–1869		1870–1879		1880–1889		Total: 1860–1889	
		M	F	M	F	M	F	M	F
Farmers	Males	33.1		29.8		33.3		31.9	
	Females		27.3		26.7		27.8		27.2
Labourers	Males	27.9		27.9		32.1		29.0	
	Females		24.8		26.0		28.3		26.1
Artisans	Males	26.9		28.5		34.5		28.7	
	Females		23.5		25.5		29.8		25.3

ers. Indeed, farmers' kin reached well into the third- and fourth-order fields and even outside the rural district. Almost half married in this wider zone in contrast with labourers and artisans where fewer than one in five or six did so.[37] This meant that farmers' networks ramified far more extensively than did those of labourers and artisans. Conversely, labourers had more of their kin nearby.[38]

If marriage choices created and responded to social boundaries, so, too, did differences in the ages at which people married. The propensity of the poor to marry young has been seen by most Irish historians as related to the 1845–9 famine. In 1834 people knew that early marriages led to high fertility and to overpopulation, underemployment, and poverty.[39] They also understood that conacre and dowries underpinned this. The former was an incentive to early marriage among labourers; the latter was a preventative among farmers. Said solicitor McEnnery: 'The man that hopes to get half an acre of potatoes thinks that he has no reason to fear for the future, and that he may safely venture on a wife.' In contrast, 'a comfortable farmer's son is very slow to marry ... He always waits until he gets a girl with a fortune.'[40]

Indeed, in Thomastown by 1860, although all people tended to marry later than they were presumed to do in 1834, people of different status-classes married at different ages (Table 3.10). Workers, both men and women, married earlier than did farmers; and artisans married even younger. However, over the next decades, these differences disappeared. In this, local people were similar to others in Ireland more generally. The change reflected the rise in living standards while, in turn, contributing to them. Such convergence of practice amongst all local people was still insufficient to dent the key marriage practice – status-class endogamy. Here, the use of cash dowries among farmers and retailers constituted an impenetrable barrier for all labourers and the vast majority of artisans. Status-class boundaries thus had an essential material dimension. They also had an ideological one, as common sense notions of 'the labourer' changed through time.

Changing Common Sense through Time:
From 'Landless Peasant' to 'Wage Labourer'

The changes in the material and social conditions of labouring people were refracted through the way in which the ideological world of labour was constructed. Higher wages and stable prices meant an absolute increase in living standards. It also meant that conacre declined and, with it, the dependence of urban workers on farmers for access to land and, most important, on land itself. Why had conacre been important?

In 1834 witnesses observed that conacre did not make potatoes cheaper. Rather, it was that their 'bulky nature' made transporting them too time-consuming and inconvenient. Conacre was also important because workers were given 'more time to pay the conacre rent than [they] would be for the value of an equal quantity of bought potatoes from shopkeepers.' Also, workers were 'sometimes allowed to pay a portion of the rent in labour.' This meant that conacre was also crucial from the supply side of the equation: farmers who had 'no money to pay labourers in the spring ... let them portions of manured land to plant their potatoes in at a reduced price.'[41]

Conacre also was a strategy though which labourers could lessen their dependence on retailers. Farmer Cantwell noted that a married labourer with children 'never takes conacre on speculation to sell the potatoes; on the contrary, he is rarely able to obtain a sufficient quantity of it to enable him to escape the necessity of buying provisions in the dear part of the year on credit, and at exorbitant interest.' However, while trying to extricate themselves from retailers, workers became dependent on farmers. For example, two witnesses said that, if his potato crop partially failed and the labourer could buy more cheaply the same quantity of potatoes as his conacre ground contained, 'he yet endeavours to pay the rent, that he may not ... be refused another time.'[42]

After 1850, and certainly by the 1870s, this dilemma that labourers faced – of needing either retailers or farmers, of exploitation either through exchange or production – had altered. The railway and better roads made potatoes easier to transport and ended dependence on the harvest of particular localities. Other foodstuffs also entered the diet. Most crucially, however, labourers had more cash, from selling more pigs and from more waged work. In any case, dependence on the potato had never been as extensive in the Thomastown area as elsewhere in Ireland. Its failure in the locality between 1845 and 1848, although significant, was decisive mainly in the 'push' effect that it had on the local population. Poverty already had been driving people away certainly by the late 1820s. What the potato failures did was accelerate dramatically the rate of emigration; and what the massive population decline did after 1850 was end the glut of labour on the market. This moderated the excessive competition for work which had caused so much distress by keeping labour casualized, wages below subsistence levels, and workers from combining for better conditions.[43] Said farmer Cantwell in 1834: 'Such is the competition for work that, when farmers ... lowered ... wages, they ... never experienced any cessation of labour, nor found any difficulty in getting labourers ... While combinations have existed in all trades, either to check the fall of wages, or ... to raise them, such has never been the case among the agricultural labourers ... in consequence of the great numbers who are always eager to accept employment.'[44]

The massive emigration after 1845 also precipitated a large decrease in the number of smallholders (Table 3.11), that is, those whose shortage of capital inclined them to accept labour as part-payment for conacre. After 1850, wages were paid in cash and all labourers worked for cash. In other words, the decline of conacre signalled alterations in class relations.

Extensive emigration also altered the relative distribution of people inside the local class-structure. As of 1845, people were clear about the size of a viable farming unit. In appearing before the Devon Inquiry, several county Kilkenny witnesses insisted that a smallholder was a man who had less than ten acres, and that it was a 'struggle to live' with less.[45] For them, in other words, ten acres separated the smallholder from the 'farmer,' the subsistence peasant from the commercial farmer. It was a view based on perceptions of efficiency and profitability as well as viability. It reflected differential access to the means of production and to decent living standards.

In the aftermath of extensive emigration between 1845 and 1857, in

Table 3.11: Landholders in the Thomastown area, 1845 and 1857

Holding: Status:	House Labourer	−1 acre Cottier	1–5.9	6–9.9	10–19.9	20.0+
			.......Smallholder.......|----Farmer--------			
*Rural townlands***						
1845 (*n* = 547)	23.6%	8.0%	23.2%	7.9%	16.3%	21.0%
1857 (*n* = 385)	24.1	8.3	20.0	4.7	13.0	29.9
% decline	27.9%	27.3%	39.4%	58.1%	43.8%	+
*Peri-urban townlands****						
1845 (*n* = 107)	47.7	4.7	22.4	8.4	6.5	10.3
1857 (*n* = 70)	28.6	8.6	27.1	4.3	11.4	20.0
% decline	60.8%	+	20.8%	66.7%	+	+

Source: *Griffith's Valuation*, 1849 (for which the surveys were made in 1845) and the Valuation Office, Dublin.
*See Table 3.5 for a definition of 'valued acre.'
**42 townlands were used, all in Thomastown Catholic parish. These contained 18,268 statute acres or 9734.3 'valued acres.'
***Occupiers who lived on town streets that extended into these townlands are excluded.

rural townlands, the proportions of people in these categories had changed little (Table 3.11). Prior to 1845, labourers and cottiers formed somewhat less than a third of the rural population, as did the smallholders. Farmers (those with at least ten valued acres) formed slightly less than 40 per cent. Emigration had little effect on this landholding and class structure even though the total number of rural holders decreased by almost a third. By 1857, a third of rural dwellers were still landless labourers and cottiers. The proportion of smallholders had declined slightly, to form about a quarter of the rural population, and the proportion of farmers had increased to form somewhat over 40 per cent. What this meant was that the status-class hierarchy, and the structure of landholding in Thomastown's hinterland, pre-dated 1845 and remained virtually intact after.

This was not the case close to the town, in peri-urban townlands. In 1845, almost 50 per cent of holders had a house without land. They were industrial or casual workers. Smallholders comprised slightly less than a third of the occupiers, as they did in the rural townlands. However, farmers formed only about a sixth. By 1857, the proportion of smallholders remained virtually intact while the landless labouring population had declined dramatically. The proportion of farmers had increased and, along with them, the proportion of cottiers. The peri-urban townlands, in other words, became more agricultural as the urban-oriented, landless, and occasional labourers were displaced. The agrarian structure of the peri-urban townlands thus came to resemble more closely that of rural locales – with farmers and their cottiers and without a superabundance of casually employed, landless labourers.

Such change cum continuity invariably implicated the *mentalité* of workers as well as others. In 1834 both farmer Keefe and a land agent had noted that employment was so 'precarious' that 'the labourer looks to the possession of land as the only sure mode of existence. To obtain it, cottiers consent to work at any wages, however low; and, as they form the most important class of labourers, they contribute to keep down the wages of all.' Indeed, the common view was that 'land is the peasant's only sure mode of subsistence, and he will take is at any price.' So said McEnnery and brewer Splint. 'A man that has land,'observed labourer John Brophy in response, 'is always sure of a meal of potatoes at any rate.'[46]

In these views, the labourer was a landless peasant whose aim was to obtain land in order, at a minimum, to ensure subsistence. Moreover, as retailer O'Connor noted, that 'even if permanent employment at wages could be had, it would not immediately ... withdraw ... the competition for, and reduce ... the rent of land. [For] at first the labourers would prefer the land ...; they were so accustomed to consider the possession of it as the most desirable, as well as the most certain, means of obtaining a livelihood. However, if they were convinced that the employment were ... permanent ... they would, of course, prefer it to holding land upon terms not affording them as good a subsistence.' David Brophy, a labourer, 'who heard Mr O'Connor express himself in these words, exclaimed, 'Aye faith! that's just what I think myself.' 'For my part [added landlord E. Robbins], I think they would soon learn to prefer the wages; but at present, their greatest ambition is to get a bit of land.' Labourer Brophy also said that 'if a labourer could obtain public employment, and were convinced of its permanence, he would not work for a farmer at wages lower than it would afford him.' Indeed, landlord Davis insisted that 'constant employment is of more importance than a rise in the rate of wages.'[47]

After 1850, as these conditions were slowly realized – as more waged work and more constant work became both goals and possibilities – and as wages rose along with consumption levels, landless people came to see themselves, and were seen by others, as permanent wage labourers rather than as temporarily landless peasants. Indeed, the emic idea of the so-called poorer classes was transformed into the idea of the labouring classes. Waged work, not land, became the basis for survival and access to work became a central trope. In such material and ideological ways, a working class was realized.

At the same time, other components of common sense remained. Most important was the idea that wage levels should depend on the costs of shelter and food. Although wages might depend on the availability of labour, and although what was defined as an acceptable standard of living might rise, a fair wage was still defined by the costs of a worker's subsistence and, in turn, the costs of a worker's sustenance were still seen as the maximum level to which wages should rise. Severe ideological constraints were thus put on a worker's ability to accumulate wealth. Dowries could never become part of working people's lives.

Other, older ideas were also reproduced. Those who owned the means of production had a right to profit and, should this require wages to be lowered below subsistence levels, such dearth could be alleviated by charity. Ideas about donors as subjects and recipients as objects were thus reproduced. Givers still had to be generous and, through their generosity, could enter into and alter the lives of working people. Workers, as recipients, still had to be 'deserving.' Yet, alongside this older paternalism, the state's incursions into poor relief were also being experienced. The idea of 'deserving' was slowly to be amplified into a far broader notion of 'respectability.'

Also reproduced was the idea that labourers' ties with landlords were different from their relations with farmers. This came from the ways in which landlords were connected to the labour process, the law, and charity. It was only on landlord's demesnes that married women and children might obtain waged work outside the harvest season. Landlords also employed more labourers than did farmers and provided more permanent work. Indeed, mere residence near a demesne lowered the competition for work. Labourers' houses on such estates were better, with moveable sashes providing ventilation that relieved the 'positively unwholesome atmosphere' characteristic of labourers' cabins elsewhere. Landlords provided relief in times of dearth and, as magistrates, mitigated fines for trespass. The vast social chasm between landlords and workers, mediated by estate agents, stewards and keepers, limited close interaction and allowed conflicting interests to be masked by generosity. In contrast, labourers interacted directly with farmers; and implicated with conacre, the wage nexus, and working conditions was the constant potential for conflict.

The Tenor of Labouring Lives

The 'wretched' living conditions described in 1802, and the misery portrayed by the witnesses in 1834, were somewhat alleviated after 1850 and continued to be so after that time. Yet labouring lives remained precarious and bleak in terms of access to work, life chances, and working conditions. The employment career of Edward Long is an example (Case 3.3). Born in 1828, he married a labourer's daughter in the mid-1850s. His children were born between 1856 and 1864. His working life, as he described it when he was a witness in a court case in 1868, illuminates the insecurity at the time. Long moved between gentlemen employers and day labour, types of jobs (herding, spade labour), and tied houses. His wife worked when possible.

Case 3.3: The Employment Career of Edward Long

'I am in Sir John Power's employment as a herd; [I] was with him last October, and over half a year before that; ... I had been in the employment of Mr Davis, of Summerhill; after that [I] was working by day, as a [day] labourer, not as a herd but with any one that employed me at spade labour; I was not with anyone as a herd since I was a young boy. I was in Captain Butler's employment about 12 years ago [and] was for a time living a quarter of a mile from his lodge-gate; I remained there until I went into Sir John Power's employment; I was hired by Sir John Power by the day at 7s. per week [but] was not fed beside; my wife lived 12 or 13 years ago in Captain Butler's employment – not since. I lived at Ballyroe which was a quarter of a mile from Captain Butler's; my wife was not employed in Captain Butler's this 12 or 13 years; my experience of sheep was when I was a boy; I am now pushing up to 40.'[48]

Long's description of his peripatetic life omitted reference to what were desperately poor working conditions. Fishers were drowned in cot accidents; workmen fell from scaffolding that was too narrow. Labourers were hit by falling roof slates, drowned while transporting materials to the railway viaduct, and thrown from, or run over, by carts. They received accidental shotgun wounds and they attempted or committed suicide. They were killed when caught up in mill or harvest machinery.[49] Labourers also lived very close to abject poverty (Case 3.4).

Case 3.4: The Hudsons, 1856 and 1861

Some Thomastown men had found work re-laying railway ties. Picked up by a ballasting train heading for the works in Dunkitt, County Waterford, the labourers were dropped on a siding to load ballast waggons. As they worked, an incoming 'mail train was mistakenly diverted to the siding. Several men on the waggons were immediately crushed to death.' Five were from Thomastown, 'able labourers in the prime of life.' The only one unmarried 'was a disbanded militia man of the Kilkenny Fusiliers.'[50] One of the deceased was John Hudson. He was in his mid-thirties and married with two children.

Five years later, 'a wretchedly poor man named Michael Hudson was found suffocated and much burned on a lime kiln ... near Thomastown, to which he had gone for shelter and warmth the previous night. He was the father of one of the five men killed in the Dunkitt railway accident ... and having reared a numerous family decently, was for some years supported by their remittances from abroad, all the survivors having emigrated. No remittance having been received for some time back, he was in a deplorable state of destitution.'[51]

Service in the British army and remittances from emigrant kin were natural parts of working-class life in the nineteenth century. So, too, for many, was alcohol abuse. Two of the above-mentioned suicide attempts, and cart accidents, were related to drunkenness.

Such precarious life conditions often brought labourers into contact with those who managed the Poor Law Union and its workhouse. Out of such situations, labourers experienced directly the powerlessness and circumscription of their lives. When Margaret Connors asked the guardians for the meagre six shillings 'left her by her aunt, who died lately in the workhouse,' the board replied that the money had already been 'impounded' to pay for the aunt's maintenance.[52]

Out of such conditions and treatment, other agents could build political viewpoints. In 1879, a 'year of dire agricultural depression,' the Kilkenny *Journal* editorialized on the evictions of farmers: 'It is a cruel position to have occupier, wife and children cast out of an old home, raised by the hands of forefathers, upon the wide world – to enter the workhouse, with the disruption of all social ties involved, the degradation experienced, the hopeless feeling of despair engendered; that all independence is gone, and demoralization of a decent family by abject poverty has been the outcome of a life-struggle of toil, poverty, and self-denial!'[53] That the editor saw fit to comment on the plight of long-time farmers, while ignoring the conditions of labourers, was a telling point indeed. It reflected political aspects of the labouring experience during the nineteenth century which formed part of how the working class was realized. It is to this that I now turn.

4. Political Domains and
Working Combinations after 1815

*'None of the witnesses are aware of any combination having existed among ...
labourers.'*

– HC 1836, Appendix D: 22

*'The outrages ... and the defiant manner in which the mobs ... paraded our
streets at will, were ... most alarming ... If the mob be allowed to have its triumph,
adieu to freedom and civilization.'*

– Kilkenny *Moderator*, 11 August 1858

By the early nineteenth century, labourers were a necessary and naturalized part of the social landscape. Yet, if they became too numerous and
wages fell too steeply and/or if prices rose, subsistence crises might
ensue. Conversely, if labour became scarce, wages might rise beyond
what employers perceived to be the costs of subsistence. To maintain the
balance, charity from gentry in times of dearth was key. Labourers, however, also were learning that, in addition to being deserving and defer-
ent, it was sometimes useful to combine. After the 1815 peace, as the
condition of labour deteriorated, such political action took several
forms.

Defining Political Domains

Historians have tended to see Irish politics through a modernization
lens. Individual acts of banditry in the mid-eighteenth century were

displaced by agrarian protest groups which, in turn, were superseded by organized, broad-based nationalist movements and, then, by formal electoral politics. The evolutionary assumptions in this model are clear: from unorganized protest to orchestrated representations, from agrarian outrage to non-agrarian issues (nationalism, political independence), from local disturbances to national movements, and from violent resistance to non-violent politics. Such macro-trajectories, however, tend to sideline the particular experiences of both labour and particular localities. They also make assumptions about what politics are and, in so doing, they obscure the changing nature of the colonial state.

Prior to 1800, all local politics were elements of colonial state formation, a process being overseen by those who sought legitimacy through both coercion and consent. At different times, a segment of those who formed the dominant classes comprised the ruling faction or government. The state, however, also was comprised of a bureaucracy. Peopled by those with technical expertise and/or political partialness, the function of bureaucracy was 'to structure and stabilise relations between the leaders and the led' – between the dominant and subordinate classes.[1] Labouring people were clearly among those to be led.

To explore how this hegemonic process worked through time, it is useful to distinguish two types of political domain. The first is where labourers were the subjects of their own political action. They aimed to be leaders, to devise ideological alternatives, and to alter relations of domination and subordination and thus ameliorate or change the condition of their lives. These are the *politics of combination*. Second, labourers were also the objects of political actions and became enmeshed in contests waged by agents from other classes. I call these the *politics of dependence*. Here, the lives and experiences of labourers were used as *rhetorical devices* or as *resources* by those who had their own ends in mind. Labourers also became the *educational targets* for those of the dominant classes who would be leaders.

Clearly the two domains overlapped. Indeed, the character of their conjoining at certain moments was important for constructing ideologies, the activities of formal organizations, and the outcome of events. Initially, however, the distinction between subject and object provides two broad ways for exploring aspects of the hegemonic process during the nineteenth century. In this chapter, I look at the politics of combination. In the next, I explore the politics of dependence.

Combinations in the Trades

In Ireland and England, trade unions or associations had been illegal since the sixteenth century. Later anti-combination acts during the eighteenth century further suppressed them by applying ever more drastic penalties. Yet, by the second half of that century, associations had emerged in the larger Irish cities of Dublin, Belfast, and Cork. They were, however, highly localized, and no overarching organization linked them.[2] Because of this as well as the small numbers in each trade in small towns, it is unlikely that such associations emerged in Thomastown. What did appear were benefit societies. In Thomastown in the early 1830s, two such associations were extant. Witnesses at the 1834 inquiry mentioned one society 'belonging' to artisans who subscribed 1s. per month and another, gentry-run, for artisans, labourers, and farmers. Both gave support to sick members and paid funeral expenses.[3]

Legislation in 1824 and 1825 eased sanctions against tradesmen's combinations. Artisans could now meet to discuss working conditions and wages and present their combined demands to employers. However, they could not control the ratio of higher-paid journeymen to lower-paid apprentices and they could not intimidate or interfere with those who were working.[4] All this, of course, mirrored a dreadful fear which the propertied had of combinations. In 1828, for example, when journeymen coopers in Kilkenny city 'turn[ed] out against some employers who resist[ed] their demands for an increase in wages,' the *Moderator* announced that 'the baneful spirit of combination is spreading.' A local cooper was attacked by other coopers for continuing to work for his employer and, the following week, the *Moderator* reported that the Waterford Chamber of Commerce had 'resolved to protect their members and those employed by them against any illegal acts arising out of the present combination among the coopers.'[5] Such pan-regional outlooks and coverage continued. In 1833 the *Moderator,* in Kilkenny, detailed how boatmen in Waterford and Carrick-on-Suir were refusing to work without a wage increase and were preventing boats from passing between the two cities.[6] In 1834 the *Journal* told of a coach makers' combination in Kilkenny city and, in 1837, of journeymen printers in Waterford: 'We regret exceedingly that the fatal system of combination ... has spread its deadly root far and wide. In [Waterford] ... the pestilence has arrived at ... an alarming height ... Misguided men ... the journeymen printers ... under the name of the "Typographical Society" have formed a combination with a view of forcing upon the employers certain regulations, the result of which would be the destruction of their property, and consequently the ruin of those very men who depend upon them for employment.'[7] This imagery and discourse of combination as contagious, pestilent, and deadly, as an epidemic infecting misguided men and as destroying both property and jobs, highlights the deep hostility which could divide capital from skilled labour and the fear which the former had of unfettered, poorly educated artisans who did not comprehend how the civilized world worked.

Agrarian Combinations

In reporting on the coach makers' combination in 1834, the *Journal* noted that 'most, if not all, the combinators are strangers from other parts of Ireland.'[8] This view of outside agitators was also expressed in relation to agrarian outrages in the Thomastown area: they incited locally evicted, tenant-farmers to take action (murder, arson, cattle mutilation, and threatening letters) against landlords, middlemen, and new tenants. Such rural violence in the early 1820s had prompted an Insurrection Act through which landlord-magistrates could 'proclaim a barony' if the barony were particularly disturbed and impose a curfew, outlaw meetings, and increase the severity of penalties.[9] Often, however, it was the fear of strangers that led to the proclamation. Certainly William Tighe believed this in 1824. In his evidence before a House of Lords committee, Tighe said that he 'knew the country near me, both in the baronies of Gowran and Ida, was not disturbed.' Yet several landlord-magistrates told him 'that if they did not proclaim them [the seemingly disturbed baronies of Gowran and Ida], the disaffected would take refuge there.' The inspector of constabulary, Leinster Province (Major Thomas Powell), agreed. Ida, he said 'was put under the act because of its location – to prevent it being a place of refuge.' The only violence that locals engaged in was 'faction-fighting.' These malefactors were not labourers: they were smallholders caught up in family feuds.[10]

What, then, of labourers? At times, workers were caught in the middle. Edward Murphy was an extensive middleman near Thomastown, sub-letting land from which tenant-farmers had been evicted. For this, he had been shot and badly wounded. In 1833 two notices were posted 'ordering no person, on pain of death, to work for Murphy or any of his family.' A week later, another notice reiterated the message, adding that this was the last warning which labourers would receive.[11] Clearly workers were not part of this combination although they were overtaken by its actions. In contrast, how labourers were directly implicated as political subjects was early on exemplified by 'a riotous and formidable' situation which occurred in 1832 (Case 4.1).

Case 4.1: An 'Assemblage of Country People,' 1832

In August 1832 a threatening notice *appeared on the church gate in Thomastown: 'Any person ... employing Mowers this season for ... Cuting Cawron [sic] may mark the consequences.' Three days later, 'an assemblage' of 250 'country people, ... armed with reaping-hooks, entered a field where five men were mowing oats in Mount Juliet demesne, the seat of the earl of Carrick. They 'attacked' the mowers 'with a great violence, breaking their scythes and almost ... tearing the clothes off their back. Before they left the unfortunate workmen, they* threatened, *in case they again dared to mow oats in any part of the County to visit them with the severest punishment.' The earl's steward 'was summoned ... They ordered him not, at his peril, to employ any of the men whom they found cutting the oats.' The party then left Mount Juliet and entered William Bayley's demesne (Norelands) 'where, not finding any mowers at work, they left ... without doing any injury.' Bayley's steward, 'on observing the country people ... [had] prudently sent' his workmen 'out of the corn field before the arrival of these rural legislators.'*

The Moderator's editor described the event: A 'formidable display of numbers was made by the harvest labourers ... and a system of combination ... enforced under ... direct intimidation. *The agricultural labourers of this county compelled the farmers who were about to hire them ... to submit to their demand of 2s. per diem [with] diet. The argument of the labourers was: "You pay no Tithes and [at] the least you may give something to us who ... helped you to get rid of them."' In a subsequent inquiry by local magistrates, the testimony of several labourers 'left no doubt ... that the attempt to* intimidate *the workmen did not proceed from any ... in the employment of either Lord Carrick or Mr Bayley.'*[12]

The use of new labour-saving technology impelled combination. A mower with a scythe was said to harvest an acre of wheat in a day whereas it required six men with reaping hooks to do that amount in the same time.[13] The new technology directly threatened livelihoods. So, too, did the fall in wage rates that accompanied it. These decidedly working-class issues not only suggested a very real antagonism between those who hired labour as opposed to those who sold it, but they signalled that workers had clear political views and claims. They said that they had helped to end tithing. Were they not, then, entitled to a share of the increased profits? However, their claims were ignored and, instead, much was discursively made of labourers who intimidated others workers. As in the coalition against middleman Murphy, some labourers were again stranded in the middle. But this time, because it was a labourers' combination, the middle-ground was potentially divisive. Meanwhile, the magistrates never found out who the leaders were, or so we are told. On the one hand, it was 'the labourers of the county who combined.' On the other, they agreed that none was employed by either Carrick or Bayley. They thus accepted that the combination was made up of those without local roots or known employers.

Such viewpoints continued, as evidenced in a similar incident twenty-six years later when new reaping machines were introduced and harvest wages fell. Each machine reputedly displaced the labour of forty men. When workers from both the city and the surrounding countryside, as well as migrant workers from adjacent counties, came to the hiring fair in Kilkenny city and discovered the new technology, combinations and disturbances ensued (Case 4.2).

Case 4.2: The 'Mob' of Agricultural Labourers, Kilkenny City in 1858
On Sunday, 'as the market was glutted,' farmers came to the hiring fair thinking that labour would be cheaper than for the previous harvest. However, 'a combination had been entered into ... and those few ... labourers ... inclined to accept ... moderate wages ... were set upon and intimidated *by the others, so that the city was ... in a ... state of noise and turmoil throughout the day.' There was no 'overt violence' until evening, when James Walsh, 'an extensive and respectable farmer ... and ... Poor Law guardian' from Outrath townland, came in 'to hire women as binders ... having supplied himself with a reaping-machine, and therefore not requiring reapers. He was ... assailed by the* mob, *hooted ... in the most violent manner, informed that his machine would be broken to fragments, and threatened with serious pain ... if he dared to set it to work.' The labourers also threatened farmers who were offering from 1s. to 1s.6d. per day for reaping.*

On Monday morning, the labourers gathered and 'marched' towards Outrath. The 'mob' was made up of 'about 300 persons ... of whom nearly one-third were females.' James Walsh was with 'his workmen ... some being engaged with the ... reaping machine, and others mowing a portion of the crop with scythes ... the rioters ... broke through fences and ... hedges ... but seemed careful not to trample on the corn crops. [They] marched directly to ... the machine and with loud cheers ... proceeded to its demolition.' The workmen did not resist 'but asked to ... remove the horses lest the animals ... receive injury ... The mob ... grant[ed this] and then wreaked their vengeance.' *Workmen who had been mowing took 'the opportunity ... to slip away with their scythes, which were sought by the* mob

before departing ... as they had, it appears, resolved to permit no reaping ... with anything but the hook.'
   Part of the mob *then moved to where there was another reaping machine. This farmer, Howison, had armed himself and his son. Seeing this, the mob sheltered behind walls and threw stones. Howison was struck and his sons ran off, 'pursued by a portion of the* mob *whilst ... the others rushed upon the machine and commenced its destruction.' Others 'attacked Mr Howison, whose daughter ... states that but for the interference of two ... members of the* mob *... he would ... have been murdered.' The five workmen employed by Howison 'do not seem to have done anything whatever to assist him, although in the field where the out-rage took place.' Another part of the mob had meanwhile left Walsh's farm 'in search of corn-mowers.' At two farms, 'they seized the scythes and "cradles" of men mowing corn and broke them.' They then searched other farms, 'but the owners had contrived to hide the implements.'*
   'Both bodies ... united again ... and ... marched into town cheering ... triumphantly. Mr Walsh's men stated that there were a few Kilkenny people in the mob; *but that the great majority, and all the ringleaders, were* strangers.' *The sub-inspector visited Outrath and 'pressed the persons who had ... made this statement' to identify the Kilkenny people, 'but the men ... alleged that they could not swear to anyone who was in the* mob.' *The next day, fewer 'reapers [were] in our streets ... but such as there were ... refused all wages lower than the prices they chose.' They said 'that if they did not get employment on their own terms, they knew where bread was to be had ... There was a considerable ... uneasiness amongst the provision dealers of the town, but no overt act ... took place.'[14]*

A meeting of county magistrates in Stoneyford, four miles from Thomastown, endorsed the action of the resident magistrate in applying for more troops and decided also to request more police.[15] These arrived but had little to do since their mere presence was reportedly 'sufficient to repress ... further violence.' The only other events were 'the forcing of labour on some farmers' and the breaking of several scythes in the Thomastown area. The *Journal's* editor observed: 'While the labouring classes are organising on one side, the gentry and the farmers are organising for self defence on the other. Every reaping machine in the county is now in operation, and those of the gentry who have cut down their corn are lending their machines to the farmers to enable them to dispense with the labour of the rioters.' The *Journal* and the Dublin *Evening Mail* said this action was 'bad' because 'gentry and farmers should show more sympathy to those who ... help to make their wealth.'

Wages of 1s.6d. were known to be insufficient to maintain a labourer. The workers had in any case planned 'no personal violence nor destruction of property beyond the obnoxious machinery.' Their acts were those of 'disappointed, hungry and perhaps hopeless men, and not those of lawless desperadoes.' Even farmer Howison's injuries were not serious. The *Journal*, in urging labourers 'to refrain from violence' since it only could bring 'ruin upon themselves and their families,' also suggested that the 'gentry and farming classes be more generous ... to the ill-fed, hard-worked, much enduring Irish labourer.' Yet, underlying it all, the editor's views were the same as those of the *Moderator* and of the members of the Thomastown Farming Society: 'Men will not be deterred by the violence of foolish multitudes from doing what ... consists with their interests ... Every man has the right to make the best use of his capital. The farmer has a right to employ ... machines ... and the labourer has a right to set any price he pleases on his labour ... Experience has [also shown] that ... agricultural machinery creates an increased demand for constant labour ... Combination to prevent [its] use cannot succeed. The law is too strong and the constabulary too vigilant and diffuse.' In any case, continued the editor, 'the value of wages ... is enhanced by ... improved machinery' because 'the community at large is served by whatever contributes towards the cheapness of articles in general use and demand.'[16]

Only four labourers were charged. All were locals. This was because, said the *Moderator*, they were known whereas 'the *strangers* who formed the chief contingent amongst the rebellious reapers were not.' At the same time, however, the *Moderator* warned that the strangers had likely been encouraged in their 'mischief by natives who prudentially kept in the background.'[17] The four charged were accused of breaking the scythe of local labourer Michael Kavanagh, who offered information to the magistrates and identified three of them. At the petty sessions, Kavanagh softened somewhat, saying that the 'boys said not to break the scythes but the cradles.' Two other locals were examined. They admitted to being in the field but would not swear that any of the four were in the mob. The magistrates, however, accepted Kavanagh's evidence and the three were sentenced to a month in county jail. Their premise was that 'this frantic *insurrection* ... must be dealt with by a strong hand' before it becomes 'formidable.'[18] A week later, in both Kilkenny city and Thomastown, the hiring of harvest labourers by farmers was reported as 'orderly' and the reaping machines were 'everywhere at work in the county.'[19]

That strangers were the majority of the combination but *perhaps* were incited by locals was a compelling interpretation because both the leaders and the local perpetrators were invisible, rendered so because workers refused to identify the agents. Thus, it was concluded, workers were not only ignorant but they also colluded. Therefore, they had to be coerced: 'A man starving, while ready and willing to work, will not be likely to understand the obtuse theories of political economy; and if you tell him, while he sees the machine sweeping the corn field, that such inventions ultimately increase rather than diminish human labour, he will consider you a fit subject for the lunatic asylum.'[20] It is therefore 'fair to judge the guilt of those men ... rather by their ignorance than our knowledge of political economy.'[21] For, ultimately, 'capital is powerful, and every effort on the part of mere labour to check the means of its increase is [in] vain.'[22] In any case, it was well known that when a labourer has 'a few additional shillings ... he feels justified in spending [them] on whiskey ... The consequence' is that the farmer is impoverished and this 'reduces the wages of the labourer during the [rest] of the year to that lamentable point which would scarcely give him the bare means of existence.'[23] Labour, therefore, must be made to desist from pointless violence while capital managed both them and the economy. The ideas of dearth, paternalism, and deference were reproduced in the light of agrarian combination.

Assemblages, Crowds, and Mobs: The Political Discourse of Combination

Several key words permeated the reports and the perceptions of those who wrote and read them. The 1832 combination was repeatedly called an 'assemblage' whereas the 1858 coalition was a 'mob.' While both 'threatened' and 'intimidated,' it was only the latter that 'rioted.' What were the material differences? The former broke the tools of workers; the latter destroyed the property of capital. The former attacked only machinery; the latter also attacked persons. The former claimed a political entitlement; the latter were only ignorant workers who, like the artisans in the 1830s, failed to comprehend how the world worked.

However, the fact that both combinations were seen as comprised of strangers meant that local norms and values, and local gentry, could be perceived as uncontested and unmolested. Yet two unknowns remained: the intentions of the outside agents and whether or not the riot was part of a broader 'state of insurrection.' For so-called riots were not uncommon. They were, for example, a 'normal albeit sporadic' feature of Irish elections. This was because, until 1885, the franchise was extremely limited and the 'mob represented the chief electoral power of the poor.' Candidates were often 'obliged to deal with popularly recognised mob leaders who negotiated pay and contracted to supply crowds.'[24] The 1852 parliamentary election was especially disturbed.[25] In Thomastown, 'thousands of ferocious looking fellows' poured in from as far away as New Ross and a 'mob' gathered. It was ostensibly incited by one of the candidates, William Shee, a sergeant-at-law (Case 4.3). His mother lived and held land in Thomastown. Shee, a Catholic, ran for the Independent Irish Party, as did the incumbent, Captain John Greene, a Protestant. They soundly beat the Tory and Whig candidates.[26]

Case 4.3: Who Was the Thomastown Mob on Election Day, 1852?

An agent for the Tighe estate in Inistioge, Alexander Hamilton, and a friend of his were visiting Tighe's tenants to 'inform' them that they should vote for the Tory candidate. According to his own description, Hamilton and the friend 'met no kind of insult or opposition, until we came upon a large crowd which Sergeant Shee was addressing from his tallyroom window.' On seeing them, Shee 'shouted at the top of his voice, "Groans for the enemies of the church" [and] we were immediately struck with sticks and stones ... I [then] saw the exciter of that maddened rabble waving his hat and cheering lustily. We at last got shelter in a house, the doors of which the mob did not leave for half an hour ... Some time after, when ... walking alone through another street and another crowd, I was treated not only without insult, but with respect; but when I again came into contact with the mob who had first attacked me,' I was again 'assailed with stones, and mud, and had to require an escort of dragoons to conduct us safely out of the town. Excitement ... perhaps is unavoidable at a contested election; but that an infuriate mob should be excited to beat and insult unoffending men, and that by a person in the position of a gentleman thought to be well-versed in the law, cannot be excused, and can hardly be understood.'

Shee responded from London, stating that he 'never used the words, or words to the same effect, as those reported' by Hamilton. He 'never instigated the people to acts of violence or insult against him or any other person.' In fact, when 'Mr. Hamilton and his friend entered the crowd, I made no allusion, direct or indirect, to their presence, and what they heard of my speech has been misunderstood by them.' Hamilton's companion wrote back, confirming 'in every respect' what Hamilton had written.[27]

Meanwhile, in other parts of County Kilkenny, magistrates, landlords, and tenant farmers also were being 'assailed with sticks and stones,' 'attacked by the mob,' or 'severely beaten.' The 'ferocious mob' also 'broke shop windows,' burned an effigy of the Whig candidate, and set fire to a jaunting car which took the Tory's tenants to the polls. Among those brought to the petty sessions for election outrages were six men from Kilfane townland, two miles north of Thomastown town. They were charged with 'riot and assault on the horse' which was harnessed to the jaunting car. A witness passing by said that he saw the horse and cart 'but saw no violence of any kind.' He did see one of the accused, John Holland, 'with a bit of a stick and exhorted him to keep the peace and he felt that Holland took his advice.' Several other witnesses said that they saw Holland with a stick 'but did not see him use it or flourish it.' Holland was found guilty. The others were released for lack of evidence.[28]

Shee and Holland were seen as inciting a 'crowd' which, through its assaults on other men or objects, was transformed into a 'mob.' In this emic view, a mob had no ideology, only targets (for example, individuals, machines, cars). It was impelled to violate these targets, not by legitimate leaders, but by instigators. On the one hand, gentlemen such as Hamilton were contemptuous of mobs and their instigators, such as Shee and Holland. On the other hand, mobs could spiral out of control and threaten to overwhelm the abilities of local coercive agents to curb them. Yet mobs remained local problems, containable by force. They were therefore different from insurrectionary groups – from organized, trans-local agency which challenged the colonial state.

What had thus emerged in Thomastown by this time, and in County Kilkenny, was a typology of combinations and of appropriate responses from the military, police, and courts. At one extreme were *insurrectionary actions*. At the other were *breaches of public demeanour*: the actions of individuals or small groups which comprised a temporary fracas in a highly localized setting. Faction fights were an example, as were brawls. In between were, on the one hand, *mob actions* which caused short-term turmoil and attacked persons and/or property. On the other hand were *crowds*, also short term but certainly more orderly and, most important, directed at neither individuals nor the property of capitalists. What a crowd looked like, and how it was perceived, is visible from a 'riotous demonstration' in 1870 which occurred because some local people wanted 'to testify their sympathy with the French nation, in consequence of some report which reached Thomastown ... that the army of the French had gained a victory' (Case 4.4).

Case 4.4: The 'Night of the French' in Thomastown, 1870

Twelve men were charged with illegal assembly: four general labourers, a millworker, a carpenter-fisher, a blacksmith, a cooper, a tailor, and, finally, a retailer's son whose family had known Fenian connections. The men were all in their twenties.

The crown solicitor stated that several men and the Thomastown Band had marched through the town streets, with banners, calling on 'the inhabitants to illuminate and otherwise annoying the respectable portion of the community; but not stopping at that, they ... proceeded to break the windows of the houses of those who did not comply with the demand to "light up" ... This should not be tolerated ... if persons assembled in a tumultuous crowd *to the annoyance and terror of the neighbourhood, they should be convinced that there was a law to punish them. He had not proof against any one of the men as to having broken the windows, but he had proof that they were ... taking part in the general row, and that ... was sufficient to convict them of an unlawful assembly.'*

Head constable Kelly stated that there were 'about 1,000 persons in the crowd.' *He saw defendant Kelly [carpenter/cotman] beating a drum and recognized Neill [unknown] and Murphy [cooper]. 'Neill had a banner; it was either the tri-colour or black and green.' Sub-constable Nugent saw 'women and children running before the band and shouting.' Other sub-constables identified the defendants as having been part of the crowd and several townspeople deposed that their windows had been broken. No one knew who had broken the windows.*

The defence asked the court to dismiss the case for lack of evidence. 'Every one of the constables stated ... that no fear of disturbance had been apprehended.' The crowd had dispersed when requested by the constabulary. The crown replied that 'it did not require the town to be shelled ... to constitute an illegal assembly; if persons held opinions, ... let them indulge ... in those opinions, but not to the destruction of other persons' property.'

The magistrates sent the case to the quarter sessions. The defendants pleaded guilty. Their solicitor said that 'they were all foolish young men' carried away by 'the excitement of the moment ... Glass had been broken, but there was no proof that any of the men charged had taken part in this ... they had dispersed when told to do so by the police. Neither was there any ... insolence to the police.' He asked that they be allowed out on their own recognizances. The crown agreed: 'They were all quiet young men, in respectable *employment and this would be a lesson to them.' The chief magistrate warned of the 'severe punishment' the men would have received had the trial gone on and they were convicted. 'The mere fact of their having been ... with the* crowd *would render them liable ... [But] they were all* respectable *young men, and he would ask them to go home and pursue their usual avocation peaceably for the future.' The prisoners were then bound over in £10 each.'[29]*

Young men who were well known locally and respectably employed constituted a 'crowd,' not a 'mob' and certainly not an insurrectionary force. This 1870 assembly was therefore perceived differently than were the agrarian combinations in 1824 (insurrection), the artisans' combinations in the 1830s (insurrection), the labourers' combination against machinery in 1858 (mob), and the election fracas in 1852 (mob). However, the 1832 agrarian combination was also designated a crowd. What did it have in common with the 1870 combination? Both were relatively localized in time and space, and neither was seen as coordinated over a large region. Both were also perceived as impelled by what at least some outsiders could define as reasonable motivations: national sentiment in 1870 and fear of below-subsistence wages in 1832. Neither challenged capital, physically attacked individuals, or interfered with vital property. Window panes and workers' scythes were not crucial components of any production process. They therefore were not mobs. Nor were they insurrectionary combinations: widely dispersed yet seemingly coordinated and ideologically motivated actions which threatened order, either implicitly, via a steam-roller effect, as in the case of the trades or agrarian combinations in the 1830s, or, explicitly, as in the Fenian uprising in 1865 (Case 4.5).

Case 4.5: The Fenian Insurrection in Thomastown, 1865

Two Thomastown men were charged 'with being connected in the Fenian conspiracy.' James Connors, age twenty-six and a sawyer in Market Street, was described as 'a rather intelligent man who can read and write very well.' James Nixon, a carpenter in his mid-twenties, lived in Low Street. They were taken to the Kilkenny jail. 'No popular excitement' was 'aroused in the locality by these arrests, but a slight manifestation of feeling [took] place' when the prisoners were removed: 'some hooting – we presume directed against the police – was indulged in by the crowd of spectators.' Connors was charged with having administered an illegal oath; Nixon with having drilled a Fenian squad. Soon after, 'three or four young men, considered to possess very strong political opinions, left Thomastown' for the United States.

The Journal added that 'when it became known ... this morning that arrests had been made, there was not that excitement' which typified 'like proceedings in other places.' The Journal then named the informer, adding that 'hardly anyone suspected him as capable of doing anything so unmanly ... Much sympathy is felt here for the friends of Nixon and Connors. But how often has the public been warned of such delusions as Fenianism!'

At a hearing in Kilkenny city, Nixon was allowed bail. His sureties were two large-scale, local farmers. Magistrates Connellan and Hamilton 'expounded on the enormity of ... swearing allegiance to the Queen and then joining a secret society' which aimed to subvert the queen's authority. The two men were removed to Dublin, 'the arrangements' being so quiet 'that not a single person [was] in the street.'[30]

The Fenian rising was national and insurrectionary, actualized through the activities of a network of individuals in dispersed local places. From an evolutionary, macro-perspective, it was a complex combination: trans-local, national, ideological, and organized. Yet, as an insurrectionary coalition, it was a secret organization. The vast majority of people could only glean bits about its agency, regardless of their sympathy or antipathy for its unmasked activists and ideology. From a local position, then, and in terms of actual experience, the drama enacted in the 'night of the French' was far more immediate for Thomastown's labourers. Yet, on that night, the appearance of a Fenian's son and the tri-colour suggests that working people's sentiments were woven, at least in part, out of earlier and failed Fenian ones. Such *metissage* was further entwined in the light-handed treatment later given to the respectable young men by state agents who saw no insurrectionary ideals in the drama but, rather, an opportunity to educate labourers. In other words, a so-called national event becomes highly nuanced and indeterminate when painted on a locally focused and labouring people's canvas in the context of a wider hegemonic process.

The Material Bases of Combination

As workers formed combinations, agents from other classes advanced a central counter-lesson: people who combined were wrong in their understandings and unrealistic in their goals. How could strangers comprehend local conditions? Did artisans and reapers think that they could turn back the forces of capital? Did 'quiet, young men in respectable employment' not understand the moral opprobrium of taking a false oath? All these ideological viewpoints, iterated through public discourse and the actions of the courts, military and police, were also sustained through the schools, pulpit, and, ultimately, the realities of the labour market. For a pre-eminent constraint on combination, and a determinant of its nature, was the dependence of labourers for their

material sustenance on the attitudes, interests, and actions of people
from other classes: on farmers, retailers, gentlemen, and industrialists
who hired workers; on farmers and gentry who manned the Board of
Guardians and managed the work house; on gentry who formed the
grand jury which allocated public funds for public works; and on gentlemen anglers who sat on the Waterford Board of Fishing Conservators.
What work did they offer and how?

Guardians and grand juries always called for tenders for particular
projects. As a result, jobs would often not come to Thomastown at all.
When the workhouse opened in 1853, local cabinetmaker Henry Duffy
and sawyer Richard Dawson submitted a tender to build the furniture. A
Carlow firm received the contract.[31] However, the ongoing need to
maintain the workhouse provided steady work for some local tradesmen. In 1867, for example, a mason was contracted for a year to keep
the roof in repair, an ironmonger to maintain the keys and locks, a carpenter to build coffins, a nailer to make nails, and a baker to provide
daily rations. All acquired this work by competing with other artisans.[32]
Even when the jobs were one-off, as when a painter was hired for all the
external wood and ironwork, competitive tendering was required.[33]

A few appointments were permanent. These, too, were highly competitive. The selection of a summons server by local magistrates elicited
applications from at least 'three able men' (the civil-bills officer, a water
bailiff, and an ex-army corporal).[34] Moreover, after a selection, competition often continued. Such was the situation for water bailiff Unkles
(Case 4.6). It all meant that workers had always to keep their micro-
political fences mended.

Case 4.6: Retaining a Head Water Bailiff in 1873

*Some of the Waterford Board of Fishery Conservators were responsible for the River
Nore. Eleven members met, including John Doran who was himself on occasion
accused of illegal fishing with his salmon weir. The issue was whether to retain
Unkles as head water-bailiff. The chair said that he thought Unkles a very good
man. Mr Colles disagreed. Mr Doran agreed with the chair but 'thought so long
as they were suspicious of each other they could do nothing.' Mr Strubber suggested that they keep on Unkles. Colles then moved that the bailiffs under Unkles
be discharged and that Unkles be removed to Thomastown. Doran added that he
'had a house and if Unkles would live in it, he would give it to him for free.' Colles
then suggested 'putting him in Durrow for the present season and then to let him*

come down and watch Mr Doran.' Major Hayes was 'against shifting a bailiff about from post to pillar. They should give him his post and make him do his duty ... The chair thought Kilkenny was the best place for Unkles. He would however put it to the Board.' A motion was passed that Unkles be moved to Durrow.[35]

For casual workers, the most important tenders were those that came to the grand jury from farmers who earned extra cash by maintaining or building roads, footpaths, bridges, and ditches in their local area. For example, in 1858, the jury allotted £200 to a farmer-contractor for extending a section of road. Generally, however, the monies and projects were not large: £20 to repair a country bridge, £10 to build a footbridge, £15 for constructing a trench at the railway station, £17 to repair Thomastown's courthouse, £12 to build a protecting wall near a lime kiln, £3 for paving a bridge,[36] and so on. Through such bits and pieces, farmers added to their incomes and local labourers received work. However, the competitive tendering meant that wages were extremely low and labourers had to maintain good relations with a multitude of non-labouring people in order to get work and hold on to it. This was often both difficult and beyond their control. For example, when the errant son of a local farmer was caught stealing four heifers from a neighbour, it was the caretaker whom the farmer-victim fired the day after.[37] Or, in 1881, when seven large farmers who belonged to the Land League staged a boycott of another farmer who had rented a farm from one of their evicted colleagues, the farmers paid labourer William Langfry, the town's bell ringer, to announce through the town streets that the 'grabber' was to be 'boycotted.' A constable came up to Langfry and told him that such denunciations were not allowed and that if he continued he would be arrested. One of the boycotting farmers, near to Langfry, told him 'to ring on.' Langfry presumably chose what he saw as the better option, rang the bell, and, with the seven farmers, was arrested and tried at the assizes.[38]

This problem of multiple loyalties and demands was compounded by the need for careful behaviour once employment was obtained, particularly when it was constant. Workers quickly learned that if they 'abused good employers' they were severely dealt with, both corporeally and morally. In 1862 mill owner Innes complained to the quarter sessions that one of his workers had taken a thirty-pound bag of flour. The 'magistrates commented ... on the ingratitude exhibited in Mr Innes being

subjected to pilfering by any of the men employed by him, as he supplied bread to so many by constant employment.' The worker was
imprisoned for one month with hard labour. [39]

Permanent work was difficult to get and to keep. The employment
career of Edward Long is an example (Case 3.3), but even his history
compares positively with that of many day labourers who lived far closer
to dearth. They were restrained by the seasonality of various labour processes, particularly in agriculture, and they were much affected by
weather conditions which regulated how much outdoor work could be
done. In 1853, for instance, difficulties for labourers were anticipated
because the wet weather might lead to both a scarce harvest and less
work. [40] Indeed, the harvest was a focal time: all able-bodied, workhouse
inmates were discharged both to provide labour for local farmers and to
relieve pressure on local rates. [41] The rhythm of the workhouse in fact
hummed in tandem with the harvest. Wrote a Thomastown correspondent in 1867: 'Admissions [to the house] this day were beginning to be
somewhat stirring, as the harvest has been cut down; and the "poor"
having no more to do, bend their steps to the home of the widow and
widower, father and fatherless.' [42]

'To Challenge, Organise and Improve': [43] Petitions, Strikes, and Blocs

In the context of the dearth and uncertainty that typified so many
labouring lives, other combinations occasionally emerged during the
nineteenth century. All were circumscribed in space and time and all
were dedicated to the materiality of living and working conditions (Case
4.7).

Case 4.7: A Petition (1830) and a Strike (1851)

*(A) In 1830 local industrialists and professionals met in Thomastown to protest
a new stamp and spirits tax. As the meeting ended, chair/landlord Sydenham
Davis said that he had a petition from 'about 200 of the labouring classes, who in
a few moments, filled ... the court-house. He most humanely advocated their most
wretched situation, starving as they are now, and succeeded in forming a committee to collect money to buy provisions for them.' A few days later, over sixty were
employed in repairing the town streets. The 'charity is intended to give employment to such as are able to work, and to give bread and soup to such as are
unable, through age or infirmity, to support themselves.' [44]*

(B) In 1851 'there was a strike among the operatives employed in building the

Thomastown workhouse. On Saturday last, Mr Ryan, contractor ... disemployed one of the men, which caused the great majority of the rest to turn out and refuse to work unless the dismissed operative was re-employed. As a result, work was stopped for the day. The contractor was about to take steps for prosecuting the ringleaders when, at length, the workmen seemed restored to reason, and returned to work. Over 100 men have been employed for some time past at this building.'[45]

Little additional information was given on either the petition or the strike. They obviously were not considered sufficiently important. Why? First, the highly localized combinations seemed to pose little threat, even if a 'great majority' of one hundred men were on strike. These workers were clearly perceived as having little tactical power. Second, both combinations were rapidly diffused. The building labourers were coerced – 'restored to reason' after being threatened with prosecution. The hungry labourers consented to have work or food, according to their perceived physical abilities, funded in typical fashion by a local charitable collection.

The limited impact of these two combinations contrasted with a coalition in 1832 when, during the Tithe War, four local men and thirteen police were killed at Carrickshock, several miles from Thomastown. Here, a process server, protected by police, persisted in trying to collect tithes. A large crowd gathered, a fracas erupted, and the deaths ensued. Eleven men were charged with murder. Money was raised in the vicinity to defend them. William Hunt, a Thomastown landlord, was one of the jurors at the assizes. Because it was unclear what in fact had happened, he voted to acquit. Several days later, nearly 2,000 men and women from the neighbourhood harvested, *gratis,* forty acres of his corn, in thanks. In contrast, the editor of the *Moderator* saw Hunt as a self-interested landlord more comfortable receiving accolades from rabble and radicals than with buttressing the authority of the regime and his fellow landowners.[46] In this case, then, was reflected the potential for class alliances as well as the fragility of the hegemonic order at any given moment. Personal networks might intersect with and mediate the actualization of class identities. Or class loyalties, never homogeneous, might allow various options. As a gentleman, landlord, and magistrate/juror, Hunt believed that he was obligated to ensure fair play. It was precisely this agency from within the paternalism-deference code which led him to acquit. In that moment, relations within civil society prevented the application of force by political society even as Hunt and the Carrickshock events reproduced the paternalism-deference code. Labouring people thus learned that the efficacy of political combination might depend on the agency of those from other classes and on the formation of political blocs.

Political Subjects and Hegemony in the Nineteenth Century

In exploring hegemony and the political domain, it is necessary to bypass such common dichotomies as collective action versus quiescence and resistance versus consent and to probe instead how experiences of the political – as combination and bloc/alliance – became part of accumulating understandings and how these, in turn, were manifested through the political. In other words, how were Thomastown's labourers implicated as political subjects? This question leads to a focus on how labourers and their combinations were perceived by others and to an effort to comprehend the intentions of labourers themselves. Clearly the documents, produced mainly by others, yield up far more about perceptions than intentions. Moreover, intentions were often clouded, as when workers found themselves caught in the political middle. When this was created by their own agency, labourers had to intimidate their own kind as well as others. This, however, was a crucial aspect of combination. So, too, was the wilful silence of those workers who stood by, uninvolved yet unwilling to bear witness. Clearly, then, some idea of the intentionality of labour can be deduced from the perceptions, categories, and discourse of others.

It thus emerges that technology and wages were central labouring concerns from early in the century. These were accompanied by gradual, perceptual shifts: from landless peasant to wage labourer, and from the idea that combination was pestilent to the belief that it was potentially efficacious. Combination also became understood in relation to alliance: when agents from other classes followed their own bent and, in so doing, ameliorated the condition of labour. The idea of the stranger, too, highlighted an ideological convergence whereby both local workers and magistrates kept the coercive agents of the state at bay. When outsiders could not be blamed, locals could be defined as 'respectable,' thereby allowing, yet again, local magistrates to collude. Paternalism and deference were thus reproduced through combination and alliance. Indeed, that people in local places had to interact with each other or, at least, choose not to do so, underlay in large measure the (re)formulation of political meanings and the application of force.

Most generally, the issue is how the *metissage* of labouring experience was braided through political action. I therefore turn now to the ways in which labourers and labour were objects – how they were viewed and used, both in political practice and in discourse, by people from other classes. For such actions and outlooks also entered the awareness and common sense of workers, affecting their assessments of the choices that they had and of the possibilities that existed.

5. The Political Domain:
Labour as Device, Resource, and Project

The earl of Carrick 'gave a ball to the tradesmen of the family and the respectable farmers ... of the neighbourhood.'

– *Finn's Leinster Journal*, 7 September 1811

The chair of Thomastown's guardians said that 'there was no unusual distress ... There are always odd jobs going for labourers in Thomastown.'

– Kilkenny *Moderator*, 17 January 1880

There also 'will be the ordinary charity by which those who have no regular employment contrive to live.'

– *Local Government Board Report*, HC 1881 xlvii:54

During the nineteenth century, labourers were objects whose presence and condition were of concern to non-labouring people for varying reasons: economic self-interest, charitable impulse, Christian morality and notions of self- improvement, aesthetic values, and public health. This concern also emerged in the political domain, where labourers were used, through action and talk, in the political machinations of others. These experiences, as discursive political devices, competitive resources, and educational projects, invariably infused the common-sense ideology of labourers while reproducing relationships between labourers and the people from the dominant classes.

The Politics of Argument: Labourers as Discursive Devices

From at least the early years of the nineteenth century, the organic attachment of labourers to a notion of the common weal was often used in political debate. As labour power, they were seen as needing work. As consumers, they were viewed as requiring cash and cheap food. As the poor, they were seen as needing relief in times of dearth. All these angles provided a good deal of scope for discursive embroidery by people from other classes. The needs of workers and the poor could thus be used as ammunition in various kinds of political endeavour by people of other status-classes (Case 5.1).

Case 5.1: Exploiting Labour and the Poor in Political Argument, 1816–40
Road building (1816): In arguing that government should fund a new road near Thomastown, grand jury members/landlords noted that the 'new road, and the easy access to ... Waterford will help farmers and ... merchants.' So, too, would 'the benefits that will follow ... from the circulation of so much money among the labouring classes who are at present so destitute of employment ... This project will not draw ... from the pockets of the farmers [but] will circulate near £5000 among the working classes.'

Canal building (1831): Some merchants and landlords wanted a canal built from Kilkenny city to the sea. The Earl of Carrick was very much opposed since the canal would pass through his demesne, and so it was noted that 'the merchants and traders of Kilkenny and Thomastown are to be prevented from increasing their commerce, the poor to be left unemployed, and the country unimproved.'

Tithes (1838): A motion passed at an anti-tithe meeting near Thomastown stated: 'People who needed legislative relief for their poor cannot afford to maintain a useless ... Church establishment.'

Railway building (1839): In seeking parliamentary approval for the Great Leinster and Munster Railway, the Journal argued that 'the labouring classes would find employment' and that this would 'relieve the poor laws.'

Irish industry (1840): The Protestant and Catholic clergy, gentry, and industrialists, at a meeting in Kilkenny city, argued that Irish exports to England were hampered by a heavy tax while Irish manufacturing was inhibited by a prohibition on the export of manufactured goods to any place other than England. It was therefore resolved (1) 'to encourage home manufacture' because labour 'resulting from manufacture was more permanent than that arising from public works'; and (2) 'to bring back the former situation of supplying Dublin markets, and thus giving local artisans employment.'[1]

The use of labour as a rhetorical device in political argument occurred in part because workers were seen as integral components of the body politic. This view received a fillip with the 1838 Poor Law. Its promulgation had been contested by those who believed that it would cost too much and that the rates on property to fund it would impoverish both landlords and tenant-farmers.[2] Through both the debate and the imposition of rates, the condition of labour was moved to centre stage. What happened to labour now implicated all other classes in a direct, material way. This, in turn, contributed to the shifting alliances among different classes in local arenas.

A telling Thomastown example was during 1840–1 when a combination of the town's notables challenged the authority of the landlord and town sovereign, Sydenham Davis. In the ensuing dispute, the condition of labouring people was discursively central. When the notables brought Davis to the petty sessions for building a weir which prevented navigation and caused flooding, they said that Davis, 'far from being moved by the plight of those he reduced to poverty had, when he advertised the letting of his mill ... put down as an advantage that there was large unemployment in the area and thus workers could be found cheaply.' When the notables petitioned the lord lieutenant about the weir, they pointed out 'the great hardship caused to the poor' by the flooding and unemployment 'attributable to the obstruction of navigation.' In fact, the navigation had been declining for decades and it had been Davis who had tried to raise funds to revive it. The charge was simply a round in a wider competition, with the plight of labourers forming the discursive ammunition.[3]

Such ammunition might even be fired in the worst of times. After the partial failure of the local potato crop in 1845, the clergy, notables, and retailers of the town wrote to the grand jury requesting funds for relief works: 'There is at present a most alarming and unprecedented number of the labouring classes now unemployed,' they wrote, who were 'rendered doubly destitute' owing to 'the total failure of the potato crop.' They ingenuously asked for funds to revive navigation.[4] In a similar vein a dozen years later, when tenant-right agitation was beginning among farmers, a letter to the editor of the *Journal* described the material interests of tenant farmers through the idiom and life of 'a humble labourer' (Case 5.2).

Case 5.2: The 'Humble Labourer' and the Rights of Tenant Farmers, 1857
'*Sir,* ... tenant farmers *are looking forward to you in their fight against* landlord *tyranny. At present, there is a threat to raise rents even though prices are*

rapidly falling ... There is a particular case I would like to mention of a humble labourer *who had a patch of ground at a cheap rent. He spent £50 erecting a cottage on this land thinking that his rent would remain low and that he would have it forever. As long as his old landlord remained this was the case but in the property changing to another owner the rent was increased 25% in the first year and the same the second, the case ending in ejectment. This is not justice ... When will the farmers look to their ... interests and take some steps towards the procurement of tenant right?'*[5]

The writer clearly appropriated a labourer's experience, whether actual or imaginary, for other political purposes. Indeed, the inclusion of labourers as part of farmers' agitations became common. At an 1869 meeting to found a Thomastown branch of the Tenant Rights League which aimed to press for legislation to protect tenant-farmers, the rhetoric conflated labour's needs with farmers' goals. Farmers' rights would encourage industry and provide jobs and, by freeing all Irishmen, capital and labour would co-exist without conflict. Said Mulhallen Marum, Kilkenny MP: 'The insecurity and uncertainty of ... land tenure ... is one of the main causes of the industrial resources of the country not being fully developed ... They should not forget the brawny arm and sweat of the brow of the honest labourer.'[6]

The use of labour as a rhetorical device in debates which were either unrelated or only marginally linked to labourers' interests occasionally saw labourers or artisans taking part. In 1831, during the agitation to repeal the political union with Britain, the town's artisans were brought in as a physical presence as well as a discursive device. Four shoemakers, two smiths, and a baker, carpenter, mason, stonecutter, brazier, and butcher met to sign a petition for repeal. The meeting had been organized by those active in O'Connell's repeal campaign, and tradesmen in numerous parishes were meeting at the time and passing the same motions. In Thomastown, a local retailer cum political activist told the audience that the 'time has come when the working classes will no longer submit to be trampled on by men who wallow in the riches annually drained from an impoverished and insulted land.' Workers 'were not beasts of burden ... they knew their rights and should have them.' Motions were passed that the union with Britain caused misery; that a resident Irish legislature would allow them to work as tradesmen and not force them to work on the roads for 6d.; and that repeal was the only solution to current problems.'[7]

In this situation, local artisans were clearly being organized as a combination by others. What sometimes also occurred was that a labourers' combination might be penetrated by outsiders and redirected. Five decades later, in 1882, some Thomastown farmers and retailers tried to bolster the local branch of the National League, an association that agitated for tenant-farmers' rights. To do this, they tried to create alliances with people and organizations in other classes. They therefore attended a meeting of the Thomastown Labour League. A large farmer cum town retailer gave a 'forcible' speech. Then, he and another farmer proposed that 'as the interests of the labourers are identical with [those] of the agricultural occupiers, we pledge ... to do no act antagonistic to the interests of either parties.' A joint motion was also passed, suggesting a successful penetration of the Labour League: 'We, tenant-farmers and labourers, hereby signify our full determination to ... abide by and carry out the rules of the Labour League.'[8] In subsequent meetings of the local National League branch, however, labourers' interests received no attention.

Labourers as Resources: Private Authority and Personal Interests

As well as organizing labourers or penetrating their organizations in formal ways, the politics and political interests of agents from other classes implicated labourers as individuals. For example, labourers were called upon to give evidence when landlord Davis was charged with the above-mentioned weir violation. Some gave testimony that supported Davis's position; others refuted it. Clearly, labourers had political agency, not only in combination but as individuals vis-à-vis private authority and personal interests. Several incidents during 1853–4 illustrate how this formed part of common sense (Case 5.3).

Case 5.3: Flour Millers and Their Labourers, 1853–4
The owners of the two modernized flour mills in Thomastown, Harry Innes (Island Mill, Little Mill) and Robert Pilsworth (Grennan Mills), competed in the market: buying wheat from farmers and selling flour locally and to Dublin factors. Given the relative locations of their respective weirs, mill races, and water wheels, Pilsworth could alter Innes's water supply. In 1853 Pilsworth repaired his weir. Later that year, he charged two cotmen, Richard Hutchinson and James Kelly, for tearing down his repairs. He said that Innes had ordered them to do so.
    John Dawson, a sawyer cum fisher, deposed that he had been in a cot when he saw Hutchinson and Kelly in an Innes boat at Pilsworth's weir. He saw them

pull a stone off the weir and 'work at the weir ... for about three-quarters of an hour.' On his later return, he 'felt a great suction of water [at] the weir where gaps had been made.' In contrast, Pilsworth's employee, Harry Culleton, said that he 'recollects the weir for 36 years' and that it was Innes who had raised the height of his own weir whereas Pilsworth's weir was 'under the level of its ancient height.' This was corroborated by James Freeney, a mason. Both knew this because, as Pilsworth's employees, they had helped to repair his weir.

Meanwhile, Innes sued Pilsworth for diverting the course of the river that supplied his mill and for raising a bank which obstructed the flow of water. He also claimed that Pilsworth, on an earlier occasion, had cut the bank and diverted water. Innes asked for £2,000 in damages; Pilsworth denied the charges. At virtually the same time, Innes was summoned to the petty sessions for 'allowing a net to be set on the Queen's gap' of his mill-weir. Two witnesses, both named Cotterall, said that they found a net set in the gap on three occasions during the previous few weeks and that salmon were in the nets. They added that if the two water bailiffs, Elmes and Dawson who lived on the spot, did their duty, this would not occur so often. The defence solicitor argued that Innes 'did everything he could to prevent the poaching in the gap of his weir, and if there was any neglect it was with the water bailiffs.'[9]

Had Dawson and Elmes's neglect been intentional? Had they even placed the nets in Innes's weir? Clearly, the various workers saw themselves, as did others, as carrying out the instructions of, and as helping in the political contests that engaged, their capitalist employers. Given that the locations of the two mill weirs created a highly charged material context, the good will and loyalties of workers were essential to the owners. In their turn, labourers were loyal because their employers fulfilled certain obligations. In 1866 a fire destroyed Innes's Island Mill. A journalist noted how the 'working classes will suffer severely by the suspension of employment.' For 'the supply of flour ... far exceeds the demand and Mr Innes kept a good many persons at work' despite this.[10] He also was charitable. In 1859 he gave a barrel of coal 'to each family ascertained to be in need ... during this ... inclement season.' A year later, a local Catholic landlord and his MP brother contributed £50 towards building the new Catholic church. Innes, a Protestant, had given £20.[11]

Thus, loyal workers and good employers were mutually interdependent and constitutive in both public and private domains. Personal and class interests might thus conjoin through the exercise of private authority. This was apparent when Unkles was retained as bailiff (Case

4.6), when labourers gave evidence both for and against Davis during the weir dispute, in the idea that an 'old landlord' would not raise the rent (Case 5.2), and in the Pilsworth-Innes disputes (Case 5.3). Imagery of good relations, however, also implied the opposite: bad employers and disloyal workers who failed to set up and sustain the requisite obligations and responsibilities, such as the millworker who pilfered a bag of flour. People were also aware that these asymmetrical relations might become coercive. Indeed, the very notions of what was good and bad might themselves become contested. All this was illustrated in 1882 when Thomastown's Catholic clergy became concerned with a new school which a landlord had set up for the labourers on his demesne. The editor of the *Journal* wrote: 'It appears that a school in charge of a Protestant teacher and under the patronage of a local squireen has been established, and this school the non-Catholic employer ... compels the children of the labourers engaged on his estate under pain of dismissal to attend ... [But] the ... Proselytizers will learn ... that the discreditable campaign they have engaged in will be ... so dealt with that no attempt will be made to renew it there or elsewhere.[12] Clearly, ties between employers and workers went well beyond the cash nexus, and the moral and material influence of the employer, both real and symbolic, was seen as highly potent.

More typically, however, the employer-worker tie was simply naturalized: labourers were seen as part of the anonymous forces of production. In 1860, in a speech to the Thomastown Farming Society, Sir John Power reviewed the aims of the Society: 'To foster a better class of cultivation, to extend a superior breed of animals, and to induce the working classes to adopt more cleanly habits.' Clearly, labourers, along with tillage and livestock, were improvable. Moreover, in the Society's annual ploughing competitions, the listed competitors and winners were all gentry, both male and female, even though the actual ploughing had been done by their unnamed employees.[13] Labourers were anonymous, their public identities constructed through the mediations of their employers.

The asymmetrical relations between labourers and employers were thus underwritten by reciprocity and coercion, material exchanges and symbolic meanings. In these ways, personal interests and private authority were intertwined. Such mutuality was, in turn, expressed through the discourse and practice of charity and relief. For charitable works and representations not only expressed the asymmetry of the employer-worker tie, they also expressed the dependence of employers on labourers for constructing their own public identities, for exercising personal authority, and for masking exploitation.

Labourers as Educational Projects: Occasions and Charity

During the nineteenth century, charitable and benevolent acts towards labourers became essential components in how the gentry constructed their public selves. The 1841 eulogy for the Countess of Carrick told how 'this exemplary Lady' never withheld 'kindness and relief' when confronted by 'distress and suffering.'[14] The notables absorbed this style. The 1870 eulogy for mill owner Robert Pilsworth told how 'he was deservedly held in high estimation by all classes ... in the community' but 'amongst the humbler classes ... in particular will his loss be long felt ... He gave most extensive employment ... and was always most kind and indulgent to all connected with him in whatsoever capacity.'[15] Through such discourse, labourers were continually folded into the identities of benefactors from other classes and presented with images of their own symbolic and material subordination. At the same time, the actual acts of charity that underlay this imagery did alleviate somewhat the dearth and drudgery which the benefactors had created in the first instance. So, too, did such ritual occasions as the 'harvest home' (Case 5.4).

Case 5.4: Gentlemen, Labourers, and Harvest Home, 1849 and 1866
In 1849, at Kilmurry estate, the owner's birthday provided 'a most suitable' date 'for the harvest rejoicings by his numerous farm labourers.' For the occasion, 'the barn was beautifully decorated with laurels and flowers tastefully arranged' by the steward.

In 1866 the harvest home ritual at Kilfane was described. 'There is in the giving of a harvest home an act of kindness performed by the employer to the employed, that is remembered by the latter long after the festive evening has passed.' On this occasion, the 'work-people' were given 'a substantial dinner' and then 'were joined by the sons and daughters of the neighbouring tenantry [farmers] in footing the jig and the reel.' A few hours later, the younger generation of the owners 'entered the room. The arrival of this amiable party was greeted with three lusty Irish cheers from the country folk ... They joined with a joyous spirit in the dance until midnight, when they retired, admired and beloved by all for their kindness and amiability.' The land agent and steward then 'addressed the people in ... discourses bearing on the happy location ... which they enjoyed in this par-

ish under [their] good and humane landlords ... The grateful expressions ...
uttered on the conclusion of his address bore ample testimony that, as an agent
and extensive employer,' the agent 'himself is highly popular.'[16]

The harvest home ritual, as represented by the *Moderator*, highlighted
the separation of classes, lauded good landlords and employers, encouraged hard-working and grateful labourers, and displayed the mutuality of
paternalism and deference. Sometimes, too, public rituals served as
object lessons in the unity of the dominating classes. At the 1837 funeral
of Thomastown's parish priest, more than 400 people attended the procession, 'Catholics and Protestants, dressed in scarves and hatbands,'
with the carriages of all the local gentry following the coffin. The priest,
it was noted, 'was beloved by men of all classes and creeds in his parish.'[17]

Such occasions, however, were secondary to the numerous charitable
acts of individuals and organizations. Nonetheless, major changes were
afoot. In the 1830s, the Charitable Society and the Benevolent Society
mentioned by Tighe in 1802 were still relieving 'sick and bed-ridden
objects' in Kilkenny city.[18] In Thomastown, in 1837, such a Society also
was formed for those resident in the locality for at least a year. Its ideological mandate was strikingly familiar: to 'lessen pauperism without
increasing its amount by encouraging idleness,' to stop those 'petty
thefts, so frequent in spring and summer months,' and to demonstrate
'to the vicious, immoral and irreligious, one of the rewards due to a
good character.' The Society's regulations thus refused 'charity to any
who can, but do not labour, however small the remuneration' and to
those who 'misbehaved in a moral or religious sense.' Those relieved
were not permitted 'more of the necessaries of life than the poorest who
support themselves by their own industry.' Members contributed from
1d. to 1s. and met weekly to allocate relief.[19]

This Society, however, was explicitly mandated to run only 'until the
government plan will come into operation,' that is, until the 1838 Poor
Law came into effect. This suggests that the state was seen, at least by
some gentlemen, as the legitimate heir to the formal associations, the
ad hoc relief, and the fever hospitals which they had overseen since at
the least the late eigtheenth century. Indeed, in agreeing to sit as Poor
Law guardians, members of the gentry became agents of the state, along
with large farmers. The new Poor Law thus rendered the benevolent
societies obsolete while circumscribing dramatically, but not displacing,
individual gentry charity.

All this became apparent during the 1845–9 famine when it was the state that provided the impetus for the formation of a Thomastown Relief Committee. Wrote Sir John Power to Dublin Castle in June 1846: 'I formed a committee as directed by the Government for the Relief of the Poor.' That committee ascertained, as ordered, that the district had 1,944 'destitute poor' and 784 'able-bodied men requiring work.' Sir John enclosed a list of 62 landlords, notables, and retailers who had subscribed a total of £449, adding that, 'to this we hope, in a short time to add subscriptions from the Farmers.' He pointed out that the 'Committee have a number of able-bodied labourers, old men and boys employed for some weeks upon two of the works for which I forward the plans' and that the 'Committee also distribute Indian meal twice a week.' However, 'only when the parties cannot from circumstances leave their homes and therefore do not get relief from the Poor House, is meal given gratuitously.'

The amounts that individuals subscribed to the Relief Committee corresponded to the local status-class hierarchy, moderated somewhat by relative prestige and residential proximity.[20] This generosity was not, however, based solely on moral impulses. During 1846, combinations of workers were seen to be forming. Mill owner Innes wrote Dublin Castle about the 'unprotected state of this town' and 'the threats to attack' of the flour sent weekly to Dublin and Liverpool from 'five large flour mills.' Apparently, too, the town had 'been in the possession of a riotous mob, threatening the property of the inhabitants.' A few months later, Innes wrote that 'large gangs of railway labourers' posed a threat to the flour transports. Also at that time, a landlord in Jerpoint townland deposed that twenty men broke onto his land and took twenty-five sheep and six cows. Although his labourers gave chase and retrieved the animals, he expected a repetition of this kind of theft given the 'very disturbed state of the country at the present time.' A year later, in early 1848, the jury at Thomastown's quarter sessions objected to a reduction of police and removal of the military. The jury had been informed 'by members of their body that a riotous disposition of a serious nature exists amongst a vast number of the unemployed inhabitants of the town.' The jury was made up mill owners, the Jerpoint gentleman, and a large farmer living near the town.[21]

Partly out of fear of workers' combinations, then, local gentry and notables ceded famine relief to the state. It was the government that organized employment on public works in 1846, ordered outdoor soup kitchens in 1847, set up matching relief funds, demanded reliance on the Poor Law and workhouse for relief in 1848, and fixed the rates to be levied for relieving distress. Local committees of gentlemen, priests, and notables were told what was expected and responded accordingly. In such ways, the initiative and means for relieving subsistence crises was taken out of their hands.[22] Three features remained. First, in taking over relief administration, state agents reproduced the narrow-minded morality that underlay the idea of charity and relief. Second, people from the landed, professional, and capitalist classes continued their charitable endeavours through individual acts and, also, through new organizations which had a wider class base and a more sociable hue. Third, farmers remained alienated from charitable works. Sir John Power failed to collect famine-relief monies from local farmers.

Under the 1838 Poor Law, relief was given only in a workhouse. In 1880, a time of high unemployment, near-famine, and great distress, a reporter described scenes of dire poverty in Thomastown. Through these, he tried to show the limitations of the Poor Law: how labourers, once they entered the workhouse, become stigmatized as 'paupers.' He quoted a town labourer named Kearney who, in answer to a question as to why he did not enter the workhouse, said: 'Well sir, I have a few sticks of furniture and if I left this place the house would be knocked down, and I'd never see them again; times won't always be so bad.'[23] In this was the echo of the economic and political times. The government had prepared a Relief of Distress (Ireland) Bill to enable Poor Law Boards to take out government loans for public works and so to hire the unemployed. Its provisions were discussed at a Thomastown Board meeting in March 1880. To give outdoor relief made people lazy, said several members; it also interfered with the labour market. In any case, like labourer Kearney, they believed that the bad times were only temporary. Most also agreed that there was no work to be had, although two did claim to know gentlemen who needed workers but could not get them. This raised the issue of whether labourers really wanted to work at all. The tenor of discussion changed somewhat after several 'labouring men, waiting outside [and] anxious to appear before the board,' were allowed to enter the meeting room (Case 5.5)

Case 5.5: 'Eight Men of the Labouring Class' at a Meeting of the
Thomastown Board of Guardians, 1880
'Eight strong, healthy-looking men of the labouring class entered the room ... One put himself forward, and intimated that he was prepared to answer ... questions.

'Mr Hamilton [land agent for Tighe, Protestant]: Have you consulted with your comrades as to the statement which they wish to make to the board to-day? – I have, your honour.

'Mr Hamilton: Now, what do you wish to say; what is your object in coming? – Our object is to try and get work, or some relief that will pull us over the next fortnight ... We have been looking for work among the farmers, but they have none ... We would be satisfied with three days' work in the week ...

'Mr Hamilton: Are all you men married? – We are, your honour, and have families depending on us for their support. If we could get work we would not come here to-day.

'Mr Hamilton: That is very creditable to you, I must say. However, the Government have brought in a [Relief] Bill, which ... will, very likely, be passed in a fortnight, and then the board of guardians will have power to provide work for you. – (laughing) But sure, sir, we might be all dead in a fortnight.

'Mr Hamilton: No fear of that, I hope. You are too cheerful to think of dying so soon (laughter).

'Chairman Connellan [gentleman, Protestant]: I must say that the conduct of these poor men ... has been very creditable to them. – Sure we know that if any work was going we would get our share of it.

'Mr Hamilton: I should like to know if there are any other labourers in Thomastown who are unable to find work as well? – There are plenty besides us, your honour.

'Mr Hamilton: Did they know that you and the men with you were coming here to-day? – No. As for myself, I know I'll get work in a fortnight, and all I want is a little relief that will help me on till then.

'Mr Hamilton: If work was to be had within four miles ... would you go to it? – We would, sir, and six miles. Sure we worked on the railway at Bennettsbridge, and used to walk all the way there and back.

'Mr Blake [landlord, Catholic]: At present the law, unfortunately, will not allow us to provide work for you, but the law will be changed ... and then we shall do what we can for you.'

Mr MacCartan (clerk to the Board) interjected that 'if you pass a resolution ... that exceptional distress exists and request the Local Government Board [LGB] to anticipate the ... Bill, probably they will do so, and then you could provide work for these men at once.' Hamilton said that he 'was quite prepared to move that the men before the board should be employed immediately on some work ... on ... workhouse land. In fact, he was prepared to anticipate the passing of the Bill ... so far as providing immediate employment for the labourers of the union.' Discussion ensued on draining a part of workhouse land which would 'give work to those men for a week or two.'

'*Mr Hamilton: Is there any scarcity of fuel in Thomastown at present? – No, sir, there is plenty of "firin," but 'tis the money we want to buy it ...*
'*Mr Hamilton: You surely can get fuel at Dangan wood without money? – Oh, indeed we can, sir.*
... 'The labourers then retired.'

Gentlemen Hamilton and Blake then moved that twelve workers be employed at once to drain the workhouse land and be paid 1s.2d. per day. One of the large Catholic farmers on the board commented: 'They won't earn fourpence a day at it, Mr. Chairman, for they will not do much while they are at it (laughter).' Countered another: 'Anything in the shape of work is better for them than out-door relief.' As to the idea of adopting a motion that 'exceptional distress' existed and thus to request immediate funds for public works, the clerk pointed out that the number of paupers in the workhouse was actually less than in the previous year and that, in any case, the Local Government Board was only loaning funds for relief and these would have to be repaid. The subject was dropped.

The combination of labourers who approached the Thomastown Board of Guardians for work included eight married men with families. They did not attempt to obtain benefits for any others nor did they try to get outdoor relief. Rather, they said that they needed to buy food and wanted to work for the money. Only if that were not possible would they take outdoor relief to tide them over. These unnamed workers were then asked about their willingness to travel distances to work. Their 'creditable' answers, being those that the guardians wanted to hear, led to a small drainage project being formulated for them and, as it turned out, eight others. In all this, the lead was taken by the gentry who unanimously agreed that help should be given to married, hard-working labourers. Indeed, it was the gentlemen who addressed the labouring spokesman and injected humour. In contrast, the farmers dithered. They did so behind closed doors, without talking to the workers directly. At the next meeting, they continued to dither (Case 5.6).

Case 5.6: A Second Meeting of the Thomastown Board of Guardians, 1880
It was reported that twenty men were employed on the drainage scheme and that £9.17s. had been spent. A large-scale farmer/guardian, Richard Murphy, complained that little work was being done. He added that it was unfair to have the

*cost borne by the 'Union at large' because those employed were from the Thomas-
town DED. The clerk, MacCartan, disagreed and the chairman added that 'he
had once come upon them by surprise and found them working very hard.' Murphy then asked: 'Why could this work not be given to a proper contractor [that is,
farmer]; had this been done the expense would not exceed one half of that already
incurred.' The chairman explained that 'the sole motive in reclaiming this land
was to give employment to as many poor starving people as possible.' Had a contractor been used, he would have hired 'only a very limited number of men, and
those of his choosing, and very probably too not of the most needy.' Murphy sarcastically retorted that he would prefer giving outdoor relief.[24]*

In capturing the divisions between gentlemen and farmers, these
voices also captured some of the common-sense notions that all guardians held: labourers were intrinsically lazy and untrustworthy, unless
proven otherwise. In turn, the labourers' view was likely paraphrased by
the above-mentioned journalist from his conversation with Father
Delahunty, the parish priest, who insisted that 'the distress in his parish
was most severe and no real or practical steps were being taken to meet
it. Unless a man dies, they won't believe he is in want. But for the charity
of Mrs Pilsworth he does not know how the people would fare.'

Indeed, individual acts of kindness were not uncommon although,
unfortunately, virtually all were unrecorded. However, more formal
charitable donations were occasionally reported, as when Sergeant Shee
gave £25 to the parish priest 'for the poor of Thomastown,' when a gentry lady gave £2 to the Thomastown Relief Fund, or when the Board of
Guardians paid for Johanna Ryan, aged seventeen, to emigrate and two
members of the gentry 'assisted Ryan by providing her with clothing
and sea stores at their own expense.'[25] In all this, however, class-based
differences were striking. In 1868 several sheep robberies occurred.
Local gentlemen and government each contributed £100 to make up
two rewards. The thieves were caught though the efforts of Thomas
Seigne (land agent) and John Cronyn (large-scale farmer), both Protestant. A meeting was held to hand out the rewards. The lord lieutenant
directed that £60 of its money should be paid to Cronyn and £40 to
Seigne. Seigne declined the money. He proposed instead to apply £15 to
a coal fund for the poor and to give the rest to the farmers and labourers
who had aided him. Farmer Cronyn took his £40 as well as the £100
made up from private gentry subscriptions.[26]

Such contrasting responses highlight important differences among those who had wealth. Farmers, as rural-dwellers, disdained the so-called politics of reputation which came to typify town life. By the early 1860s, charitable impulses had expanded from the gentry to include the notables and, soon after, to become part of the public personae of town retailers who began to compete for prestige and reputation by the public giving of charity. This sometimes added to the town's social season, providing a social site in which gentry and retailers could meet. One example were the collections held in times of dearth. In 1867 town inhabitants met in the courthouse 'to devise means' for relieving 'the poor of the town and neighbourhood.' Organized by mill owner Innes, the doctor, and the Protestant and Catholic clergy, 'a subscription list was opened' and, soon after, the names of those 'ever-generous people' who had contributed were published in the county newspapers, along with the amounts they had donated. The list included Protestants and Catholics, notables, clergy, and retailers. Five years later, another meeting had an even more illustrious attendance, with numerous, locally resident landlords present alongside retailers. The newspaper praised them all.[27]

A second example, and equally ubiquitous, were the amateur musical concerts held both to relieve 'the destitute poor of the town' and to praise the 'ever-generous people of this town and its vicinity.' In 1862 the performers were retailers and notables. An 1879 recital reportedly had an audience of five hundred, all under the patronage of landlords, notables, and clergy. The next year, landlords and gentry, men and women, were participants.[28]

Cleanliness, Thrift, and Respectability: Labourers as Educational Projects

Ritual occasions and good employers rewarded labourers for their loyalty and hard work. Charitable largesse, in its turn, helped those who were temporarily out of sorts while Poor Law administrators provided for those who would not or could not work, thus keeping the truly destitute from starving. All such practices, and its associated imagery, brought together numerous people from the non-labouring classes and augmented their common perception that workers were inclined to be lazy and feckless. This raised the question as to how they could be improved. The answer for many was to make them literate, clean, thrifty, well-behaved, and respectable.

Much was seen as possible through the schools. Thomastown's National School was built in 1839. In 1873, the first year for which records survive, the forty-nine boys in the graduating class (age four-teen) came from all status-classes. Twenty-eight were sons of labourers (eight artisans, one soldier, three fishers, sixteen labourers), twelve were sons of farmers, four were sons of retailers, three were sons of constables or clerks, and two were sons of widows. Of the forty-nine, twenty-four lived in the town, twenty-five in the countryside. Such proportions, of course, varied from year to year, but the point is that the sons of labour-ers and artisans consistently formed a large proportion and, often, the majority of students in a cohort. This meant that the school brought labouring boys into contact with those from the better classes and sub-jected them to common education. At the same time, one of the central precepts of that education was the natural order of the class hierarchy and the place of labourers at its bottom.

The lack of cleanliness among workers had long been noted and was an obvious focus for intervention. Yet this was a difficult task for, as wit-nesses noted in 1834, dirt was caused not only by the intrinsic indolence of labourers but also by their material conditions: their poverty, the excessive labour time required to dig and prepare potatoes, and the lack of fuel.[29] One multipronged solution was to inculcate thriftiness in order to improve consumption levels. Here, both state and local agents intervened. In 1837 a Loan Fund Board was established by government to undercut the 'pernicious system of money-lending at rates of enor-mous interest, as practised by the small usurers throughout Ireland.' In Thomastown, two local branches were set up. One, the Marsh's Street Benevolent Loan Society, was operated by the Protestant rector and audited by the manager of a local bank. In the last week of November 1839, £323.0.6 was 'in the hands of borrowers.'[30] Indeed, by 1843, County Kilkenny had seventeen local societies, generally overseen by local clergy and often capitalized in part by locally resident landlords. The capital circulated in the county in 1842 was £51,495 via 16,556 loans. The average amount of each loan was £3. As part of reports from various localities in 1843, the Kilkenny city branch noted that the 'con-dition of the Borrower is improving ... some having one or two cows that had none before; and some have been enabled to buy horses and become carriers, thereby supporting large families that would otherwise have become destitute. Various small dealers, broguemakers, shoemak-ers, victuallers, collarmakers, weavers, and smiths have been very much assisted. The great majority of Borrowers obtain loans to buy pigs, seed, potatoes, to pay for rent and quarter ground, or to obtain necessaries for their families.'[31] In 1865, when Thomastown's rector resigned as secretary of one of the Loan Funds after twenty-six years of 'efficient and gratuitous service,' the Society had circulated more than £44,000 in over 11,000 loans. It had distributed £290 of its profits to charity and had an additional £291 of profits which was being used as capital for loans.[32]

More locally rooted initiatives also emerged and some, in combining charity with self-help, mirrored the benevolent societies which were common in Kilkenny city in the late eighteenth century and in Thomastown in the 1830s. For example, a Penny Club was founded in Thomastown in 1868, financed by membership dues 'from the very poorest in the community' and by 'subscriptions from friends in the locality.' Its funds were spent on fuel, clothing, and food for members. In 1876 the club was deemed more successful than ever: £66 had been spent. Of this, £29 came from subscriptions while the remainder had been 'paid in at a penny a fortnight by the 150 members, the poorest in the town.' The 'success of these institutions,' said the report, is 'an argument against any feeling of despair as to the possibility of thrift among the poor.'[33]

The data on such local organizations, particularly those relating to their daily operations, are unfortunately sketchy. Yet it is clear that the idea of thrift as uplifting, and the practices attending this belief, had been extant since at least the turn of the nineteenth century. After 1838, when the state institutionalized its own poor-relief system and marginalized the landed in relieving dearth and periodic subsistence crises, personal charity continued and so did its association with elevating recipients. The giving of such charity, however, expanded beyond the gentry and became part of the social life of the town and its politics of reputation. This in turn gave a fillip to associations that aimed to improve and uplift working people.

Several such societies became linked with recreation because thrift, like other forms of good behaviour, was associated with suitable leisure activities. For example, the Thomastown Band, which led what was seen as an unfortunate riotous crowd in 1870, was also, at other times, an acceptable body which played at formal dances with permission from the parish priest.[34] In 1883 a concert was held to raise funds for 'a reading room, library and billiard table for the benefit of the artisans and working class.' It was organized by the bank manager and retailers. Within a month, seventy working men had reportedly enrolled even though the 'original intention ... to provide a billiard table ... was opposed by the clergy of both denominations.' As the editor of the Kilkenny *Moderator* put it:

The benefits to be derived from such an institution in a small place like Thomastown are incalculable. It brings together a number of working men who might otherwise spend their evenings in a profitless, if not worse manner; it improves their mental condition, thus raising them in the social scale, and as the reading-room is not confined to any class in particular, a liberal interchange of opinions and feelings dissipates that narrow bigotry which is too often a conspicuous element in small communities. It is a pleasing feature to see people differing in religion and politics uniting in the common cause of improving the condition of those amongst whom their lot is cast.

Not be outdone, local landlords formed 'a large and fashionable audience,' along with the town's notables, at a concert in the courthouse to raise funds to establish a coffee house.[35] Both the reading room and coffee house were responses to the number of pubs in the town. In the mid-1870s, a visitor to the town came 'by the early train (too early for the business hours of the place).' He 'found the town in the silence of slumber, doors closed with the important exception of those of the 13 public houses, which stood invitingly open to supply the wants of the thirsty.'[36]

Clearly, public houses and gambling at billiards were seen to dissipate money which workers should spend in more responsible ways. Ultimately, the views that non-labouring people held of alcohol use and recreation, thrift, and cleanliness all conjoined into a singular notion of what constituted proper, public behaviour. This notion was the trope of respectability. It was already developing in the 1830s when, at a Thomastown petty sessions, sixteen men were fined for drunkenness and thirty-four artisans and labourers for having their pigs on public streets. Eight labourers were charged with assault, two with breaking windows, and two with drunkenness.[37] Clearly, there was a lot of raw cultural and social behaviour which, it was thought, needed educating and improving.

Conclusion: Subjects and Objects in the Political Domain

In an organic view of society, labourers were both inevitable and necessary. They thus became political objects to be used as rhetorical devices, competitive resources, and educative targets for agents from other classes. This sometimes reflected shifting alliances amongst the non-labouring classes in the colonial state and/or the agency of labourers themselves, as combinations organizing or being organized for particular ends. Out of such processes came the mutually constitutive notions of private authority cum personal interests, reciprocity cum asymmetry, and consent cum coercion. Through these, the identities and material interests of employers often assimilated those of workers. Meanwhile, the colonial state began to displace much of the ritual, imagery, and charity that had previously fallen under the purview of civil society. Nonetheless, feckless and lazy labourers were still seen by local agents as improvable. The activities associated with this view slowly became part of the social and political fabric of the town.

However, the experience of labourers during the nineteenth century came not simply from the political domain, out of their agency as subjects and objects. It also came through the law and the varying and sometimes contradictory actions of its agents. This, too, was related to the changing ways in which labour was viewed by those from other classes and in which labour saw itself. I discuss this issue in the next chapter.

6. Custom and Respectability: The Petty Sessions

'The fullest possible publicity should be given to all magisterial proceedings in petty sessions. The administration of justice should not only be pure, but it should also be unsuspected.'

– Nun and Walsh, 1844:45

That the Irish poorer classes were seen to be unruly and disorderly was expressed during the 1834 parliamentary inquiry when a landlord/ magistrate, resident near the town, said: '*To this habit of making their own regulations, and combining for the revenge of private injuries, may be traced much of the lawless habits of life so prevalent among them.*'[1] Ironically, this view was in turn mirrored in the attitude that state agents had of Irish landlords: as inept and shoddy agents of law and order. The 1827 Petty Sessions Act thus aimed to domesticate both the landed magistrates and the poorer classes by institutionalizing public legal proceedings. The ensuing process comprised both coercion and consent. It embroiled varying agents, class alliances, and class experiences. One of its seminal outcomes was to help fashion a trope of respectability which gained a profound legitimacy in the lives of working people.

The Nature of the Law: The View in the Sessions House

The definitive characteristic of the state, that is, of political society, is coercion.[2] Not surprisingly, then, constructing hegemony (consent) always occurs in dialectic with applying coercion or punishment (domination). Consent is built through the organs of 'civil society' such as church, trade unions, schools. Coercion occurs through 'political society,' via the actions of the police, military, and the law.[3] But the law in fact has a dual character. Located in the interstices of civil and political society, it is both coercive/punitive and educative/civilizing. According to Gramsci, every state uses the law to create and maintain both 'collective life and ... individual relations' by eliminating certain customs and attitudes and disseminating others. At the same time, it cannot be assumed 'that the state does not "punish" ... but only struggles against social "dangerousness" ... For once the conditions are created in which a certain way of life is "possible," then "criminal action or omission" must have a *punitive sanction, with moral implications*, and not merely be judged generically as "dangerous."'[4]

This dual character of the law, as both educative and coercive, is not typically addressed in anthropological studies of law and hegemony.[5] In part, this is due to the way in which law, hegemony, and class have been conceptualized. Anthropologists have put law into a cultural world – as code, practice, discourse, and communication which shape common sense and consciousness through legal processes (for example, enfranchisement, discourses of entitlement), legal procedures (for example, courts), symbols, and legal institutions. Law is thus 'a maker of hegemony'; it is also a means of resistance which subjugated peoples may use. Courts have often been used to explore these themes. As 'critical sites for the creation and imposition of cultural meanings,' courts are also seen as 'sites of resistance' and of 'oppositional practice.'[6] The paradox is that people who challenge meanings through courts are simultaneously implicated in the power relations and hegemonic categories which are embedded there.[7] Yet, it is argued, courtroom practices can have cumulative effects because meanings and discursive alignments may be (re)created and/or altered there. In such ways, law is central in the 'making of subjectivities.'[8]

This focus on the manufacture of consent/hegemony through the negotiation and struggle over meanings invariably sidelines the coercive nature of the state and of the law and obscures the dialectic between consent and domination.[9] Moreover, although much empirical work has focused on courts and on legal cases and actors (as participants, intermediaries, or professionals), people's involvements with the law have been individualized. This means that subalterns have been seen as having class-based identities or positionings but hegemony, coercion, and the law have not been linked to ongoing processes of class or group formation.

Yet courtrooms do yield rich data for exploring the 'articulation between the state and civil society'[10] – as long as individuals and ideologies are analysed as class-based, coercion and social relations are included, and a diachronic approach is used. For hegemony is a never-finished political project of state formation which is directly implicated in the material bases and relations of society.[11] Moreover, although Gramsci never theorized the role of law or included it in his discussions of political strategy, he did note the importance of law in creating homogeneity within the ruling class. For him, law played 'a part in the creation of both the political and the ideological elements of hegemony, first by unifying the emergent directive class and its allies, and then by bringing the masses to conformity.'[12]

County Magistrates, the Colonial State, and the Petty Sessions

Since the early fourteenth century, magistrates had been appointed by Parliament or the lord chancellor 'to keep the peace in their respective counties.' Acting on their own and in private, albeit ostensibly 'guided by the rules of law and reason,' they were responsible for suppressing riots, binding people to the peace, and apprehending and committing criminals to trial in cases of indictable felonies and misdemeanours or, alternatively, discharging or summarily convicting those charged with offences which statutes had placed under their jurisdiction. Property qualifications ensured that magistrates would only be 'the most sufficient persons'[13] and, by the early nineteenth century in County Kilkenny, such persons were invariably locally resident landlords.

Despite their legal role, magistrates had a long, uneasy relation with the British state. Disturbances during the 1780s had led the British government to extend the Riot Act to Ireland and to try to reform the magistracy and police. Opposition to the reforms from the Irish gentry was 'intense' and 'bitter,' based on the belief that 'hirelings of state despotism would usurp the functions of local gentlemen' and 'strengthen England's control' of Ireland.[14] That is, both localism and nationalism fuelled ongoing opposition to the British state. However, insurrection in 1798 and recurring agrarian violence continued to raise questions about the efficacy of Irish magistrates and of piecemeal policing. On several occasions, therefore, the British regime acted both to educate and to coerce the magistrates. The 1814 Peace Preservation Act tried 'to coerce cowardly or corrupt magistrates into action' and 'to reactivate the magistracy' by setting up a police force; but this failed because local magistrates did not support it.[15] In response, an 1822 act established a county constabulary, partly paid for out of central funds, and, although under the direction of local magistrates, a 'stipendiary' (paid government) magistrate could be appointed if local magistrates did not co-operate.[16] To allay this possibility, the Irish magistracy was reformed at the same time. 'All existing commissions were cancelled and new ones issued.' Along with this 'purgation' of the 'old, the enfeebled, and the unfit,' the government began to encourage an informal practice which had been emerging, that of 'neighbouring Magistrates meeting on a given day in each week at Petty Sessions.'[17] The 1827 Petty Sessions Act formalized this practice. This, and the reform of the magistracy lists, thus reflected the ongoing, equivocal relation of Anglo-Irish magistrates to the British state and to the efforts of various regimes to subvert Irish attitudes and customs.

The 1827 act neither took away any rights that magistrates already had nor gave them any 'greater authority than each member acting in private would have.' The act, however, did put great moral and administrative pressure on magistrates to cease acting on their own, in private, and to act instead collectively, in public, at the petty sessions. New links were thus forged not only among landlord-magistrates but also between them and people from other classes. According to a barrister at the time, 'when magistrates act separately and in private, they are ... more accessible to undue influence, and are more liable, if not to partiality and prejudice ... to suspicion and misrepresentation. It cannot, therefore, be less satisfactory to themselves than to the community ... that they should act under the eye and observation of the public ... A confidence in the law, and in the magistrates who administer it, will thereby be created.' Moreover, if magistrates acted collectively in petty sessions, they would benefit from 'mutual advice and assistance' and develop 'a uniformity of practice.' Indeed, such were the presumed advantages of this that they were strongly advised to 'decline acting singly or in private' except in emergencies.[18] Landlord-magistrates, along with all other Irish, were to be coerced and educated.

The 'Eye of the Public'

Magistrates at petty sessions took part in a summary process. After determining questions of fact and law, they could dismiss a complaint, impose a penalty, or pass the case to a higher court.[19] The matters assigned by statute to their jurisdiction were broad, potentially involving people of all classes. They included employer-worker relations (wages, work conditions), combinations and unlawful societies/assembly, weights and measures, the licensing and operation of pubs, cruelty to animals, salvage, trespass, poaching (fish, game), forcible entry, petty larceny, malicious injury, simple assault, and the Poor Law. Complaints could be brought by three agents: a constable, an aggrieved party, or an informer who became entitled to part of any fine.

From their beginnings in 1828, Thomastown's petty sessions were indeed public, not only in their sittings but also because county newspapers became increasingly concerned to report on them. Between 1828 and 1853, lists of offenders' names, offences, and fines were published biannually. Then, as if such rosters contained too little of the moral lessons to be learned, reporters began to provide detailed and often verbatim coverage of those cases which they deemed, in their own words, to be 'of public interest.' Although this reporting style prevents our knowing all the cases which came before the bench after 1853, it amply compensates by providing a wealth of detail on those incidents deemed sufficiently important and interesting to catch the public eye. These reports therefore reflect the central and changing concerns, interests, and viewpoints of local people – as journalists, participants, and readers.[20] As a result, they allow the petty sessions to be used as a point of entry into the hegemonic process as it was actualized over time through the educative and punitive roles of the law and its courts.

Thomastown's Petty Sessions after 1853

In looking at the complainants and defendants whose cases were deemed to be of public interest, it is clear that the petty sessions, in their coercive/punitive capacity, were mainly directed against Thomastown's populous working class. Taking as an example the fifteen years between 1854 and 1869, 253 cases were reported. Tellingly, labourers and artisans were defendants in 68 per cent of them but were complainants in only 11 per cent. Farmers and retailers, in contrast, were plaintiffs as often as they were defendants. Yet, varying agents, with different and often divergent interests, had charged labourers/artisans during 1854–69: landlords (nineteen cases), constables (thirty-four cases), fishing bailiffs (forty-five cases), Poor Law guardians (forty cases), farmers (eight cases), retailers (two cases), and, not unimportantly, labourers themselves (twenty cases).[21] This suggests that the nature of the law as coercion must be examined more closely. In what areas of life were labourers defending?[22]

In the thirty years between 1854 and 1884, 279 cases were reported which involved working people as complainants or defendants (Table 6.1). Of the eighty-five cases that constables brought against labourers, the majority (forty-five cases) were for offences against public propriety (drunkenness, nuisance), licensing regulations (drinking after hours, selling salmon out of season), or trespass (theft, poaching). Clearly, public demeanour and private property were of great concern to the constabulary. Yet, a large minority of the eighty-five charges (that is, twenty-five cases), came from situations in which labourers committed delicts against each other: assault, fighting, intimidation, manslaughter, attempted murder. Workers themselves were also only somewhat less active than the constabulary in bringing complaints. They were plaintiffs in seventy-two cases and, in fifty of these, they plainted against each other: for assault (thirty-six cases), theft (seven cases), and abusive language/threatening behaviour (seven cases). In short, 75 of the 279 cases concerned intra-working-class interaction.

Inter-class delicts also came to the petty sessions, although far less often. Workers plainted against those in other status-classes in twenty-two reported cases. They did so mostly against farmers and usually for assault.[23] As well, fifteen of the eighty-five cases that constables brought against workers were because labourers obstructed or threatened constables (nine cases) or assaulted or intimidated farmers (two cases), publicans (two cases) or a lodging-house keeper (two cases).

In short, the variety of complainants, the involvement of labourers in this role, mainly against each other, and the general patterning of inter- and intra-class complaints, suggest that a complex process typified the petty sessions. In a context in which labourers were certainly being coerced in terms of public demeanor and private property, they also were consenting agents. Moreover, the reporters occasionally described the audience that came to the petty sessions. It was mainly made up of labourers. This reflected their numerical dominance in the town. It also reflected the interest that working people had as to what went on there. For the petty sessions were a twice-monthly source of gossip and, according to the reports, of entertainment.

What occurred after 1828 through the law and its petty sessions was therefore neither forthright coercion nor clear-cut moral education. Nor was it a singular imposition of law and/or resistance. Rather, it is best seen as an intersection of three political meanings and processes. First, the petty sessions were sometimes constructed by the participants as a *theatre* in which the power of the state to punish and educate was

Table 6.1: Petty sessions complaints involving labourers, 1854–84

	Number of Complaints ($n = 279$):
Labourers as complainants against others:	22
Complaints against labourers brought by:	
Constabulary	85
Labourers	50
Board of Guardians	47
Landlords	28
Water bailiffs*	18
Farmers	12
Retailers	7
Others**	10

*These complaints exclude fishing/poaching complaints. They include complaints brought by bailiffs for possession of fish out of season, assault, and threats.
**There were four complaints from professionals, four from the railway company, and two from the sheriff's bailiff.

starkly dramatized. Second, the experiences of labouring people as defendants were effected by different agents who had diverse and perhaps conflicting material interests and ideological outlooks. Labourers also had personal relations to people from other classes and with varying reputations. The petty sessions were thus a *forum* in which interpersonal ties were (re)created, class relations reproduced, and class experience made manifest. Third, the petty sessions were an *arena* which working people gradually appropriated in order to pursue their private quarrels.[24] The intersection of these various meanings, uses and occasions in turn propelled a process in which agents of all classes came to define the customs and crimes which comprised the grist of the court and its educative and coercive functions. Yet this state organ was geared to repress dangerous behaviour, punish anti-social actions, and inculcate civilized values in *all* classes. The resulting acculturative process was complex indeed.

Guardians and Labourers: The Petty Sessions as Theatre

The workhouse was a 'total institution.'[25] The daily round was regulated, deviance was severely punished, and exit forbidden. In such a setting, Gramsci's view of the law was most closely approximated: punishment and moral education went hand in hand, wrought not simply by the state through the Poor Law itself but through the locally sited actions of the guardians who, as ratepayers, aimed to administer the workhouse with minimum cost and bother to themselves.

In this total institution, workhouse authorities had ways of struggling against social dangerousness and of educating and punishing. At every biweekly board meeting, a punishment book was brought forward by the workhouse master. It listed the offences committed in the previous weeks by resident paupers and the punishments he had meted out. At an 1863 meeting, the 'following offences and punishments appeared in the punishment book: Pat Finn, Michael Purcell and John Neill, not working. Milk stopped at breakfast. Finn and Purcell for speaking to women in the dining hall – three hours each in cell.'[26] Beyond that, the board could turn to the petty sessions if punishment failed to stop unwanted behaviour, if the board wished to expel an inmate, if a pauper committed an indictable offence, and if the board wanted to pursue those who were shirking their financial and moral obligations to support their spouses and/or children, thus forcing ratepayers to relieve them in the workhouse.[27] At a board meeting in 1865, it was decided that 'William Matthews, Roger Tobin and Pat Comerford ... be discharged [from the house] if they continue to refuse to clean the [septic] tanks.' Apparently they continued to refuse. They then refused to leave the house when ordered by the guardians. The magistrates at petty sessions ordered the 'sturdy rascals' to be imprisoned for a week with hard labour. A month later, the master again prosecuted Tobin for the same offence. He was imprisoned for a month.[28]

The severity of punishment is striking: non-conformity could not be tolerated. However, local meanings went further, for the exact nature of the petty sessions as theatre lay in the fact that it was not just the offence that had to be punished but the status category of pauper itself (Case 6.1).

Case 6.1: The Theft of Union Property, 1863

Patrick Ennery, a carpenter, was prosecuted 'for having a pair of blankets in his house ... the property of the Union.' He claimed that these blankets 'were sold by some ... paupers to [his] wife, without his knowledge ... On the Bench considering this, they adjourned the hearing, so far as this man was concerned until next court day.' It was by then 'ascertained that a pauper, William Whelan, then in

the workhouse, with another pauper, who the day before had taken his discharge,
sold the blankets to Ennery's wife. This Whelan did not deny, saying he found
them rolled up in some straw, which was taken out of the poor house. He expressed
a wish to be tried by the Bench in preference to being sent to the Quarter Sessions.
He was ... imprisoned for 3 months.'

'Further information' was then received 'about Union property being concealed
in the houses in Chapel Lane and a search warrant was placed in the hands of ...
a constable ... who, on coming near Ennery's house ... saw Ennery's daughter
about to start in with a bundle, which he saw concealed by her ... He found it to
consist of a blanket and a sheet, with the Union brand cut out, and which ... the
Master of the Workhouse said were the property of the Union ... She also wished to
be tried by the Bench and was ... imprisoned for a fortnight.'[29]

Workhouse property (boots, blankets, furnishings) were highly sale-
able commodities and their theft severely punished. Yet Ennery's denial
was readily accepted: he was a carpenter, not a pauper. Moreover, the
jailing of his daughter for two weeks for concealing what she knew to be
stolen property contrasted with the sentence received by 'pauper'
Whelan who claimed that he did not even know that the blankets were
stolen.

All this reflected how the law's application was mediated by what magistrates presumed to know of the locality and its offenders and by their
belief that pauperism, as a condition, was a moral and material danger.
Landlord-magistrates thus made the petty sessions an arm of the Poor
Law and turned it into a theatre through which the law was demonstrated to be a coercive instrument of the state. At such times, the petty
sessions most closely resembled Gramsci's notion of the law as 'punitive
sanctions with moral implications.' However, most complaints at the
petty sessions did not involve paupers; nor were they brought by agents
of the Poor Law. The petty sessions, in short, were only in part a theatre.

The Petty Sessions as Forum

The magistrates were landlords who owned land tenanted by farmers.
They also hired labour. With both their persons and property requiring
protection, it might be expected that landlords would often appear as
complainants. This was not the case. Between 1854 and 1869, landlords
brought 21 of the 253 complaints to the petty sessions. Of these, nineteen were against labourers who, in their turn, never plainted against

landlords. Between 1854 and 1884 (Table 6.1), landlords prosecuted only twenty-eight cases against labourers. In twenty of these, the complaints were in fact pursued by the landlords' stewards, caretakers, and servants. This means that most delicts were against the landlord's property rather than his/her person. What were they? Usually trespass or petty theft: food (rabbits, apples), fuel (wood, timber, branches, fencing), and fodder (grass). These comprised sixteen of the twenty-eight cases. The majority involved women (in nine of the sixteen cases, fourteen women were charged). Only one assault against a landlord was reported. It occurred during an election fracas in 1859. However, the landlord 'did not want to press the matter' and only a nominal fine was imposed. Indeed, in two of the trespass/theft cases, the landlords withdrew. In one, it was reported that the landlord's agent 'had forgiven the defendant.' In the other, Sir John Power, with his well-documented reputation as benevolent, 'did not wish to press the charge.'[30] Perhaps, too, landlords simply deemed it sufficient to register the charges. For in all this was reflected the general tenor of landlord-labourer relations in Thomastown at the time: as paternal and educative rather than penal. How this played out at the petty sessions is apparent from two trespass complaints (Case 6.2).[31] The first combined trespass with a political challenge; the second involved youthful enthusiasm. Labourers in both cases were gently treated by the bench.

Case 6.2: Two Cases of Trespass, Mount Juliet in 1849 and 1863
In 1849, the Earl of Carrick's caretaker, Thomas Bate, charged seven young, unmarried labourers with 'malicious trespass.' He said that they had made a 'great noise' with a drum and fife near to Mount Juliet House where the earl's brother-in-law was indisposed. Despite being told this, Bryan and Phelan 'refused to abate the nuisance, declaring that from time immemorial a band was allowed to proceed along the river bank ... and that the path was of right, open to the public. Upon further remonstrance, the same two men threatened to throw Bate into a sunk fence.' After a time, 'the whole party turned back towards Thomastown, but Bryan and Phelan immediately called on the musicians to "rise the music," for the mere purpose of giving annoyance. The only defence was that the path was always open and that it was the custom for a party with music to pass there every Sunday evening.' Said a magistrate: 'There was no right of passage ... and ... musical parties ... were only allowed on sufferance. During the illness of a gentleman, the defendants ought to see the impropriety of making any noise ... which could disturb him.' Phelan and Bryan, 'for their very improper conduct and

threatening language,' were fined 2s. each or forty-eight hours in the bridewell. The others were fined a nominal 1d.

In 1863 Carrick's steward summoned 'a number of young people' for trespassing on the demesne. 'But it having transpired that the steward had allowed them to pass on, they alleging they were going to a funeral, the cases were dismissed. The Bench, however, cautioned the parties against going there any more, which they promised not to do.'[32]

The 1849 complaint had political undertones. Yet the disposition of the case was uncoercive, ameliorative, and educative, particularly when compared with the legal treatment of paupers. In large measure, the reasons were sited in the social relations that inhered in the political economy. After 1850, labourers posed little danger to landed property or landlord persons while being fertile ground for moral improvement. Petty theft from the demesne by poor women did not threaten landed authority. Nor did exuberant youths who, even if politically inspired, were demanding a right of way across the land, not the land itself. These contrasted with the gradual but extensive growth of tenant-farmers' organizations after 1860 which were posing ever-increasing threats to landed property. As this tenant-farmer agitation increased, the logic of tripartite relations emerged: the enemies of my enemies are my friends.

This logic was buttressed by the material cum ideological relations between tenant-farmers and labourers. Between 1850 and 1884, farmers came to dominate the seats on the Board of Guardians. From there, they learned to ascribe to labourers the stigma of pauperism. For were labourers not simply one wage packet or illness away from the workhouse? What this reflected, of course, was that labourers were without land or capital. Because of this, they were ineligible as marriage partners. The resulting class endogamy led to a virtual absence of kin or affinal ties between labourers and farmers and reinforced the very clear ideas which both held about their relative positions in the status-class hierarchy. This socio-economic and cultural distance was exacerbated because farmers, unlike landlords, had little charitable ethos. They were not implicated in the deference and paternalism that underlay the various charitable works and committees which centred on landlords and labourers and, later, on town life. Farmers, too, had the turnips, furze, and pasture that were open to trespass and small-scale theft. At the same time, it was farmers and labourers who were forced into daily interaction. Unlike landlords, tenant-farmers did not have stewards to mediate either daily relations or conflicts with their labourers. In the farmer's view, labourers were an economic necessity because of the work they did; but they were a drain on household and public finances as well as a potential threat to property.

From the labourer's perspective, both farmers and landlords had land and capital. But it was the farmer whom s/he met everyday, who provided largely seasonal and not permanent work, and who insisted, if the work were permanent, that the labourer live in a 'tied cottage' from which s/he would be evicted if the job did not work out. It was the farmer who directly exploited his/her labour, who did not moderate the wage nexus and dearth through charity, and who asserted a social and ideological superiority despite daily interaction. In contrast, the immense social chasm that separated a landlord from a labourer was seldom made manifest through daily interaction. In any case, the distance was occasionally bridged by the charitable relations that obtained between the classes and/or the paternal ties that sometimes obtained between individuals.

All this was reflected at the petty sessions, which became a forum through which everyday relations between all three classes were negotiated. Indeed, it was the only such formal site in the locality. Between 1854 and 1884, farmers reportedly brought a dozen cases against labourers. These were mainly for trespass and theft. In turn, workers brought fourteen cases against farmers. Only one was about wages; eight were for assault. Five were brought by women and one was brought by a young boy. The details of this last case suggest how workers used the court as a weapon against, and refuge from, farmers' violence (Case 6.3).

Case 6.3: A Young Farm Labourer versus a Powerful Farmer, 1865
Martin Ryan 'appeared to prosecute a powerful man ... for assaulting him.' He had been sent by his own farmer-employer to a neighbouring farmer, James Power, to return trespassing cattle. His employer and Power were often in dispute over this issue and 'were not on the best of terms ... Some words passed' between Ryan and Power 'which were anything but complementary when Power kicked Ryan.' Power admitted this to the bench 'but said he was provoked' by the boy's talk. The magistrate 'said that no amount of bad language coming from the boy could justify him in kicking him. If he was insolent, other means ... could be resorted to for removing him from the premises.' Because Ryan 'was not much hurt,' Power was fined. If it happened again, he 'would be sent to gaol.'[33]

Landlord support was not unequivocally given to labourers, however. This was apparent from the fact that only two of the seventy-two complaints made by labourers between 1854 and 1884 involved retailers. Wor-kers quickly learned that, against retailers, they fared poorly (Case 6.4).

Case 6.4: The Two Complaints against Retailers, 1876 and 1877

In 1876 fisher William Dunphy accused Patrick Hayden, a timber merchant, of theft. Hayden had bought some timber from Carrick's steward and some of it which had been felled near the river floated away. Dunphy salvaged it, 'believing he had as good a right to it as anybody else.' Hayden later learned where the timber was and removed it. The case was dismissed. The magistrates said that they were 'confident that there had been no intention on Mr Hayden's part to steal the timber.' They suggested that 'Mr Hayden ... pay Dunphy the amount of loss he had sustained by recovering the timber and taking care of it.' In 1877 farm worker David Phelan sued retailer Patrick Hoyne for £5. Phelan said that he had given Hoyne £5 to 'pay off his account' but was told several weeks later that he still owed £7.12.6. Hoyne deposed that Phelan had only paid off £1. The bench found for Hoyne.[34]

Such outcomes in labourer-retailer complaints, discursively expressed in the naming of 'Mr Hayden' as against 'Dunphy,' contrasted with those in landlord-labourer and labourer-farmer complaints. They therefore highlight the way in which the court was implicated in class interests and class politics. In proceedings that touched on relations among landlords, farmers, and workers, class alliances/cleavages were played out. When they involved labourers and retailers, private property was favoured. However, what also emerged was the role of the court in the formation of class experience itself. For in insulating retailers from labourers, the landlord-magistrates were preventing the kind of interaction with which they colluded when the petty sessions served as a working-class arena. What did this arena look like?

The Petty Sessions as Arena

Gramsci noted that, as part of the civilizing process, the state uses the law to eliminate certain customs and to disseminate others. However, in Thomastown between 1854 and 1884, the petty sessions reflected far more about reproduction: of customary magisterial discretion and of labourers' customary concern for the 'revenge of private injuries.' This came out of two seemingly contradictory trends. On the one hand, labouring people continued to define their quarrels as private. On the other hand, working people appropriated the public petty sessions. It was all made possible because the magistrates colluded.

Between 1854 and 1869 (Table 6.1), eighty-five complaints were laid against labourers by the constabulary. All concerned public demeanour: drunken or disorderly behavior and assault, mostly against other labourers.[35] In only nine of the eighty-five cases were labourers charged with assaulting or obstructing the constabulary. Case 6.5 illustrates how these latter delicts could come about.

Case 6.5: Connors and the Constable, 1863

After it was reported that Michael Connors broke a pub window, a constable came and told him to leave. After much remonstration, Connors moved 'a few paces towards the door for the purpose of leaving the house, as the constable thought.' Instead, Connors 'caught the constable and thought to trip him. The constable then seized the defendant, with the view of bringing him to the barrack.' As he did so, Michael's brother Peter, a shoemaker, 'interfered with' the constable. Peter was charged and found guilty of 'obstructing ... a police officer in the discharge of his duty' and was fined 5s. and costs or jail for forty-eight hours. Michael Connors was imprisoned for six weeks with hard labour.[36]

In this case, as in many others, drunkenness escalated into a minor brawl; kin or friends became involved; and the constable was assaulted, usually when trying to convey the parties to the barracks. Indeed, most charges against labourers for assaulting constables occurred while a constable was trying to make an arrest for public misbehaviour. Yet very few such altercations were reported. Why? Because a coalition among working people to withhold information from the police caused prosecutions to fail (Case 6.6). This constrained constables from becoming involved in labourers' private quarrels and the incidents from entering the newspaper.

Case 6.6: The Coalition of Silence

In 1866 a constable charged blacksmith Michael Rogers with assaulting carpenter James Mohan 'by striking and cutting him with a half-gallon on the face.'

Prosecution witnesses said that they were in the room at the time and saw Mohan knocked down but 'they did not see by whom the blow was given.' Similarly, in 1877 a constable charged a small boy, John Meany, with assaulting another boy, John Miller. Labourer Patrick Dempsey, a witness, 'swore that he saw a portion of the row between Meany and Miller, and that the latter "shoved" the defendant, knocked him down and kicked him.' But Dempsey 'could not say who commenced the row.' The case had to be dismissed. In 1883 a 'drunk and disorderly' charge was brought by a constable against blacksmiths Pat and Thomas Lonergan. The 'constable said that he saw both parties fighting at their forge. Mrs Lonergan sent for the police and said her son was killing his father. Pat Lonergan appeared and said it was a family row.'[37]

Clearly, for working people, disputing and fighting were private concerns. The coalition of silence that came out of this viewpoint meant that the constabulary could successfully intervene in only two contexts. First, they could intrude when events actually took place in their presence. Second, they could intercede when indictable offences occurred, such as manslaughter or serious wounding. In other words, although labouring people treated their quarrels as private, the constabulary would move in if and when workers allowed their disputes to escalate (Case 6.7).

Case 6.7: Richard Hale and the Whelan Family, 1866

Labourer Richard Hale was 'allegedly assaulted by James Whelan ... and Arthur Whelan, both labourers' who struck 'him on the head with a pitchfork, thereby knocking him down and injuring him very much.' James Whelan was remanded by the magistrates until Hale recovered. Seemingly, Hale had been drunk. He 'went into Whelan's house to light his pipe, and as the parties about 12 months since had assaulted each other, his presence there in the state he was in, was not pleasing to Whelan, and an altercation took place out of which the assault arose.' The Moderator *added: 'The case will be fully inquired into at the next petty sessions when it is possible that the accused may be able to show that he was not the actual aggressor in the affair.' It was two sessions later before Hale recovered. Whelan was charged with 'dangerous assault.' However, a 'cross-summons had been issued by James Whelan against Richard Hale for having entered his house in a riotous manner ... asking for James Whelan or his sons to fight; and also for having ... then pulled and dragged Whelan's wife and daughter.'[38]*

The escalation of violence in this case allowed the constabulary an entry into a private dispute which in turn permitted the court to intervene and convert labourers' private concerns into public delicts. However, the case also shows that labourers did not eschew the petty sessions. Rather, even as they formed coalitions to keep the constabulary out, they came to the petty sessions, on their own terms, with their own complaints, meanings, and practices. Thus, many of the cases involving workers between 1854 and 1884 (Table 6.1) were ones in which labourers charged other labourers or, as often occurred in the numerous cross-cases that were heard, to charge each other. Of the seventy-two cases reported in which labourers were complainants, fifty were brought against other workers. The petty sessions thus became part of the custom of 'revenging private injuries' and pursuing private interests. What were these?

Of the fifty cases, thirty-seven were for assault. The rest were for threats and abusive language (five cases) and for theft or nuisance (seven cases). They were occasionally provoked by property claims and were often *simple disputes*. That is, they led to one-off appearances at the petty sessions to resolve a particular issue; they did not bring in other parties as disputants. Thus, Anty Byrne summoned Mary Doran for assault because Byrne 'went to Doran's house and demanded some furniture, which belonged to [her] sister, now in England, and who had written ... wishing her to get the articles.' On the demand being made, Mary Doran struck her.[39] Neither Doran nor Byrne appeared against each other at any other time. However, when interest was linked with physical proximity, disputants often engaged in a series of cumulative altercations. Indeed, as time went on, there was an increase in cases of this kind. These *complex disputes* involved women as well as men. Often, too, by the time a complainant reached the petty sessions, the original cause was deeply obscured by the history of the dispute itself. In 1882 Mary Ryan (Ladywell Street), summoned Mary Costigan, also of Ladywell, for assault. Ryan 'said it was almost 4 years since she had last to prosecute the defendant and since then she had "neither rest nor aise."'[40]

If proximity led to ongoing disputes and the entry of the constabulary when violence escalated, it also was likely to bring in kin, as did the Hale-Whelan quarrels (Case 6.7). Yet what is striking about all the reports is the almost total absence of complaints between kin. It was not that intra-familial disputing and violence did not occur, for the constabulary were reported as prosecuting several cases such as the Lonergan altercation (Case 6.6). However, labourers did *not* bring their kin or their affines to court.[41] The corollary, of course, was that kin were likely to enter or be brought into disputes as co-protagonists and/or witnesses. At such times, when complex disputes, convoluted issues, and numerous people came before them, the landlord-magistrates took it upon themselves to explore and interpret local, social relations. In exercising this customary independence, they invariably became enmeshed in local meanings and practices (Case 6.8)

Case 6.8: Investigating Local Relations at the Petty Sessions
(1866) Labourer Patrick Hurley was put on bail for having assaulted Michael Walsh. The magistrates commented: 'These parties have before manifested a love for litigation.'

(1876) Anne Reilly 'charged Mary Kerevan with having assaulted her and made use of threatening language towards her ... A good deal of evidence was taken and after a patient hearing the worships decided that it was "a woman's quarrel" and dismissed the case.'

(1883) Anastasia Murphy, Ladywell, summoned Ann Murphy, also of Lady-well, 'for having assaulted her by striking her on the head with a tin quart.' The constable provided the bench with the information that 'these women in Ladywell were always quarreling and causing much annoyance.'

(1877) Simon Grace said he was 'a road contractor's man,' in the 'habit of scraping the roadway in Low street.' He 'had a heap of stuff collected ... but when he went to remove it ... he found that William Finnegan had removed it to a heap of his own ... Grace then made use of very strong language towards Finnegan who thereupon (according to Grace) struck Grace a blow on the head with the handle of the shovel.' James Madigan was called by Grace to support his case. But Madigan swore that Grace had first struck Finnegan's donkey on the neck with a shovel and that Finnegan then pushed Grace.

'Complainant [Grace] – Did you not see him knock me down dead (laughter), and then didn't I say to you "witness that James Madigan"? (much laughter). Witness [Madigan] – Now Simon Grace, I am sworn to tell the truth, and I must say you did nothing of the kind. Sure if you were knocked down dead and "kilt" entirely, you could not say "witness that James Madigan" (laughter), and more than that, Simon, if you were "kilt dead" you could not be standing on that "binch" today (laughter).'

Finnegan had a cross-case against Grace for assault. Finnegan swore that he 'had liberty from ... the road contractor to scrape the mud off the roadway in question, and further, that he has been in the habit of doing so for the past 24 years.

He also swore that Grace brandished a shovel and threatened to cut him in two with it.'

The magistrates 'said that both parties ... were old men and it was a shame to see them bad friends. Grace seemed to have been in default,' but the court decided to dismiss both cases.[42]

The nature of the proceedings, with their use of and deferral to local knowledge, norms, meanings, and relations is striking. So, too, is the everyday language and interests of working people, the informal ambience of the courtroom and the magistrates' paternalism. Clearly, the petty sessions were an arena in which working people voluntarily participated. They used the court to pursue private concerns: to seek compensation for damages inflicted, to air and intensify accumulated ill-feelings, and to bring magistrates in as allies for their interests or as referees for their disputes. The petty sessions were oftentimes, therefore, an arena for negotiating interpersonal and neighbourhood relations which included the landlords who sat on the bench as well as the labourers who brought the complaints. The constabulary was excluded from this public pursuit of private grievance while the landlord-magistrates, in pursuing their own customary, independent action, colluded. In part, then, the petty sessions were appropriated by workers to reproduce their own, customary disputing style even as the institution was sited in political society, overseen by men of the dominant classes and intended to educate.

The Hegemonic Process: Abusive Language, Respectability, and Informers

As a theatre, forum, and arena, the public proceedings established by the 1827 Petty Sessions Act had multiple and interdependent consequences, both intended and unintended, as the colonial regime struggled against social dangerousness while simultaneously trying to educate and punish. The petty sessions forced landlord-magistrates to act in concert, develop common norms and practices, and learn what were considered by colonial agents to be proper ways of administering British law. They were being taught to be colonial agents themselves. Yet what simultaneously occurred was the reproduction of their particularistic, locally sited, and landed interests as these interfaced with the customs and concerns of labourers. As paupers, political clients, and/or self-interested agents, labourers continued to combine to redress private injuries in the context of kin and neighbourhood relations. Thus, coalitions that insulated certain of their practices from the state were reinvigorated even as ties between labourers and colonial agents/landlord-magistrates were intensified. In this process, workers obtained greater leverage against farmers while being taught to respect the private property of retailers, landlords, and guardians.

There were, however, certain cumulative aspects to this reproductive process. The petty sessions introduced new ways for locals to interact with state agents, people from other classes, and those of their own kind. Class distinctions were sharpened. The process also led to new discursive categories. This was instantiated in the idea that language could be 'threatening,' 'insulting,' or 'abusive' and that this constituted an offence for which restitution could be demanded. This notion only gradually emerged in Thomastown, however, dating from the second half of the nineteenth century. Two cases were reported before 1858 and three between 1859 and 1861. The next reported case was in 1869. Between then and 1884, nine more cases were reported.

In four of the earliest five cases, all before 1861, labourers were charged by people occupying superior status categories: a landlord, a gentleman, the station master, and a water bailiff. Then, in 1869, on the complaint of Margaret Delahunty, a labourer's daughter married to a shoemaker, labourer Catherine Murray 'was bound to keep the peace, for 12 months ... for having repeatedly *abused her, and used language calculated to lead to a breach of the peace.*'[43] From that point on, the numerous newspaper reports suggest that not only had abusive language entered the disputing repertoire of the working class, but it had also become the exclusive idiom of workers, used equally by men and women. This meant that labouring people could pursue quarrels into the petty sessions without actual physical violence having occurred. It meant, too, that women and children could enter a dispute more freely and this, in turn, reinforced the notion of quarrels as both private and familial. The jurisdiction and scale of the petty sessions as an arena were therefore expanded even as physical violence was displaced as a disputing device, appropriated by the state in its educative mission. Meanwhile, as working people continued to grab hold of the legal process and rework it into their customary way of 'making their own regulations' and of seeking private restitution, the law, the state, and 'civilized customs' became more profoundly implicated in their lives, experiences, and notions of legitimacy.

This was exemplified further by a key contradiction that emerged from within the workings of this hegemonic process. Those workers who appeared once before the magistrates were seen as dealing with interpersonal difficulties that might beset anyone. However, if quarrels were continually pursued or allowed to escalate, 'bad friends' might become seen by magistrates, constables, and, importantly, other labourers as quarrelsome people or litigious neighbours. They risked the interference of the police, public reprimand by impatient magistrates, and avoidance by other labourers. Similarly, those who were arrested once for public misconduct were punished and forgotten. However, repeated appearances connoted personal and moral weakness: this was a person who 'drank too freely' and became involved in what the press described as 'those disgraceful rows.'[44] The fineness of the line between legitimate cause and unrespectable public exposure was part of the reason why not all labourers were reported as taking part in the petty sessions. Richard Donnelly's career is a case in point (Case 6.9).

Case 6.9: Richard Donnelly at the Petty Sessions, 1844–79
Apart from his numerous appearances for salmon poaching, Donnelly came before the magistrates seven times between 1844 and 1879: for trespass, petty theft, assault, and fighting. These appearances affected his reputation and credibility and this, in turn, affected how his kin acted and were perceived to act. In 1873, when hotelier Mrs. Bishop was charged by Donnelly's enemy, water bailiff William Murphy, with buying salmon during the closed season, one of the witnesses was Donnelly's wife. She was asked by Murphy if she delivered any fish to Mrs. Bishop during the closed season. 'I did not,' she replied. 'I was not in Mrs. Bishop's for the last 16 years.' Murphy then asked: 'Do you remember the 16th of September?' Mrs. Donnelly retorted: 'I will not remember anything for you, Billy.[45]

Labouring people and their kin who had repeatedly appeared at the petty sessions treated facts as relative to the state of their interpersonal relations at the time. The magistrates knew this. In 1878 fisher James Kelly was charged with assaulting water bailiff Ryan. Kelly sought to prove an alibi by producing Richard Donnelly's nephew, Thomas, who swore that it was he, Thomas, who had assaulted Ryan and that Kelly was not there at all. The chairman said that he 'did not believe a word of it' and Kelly was fined.[46]

This lack of credibility signalled a too-public reputation which had been achieved, in part, by too many appearances of oneself and one's kin at the court. The equivocal meaning that gradually became attached to such a reputation was engendered in part because few people from other classes came to the petty sessions to pursue their quarrels – a feature that the landlord-magistrates tended to encourage when, for example, they privileged the private property of retailers over the private interests of labourers. Indeed, it was probably because the petty sessions had been so successfully appropriated by working people that members of other classes came to eschew both the court and the kind of interaction that brought people there. This, in turn, helped local people construct notions of what constituted respectable behaviour. Over time, respectability for people of all classes came to be associated with *not* using the petty sessions – with *not* 'combining for the revenge of private injuries.'

Thus, the delict of abusive language expanded the capacity of labouring people, along with their kin, to pursue private injuries into a public arena even as it allowed the state to appropriate the means of violence and even as the importance of reputation and respectability came to constrain such participation. All this signified several, seemingly contradictory processes: the intensification of labouring custom alongside its displacement; the increasing efficacy and legitimacy of the court, an organ of political society, alongside its avoidance; and the growing independence of landlord discretion inside the court alongside landlord collusion with the colonial state. That all this could occur simultaneously was because the working class had become differentiated – socially as a result of accumulated disputes and culturally because of assignments of relative respectability. Nevertheless, the coalition among labourers to protect themselves from the intrusions of the police was reproduced at the same time, a product of the antipathy that slowly emerged towards key roles associated with the petty sessions – that of 'informer' and 'perjurer.'

For labourers to inform was occasionally a material necessity. Thus, when an excise officer charged rural, lodging-house keeper Patrick Burke with 'selling tobacco and spirits without a licence,' it was two labourers, Daniel Fleming and James Magrath, who deposed that they had bought the items from Burke. Under cross-examination, it became clear that they were being paid by the excise officers for their 'swearing,' that they were casual labourers, and that Magrath's brother had 'absconded to America' under suspicious circumstances. Burke's solicitor maintained that the case was 'one perfect tissue of falsehood and perjury by Fleming' and that he 'would produce three witnesses of unimpeachable character' to 'contradict the evidence of the Informer Fleming.' Thus, a servant in Burke's house, a wheelwright who was boarding there, and a millwright all swore that they had never seen 'a drop of whiskey.' The excise officer interjected that Burke had already been fined twice before for this offence. Burke was a found guilty and fined a hefty £12.10s.[47]

Through this case, three labouring witnesses, self-defined as being of 'unimpeachable character' and gainfully employed, were ignored by the magistrates while the evidence of two casual labourers who had been denounced as 'perjurers' and whose kin were suspect was used by the magistrates to decide in favour of what they already knew about Burke, in favour of the state. Through the process, respectable people had been denigrated and, perhaps, tainted with the implication of perjury themselves. It was all because Fleming and Magrath were trying to earn a few shillings from the excise officer. Out of such collusion, however, the terms 'informer' and 'perjurer' came to be seen as synonymous epithets. They also came to be part of the abusive language for which a complaint could be made at the petty sessions, as part of the expansion of the jurisdiction of the court and as part of local constructions of respectability.

This was the situation when water bailiff Sherwood charged Bridget Carroll with 'threatening and abusive language' because she had 'met him within the precincts of the court,' that is, in a very public place, 'and called him a perjurer.' It was also the case in 1883 when labourer Thomas Raftice charged Andrew Walsh, a victualler and rural publican, 'with using abusive language towards him' because Walsh had 'called him "Tom Raftice, the informer."' In these cases, the magistrates concurred. They also regarded the charges as sufficiently serious to remand the perpetrators for twelve months on bail set at the high figures of between £10 and £12.[48] Thus, both labourers and landlord-magistrates contributed yet again, through the petty sessions and political society, to framing the cultural boundary around Thomastown's working class, to defining the nature of working-class experience, and to constructing the hegemonic process itself.

Conclusion: Custom and Respectability through the Petty Sessions

Through the variable meanings that the petty sessions took on between 1828 and 1884, as theatre, forum, and arena, the court proved to be a highly successful 'civilizing' device. The vitality of labouring culture appropriated the petty sessions while simultaneously allowing the hegemonic process to operate through other, more micro-level, processes: the stigmatization and punishment of paupers; the ongoing politics and differential paternalism of landlords, farmers, and retailers; the intensification of labouring custom; the changing relations of landlord-magistrates with the state; the state's appropriation of violence; and the emergence of 'respectability.' At the same time, class differences and boundaries were reproduced via the different roles, treatment, and involvements that people from varying classes had at the petty sessions and through the emergence of such discursive categories as 'informer' and 'perjurer' which excoriated collusion with certain agents of the colonial state. These agents, the constabulary, were outsiders. In contrast, the landlord-magistrates were locals, enmeshed in social relations and shared meanings with other local people from other classes. It was largely through the agency of the magistrates, as members of the dominant, propertied classes but also as uneasy allies of the colonial state, that the education of people from all classes took shape through the petty sessions and the law.

7. Privatizing the River: Politicizing Labouring Fishers

There is a general complaint of the diminution of the salmon fisheries. In the ...
Avon, the Severn, and the Trent, it is becoming ... a scarce fish. The great north-
ern fisheries, and the Irish fisheries, are much less productive than formerly.

– Sir Humphry Davy, IUP 1824 [427] vii:145

In 1802 the rivers Nore, Barrow, and Suir and the Waterford estuary were 'celebrated' for their salmon while the fishing itself was 'free by custom' to those who lived along the banks.[1] These resources and rights, as well as the rivers themselves, became highly contested during the nineteenth century. On the upper, non-tidal portions of these rivers, the prerogatives of private property began to usurp and, by 1884, had criminalized the rights of custom. The process was complex, woven out of parliamentary legislation, case law, policing policies, administrative priorities, and market exigencies. Also crucial were political combinations, alliances, and oppositions which came out of the various and often opposing interests in the salmon fisheries themselves.

Fishing did not provide full-time work in Thomastown nor did it form the basis for an occupational group. However, as time went on, more local people began to fish while others occasionally entered the contest in pursuit of other material, personal, or ideological interests. Far more importantly, however, the decades of public argument, hostility, and often violent confrontation made the inland salmon fishery a powerful symbol which incorporated, in various and often conflicting ways, the interests and ideologies of most local people. For labourers in particular, the political-legal process and its outcome became a profound strand in the *metissage* of their experiences as subjects and objects.

The 'Declining Salmon Fisheries,' 1800–42

Although the right to fish was 'free by custom,' the fishing itself was not free from legislative interventions. Importantly, these had never been linked to the ownership or occupation of property. However, the failure to enforce these laws, said Tighe in 1802, meant that the 'quantity of salmon has ... very much decreased within the last forty years.'[2] Indeed, little was even then done until the decline became 'a general complaint.' Parliamentary inquiries ensued. In 1825 C.H.B. Clarke, a Kilkenny MP, said that illegal weirs had been erected on the upper Nore and that the owners of all weirs, including millers, had blocked the requisite fish passes. In short, said Clarke, the law existed but was evaded.

Clarke's inland view, however, could not entirely explain conditions there. Salmon are a migratory species. After spawning in the upper waters, both the 'spent fish' and young 'fry' swim downriver, through the tidal waters and estuary, to the sea. They return after several years to the upper waters to spawn again. This meant that agency in the lower reaches was key. There, said activist Patrick Magee, landed proprietors had set up fixed Scotch weirs after 1807 and had virtually destroyed the tidal fishery. The law in all this 'remained a dead letter,' he said. 'The magistrates who should have enforced them became weir owners, and in receipt of great revenues therefrom, allowed the fishermen ... to dwindle away into ... poverty.'[3]

In response to the decline, 'gentlemen interested in the protection of the fisheries' began a fund in 1828 to hire a fisheries inspector. Over the next few years, Patrick Kelly brought suits against inland weirs which did not conform to legal regulations, causing gentlemen such as Tighe, the Earl of Carrick, and Hunt at Jerpoint to put in salmon passes, to remove fish traps set in their weirs, to fish only during the open time, and to shorten the lengths of their weirs. In tidal waters, Kelly levelled illegal nets, including the new Scotch weirs which had been found by the courts to be illegal. In both tidal and non-tidal areas, Kelly seized the cots and nets of fishers who were netting in the closed season. He also talked to mill owners about removing traps from their weirs. Finally, he appointed water keepers to watch the upper waters during the spawning season.[4]

Almost immediately, optimistic reports came in about the increase of salmon and breeding fish. Yet, although some gentlemen attended meetings, gave money, and continued to urge the removal of all illegal obstructions to the salmon migration,[5] others among them who held inland weirs or tidal nets were concerned to maximize the returns on their property. By 1830, these owners had re-erected or altered their weirs and nets to their former state, and Kelly found himself levelling, seizing, and shortening the same 'fixed engines' that he had the year before. These failures 'induced' cot fishers 'to try the only means left, that of forming a society.' This, said Magee, was St Peter's Society, a pan-regional combination formed by the fishers of the rivers Barrow and Nore at a meeting in New Ross in late 1835. Its aim, to 'protect' the fisheries, meant opposing the gentry-owned fixed nets and weirs. Magee explained how 'we discovered many old Acts ... in force against those weirs [and] commenced prosecuting and taking them down.' A solicitor 'gave ... his time ... gratis ... At the last assizes of Kilkenny, he proceeded against weirs on the river Nore.' Yet, although 'the parties pleaded guilty ... the weirs are kept standing, and fishing.' The Society also sent petitions to the Waterford MP regarding 'their rights as fishermen.' But the ineffectiveness of subscriptions, courts, and petitions led to violence. In 1834 tidal weirs were destroyed 'by a mob from the interior of the country.'[6] Again in 1837 and 1839, cotmen tore down tidal weirs that had been re-erected.[7]

On the inland Nore, conditions also were worsening. By 1834, a fisheries inspector no longer was hired by private subscription and a petition from Barrow and Nore fishers, presented to the House of Commons by Daniel O'Connor and signed by 1,000 people, complained of great distress. Police were also reported as guarding the weirs at Inistioge and Mount Juliet which, according to the nationalist owner-editor of the *Journal* at an 1835 commission of inquiry, had 'usurped' the fishing rights on the inland Nore, a river on which 'there are no private rights of fishing.'[8] As a reflection of this, the cotmen who joined St Peter's Society were soon aided by a new society to protect the Nore fisheries. Founded in 1835 by 'gentlemen (not being weir-owners),' it sent circulars to millers requesting cooperation and laid charges against weir owners. Water bailiffs were hired and, by 1837, Thomastown petty sessions had dealt with a large number of local, inland gentlemen who were had up for weir violations.[9] A year later, however, all had to be prosecuted again because the owners kept 'constructing fresh and illegal obstructions for the take ... of ... fish.' In early 1842, the water-keepers wrote that they were heavily in debt because convictions did not mean that costs were recovered. When Lady Carrick appealed her second conviction, not only was her fine lowered but she was released from paying court costs.[10]

The battle was thus unremitting, landlords were deeply divided by the issue, and cotmen in the tidal and inland waters shared both common sentiment and organization. By 1842, several other features were also central. On the one hand, it was a 'golden age' for fishers. The alliance of cotmen and anti-weir gentry had ensured, according to Magee, that 'our rivers were open to the free passage of the salmon. The fishery increased 100 per cent by our perseverance.'[11] It was likely at this time, in fact, that cot fishing in the Thomastown area became a more common activity for labourers. Yet, on the other hand, it was a continuous effort for the regional combination to keep the inland weirs fair and the tidal nets levelled.

Through all this, public interest in the fisheries had been made manifest through the media. After 1828, editorials, letters, reports, and prosecutions heightened public awareness while, a decade later, when new fisheries legislation was being considered, the reports, including parliamentary deliberations and news from all parts of Ireland, became incessant. The local discourse reflected the intense sentiment and grave material concern (Case 7.1).

Case 7.1: Discursive Views from the Southeastern Fisheries, 1829–40
Kilkenny Moderator, *27 June 1829. A motion passed by a meeting of gentry, chaired by the Earl of Carrick, said 'that the alterations lately made by Mr Kelly in the fishing weirs on the Nore will ... be of considerable advantage to the Upper Fisheries, and ... an equal share of salmon will be insured.'*

Kilkenny Journal, *29 March 1837. 'When Ireland was a nation and had a parliament,' there 'was ... fish in our rivers for the common benefit of all. Now there is none but what is entrapped ... [by] a few monopolists' who erect illegal weirs and nets; 'and those who ... send to gaol a poor man for "illegally" taking a few potatoes to sustain life ... scruple not to violate the fishery laws with impunity by appropriating ... common property.'*

Kilkenny Moderator, *15 July 1839, New Ross. 'A vast fleet of cots ... to day proceeded in warlike array to extirpate the salmon-weirs erected along the banks ... The authorities were on the alert and the proprietors of the weirs were alive to the mischief meditated ...; but what could they do? New faces, placed ... judiciously to perpetrate the overt acts, baffled the skill of the police to identify the delinquents ... Shame upon the government to allow matters to attain such a height without repelling them by force.'*

Kilkenny Journal, *14 March 1840. The mayor of Waterford wrote to Dublin Castle: 'My Lord – As it has been the practice for the last few years for the cotmen to come down this river ... in almost overwhelming numbers [to] ... destroy the*

*various salmon weirs ... I beg ... to be informed ... what steps I shall be authorized
... to take to prevent a recurrence of these assemblages, in which the peace and
tranquility of the country is violated, and life often endangered.' Dublin Castle
tersely replied: 'The proper course is to prevent the erection of those weirs, which
have been repeatedly pronounced illegal. If erected, they become a public nuisance
and may be abated by any persons with impunity. Informations should be taken
and returned to the Assizes against those who erect the weirs.'*

For many, complaints about the fisheries challenged the legitimacy of
law and, even, the state. Landlord-magistrates cum weir/net owners
were not only refusing to enforce the law but were explicitly breaking it,
while combinations of cotmen were destroying private property and
threatening 'peace and tranquillity.' The price of salmon had made it a
luxury in Ireland instead of a staple, petitions were arriving at the
House of Commons, a private member's bill to privatize Irish rivers was
barely defeated, and fish markets in Liverpool and Manchester were
teeming with Irish salmon, exported via the exertions of illegal technologies. The issues seemed complex. Were new laws required to protect
the fisheries or would old law suffice? How could the law be enforced;
who should pay? What, in fact, did 'protection' mean? To answer such
questions raised a key issue: what was the purpose of the fisheries? To
supply the lucrative export market and profit capital or to provide food
and work for local people? What technology should be allowed: the efficient, but illegal, fixed engines or the less productive, but legal, moveable nets and rods?[12] Ultimately, who was protection for? Who had the
right to fish? Who owned the salmon?

Viewpoints of the State: The 1835 Commission and the 1842 Act

Years of political argument and combination culminated in the 1842
Fisheries Act which was in turn rooted in the understandings and the
language of class which informed the findings of an 1835 inquiry. Simply put, all problems were seen as coming from the 'natural conflict'
engendered by the location of private property. The 'most productive ...
fisheries were in the lower [tidal] reaches ... whereas the function of
protecting breeding salmon, spawning grounds and salmon fry were in
the [inland] upper reaches.' This meant that inland/upper proprietors
had little 'pecuniary interest in the fisheries' and were thus 'indifferent
to poaching, and unwilling to co-operate, either in purse or in person,

towards its abatement.' The solution, like the problem, was equally simple: ameliorate the 'natural conflict' by allowing the upper proprietors more fish. This could be done by eliminating 'poaching in Ireland [which], though in part attributable to the circumstances and habits of the peasantry, is principally encouraged by the absence of an efficient Police.'[13] The upper proprietry were to be co-opted, the so-called peasantry were to be coerced.

The mechanism was the 1842 act which replaced all prior laws and had three ambitious but contradictory aims: to increase productivity, to allow everyone to fish, and to preserve the stocks. Two aspects were crucial. First, to ensure market supplies and mollify lower proprietors, the 1842 act legalized Scotch nets and fixed engines if the proprietor had used them in the twenty years prior to the act. However, before 1842, most weirs and fixed nets in the estuary were illegal. The 1842 act legalized them. Second, to induce upper proprietors to improve preservation, the act recognized private property in inland waters ('a several fishery'). Yet chapter 106, section 65 also recognized the public's right to net in such waters ('a common of piscary') if such a right had 'been enjoyed for ... twenty years before ... this Act.'

Two problems ensued. First, it was assumed that private property and public rights could co-exist on a daily basis. Second, the meaning of 'inland' was unclear. The case of *Murcott* v. *Carter* (1768) distinguished navigable from non-navigable waters and the kinds of fishing rights in each. Along non-navigable rivers, the owners of the land owned the fishery and this ownership extended to the middle of the river. Along navigable rivers, however, 'the fishery is common. It is *prime facie* in the king, and is public.'[14] The 1842 act added that navigable/public waters were tidal and that non-navigable/private waters were non-tidal, inland waters. However, the River Nore where it flowed through Thomastown was an anomaly: it was inland/non-tidal yet navigable. It had also been labelled, along with the Barrow and Suir, a 'royal river' in 28 Henry VIII.c.22. It thus seemed to belong to the crown and, hence, to the public. Until 1868, the anomalous Nore (navigable, royal but non-tidal) and an act that recognized the public right to fish in private fisheries formed the context for contest and combination in the Thomastown area.

Irreconcilable Conflicts: The Evolution of Combinations and Fisheries Policy, 1842–63

The 1842 act explicitly stated that enforcement of its provisions was to be in the hands of the interested parties, under the eye of fisheries com-missioners.[15] Over the next few decades, this policy slowly unravelled under the pressure of irreconcilable conflicts which, although existing prior to the act, were aggravated by it. Succinctly, the dynamics of class-biassed enforcement, class-based combinations, and regionally rooted class factions overwhelmed the Fisheries Act.

Class, Faction, and Region

As soon as the act was passed, inland proprietors on the Nore formed an association to enforce it. They collected subscriptions to pay for water bailiffs and prosecutions. By late 1844, reports of fishery cases at Tho-mastown's petty sessions were telling. Instead of weir owners being charged, it was a cot crew, a labouring fisher, and local fishmongers. Such class bias had quickly become a general feature, as the fisheries commissioners noted: 'The new fishing associations ... were composed chiefly of ... proprietors ... and their efforts ... against offences ... caused many of the poorer order to be convicted ... and thus created an impres-sion, an erroneous one certainly, that the law was one for the advantage of the rich, and an additional source of coercion on the poor.'[16] This occurred in a context in which illegal technology had been legalized, thus encroaching on the public fishery in tidal waters. Moreover, land-lords erected new fixed engines 'under the assumed protection of ... the Act.' Class conflict in the tidal waters, manifested in the clash over tech-nology, was exacerbated. The Waterford estuary was an important site (Case 7.2).

Case 7.2: Combination and Confrontation in the Waterford Estuary

Before the act, very few fixed nets remained in the estuary; however, by the spring of 1843, 'all the weirs sprang up again.' A regional coalition arose again in response, made up of drift-net fishers in the estuary, a preservation society of gen-try on the Suir, and cotmen from the Nore, Barrow, and Suir. They prosecuted the fixed nets for fishing in the closed time. But the owners were simply fined £5 and continued fishing. Shortly after, the secretary of the Suir Society described how he had come to Waterford to find 'the bridge lined with police, the military and the magistrates all out, a descent of cotmen having been threatened.' The last 'were dissuaded from going to prostrate the weirs,' and the Society, along with the fisher-ies commissioners, jointly charged the owners with using illegal nets. The bench on the Wexford side of the estuary indicted them but the Waterford magistrates at both the petty and the quarter sessions refused to do so. 'The peace of the whole country was at stake' as 2,000 fishermen then took 'the law into their own hands and openly prostrated the weirs.' [17]

With the gentry still breaking the law, fishers rioting, and loud complaints being made by numerous interests, the commissioners increasingly had to intervene. In Waterford over the next years, the crown was called on to indict weir owners. They were tried by juries at the assizes. However, the act allowed action only against a particular fixed net and, as fast as convictions were obtained and the weirs levelled, the gentry re-erected them. The crown then had to, and did, begin the legal process again. Funds for enforcement were also a problem. Not only were voluntary subscriptions insufficient but a 'hostile feeling' was produced by the common belief that 'upper proprietors paid while lower proprietors fished.' In any case, more enforcement was clearly needed. In 1845 the commissioners were successful in having the Constabulary Act amended to allow the police to act in fishery offences. [18]

In late 1844 the commissioners held an inquiry into the closed season, another source of conflict. The 1842 act required a 124-day closed season and it had become policy to make the dates uniform everywhere to ease enforcement. However, because salmon migrated downriver in the autumn, tidal fishers wanted a longer autumn season whereas inland fishers, because salmon migrated upriver in early spring, wanted to fish before February. The 1844 inquiry was an effort to find solutions. In Thomastown, two witnesses appeared. Major Izod represented the gentry's association, complaining that angling had deteriorated since the 1842 act because of the tidal nets, the non-observance of the closed season, the failure of protection efforts, and a lack of help from tidal gentlemen. As an angler, he wanted the closed season to be from 1 October to 1 March. His grievances contrasted starkly with the evidence from water bailiff Edward Bryan. In 1843, said Bryan, eighteen water bailiffs were on the Nore and its tributaries. It was 'a very valuable year because a man could well support his family by snap net fishing.' No weir extended entirely across the river nor was there any weir that had not a gap. There was thus 'no hindrance to angling.' [19]

These two interpretations of local conditions, from a gentleman angler as opposed to a man concerned with cot fishing, were rooted in material differences. A petition signed by 108 Nore cotmen, which duplicated one sent in by 74 Barrow cotmen, made this clear. All these inland netmen requested a different closed season (30 August to 31 January) from the one proposed by inland angler Izod. Importantly, too, the inland cotmen's request differed, as they pointed out, from estuary cot fishers who wanted September open. In short, the concerns of fresh-water fishers had begun to link inland localities at the same time that their interests began to diverge from those of tidal cotmen. Yet the inland cotmen's last request kept alive the alliance with cotmen everywhere and all upper proprietors: 'That the Board will not neglect the prosecution of the illegal ... Scotch weirs.'[20]

Orienting Fisheries Policy

By 1845, the commissioners noted that 'the commercial value of the Irish Fisheries' had improved because of individual enterprise, an expanding English market, better fishing technology, and railways. In this expansionary context, they proclaimed that the priority should be to ensure a 'maximum productiveness of food.' This meant, for them, that 'commercial value ... and not ... private or local ... interests' was central; so, too, was specialization. Coastal and tidal fisheries were to be 'the entire of the commercially valuable ... fisheries' while the fresh waters were to be 'the natural nurseries' which had to be regulated.[21] Their view received considerable fillip with the potato failures between 1845 and 1848. That the fisheries had not provided an alternate food supply for Ireland seemed to confirm the need to develop the fisheries 'as a source of industry and trade, and consequently of food.' Ironically, what they saw as disorder during the famine years (ignoring of closed times, killing of breeding fish and fry, attaching nets to weirs) was what in fact fed people in such localities as Thomastown. For the commissioners, however, the absence of enforcement was a sign of breakdown.[22] The 1849 act came out of this view. Ireland was divided into seventeen districts. In each, a board of conservators was to be elected by licence holders. The licence fees were to pay the costs of protection, with each board enforcing the Fisheries Act in its district and, if needed, passing by-laws subject to the approval of the commissioners. Thomastown became part of Waterford District, an area of 3,400 square miles, comprising the tidal and inland portions of the rivers Nore, Barrow, and Suir along with the Waterford estuary and coastline. Its new board inherited the problem of proliferating, illegal stake nets in the estuary and the fact that these were the most 'conducive to the supply of good fish to the market.' It also inherited interest groups which were demanding changes to the closed season. It was told that it 'must be guided solely by the ... dispassionate consideration of what is good or bad for the fisheries, as regards their permanent productiveness to the public.'[23]

Over the next few years, although the commissioners observed that 'all the old complaints are repeated,' they continued to insist that 'the law, if faithfully observed, was sufficient.' Inland proprietors/anglers would obtain 'a sufficient share of fish ... to enlist their cooperation in close-time' so that the tidal fisheries could then produce the requisite fish for market. This view was aided by increased catches which began in the mid-1850s and which were attributed to greater cooperation by these 'interested parties [who] allowed each other a fair participation.'[24] The meaning of participation, however, still included only proprietors; and the common-sense logic of this now began to work itself through the bureaucracy, particularly when it became associated with the belief that there never could be commercial value in fresh-water net fishing. It was thus concluded that it would be 'far more remunerative' for proprietors of the inland waters to lease angling rights rather than to sell the fish. The inland fisheries, not the inland fish, could be commoditized. In fact, this was occurring at the time: the 'exclusive fishing right upon Mount Juliet property' was being 'let for profit' annually to the 'best bidder.'[25] Of what use, then, was inland netting by cot fishers? Indeed, in 1856, the commissioners suggested that the abolition of inland netting would be 'a general public good.' Why? Because poaching, or unlicensed fishing, was still seen as a problem among the so-called peasantry. This common-sense view was then extended: 'It is notorious that from one end of the river Nore to the other there are innumerable cot-owners whose sole occupation is the netting of ... salmon.'[26] In this view, unlicensed fishing/poaching had become synonymous with cot fishing.

The rhetoric subsided but the number of prosecutions slowly increased. There had been one in 1851, none in 1852 or 1853, and one in 1854. In 1855 there were five; and in 1856, three. None involved weir violation. These prosecutions, in number and class bias, were linked to a fishery which was seen as 'steadily progressing.' More fish were being caught, their value had increased, and fishing rights had become objects 'for profitable investment of capital.' By 1860, two-thirds of the salmon catch was exported. 'With such demand and no possibility of an over supply,' the commissioners happily declared that the interests of private property and public right were 'really identical.'[27] The bubble burst in 1860 when the catch fell dramatically. The commissioners concluded that too many fixed nets were fishing in tidal waters and that inland rivers were 'too closely fished.' Apparently the high price of salmon in the previous five years had induced landowners in the estuaries to erect fixed nets 'to procure fish for such profitable disposal.' As the fixed nets proliferated, upper proprietors complained that they were overfishing and evading the closed times. The commissioners now suggested that measures be adopted to control the fixed nets and, again, that inland netting be banned. This latter idea had previously been mooted to mollify upper proprietors. Now it was used to alleviate declining stocks.[28]

Within two years, the crisis was otherwise contained. An 1863 act proscribed all new fixed nets and set up special commissioners to investigate the legality of all fixed engines. Those found 'in contravention of the common ... [or] statute law' were to be levelled. By 1865, 204 fixed nets had been levelled. The value of fishery property increased as a result.[29]

Class and Faction in the Inland Salmon Fisheries

In 1861 cotmen and anglers along the inland Nore were reportedly fishing illegally in both the closed and open seasons. So, too, were there demands for bailiffs 'who will do their duty without favour or affection to any person.'[30] In such ways did the editor of the *Moderator* try to incite public concern. For, in fact, enforcement was light – bailiffs colluded, local interest was muted, and the inland Nore fisheries were not yet of great economic value. Certainly few poaching cases were reported before 1862.[31] This reflected the gentry's inability to maintain subscriptions and, later, the conservators' interests in policing mainly the tidal fisheries.[32] Only two landlords tried to claim exclusive rights to their fisheries. Davis and Marsh each charged cot crews for netting without permission on the waters adjacent to their properties. Despite 'a crowded court ... as all the cot fishers were interested,' no details were given.[33] Clearly, this issue was not important at the time. Instead, the eye of the public was on the contests between millers Pilsworth and Innes over water (Case 5.3) and among the gentry over fixed nets. Both sites implicated labourers as rhetorical devices and political resources (Case 7.3).

Case 7.3: Landlords and the Inland Fisheries – Labour as Objects

(1) When a constable brought a possession charge against the mother of Martin Murphy ('the notoriously frequent transgressor of the Fishery Laws'), the magis-

*trates, 'in consequence of the woman's poverty, decided that she would be suffi-
ciently punished by the forfeiture of the fish.'*

*(2) At a meeting of the Waterford Board of Conservators in 1856, a landlord/
conservator opposed raising the cot-licence fee because cotmen 'were not able to pay
the small sum asked of them now.' The landlord/chair added: 'The gentlemen
who have weirs are the persons opposed ... to the only class who live by fishing ...
it was ... the strength of wealth against the poor man.' The chair went on to
admit that he was paying personally the licence fees for several cotmen.*

*(3) A labourer on Mount Juliet estate was convicted for illegal fishing. The earl
wrote that 'he did not wish [him] to be dealt with severely.' The bench complied.*[34]

Such paternal concern from particular landlords, and the support
that cotmen gave to certain millers (Case 5.3), meant that cotmen were
divided among themselves. This was seen at the petty sessions in 1844
when a cotman charged another with 'assault and threatening language
over fishing.' The witnesses for both were other cotmen. Or, when the
'fishmonger of no small notoriety' was charged by a brewer for assault,
witnesses for and against were fishers.[35] Cotmen were also fragmented
by occupation. Many were millworkers; others were artisans or casual
labourers. Finally, cotmen were divided by kinship and, thus, by crew
membership. For cotmen, between 1845 and 1865, generally tended to
form most of their four-man crews with kin (Table 7.1).[36]

Nevertheless, there were links that cut across and moderated such divisions. For example, some cotmen did not have kin who fished; they
joined kin-based crews and/or were joined by those who did have fisher
kin (Table 7.1). Such cross-cutting ties were reinforced by the fact that
cotmen's links to gentlemen were necessarily fragile, emanating from a
situationally circumscribed factionalism. Moreover, all cotmen were
seen by all non-labourers as natural poachers. At the 1856 meeting
(Case 7.3{2}), even the sympathetic chair said that he would reduce the
cot-licence fee only if cotmen surrendered their cots during the closed
times. Such common sense was firmed up by the actions that fishers
sometimes took against those of other classes. In 1859 a cotman threatened a water bailiff and, a year later, a constable. In 1861 the station
master summoned 'the notorious fishmonger' for the same offence.[37]

Conclusion, 1842–63
The 1842 Fisheries Act actualized a broad alliance of anti-tidal weir interests while both faction and collusion marked the local arena. As the mar-

Table 7.1: Thomastown Cot Crews, 1845–65

	1845	1855	1856	1863	1864
William **Dawson**	x				
Mathew Dawson	x				
Martin Dawson, Sr	x				
Martin Dawson, Jr	x	(x)*			x
Patrick Dawson			(x)	(x)	x
Thomas **Donnelly**					x
Maurice Donnelly		x			x
Richard Donnelly		x			
John **Kelly**				x	
James Kelly				x	
Michael **Clooney**		(x)		(x)	
Patrick **Connors**			(x)		
Thomas **Holehan**			(x)		
John **Cotteral**			(x)		

*Brackets indicate that a cot-crew member was not linked by kinship to any of the other three crew members.
Source: These are the cases in which complete crews were named in the fishery prosecutions.

ket for fish and fisheries expanded, so, too, did the varying and often opposing interests in the salmon fisheries. The public became increasingly involved and, in later years, when fishery cases were entered for hearing, 'they excited much public interest.'[38] The conflicts also increasingly brought in the state, through legislation and its administrative agencies. Meanwhile, a slow divergence of political interests and organization was apparent. A pan-regional alliance dissolved as the interests of inland cotmen diverged from tidal ones over the closed season. In the inland fishery, the common opposition of some proprietors and all cotmen to coastal nets and inland weirs was also fragmenting into an angling (gentry) versus a netting interest (labourers). What happened after the 1863 act removed the common enemy of all these interests?

Poaching and Identity: After the 1863 Act

The 1863 act revolutionized salmon technology by allowing most fixed engines in the tidal areas to be removed and by certifying the dimensions of legal inland weirs. Not only did this increase the number of fish that reached the upper waters, but more fish produced more fishers. In Waterford District between 1853 and 1865, the number of cots increased sixfold and the number of cotmen twelvefold. In the latter year, the 'demand for cots was so great ... that the builders could not supply it.'[39] More Thomastown cotmen, netting to augment wages, now faced landlords who were no longer divided on the issue of fixed tidal nets and inland weirs and who, if interested in the fisheries, fished as angling sportsmen or rented their fisheries to rodmen.

Each side was quickly mobilized. Said the *Moderator*: 'The clearing away of the obstructions ... will but provide a larger quantity of salmon to fall ... into the nets of the many cot-fishers ... who habitually act in the most illegal manner.' The editor was somewhat mollified by section 24 of the act which banned fresh-water netting every night between 8 P.M. and 6 A.M. To prohibit an activity, however, raised the problem of enforcement. This was exacerbated because, for cotmen, the only worthwhile fishing was at night.[40] The annual closed time was tolerable because the salmon were of poor quality, often inedible, and virtually unsaleable. The weekly closed time (from Saturday night to Monday morning), introduced in 1842, was inconvenient. The new nightly closed time, however, was a drastic limitation on the public's right to net on the upper waters. Because it coincided with a larger number of cotmen and a revitalized concern by proprietors to take advantage of both the sport and the increasing rentability of their fisheries, conflict escalated. This was manifested in proprietors' renewed organizational efforts, cases at the petty sessions, the interest that the public now exhibited, a new discourse of opposition, and a new cohesion and identity for fishers.

Two days after the *Moderator*'s editorial, a meeting was held for land/ fisheries owners, weir owners, gentry members of the Suir Protection Society and of the Barrow Protection Society, and 'a number of fishermen from the locality [who] evinced a lively interest in the proceedings.' The chair announced that 'cot fishing in the fresh waters ... was virtually done away with, as ... it was useless to draw a net in clear daylight.' Thus, the object of the new, amalgamated Suir, Nore and Barrow Association was 'to maintain the interests of fresh water proprietors.' Only M. Marum, MP (Irish Party), gave a desultory nod to other rights, and, in so doing, he pushed them aside. Cotmen, he said, would 'benefit' because they could 'have the fishing of the river at a reasonable rent from the owners of the several fisheries.'[41]

Thomastown's petty sessions soon reflected the owners' outlook, their organization, and the fact that productive cot fishing now was poaching. No charges were laid against inland weirs, not even for fishing in the closed time. Charges against cot crews increased – because there were more enforcement agents, more crews, and more activities which now were offences. Conflict escalated, reflected in the *Moderator*'s numerous and graphic accounts of 'exciting chases after salmon poachers.' Cotmen, fishing in disguise, were trailed on land and water by the head constable, police, and bailiffs who crept for hours along damp riverbanks in the middle of the night. Such effort by enforcement agents was matched by rising public interest and rousing discourse. At an 1864 petty sessions, it was reported how 'the court-house, on being ... open, was immediately filled, the interest being, doubtless, to hear the result of a fishery case.' A cotman, charged with 'aiding ... a party who had been illegally fishing,' asserted 'that the next time he met the police at the river, or that they gave him any trouble, he would throw them into the water.'[42]

Such aid and rhetoric points to the growing ability of cotmen to mute their differences. A crew was charged with night fishing because 'a squabble between two ... crews ... caused ... one of those crews to go to the head constable and say they were ready to prosecute the defendants.' However, when the case came before the bench, 'nothing could be elicited from these witnesses.' Such consciousness also created active combinations, as when a cot fisher charged a weir owner with angling in the closed season. Violence began to follow class lines. Between 1865 and 1867, cotmen were prosecuted for assaulting a watchman, a publican, and a housing agent. Only one assault was reported among cotmen themselves. Such agency meant that cotmen became a recognizable political category. Parliamentary candidate George Bryan, when addressing Thomastown's electors in 1865, 'in reply to ... fishermen ... promised that from henceforth he will have no one prosecuted ... on his property ... for fishing.'[43]

The Course of the Law: From 'Public Right' to 'Private Privilege,' 1866–71

In 1866 the Waterford conservators passed a by-law to prohibit netting in the upper Nore. That it did not cover the Barrow and Suir shows that some Nore owners were pressuring the board. As the by-law went for approval to the fishery commissioners and was refused, the Barrow Society received legal advice that netting in fresh waters was illegal. Using this, landlord Marsh posted a notice 'forbidding' cot fishing 'under penalty of a criminal prosecution.'[44]

All this activity reflected an interest among certain landlords to gain, finally, unfettered control of their properties. They were stymied by the 1842 act, which gave fishing rights to the public on navigable rivers. This right, however, was checked in early 1868 by the decision in *Murphy v. Ryan*. Barrow cotmen appealed after being found guilty of netting on the river abutting a proprietor's property (a 'close'). They argued 'that the close ... from time immemorial has been part of ... a royal river ... and ... a public and navigable river ... in which every subject ... had ... the liberty ... of fishing.' The decision upheld the landlord. It said: 'A navigable river must be a tidal river.' Nor does 'the designation "royal" ... indicate a river of which the fishing is in the public.' The defence alleged 'a custom' that the public had 'a *profit a prendre* in ... private property.' Yet 'it is quite settled that such a custom cannot legally exist ... A right of way upon the land [or] ... upon the water ... may be established by usage because they are ... easements ... But no usage can establish a right to take a profit in another's soil ... and such a profit [is] the taking of fish.'[45]

In a state increasingly dedicated to the rights of profit and private property, Lord Carrick could then announce from the bench at the next petty sessions that 'cot-fishing, except in tidal waters or by the owner of a several fishery, was illegal.' Marsh, too, like Carrick, acted quickly. At the first petty sessions after the season opened, the 'court-house was filled with spectators very early, it being ... known that a number of fishermen were summoned for fishing in the fresh water ... with cots and nets.' Six cases were brought by bailiffs; all crews were found guilty.

However, the certainty of the *Murphy v. Ryan* decision dissolved as new cases and new defence arguments were made. At an appeal by a cot crew found guilty of fishing on Marsh's property, the defence cited the 1842 act. An elderly Thomastown man said that he knew the men had 'fished in that part of the Nore for more than 46 years without hindrance.' The bench held over the decision. In 1869 another crew won an appeal against Marsh because 'the lands adjoining the fishery were not the property of Mr. Marsh as they were tenanted.' Marsh persisted but the bench continued to demur. In two cases in early 1870, one crew was only nominally fined while the other case was dismissed without prejudice. Legal advisers to the fisheries bureaucracy were equally unclear. A sympathetic reporter noted: 'This question has been before Petty Sessions,

Civil Bill and Superior Courts for several years, and if the prosecutors succeed it will prevent these poor people fishing altogether, and probably drive them into the workhouse.'[46]

In early 1871 an appeal to Thomastown's quarter sessions clarified the situation. A crew admitted to fishing in a private fishery but claimed they had fished there 'uninterruptedly for the last 50 or 60 years.' The chair noted this, adding that no exception could be made to the decision in *Murphy v. Ryan*. However, he said, this was a decision taken 'by a civil court in reference to civil rights' and the legislature in 1842 'can hardly ... have been ignorant of the ... law in reference to the rights which could be claimed by the public by custom.' What, then, did the act mean when it allowed 'a general right of fishing with nets in the nature of a common piscary if these had been enjoyed for twenty years before the passing of this act?' The chair concluded: 'It appears to me that the Legislature intended ... that when such a public right, or perhaps more strictly speaking, "privilege," had been enjoyed or tolerated for 20 years, the proprietors of the ... banks [must] ... assert their legal civil rights by the civil remedies ... but that the public were not ... to be handed over ... to the administrators of the criminal law.'[47] Inland cotmen, having lost the right to fish, retained the privilege of doing so provided the owner of the fishery did not enforce his exclusive right to his private property through the civil courts.

The 'Privilege' of Cot Fishing, 1868–84

The 1868 decision in *Murphy v. Ryan* inflamed, personalized, and polarized local sentiment as it factionalized the landlord bench and turned the fishers into a political force. The depth of emotion was apparent early on, in 1869, when a cot fisher 'before the court, wilfully insulted the Justices' and was jailed for a week. Another, for the same offence, was jailed until the magistrates rose.[48] This intense sentiment in turn reflected escalating violence as animosities accumulated. A bailiff was caught with an unlicensed gun while another summoned two cotmen, each of whom had, on various occasions, 'threatened to drown him.' In court, the bailiff refused to testify: 'he was afraid the defendants would do him some corporal injury.'[49] As such complex rows increasingly required people to serve as 'impartial' witnesses, 'facts' became more relative and perjury increased. At an 1871 petty sessions, a magistrate 'spoke ... on the nature of an oath – invoking the name of God ... to witness ... truth.' He 'exhorted all to remember what ... it involved.'[50]

In the context of this escalation, only two proprietors, Marsh and Hunt, tried to claim exclusive rights over their fisheries. Neither lived locally. This was important, as was clear from a letter written by a local gentleman in 1869 to correct a report in the *Moderator* that miller Innes had charged his son with a fishing violation. 'The prosecution,' he said, 'was instituted by a bailiff named ... Read.'[51] Clearly, it had become important for local people to assign responsibility to the exact person. One such person was Thomas Doran, the lessee of the Hunt weir at Jerpoint, conservator, employer of private water bailiffs, and occasional poacher. Over the years, a feud between him and local cotmen helped to fuel broad, local sentiment in the inland fishery (Case 7.4).

Case 7.4: The Cotmen's Combination, the Conservators, and the Inhabitants, 1868–73

In 1868 the 'court-house was ... filled by fishermen' to hear a case brought by William Murphy, cotman, against Doran for fishing in the closed season. Doran was fined. In 1872 two conservators inspected Doran's weir, bringing cotman Dawson along to point out its defects. For his efforts, Doran charged Dawson with trespass: Dawson had likely reported the weir in the first instance. The bench dismissed the trespass charge as well as one brought by Doran's son that Dawson had used threatening language. A few months later, Doran was again charged with illegally altering his weir and had to fix it.

A cotman's combination clearly was watching Doran. On occasion, they probably framed him. A Thomastown hotelier was charged with possession in 1872 after Doran's son stated, during a court case, that he saw salmon in her hotel during the closed season. The defence solicitor asked Doran Jr if he knew what kippered salmon was. He did not. The solicitor informed the bench that Mrs Bishop bought a large amount of salmon for the hotel during the open season and pickled it for winter. The case was dismissed. A month later, Mrs Bishop was again charged, this time by cotman Murphy who was now a water bailiff. Murphy admitted that he had used Doran's money to pay for the prosecution. The case was dismissed. Two months later, 'the most respectable inhabitants of Thomastown' were had up for buying salmon out of season. The first case was dismissed and the conservators hurriedly withdrew the others when they found out that the charges 'had been brought entirely on a statement made to Mr Doran ... by William Murphy.'[52] Murphy was fired. The conservators had probably hired him only to inform. But had he also been set up by the cotmen, to embarrass Doran and the conservators?

More generally, these prosecutions for possession show that bailiffs were not able to catch cotmen. By the mid-1870s, no fishery cases appeared at the petty sessions. Yet 'salmon was never so plenty' and prices, too, were good.[53] As the cotmen prospered, public interest was kept up by weekly reports in the *Moderator* on the poor state of the fisheries owing to chronic poaching. Some gentlemen, because so little had been gained from judicial efforts, turned again to the Waterford Board for a by-law prohibiting nets on the inland Nore. In March 1875 the fisheries commissioners held an inquiry to decide whether to approve it. The evidence taken shows clearly that bureaucratic common sense had radically altered since 1863. Then, a weir-owning gentry had combined to oppose officials who were defending the rights of humble fishers. By 1875, these officials saw cot fishing as an anathema and the proposed by-law as a way of ensuring that the fish went to market and the fisheries to proprietors. Indeed, the evidence showed a deep antagonism of some towards cot fishing. Several memorials sent in 'from certain owners' insisted that the river was 'continually poached ... they fish at night with cots constantly; the weekly close season is not observed.' Some constables then described poachers they had seen but failed to catch because fishers had trained dogs to raise the alarm. The cotmen's solicitor insisted that such testimony did not prove illegal fishing. The chair of the inquiry, Major Hayes, countered that they had 'proved the next thing to it. Men do not go out at night in cots for their amusement.'

The structure of this opposition emerged from the evidence of Captain Forster, lessee of a house and fishery north of Thomastown. 'No one has a right to intrude on private property.' [He] 'has advocated putting down cot-fishing [and] has written a letter in the paper ... Mr Tighe has not endorsed his opinion nor Lord Carrick.' Clearly, Forster had tried to activate the gentry with only limited success. Those who joined him shared two features. They were either non-residents (Marsh, Hunt) or outsiders who had rented a house and fishing (Doran, Forster). In contrast, such resident landlords as Tighe and Carrick, the latter of whom was no supporter of cotmen, had not signed his memorial. Very likely, they wished to avoid the public confrontations which came from opposition. They probably also wished to avoid the likes of Doran and Forster themselves.

To Hayes, however, cotmen 'were violators of the law.' His view of Thomastown society was equally disparaging: 'The more they encouraged gentlemen to settle among them the better.' In this, he clearly misunderstood local class relations and sentiment. First, outsiders and absentees, concerned with sport and rents, were not part of local gentry society. Second, a fishmonger gave the retailers' position. He 'can't answer that cotmen keep the close season' nor could he say that the fish he bought was caught legally.[54] Then there were the millers. An act in 1869 specified the lattices and bars that had to be attached to mills to aid salmon migrations. The commissioners began immediate enforcement. At Innes's mill, 'short work they made of it. Trial, conviction ... and order for works to be done occupied just ten minutes ... A public meeting of Nore millers is fixed ... to protest against future action of the Commissioners.'[55] The millers, in other words, were wary of fisheries officials. Millers also had personal ties to cotmen (Case 5.3), manifested in the common belief that poaching was carried on at mills with their connivance.[56]

Fourth, absentees and outsiders were cut off from farmers by an ideological twist made explicit by William Deady (large-scale farmer, corn miller, guardian). Deady objected to the idea that custom had no value and that cot fishing was poaching. 'As demonstrated by the Ulster tenants [land] right,' he wrote, 'what is law but custom perpetuated legally? which in this case is tacitly admitted by having a special licence ... for this very mode of taking fish.' Indeed, as tenants-rights agitation became part of growing national sentiment, farmers such as Deady took note of cotmen. Fisheries law, like land law, was British. So, too, was the ideal that the *Moderator* painted of a local lessee who 'generously distributes the salmon caught with his rod among the gentlemen ... in Thomastown, in the true spirit of a sportsman.' In contrast, locals defended the cotmen's right to a livelihood, even if the more cynical held this view because of a concern with their rates. Said farmer Deady: 'Cotmen cannot be ... compelled to relinquish ... the means of providing their daily bread ... unless it can be positively shown that they are ... injurious ... to the increase of salmon.'[57]

The fisheries had clearly become a site for many contested rights and, as such, a site of intense sentiment and argument. At the 1875 inquiry, for example, cotmen took part from the audience, yelling out that Forster 'poached himself ... but there is no one to summon him' and accusing him of doing 'all in his power to take bread out of their mouths.' Then, while the parties awaited the decision from the inquiry, discursive battle continued. The *Moderator* noted that, in the 'three great centres of poaching on the river, Instioge, Thomastown and Bennettsbridge,' the practice was an 'evil' that required 'an organised system of repression.'[58] Such rhetoric led to action as the cotmen took the offensive,

sending a memorial to Tighe 'signed by upwards of 100 fishermen ...
urging him to discontinue his sweep net fishing ... as it impeded the
progress of the salmon up the river.'[59]

A week later, however, cotmen were on the defensive. The commissioners had approved the by-law prohibiting nets on the inland Nore.
'From Thomastown, where the main strength of the netting interest
lie ... a petition is being organized to the Lord Lieutenant.' Patrick
Martin, MP, was asked 'to fight, on behalf of the fishermen's interests.' It
is not known what pressures were brought or by whom, but the by-law
was refused. Cotmen held a meeting with farmers who had 'ground on
the rivers banks' and passed a vote of thanks 'to all those around the
county who had supported the cot men in their successful action against
the by-law.'[60]

If not among these supporters, then certainly not among their detractors, were some of the local gentry who sat on the Thomastown bench
and who, throughout, preserved an impeccable fairness (Case 7.5).

Case 7.5: The View from the Thomastown Bench, 1877

*A fisher was charged with obstructing the bailiffs. A bailiff swore that 'he saw a
crew fishing on the river.' When he moved closer, 'the defendant met him, and
asked him in a loud voice so that the men on the river could hear him "Who the
d—l are you at all?" and then struck a match ... to give notice to the men fishing.' In the chair was James Blake, a resident Catholic landlord. Like him, two of
the other magistrates held no fishery. The fourth magistrate was Tighe's agent at
Inistioge. Blake's response to the bailiff's evidence was that 'there was no law to
prevent a man from lighting a match on the bank of the river. The suggestion ...
was perfectly ridiculous.' The case was dismissed.[61]*

Clearly cotmen, as fishers, had the support of local people and, as
poachers, the tacit approval of most. For despite the *Moderator* and those
who supported its sentiments, such as Doran, Hayes, and Forster, most
segments of local society were unwilling to sacrifice the cotmen to
increase the profits of absentee landlords and the sport of foreign gentlemen. In any case, as the fish dealer said, he never asked whether the
fish was legal or not. With heavy demand and high prices in the export
market, locals depended on the cotmen to supply their needs. Indeed,
the cotmen wisely kept that local market well stocked, judging by the
quantities that Mrs Bishop pickled in her hotel.

In late 1877 Marsh again entered the fray with two civil suits against cot crews. 'It is our right to the fishery ... that we are here to protect,'said his solicitor.[62] Within a few months, violence escalated as the 'feud of water bailiffs against cotmen' intensified, spilling into the streets and bringing women into the fray (Case 7.6)

Case 7.6: Escalating Conflict in the Late 1870s

Two cotmen, interrupted one night by bailiffs, threw stones. One bailiff then 'fired his revolver ... which brought [the] cotmen to the bank, armed with paddles and threatening ... vengeance.' The bailiffs withdrew. All were ordered to the assizes. There, the bailiff denied firing at the fishermen and the cotmen said they had only thrown small stones. All were let off 'on their own recognisances.'

Through such episodes, conflict again spilled onto the streets. On the evidence of two cotmen, the constabulary charged Doran's bailiff, John Cotterall, now 'an old man,' who maintained that the case 'was got up ... through spite.' It was dismissed. As he left the court, he 'was attacked ... by a crowd of fishermen and their wives.' Violence escalated. Less than two months later, two cotmen were shot and wounded by a water bailiff. The cotmen were charged with assault and the case sent to Killkenny assizes. The bailiff swore that he fired only when the fishers beat him with a paddle after he was thrown into the water. In stark contrast, the cotmen said that when they came near the bailiff's cot, the bailiff struck his cot against theirs and fired his pistol. The jury refused to convict the cotmen despite instructions to do so from the bench. 'They believed the cot men assaulted [the bailiff] to prevent him firing on them.' At the next petty sessions, and stemming from the same incident, the same cotmen were up for illegal fishing. The defence asked the magistrates to 'consider the hardships to which the men and their families had been subjected.' In fact, the bench had already decided not to inflict any penalty.

The bailiff now had enemies. He charged a cotman with calling him 'a perjurer on the public streets' and, after a fisher had apparently threatened him, he pulled his revolver. The cotman brought a complaint to the petty sessions. Women entered the conflict. After a bailiff prosecuted a woman for possession, he later charged her with using abusive language because on four occasions after the case, she met him in the courthouse and called him a perjurer.[63]

Yet the issue of private property did not abate. Landlord Davis's heirs lived outside the parish and rented out their house and fishing. They brought three cases in 1880 against cotmen for netting in their fishery without permission. Davis's solicitor said that, if the cotmen agreed not to repeat the offence, he would accept a nominal penalty. The cotmen were Davis's house tenants and he did not wish to deal harshly with them. In any case, if they had asked for permission to net occasionally, Davis would have granted it. Fisher James Kelly led the defence, admitting to the charge 'because we had a perfect legal right.' The magistrates disagreed but, at Kelly's request, inflicted a penalty sufficient to allow an appeal. The two other cases ended the same way, with the cotmen asked by the magistrates not to fish in Davis's fishery until after Kelly's appeal.

> Colleton [fisher] – Well, we won't fish there – until it is dark (loud laughter).
>
> Mr. Boyd [for Davis] – Now, I shall prove the case against you, and I shall ask the magistrates to inflict the full penalty.
>
> Colleton – Very well, Mr. Boyd, sure we are all monied men (renewed laughter), and this is a good season.[64]

The cotmen were playing to the audience; and it was located both in and outside the courtroom. At an 1880 Land League meeting, M. Marum, MP, put on a very different guise than the one he had displayed in 1863 when courting the gentry. 'Did not the fishermen of Thomastown know that they were begrudged even the fish ... in these waters?' The nationalist *Journal* added that, because of 'the greed ... for property ... the humble descendants of fishers who trolled in these waters ... before the abbey lands [were] parcelled out to Hanoverian rabble,' could 'be banished now. Even the water-bailiffs say that their hardship is a great one.' Indeed, the fisher who had been shot was given outdoor relief by the guardians, with the chair noting that there was 'great distress existing among them.'[65] In contrast, the commissioners noted the 'valuable rod fisheries for which large rents are obtained'[66] and Bassett's 1884 *Guide* reported that Thomastown had 'splendid salmon and trout fishing.'

The cotmen had little option but to continue poaching. When caught, they sometimes got off or had the penalty reduced because of a technicality.[67] The major tactic, however, was evasion. Alibis became central. A case was dismissed after a woman swore that a fisherman 'was in her house, beastly drunk ... on the night of the alleged occurrence.' It was also possible to torment Doran, who was had up for more weir violations, and to take symbolic action. Two cotmen were fined for obstructing Davis's tenant while he was angling 'by paddling a cot across his line.'[68]

In 1884 four cotmen were summoned to Thomastown's petty sessions by the head water bailiff for entering a fishery rented to an outsider gentleman. Convicted, they appealed to the quarter sessions, maintaining that the bailiff had no right to institute the proceedings. Their conviction was confirmed. An appeal was made to the Queen's Bench. It held that 'it is clearly settled that use by the public, no matter how long, will not confer a right to take fish in inland waters. An action by a proprietor must succeed.' Therefore, 'why should the owner be put to the necessity of bringing civil action against trespassers?'[69] The new criminality was promptly confirmed. Bailiffs brought two cases against cotmen for fishing in Marsh's fishery. They were summarily convicted and did not appeal.[70]

Conclusion

The fifty-year process through which the rights of private property slowly usurped and finally criminalized the rights of custom was woven out of complex agency emanating from multiple sources and intentions which changed through time. Such agency was partly comprised of political combinations, alliances, and oppositions which implicated labourers as both political subjects and objects. Equally, the process invaded the awareness and sentiments of most local people and turned the inland fishery into a powerful and broad-based political symbol.

PART III

At the Turn of the Twentieth Century, 1885–1901

'There could be nothing done for the ... farmer that would not be for benefit also of the farm labourer ... If the effect of the present agitation be to make peasant proprietors, there would be no farm on which a labourer would not reap some substantial benefit.'
    – Mulhallum Marum, Kilkenny MP Irish Party (Kilkenny *Moderator*, 1 December 1880)

Inside a hierarchy of exploitation and domination wrought by capitalism and colonialism, the structure of common sense – that is, of everyday ideology – in Thomastown during most of the nineteenth century was discernible in the changing colouration of three interrelated *cultural codes: status-class, respectability,* and *locality.* These codes were in turn sited in the material and economic structure of society, in *property relations and labour processes.* An essential part of this was the process of *state formation* through which coercion and hegemony were actualized by the *agency* of individuals, combinations, and *organizations.* All these topics form the lenses through which the experience of labour and labouring people can be viewed.

The awareness and experience of *class,* intrinsic to local society by at least the beginning of the nineteenth century, were reproduced during the course of it: exploitation (via production) and appropriation (via consumption); paternalism, deference, and dearth; and the dyads that made up the class hierarchy. This reproduction often was the result of change: in the dependency of labourers on farmers, in the expansion of deference and paternalism to include a notion of 'good employers,' and in the distribution of people within the class hierarchy, as when the glut of casual labour was displaced. Changes also took place, in how status-class and class boundaries were conceptualized and maintained, in how recruitment took place and in the languages of class which were extant at particular times. The so-called poorer classes grew into the 'labouring classes,' 'landless peasants' became 'wage labourers,' and 'fishers' were transformed into 'poachers.' Marriage preferences and dowries altered the position of artisans in the status-class hierarchy and a 'cottager' who needed five acres in 1805 required ten by 1845.

Central to this reproduction process was the emergence of the code of *respectability.* It was, in itself, a cultural conjuncture, reflecting the efforts of labourers to improve their material conditions and of non-labouring agents to reform their moral ones. The non-labouring agents were both local and supra-local, emanating sometimes from the state and sometimes from private interests: magistrates at petty sessions, farmers and gentry acting as guardians, gentlemen dispensing charity and relieving distress, teachers in the national school, fisheries inspectors enforcing regulations, employers ensuring a loyal workforce, proprietors managing their inland fisheries, and so on. Ultimately, the code of respectability emerged out of the intersection of coercion and education, via the institutions set up to force workers, and the *organizations* set up to teach them, how to be peaceable, moral, honest, sober, industrious, and clean. For, although the intrinsic nature of labourers was seen as wasteful, impetuous, ignorant, rebellious, disorderly, and suspicious, these traits were also seen by many as honed by external conditions. Nature, therefore, could be altered, labourers could be taught. In this, of course, was an effort not only to alter values and demeanour but also to increase the productivity of labour power.

Throughout, labourers were political subjects and political objects. As objects, they were discursive devices and resources as well as educational targets. They thus were assimilated into the arguments and contests which enmeshed people of other classes. As subjects, workers formed combinations and organizations which, when acting to alter the materiality of their daily lives, also affected the trajectory of reproduction itself. This often occurred because their combinations either fragmented other classes or forced alliances. The Carrickshock acquittals, St Peter's Society, the antipathy between resident and non-resident landlords in the fisheries, and the negotiated relations through the petty sessions were all examples of how factions and/or alliances emerged and how these, when intersecting with labourers' active combinations or coalitions of silence, altered the trajectory of change, hegemony, and coercion.

Throughout, too, class awareness and experience were inscribed in the built environment and in spatial allocations. They were also inscribed in sentiments about the *locality* which people of all classes shared and which intersected with their ideological or material concerns. For much common sense and class experience was absorbed through parochial eyes and local knowledge. The so-called night of the French in 1870, for example, was interpreted by the magistrates as being about working-class respectability, not Fenian insurrection.

Underlying the working of cultural codes was a stable system of *property relations. Labour processes*, nevertheless, altered: in agriculture (tillage to livestock), fishing (increase in netting, criminalization), industry (contraction), and household production (conacre, pig rearing). What was reproduced, however, was competition for work, a dearth of permanent employment, and the idea that wages had a ceiling dictated by the costs of subsistence. These ideas remained in place even though the glut of labour declined with emigration and living standards rose. Thus, throughout the nineteenth century, as labourers formed combinations or were constructed as political objects, certain material issues were clear: access to permanent work, the impact of technology, and wages and welfare during times of dearth or personal crisis. At bottom, what was necessary was to limit the impact of competition for work in the local labour market. Equally necessary was what workers had learned through the course of the century: that they had to be, or seem, honest, sober, and industrious in order to improve their life chances. Overall, then, the tenor of labouring lives remained precarious, uncertain, and poor – features ironically appropriated by farmers to formulate their own ideologies and propel their own combinations.

The process of *state formation* provided the umbrella under which all this occurred, unfolding in part through the creation of law: the Act of Union, the Poor Law, fisheries acts, electoral law, the Constabulary Act, insurrection acts, Catholic Emancipation, the Petty Sessions Act, the National Schools Act, the Loan Fund Act, and so on. Equally important, it unfolded through the regulations, administration and bureaucracy associated with this law. Institutions were thus constructed and *agents* given formal roles in various bureaucratic hierarchies. Such agents operated at different levels in the hierarchy, they invariably held different viewpoints and interests, they developed diverse everyday practices, and they had various kinds of connections to those of the dominant class. Guardians and conservators, for example, were local and regional agents respectively and they only were partly derived from the landlord class. That latter class, in any case, was factionalized. Not only did one segment control the physical apparatus of the state at any time, but it was divided by kinship, ideological and political allegiances, and material interests. The anti-union, pro-O'Connell attitudes of some cousins and in-laws among local gentlemen in 1800 set the tone for what was a 'good landlord' in Thomastown. Yet new interests might yield new alliances as, for example, when landlords Tighe and Carrick avoided the petty sessions when defending their private fisheries.

Agency, however, was not only actualized by those who directly represented the ideological and coercive concerns of the state and/or the dominant classes. Agency also came from the actions of those from other classes and *organizations*. Charitable and benevolent societies, fisheries associations, farming societies, St Peter's Society, penny clubs, and artisans' guilds were examples of ideologically based and materially rooted intentions. Agency also came out of talk: parliamentary inquiries, newspapers, petty sessions, public meetings, and ad hoc gatherings. The interaction of such agents among themselves sometimes led to a homogenizing of viewpoints, as when landlords sat together on the bench, or it sometimes led to alternative or conflicting interpretations, such as whether gratuitous relief should be given and when.

At the Turn of the Twentieth Century, 1884–1901

By 1884, from the position of hindsight, a conjuncture can be seen in the political economy of Thomastown. On one level, it came out of the accumulated experiences, ideas, and practices of the previous decades: the improved material conditions, people's experiences as both political subjects and objects, the processes though which the law was experienced, and the associated (re)production of cultural codes and long-held notions of paternalism, deference, and dearth. At a second level, it came out of current trajectories in the history of agrarian unrest and Irish nationalism. By the last third of the nineteenth century, a growing combination of farmers, via the Land League and, later, the National League, was pressing forward its claims for changed tenure regulations and, soon after, for the rights of tenants to purchase their lands. Agrarian violence in the late 1870s in the west of Ireland and Land Acts in 1881 and 1885 became the dominant themes in both Irish historiography and Irish public discourse, along with, after 1870, the growing demand for 'home rule' for Ireland. Both farmers' interests and nationalism became the basis of massive electoral support for the Irish Party, particularly after the franchise was extended in 1884 and the Catholic hierarchy endorsed home rule for Ireland in 1886.

In the last few decades of the nineteenth century in Thomastown, the farmers' surge led to farmers gradually replacing landlords and gentry on Thomastown's Board of Guardians, as the organ itself slowly became a vehicle for farmers' material and political interests. At a board meeting reported by the *Journal* on 31 May 1877, for example, the farming majority passed a motion supporting a land tenure bill, despite the objections of a landlord that 'the subject is entirely outside the province of boards of guardians, who have no business to discuss in the board room a political question of this kind.' This expanding agency of farmers in Thomastown not only circumscribed the gentry's agency but, also, the interests of labour. The organic intellectuals who comprised the farmers' leadership at the time did not, of course, represent it that way. At the December 1880 meeting in Thomastown to establish a local Land League branch, Mulhallen Marum spoke of the mutuality of interests among farmers and labourers: 'Anything that tended to give the farmer security of title in his holding ... would stimulate industry, and one of the very first results would be to throw money into the pockets of the labourers.' Among the resolutions passed were to reform the land laws and, as part of this, to ensure that 'the labouring classes ... be provided with suitable residences.'

The colonial state, however, was also vying for the support of the labourers at the end of the century. Its agents saw housing as a key point of entry. Thus, the Labourers (Ireland) Act of 1883 allowed poor law unions, through their boards of guardian, to take out loans, secured by future rates, to build 'labourers' cottages.' This measure, said the clerk of the Thomastown union, according to the *Moderator* on 27 October 1883, was 'a humane and kindly-conceived effort to legislate for the promotion of the comfort, even in a limited way, of a very wretched and struggling class of the community.' With great prescience, he added that 'the prosecution of the provisions of the Act by a public body ... whose hands are already so full ... will be troublesome.'

As part of the *metissage* of the past as it became the present, and along with the political trajectories impelled by farmers' interests, a third level of Thomastown's political economy became relevant as the nineteenth century drew to a close. It was made up of several, interrelated strands. The structuration of political sentiment, knowledge, and material concerns through the inland fisheries after cot fishing was criminalized in 1884 was central. So, too, were the kin networks, occupational affiliations, and neighbourhood ties which came to operate by that time and the ways in which an explicit ideology of the working class, in conflict with capital, entered the locality. It also was made up of the ways in which the new housing act became 'troublesome' for local agents. It is this third level that I discuss in Part III.

8. Political Sentiment and the Inland Fisheries

Eliza Cody and Joanna Kelly were found guilty at the petty sessions of assaulting bailiff Cotteral. Eliza Cody admitted to striking him, saying 'I did it for my little boy that he is persecuting. I would take his life if I were able.'
– Kilkenny *Moderator*, 4 February 1885

'I consider that fresh water netting is one of the main factors in the decline of the salmon fisheries.'
– J.H. Jones, Waterford conservator (IUP 1901 [Cd.450] xii:2188–92

Between 1884 and 1901, the inland fisheries remained a focal point around which local, labouring political sentiments and understandings were created, experienced, and mobilized. Most tellingly, the fisheries also served to structure, both discursively and materially, categories of opposition and alliance within the wider region and colonial state. The result was a complex world view of contradictory and occasionally contested sentiments and interpretations. The political economy and politics of this structuration process comprise the focus of this chapter.

Structuring Polarities of Political Sentiment in the Region and Colonial State

In 1886 a labourer's weekly wage in Grennan Mills was 10s.2d. The price of salmon that year went as high as 2s.6d. per pound while its low was 9d. The average salmon weighed ten to twelve pounds. At worst, then, a fisher received 7s.6d. for a salmon. One and a half salmon equalled a

Table 8.1: Oppositions in the Irish fisheries, 1880–92

[A] 1880	Poor	vs.	Rich
	Lower/tidal waters	vs.	Upper/fresh waters
	Working fishermen	vs.	Angling gentlemen
	Public fisheries	vs.	Private ('several') fisheries
	Landless	vs.	Landowners
	Nets	vs.	Rods
	Those who sell fish	vs.	Those who rent out their fisheries
[B] 1885	Nationalist	vs.	Ascendancy
	Poor fishers	vs.	Landlords
[C] 1892	Mill owners	vs.	Landlords
	Mill owners	vs.	Fisheries administration
	Millworkers	vs.	Landlords
	Millworkers	vs.	Fisheries administration
	[Inland cotmen and 'poor anglers']		

week and a half of work in the mill. This arithmetic, and decades of coercion, kept cotmen netting on the inland Nore despite the illegalities and continuing pressure from conservators. The latter, in 1885, introduced three by-laws. Beating the water to drive fish to the bank was prohibited. Every cot had to have its licence number painted on its bow. Having a gaff or spear near the banks of an inland river was proscribed, except when angling. The mandatory fine for either of the first two delicts was £2. The penalty for the third was forfeiture of the gaff and a £4 fine.[1] A fisher found guilty of one of these infractions would pay a fine equal to four to eight weeks of work in the mill.

That same year, a parliamentary committee obtained opinions on a new fisheries bill which was then before the Commons. The proposals would open Saturday for tidal nets and allow fisheries inspectors to set different closed times for different parts of a salmon river. In giving evidence, Major Hayes admitted that these were efforts to deal with the ongoing conflict between inland anglers and tidal fishers. Indeed, by around 1880, such antagonisms were contained in a series of linked dichotomies which had emerged through time (Table 8.1[A])

These oppositions, however, excluded two anomalous types of local fishers. The first were the inland Nore and Barrow cotmen: landless, poor fishers who netted in fresh, private waters (with permission from landowners). In national debates, they were seen as an anachronism and nuisance. In his evidence on the proposed 1885 bill, Thomas Brady, fisheries commissioner, said that the 1862 legislation to open gaps in weirs was not intended so that salmon could then be netted by cotmen in the upper waters. It was, rather, to 'afford the upper proprietors sport' and make them interested in protecting the fisheries. This, view, of course, was from 1835: the fisheries and fish were property. The upper waters were to produce rents, and the lower waters were to produce fish. The other anomalous type, by now distinguishable on the upper waters, was the 'poor angler' who caught and sold salmon and trout using rod and line. Said a witness in 1885 from the Blackwater river: 'I have many hardworking men in my district who supply the public with fish by the rod.'[2] In Thomastown, their presence was signalled in 1869 when Richard Hutchinson was summoned on a angling charge by bailiff Read.[3]

The political economy that gave rise to these oppositions and anomalies continued apace after 1884 as the fisheries remained a contentious site for both the bureaucrats who administered them and the landowners. Opening Saturday to the tidal nets, for example, was divisive. Brady believed that the upper waters were sufficiently stocked with salmon and breeding stock. He supported the open Saturday because it would give 'employment and ... bring a much larger quantity of fish into the market ... to the consuming public.' In contrast, Hayes supported the status quo: 'Many ... men have told me that they require Saturdays for ... cleaning and drying their nets.' Several of the parliamentarians laughed at the 'picture ... of the fishermen debarred from fishing' as one in which 'they spend their day, contentedly ... making up their accounts and mending nets.' Importantly, however, such division articulated with wider parliamentary contests. An inspector was accused by an MP of condemning the proposed bill because it was being promoted by the anti-landlord, pro-farmer Irish party.[4]

That such politics had entered the inland fisheries was otherwise highlighted at the 1885 inquiry. Private inland fisheries belonged to landowners who also held tenanted lands. As landlords, they were under political attack from tenant farming interests and organizations. At the 1885 inquiry, poor fishers who netted in the tidal public waters were invariably seen as opposing inland, landed anglers. The dichotomy of 'tidal water vs. upper/fresh water' thus became 'nationalist versus ascendancy' and 'poor fishers versus landlords' (Table 8.1[B]).

This received a fillip through the everyday conflicts that took place in regional-fisheries administration. Brady, for example, noted that boards of conservators seldom had an adequate representation of poor fishers/ tidal netmen. Although conservators were elected by all licence holders, more expensive licences (weirs, seine nets) entitled holders to multiple votes. Moreover, every landlord/magistrate who bought a licence was an ex officio member. Poor fishers, even if elected, were grossly outnumbered. Major Hayes, in contrast, did not see a problem. He believed that the poor fishers were not being sufficiently active on their own behalf. Regardless of why, said Brady, most conservators were landed, upper proprietors. This meant that the rates on their valuable fisheries were never collected and they were never summoned for illegal fishing. Clerks, hired by the boards and needing their jobs, colluded. Further, said Brady, landlords who ran the boards used its money, including the fees collected from poor fishers, to hire bailiffs to protect their own private fisheries.[5] The data bore him out. The Waterford board spent increasing proportions of its protection monies in the open season (49 per cent in 1886, 64 per cent in 1896).[6] This meant that the conservators were chasing cotmen in the open season rather than protecting spawning grounds in the closed time.

The contrasting sentiments expressed by commissioners Brady and Hayes highlight the discord inside the state bureaucracy and the pro-ascendancy versus anti-ascendancy ideas that permeated it. The resulting subterfuge had serious implications. The clerks of the regional boards sent both data and interpretation to the fisheries commissioners in Dublin who used these to prepare annual reports on the state of the Irish fisheries for Parliament. Between 1881 and 1900, the conclusions of the reports from Waterford district were invariably positive. Yet, in all those years, the catches were 'not as great' as in the preceding year, and, always, the vagaries of nature could explain why. In 1894, for example, the Waterford clerk's report stated: 'Were the state of the fisheries to be judged by the relative capture of salmon in 1893 to that of previous years, it would be described as declining, but such a criterion would be fallacious as the exceptional climatic influences of 1893, and the consequent low state of the rivers, militated against the run of salmon. Judging, however, from the vast run of fry in the spring of 1893, it is concluded that the fisheries are improving.'[7]

To an unbiassed eye, a series of such reports shows clearly that a crisis was unfolding. Yet, at the time, either it was perceived but purposefully left unstated or knowledge of it was blunted by optimism, inadequate understandings, or politics. The main result was to allow human agency and conflicting interests to be ignored. This, in turn, left a regional administration, such as the Waterford Board, to administer on its own, using the one policy tool it had, the passing of by-laws. All these, as has been seen, were framed to contain poor fishers in both tidal and inland waters and to restrict inland netting. The one exception proved the rule. It added a month to the angling season on the upper Suir.[8] By 1901, as a result of the coercion of poor fishers, the state's fisheries agents, the board, and the ascendancy were seen by local people as allied.

In all this, concern began to focus on obstructions to salmon migrations. Several weirs on the Nore no longer had fish passes and those on Barrow navigation weirs were poorly built.[9] What about mills? Fisheries inspectors could order millers to erect grates to prevent salmon from entering the mill race, to be destroyed by machinery or trapped by poachers. Yet, if a miller could show that grates would damage his water power, the inspectors could grant an exemption. In 1888 the Waterford conservators took on miller Pilsworth, Grennan Mills (Case 8.1).

Case 8.1: The Black Arch at Grennan Mills, 1888

The Waterford conservators and several, inland fisheries owners complained about the exemption from erecting grates which had previously been granted to Grennan Mills. An inquiry was held by three fisheries inspectors, including Thomas Brady and Major Hayes. The other interests represented were: the conservators, by the head bailiff (Samuel Ireland) and its solicitor; mill owner Pilsworth accompanied by two solicitors; and the fisheries owners by Thomas Doran. Apparently, Pilsworth still refused to erect grates. The bailiff explained how the mill was worked by two wheels and that the larger one was located under a so-called black arch. A man could pass through a gap in the wheel to poach the many salmon which lay under the large wheel because the fish were unable to pass through when the water was low. 'From the position of the place,' said Ireland, 'it was impossible to watch it or prevent the fish being destroyed' by poachers. He said that his bailiffs had many times seen, from outside the mill, the fish in the black arch at night. Pilsworth's solicitor retorted that 'there was not a shred of evidence that there has been fish killed in the black arch.' The inspectors continued the exemption.[10]

Mill owner Pilsworth was made to oppose local, landed anglers and conservators. Yet state agents were only following well-known procedures under the 1863 and 1869 acts and they were usually sympathetic to millers' needs. In the 1880s, however, turbines for milling were being introduced at a rapid rate. Fish could travel through mill wheels without injury, but could they travel through a turbine and live? Experiments were unclear; and in the face of proposed new legislation in 1892, Irish millers formed a national coalition to prevent any further interference with their water power. They gave numerous arguments. If turbines did damage, it was not their responsibility. Any laws could be enforced arbitrarily against any of them at any time if the personal relations between conservators and a mill owner deteriorated, as was likely because the sympathies of the boards were 'more with the sporting world than with the commercial world.' In any case, fisheries inspectors were biassed and could not judge whether gratings were needed.[11]

Irish millers clearly saw themselves as aligned against the fisheries bureaucracy in Dublin and, locally, in Waterford. Indeed, Sir Thomas Brady took the view that 'proprietors of mills can look to their own interests, and proprietors of fisheries also; but I say it is the duty of a Government Department to look to the public interests,' that is, to 'the consuming public' and 'those fishing under their common law rights in the public waters.' In such a tripartite structure, the mill owners put government agents and proprietors into a common category of opposition. In so doing, they brought with them the loyalties of both their workers who fished and their workers who objected to being labelled poachers. Indeed, that owners everywhere were seen by most conservators as colluding in poaching inside mills, in turn, outraged the millers. They had recently achieved a new respectability wrought by their recent appointments to the magistrates' bench, as the number of landlords living locally declined. Pilsworth had been made a county magistrate in 1898. His being identified with workers, as a poacher, appalled him. Such viewpoints necessarily inserted both millers and their workers into the dichotomous structure of opposition and alliance which typified general sentiment within the colonial state (Table 8.1[C]).

The Local Politics of Inland Fishing in Thomastown, 1884–1901

The increasing legal constraint in the inland fisheries, and the polarizing of political sentiment, were dramatized by the outcome of two fisheries cases in 1893. The magistrates at Thomastown's petty sessions had dismissed the charges but the conservators appealed to the quarter sessions, chaired by a county court judge (Case 8.2).

Case 8.2: Two Appeals to the County Court Judge, 1893

[1] Cotmen James Cody and William, John, and Thomas Dunphy claimed that they were fishing on the side of the river belonging to farmer/miller Deady and not on Marsh's side. The judge insisted that the defence prove that Deady was the owner 'before his licence [permission] is any good to you.' The defence countered that 'it is as good as the ownership of the ... fishery established by the other side.' The judge concluded that 'no proof was given of Deady's ownership nor of his permission and, in any event, the cotmen were on Marsh's side of the river.' The decision was reversed in favour of the conservators.

[2] A constable swore that he saw the same four cotmen beating the water (to drive salmon to the bank where they could be gaffed/speared). Four mill workers, (James Burris, Patrick Byrne, John Hayden, and Peter Brien) all swore that they were on the bridge at the same time as the constable and saw no beating. With only one magistrate dissenting (Andrew O'Donnell, a very large-scale farmer and occasional chair of the Thomastown guardians), the judge and the jury decided against the appeal.

For the sentencing, the defence solicitor asked 'your lordship to take into consideration that they are licenced fishermen, and if anything did occur it was of a trifling nature. Would the court be in favour of signing a memorial to refute the fine? It would be utterly impossible for these men to pay a fine of £8, and it would be a question of going to gaol.' His Honour responded: 'I am myself dead against it.' A few months later, the constable informed the conservators that the fishers had gone to gaol for defaulting on their fines and that he was due 'bonuses' of £8 for securing their convictions.[12]

The public sentiment elicited by these cases was summarized by the *Journal*'s editor. Both the reversal of the decision and the substantial penalties had 'created considerable comment, and ... one is struck with the excessive punishments to which the unfortunate men were subjected. Whatever the justification for fines counted in pounds when the by-laws were framed by the Irish Fishery Board ... *their continual enforcement is an oppression as great as the operation of the most insidious land laws.*'[13] Moreover, with tenant farmers now buying up their farms from landlords under the Land Acts, it could not be known, without proof of title, who was the owner of the land along the river on any given date. Equally, some of the land sales did not include the fishing rights. This, too, required proof. Yet, at the appeal, landlord Marsh was assumed to be the owner whereas farmer Deady's ownership had to be proved. This angered the fishers and alienated the farmers.

Indeed, at the time, farmers and fishers, both net and rodmen, found that they had few interests either in common or in conflict. Farmers were winning their rights and their land and no longer needed labourers' support. Status-class endogamy had precluded kin or marriage ties between them while the accepted hierarchy placed fishers on a distinct, separate, and inferior level. In turn, virtually no cotmen were agricultural workers. None was employed by a farmer. Cot fishers, too, lived mainly in the town or its outskirts and did not depend on farmers for housing. Finally, farmers seldom fished and were therefore quite unconcerned to give cotmen permission to net on their parts of the river.

At the same time, the agency of opposition to the cot fishers was progressively less rooted in the locality. This was because the Waterford conservators were now sufficiently organized and funded to appeal all adverse decisions made by local magistrates at petty sessions. By moving cases to the county/regional quarter sessions, the conservators usually obtained reversals. This was because local norms and practices, which petty sessions magistrates had long subscribed to, were not part of the regional site. One key feature, 'the benefit of the doubt' (Case 8.3), had made the petty sessions, in fisheries cases, into a 'forum' for negotiating local class relations.

Case 8.3: The 'Benefit of the Doubt' at the Petty Sessions

[A] In 1891 James Cody, Jr and Sr, were charged by bailiffs Cotteral and Armstrong with possessing a gaff and beating the water. A witness for the defence said that he saw Armstrong go up to Cody Jr and demand a gaff from him. Cody then 'said he had no gaff, and Armstrong said that no matter whether he had or not he would swear he had one.' The magistrates 'gave the defendants the benefit of the doubt and dismissed both cases.'

[B] In 1895 John Langfry was charged with possessing a rod and line on the riverbank. He said that he only was carrying the rod for his father who was a licensed fisherman. He did admit that he had been convicted for a similar offence in 1891 and that he 'knew that he was doing wrong.' Samuel Ireland, for the conservators, however, insisted that when he came up to Langfry, he found that the fishing line was wet: 'There was no doubt but the rod was fishing.' William Langfry, the father, said that he had been delayed in town and could not go with his son but that he, William, had a licence.

'Mr. Newport [estate agent, Instioge] – We quite believe that you are licensed but at the same time we quite believe that your son was fishing.

'Defendant – I was only carrying the rod, sir.

'Newport – Was there any fly or footline on the rod?

'Complainant Ireland – No sir, it was taken off.

'Defendant [to Ireland] – I suppose if I had not stood for you, you would have fired at me.'

The chair (Lt.-Colonel Butler, landlord) said that because there was no footline on the rod, there was no evidence that the man was fishing. Ireland insisted that 'the man had a gaff in his possession, and the line was wet.' The chair said that 'there was some doubt about the case, and the defendant would get the benefit of it.'

[C] John Cotteral charged John Kelly with snap-netting in a private fishery. Kelly led his own defence and called fisher John Cody as his first witness. Cody swore that there was only one crew on the river at the time and that he, Cody, was there but not Kelly. Said Cody: I came here to prove that [he] was not there. I am not going to say I was fishing ...

'Chair: Were you disguised? – I never go out to fish without being well-disguised. (laughter)

'Chair: Was your brother disguised? – He was always disguised any time I went with him.

'John Foley (from the body of the court) – I was disguised. (laughter)

'Witness – I want the protection of the bench. We were all disguised, and Kelly was there, between man and God, as much as you were in it.'

Another of Kelly's witnesses, Patrick Gorey, said that he was not fishing that night but 'was in the boat and saw John and James Foley in the boat; he did not see John Kelly there ...

'Poe [solicitor for the conservators]: Were you disguised? – Yes.

'Poe: Were you holding the net or paddling? – I am not going to tell you what I was doing (laughter).' John Buckley was then sworn.

'Chair: Were you out in the boat that night? – Yes, I was.

'Chair: Were James Cody, John Cody and Patrick Gorey with you? – Yes.

'Chair – Did you see John Kelly that night? – I never laid my eyes on him.'

'In view of this evidence,' the bench gave Kelly 'the benefit of the doubt and dismissed the case.'[14]

Part of the reason why the benefit of the doubt was adhered to was because local magistrates had indigenous knowledge and were aware of the fragility of testimony in fisheries cases. They knew that long-term relations between bailiffs and fishers had led to deep grievances, that all fishing cases were connected, if not in fact then in sentiment, and that kinship among labourers conferred moral obligations. They also knew who were kin (Case 8.4).

Case 8.4: Local Knowledge at the Petty Sessions, 1898

In 1898 fisher John Kelly summoned bailiff John Cotteral for beating the river, swearing that he saw Cotteral do this. However, in response to a question from the chair, Kelly admitted that he and Dunphy, the defendant in a previous case, were first cousins. The chairman remarked that it was only after Dunphy was summoned that Kelly brought his charge. Bailiff William Ireland then swore that Cotteral was with him at a conservators' meeting at the time. The defence solicitor remarked that 'the prosecution was most vindictive.' The case was dismissed and Kelly was charged 20s. in costs.[15]

Such local knowledge, and its application, contrasted sharply with the 1893 appeals (Case 8.2) when the evidence of four workers was ignored in favour of one constable who stood to gain financially from his testimony. This was particularly important because the wider context was one in which, as the *Journal* noted, mandatory penalties for infractions were exceptionally severe. This had implications not only for fishers. On the one hand, it meant that the *Journal* editor in 1893 could explicitly include fishers within common nationalist sentiment. High fines were being imposed on licenced Irish fishers by a colonial state which defended the rights of absentee landlords who did not have to prove title to their properties. Irish fishers could not fish in Irish rivers. This was indeed 'an oppression as great as the ... most insidious land laws.' On the other hand, the mandatory fines alienated local magistrates. By the late nineteenth century, none of the new magistrates, being estate agents and notables, held valuable fisheries. Their interests were thus straightforward: to maintain intact their local relationships and to keep a few salmon in the river for their own sport. Since the magistrates had little interest in coercing the cotmen or seeing them in gaol, local norms and practices in the petty sessions remained viable. These were buttressed by an antipathy that the magistrates quickly developed to the conservators, the county court judge, and all those who sought to circumscribe their integrity in their own bailiwick. For mandatory fines and jail not only punished those found guilty in ways that members of the local bench did not necessarily condone but, more importantly, mandatory fines removed the assessment of damages and the application of fair punishment from the jurisdiction of local magistrates. All this was apparent in a discussion that the local magistrates had at a petty sessions in 1895 (Case 8.5).

Case 8.5: Discourses of Magisterial Dissent, 1895

On the bench were Peter Connellan as chair, Lieutenant-Colonal Butler, and William Pilsworth. The bailiff had successfully prosecuted a cot crew for fishing within 200 yards of a weir. Connellan said: 'They were convicted before ... and we can't fine them less than 10s. apiece – the nets to be forfeited. Mr. Poe [solicitor for the prosecution] said he did not think the defendants could be fined less than £2' according to the by-law.

'Mr. Buggy [solicitor for the defence] – It has been settled that it was £2 for the whole crew.

'Mr. Poe – Not at all ... County Court Judge Fitzgerald held that it was £2 each. It was all thrashed out a short time ago in Kilkenny ...

'Chairman – Well, we have never held that here, and will give only the 10s. each with costs.

'Mr. Poe – Will you give special costs in this case? I am instructed by the secretary to apply, as there was a solicitor down the last day about it.

'Mr. Buggy – The solicitor was down for other cases as well.'

The bench allowed only the ordinary costs.

Yet at other times the bench had no choice. John Buckley was found guilty of snap-netting in the closed season. Connellan, in thinking about an appropriate fine, said, 'The defendant was fined 10s on last court day.' Solicitor Poe, for the board, immediately interjected that the minimum penalty for the offence was £5. Connellan had to agree:'There seems to be no option. We can't fine him any less than that.' However, at the same petty sessions, when another cotman was found guilty of fishing during the weekly closed time, Connellan said: 'Well, we can't fine you less than £5. Of course you know there is a way for petitioning [to the lord lieutenant] to get it reduced.'[16]

The local magistrates' disgruntlement with mandatory fines and the regional court were important in protecting fishers against over-zealous conservators and biassed evidence. It gave a fillip to the idea of the 'benefit of the doubt.' Moreover, given the local magistrates' concern with apportioning blame in the context of local life, many cases did not turn out as badly as might otherwise have been the case. Fines, too, were likely to be the minimum allowed. Of course, everything could be undone if the conservators pursued the case to appeal.

All this meant that, even as categories of opposition and alliance were being forged through the broad interactions which occurred in the region and state (Table 8.1), local life included many from both the dominant and subordinate classes whose local relationships, viewpoints, and allegiances cut across these categories. Indeed, as the anti-landlord sentiment of farmers was being slowly transformed into a broader nationalist ideology at the turn of the twentieth century, cotmen and labourers still retained a local perspective in which personal sentiments and loyalties linked them in positive ways to gentlemen, landlords, and capitalist employers.

Everyday Rancour and the Sentiments of Labourers

The fisheries, however, and what went on around them did not affect only those who were directly implicated in them. Rather, most local people held opinions and sympathies in relation to the agents, rules, and outcomes. That this was particularly the case among labouring people was apparent from their relations with bailiff William Murphy. The rancour involved shows clearly that the fishers' experiences extended well beyond the river and into the town (Case 8.6).

Case 8.6: The People versus William ('Billy Arrigle') Murphy in 1895
Murphy summoned two boys, Samuel Lamphier and John Burris, for having used abusive and threatening language towards him. Murphy lived at the top of Ladywell Street, less than a ten-minute walk to the shops in Market Street. He explained to the bench that 'his wife could never go down the street without having a lot of chaps following her and shouting at her and hopping stones off her back.' He now had to buy bread himself. In late May he was going down the street when 'a whole crowd of chaps followed him shouting and calling him "bailiff" and a lot of other names. They threw stones at him and one of them nearly cut the ear off him.' He said that Lamphier and Burris were in the crowd.

Both boys denied the charge. The sergeant said that he knew that Murphy 'was given a lot of annoyance. He had made several complaints about the conduct of a lot of boys living in his locality.' Chairman Connellan said there was 'no doubt these boys were in the crowd and that they did follow the complainant and shout at him.' He fined them 6d. each, with costs, saying that 'if any more of this thing goes on, they will be made an example of.'

At the same sessions, John Burris's mother summoned Murphy for using abusive language on that same day. She said that her son 'was on the street' and Murphy 'came and caught him.' She told him to stop but Murphy 'began to abuse her [and] told her that he would spill blood in the place and that he would kill her.' Murphy admitted to catching some boys in the street on the evening they had abused him. Mary Brennan was then sworn. She said that Murphy came to her door where she was sitting and 'abused her,' saying 'he would pull the brains out of her.' The chair told Murphy: 'There is no doubt you abused her but I think you got a good deal of provocation.' Murphy was fined 2s. and costs.

A month later, Murphy was had up by the constabulary for being drunk and disorderly. He said that 'a mob followed him up to his own house threatening to beat him and pull down the house.' He said they 'were following him for the last 6 months since he became a water-bailiff.' The resident magistrate asked if he was drunk. Murphy said he was coming to the police station 'to get a warrant for the mob that broke into my house before. It is my second offence in my whole life.' Murphy was fined 2s.6d. and 1s.6d. costs. He then faced a charge brought by John Burris for abusive and threatening language on the same day. Burris claimed that 'Murphy came to his door and abused him, and swore that he would knock the other eye out of his head; he was always at it, just because he [Burris] was a servant with the Archdeacon.' Murphy, however, had a cross-case against Burris for the same offence on the same occasion. Murphy claimed that 'Burris came up to his door and called him a robbing, water-bailiff and an informer; he abused his wife also in a filthy manner.' Murphy's wife corroborated this. The magistrates dismissed the case of Murphy against Burris. In the case of Burris against Murphy, they ordered Murphy to post £5 bail 'to be of good behaviour for twelve months.'

At the same sessions, Murphy summoned Philip Cahill for abusive and threatening language on the same day. The chair asked: 'Why do you not summon the whole town?' Murphy said: 'Only I have no means I would do it (laughter).' Murphy said that Cahill was one of the mob who followed him up to his house trying to beat him and his wife. She corroborated this. John Burris said that he was present at the time and that Cahill never abused Murphy. 'The chairman said a stop should be put to such conduct. No matter whether Murphy was a water-bailiff or not he should be left alone.' Cahill was ordered to post bail of £5 for his good behaviour for twelve months.[17]

The combination against Murphy was made up of his non-fishing, labouring neighbours who were responding to his being a bailiff, an informer, and a persecutor of cotmen. He was subjected to abusive language, threats, and stone throwing. That so many took part, both adults and children, men and women, highlights the importance that cot fishing had for local working people. It also shows that the political experiences engendered by cot fishing over the previous six decades had been passed on, as of 1895, to yet another generation of Thomastown labourers.

Changing Common Sense: Combinations and Alliances in the Late Nineteenth Century

The recent experiences of inland cot fishers induced them to try to change the anomalous position that they occupied in the structure of common-sense opposition in relation to the salmon fisheries (Table 8.1) and to create a legitimate role for themselves in the eyes of both state and regional administrators. They tried to do this by forming a formal association. In 1899, at a parliamentary inquiry held into the declining salmon fisheries, the evidence of Thomas Pender, cotman and secretary of the new association, indicated that the new body's aims were to limit the workings of the 'big net' at Inistioge,[18] to divert conservators from protecting private fisheries and increase protection of the spawning grounds, and to prevent poaching. In expressing these aims and how they might be achieved, Pender also tried to gain legitimacy for inland netting and to undercut the dominant view of people like gentleman angler and conservator H.C. Fitzherbert, who rented Marsh's fishery each year, that 'netmen and poachers' were indistinguishable. To do this, Pender first presented a *mea culpa*, conciliatory posture. Then, in concurring that the fishery was declining and that human agency was the cause, he insisted that it was the poaching from all types of fishermen that was responsible and not, as the conservators and administrators would have it, the result of inland netting, whether legal or illegal. He also claimed that cotmen could play a positive role in protecting the rivers if they were granted 'warrants' by the authorities to do so (Case 8.7).

Case 8.7: The Cotmen's Association and Thomas Pender's Evidence, 1899
'[Questioner] Your present evidence is that the snap net men poach?
[Answer] All class of nets poach ...

'[Q] Snap net men, you say, poach the most? [A] All the fishermen poach; but the snap net fishermen poach bad; that is, all that is in our district.

'[Q] I want to get at what is in your mind. What is the reason salmon have decreased in your district? [A] On account of constant poaching.

'[Q] By whom? [A] By every class of fishermen – rod fishermen, snap net fishermen, trawler fishermen ...

'[Q] And you would put that down by what? [A] By paying water bailiffs.

'[Q] How would you get money for more water bailiffs – have you any suggestions about that? [A] The District Councils will supply, and the Fishery Organization will assist in every way we can. If we could get warrants – I applied, myself, at the inquiry in New Ross, and they would not grant it. They said it would be a revolver I would want next if I got a warrant ...

'[Q] Has your Association ... subscribed for bailiffs to the Conservators? [A] Oh, no, sir.

'[Q] Why not? [A] They don't like the class of water bailiffs that is in it, or the Board of Conservators that is in it either.

'[Q] They want water bailiffs of their own? [A] They will send men out of the Association to protect it if they get warrants, and let the Conservators select their own water bailiffs.

'[Q] How would you pay these men? [A] The fishermen ... in the organisation want no payment.

'[Q] How are they to live? [A] They want to put into the river what will make them live. If they get plenty of fish in the river they will be able to profit by it ... In any organisation there will be 10 or ... 20 good men picked to do good work, that will benefit everybody. It is a prosperous industry if it can be protected.

'[Q] Did you hear evidence here that the snap net men are the principal poachers, and would you appoint them to preserve the river? [A] Good men will be picked out of them. Of course there are rotten men in every agitation that will break away and do everything contrary to the right man; but we will be prepared to watch these men.

'[Q] Is it not possible for the fishermen who are so anxious to protect the river to give evidence about poaching even without a warrant – to give information to the police? [A] If you take it in that light you will be called an informer; but if you have authority to do it you won't. I was a poacher, myself, and poached a good deal – I never poached for the last two years ... since we started the Association ...

'[Q] You are on the river daily? [A] I did not fish for the last six years, because it would not support me. Myself and my father and five brothers were at it, and there are only two of us fishing now; it would not support any family ... I fished pretty well up to seven or eight years ago, and I found it would not pay me.

'[Q] You are firmly convinced that this organisation would help the fishing *very much? [A] Yes, sir. There is another thing we would wish – the rod fishing to be stopped the very same time as the nets. Then there is ... a big net up there – Mr. Tighe's net. It is about 100 yards long, and the river is only about ... 45 where it makes the sweep, and 57 where it hauls in ...*

   '[Q] Anything else? [A] We are after getting the organisation together, and we intend to send down the fry to them, and let the seine nets protect them out to sea, as well as they can, and if we find any fault in them we will attack them again.

   '[Q] You know the advantage of having a large amount of fry? [A] Yes, and there is a large amount of fry gone out, this year, on account of the organisation ...

   '[Q] How did your organisation cause more to go out? [A] Because there never was a man went out from the 15th of August, nor did they kill them on the streams. Several saw them on the streams; but on account of the talk of the people and the police they were afraid to go next or near the streams.' [19]

The cotmen's combination aimed to remake their public image, to create a niche that would allow them to continue netting in the upper waters and to offer to police themselves so as to moderate the coercive forces now arrayed against them by conservators, bailiffs, constables, absentee landlords, and the county court judge. Yet, despite their conciliatory stance, their efforts failed to dent the common sense of commissioners who did not understand why cotmen, who were concerned with prevention, did not simply pay money to the conservators and inform on poachers. Nor, in the face of such bureaucratic outlooks, could a local association have value. When Pender was asked if he knew the advantage of large numbers of salmon fry, the implication was clear: there was no indigenous knowledge and cotmen were ignorant. Then, when bailiff William Ireland was asked whether the new association 'was an advisable thing,' he said: 'You can hardly make a leopard change his spots very quickly: if a man is poaching all his lifetime it is hard to expect him to protect fish.'

The association was too little, too late, in the face of common sense and overwhelming opposition. Pender's evidence, however, did point to an important change after 1884. Decreasing stocks meant declining living standards for those who fished. This was, of course, offset by the fact that most cotmen were waged workers. When John Kelly was asked if he was a fisherman, he said: 'I am a labourer. I don't earn my living by fishing.' [20] At the same time, many labourers, including cotmen, began increasingly to avoid both the coercion and declining stocks by angling for trout, as well as salmon, for both food and cash. On the one hand, this provided new challenges for the bailiffs. Angling infractions were more difficult to prove because they were more easily covered up (for example, Case 8.3[B]). In 1897, when cotman Edward Foley was charged with illegal salmon angling, he maintained that he was fishing only for trout and pike and that no licence was required for that. He said that the salmon flies that he had with him were only part of his 'ordinary fly book' and that he was not using them at the time. In other words, not only were angling offences difficult to prove but angling technology could cover up illegal salmon fishing. It could also provide an alibi for illegal cot fishing. In 1897, at the same petty sessions, Peter Cody's mother told the bench that her son could not have been cot fishing at night because 'he does no fishing now only with a rod.'[21]

On the other hand, angling was not simply a cover. It was a fairly reliable way of fishing and certainly less risky than snap-netting. It also was accessible to all interested working people and thus came to include many men who were not cot fishers. This had the effect of amplifying common sentiment and the experience of oppression in the fisheries. In 1898 owner Marsh summoned a publican's son and a shoemaker for angling on his property 'without being duly authorised.' The defendants said that they had a right to fish on the lands because no prohibitory notice had been placed in the newspapers or on the property. Marsh's solicitor insisted that such notices were not required and the anglers were fined £1 each and cost or a fortnight in jail.[22]

In such ways, repression in the fisheries extended outward to incorporate those who fished with rod and line, both poor anglers and local sportsmen from all classes. Repression also extended outward, across class lines, to local mill owners. A dramatic example occurred at an 1899 parliamentary hearing when evidence from gentleman angler Fitzherbert threatened the reputations of mill owner Pilsworth and his workers in front of the entire nation (Case 8.8).

Case 8.8: Locality and Mutuality – Fitzherbert and Pilsworth at the 1899 Parliamentary Inquiry

H.C. Fitzherbert, who rented Marsh's fishery, lived in Thomastown only for one month during the open season. He complained, as had Samuel Ireland in 1888 (Case 8.1), about the black arch at Pilsworth's mill and how millworkers poached there. The black arch, he said, 'was a celebrated place ... Mr. Pilsworth is a good fisherman [angler] and a friend of my own, and I spoke to him privately, and I thought he would have met me, but nothing has been done.' W.E. Shackleton, secretary of the Irish Water-Power Industries Association, was monitoring the proceedings. He hurriedly wrote to Pilsworth about Fitzherbert's testimony, saying that his evidence 'either had to be contradicted or the poaching stopped.' Shackleton happily noted that at least 'no allusion was made in newspaper reports to his evidence regarding your mill.' He asked Pilsworth if he wanted to appear to refute Fitzherbert's evidence. Pilsworth agreed and Shackleton offered lengthy advice on what he should say: 'Give general evidence ... as the commissioners are only allowing us to send ... a limited number of witnesses.'

Pilsworth's evidence, however, was brief. He read a prepared statement which addressed itself directly 'to some statements that Mr Fitzherbert made about alleged poaching on mill premises.' He added briefly that 'numerous statements have been made to this Commission that poaching is habitually practised in mill races and our association denies that this takes place to any great extent.' He then returned to Fitzherbert's testimony, saying that it was untrue that the archway was hidden from bailiffs. He also 'emphatically' denied that 'any men employed in the mill during the last 30 years ever took fish out of the archway.' His foreman was 'prepared to swear that during the 12 years he has been in my employment no fish were taken by my men.' His night foreman of twenty years was prepared to give the same evidence. Pilsworth said that he lived beside the mill and could hear if it stopped. When it did, because he feared something was wrong, he went out, 'even in the middle of the night.' Poaching was therefore impossible without his knowledge. Indeed, 'where the water emerges ... is a public right of way, giving the bailiffs access to it at all times ... A grating such as Fitzherbert requires would interfere very seriously with the working power.' He also pointed out that 'the archway in question was the subject of inquiry' twice, and the conservators 'tried to get a grating put there. On both occasions the Inspectors decided that ... the grating would be injurious ... As regards the decrease in salmon, ... my opinion is that it was caused ... by the wholesale slaughtering of the spawning fish in the ... upper reaches ... It is not regular poachers who do it. It is country people – farmers and people of that class, I understand ... The Conservators should employ extra bailiffs during the close season to watch the spawning beds, and I understand that during that season the staff is reduced rather than increased.'
Pilsworth concluded that 'a statement of that sort, coming from a man of Mr. Fitzherbert's position with regard to the mills, might have a very injurious effect.' The chair responded: 'You are quite right to vindicate your employees and yourself if you thought it necessary.'[23]

Clearly, Fitzherbert had assumed that a word between gentlemen who fished would put an end to labourers who poached and fish that entered a tail race. His confusion as to why this did not happen brought him to the commission. Pilsworth immediately moved to limit what was seen by his colleague as damage. When so doing, he placed his own interests first and those of his workmen a very close second. He proffered the local cotmen's view of what caused the fisheries to decline; he refrained from dealing with the 'general issues' which Shackleton had asked him to raise; he explicitly refuted the evidence of a gentlemen angler; and he defended his labourers from this outsider's attack. Interestingly, when asked by the commissioners to describe the size of his enterprise, he answered: 'There are about twenty families employed.' Neither the interests of angling gentry nor Irish millers superceded Pilsworth's immediate, local concerns with his mill and his labouring families. Equally interesting is that 'blow-in' anglers, such as Fitzherbert, could not comprehend how Pilsworth failed to put his sporting interests before his commercial ones and his Protestant gentleman's ties before his local ones.

Modes of Knowing and Political Sentiment through the Inland Salmon Fisheries

When Pilsworth in 1899 attributed the declining fisheries to a lack of protection on the spawning beds, he was simply reiterating what many people in Thomastown 'knew' and what his workers cum local cotmen had told an 1891 inquiry. This suggests the significance of local knowledge, regardless of class. Yet the data also suggest that local people of different status categories might equally have held diverse understandings (Case 8.9). What all this means is that Thomastown people held generalized local opinions in tandem with the common-sense categories of alliance and

---

Case 8.9: Why the Salmon Fisheries Declined, According to Thomastown Witnesses in 1891

Occupation/status of witnes	Cause of the Decline
Gentry angler	*Netting in February.*
Gamekeeper, Mount Juliet	*Low water and the draft net ('big net') at Inistioge.*
Cot fisher	*Illegal constructions on weirs (for example, Doran/Jerpoint weir)*
Cot fisher	*The destruction of spawning fish by poachers in upper waters*
Grennan millworker	*'The tributaries not being properly attended to.'*[24]

---

opposition that had been constructed through the agency of state and regional administration. These two modes of knowledge also meshed with what local people grasped about their personal, material interests. Thus, at least three systems of knowledge, and three kinds of consciousness, had been structured by the turn of the twentieth century through the politics of hegemony and coercion associated with the inland salmon fisheries.

9. Social Organization and the Politics of Labour

Among both workers and cotmen, the material experiences and systems of knowledge that grew out of the late nineteenth century were sustained by local networks of kinship, occupation, and neighbourhood. These slowly merged with the growth of formal, working-class organizations and ideologies after 1890. Less than a decade later, the franchise was extended. Local and regional government was reorganized and a new frame was provided for labourers to pursue their interests. One of these interests was subsidized rural housing. Created through the agency of the state, the Irish Party, and public health officials, housing became a focal point through which cultural codes and labour processes became further implicated in the *metissage* of labouring experience.

The Children of Fishers: Kinship, Occupation, and Locality

After 1884, Thomastown's cotmen continued to fish. To do so profitably, they had to poach at night, taking fish from waters that were part of privately owned lands. Yet the political economy of the fisheries continued to change, affecting the structuration of sentiment and social relations in the locality.

Kinship Networks and Household Reproduction

By the late nineteenth century, kinship and affinal connections among fisher households had become more dense while ties with local labouring families increased. The Catholic ban on marriage up to and including third cousins, and its ban on marriage between affines, prevented the practice of endogamy which might have intensified blood ties

Figure 9.1: Genealogy: The kinship links of selected fisher households

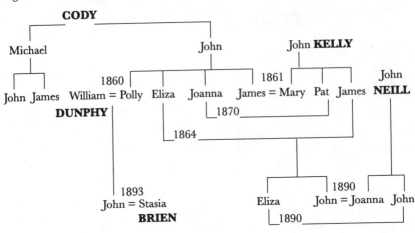

among fisher kin and perhaps marked them off as a bounded status or occupational group. Instead, a fisher accumulated a maximal number of first, second, and third cousins because all of these had to marry non-cousins. The church, however, did not forbid marriages between the siblings of affines. Fishers thus were able to achieve a greater density in their kin nets through 'sibling exchanges,' that is, by the marriage of the siblings of a married couple. Figure 9.1 shows how such marriages in 1861, 1864, and 1870 linked the fisher Kellys and Codys and how they tied the Neills to the Kellys in 1890 and thence, to the Codys.

When tracing kin, Thomastown people in the 1980s said that certain people were 'double first cousins.' The expression contained the clear implication that such relations were particularly close, certainly more intimate than if the doubling had not occurred. For some fishers, then, sibling exchanges created a dense web of affinal ties within the generation in which such marriages occurred and, also, extremely close cousin relations in the next. At the same time, however, the ban on cousin marriage did force fishers to look elsewhere for partners because not every fisher could or would marry the sibling of an affine. So, at the same time that relations between some fisher households were compounded, marriages into other fisher households also took place. This had the effect of broadening the reach of fisher nets and of incorporating most fisher households into an interlinked network of kinship and affinity (Figure 9.1). It also had the effect of absorbing newcomers. This aug-

Figure 9.2: Genealogy: Incorporating newcomers into the fisher kinship net

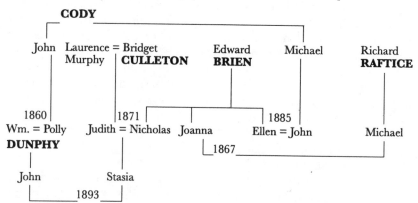

mented the number of fisher households and allowed for the replacement of those that had not reproduced locally. Both the fisher Briens and Neills came to Thomastown from other parts of Ireland. The Briens arrived earlier and quickly married in, connecting themselves to the Culletons, Raftices, and, later, Codys (Figure 9.2). The Neills were also linked in through a sibling exchange in 1890 (Figure 9.1).

At the same time that newcomers were incorporated, many of the old fisher surnames, so prominent in the petty sessions records before 1884, were no longer in Thomastown by the 1901 census. Known from poaching charges, fisher surnames, such as Clooney, Connors, Culleton, and Donnelly, simply disappeared from archival records. That their children never appeared as heads of households in the parish records or censuses points to the importance of emigration, which halved the parish population between 1851 and 1901. However, there were other reasons for the failure of fisher households to reproduce. Cotmen Kennedy and Mathews were drowned in 1846 and their young wives and children emigrated. Gender, too, was important, as were the implications of only girls being born in a fisher household. For snap-netting was a skill passed from father to son. Female births precluded not only passing on the surname but also passing on the skills. In Thomastown, the sons of fisher daughters did not become cotmen unless that daughter had married a fisher. Thus, the surname of Curran disappeared. The fisher surnames of Dawson and Dempsey also vanished because their sons, although remaining in the locality, chose not to follow their fathers. 'Cot fisher' was an achieved rather than ascribed status.

By the late nineteenth century, then, the kin nets of local fishers showed an accumulation of cousins as far as was possible in the context of high emigration and the failure of household reproduction. These nets also contained numerous links to other fisher households as a result of a marriage or a sibling exchange. Indeed, particularly close relations were created among the many who had 'doubled' relations. Thus, through the proscription on cousin marriage and the use of sibling exchanges, fisher cousins accumulated and fisher kin links were both extended outwards and internally reinforced.

Fishers as Labourers: Emic Categories, Occupational Strategies, and Kin Nets

The extension of fisher kinship outwards had an important dimension. Given that not all fisher people could marry other fishers, whom did they marry? In 1864 a civil-marriage register began. It recorded the 'occupation or status' of each of the marrying pair and each of their fathers. The earliest fisher marriage in this register was John Donnelly's marriage to Kate Traynor in 1864. The occupation of each, and of their fathers, was given as 'labourer.' Similarly, ten marriages of fisher males who are included in the above genealogies took place between 1864 and 1897. The occupations of the grooms were as follows: seven were 'labourers,' two were 'millers,' and one was a 'shoemaker.' Their fathers' statuses were also given: seven were 'labourers,' one was a 'mason,' and one was a 'fisherman.' Clearly, cotmen were seen as part of the category of labourer. Importantly, this had a material component. Cotmen were labourers/artisans by occupation as well as by classification. Wage books for Grennan Mills survive for the years 1876 to 1886. Between twenty-four and thirty-four men were employed at any one time. Figure 9.3 combines the genealogies of fishers and those of millworkers. The names of cotman cum mill worker are underlined and the dates during which all workers laboured in the mill are given. Cotmen thus worked as labourers and, importantly, their non-fisher kin were working in the same enterprise. The wage books also show that cotman Pat Dawson worked in the mill until the late 1870s, as did Martin Dawson. So, too, did fishers Richard Donnelly and John Donnelly, both of whom worked, off and on, until the late 1870s.[1] Yet how could millworkers both fish and labour?

The wage books show that there were various labour processes in the enterprise. First, the owners held a large farm for which they required labour, some of it seasonal, for lambing and harvest. Second, flour milling, too, was somewhat seasonal, requiring more labour in the autumn

Figure 9.3: Genealogy: The networks of fisher and millworker kin

[A] The Cody-Brien Segment

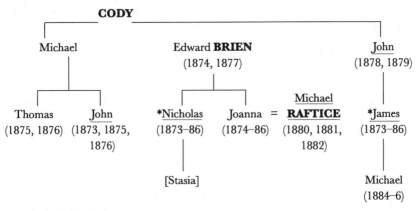

[B] The Kelly-Neill Segment

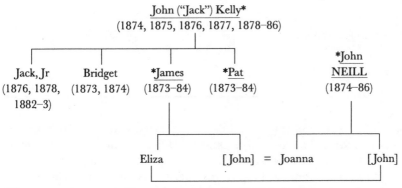

*The names of cotmen/millworkers are underlined and their employment dates in Grennan Mills are given for all those who worked between 1876 and 1886. Their work histories are given in Case 9.1.

[ ] We know from interviews that the people bracketed were millworkers after 1886.

and early winter. Third, the mill required artisans (carpenters, masons, blacksmiths) who did task work which might take a day, a week, or a month. All this created different work patterns depending where labourers worked and whether they were permanent or casual (Table 9.1)

Long-term, full-time, and permanently employed workers formed a core in the mill and a small core on the farm. At the other extreme were

Table 9.1: Work patterns and workers in Grennan Mills, 1873–86

	Location Worked:		
Permanent Workers	Mill	Farm	Mill & Farm
Worked 3–13 years:			
Still working in 1886	15	2	–
Left before 1886	11	–	–
Worked 1–2.9 Years:			
Still working in 1886	2	–	–
Left before 1886	7	–	–
Worked 1–11 months:			
Still working in 1886	2	–	–
Left before 1886	22	4	–
Worked –1 month:			
Still working in 1886	–	–	–
Left before 1886	12	7	–
Casual: Worked more than twice in a 5+ year period	–	3	16
Casual: Worked more than twice in a –5 year period	–	2	7
Artisans (on contract)	9	–	–
Total:	80	18	23

those who worked in the factory or farm but who gave it up after several weeks or months, for reasons unknown. However, there also were men who worked off and on over various periods of time, from under five years to over the entire thirteen-year period. Almost all of these were 'mill and farm workers,' obviously assigned where and when they were needed. In contrast, 'mill-only workers' never worked as casuals.

The work patterns of some of the cotmen were different than those of the workforce in general. Of the nine cotmen/mill workers in Figure 9.3, five were permanent. They worked only in the mill. The other four were casuals who worked on farm and mill. They put in most of their time (64, 83, 88, and 92 per cent) in the closed season (15 August to 15 February). This was possible because the seasonality of milling and fishing dovetailed neatly. Grain harvests began at the end of July, just before the closed season, while the slack milling period, from January to June, corresponded with the opening of the salmon season and the best

Figure 9.4: Genealogy: The Fisher-artisan Kellys

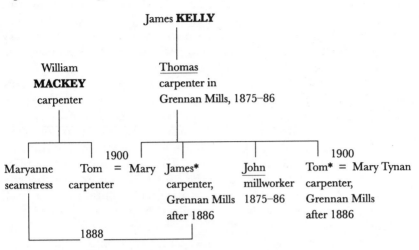

The genealogy contains information from the Grennan Mills wage books (1873–86). Names of the cot fishers are underlined. Asterisked names are of those who became cotmen after the period covered by Grennan Mills wage books.

of the early fish. Yet the best cot fishing was at night. A cotman working full-time in the mill during the day would be hard-pressed to fish all night and then return to the mill in the morning. Several managed to do this, often by confining their fishing to Saturday nights. All this meant, however, that casual mill work fit best with fishing. Owner Pilsworth supported such labour practices. It provided him with casuals in season, lowered his wage bill, and sustained the ideology of paternalism and deference.

The above genealogies not only contained cotmen who were mill-workers but millworkers who were not cotmen and men who were neither. It also included cotmen who did not work in the mill.[2] John Dunphy was the fisherman for Mount Juliet estate; others worked 'casually around.' Some were artisans: they formed a single kin net with the surname of Kelly. This net, in turn, connected to other artisanal households. The sibling exchange between the Kellys and Mackeys in 1888 is an example of links extending into non-fisher, artisanal households.

That there was no connection between the mill-working Kellys (Figures 9.1, 9.3) and the artisan Kellys (Figure 9.4) is striking. It was likely the result of one of two factors. The earliest male Kellys in both networks, John and James, may have been brothers or cousins and this would have precluded marriages between the people in the two nets after 1860. Given the similar Christian names in each net, this is very possible. Alternatively, the higher status of the artisan Kellys may have discouraged marriages between the two nets.

The wage books from the mill show that carpenter Thomas Kelly worked casually on the mill and farm in the 1870s and did half his time during the open season. Either he was less inclined than non-artisanal casuals to concentrate his mill work during the closed season or, more likely, as a carpenter, he had to be available whenever needed. Indeed, when blacksmith 'Jack' Kelly (Figure 9.3[B]) was a casual before 1878, only 60 per cent of his work was in the closed time. Moreover, that cotman John Kelly (Figure 9.4) was not a carpenter but a full-time mill-worker points to the fact that some fishers chose, or were forced, into that work pattern. In any case, as elderly people in the 1980s recollected, the 'carpenter Kellys' were always kept busy building cots for the fishers, poaching, and doing carpentry for anyone who had work.

In addition to all these fishers, other households in the 1901 census were headed by men charged with poaching. What they had in common was that they were unconnected to other fisher networks. This resulted from technology, generation, and geography. Two of those charged were rodmen. Of these, Patrick Magee worked casually, on mill and farm, at Grennan Mills while William Langfry, who called himself a 'labourer' when he married in 1870, did casual work around. Another fisher household was headed by Billy 'Arrigle' Murphy, cotman and sometime water bailiff (Case 8.6). Two other households were headed by elderly fishers: Richard Hutchinson, born in 1825, and James Carroll, born in 1831. Finally, John Buckley's household was in an outlying townland down the Nore which linked Buckley and Thomastown cotmen to those fishers resident south of the parish, on the way to Inistioge and the tidewater.

By 1901, Thomastown thus had kinship networks of labourers and artisans who fished by net or rod and who formed, emically and occupationally, part of the working class. Through ties of blood and marriage, and wage work as non-fishers, such households were connected to non-fishing households made up of labourers and artisans. Kinship, affinity, and occupation thus linked cotmen, millworkers, labourers, and artisans.

Fishers as Labourers: Locality, Distance, and Proximity

In the 1980s Thomastown people classified locality in various ways, depending on who was talking, the topic, and the familiarity that the speakers had of the locale being discussed. On the one hand, gossip shared between two people who lived near to each other and the event being discussed elicited a minute categorization of space. In the appropriate context, every house, shed, street, footpath, and field could be differentiated from every other. On the other hand, gossip about people living distant from the speakers elicited spatial categories of a general and even ambiguous nature.[3] However, one key physical feature was the River Nore. It cuts through the parish, town, and countryside, making various places somewhat more or somewhat less known and accessible. This is in part because, for a distance of two and a half miles from the town's bridge, no other bridge crosses the Nore. The river was thus a physical divide. It also was a socio-cultural one. It influenced the residential, marital, and occupational choices of workers and it became implicated in their world-views.

For the years 1895 to 1931, wage books for the tannery survive. In 1895, it employed thirty-two workers of whom sixteen worked the full year. The total numbers were down to twenty-one by 1901; of these, fifteen worked full-time. The tannery was located north of the River Nore, on Ladywell Street, a ten-minute walk from Grennan Mills on the south side (see Map 2). This walk took a person through Market Street and the shopping area and, thence, across the bridge to the south bank and along Mill Street to where it joins the Mall. In Thomastown in the 1930s, people who lived in Mill Street and Mall referred to people across the river as 'townies.' The townies responded with the epithet of 'Mill Street crowd.' One man, born in 1913 and living on Ladywell, recalled how his mother did not let him to go to Mill Street until he was sixteen years old. She considered the place too dangerous. Clearly, Thomastown was divided into micro-neighbourhoods which were categorized and stereotyped in particular ways. How was this expressed among labouring people in the late nineteenth century?

The households of forty-four tannery labourers, working full- or part-time, listed in the tannery wage books for the 1895–1901 period, could be located in the 1901 census. Of these, forty-three lived north of the river – in Ladywell or adjacent streets or, occasionally, in northern peri-urban, or rural townlands. This residential segregation did not occur because of artificial constraints such as tied housing in either mill or tannery since all houses were held by head landlords or local middle-men unconnected to either industry. The marriage patterns of the tannery workers reflected this residential segregation. Of the fifteen tannery workers for whom complete civil-registry data were available,[4] twelve married women from north of the river. One of the dissenting three was Patrick Murphy, the lone tannery worker who crossed the river daily to and from work. Generally, the outcome of such marriage choices, of course, was that tannery workers had virtually no kin links on the south side of the Nore.

This stark spatial and social circumscription was reflected in an occupational segregation. The wage books from both mill and tannery, although somewhat separated by time, permit a comparison of personnel. Together, the books contain entries for 182 workers: 121 in the mill and 61 in the tannery. A large number were casuals who likely would have worked wherever they could. It thus seems plausible to expect that numerous labourers should have worked for both factories at different times. In fact, only 4 labourers of the 182 worked in both places. This was the same for artisans. Each factory required them. Some were, of course, only relevant to the particular production process in each enterprise. Curriers, tanners, and coopers were needed in the tannery; millwrights and wheelwrights were needed in the mill. Yet both factories hired masons, carpenters, and blacksmiths, usually for task work. However, the mill and tannery used, apart from the one harness maker in the town, an entirely different pool of artisans. The labour forces of the tannery and mill were thus virtually distinct. Indeed, from the view of those who lived and worked north of the river, Thomastown barely had another side and other labourers. How did it look to those who lived and worked on the other side, in Mill Street and the Mall?

Unlike those north of the river, Mill Street people had to cross the river often. They went every Sunday to Mass. After 1840, when the first National School was built, their children crossed every day. After 1853, they came to get medical aid from the dispensary at the workhouse and, perhaps, they crossed to go, for a time, to the workhouse itself. They went to the courthouse to be the audience, plaintiffs, or defendants. After 1853, they crossed to the railway station to send their salmon to Waterford's markets. They went to the poultry and pig markets held weekly in Market Street. Perhaps they crossed also for some shopping, although the three pub-groceries in 1880 on Mill Street may have sufficed. The drapers, however, and the hardware merchants, were located

Table 9.2 Residence and marriage among millworkers and fishers

Residence of Bride:	Residence of Groom:							
	Millworker		Fisher/millworker		Fisher		Others from Figures/ Genealogies 9.1, 9.2, 9.3, 9.4, 9.5	
	North	South	North	South	North	South	North	South
North	3	2	1	–	4	–	–	1
South	1	2	–	6	–	5	3	–

in Market Street. Indeed, as the nineteenth century amplified the institutions and services of state, market and church, Mill Street and Mall people became increasingly linked to the other side of the river. The residential and marital patterns of the millworkers reflected this wider horizon.

The residences of sixty millworkers, who appear in the 1873–86 mill records, were located using parochial, civil, and valuation records. Of these, forty-one workers, or 68 per cent, lived south of the River Nore. Over a quarter (28 per cent) lived north of the river; and two workers moved between. The marital choices of millworkers also suggest this broader outlook. Here, however, data are limited because the civil registry, with its detailed information, began only in 1864 and most millworkers in the 1873–86 mill books were already married. However, through the inclusion of fishers who did not work in the mill and the kin of fishers noted in Figures 9.1 through 9.5, data are available for twenty-eight marriages (Table 9.2).

The number of spatially exogamous marriages among all millworkers was fairly small: three out of 15, or 20 per cent. Yet this was greater than among tannery workers (13 per cent). Importantly, however, Figure 9.2 shows that exogamous unions involved only non-fishers. That is, only non-fishing millworkers sometimes chose spouses from across the river, whereas cotmen, whether or not they were millworkers, chose wives from their immediate locality. This fisher parochialism was offset by some of the women, four of whom married across the river (Case 9.1).

Case 9.1: Marrying across the River – The Daughters of Fishers
Two spatially exogamous marriages (Figure 9.5) created a cyclical pattern which linked and relinked the north and south banks and the dense kinship connections

Figure 9.5: Genealogy: Cody-Brien relations across the Nore

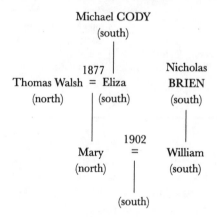

in the fisher net. In 1877, Eliza Cody married out, both to the north and to a non-fisher. Her daughter not only married back south, she also married a fisher who already was linked to the net.

In 1891 the daughter of fisher Patrick Kelly married the son of a tannery worker from the north side of the river. In 1900 the daughter of fisher-carpenter Kelly, whose kin net was based in Grennan Mills, married into carpenter Mackey's net based in the tannery. Both new households were set up in the north.

Three of the above four cross-river marriages occurred late in the 1884–1901 period. As well, given the local bias towards patrilocality, women moved to the north side of the river after three of the four marriages.

Thus, while fisher-men married locally, some of their daughters married outward, linking other places, industries, and occupations. These marriages marked a widening spatial and class awareness at the end of the century which complemented the daily migration of numerous mill-workers from their homes north of the river. Relative to tannery workers, millworkers were cosmopolitan indeed. At the same time, the kin nets of fishers/cotmen continued to constitute tightly knit segments of a wider labouring network. Thus, the broader horizons of Mill Street and Mall workers were associated with the narrow kinship horizons of cot fishers who, perceptually and structurally, shared their working-class milieu on both sides of the river.

Elections and Organizations after 1884: Experiencing the Political as Labour and Capital

Historians have generally focused on the impact of two key changes after 1884: the extension of the franchise and the growth of formal, national organizations.[5] Such foci, although correct, err by privileging the chronologies and agents in national and institutional sites, obscuring how the *metissage* of locally lived experience formed an intrinsic part of these sites by being implicated in processes of state formation via hegemony and coercion. In other words, a focus on administration and formal organization provides only a partial view. It must be complemented by a focus on other dynamics which underlie the reproduction of the colonial state: local understandings, awareness, and experience; the political as both common sense and articulated ideology; and the nature of consent cum coercion. In the late nineteenth century in Thomastown, these dynamics became implicated in a newly acquired right to vote and in formal organizations. It was immediately clear to people at the time that these were crucial changes. The editor of the *Moderator,* for example, was quick to point out the potential leverage of an enfranchized labourer and the importance of enticing labour away from its apparent alliance with farmers (Case 9.2).

Case 9.2: The Franchise and Labour – A Tory Voice in 1885

'The party which can secure the labour vote in Ireland will hold the situation, and the leaders of the Conservative Party ought, in our opinion, to so guide the policy of the party as to unite with its interests the interests of the Irish labourer. Such a union is far from impossible.

'It is quite plain ... that, as the dominant political power, the sovereignty of the tenant farmer class is no longer unchallenged or secure. The labour vote of Ireland, at least if it were organized and stood up for ... its own interests, is stronger than the farmer's vote. True, the former class ... has chosen so far to merge itself, its interests and its future in those of the farmers. The National League as an organization is a farmers' organization ... The popular press of this country is in the hands of the farmers' representatives ... and accordingly while we hear on all sides the most frightful lamentations over the woes of those who have farms, stock, homes and abundant credit with shopkeepers and banks ... we hear nothing ... about you who are far poorer and more dependent and far better acquainted with poverty, hardship and wrong.

*'The labourers constitute a class which we regard with the utmost sympathy ...
They have much concerning which they might complain, and they have hitherto
complained but little. They have been deluded ... by the Land League and
National League ... None can know better than the people of this County that ...
we have laboured to impress upon the government the duty incumbent upon them
of so governing ... Ireland ... that the hands of the labourer shall ever be full, and
that he shall not know what lack of employment means, and that for his labour he
shall have a fair and adequate recompense.'*[6]

In Thomastown, in February 1891, a United Trades and Labour Club
held its founding meeting in the 'band room' in the national school
where the Thomastown Band had met to practice. It is unknown if this
new club was affiliated with any of the other, numerous labour organizations which dotted the urban landscape at the time.[7] However, its composition and stated program say much about the organizational and
ideological state of local labourers as well as of the nature of the 'numerous small rural unions' which were extant at the time.[8]

Unlike the unions in larger centres which divided the varying skilled
workers from each other and from unskilled labourers, both artisans
and labourers together joined Thomastown's club. The men named in a
newspaper report included several artisans: a waged journeyman tailor
(Tynan), a self-employed mason, a shoemaker, a baker, and two carpenters. Several of the latter did occasional contract work for the tannery.
Eight of the men were tannery workers and two were general labourers.
No millworkers were listed in the report. Partly this reflected the north-
south divide; partly it resulted from the wages in each industry. In 1895
the tannery paid an average of 10 and 12s. per week. Grennan Mills had
paid this ten years earlier. Such different conditions of work elicited
multiple and conflicting discourses (Case 9.3).

Case 9.3: Two Discourses at the United Trades and Labour Club, 1891
*[A] 'Mr J. Tynan ... in the chair ... said that ... the society was intended for
mutual help and support. If a member fell sick or was disemployed through no
fault of his own, all the members would rally round him ... There were remarks
made about the town that the society would be a menace to the employers and that
it would cause strained relationships between the employers and their workmen.
That would not be so. This society had nothing to do with strikes, and the work-*

*ingmen would deprecate them as much as possible … Several of the workmen from
the different parts of the town [then] said that they had no grievances to complain
of and had no fault to find with their employers. The Messrs. Pilsworth were gentlemen who looked specially after their workmen, and when any of them fell sick,
which often occurred, and remained sick for a considerable time even, there was
no cessation in the payment of their wages. Those gentlemen, too, always provided
for those who had grown old or infirm in their service. The other employers, too,
dealt fairly with the men.'*

*[B] At a meeting of the 'organising committee' of the club a month later, a
general labourer chaired. A shoemaker made 'a speech urging the working class
to unite against the capitalists.' Discussion then took place as to whether the
club could continue to meet in the 'band room' in future. Shoemaker David
Shea said that 'he had been speaking to one of the members of the band about
the matter and he had said that the club could meet there as often as they liked,
as the National League didn't meet there any more – "it is … a thing of the
past" (cries of "Bravo David" and a voice "Put that down" [in the minutes]
and laughter).'*[9]

It was not surprising that the tannery workers showed themselves to
be aggrieved yet wistful when they described the millworkers. Clearly,
even though all was not well in the tannery, the paternalism in Grennan
Mills was functioning smoothly. In such a context, Tynan was a conservative intellectual, representing the club as a self-help association, deni-
grating industrial action, and content with employers. This contrasted
dramatically with shoemaker Shea's radical call and the humour that
the committee found in the difficulties that farmers' organizations were
having at the time. Clearly, then, at least two views of working people's
organizations were being expounded; so, too, were there at least two
responses to such views 'about the town.' All this added to the kaleidoscope of ideologies being formulated by diverse organic intellectuals
in the period after 1889 when numerous unions, comprised of the
unskilled, semi-skilled, and trades, surfaced in the larger centres of Ireland.[10] Kilkenny city was not exempt. In June 1890 a branch of the
Amalgamated Society of Railway Servants was formed and, a few months
later, a branch of the Union of Gas Workers and General Labourers of
Great Britain and Ireland met. At that latter meeting, a speaker made
two main points: that 'the union is purely a labour organization … politics should not be introduced into trade unionism,' and that 'nothing

foreign should be introduced into it.' He added his support for Parnell and the Irish Party because they had agreed to support the eight-hour work bill 'now that labour is organised.' He urged the audience not to endorse a party: 'Only endorse those who will do something for labour.'[11]

What all these voices from both Thomastown and Kilkenny city point to were the kinds of centripetal issues that were emerging out of the organizational impetus at the time. Should workers' organizations aim for self-help or class warfare? How should artisans fit in? How should labourers relate to British-based unions? Should unions be involved in political activity? How should labourers relate to political leaders who privileged farmers' interests? Should workers support the Irish Party?

There were no further reports on Thomastown's United Trades and Labour Club and no local memories of it in the 1980s. Like so many other clubs in Ireland in the 1890s, it probably died away. In fact, the organizational fervour of early 1890s generally quieted down until the 'renaissance of general unionism' with James Larkin in 1907.[12] However, political sentiments of various kinds continued to be stirred into the local *metissage*. For example, unskilled workers in Kilkenny met in 1897 to hear a Railway Society organiser and to pass a resolution approving 'the principle of trade unionism and calling upon all those who are not organised to become members of the trade unions and labour societies.'[13] The period at the turn of the century, then, was a time of organizational building and of heightened, yet competing, ideological views. However, the general position of all labour organizations and all voices was that workers could be subjects, that is, the working class could be an agent for its own objectives and interests.

In this context, a new local government act was passed in 1898. It gave over the grand jury's responsibilities for public works to new, elected county councils; it extended the franchise to all male householders or occupiers; and it assigned the tasks of the Poor Law guardians to new rural district councils.[14] Thomastown Poor Law Union became a rural district with a council and with broader powers. Its seat remained in the town. With the first elections to both the county and rural district councils to be held in 1899, something called 'labour' was immediately mobilized, not only in Thomastown but throughout the country. What this label meant, however, was unclear. Some candidates simply called themselves 'labour,' others were nominated by trade unions and trade councils or by 'Land and Labour' bodies, and some were put forward by previously unorganized groups of workers. There was no central agency or party approving the designation. Nor did any trades council or the national congress try to formulate a program for local government. However, the Irish Party, led by John Redmond, did urge 'workers not to form separate political organizations because they might disrupt the Home Rule movement.'[15]

In Thomastown, however, there was no confusion about whether or not workers should vote for so-called labour candidates. In the county council election, voters gave 507 votes to Richard J. Ryan, spokesman for labour and cotmen and an ardent nationalist.[16] The other candidate, a landlord, received 71. For the rural district council, however, those south of the river proved more radical than those north of it. In the Jerpoint electoral division which included the millworkers and cotmen, 'labour' tried for two seats and lost the second by only four votes. In all, labour polled twice as many votes as the farming candidate (Case 9.4). In the Thomastown electoral division, covering the tannery, there were no reported labour candidates. A large retailer (P.T. Kelly) and medium-sized farmer (William Bookle) won.

Case 9.4: 'Labour' in the Rural District Council Election, 1899[17]
Jerpoint Electoral Division (south of the river; included Mill Street, the Mall and a rural hinterland).

(1) John Magee, millworker	'labour,' 51 votes (elected)
(2) Edmond Forristal, very large-scale farmer/Land Leaguer	43 votes (elected)
(3) James Cody, labourer/cotman	'labour,' 39 votes
(4) James Power (unknown)	3 votes

At the first meeting of the new Thomaston Rural District Council in April 1899, members dealt with organizational business. They had to co-opt onto the council three magistrates who had been members of the old Board of Guardians; they had to elect a chair; and they had to co-opt three additional members. For the first magistrate's position, farmer Andrew O'Donnell was voted in unanimously. Nominations were then taken for the other two magisterial positions. The key to the nominating patterns was locality and propinquity (Case 9.5).

Case 9.5: Co-opting Magistrates onto the Rural District Council, 1899

Nominee	Locale	Status	Nominators	Locale	Status
P. Connellan	Coolmore	Gentry	Col. Butler	Ennisnag	Gentry
			Pat Prender	Ballyvool	Farmer
W.T. Pilsworth	Jerpoint	Millowner	John Magee	Jerpoint	Mill-worker
			William Bookle	Thomastown	Farmer

Nomine					
Richard Doyle	Castlegannon	Farmer	Ed. Fitzpatrick	Castlegannon	[?]
			James Rice	Knocktopher	Farmer
John Murphy	Graigue	[?]	Edward Walsh	Bennettsbridge	Farmer
			Nich. O'Donnell	Ullard	Farmer
J.T. Ryan	Thomastown	Tannery Owner	Ed. Forristal	Thomastown	Farmer
			Walsh	Cappagh	Farmer

(1) Pilsworth, Magee, Forristal, Bookle, and Ryan, together with Walsh of Cappagh townland, a part of Thomastown parish, formed a locally rooted combination which cut across class. (2) The Walsh-O'Donnell-Murphy combination came from a small area in the north of the rural district and the Fitzpatrick-Rice connection was from the south. (3) Only the Butler-Connellan connection was class-based but (4) the Prender-Connellan link was local.[18]

Pilsworth and Ryan were elected. The massive farmer majority on council had rejected Connellan, a 'good' landlord and magistrate who had served for many years on the old board, in favour of two urban capitalists and a large farmer. In the election for chair of the council, the entire Thomastown cohort voted for the same candidate (from nearby Woolengrange, adjacent to Thomastown) and against a candidate from the town of Graigue, ten miles to the east. Then, in co-opting the three councillors, all nominations were again entirely along lines of locality. For example, retailer Kelly and farmer Bookle once again nominated tanner Ryan. Labourer Magee and retailer Kelly nominated their newly elected, county councillor, Richard Ryan. Then Bookle, with another Thomastown parish councillor (farmer, Pleberstown), nominated another Pleberstown farmer, Patrick Murphy. Similarly, two councillors from Knocktopher nominated another from their division, as did those from Bennettsbridge, Kilkeasy, Graigue, and so on.[19]

In the above proceedings, labour councillor Magee had little choice but to vote for and with the farmers and the one retailer because there were no other labour people on council. On the other hand, he might have voted *against* those in his immediate locality on the grounds that they were the closest opposition. However, this logic did not operate, neither for labourers nor for farmers. Instead, at the end of the nineteenth century, the idea of locality and the ties generated by propinquity conjoined with class to form complex ties of allegiance, alliance, and opposition.

The Politics of Housing after 1884

The Labourers (Ireland) Act of 1883 aimed to improve the housing of rural, agricultural labourers by providing local governments with the legal and financial means for building subsidized cottages. By 1887, Thomastown's guardians had applied to the Local Government Board for permission to build seventy-two cottages of which forty-five were authorized. A year later, eighteen had been built and four were in progress. By 1903, 131 had been built and four were in progress. The Thomastown Union had borrowed £17,072. To repay this, £752.13.0 had to be raised annually from rates. The rents received from tenants of the cottages amounted only to £228.2.8.[20] Clearly, ratepayers were subsiding housing for agricultural labourers. This raised issues as to how decisions should be made about if and where to build and who the tenants should be.

From the beginning, it seemed self-evident to the guardians that those who paid were the ones who were to make these decisions. The clerk of the council, Mr MacCartan, made this clear in 1883 when he advised members on how to proceed. He suggested that the ratepayers in each electoral division 'confer among themselves as to the wants of their divisions in respect of the accommodation of labourers, and make up their minds as to the number of cottages that might be required, and as to the position they should occupy within the division.'[21] But who would choose the tenant? The landlord from whom the site had been bought, the tenant-farmer who had to give up the site, or the Poor Law guardian who represented the division in which the cottage was built? MacCartan believed that it should be the guardian. But what if the guardian approved someone unacceptable to the local ratepayers? MacCartan's response was that the guardian should consult with the ratepayers in his division before supporting an applicant.[22]

From the beginning then, labourers were entirely dependent not simply on a particular guardian but on the good will of an entire neighbourhood of farmers. Such farmers were often antagonistic to the cottage in the first instance. Typical objections in the early years were that the labourer would have to cross a farmer's land to get to work or that a farmer simply did not want a site near him. One farmer had his landlord's agent write that he 'objected to pauper squatters' on the estate.[23] Disputes among councillors also emerged over which administrative unit should pay the cost: the ratepayers from the division in which the cottage was built or from the union at large. Why should ratepayers in a particular division, which received fewer cottages, pay for a greater number received by another division?[24]

The cottages were not particularly grand, but they were dry and clean and sited on a half-acre of land. Each cottage had a loft, a kitchen, and three sleeping rooms. The last included 'a bedroom for the father and mother, a boys' room and a girls' room.' The width of the cottage was ten feet. The upper room was reached by ladder. The cost of each cottage in 1884 was £64.12.7. What, therefore, should be the rent? What was a 'fair rent?' How much of the cost should the rent cover? And what happened as building costs increased over time? By 1895, a cottage cost £120. Should labourers in new cottages pay more than older tenants? The latter were paying 9d. per week. The former would have to pay 2s.6d. to cover the costs.[25] The guardians decided this issue, as they had all others. They also decided who was to receive a cottage once it was built. This gave rise to contests in which the labourer was yet again an object and seemingly deprived of virtually all agency (Case 9.6).

Case 9.6: Allocating a Labourer's Cottage in Jerpoint, 1887

A meeting of the Thomastown guardians considered a letter from William Deady, farmer and miller. He referred to a cottage which had been built on his land. 'As one of the largest ratepayers in the division I asked the board to sanction ... a man of mine, who I know would make a good tenant, and who is an agricultural labourer of the first class ... For some reason, not only this cottage but another built on Mr Frank's [gentleman] land have been given away to two men ... [who] are not agricultural labourers at all – one being an old man without family, the other a young fellow who has not been brought up to farming, and neither of whom would make a suitable hand for a farmer to employ. As I understood, these cottages were built for the accommodation of agricultural labourers, whose work would be a benefit to the locality, and who always would be sure of employment.'

Another letter had been received from Mr Franks's steward: 'James Spillane has been in Mr Franks's employment for the last three years. I have found him to be a first-class man at all sorts of farm work (unless ploughing) which he has been required to do as yet, and bears a good character.' Deady then came before the board. He 'thought it wrong that Mr Franks's two men should have been placed in those cottages, while the suitable man he had recommended for the cottage built on his own land was passed over.' The chair then 'asked what description of labourers were the two men.'

'Mr Deady – They were not general farm labourers at all. They could cut furze, herd cattle, and such things but were not able to plough or do general agricultural work. The man Cullen, whom he had recommended for the cottage on his (Mr Deady's) holding was thoroughly competent and would be most useful. He was himself the largest employer ... in that locality, except for Mr Franks, and he thought his claims in this case ought to be considered ...

'The chairman said that the ratepayers were directly concerned in the putting of a man in a ... cottage who would be ... useful to the farmers in the locality, for that was the best guarantee that the rent of the plot and house would be paid without needing extra taxation.

'Guardian Doyle thought the man recommended by Mr Deady was more suitable than the others. They should give fair consideration to his representations when the site was on his land, and when he did not oppose the building of the cottage there.

'Chairman – This is essentially a ratepayers' question, for the ratepayers will have to pay two-thirds of the cost of the erection of those cottages for 49 years.

'Guardian Corcoran considered that the guardians should give the preference to the best man, the man who would have constant employment ... Then the guardians would be sure of the rent. The man on whose land the house is built should have a voice in the selection of the tenant.

'Chairman – Otherwise there would be constant disputes about trespass and other things.

'Guardian Corcoran – I must say for myself that if I knew that an objectionable man was to be put on my land in spite of me, I would oppose the building of such a cottage ... instead of agreeing to it as Mr Deady did. If Mr Franks's place was closed, these other two men would not get employment in the place.

'Mr Walsh, guardian for Jerpoint, said that he had supported the selection made on the last day at the request of the local ratepayers. The two tenants selected were very good working-men.

'Mr Deady – Will you employ them? Mr Walsh said that he did not want them.

'The chairman thought that the labourer who had exerted himself to get up the original representation on which the cottage was built, when he was found to be a

good and useful man, should have a preference. Such was the case of the man Mr Deady recommended.

'*Mr Deady – He got the names of 17 resident ratepayers signed to his petition.*

'*Mr Walsh – The petition of the other men was also largely signed.*

'*Mr MacCartan remarked that some of the same names appeared on both documents (laughter) ...*

'*The chairman asked why ... the man ... in Mr Deady's case [did] not get the cottage.*

'*Mr Walsh replied that there were ... many reasons ... The neighbours did not like him.*

'*Mr Doyle – It is hard for the man who gave the site to have a labourer put on him that he does not like, and the man he recommends passed over.*

'*The chairman said that it looked strange ... to see two men selected from one man's employment.*

'*Mr Walsh – That was not the view taken at all. The surrounding neighbours preferred these two men, and they are men of good, honest character.*

'*Chairman – It looks as if the guardians built the cottages for the gentleman's labourers ...*

'*Mr Doyle moved that the matter be re-considered on that day fortnight. Mr Leahy seconded ... On a show of hands this motion was passed by a large majority.*'[26]

Labourers had two bureaucratic allies in this process. The Local Government Board reviewed all decisions made by the guardians and, in the case of cottages, had its inspector hold an inquiry into the location and tenant of each new cottage. The second ally was the local doctor who was responsible, as the medical officer for the union, for assessing whether a labourer's house was 'unfit for human habitation.' This entitled the labourer to apply for a cottage. Even this, however, could be contested (Case 9.7).

Case 9.7: Contesting the Allocation of Cottages, 1895

The Thomastown guardians read a letter from solicitor Shortall. His client, labourer Thomas Skehan, had applied for a cottage, attended the inquiry, and satisfied the inspector that he was a farm labourer. However, the cottage was given to John Brady who had a house and a small portion of land. Although Brady's house had been deemed unfit and he had attended the inquiry, the inspector had rejected his application. Two other letters were read. One was a 'protest against this man Skehan getting the cottage ... as we the ratepayers [farmers] of that part of the division don't want him.' The other was from farmer Gorman: 'When we signed the paper for him we thought him a trustworthy man, but ... he tells every place he is that if he gets the cottage he will be a torment to me all my life.'

The chairman suggested that it would be best to send all the letters to the Local Government Board. Clerk MacCartan explained that farmer Gorman 'objected to Skehan on the ground that the man used threatening language towards him.' Councillor Bookle stated that he understood that 'that is a false statement, and that the man never met Gorman at all that day.' MacCartan suggested that the Local Government Board 'inquire into it themselves.' The council agreed.[27]

In such ways, the guardians dealt with both the local government board and the ratepayers whom they represented. To industrious and honest labourers, however, it was being made clear, from the beginning, that local power hierarchies, patronage, and political sentiments affected their access to decent housing along with their personal traits and the good will and material priorities of farmers. The essential contradiction here was that, whenever one labourer was given a cottage, another labourer was refused.

Thus, by the 1899 local elections under the new franchise, an important reason why labourers voted, first, for so-called labour candidates, and second, for local candidates, was because of their concern with housing. Indeed, the 1883 act was rapidly becoming a cornerstone of political agency and ideological conflict. As it did so, it became implicated in the cultural codes of status-class, respectability, and locality which informed social life and in the working-class organizations and ideologies which had begun to compete for the sympathy and support of labourers. This articulated with the 1899 county and rural district elections as labouring men, some of whom were cot fishers and all of whom were connected by ramifying ties of kinship and marriage, voted for the first time. They did so using three types of knowledge: their personal interests, the polarized sentiments that had been emerging through the inland salmon fisheries since 1884, and the norms, practices, and relations that linked people of all classes in Thomastown by virtue of living in a shared locality.

PART IV

Metissage and Hegemony, 1901–50

*Labourer John Hennessy applied for a cottage site on the land of a large farmer.
Hennessy said that he had a family of six and he occupied a dwelling condemned
by the medical officer. The farmer said that Hennessy had a good slated house,
with two rooms and a kitchen, and he thought that 'the house was good enough
for any poor man to live in.'*

— Kilkenny *Moderator*, 19 October 1895

Providing subsidized housing for labourers was part of the common-
sense view that wages should be linked to the costs of a labourer's subsistence and, specifically, that such costs formed a ceiling on wages. Thus,
the 1883 Labourers Act tackled many issues. It aimed to obviate a farm-
labour shortage, keep a labour pool in rural areas, restrain wages levels,
and alleviate what had become an unacceptable living standard and
public-health problem. Simultaneously, it gleaned political and ideological support for the colonial state even as the Irish Party claimed some of
the credit for the act. Indeed, even landlords could be fitted into the
equation. The *Moderator* pointed out, on 16 March 1895, that houses
'erected for labourers under the Act ... are the work of the State' while
'all others are the result of private enterprise ... in order to make money.
On the other hand, [on] hundreds of Irish estates the landlords ... have
expended large sums for the housing of labourers ... Property has its
duties as well as its privileges.'

By the turn of the twentieth century, the material and ideological
realities of housing had become implicated in common sense and, also,
in daily experience. A picture of this experience, or what can be called
the 'political miscellany of everyday life,' can be seen by taking a series
of local events which were reported by the press in a given week (Case
IV.1).

***Case IV.1: The Political Miscellany of Everyday Life – The Week of
10 September 1898***

*At a 'harvest home' at the Franks's estate, the steward 'entertained his workmen
and some neighbours.' A 'sumptuous meal was served,' followed by dancing until
dawn in a 'well-decorated room.' The 'custom of entertaining farm workers is one
of the most pleasant events of the agricultural year,' said the reporter, and the
workers were 'deeply grateful to their employer and his good steward.'*

*Thomastown's councillors discussed the need to hire a new lamplighter for the
town. The previous man was also a summons-server and worked as well for a*

retailer. He would no longer do the work for 6s. per week. The relieving officer said that 6s. 'was not enough pay for the job.' It was decided to ask the lamplighter to continue working for a week and to advertise for a new lamplighter at 6s.

Anne Murphy, from the town, summoned farmer Patrick Aylward, to the petty sessions. She said she was owed 14s. as wages. Murphy said 'she was binding' corn for seven days but 'had no agreement with him. Other women binders had 2s.6d. a day. She got paid only 6s. for the week's work.' Aylward said that he had 'agreed to pay her 1s. a day and that she had worked only 4½ days, the rest being wet. His wife corroborated this as did his servant Ellen Shannon. The case was dismissed.'

Collections were being made for the new convent in Thomastown. The bishop of the diocese, at a public meeting two years before, had urged local people to donate: 'The nuns ... will ... have the ... education of your children in their hands.' They also 'propose to develop ... [a] middle-class benefit school, in which the children of shopkeepers and well-to-do farmers will find nearly all the benefits of a boarding school.' Therefore, 'I will ask wealthy people ... to be generous, middle-class people to be charitable, and the poor out of their poverty to give even a little for this high and holy work.' Donations in the autumn of 1898 ranged from £25 to the 2s.6d. given by Patrick Magee (Mall), the 2s. from John Kelly (Mall), and the 1s. from John Hennessy. Every household in the parish contributed.

The week of 10 September 1898 saw capital, state, and church directly involved in the daily lives of working people and in ways that manifested and reproduced status-class differences. Some workers, however, were very busy, judging from the multiple occupations pursued by the lamplighter. Others, such as casual worker Murphy, were caught out by the weather. To ease her poor luck, she appealed to the magistrates who took the word of a permanent labourer, working for the same farmer, to rule against her. Yet others, such as Hennessy, perhaps saw a link between their struggles for cottages and their financial support of Catholic institutions.

The Parish Population in 1901

The availability of household returns from the 1901 census permit a look at aspects of local life not accessible from the published aggregations in other census years. In 1901 there were 473 households in Thomastown Catholic parish. Of these, labourers headed 227 households or 48 per cent of the total. Forty-five per cent (n = 103) of these 227 households

Table IV.1: Occupational distribution, Thomastown parish in 1901

	Males	Females	Total	Per cent
1 *Agricultural Sector*				
Farmers			193	
Farmer's son/daughter			310	
Farm labourer	198	46	244	
				747 (53.5%)
2 *Non-Agricultural Sector*				
(a) *Labourer*				
Non-farm labourer	155	77	232	
Artisan, trades	116	33	149	
Domestic servant	12	98	110	
				491 (35.2%)
(b) *Commerce, professional*				
Retailer, business	28	26	54	
Shop assistant*	30	23	53	
Teacher, professional	32	19	51	
				158 (11.3%)
3 *Other*				
Homemaker, pensioner	3	296	299	
Non-working 'child' (16+)	12	90	102	
Gentry	9	7	16	
Clergy, nun	6	19	25	
4 *No answer*	11	48	59	
Total:	926	971	1897	1396 (100.0%)

*Shop assistants are included here because the occupation, in 1901, was regarded as an apprenticeship and as a first step to becoming a retailer.

were headed by 'general labourers; 'the remainder were headed equally by farm labouring heads (n = 62) and artisanal heads (n = 62). Most households, however, contained more than one wage earner: adult children and sometimes wives did waged work. In the parish in 1901 were 1,396 adults who declared an occupation in the agricultural, non-farm, and commercial sectors (Table IV.1, sections 1, 2[a], 2[b]). Of these, 193 were farmers and 244 were farm labourers. The 310 self-designated 'farmers' sons or daughters' invariably did unpaid work on the home farm and the vast majority, as non-inheriting children, would be given their cash 'fortunes' out of the farm and would leave. If these children are omitted, waged farm workers clearly outnumbered farmers in the

Table IV.2: Household composition of Thomastown parish labourers, 1901

Household Type	Occupation of Household Head:		
	General Worker	Farm Worker	Artisan
Nuclear Stages:			
Conjugal pair	5%	8%	11%
Pair + children	41	53	43
Widow(er) + children	13	15	15
Single person	8	11	11
	67%	87%	80%
Non-nuclear types:			
Sibling	3%	0%	7%
3-generation stem*	3	3	1
2-generation sibling**	0	3	2
Other	17	7	10
	100%	100%	100%
Total number of households:	103	62	62

*A conjugal pair, their children, and the parent(s) of either the husband or the wife.
**A conjugal pair, their children, and sibling(s) of the married pair.

farm sector. More generally, in the three sectors, people who worked for wages or were of the labouring status-class (n = 839) comprised over 60 per cent of Thomastown's working population (n = 1,396).

Some of these labouring people lived in the kinds of households that are associated with precarious employment. In Ireland, the ideal household for respectable working people, as had long been promulgated by state and church, was the nuclear unit: a married couple and their children in their own home. Through time, of course, such a structure necessarily alters: one of the conjugal pair dies, leaving a 'widow(er) and children,' or the children depart, leaving behind the 'conjugal pair,' and, when one of these dies, the household is inhabited by a 'single person.' Table IV.2 shows the percentages of labouring households in each of these nuclear phases and the proportions that had non-nuclear formations. The households departing most dramatically from the nuclear ideal were those of general labourers: urban-based and often casual workers. It was the farm workers who most conformed to the respectable ideals.

At the Turn of the Twentieth Century

The growth and character of nationalism, and its relation to socialist ideology, policy, and organization, form the central and often the only foci for Irish historical analyses of the final years of the colonial state (1880–1921) and the early decades of the Irish Free State (1922–50). These topics and chronologies are important. Yet their usual purview is narrow, fixing on the national or sometimes the regional levels and on dramatic events, great men, and big cities. However, the Thomastown lens allows an expansion of this approach and a contextualization of its findings. Indeed, by siting the contradictions of socialism and nationalism in the local and experiential domains of socio-cultural life, the complexities of political domains and of colonialism take on a different hue. To see this in Part IV, I continue to explore both the material and ideational aspects of local life (cultural codes, labour processes, organizational dimensions), the nature of agency, and the role of the state. I look also at the *metissage* of experience as it informed the hegemonic process and the application of coercion in the first half of the twentieth century.

10. The Organizational Impetus: Class and Nationalism before the War, 1906–14

'The benefits of belonging to the Trade and Labour League are many and any worker in Thomastown district would do well ... to join in order to avail of the benefits and help promote the spirit of democracy and self-reliance.'
— Kilkenny *Moderator*, 16 October 1909

In 1908 a 'cruel incident' was reported, an incident 'too inhuman and tyrannical to ... pass without being brought under the public gaze.' So stated the Kilkenny *Journal*, the nationalist county newspaper, when it conveyed the story of labourer-cotman Edward Wallace (Case 10.1).

Case 10.1: The Life and Death of Cotman Edward Wallace, 1908
In a letter to the editor, a 'Thomastown correspondent' told how Wallace, unable to work owing to 'an affliction to his eyes, was convicted for the awful crime of trying to earn his bread and butter honestly in the sight of God, but illegally according to English laws made in Ireland. The terrible offence consisted of looking for salmon ... a vocation he followed during his life. The poor old desolate creature who lives in a barn without any friends, was convicted and fined £10 for one offence, with the alternative of three months imprisonment. For the whole winter he has been ... in Thomastown Workhouse, too unwell to be discharged ... On coming out ... he was lodged in Kilkenny jail to mix with ... criminals for three long months ... My reason for calling attention to poor Wallace ... [is] to ... catch the eye of the ... [MP] for North Kilkenny, Mr. Meagher, in whose division [Wallace] resides, in the hope that he may ... secure his ... release. The magistrates who convicted may also memorialise the Lord Lieutenant for his release.'

An editorial added: 'How is it that, notwithstanding all those years of ceaseless agitation ... the Irish fishery laws are still permitted a place on the statute book? ... So ruthless are they and so ... unjust that the magistrates themselves, largely taken from among the very class whose ... interests those laws are designed to uphold, are ... ashamed to enforce them. A poor fisherman is hauled before a petty court of law and charged with some absurd antiquated statute. The magistrates [say] the case is proved ... They turn to the statute ... to ascertain the lightest possible penalty ... and discover that it is a fine of £10 with an alternative of 3 to 6 months imprisonment ... The chairman [tells] the trembling culprit who ... in nine cases out of ten, is not aware that he has even transgressed ... that a recommendation will be made to the Lord Lieutenant ... to reduce the fine to 10s. Generally, the magistrates sign this memorial.' The editor then denounced the hypocrisy of reducing £10 fines to 10 shillings and went on to observe that the 'fishery laws are among the last survivals of cruel and arbitrary class rule in Ireland ... With class rule ... the land ... [and] waterways [were] grabbed and property was even established over the birds that fly through the air.' Thus, the 'case of Wallace will, we hope, be a rallying centre from which will spread an agitation which will destroy once and for all the almost inhuman power vested in petty courts of law ... [and] ... place the inland fishery industry as a valuable national asset.'

A month later, Wallace was released. He wrote to the Journal *to thank people for their support and for signing his petition: MP Meagher, members of Kilkenny city corporation and Thomastown's rural district council, the chair of the county council, Thomastown's doctor Murphy, a local land agent and a bank manager, district councillor J.T. Ryan, county councillor R.J. Ryan, and 'the merchants and others in Thomastown.' He added that 'the Irish Party would be sure to get the support of the labour and radical party in any attempt to remodel the fishery laws enacted ... towards the poor for the benefit of the upper class. God knows we have suffered such tyrannical laws long enough.'*

Within the week, Wallace was dead. Thomastown district council passed a motion condemning 'the unjust fishing laws ... which consigns to an early grave ... men like Wallace, who is a corpse in our hospital today, by tyranny for his honest endeavour to reap the fruits of the Almighty. We call upon our representatives in Parliament to abolish the unjust fishing laws ... which are tyrannical and cruel.' [1]

The powerful narrative of Edward Wallace's last few months resonated with diverse and even contradictory strands of deeply rooted common sense at the time. Because his plight could be differently construed, it mobilized people of all classes and allied them in common effort. In the tale of a person, Wallace was a poor labourer cum fisher who was ill and fallen on hard times, through no fault of his own. Certainly this called for charitable relief. As a metaphor, Wallace was Ireland: powerless before arbitrary laws and trembling before the magistrates. That this had not changed had to be condemned. As a morality tale, Wallace's story was about what might happen to a good labourer who had been denied the accoutrements of respectability, such as job, cottage, and family. This demanded change. Thus, Wallace was a multifaceted symbol, evoking responses from all parts of the political and socio-economic spectrum.

The *Journal*, for example, used Wallace as a vehicle for expressing nationalist sentiment, an occasion to attack English laws and 'class rule.' The latter was defined as the appropriation of Irish property (land, fisheries) and the rights thereon (hunting, fishing). According to the editor, however, only the laws surrounding fishing survived while the others had been obliterated through the various land acts. In any case, for the *Journal*, English class rule was contrary to divine will: law itself was valid, but only when it was not English and not burdened by extralegal practices, such as appeals for remissions of fines by those who had created the law in the first instance. For Wallace, however, and those who helped him write his letter, the world was differently structured than it was for the *Journal*'s editor. They supported the 'labour and radical party,' voting for the Irish Party only insofar as it responded to their interests. For them, tyrannical laws had no nationality; they were simply laws enacted by the rich against the poor.

In all this discourse were summarized many of the conflicting sentiments, interests, and relationships embedded in local experiences of class and nation. Indeed, the *Journal* had no solution for the fisheries. That they were to serve the so-called national interest had long been espoused by many, even as they disagreed on what comprised the nation. In any case, not all tyrannical law in Ireland concerned the fisheries; not all class rule emanated from English agents; and the precise intentions of God could be known only through human mediation.

Into the Twentieth Century: Macro-Narratives of Nationalism and Labour

Irish histories of the period generally have had two plots. The political narrative, which is predominant, has traced the key events and national agents canonically defined as integral to the growth of nationalism and the fight for Irish independence. The labour narrative, always framed through the chronology of the political tale, has explored the role of formal labour organizations, socialist ideology, and dramatic events as these were actualized through the machinations of key labour leaders. Although it is indisputable that both nationalist and labour ideologies and combinations were key, it is also clear that the two dominant narratives obscure other viewpoints. Such alternatives would privilege labour history in order to provide insight into nationalism; provide more nuanced understandings of both by exploring the agency in local sites which underwrote so-called nationally significant events; construct a chronology out of the awareness and experience of people in local places rather than in the meetings and deals in Dublin and London; and, finally, site these alternatives in an analysis of the hegemonic process.

In Thomastown and elsewhere, this process was fuelled by the nature of common sense and class awareness, by the efforts of agents from other classes to influence labour in certain ways, and by the attempts of labourers to carve out an ideological, economic, and political space for themselves alongside the determined and often conflicting efforts of farmers, landlords, nationalists, and colonial agents who were trying to appropriate the electoral, moral, and economic potential of labour for themselves. What textual strategy can be used to describe this? An oft-used but inadequate method is to take the key events, leaders, and formal organizations from the dominant, macro-narratives and fit a locality in as a footnote. Far more innovative and productive, however, is to derive chronology and themes from the locality and to look at how the hegemonic process and the *metissage* of local experiences of nationalism, trade unionism, and socialism accumulated through time and meshed with the experiences of the previous century. It is this that forms the subject matter of chapters 10 and 11.

Before the Great War: The Organizational Impetus

A striking feature of local political life by the turn of the twentieth century was the tendency of people to form or join organizations because of perceived local needs or in response to other organizations. Often, they formed branches of national associations (Case 10.2).

Case 10.2: Four Thomastown Organizations, 1900–7
In 1900 a branch of the United Irish League *(UIL) was founded. Concerned largely with agrarian issues, it attracted mainly rural-dwelling farmers. However,*

a retailer was branch secretary and a labourer was put on the executive as part of an inclusionary strategy which the UIL was pursuing. Soon after, numerous local retailers joined the League in response to a series of urban evictions. They soon became dissatisfied with the UIL agitation on their behalf and formed their own Town Tenants League *in 1905. The local curate was president. It, too, failed to resolve the issues and dissolved. It was re-formed in 1911, again under the guidance of the curate, Father O'Shea, who, in urging the association to re-form, said it would 'assist the Irish Parliamentary Party ... to obtain proper legislation.' Millworker Patrick Magee was on the executive. At the same time, O'Shea and several retailers revived the UIL. At its first meeting, O'Shea 'said the Parliamentary Party in its fight was never more deserving of support ... Every man in the district, be he working man, farmer or shopkeeper, should continue to contribute to the fund.' Millworker and rural district councillor John Magee joined.*[2]

In mid-1907, the Thomastown Teachers' Association *held its quarterly meeting. A motion called on the Irish Party in Parliament to improve working conditions to the levels enjoyed in England and Scotland. Around the same time, at a public meeting in Thomastown, a* Sinn Fein *branch was formed. Members included two retailers, two retailers' sons working as artisans for their fathers, three artisans (including baker James Cahill, rural district councillor), and Sean O'Mahoney (tailor's son, commercial traveller).*[3] *The tenets of Sinn Fein were radically nationalist. Native language and industry were to be encouraged, the British armed forces were to be boycotted, and county councils were to form the nucleus of a new 'national authority.' A meeting later in the month was reportedly attended 'by the young men of the district.' Eight months later, notwithstanding its position supporting Irish independence, the branch accepted a national directive that Sinn Fein support Irish Party candidates in parliamentary elections. As part of the cultural nationalism extant at the time, member Kelly (carpenter) now was recorded as O'Kelly and grocer James Ryan as Seamus Ua Riain. The branch also congratulated politician James O'Mara for joining Sinn Fein and announced its support of him as the Irish Party candidate for south Kilkenny. This was the last reported meeting of Thomastown Sinn Fein for a decade.*[4]

These abbreviated histories display several aspects of the period. During the latter nineteenth century, tenant farmers had met with great success in agitating for their land, an achievement orchestrated largely through various formal combinations such as the Land League. In direct emulation, there was a flurry of organizational activity both by labour in the 1890s and by those (for example, retailers, teachers, town tenants) concerned with their own causes. Constructing formal combinations had clearly become an accepted way of fomenting change. Moreover, change was defined as obtaining ameliorative legislation through pressures exerted by the Irish Party on the British Parliament.

These formal combinations generally declared themselves to be inclusive while aiming to better the special interests of particular classes or groups. Often, too, they were national in scope, with local agitation on particular issues being harnessed by outside activists via the agency of numerous local branches acting in concerted ways. Crucial among such agents were the Catholic clergy. Finally, these formal combinations often had an ephemeral existence, a branch being formed when a particular issue was relevant in the locality (for example, an eviction, an election) and abating as the issue receded. Irish nationalism at the time, therefore, from a Thomastown perspective, was formal (via organizations), sectional (privileging particular interests), rooted in local concerns, linked to the Irish Party, and dependent on support from the Catholic hierarchy. Conversely, and importantly, all political agitation at the time always implied or contained elements of nationalism. For some in this Thomastown area, where English had long been the language of everyday life, political activism also incorporated a nod to Gaelic or Irish language and culture, even if local people were able to carry it off only in a symbolic way.

Thomastown Trade and Labour League

The same organizational fervour, with similar features, typified labouring life and the pursuit of labourers' interests. It was impelled by legislation in 1876 which allowed unions to register more easily[5] and by artisans' guilds in larger centres which aimed for self-help and better working conditions. In early 1908 Father Fitzgerald, Thomastown's parish priest, chaired a meeting to 'organise the tradesmen and labourers of the district.' A Thomastown Trade and Labour League/Union was established and Fitzgerald informed the audience of its purpose: 'To create harmony between employees and employers, to support and foster home industries and to ... stem ... emigration.' These aims, he said, 'were compatible with those of the United Irish League, although it was stated that this meeting was got up to be antagonistic to the U.I.L. He was glad that such was not the case and if it were he would not touch it with a 10-foot pole.' Officers were then elected. They worked in various places: tannery, mill, Mount Juliet estate, and other smaller enterprises. They included millworker Patrick Magee, fisher John Dunphy, carter

Pat Ryan, and baker James Cahill. Over one hundred men were reported as handing in the entrance fee of one shilling.[6]

The League was linked to the Kilkenny Trades and Labour Council (KTLC) and to a broader-based ideological purpose. This purpose very soon created local divisions (Case 10.3)

Case 10.3: Thomastown's League and the Kilkenny Trades and Labour Council

A League meeting two weeks after its founding unanimously supported a KTLC motion that the contract for putting electric lighting in public buildings should be advertised 'in Irish papers to give local firms a chance of competing.' Two months later, 'enthusiastic' public meetings in Thomastown and Inistioge, addressed by the secretary of the KTLC, explained to workers and artisans the importance of electing their own representatives onto the rural district council. 'As ratepayers,' he said, they 'had the right to be represented by one of their own class.' A motion was passed that 'this meeting of citizens and labourers claim the right to just and equitable representation on the rural district council, and endorse the candidature of the men put forward on behalf of the Thomastown Trade and Labour Union [League], and pledge themselves to secure their return at the head of the poll on June 3rd 1908.' At that point, local labourer and member John Breen dissented. He said that they owed a debt of gratitude to Michael O'Neill (farmer), current chair of the rural district council, 'for the manner in which he had conducted the business.' The KTLC secretary retorted that Breen had not addressed the meeting with the authority of the KTLC and that 'they desired to disassociate themselves from the remarks he had made. The Labour platform,' he reiterated, 'could not be utilized by any person but a genuine Labour candidate – a man who was considered such by the trades and labour bodies of the district.'[7]

Labourers, as 'citizens' and 'ratepayers,' with their 'claim' to representation, were divided on how their franchise should be exercized and who should influence it. A few months later, Patrick Ryan, secretary of the League, in fact had to clarify the League's position 'with regard to certain points that have recently arisen in reference to its power and scope as an organized body, and ... to the attitude it has adopted regarding ... the rural district council.' He wrote that the 'first object of the League was the general advancement of the principle of Trades Unions. The only effective way to carry out this idea ... was to secure as far as possible ... the election of labour representatives who would voice their opinions.' Why? 'It is quite clear ... that, since the passing of the Local Government Act, 1898, the affairs of the council were carried out in anything but a satisfactory manner.' Rates were rising and the contract system for public works, such as building labourers' cottages, had resulted in houses which were 'poorly constructed and expensive for the council to maintain.' The town's water supply was both 'a disgrace and also a ... menace to the public health,' even though £144 had been spent on a useless pump 'by giving away contracts without advertising' for tenders. At the same time, 'our representatives are out-voted in a hopeless minority to do what they consider fair.' For example, despite criticism, the League supported increased salaries for the county council's medical doctors whom labourers, by virtue of their wage levels, were able to consult free or at a low fee. He concluded that, 'as ratepayers, both the tradesmen and labourers are in the majority, as it is they who are paying the rates; if the same be indirect, it is through their work and toil that they are paid. So ... it is our interest, as representing them, [to] ... forward all employment on their behalf.' [8]

Thomastown's labour leaders, through the League and the Kilkenny city-based Trades Council, defined local labourers as ratepayers or, importantly, as those whose labour allowed people from other classes to pay their rates. With this definition of ratepayer and citizen, they claimed the right to self-representation. They thus entered local, electoral politics using issues that concerned both the governing of the locality in general and the specific needs of labourers. That this viewpoint was not uncontested was apparent in the disagreement expressed by worker Breen. (Case 10.3). Indeed, the issue arose again at a meeting to decide which of the two candidates for the chairship of the rural district council should be supported by the League's representatives on the council. For whom should David Murphy (victualler), James Cahill (baker), and Patrick Magee (millworker) vote? A member proposed that they vote for whomever they thought best. Another proposed that 'they vote according to the decision of the committee.' The latter was passed, but only by eight votes to six.[9] The League's political jurisdiction was clearly disputed. Yet there was unanimous sentiment on economic nationalism and support for local workers (Case 10.4).

Case 10.4: League Policy on Economic and Local Needs

At a 1909 meeting, the chair of the League reported that the slates supplied to Thomastown's rural district council for roofing labourers' cottages were imported from Wales. 'He could not see ... why the Thomastown council – or any other council in Ireland – should use Welsh slates when they could procure them at home and ... give the Irish worker a chance to earn a livelihood in his own country.' A resolution was passed, in the name of the League, 'comprising a membership of close on two hundred,' condemning the action and calling 'on the council to see that ... there will be no repetition' of this. The secretary added that 'they had been hearing a lot of preaching ... against emigration, but what alternative had the youth of the country but to emigrate or, worse still, join the British army, when our councils are content to let the ratepayers' money go out of the country for foreign articles that can be got at home?' Copies of the resolution were sent to the rural district council.

In 1910, the League passed 'vigorous resolutions ... against the action of the Local Government Board in attempting to coerce the rural district council into raising the rent of cottages ... and thereby inflicting a great hardship on the labourers.' Indeed, 'by their timely action,' the board's attempt 'to force the peoples' representatives to raise the rents of houses and plots to an exorbitant pitch, on the labourers of the locality, has been frustrated; and by the vigorous protests they have made in the matter of foreign slates, it is to be hoped, that no such attempt will ever be made again.'[10]

In fighting the rent rise on labourers' cottages, the farmers on the council colluded. Higher rents could lead to demands for higher wages. It made more sense for large scale farmers, who formed the majority of councillors and who hired a good deal of labour, to keep wages low and the cost of cottages distributed among all the ratepayers. As to foreign slates, they were simply cheaper.

Two trends emerged in such a context. On the one hand was the problem of retaining local enthusiasm for the League. At its 1910 annual general meeting, it was noted that 'while in many respects the work has been so full of promise, we cannot but regret that some of our members have lately shown a tendency to lose interest in the organisation ... This is deplorable.'[11] On the other hand was the accomplishment of being accepted by the farmer councillors as a legitimate presence. The rural district council also acted as a board of guardians, managing the workhouse and fever hospital. As the board, it had different officers than did the council. In 1911 councillor-farmer Michael O'Neill proposed that 'one of the newly-elected labour representatives' be vice-chair of the board. He proposed fisher John Dunphy who was elected unanimously, as was Patrick Ryan for the deputy vice-chairship.

Ryan then 'thanked the members for the honour conferred on him as a representative of labour.'[12] Note, however, that labourers had not been elected as chair, but as vice-chair and deputy vice-chair, and not for the council, but only for the board.

Thus, within a very few years, labour had inserted itself through the League into the local public, political domain. It had fashioned a broad economic and nationalist position and had set itself up as the agent for labouring interests in the locality. Although this was not uncontested among labourers themselves, the League had acquired a distinctive political identity, separate from farmers and the UIL. It had achieved a respectability which farmers were willing to acknowledge while ensuring that this did not circumscribe, to any real degree, their own authority. The League had also tried to appropriate for itself the role of legitimate representative of the locality's interests on the grounds that labourers formed the majority of ratepayers or, alternatively, the means by which most rates were paid. At the time, this claim remained muffled in other, more timely issues.

The Election of Captain Walter Lindsay, 1911:
Class, Locality, and Nationalism

Walter Lindsay was married to Lady Kathleen Butler, the daughter of the now deceased 6th Earl of Carrick. The tenanted lands belonging to the Carrick estate had been sold off in the 1850s. What remained were 1,500 acres of demesne lands a few miles from the town. Lindsay had recently become manager of this large agricultural estate and an extensive and benevolent employer of Thomastown labour. Lindsay's sister, married to the 7th Earl of Carrick, was much involved in the Gaelic cultural revival,[13] while Lady Kathleen was an activist in the Irish Party and a supporter of home rule. She was also an indefatigable organizer of local good works, having gleaned the funds, from both gentry and local labourers, to build a public concert/meeting hall in the town. In April 1911 Walter Lindsay was nominated for a seat on the county council by no less than four sets of Thomastown nominators and seconders: (1) John Murphy, tanyard worker and president of the League, seconded by an outlying farmer; (2) two Thomastown retailers; (3) Grennan Mills owner Pilsworth, seconded by Protestant farmer William Cronyn; and (4) tannery owner Ryan and hotel owner James Walsh. Clearly, Lindsay had broad support which cross-cut class, status-class, religion, and town and country. The response of the *Journal*, a supporter of the nationalist

Sinn Fein, was highly critical of Lindsay. He was a gentlemen and, thus, a unionist, a Tory and anti-labour while his wife was a member of the Irish Party. The brouhaha that ensued said much about the articulation of local labouring interests and nationalist ideologies (Case 10.5).

Case 10.5: Competing Ideologies, Interests and the Election of
Captain Walter Lindsay, 1911

The Journal *described Lindsay as a 'unionist, outsider, Victorian and upstart' who was taking advantage of his wife's popularity in this 'age of Nationalist and Catholic toleration' to enter 'the esteem and confidence of the nationalist electors of Thomastown.' In contrast, the 'mantle' of former councillor Richard J. Ryan had passed to John Barry, a large-scale Catholic farmer and 'member of a family identified for generations with the Irish National Cause.'*

A week later, a letter to the Journal*'s editor appeared from six 'large ratepayers, representing the League.' It protested 'the introduction of Lady Kathleen's name into this contest' as a 'glaring piece of bad taste.' It said that they had asked Lindsay to stand because 'we know him thoroughly, have absolute confidence in his honour and integrity, and are convinced that he will look after our interests on the County Council independently and honestly.' The* Journal*'s editor responded, reminding the 'Nationalist electors of Thomastown' of Lindsay's patronizing attitude to home rule: 'I pledged myself to look after the ... interests of the Thomastown division' so that, 'should the measure of self-government desired by the majority of my constituents be granted by parliament ... I shall have assisted the County Council ... in proving ... that Ireland is ready for such a measure.' The editor noted the 'audacity of this claim to act as a ... headmaster to the untutored people' on the county council. He wondered whether 'centuries of serfdom have left an irradical mark on the Irish character' and whether the 'influence of the lord of the manor is still potent.' For 'we seek in vain for another explanation of the support which Captain Lindsay ... has received among people who should be instinctively nationalist and democratic.'*

A week later, the Journal *published a letter from John Kelly, one of the very few Thomastown retailers whose parents had been labourers and, in his case, fishers. Kelly wanted to inform 'the public' about 'the treatment meted out' to him because he was actively supporting Lindsay. The 'boy in my employ was going his customary rounds delivering bread' when he met up with councillor/farmer Mr Hughes who 'told him to be gone out of the place ... Mr Barry also informed one of my fellow townsmen that he would not allow a bit of my bread to be bought. If these are the men who are to administer Home Rule and if this is the treatment we are to receive because we choose to exercise freedom of opinion, then home rule would be a curse instead of a blessing.' The editor tartly responded that 'the custom of Cap-tain Lindsay and those of that ilk will more than compensate [Kelly] for the loss of business ... We have nothing but contempt for his communication.' The* Jour-nal *soon after printed 'a rallying letter from former councillor Richard. J. Ryan' who was living in London and working for Sinn Fein: 'Having the interests of the old division at heart, I [cannot] ... believe that the reliable old nationalist vot-ers of Thomastown ... who gave such a fine dressing to a unionist candidate at the first election [chapter 9], have become so absorbed in ... unionism as to return Captain Lindsay ... At this side of the water, the [Tory] party which Captain Lindsay belongs to are sworn enemies of ... labour representatives ... I [therefore] appeal to every voter ... [to] ... remain true ... to Ireland's cause ... by voting for Barry.'* [14]

The *Journal* tried to define the regional, county council election as part of a broad nationalist struggle which required de-legitimizing the Irish Party and fighting the unionist and anti-labour Tory Party. How-ever, many Thomastown people from all status-classes, but especially labourers and the Labour League, perceived the election differently. They saw the need to have a representative who would privilege the needs of the local economy; they believed that they had some reciprocal obligations towards a good and extensive employer; they valued Lady Kathleen's local good works; they were suspicious of large-scale farmers, their interests, and their organizations (for example, the UIL); and they supported the Irish Party and home rule. For Thomastown's workers, supporting Lindsay, labour, and nationalism was not contradictory, even if the *Journal* and Richard Ryan, one of their former intellectuals, dis-agreed. Walter Lindsay was thus elected county councillor for the Tho-mastown electoral division. He received 390 votes; Barry received 283. [15]

The 1911 Strike and the Trade and Labour League

A month later, the *Journal* sarcastically noted that the 'rumour that Tho-mastown is to have its name changed to Walter's Town is said to be false.' [16] The irony was elicited because of Lindsay's effort to mediate among the parties during a strike in Thomastown. It had been orga-nized by the League which, despite its constitutional focus and new respectability, or perhaps because of it, took on the main employers in the town. With complaints common about working hours, a motion was passed at a League meeting 'that a deputation be appointed to wait on the principal employers in the town with a view to allowing their work-men to cease work at 2 o'clock on Saturdays.' A month later, the tannery was on strike. So too, ironically, was the currier's firm next door, owned by the father of Richard Ryan, the pro-labour and Sinn Fein activist (Case 10.6).

Case 10.6: The Strike in the Tanneries

League members had approached the tannery owners with their requests and been refused. At Grennan Mills, 'after a few days to consider,' the owner 'informed the representatives of the men that they would accede to their request, or if the men wished to work all day on Saturday their wages would be increased by 1s. weekly. The latter offer was accepted.' In the tanneries, however, 'the men were not seeking any concessions as to time, as they are willing to make up for the three hours off on Saturday evening by a curtailment of the meal hours during the week. The employers on the other hand, state that there is special work to be got through on each day. A large force of extra police have been drafted into the town ... but up to the present no untoward incident has occurred. The tanneries are constantly under the supervision of police patrols. On Monday last, Captain Walter Lind-say, M.V.O. ... interviewed the employers and the men's representatives, with the result that a conference was held, but up to the present no understanding has been arrived at.'

In the interim, a League meeting had been held. 'It was decided that the men on strike should be maintained out of the funds of the organisation.' In addition, workers employed by James Walsh, owner of the Commercial Hotel, had their wages increased by 1s. The Kilkenny People *noted that 'Mr Walsh was not approached on the matter, but on being informed that Mr. Pilsworth had increased the wages he decided to put his men on a level with them.'*[17]

The tannery and currier workers won a shorter work week and, according to the tannery wage books, no change in basic pay. They had not achieved, however, what the mill and hotel workers had gained with-out a strike. Yet, because of its success, the League prospered. Its finances steadily improved,[18] and its membership remained broad-based as it addressed itself to practical, local concerns. A death-benefit scheme for members was established in 1910 and Rooms were set up in Market Street for relaxation and education. The Rooms were an 'attrac-tive place ... during the winter evenings,' with facilities for cards, bil-liards, and reading. The League and its Rooms also aimed to educate.

According to its charter, no member could enter while intoxicated, speak 'after order has been called three times, curse, wager more than a ha'penny per game,' offer to fight, urge any other member to strike him ... vilify another.'[19] The League also offered political education, as when it stopped its subscription to a particular Irish newspaper in 1913 to 'protest against the treatment of the locked-out tramway men and other employees in Dublin.'[20] Indeed, by juxtaposing itself spatially to the retailers' Reading Rooms, which had been founded in 1891 on an adjacent town street, the League not only emphasized but also formalized the fact of status-class difference and offered a new means by which such difference could become part of everyday practice.

The League also educated by directing labourers into entertainment and sport. It revived the brass band, organizing band concerts and raising funds.[21] It planned annual sports days, with cot, swimming, and bicycle races and dancing competitions 'in a splendid field kindly given for the occasion by Mr. Pilsworth.'[22] Ultimately, the League provided access to the media by virtue of its formal status. This allowed it to represent and further the respectability that workers cultivated as a class and as individuals. Major life passages, for example, could now be publicly marked. An obituary for James Grace, saddler and insurance agent, noted that he was a 'popular and talented young gentleman' who had 'held the post of secretary' in the League. It was noted, too, that he had a 'deep interest in the [Irish] Language revival, as well as the Industrial Movement ... He was an ardent Nationalist, and was remarkable for sincerity and honesty of purpose in everything he took in his hands.'[23] As for many labourers at the time, identity was a *metissage* of many threads.

In mid-1914, local elections were again held. Walter Lindsay, nominated by labourer Patrick Magee and a local farmer, quietly and handily retained his seat with a larger majority. For the rural district council, League member Pat Ryan was re-elected for Thomastown electoral district, along with a local farmer. League member John Dunphy was re-elected for Jerpoint. The second Jerpoint seat, however, was won by a farmer because John Kelly, former labourer/now retailer, nominated by a publican and John Burris, the night miller in Grennan Mills, ran against Patrick Magee, splitting the labour vote.[24] Clearly, unanimity on the role of the League had proved elusive. By this time, however, the newspapers had no lengthy statements from the League on ideology, issues, and concerns. Reports on the combination had settled into a predictable round of annual general meetings and council elections. This routinization was accompanied by continuing education, an absence of political consensus, and complex threads of experience which combined political and cultural nationalism alongside a labouring radicalism.

The Irish Transport and General Workers' Union (IT&GWU)

The League's strike in the tanneries had brought out, like most dramatic events, the lines of cleavage, alliance, and contradiction which were then, in turn, made more so by the event. This also occurred with the founding and subsequent history of the IT&GWU, which, in 1912, through its unionizing activities around the country, founded a branch in Grennan Millls. There is no recorded or remembered opposition to this: it occurred smoothly and without rancour. The reasons that local people gave, decades later in the 1980s, varied along a consent-coercion continuum. Some former workers suggested that the Pilsworths were politically astute and saw current trends. Others said that 'they'd never stand in the way of their workers.' One elderly millworker said that the millers in Thomastown and elsewhere in Ireland were Protestant, and 'once the push came from above to unionise, the owners were not pressured by the Catholic Church to oppose it.' An elderly worker/fisher explained that 'workers in one mill supported another. They wouldn't unload corn from a non-unionized mill. So if one unionized, the others had to.' A young labour activist expanded that view. Irish dock workers were being unionized and the millers were afraid their grain shipments from America would not be unloaded if they were not unionized.

Regardless of their explanations, most people immediately began to contrast the mill with the other large Protestant enterprise, Mount Juliet estate. It was 'bitterly anti-union. One word about a union and you were out.' It also was never unionized, said several people, because the employees 'didn't work as a group.' They were 'scattered all over the estate,' doing different kinds of work (garden, farm, stud, hunting stables, and house) and 'they lived in different places. Not like the mill workers who lived together in a few town streets.' As well, Mount Juliet workers were never an object of a national unionization drive. As to Catholic employers, such as Deady's mill, people in the 1980s were unanimous in saying that they 'were violently anti-union.' One labourer did add that this was 'partly because they owned the smaller enterprises.'

However it was perceived at the time and in retrospect, Thomastown's millworkers had become part of an organization that was national, radical, charismatically led, and dedicated to the welfare of unskilled, general workers. The motion by Thomastown's Trade and Labour League in 1913 to boycott the Dublin newspaper was part of a wider conflict involving an IT&GWU organizing drive in the face of intense management opposition. In a general strike that occurred in the autumn of 1913, Thomastown's millworkers went on strike, as did all IT&GWU members. Seventy years later, elderly local people recalled how the Pilsworths delivered coal, free, to their workers' homes.

The Thomastown Volunteers, 1914

In June 1914 a new organization appeared on the scene. An adjunct to Redmond's Irish Party, with its headquarters in Dublin, the Thomastown branch of the Irish Volunteers was founded at a meeting presided over by Father O'Shea at which 'over 200 young men handed in their names.' A 'parade of the Volunteers headed by the local brass band' then took place. A few days later, a corps of fifty Volunteers was formed in nearby Kilfane, the home place of League member and district councillor Pat Ryan. It joined the Thomastown branch in route marches with the brass band and in drill exercises in Market Street, usually 'in the presence of a large crowd.' In a route march soon after to Stoneyford, in which the Volunteers carried wooden rifles supplied by the local sawmill, Walter Lindsay had all the gates of the estate open so that they could pass.

The president of the Thomastown Volunteers was Father O'Shea and the commanding officer was district councillor/League member Patrick Ryan. The other nine executive positions were filled by farmers and retailers. However, the seven drill instructors were labourers and former British soldiers; three were anglers. None, however, was active in the Labour League. Several months later, when Matthew Keating, Irish Party MP and UIL organizer, came to review the local corps, not a single labourer, apart from councillor Ryan, was mentioned in the newspaper report. Indeed, at a home-rule demonstration in Waterford at the beginning of 1914, various retailing and farming members of Thomastown's district council and the Town Tenants League were listed as attending, along with a residual category of 'other leading nationalists.' 'Prominent on the platform [too], convenient to Mr. John Redmond, was Lady Kathleen Lindsay.' The only labourer named was, yet again, Patrick Ryan, in his capacity as rural district councillor.[25]

Conclusion: The Hegemonic Process before the Great War

In September 1914 the news that the Home Rule Bill had been placed 'on the Statute Book was learned in Thomastown ... with great jubilation. An immense crowd, headed by the local Brass Band and ... Volunteer Corps ... paraded the streets of the town. Cheers were given repeatedly for John Redmond and the Irish Party.' Two days later, an organized celebration was held. All the 'houses in the town, Protestant and Catholic – with three exceptions – were brilliantly illuminated.' A procession was led by the newly formed boy scouts' brigade, followed by the brass band, the Volunteers, the Trade and Labour League, and the general public. Father O'Shea gave 'a stirring address' and, on the return to Market Street, 'Patrick Ryan, D.C., commander of the Volunteers, called for 3 cheers for Redmond and the Irish Party.' The procession then disbanded.[26]

Between the death of Edward Wallace in 1908 and the home-rule celebration in 1914, a great deal had happened yet little seemingly had changed. For people at the time, the two events framed answers to such questions as to how the so-called national interest could be defined, how class rule and law could be fairly administered, how English tyranny might be obviated, and how God's intentions could be interpreted. That the answers were differently perceived by various people was masked by a dominant, political sentiment held by the vast majority of local people. That sentiment cut across class lines, it was experienced through the organizational impetus after 1906, and it was built out of the oppositions/alliances which had emerged in the inland fisheries after 1884. What, however, were the particular perspectives of local labourers?

At the time, any contradiction between the experience of class and that of nationalism was masked and unarticulated. In part, this was because of the respectability that labour had achieved through the successful actions of the Trade and Labour League both in formal local politics and in relation to employers. It was augmented by the ease with which the IT&GWU had unionized the mill and the support given by the owners. This code of respectability both informed and furthered the language and actions which the League then used as it phrased its claims and those of labourers through the discourse of responsible citizenship. That this was sometimes accompanied by more radical political action, as in the 1911 and 1913 strikes, was still perceived positively because it was framed by the attitudes and actions that came out of the paternalism and deference which continued to underlie life and work in Grennan Mills. In any case, the well-recorded bitterness of the 1913 strike, both materially and ideologically, was a Dublin experience. In Thomastown, such experience was markedly muted by the tenor and actions enmeshed in local paternal relations. Thus, in 1914, a political celebration ended because the crowd simply dispersed whereas, in 1870, windows were broken and labourers arrested (Case 4.4).

The apparent unanimity, respectability, and paternalism were buttressed by the fact that local labourers remained in the background during the process of national construction which was then in train. Local labour was in any case viewed, and perceived itself, as 'honoured' by the tokenism of a few minor executive positions on government bodies or as satisfied with nominal representation on such formal associations as the Town Tenants League. The old, organic model of society was still extant. Labour was seen as integrated into the wider body politic: it supplied the muscle and music for the Volunteers while farmers, retailers, and priests provided the leadership. Thomastown labour at the time, in other words, was in step with many of the dominant viewpoints which the majority of local people held about status-class hierarchy and proper behaviour. That the labouring organizations at the time also delivered better material conditions and staked out the right to agitate for more jobs and housing only added to labour's legitimacy. This was because the means through which it chose to do this resonated with the sentiments of paternalism and good government while the idea of well-housed, hard-working workers had long been a key component in the idea of respectability held by people of all classes.

What all this signified, of course, was that, for local labourers, the experience of class and nation was a singular one. The UIL, through the agency of farmers and priests, had failed to implicate labourers in its interests and outlooks. Local labour, both agricultural and non-agricultural, had charted its own course in league with its own associations and viewpoints. In addition, the discursive style of early Sinn Fein was precisely what respectable labourers had been leaving behind: inflammatory, insulting, and threatening. It was the language that had often typified the inland fisheries, the petty sessions, and mobs. It was the discourse, too, of many of the labouring combinations as they had attempted, over the previous century, to be the determining agents of conditions and events. Such discourse by 1914, however, had been largely displaced by the language of constitutionalism, gradualism, and respectability. In any case, Sinn Fein did not directly appeal to the material interests of labour. In Thomastown, the Sinn Fein leadership was not seen as addressing the oppressiveness of class as it continued to be experienced both materially and ideologically. Sinn Fein spoke about the oppression experienced by the nation through British domination. Yet most oppression of workers in Thomastown came precisely from those agents, such as priests, farmers, retailers, and curriers whom Sinn Fein sought to liberate. In contrast, Sinn Fein defined as oppressors those who had long been labour's patrons, employers, mediators, and neighbours. Thus, it was the Labour League that represented local labour, along with the Irish Party.

Yet labour in Thomastown was also a complex amalgam of sentiments and interests which not only united workers but also led them in disparate directions. Not all workers had an interest in the League, especially those who lived outside the town. Not all agreed on the League's political jurisdiction. Moreover, the multiplex relations enmeshed in the locality, and the so-called redundancy of local life, dissipated the intensity that might have surrounded labour had its agents been able to pursue, in a single-minded way, purely labour concerns.[27] For example, friendship sometimes crossed class lines. The sons of retailers occasionally joined labouring activities before taking on the shop. In 1898 the brass band had thirteen men, two of whom were brothers and the sons of a retailer. Indeed, a few local people even straddled status-class lines. Activist Richard J. Ryan, son of an artisan and himself a victualler, was a key agent at the time, albeit unsuccessful in linking Sinn Fein and the Labour League. Ties of patronage, too, either actual or anticipatory, were important. Labourer Breen (Case 10.3) saw a large-scale farmer as more protective of his interests than his fellow labourers. Lindsay was seen as a generous employer, Pilsworth defended his labouring families from poaching charges, and hotelier James Walsh raised wages without being asked. The pull of Irish culture, too, in the form of language, music, and sports, attracted some labourers such as saddler James Grace; and this involved some in other organizations, such as the Gaelic League and the Gaelic Athletic Association (GAA), and in other networks. As well, in the pursuit of respectability, some labourers preferred the company of non-labourers and became friends with smaller retailers. Such varying ties and loyalties could lose a council seat for the League, as it did in the 1914 local elections.

In short, the cross-cutting ties, complex sentiments, and *metissage* of experience, as a result of membership in organizations, personal and/ or ideological predilections, and the many and ramifying relations of kinship, friendship, patronage, and work, could affect either the enthusiasm or the antipathy which labourers had in relation to any particular organization or cause. Yet, at a more general level, when retailer Martin Cantwell went to a home-rule meeting in Waterford, accompanied by members of Thomastown's Rural District Council,[28] it could be said that the locality belonged to the Irish Party while its workers, in the main, belonged to both the Irish Party and the Trade and Labour League.

11. From Class to Nation: National Chronology and Local Experience, 1914–23

'Let Brethren dwell together in unity. United we stand, divided we fall.'
— Charter of the Thomastown Trade and Labour League, 1908

A week before the home-rule celebration in Thomastown in September 1914, a drill instructor for the Volunteers joined the British army. Six weeks later, a meeting of Volunteers, chaired by Father O'Shea, tendered its 'deep sympathy' to Major Connellan whose only son had been killed in action. A month later, Walter Lindsay, now a colonel, left Thomastown to join his regiment.[1] In such ways was the impact of the war on local labour, its organizations, and its patrons made clear. Yet such local happenings have mostly been buried by the compelling events of macro-narratives and the nature of the records which gave rise to them. Indeed, the macro-narratives did become part of how local people constructed their world. At the same time, however, they also built viewpoints out of local agency, perceptions, and common sense and out of the ways in which these became implicated in the domestic, economic, and political cycles of local life.

Before 16 April 1916

At the 1916 annual general meeting of the Trade and Labour League, the chair stated that 'owing to the large number of their members who had joined the colours since the outbreak of the war, the receipts were not so high as previous years.' Thus, 'there was very little prospect of ... holding the sports the coming summer owing to the difficulty of obtaining subscriptions while the war was in progress.' In contrast, expenses mounted: 'Death benefits paid to members or other relatives was, he regretted to say, higher than for a number of years past.' What he did not say was apparent in the officers elected: all were older men who had been politically active since before the League's inception. With so many young labourers at the European front, how could the radicalism and experience that pre-dated the gains and respectability of the League and IT&GWU be transmitted?

The League's problems were exacerbated by national events and sentiment over the next five years. The broadly supported, counter-hegemonic ideology formulated by Redmond, the Irish Party, and the Home Rule Bill were not uncontested at the national level. Yet this only barely reached Thomastown, as was exemplified by reactions to anti-recruiting posters hung on the town's outskirts in March 1915. They 'referred to England's mis-government of Ireland ... and advised young men of the district not to join the local Volunteer corps or the English army.' The nationalist *Journal* noted that these posters elicited 'much indignation ... among the people ... who are entirely on the side of the Allies in the present war.'[2] Indeed, nine months later, the *Journal* reported that 120 men from the Thomastown district were in the British armed forces. Nine had been killed, twenty-three had been wounded, two were missing, and five were prisoners of war. It added that in the previous two weeks, eight young men enlisted after a recruiting meeting in the town, promoted by the Central Recruiting Office, Dublin. The meeting had been chaired by tannery owner Ryan who 'urged everyone to do everything possible to bring the war to an end.'[3]

From a Thomastown perspective, however, what is so striking is the way in which the experience of the war, whether in the trenches or in knitting socks at the home front, was so completely the experience of labouring people and gentry. The membership lists of Thomastown's British Legion and of the Comrades of the Great War, both formed in 1919, contain not a single member of a retailing or farming family from the area. Why did labourers enlist?

People's recollections in the 1980s ran a gamut from economic need to ideological commitment. For some, the army provided a regular paying job with a good pension after. In fact, it had long been common for labouring people to serve in the British army. Gentry employers also encouraged their labourers to join, promising support for the wives and children left behind. Some of the younger labouring men simply went along with their friends. Many local labourers also believed in Redmond and the future of home rule which was to come as soon as the war was won. Many, too, believed in an idea extant at the time that they were 'fighting for the freedom of small nations.' Regardless of why, however, the class-based nature of the experience was to be a major contradiction which heretofore had been hidden under the seeming unity of the Irish Party.

What, then, of the Easter Rising in Thomastown? In mid-1916, at an inquiry into the armed insurrection, the chief inspector of the County Kilkenny constabulary explained how the Irish Volunteers had split into Sinn Fein and Redmonite factions. He said that the former had begun to organize in the county in April 1915. This, in fact, coincided with the appearance of the anti-conscription posters in Thomastown. According to the inspector, there were only a few hundred Sinn Fein Volunteers in the county until April 1916 and no outbreak in Kilkenny during Easter week, 'although there was a considerable amount of restlessness and activity among the Sinn Feiners ... [whose] ... leaders were in constant conclave' during the week. Yet the county had done well in recruiting for the army. 'Then really it is a loyal part of the country and this was only a small body?' asked a commissioner. 'Exactly,' responded the chief inspector.[4]

It was, however, in the aftermath of the rising that nationalist and national sentiment altered throughout Ireland, as in Thomastown. Martial law, secret court-martials, internments in England, and the brutal executions of fourteen nationalists in early May have been amply described. The result was to make it clear to people that 'the military were bent on doing what the civil government had so signally failed to do – destroy revolutionary nationalism.' Thus, hatred came to be 'the chief, legacy of the Easter Rising' and 'the whole constitutional movement was the chief casualty.'[5] In August 1914, the Thomastown Rural District Council had passed a motion supporting Redmond. In June 1916 the same council passed a new resolution condemning any partition of Ireland and demanding 'an Irish parliament with full executive powers.' 'Why,' said a councillor, 'had they taken men out in Dublin and shot them without even a trial? Because they were Irishmen.'[6]

Before the Troubled Times: Competing Ideologies

After 1916, as the League continued its activities in attenuated form,[7] crucial agency came from elsewhere: the growth of a new Sinn Fein, the

activism of the IT&GWU, the founding of a Labour Party, and, ultimately, the complex relations among these.

The Players, the Drama, and the Plot

In mid-1917, some young men met in the Concert Hall to form a Sinn
Fein club, the earlier branch founded in 1906 having petered out long
before. A retailer and a large-scale farmer were elected president and
secretary. Over fifty names were handed in and it was decided to invite an
organizer from Sinn Fein headquarters to visit. He lectured on 'the most
dangerous obstacle to Irish independence,' namely, the Irish Party. It
'represented the slave mind in Ireland; its members went to a foreign
parliament and begged for doles.' A Kilkenny city Sinn Feiner described
how Thomastown had once had been 'an important' and 'prosperous'
place. Now its river, 'once busy with boating traffic,' was choked and its
many mills, breweries, tanneries, and quarries which once 'kept men
working' were gone. 'If you are men with men's minds and ... the strength
of character that differentiates men from serfs, you will work with the
movement marching for a free and independent Ireland.'[8]

This combination of economic nostalgia, personal sovereignty, and
political chauvinism was profoundly appealing to workers. Yet it was also
clear from subsequent Sinn Fein meetings in Thomastown that the club
was run by farmers, retailers, and outsiders. The space was there for a
radical counter-ideology along the lines of, but distinct from, Sinn Fein.

The Irish Trades Union Congress and Labour Party (ITUC&LP) was a
single entity and the IT&GWU was a member of the Congress. The
Labour Party section, founded in 1914, had floundered ever since over
harmonizing nationalism with workers' interests. The problems were
tactical and ideological: how to reconcile the interests and sentiments of
Protestant labourers in the north who were unionists with those of Catholic workers in the south who were nationalists; how to reconcile the
anti-war and anti-conscription stance of nationalists with the fact that so
many labourers were being called up as reservists or were joining the
British army. Then, as Sinn Fein began to gather popular support in the
run-up to the parliamentary election in 1918, the ITUC&LP leaders had
to decide whether or not to compete. The Kilkenny Trades Council
(KTC), for example, 'registered total disapproval' of fielding candidates
against Sinn Fein. It would be 'an immense disservice to Labour and the
country.' After much internal wrangling, the ITUC&LP decided to
desist, ostensibly to avoid prejudicing 'a clear expression of the people's
opinion upon the question of self-determination.'[9]

Of course, many Sinn Fein candidates had pro-labour sentiments, and the Labour Party subsequently organized industrial action which helped disrupt British authority. Labour also provided Sinn Fein with its so-called Social Programme, which gave Sinn Fein the legitimacy it wanted in the international socialist world while simultaneously enabling the Labour Party to say that Sinn Fein had adopted Labour's socialist politics.[10] However, in the light of the decision taken by the ITUC&LP leadership, Thomastown's labouring electors could choose between only Sinn Fein and Irish Party candidates in the 1918 election. They chose Sinn Fein. As a result, Sinn Fein was transformed into the legitimate carrier of the political sentiments associated with both the nation and working people.

This outcome was in part the result of the ideology that propelled the IT&GWU and its subsumption under the ITUC&LP. From this organizational position, neither trade unionists nor the IT&GWU leadership was able to produce a workers' version of nationalism or a plan of action to compete with Sinn Fein. In any case, after its tremendous surge until 1913, the IT&GWU had declined dramatically, circumscribed by its links with British trade unions and their commitment to the war and by the large number of jobs provided for workers by the British army. Half of the IT&GWU's national membership in 1914 had joined the British army by 1916.[11]

The war brought immense prosperity to Irish employers. Workers, however, faced food and fuel shortages while inflation cut into real wages, 'generating accusations of profiteering against farmers, businessmen and shopkeepers.' However, 'if the first half of the war stored up social grievances, [the] production demands and growing manpower shortages after 1916 provided the means of redress.' Union membership went from 100,000 to 250,000 by 1920. 'Labour became a nationwide force,' as did the IT&GWU's syndicalist ideology. It was expressed through a so-called wages movement by which unions, through 'incessant ... wage militancy,' would ensure 'the triumph of the working class.' The aim was to create a 'One Big Union' (OBU) made up of industrial sections serving as 'social centres' for workers around which they could construct every activity of their lives. Political parties were dismissed as irrelevant.[12]

Such industrial unionism continued successfully into the early 1920s, led by the IT&GWU in its drive to be the OBU. This left the ITUC&LP to struggle with nationalism. On the one hand, it took the view that 'nationalism was something that should be kept at arm's length' and,

'while willing to go with the flow of popular sentiment, it was not prepared to lead opinion, or bargain with the nationalists.' On the other
hand, the pursuit of a workers' republic was an aim for at least some radical nationalists, such as Cathal O'Shannon. Thus, the ITUC&LP, of
which the IT&GWU was part, backed the anti-conscription campaign
being waged in early 1918 while withdrawing from the parliamentary
election which took place in December of that year.[13]

The anti-conscription campaign began with the German offensive in
March 1918, Britain's need for more troops, and the passing of a bill
that gave the British government the power to impose conscription on
Ireland whenever it wished. The Irish Party withdrew from Parliament
and formed a coalition with Sinn Fein, the trade unions, and the Committee of Irish Bishops in a 'massive demonstration of national solidarity.' The leadership decided that each parish would form a 'committee
of defence' to obstruct the law. An anti-conscription pledge was administered after Mass in every parish the following Sunday. The ITUC&LP
called for a twenty-four-hour general strike on 23 April, the success of
which, the first in Irish history, 'made labour seem a power in the land.'
Over the next months, union membership surged, especially that of the
IT&GWU. In County Kilkenny, between April and December 1918,
nineteen local branches were founded. Thomastown's branch, reported
as 'founded' in August, had 152 members.[14]

Yet, by late 1918 and early 1919, the routinized activities of the Thomastown IT&GWU branch provided a sharp contrast to the drama that
Sinn Fein provided. At a typical meeting of the union's Thomastown
branch, members condemned the South Kilkenny Farmers' Association
for opposing efforts being made by the IT&GWU to recruit farm
workers. It was also announced that head office (HO) had sent the
forms by which members could claim back wages, according to the
minimum-wage level set by the Agricultural Wages Board. In many
areas, strikes resulted;[15] in Thomastown, the £210 in arrears were recovered without even recourse to the petty sessions. At the same meeting,
an IT&GWU organizer spoke 'on the objects of the organisation.' Chair
Pat Ryan, rural district councillor, then 'impressed on members' the
need to prepare 'for the coming county and rural district elections,
expressing the hope that Labour candidates would be put forward for
each division.'[16]

If the local IT&GWU branch was enmeshed in issues and official
directives as they filtered in from outside organizers and HO (head

office), so, too, was the local branch of Sinn Fein. However, its activities also combined high drama with bureaucratic necessity, theatre with practical action. In the process, Sinn Fein directly implicated local labourers in its performances and its sentiments (Case 11.1).

Case 11.1: The Sinn Fein Drama in 1918

A Thomastown Sinn Fein rally on St Patrick's Day 1918 was one of numerous local agitations called by the national leadership to endorse 'Ireland's claim to have her demand for ... independence heard at the Peace Conference.' Sinn Fein clubs and Volunteers came from all of south Kilkenny, as did Cumann-na-mBan, the women's wing. The meeting was chaired by the vice-chair of the Kilkenny County Council. Sean O'Mahoney spoke, as did W.T. Cosgrave, MP for Kilkenny city, and E.T. Keane, owner of the Kilkenny People. A quiet meeting of representatives from south Kilkenny did, however, follow. A priest from Callan chaired. The new franchise bill was discussed and all clubs 'were directed to open rooms at once to take the names of all entitled to vote under the new franchise.'

Sinn Fein returned to drama a month later as Thomastown's club planned the anti-conscription drive. At 'one of the largest demonstrations ever held' in the town, with contingents and musical bands from numerous nearby localities, a torchlight parade was held. In Market Street, a platform was erected and the chair was taken by the parish priest, Father Doyle. He 'congratulated the people for attending in such large numbers to protest against the most iniquitous measure that had ever been attempted to impose on the Irish people.' A week later, practically all the men in the parish had reportedly taken the anti-conscription pledge administered by the parish priest after Mass, outside the chapel gate.

A meeting in Kilkenny city two months later to protest the internment of Sinn Fein activists brought out Thomastown's brass band and the president of the Kilkenny Trades Council. As the 1918 election neared, more Sinn Fein rallies took place: for Cosgrave in Kilkenny city with the support of the Trades Council and in Thomastown where Father O'Flanagan, vice-president of Sinn Fein, endorsed the candidacy of James O'Mara. A large crowd in Market Street marched around the town, led by the brass band, pipers from Kells and Ballyhale, and 'large numbers of sympathisers ... from ... surrounding districts.' They then gathered to hear O'Mara speak. He began by reading letters from various bishops wishing Sinn Fein success in the coming election, 'handicapped though that cause is by the unjust imprisonment of its leaders.' O'Mara then proclaimed that 'the policy of "massaging" English ministers by our "expert statesmen" had had an ample trial' and had led only into 'the national degradation of partition ... The Irish Party were helping to divide and destroy the country.' O'Mara asked them to 'remember Carrickshock (cheers)' and 'to be proud of the fight, for at Carrickshock the men of Kilkenny defeated the tithes ... Landlordism was first fought in Callan by Callan curates. [And] ... you all know about Easter week ...'[17]

In the context of a stirring past and a dramatic present, Sinn Fein was offering a fourfold plan to the electorate: withdrawal from the British Parliament; use of any means necessary to end English domination; creating an assembly to act as a 'national authority'; and asking the Peace Conference to accept Ireland as an 'independent nation.'[18] Election meetings for Sinn Fein continued throughout south Kilkenny. On voting day, the constituency was 'quiet and orderly.' Volunteers armed with 'substantial sticks' patrolled polling booths and took the ballot boxes to Kilkenny city. James O'Mara, Sinn Fein, received 8,685 votes (82 per cent); Matthew Keating, Irish Party, polled 1,855.[19] In the twenty-six counties that later formed the Irish Free State, Sinn Fein received 65 per cent of the vote.[20] Clearly south Kilkenny, in the absence of labour alternatives at the polls, belonged to Sinn Fein.

Ideologies and Experience

The failure of the national executives of labour organizations to develop a political bloc and, worse, their cession of leadership to Sinn Fein have been amply deplored and explained by reference to personality conflicts, competing ideologies, and political and economic contingencies. What it meant at the local level was that the national leadership had accepted an idea that local workers had rejected for over a century: that economic and material interests could be separated from the political domain. Their experience of class, both material and ideological, had long kept workers alert to the fact that their needs and concerns were distinct from those of farmers and retailers. In the recent past, this awareness had impelled them to form a club in 1891, vote for labour candidates in 1899, reject the UIL, found a Labour League in 1908, and, then for some, join the IT&GWU in 1913. It was reflected in the different view that labourers had as to the implications of Edward Wallace's death. Why was this critical awareness and knowledge not extended to the Irish Party and, in 1918, to Sinn Fein?

The dichotomous political world that had been structured by lengthy and intense conflict in the inland fisheries (Table 8.1) had created a bedrock of common sense which put local workers in direct and natural opposition to the ascendancy and, in part by implication and in part by choice, in strong support of Irish independence. Such sentiment was buttressed by the code of respectability which directly affected access to work and patronage and which made labourers especially sensitive to approval emanating from those in other classes who, by 1918, were no longer primarily landlords and gentry. In any case, improved living standards gave labourers more flexibility and made them more alert to the resonance of political argument and ideology. At the same time, labouring ranks had been increased by local artisans whose activism on their own behalf during the nineteenth century was by now obviated by their downward mobility, as status-class boundaries tightened and pushed them into the working class. Their new position was institutionalized by the Labour League and, later, by a union that brought them all together in common cause. These trajectories were supported by the extension of kinship ties which ramified throughout the working class and which, slowly, began to break down the strictures of neighbourhoods. Then, the constitutional focus that had typified even the Labour League, and its concern to gain legitimacy through participation in formal government organs, had educated local labourers into supporting the same strategy vis-à-vis the Irish Party and Sinn Fein. This was enhanced by the dramatic public theatre and military wing which Labour was unable to counter or duplicate. The pull, too, of cultural nationalism via the activities of some of the local gentry, the Gaelic League (Irish language classes) and the Gaelic Athletic Association was relevant here, since it socialized some labourers to the idea of a Gaelic nation. Indeed, GAA sports were themselves often 'held under the auspices' of the Trade and League.[21] A push, too, was given by the Catholic hierarchy's often explicit approval of Sinn Fein and its equally blunt disapproval of labourers' combinations and the OBU. Finally, people's parochial sentiments were now being channelled into county loyalties. According to O'Mara's history (Case 11.1), it was the 'men of Kilkenny,' not locals, who triumphed at Carrickshock. Their descendants were now being organized by county affiliation via GAA sports and the 1898 Local Government Act. The idea of county, as a building block for both the Gaelic nation and the Irish state, had become part of common sense.

Thus, through both unconscious predispositions and conscious decisions, the historical bloc that formed at the end of 1918 was aligned through an experience and idea of nation and state rather than of class. Sinn Fein had rewritten the past and prepared a program for the future. Labour's factionalized leadership failed to do either. Its syndicalism, espoused by saddler James Grace (p.236), and its Social Programme provided little local drama. In any case, these were buried with the martyrs of 1916 and by the respectable constitutionalism to which workers had been educated for almost a century.

Sharing Violence: Collective Experience and Individual Encounters, 1919–23

In January 1919, after Sinn Fein's MPs withdrew from the British Parliament and formed an alternative Irish assembly (Dáil Éireann), unilateral independence was declared. Over the next months, with its members pursued by British police, the Dáil managed to appropriate the machinery of government as one local council after another declared its allegiance to the new assembly and as a separate hierarchy of courts was set up. On the same day as the first Dáil met, violence in county Tipperary signalled the start of what was to be the War of Independence.

The War of Independence

In its first phase, during 1919 and early 1920, it was mainly a guerrilla war fought against the Royal Irish Constabulary by former Volunteers who had taken an oath of allegiance to the new state and who now comprised the standing army of the republic (IRA). In early 1920, in the face of escalating violence, the British supplemented the RIC with new recruits (so-called Black and Tans), introduced Auxiliaries to the RIC, and increased the number of British regular troops. The guerrilla war continued, fought mainly in the larger cities and in the south and west of the country. The British responded with two strategies. The Restoration of Order in Ireland Act, passed in mid-1920, gave the military authorities the right to imprison without trial any persons suspected of having Sinn Fein connections. The British also adopted the unofficial policy of meeting 'terrorism with reprisal.' The war was thus marked by violence and counter-violence.[22]

County Kilkenny, however, was not part of mainstream struggle and, in the 1980s, this informed the similar stories which elderly people told of local happenings.[23] They said that 'the lads used to go out and knock trees to keep the Tans from getting through. Then the Tans would come round up the lads to clear the road.' Or, 'there were a few meetings and a lot of tree-cutting, but not much else. It was quiet in Thomastown.' Such uniform general impressions were occasionally accompanied by a more personal memory. These, however, with very few exceptions, saw the person as an object in the war, not a subject. For example, the widow of James O'Neill (labourer, fisher, district councillor) recounted that 'the Black and Tans once lined up my husband's brothers against the wall to get them to say where James was. But they never shot anyone.'

What emerges from both the memories and published records are that local people, as political objects, experienced personal harassment and the threat of violence. Rounded up to clear trees, to stand in line and be stared at, or to be arrested by armed Black and Tans was not only intimidating but also contained the potential for violence. In such a context, people observed, read, and gossiped. The railway station, for example, was a centre for police and troop movements while the newspapers brought together numerous local happenings which fuelled local conversation (Case 11.2).

Case 11.2: Experiencing the Threat of Violence, 1919–21

1919. May. Seven farmers, members of Thomastown Sinn Fein Club, were arrested. As they were to be conveyed to the Waterford jail and the police cleared the street, 'some angry conflicts took place between the police and the people.' July. The prisoners were discharged and 'a large crowd gathered. Several labourers were hurt' after a baton charge by the police.

1920. April. The manager of Thomastown Creamery, from County Cork, was arrested. In County Kilkenny, fifteen police barracks were destroyed, including Inistioge and Bennettsbridge. June. British troops took over Thomastown courthouse and fortified it with sandbags and barbed wire. August. 'Masked and armed men' were reported as 'active in Thomastown.' The pub owned by James McKenna, Sinn Fein member, was raided by the military and police. The retailers' Reading Rooms were raided. September. The pub and Reading Rooms were again raided. Several retailers, including John Kelly, were arrested for supporting the Belfast boycott. A farmer was arrested. The town streets were cleared by troops and Black and Tans. The houses of labourers James O'Neill and James Kelly and of the surveyor were raided and tarred with inscriptions. October. A news report noted that the 'methods and reprisal threats of the Black and Tans ... in south Kilkenny have created a feeling of grave alarm among the people of all creeds and politics in Thomastown and Inistioge. Raids, personal searches, arrests, the tarring of houses, gun-firing, and seizures of motor cars, these are some of their activities during the past month.' They 'tarred the fronts and some of the windows of houses of leading residents'; they rounded up all the men on the streets under the Big Tree; shots were fired and the Reading Rooms searched. A requiem Mass was said for the Lord Mayor of Cork who had died on hunger strike. All business establishments were closed and work suspended. A shop assistant had his motorcy-

cle seized. **November.** *The brother of retailer McKenna was arrested.* **December.** *The house of James O'Neill, millworker/district councillor, was raided. The surveyor was taken as a shield in a British lorry. Two Brownsbarn farmers were arrested but later released. More auxiliary police arrived in Thomastown. The fever hospital and part of the workhouse were 'commandeered ... Searches of farmhouses in the district by the new forces have begun. There is much suppressed excitement throughout the entire district.'*

    1921. January. *Blacksmith Michael Kelly, sawmill owner George Phelan, and road contractor John Gardiner were arrested.* **March.** *Thomastown was surrounded by Woodstock auxiliaries who inspected houses to see 'if occupants' names were posted as required by martial law.' Raids were made on the houses of retailer John Kelly (Market Street), millworker James O'Neill (Mall), a retailer, and journalist/League member Edward Maher (Low).* **April.** *Tom Dack, postman, was held up by masked men. The Auxiliaries searched the area with a bloodhound and visited Sinn Fein houses. Dack was arrested but released the next morning.* **May.** *Goods at the railway station from Belfast blacklisted firms were destroyed. Local retailers had refused to take delivery of these. 'Activity on the part of Crown forces afterwards took place.'* **June.** *Labourer Patrick Ryan (district councillor) was arrested and sent to the Waterford jail. While incarcerated, he was unanimously elected vice-chair of the rural district council. Father Loughry (curate), millworker/councillor James O'Neill, a retailer, and a shop assistant were also arrested and jailed in Waterford. The remains of Nicholas Mullins, a publican's son, arrived at Thomastown station. A member of the IRA, he had been killed in fighting in north Kilkenny. Only immediate relatives were allowed to meet the train. 'The large numbers who arrived ... with the intention of taking part in the funeral procession were stopped by crown forces.' Subsequently, all the men who had assembled were rounded up at the church gate and searched, and several labourers and farmers were arrested; about fifty young men were also commandeered to remove trees off various local roads. The next day, a large number of young men were arrested.* **July.** *Potatoes assigned to the Auxiliaries at Woodstock 'were found destroyed at the railway station. Later that day, all available potatoes were commandeered by the auxiliary forces.' The keeper of a lodging house was fined 40s. at a military court for failing to keep a register of arrivals and departures.* **Truce declared.** **December.** *Several Thomastown detainees were released from jail: Father Loughry, four farmers from various parts of the parish, and blacksmith William Lee. The Volunteers formed a guard of honour, as did Cumann na mBan.* **1922. January.** *A farmer and a retailer, imprisoned in England, were released. They were met by the brass band and a torchlight parade.* **February.** *The Black and Tans left.*[24]

For over a year, labourers, retailers, farmers, clerks, priests, and professionals had been enmeshed, seemingly equally and often together, in dramatic and intense happenings. Father Loughry, retailer Manogue, and millworker James O'Neill reputedly shared the same jail cell in Waterford during their three-month incarceration, although it was also said that the curate had *his* meals brought in from a local hotel. Generally, however, there had been in the locality a shared experience of intimidation and violent possibilities.

The Routinization of Revolution

Even before the military outcome of the war was known, Sinn Fein was appropriating bureaucratic structures and practices and constructing a parallel government. In June 1920 councils and courts were asked to swear allegiance to, and subsume themselves under, a new hierarchy. They all did so. This was, in part, because of nationalist sentiment but also, in part, because the legitimacy of hierarchy, regardless of what or who was the state formed an essential component of common sense. In the latter guise, it invariably affected how labourers located themselves in the revolutionary process.

An early example was in April 1920 when the chair of Thomastown's rural district council announced that he had only just learned that 'a national strike had been declared ... He thought it ... their duty as a nationalist body to adjourn.' Labour councillor Pat Ryan then moved to adjourn because the council endorsed 'the National ... protest issued by the Irish Labour party against the murderous policy of the Government towards the untried and patriotic prisoners.' The resolution passed unanimously. That the strike was called by the TUC and coordinated in some places by workers' councils has been seen as 'a spectacular demonstration of labour discipline' which pointed to 'a social revolutionary dynamic' that potentially underlay the labour movement.[25] In Thomastown, however, such origins went unreported. Moreover, the strike was simply channelled through formal institutions, bureaucratic routine, and ritual statements.

Such practice and outlook had important implications. Prior to the county council elections in June 1920, delegates from various IT&GWU branches in the area met in Thomastown to select candidates. James Lalor, president of the city and county executive, was moved to the chair. Pat Ryan spoke. He lectured on the need to have labour representatives on the county council given the poor way in which it treated workers who were hired as 'direct labour' on public works. Ryan then proposed that they select two candidates. An amendment was then put to select four. Ned Maher, secretary of the Thomastown branch, supported Ryan's proposition because '*it was a bad policy for the Labour Party to adopt to monopolise four seats.*' The amendment was withdrawn. Pat Ryan and James Ryan were unanimously selected. It was decided that each IT&GWU branch form election committees and hold public meetings.[26]

The ameliorative purposes in running for council seats, the notion of fair play, and the inability to visualize that labouring interests might differ from or conflict with Sinn Fein certainly belies the idea that there were any radical tendencies among these delegates. In the event, and not surprisingly, there were 'overwhelming republican victories' at the polls. For the county council and Kilkenny city, the headlines read: 'City and County Solid for Sinn Fein.' For Thomastown rural district council, it was: 'Labour and Sinn Fein ... Top the Poll' (Case 11.3).

Case 11.3: The 1920 Local Government Elections

Replacing the British system of single-seat constituencies and 'first past the post,' these elections were based on multi-seat constituencies and transferable votes.

   County Council. Thomastown Electoral Area *(9 candidates ran for 4 seats).* Elected: (1) Farmer, Kells, Sinn Fein; (2) James Ryan, Castlegarden, labourer, Labour-Sinn Fein; (3) Patrick Ryan, carter, Labour; and (4) Farmer, Windgap, Sinn Fein.

   Thomastown Rural District Council. Thomastown area *(9 candidates ran for 5 seats).* Elected:
– *1st* count: Patrick Ryan (carter, Labour) and William Forristal (farmer, Sinn Fein)
– *2nd* count: James O'Neill (millworker, Labour, Thomastown) received virtually all of Ryan's transfers (101 out of a possible 134) and reached the required quota.
– *3rd* count: David Holden (labourer, Sinn Fein) and Richard Moore (farmer, Sinn Fein)

   Thomastown Rural District Council. Woolengrange (Bennettsbridge) area *(7 candidates ran for 4 seats).* Elected on the 1st count were Michael Murphy (labourer, Sinn Fein), M.J. Westermann (clerk, Labour) and a farmer (Sinn Fein). On a later count, a farmer (Sinn Fein), was elected.

The newspaper accounts of the 1920 election depicted both Sinn Fein and Labour as republican. James Ryan, selected by Labour/IT&GWU as one its candidates for the county council, was in fact recorded as 'Labour-Sinn Fein.' Several other workers, too, ran as Sinn Fein, not Labour. Then, when the Kilkenny *People* reported the results of the race for the Thomastown rural district council, it stated that the 'five success-ful candidates were those sanctioned by Sinn Fein.' In fact, the three incumbents (fisher John Dunphy and two farmers) were overwhelm-ingly defeated. Sixty years later, Dunphy's son said that the 'republicans had wanted control so John Dunphy resigned.' Yet, as later events showed, Dunphy was indeed a republican. It seems, then, that Sinn Fein was creating a network of vetted men and that local labour was willing to concede to Sinn Fein's definition of credibility. Certainly they granted that Labour was only entitled to a certain number of candidates and seats. In Thomastown, Ryan and Maher held the Labour candidates to two. In Woolengrange, no Labour candidates ran who might have been elected on Westermann's surplus. In such a context, councillor Pat Ryan made the transition from the former council to the new. Presumably his republican credentials were in good order, having spent time in a Brit-ish jail. Dunphy and the two farmers had not. All this suggests the tacti-cal supremacy of Sinn Fein over Labour and, more important, its ideological supremacy. It fed on the inability of local labour to concep-tualize, let alone actualise, an alternative route.

Sinn Fein's overall success in the 1920 local elections enabled the Dáil to ask that local councils end their connection to the Local Government Board. Thomastown's rural district council complied. At the first meet-ing after the election, it declared its allegiance to Dáil Éireann and, from then on, it no longer sent its minutes or correspondence to the Local Government Board but to the relevant ministry of the Dáil. A month later, parish and district courts were being established in the county under the authority of Dáil Éireann.[27] Policing, too, passed to the emerging state. At the June local elections, no police went to polling stations. Instead, 'their place was taken in each town and village by members of the Irish Volunteers who took it upon themselves the duty of keeping order. There was not the slightest disorder in any district.' At a Board of Guardians meeting, when the master reported that vegeta-bles and potatoes had been stolen from the workhouse farm, council-lor/millworker James O'Neill said that it should be reported to the local Volunteers. This was agreed to.[28]

Such labour support for Sinn Fein and/or the republic was occasion-ally repaid. At the same meeting, Delia Larkin, daughter of union orga-nizer Jim Larkin and secretary of the Jim Larkin Release Committee, asked council members to sign a petition. They 'decided' to do so. That large-scale farmers and the few retailers on council petitioned in favour of the radical and fiery trade unionist suggests the extent to which labouring and Sinn Fein interests, beliefs, and practices were seen as overlapping, not simply among labourers but among people of all status-classes. This received an ironic fillip with the outbreak of civil war in early 1922. Thomastown's labourers divided, as did members of all status-classes, over the fact that the peace treaty which had been negotiated with Britain did not give Ireland full republic status; instead, it partitioned the island and retained an oath of allegiance to the British monarch.

The Civil War, 1921–2

Most elderly Thomastown people agreed with what labourer Josie Cahill said in 1983. 'The popular support was for the IRA. It was only after the Treaty was signed that the tragedy began. Everyone in town took sides. Even children would taunt each other ... There was an awful lot of bitterness and it goes on to this day. People back then could label every family's political allegiance.' The division caused by the civil war informed both sentiment and daily actions. For example, the efforts of some rural district councillors to protest the execution of republican prisoners by the Free State resulted in bitter argument.[29] In part, this passion was because the violence in Thomastown now was actual, not potential. The billeting of troops, shoot-outs, and executions (Case 11.4) augmented the earlier litany of harassment, arrests, and tree clearing (Case 11.2). Deeply traumatic, too, was the disruption of normal relationships and predictable patterns of behaviour across kin, neighbourhood, and status-class lines.

Case 11.4: Experiencing Violence, 1922–3

1921. December. The Treaty was signed, British forces left the town, the RIC was disbanded, and policing was handed over to the IRA who took over Thomastown's barracks.

1922. April. The new Irish government organized a police force which came to Thomastown and demanded the barracks. They were handed over, and the IRA left. May. Retailers sent a petition to the military in Kilkenny to obtain a guard to protect the town from robbers. The petitioners said that the Volunteers occupying the town declined to do police duty. The request was refused. June. Pro-treaty forces took over the Thomastown's courthouse, a pub, a big house (Millview), and *the fever hospital. Anti-treaty forces ('Irregulars') came into the town, attacked the barracks, and burned the courthouse. **July.** National troops commandeered lorries belonging to miller Pilsworth, another miller, and a retailer. One hundred National troops from Kilkenny were billeted in two Thomastown houses and 'all motorists and cyclists entering the town [were] held up and questioned.' Two small bridges within a few miles of the town, were blown up. **August.** Three houses occupied by National troops were attacked by Irregulars from a height on Mill Street. The Irregulars then retired. The rural district council passed a motion disclaiming 'any responsibility for [financial] claims arising out of the present ... warfare.' **September.** Labourer William Challoner was arrested by National troops. A shop assistant (a former British soldier) was arrested. A lorry driver who had worked for a local retailer was killed. The Thomastown garrison was augmented by troops from New Ross. 'They were billeted on ... houses in the town.' Col. Butler's car (Kilmurry) was stolen. The railway station signal box were burned by a party of armed men. Gunfire was reported in Thomastown. Railway worker Martin Drea was arrested. The Thomastown garrison was attacked by Irregulars, an event that created panic in the Concert Hall during a concert. The incident ended after fifteen minutes. National troops arrested labourer Michael Hearns, Jerpoint, and, again, Martin Drea. **October.** Major McCalmont's truck (Mount Juliet) was stolen. Pilsworth's lorry, used by the army, was damaged. National troops were ambushed in Jerpoint. A Jerpoint farmer was arrested, then released. A farmer, formerly a captain in the IRA and now an Irregular, was arrested. A farmer was arrested. James Power, a local postman, was held up. The Thomastown garrison was attacked for twenty minutes; people ducked for cover. The next evening, the town was attacked from the overlooking heights. The garrison strength was doubled. A bomb exploded in Inistioge and was heard in Thomastown. **November.** A 'large military force' was in Thomastown to recapture some escaped prisoners. National troops raided a farm and arrested three men with guns and ammunition. Shots were fired for about ten minutes at houses occupied by the Thomastown garrison. **December.** Fifteen National Army troops were attacked by thirty Irregulars near Inistioge. The Irregulars retreated. A Powerswood farmer was wounded and a rumour circulated that labourer Daniel Challoner was killed. Both, however, had been arrested after an engagement. The town was attacked by eighty Irregulars. George Phelan (miller) and John Murphy, an ex-British soldier, were arrested by Free State soldiers. Each had an illegal firearm and stolen property. They were executed in Kilkenny.*

    *__1923. March.__ Trees were felled in Jerpoint and civilians commandeered to clear them. Three men bobbed the hair of a young girl for 'associating with a member of the National Army.' Labourer O'Malley was shot at while trying to escape being commandeered for road clearing. **April.** The rate collector was unable to* *serve civil bills for rates because of intimidation. Two farmers were arrested. **May**. A farmer was arrested. A ceasefire was declared. **June**. The clerk of Thomastown court was transferred. It was noted that, during the War of Independence, he had spent twelve months in a Belfast jail and 'was one of the hunger-strikers. He is a firm supporter of the treaty.' **August**. The military left the town and the barricades around the houses where they were stationed were torn down. **November**. Notices were posted prohibiting all sports meetings until all the republican prisoners were released. J. Hennessy, gardener/farm worker, was released. Shots were fired in Thomastown protesting that a dance was taking place while prisoners remained incarcerated. **December**. Two farmers, a shop assistant, and a retailer were released. **1924. May**. Two farmers and labourer Martin Drea were released.*[30]

'We had an awful time,' said Josie Cahill. 'There were British soldiers in Millview house and the IRA would shoot at them during the night. Our house was in the direct line of fire and the shots sometimes hit the side of our house. So we lay down on the floor of the downstairs when it was happening.' Elderly people also spoke of a distraught parish priest who returned from Kilkenny city in December 1922 after giving the last rites to Phelan and Murphy and witnessing their executions. He said that he never wanted to see this again. People told how fisher John Dunphy was in the house when Phelan and Murphy were arrested but he hid under a table or he too would have been executed. Memories also touched on the intimate contradiction between goodwill and violence. A maid in Kilmurry House at the time said that she had no idea 'how Hennessy worked for Colonel Butler and yet was IRA. But Isabel Butler used to jokingly refer to the back gate as the 'Sinn Fein walk.' It was where 'the Sinn Feiners used to come to Kilmurry house and it was also a walk that had snowdrops, crocuses and greenery which gave it a lovely tri-colour look.' When pushed as to why the Butlers kept Hennessy on, amusement turned sharply serious: 'They could burn the place on them, couldn't they?'

The civil war made ordinary social relations unpredictable, precarious, and even violent. A labourer told how 'Irish soldiers once went into a little shop in Jerpoint and took all the lady's cigarettes without paying a penny.' Gruesome stories circulated: how several republican prisoners from Thomastown were in jail in Kilkenny for possessing arms and had received a death sentence from a military court. They were taken out to dig their own graves the night before their executions. They were reprieved at the last moment.

In 1922 a petition was circulated to have the remaining republican prisoners released from jail. Most Thomastown people signed, but some did not. Said an elderly worker: 'Those people had broken the law. I refused to sign the petition on principle.' Posters were then put up in Thomastown: 'Blacklist Persons who Refused to Sign for the Release of the Prisoners. 62 refused to sign; 1,742 signed.' The sixty-two people were named. They came from all status-classes.[31] The farmers were both large and small, from all parts of the parish. The workers were also diverse: artisans, both waged and self-employed, domestic servants and those who worked for farmers, the county council, the mill, and Mount Juliet. Importantly, those who prepared the petition and the poster saw the decision to sign as a highly individual one. Families were not named as a unit, signified by the husband's name and address. Instead, men were named, but only some of their wives, or vice versa; and adult children in the same household were separately listed. The poster, in short, was a statement of the divisiveness of the civil war. It reflected, too, the individualization of political responsibility. For years after, these features formed part of the world-view of workers.

Nation, State, and Class: Conclusion

Common rights, as in the workers' use of paths in 1849 (Case 6.2) and the river for fishing, national sentiments, as couched in the 'night of the French' in 1870 (Case 4.4), and class conflict, as asserted by shoemaker O'Shea in 1891 (Case 9.3[B]), had all undergone numerous permutations and accretions, as had the combinations and organizations that carried the variegated ideas held by working people. Something of these experiences, however, had woven into current material and personal interests, social relations, and cultural codes. Thus, after 1916, issues of rich and poor, dignity, and respectability came to co-exist with ideas about independence, republicanism, and Gaelic culture. This *metissage* was manifested in a material world made up of Welsh tiles, labourers' cottages, working hours, and 1s. donations to the convent. As the Troubles (1919–23) continued, however, some of the contours of this *metissage* emerged in a new light. What did this look like?

12: From Nation to Class in the New State: Replicating Capital and Labour, 1920–6

'Farmers, no matter what they have, are always complaining. And then they crucified the ones they had working for them. You wouldn't put a dog in the bed of old bags and straw that labourers were given. And the workers were so ill-educated that they thought the farmer was good.'

– Builder's labourer, aged seventy-three, 1983

The new Irish Free State incorporated the diverse and conflicting interests, sentiments, and perceptions that had long comprised local society. In part, this came from the ease with which the new state had appropriated the formal organs and agents of the British colonial administration. In part, too, it emanated from the local economy – its relations of production and labour processes which remained unchanged because labour leaders had failed to mount a successful challenge. All this became clear both during and after the Troubled Times.

The Place of Labour: The Reproduction of Experience, 1920–4

Several months after the local elections in June 1920, but before Thomastown's district council swore allegiance to Dáil Éireann, the Local Government Board objected to the price that the guardians planned to pay the contractor for supplying butter to the workhouse. The price of 3s.6d. a pound was too high. This was discussed at the next council meeting (Case 12.1).

Case 12.1: Labour, the Guardians, and the Price of Butter, 1920

Westerman (Labour, Bennettsbridge): 'The prices are certainly a bit high ... Butter can be got at the creamery at 3s.2d. per pound at the present time ...'

Chair William Forristal (Sinn Fein, large-scale farmer, Jerpoint): 'Butter may go up to 4s. during the winter months, and who are you going to get to supply it then?'

Pat Ryan (Labour, Thomastown): 'It would look very bad for us to give 3s.6d. for a pound of butter when it can be got for 3s.2d. in the town. It would look very bad for me, as a representative of the Labour Party ... because that would be an incentive to other ... shopkeepers to raise the price ... this evening.'

Forristal: 'Not at all.'

Holehan (Farmers' Party, large-scale farmer, Knocktopher): 'Mr. Ryan's remarks seem to be directed against me, as he mentioned that he represented the Labour Party.'

Ryan: 'Not at all; I am simply speaking for the class of people I represent. If we give 3s.6d. and the price was raised outside, what would the people I represent say but that I was party to [the raise].'

Holehan: 'I may tell the labour class that it was proved by statistics that it costs 3s.3d. to produce butter, and if you tell me you are able to get butter at 3s.2d. a pound, all I can say is that the farmer who is selling it at that is only a fool.'

Ryan: 'We are buying butter at 3s.2d. Of course, if any more butter is sent across channel, the price may go up to 10s. a pound.'

Forristal: 'We will have to take things as we find them.'

Ryan: 'I am not going to be party to fixing of the price of butter at 3s.6d. per pound.'

Forristal: 'You have made that objection already.'

Ryan: 'Leave it in the [waged, workhouse] master's hands to buy butter.'

Forristal: 'I would do no such thing.'

Holehan: 'I am as anxious as anybody else to get things as cheaply as we can, because I am a large ratepayer and will have to pay for the cost of any advance as well as anybody.'

Ryan: 'I quite recognise that; but you see my point.'

Forristal: 'Your view is very narrow.'

Ryan: 'It is not a narrow view.'

Forristal: 'It is frightfully narrow.'

Ryan: 'I represent the class that would have to pay the increased price.'

Holehan: 'That is child's talk.'

Forristal: 'You have no guarantee that butter won't go to 6s. per pound.'

Ryan:'Why wouldn't it go to 6s. when butter is being sent out of the country?'

Holehan: 'If we are not going to be paid for our butter, we won't produce it. There is a lot of talk about the price of butter but we never hear anything about the increased cost of production.'

Ryan:'The cost is the same as years ago. The same grass is growing now, and you have the same fields, and you haven't to pay anything more for the land. Don't tell me what it costs to feed a cow!'

Holehan: 'Will you come in and look after them for us?'

Ryan: 'Leave them in a field, that's all the looking after they want.' The matter was dropped.[1]

The Rural District Council (post-1898) and, earlier, the Board of Guardians (post-1850) had always worked inside an extremely vigilant state bureaucracy in which civil servants reviewed the minutiae of local administration. Over the years, a bureaucratic *mentalité* and a frugality, often bordering on extreme meanness, came to typify the workings of the council. Labourers had entered into this kind of administration in 1899 but had been on the receiving end of it for half a century before. With such a *geist,* plus the uncertainty of the butter market, animosity and stereotyping between agents of different status-classes received full vocal play. The only point of convergence in this debate was that farmers, retailers, and labourers would all indirectly pay for the higher cost of butter. However, some would get this back as producers and retailers. Workers simply lost. Through all this was highlighted the inherent conflicts between producer and consumer, local market and export market, and labour and capital.

These conflicts, and the general disdain of farmer-councillors not only towards the workhouse master but towards all employees, were also made clear a short time later (Case 12.2).

Case 12.2: Employees and the Rural District Council, 1921
The clerk of works, Mr. Aylward, *was dismissed by the council. He came to its next meeting to say that his dismissal was illegal because a quorum had not been at the meeting.*

William Forristal (Sinn Fein, large-scale farmer): *'Our quorum is five ...'*
... *'In reply to Mr Aylward, the* clerk *of the council stated that it required seven members.'*

Westerman (Labour): *'Apart from that question, it is quite irregular ...*

[He] was re-appointed ... for six months and before you ... dispense with him you ... have to rescind the motion re-appointing him.'

Forristal: *'It is for the Council to decide whether his dismissal was in order or not.'*

O'Gorman (Sinn Fein, large scale farmer, county councillor, Woolengrange): *'He is a weekly man and he has got a week's notice and that terminates his appointment.'*

At the same meeting, there was also 'some difficulty with the midwife *at Goresbridge.' She had been ill and another midwife (Mahon) had filled in. The council offered Mahon £2 a week for her work but she refused that amount. The council had now received a letter from the Irish Nurses' Union, having previously passed a motion refusing to pay her the amount she had requested.* Westerman (Labour) *asked to have the letter from the Union read. Chair* O'Gorman (Sinn Fein) *said that 'it would only be a waste of time. You can't do anything till you rescind your previous resolution.' The matter was dropped.*[2]

Aylward had tried to keep his job through a legal ploy. At worst, he would have been paid until the firing was legally carried out. Labour councillor Westerman pointed to an additional irregularity in the dismissal. Both their arguments were discarded. The council, with its farmer majority, had little time for employees. Even the representations of a legally constituted union, as in the case of the midwife Mahon, were considered 'a waste of time.'

In these various ways, the conflicts that informed local society continued though the Troubled Times and after. So, too, did a long-contested, key issue, namely, the labour process used by the rural district and county councils for public works. At a rural district meeting in 1924, when the county surveyor submitted proposals for 137 new works, a number of road workers from south Kilkenny, including Thomastown, gathered outside the meeting room together with Mr. Baird, an organizer from the IT&GWU. They had combined to advocate that roads be repaired by 'direct labour,' using unionized wages and workers under the supervision of a council employee. They wished to supplant farmers who took on road work to supplement their incomes using family labour, farm servants, and cheap casual labour. Such farming-contractors, using their own transport, also took work away from labourers like councillor Ryan who had an acre or two of ground and a horse and cart. Chair/large-scale farmer O'Gorman said that he would hear Baird but 'would not agree to have any road workers enter the room ... He would limit Mr Baird to 10 minutes.' Baird, was admitted, 'protesting the treatment of the other workers' (Case 12.3).

Case 12.3: The Labour Process – The IT&GWU versus the Rural District Council, 1924

Baird asked that all road works be given to 'direct labour ... On the last occasion, workers got only a share of the roads, not all ... At present, men with comfortable farms [were] doing the roads and their horses [were] carting ... He could [also] tell them that during the fine spring just passed, scarcely an extra man was employed on any farm' while only a few men were employed on the roads in the whole rural district. 'The unemployment ... was ... appalling. It would seem there was a conspiracy ... between the government, public bodies and private employers to starve the workers into subjection, so that they would be glad to work for any wage ... He warned the government and employers that if they persisted, ... workers would be forced to seek outdoor relief ... or go into the [workhouse] and become a burden on the rates. The workers had already gone through hell, [and] when the "Tan" trouble was over they were told there would be plenty of work available ... They were afterwards told that it was the ... republicans who were forcing them out of work. The road workers were prepared to give a decent day's work for a decent day's pay. He was not speaking for loafers, but for honest working men ... The Irish farmer and private employers were hoarding up their money ... which was transferred to English banks for investment. They were forcing desperate men to do desperate things ... The high cost of living did not affect men in comfortable circumstances ... He asked council members to put themselves in the place of the unfortunate unemployed workers who naturally feel sore when they see the farmers getting work on the roads while the workers' children are hungry and not properly clothed. The Irish workers had put up a fight for the farmers to become owners of their land, but all that appeared to be forgotten. In the recent fight for liberty ... the workers who did the fighting got nothing, while others who looked on got the jobs. He did not ask them to waste public money but ... if they ordered the roads to be done by direct labour, they would get a good return.'

Councillor/large scale farmer William Forristal *'denied any conspiracy between government and themselves. He also ... assure[d] Mr Baird that ... most farmers were on the verge of bankruptcy after the two bad years just gone. The labourer ... in constant employment is better off than any farmer.' Labour councillor* Ryan *then proposed that all roads be kept in repair by direct labour: 'There was an order ... from the County Council that all expired contract roads be repaired by direct labour.'* O'Gorman *'denied all knowledge of such an order.'*

Ryan *'said there was a large number of men idle and they preferred to work than draw "dole."'* O'Gorman *retorted that 'there are others besides the labourers who want work. There are many small farmers who need work ... as bad.' It was finally agreed to 'consider each road ... separately.' At the end, eighty-one roads were given to direct labour and fifty-six to contract.*[3]

The above encounter showed how explicit was the conflict between labour and capital, the latter being represented by farmers/employers acting for the new state. Baird was also suggesting a conspiracy to force wages down. In so doing, he chose words that threatened (workers would become a burden on the rates), obligated (workers had supported farmers' land agitation), appealed to nationalist sentiment (workers had fought in the War of Independence), and deferred (honest workers earned their wages). The farmer-councillors, as state agents, ignored the threats, obligations, sentiments, and deference and instead appropriated Baird's depiction of the poor worker and applied it to their own kind. It was an old tactic (Cases 5.1, 5.2) but still effective, as was the disparagement of Ryan's knowledge (Case 12.1).

Clearly, then, the tactical power lay with the farmer-councillors who controlled a majority of votes, the executive positions, and the discursive themes. The last was abetted by the fact that both sides constructed the needs and images of both farmers and labourers in terms of lifestyles rather than in terms of conflicting claims. Both sides thus spoke the same language, and this created the space for a negotiation and compromise. In this, the farmers won as labour gained ameliorative measures. Yet the encounter also suggests that past history had become important to labour. Some workers, at least, had begun to see that past, and their actions in it, as a poor investment which had not reaped its rightful returns. Again, it was an old but important theme (Case 4.1) through which some workers began to see a betrayal which continuing appeals to mutual obligation and common sentiment could not allay.

Replicating Points, Turning Points: To the Mid-1920s

The process of reproducing the labouring experience was part of a political economy whose trajectory had been foreseen by councillor Ryan's position on the price of butter (Case 12.1). In the autumn of 1920, overproduction caused a depression in agriculture. Unemployment reached 26 per cent, depressing consumer demand and contributing to recession. As Irish employers moved to cut wages, the 1921 Labour Party/Trade Union Congress renewed its commitment to industrial unionism and to the strike as the main weapon. However, the executive failed to develop a unified strategy and, by the spring of 1923, labour everywhere in Ireland had fallen victim to 'the employers' offensive.' Meanwhile, the Anglo-Irish Treaty had been ratified in January 1922 and the 'Congress executive sidled into constitutionalism as fast as decency permitted ... Neutrality on the Treaty became official policy' even though it was recognized that labour had more in common with the social, economic, and political views of the anti-Treatyites. Labour did well in the 1922 general election: seventeen of its eighteen candidates were elected. However, this constitutionalism, alongside the treaty versus anti-treaty split, coincided with the return of Jim Larkin from the United States, bitter factionalism among the national leaders of the IT&GWU, and the defeat of its radical wing and the ambition to create One Big Union and a workers' republic. Labour did very poorly in the 1923 elections. Yet Labour still had a 'structural framework developed during the post-1916 advance. Trade unions were now largely native based ... Congress had become a voice of the movement, trades councils were more numerous, and the Labour Party was in being.'[4]

This routinization of the revolution in the Free State, the conservative win among the national and regional leadership of labour, and the reproduction of older, indigenous conflicts in the locality took place alongside other events and agency during the early and mid-1920s. These emanated from, and proceeded in turn to structure, local experience, to mediate the policies and ideologies of the pro-treaty government and the Labour Congress, and to provide constraints and possibilities. They came out of political and civil society, the *metissage* of past labouring experience and the present agency of labourers and of people from other classes.

Local Employers and Labour Processes
In 1914 General Sir Hugh McCalmont, from northern Ireland, bought Mount Juliet estate (house, 1,500 acres, fishing and hunting rights, outbuildings). By 1922, the McCalmonts were in residence, bringing with them both new capital and the gentry's paternal code. A period of high patronage and deference began which lasted until the late 1980s. It was symbolized by 'the first annual sports meet' for employees in 1926, with races, high jump, cycling competitions, and donkey races.[5] Of the forty cottages on the estate for housing employees, the McCalmonts built

thirty-five between 1915 and 1928. These tied houses were rent- and maintenance-free. They were allocated to the skilled labourers who worked in the kennels, hunters' yard, stud farm, garage, and garden. Many of these workers were brought from Scotland, particularly the stewards, whips, and foresters. Others (for example, gardener, grooms, farriers) were brought from other parts of Ireland. The numerous unskilled farm workers, all of whom were from the Thomastown area, had to find their own housing.

The estate's forty houses were scattered in thirteen separate locales. One site had ten houses; another had five. The remainder had between one and four. An idealized nineteenth-century atmosphere quickly settled over the estate – a rural world of harvest homes, fox-hunting, cricket (with both gentlemen and labourers in the club), and charity from the big house in times of illness. Allowances of coal, kindling, meat, and milk were allotted from the estate farm to resident employees and, for the highly skilled, butter and fresh vegetables. Most important were the full-time jobs, numbering 170 in 1930. The big house alone, in 1924, had seventeen servants (five men and twelve women). Former British soldiers were preferred. Local retailers flourished, too, as did farmers who found a ready market for their straw (to bed horses) and beef (to feed hunting dogs).

The labour process was hierarchical, formal, and fragmented. Apart from the house, which was under the supervision of Mrs McCalmont, an estate agent managed all day-to-day affairs through five separate departments: farm, dog kennels, hunters'/horses yard, stud farm, and garage. Each had a head, subheads, and labourers. Under the 'steward' (farm head), for example, were a substeward, trades (gardener, mason, carpenter), ploughman, and farm workers. In the kennels, the huntsman was head. He had an understudy because he was out four days a week with the hounds. Below his understudy were 'kennel men.'

The workplaces were scattered throughout the estate and working hours varied depending on whether it was hunting season, hay-making season, harvest, and so on. Labourers thus worked in different places at different times with different amounts of prestige, remuneration, and perks. Alongside such formality and fragmentation, personal relations and gossip thrived. A first whip and a head groom were notorious for having the ear of 'the Major' (the general's son and heir) and for being a 'cabal' with control over information, job mobility, and perks. Generally, however, the McCalmonts were seen as 'good employers' by local labourers, who also were aware of the uncertainties and ambiguities that this invariably produced. First, the McCalmonts were 'violently anti-

union.' 'One wrong step' or 'one word about a union and you were out.'
So 'you had to keep quiet if you wanted to keep working there. The pay
was not good, but the perks were great and this made the jobs desirable.' Second, paternalistic authority necessarily privileged particular
individuals. 'There was a lot of coming and going in the house because
the McCalmonts were terribly exact. If they didn't like one thing about
you, you were sacked.' Third, hierarchical organization, tied housing,
cabals, and dependency did not appeal to all workers. 'There's no independence in that kind of work.' 'You were almost a slave.' Fourth, the
McCalmonts saw their labour regime as benevolent and long term. They
took pride in the loyalty of their employees, in their offer of long-term
service, and in their own understandings of how workers behaved and
thought. Thus, middle-management positions were given to outsiders
because, from his northern Irish perspective, the major believed that
'the Irish cannot give orders. They make good soldiers but not good
officers ... They also prefer to take orders from an outsider.' All this was
ironically summed up by one local: 'There's a slippery step in front of
every gentleman's hall door.'

Between 1924 and 1950, Mount Juliet estate, with its labour process
and cultural regime, provided Thomastown with a large proportion of
its full-time jobs. The next largest, full-time employer was Grennan
Mills. In 1926, in mid-depression, it employed only twenty men in two
shifts.[6] Normally, however, thirty men worked three shifts. In busy seasons, temporary workers were hired. There was a hierarchy of labour
inside the mill, as at Mount Juliet. Each shift had, in order of importance, an artisan-miller, a rollerman (foreman), a purifier man, and a
packer. The day shift also included a millwright and a carpenter, lorry
drivers, lorry helpers ('lads'), a receiver, several 'day workers,' a bran
packer, and two 'bag women' who sewed the full bags. Different work
yielded different wages, and 'lads' and women were always paid less.

In the 1920s most millworkers lived in Mill Street and the Mall and
drank at one of its three pubs. Unlike Mount Juliet, there were no perks-
in-kind for workers, only cheaper flour. This was obviated by union
wages (the highest in the locality) and union intervention, both local
and from head office, when a labour dispute occasionally erupted. The
workers also had an employer who regarded their welfare as a personal
concern. Numerous stories about charity in times of illness or death
were explicable by Robert Pilsworth's view in 1899 that it was not men
whom he employed but families (p.191). Thus, said several former
workers, 'there was great loyalty to the mill.'

Such sentiment was buttressed by the fact that 'only established mill families could get work there.' Even when part-time, seasonal workers were hired, the millworkers insisted that such temporaries be Mill Street locals. A common expression, that 'it was Dunphy's river and Synnott's mill,' highlighted the kin-based nature of mill employment as well as the kin-based transmission of fishing skills. It pointed, also, to the intimate link between mill work and salmon fishing. Yet, ultimately, it was all rooted in a respectability that accompanied an ideal working-class life: long-term employment, local ties, and the transmission of skills/jobs to one's children. This ethos was contained in an obituary for James Kelly (1860–1953). He 'had been employed for over 50 years as a millwright in Grennan Mills. He was a leading member of the old Thomastown tug-of-war team while his prowess in the old days of cot racing was known over a wide area. He was the father of Mr. T. Kelly who succeeded him at Grennan Mills; Pat Kelly, lorry driver, do; etc.'[7]

The high patronage and anti-unionism of Mount Juliet, and the union-neutral paternalism of Grennan Mills, contrasted sharply with the tannery, hardware, and shop owned by the Ryans It was said that 'the Pilsworths were the best employers, particularly when compared with the Ryans.' When a former tannery worker died in 1912, his daughter went to the Ryan shop to buy paraffin and a globe for the wake. Ryan charged her for the items even though her father had worked in the tannery for fifteen years. 'The Ryans would follow a crow for a crust of bread,' she said in 1983, 'but they were dead honest.' Work in the tannery reflected this, said an elderly informant. The hierarchy was simple, work unpleasant, and labour process rigid (Case 12.4).

Case 12.4: The Labour Process in The Tannery, c. 1920

'Michael Ryan managed the tannery and under him came the tanner, Tom McCrea and, before his time, Jason Wright. All workers, except those who worked "on the beam" removing the hair and fat from the hides, for which they were paid an extra 2s. per week, were "just labourers." Tom Johnstone, though, did a special job – preparing the tallow and treating the hides with it. He received no extra pay. Removing hair and fat from hides was particularly distasteful work. The hides had been steeped in a lime solution and the workers, when scraping them, wrapped cloth about their hands to protect their skin.

'Work started at 6 a.m. and, at 8 a.m., the workforce went home for breakfast. They returned at 9 a.m. and worked until 1 p.m. They resumed after lunch at two and worked through until 6 p.m – six days a week [that is, 60 hours] until 1911 when the weekly hours fell to 56 [5.5 days per week] following the strike. If a worker was more than a quarter of an hour late for any the three sessions, he *was not allowed to begin work until the start of the next session. His pay packet reflected his absence.*

'Workers also bought their groceries from the Ryan shop during the week "on the slate." This amount was subtracted from their weekly pay packets.'

The 1911 strike had lowered the number of hours in the work week but, unlike Grennan Mills, wages had been pro-rated. It was not lost on workers, when they compared the Pilsworths and the Ryans, that the former were Protestant and the latter were Catholic.

According to surviving wage books (1895–1931), the tannery workforce in 1926 was as large as it had been since the mid-1890s, with six full-time and five part-time employees. There was only one father-son dyad; they worked part time during 1926. Workers, however, did live near each other, in Maudlin and Ladywell streets. The IT&GWU never organized the tannery, nor did any other union. Indeed, former millworkers in the 1980s recalled the tannery workers with some contempt. 'The tannery workers just took what the owners offered them.' However, it was Pat Murphy, Maudlin Street, a full-time tannery worker for twenty-five years (1906–31), who had been a leader in the Trade and Labour League and who had organized the 1911 tannery strike.

The Organizational Dimension

It had also been the Trade and Labour League that had brought workers together across spatial, sectoral, and industrial divides. It had linked the skilled, semi-skilled, and unskilled; young and the old; self-employed, permanently employed, and casuals; urban and rural; unionized and non-unionized. Mill, tannery and farm workers, road and county council labourers, artisans (self-employed, waged), and carters had all belonged. The League's activities diminished during the Great War and virtually nothing was recorded about it during the Troubled Times. In 1925 the League was evicted from its Rooms in Market Street by the retailer/owner. It moved to Maudlin Street. The billiard table, however, did not make the journey, and this proved crucial. For at the time, the parish priest (Father Doyle), his curates, local notables (teachers, stationmaster, postmaster), tanner Ryan, and about twenty retailers were raising £400 from the bank and from private subscriptions to buy premises in Market Street to house a branch of the Catholic Young Men's Society (CYMS).

Originally mooted in 1922, the CYMS was installed by early 1925. It had a billiards table and, as local people recalled, its premises were very modern. The CYMS also had a curate who, as its 'spiritual director,' frequented the premises and addressed its formal meetings.[8] Formal Catholicism thus entered recreation, and recreation was a key part of local working-class life. Previously provided through a labourers' club and premises, recreation was now purveyed by retailers and clergy. No informants suggested that the 1925 eviction of the Labour League from its Rooms was related to the opening of the CYMS. Yet some collusion seems likely because the rural district council not only refused to interfere with the eviction but also refused to order the landlord to build the sanitary facilities which the medical officer had ordered if the League were to continue its tenancy. At a council meeting in early 1925, just as CYMS opened, labour councillor James O'Neill inquired what the council would do regarding the order made by the doctor. The chair said that the eviction notice had been served 'and we have nothing further to say to it.' O'Neill retorted that 'the days of landlord tyranny ought to be over ... Do you intend to do anything to compel [the] landlord to provide sanitary arrangements in [the] premises?' Chairman: 'We have nothing further to say to your dispute. You can fight it out between yourselves.'[9]

The local IT&GWU branch was also in difficulty, a reflection of Larkin's return to Ireland in 1923 and the conflict within the IT&GWU between 'the defensive, bureaucratic' and pro-Treaty wing and the radical, communist, and republican wing.[10] It was manifested locally when Larkin's radical faction obtained a judgment in Chancery (Dublin) against Ned Maher, Thomastown branch, for failing to account for money he had received as secretary/agent for the plaintiffs. The court ordered Maher to hand over all union monies and books. Ultimately, however, Larkin lost these legal battles and was expelled by the IT&GWU executive in March 1924.[11]

The Decomposition of the Labour Movement?

Such rivalries have been seen by some labour historians as a rural-urban split in that the more radical parts of the labour movement, situated in Dublin, separated from the conservative, rural parts. The latter then slowly dissolved, leaving behind 'hundreds of local and sectional power centres,' a clientelist structure with loyalties to local branches rather than to a larger movement, outlooks that were conservative and ameliorative, and local officials who aimed to be 'influential figures in their own small entities rather than being subsumed into larger organisations.' Ultimately, 'reliance on a contracting, faction-ridden trade union movement for ideological stimulus produced a pedestrian Labourism' which drove away many labour republicans.[12] They joined the Fianna Fáil party, founded by anti-Treatyites who split in 1926 from Sinn Fein over the latter's continued abstention from the Dáil.

This idea of decomposition after 1921 assumes that only a so-called national movement is relevant for history and historians. In both the Irish and English contexts, this invariably privileges the failures of labour and its leaders while ignoring how local peoples constructed their worlds and how, by implication, local experiences and consciousness in turn addressed the so-called national movement. For, in fact, the organizational base of Thomastown labour was quickly reproduced by 1926. Eviction from the League Rooms and the union/labour party factionalism created a flurry of organizational effort. In December 1925 a Labour Club was formed with a reported membership of fifty and 'new members ... joining daily.'[13] A year later, a Thomastown branch of the Irish Labour Party was founded. The club and party found new premises, called Labour Hall. All this activity again brought together diverse interests and people. Water bailiff Sam Ireland joined the Labour Party along with fisher John Dunphy. So, too, did teachers. It was a broad coalition of labouring people and unionized workers.

The need to secure the 'interests of political labour,' as stated by a teacher who addressed the founding meeting of Thomastown's Labour Party, was in fact a realistic assessment of the poor electoral condition of labour in the new state. In the 1925 Kilkenny county council elections, with eight seats in the Thomastown area, Labour ran only two candidates and won just one seat. In contrast, the Farmers' Union won six. Newly founded to secure farming representation on council, it aimed also to develop agriculture and marketing and to reduce taxation.[14] Interestingly, all candidates in the elections had been nominated by people from their own localities. This parochialism, typical since the inception of elections in the 1850s, was replicated in the new state (for example, Case 9.5).[15]

Centralizing the State: Local Government (Consent) and Courts (Coercion)

The Rural District Council had managed local affairs (roads, cottages, setting rates, and so on.) and had employed much local labour, directly or indirectly, since 1899. Even the Board of Guardians after 1850, with a restricted jurisdiction, had provided jobs for local people. In mid-1924 it was learned that local government was to be reorganized: that rural district councils were to be abolished and their authority and functions vested in the county council. The Thomastown rural council passed motions 'protesting emphatically' the disenfranchising of ratepayers and calling on 'our representatives in the Dáil ... to strongly oppose the proposed bill.'[16] Such defence of local autonomy proved futile and the Local Government Act of 1925 was passed. It meant that local people now had to access a non-local, regional arena in order to pursue parochial interests. This, in turn, required pan-local coalitions and viewpoints. An example from 1926 was the old issue of the labour process in public works (Case 12.5).

Case 12.5: Wider Coalitions and Viewpoints after 1925

The rural district council had been moving to 'direct labour schemes,' in part because of pressure from labour and in part because direct labour eliminated inefficient and recalcitrant contractors (farmers) who often did not work up to standard. Importantly, too, and as labour was quick to point out, direct-labour schemes did more to relieve unemployment. With the abolition of the rural district council, local labour came to depend on the county council for initiating public works and for recruiting workers to carry them out. The county council, however, was geographically and administratively distant. How could pressure be exerted to obtain public works for the locality and/or to get local labourers work on public-works sites? One answer could be seen in 1926 when a Thomastown *reporter used his column on local, Thomastown happenings to construct an argument about a broader locality. He thus complained of the unemployment* 'in Thomastown and throughout south Kilkenny' *because* 'a large number of road workers, who have been employed on the direct labour roads in the different districts, have been disemployed for the past 3 weeks owing to lack of funds.'[17]

The centralizing efforts of the Free State thus fomented the construction of a regional viewpoint in direct response. It also favoured farmers, marginalizing the needs of labour and, invariably, of fishers. The Tighe estate in Inistioge was dismembered by the Land Commission in 1925 and its hundreds of acres divided among farmers in the area. This change from estate agriculture meant that 'over 100 hands were formerly employed there [and] now there are none.' It also was suggested that the new fisheries ministry would take over and operate the big net 'with disastrous results' for the catches of the cotmen in Inistioge, Thomastown and Bennettsbridge.[18] Worse yet, a Kilkenny

Anglers Association had recently been formed, which brought together Kilkenny city professionals who were aiming to secure all fresh-water angling rights on the Nore between Kilkenny city and Inistioge.[19] In response to these events, a 'large meeting' ensued in Thomastown, organized by local cotmen. A County Kilkenny Cot Fisherman's Association was formed with James O'Neill and cotfisher James Long, Ballyduff, as its officials.[20] In such ways, agency stimulated counter-agency, broader spatial horizons and local organizational activity as the locality was absorbed into new and wider arenas.

The new cot association had numerous flanks to protect. Not the least of these was the Free State district court. It replaced the petty sessions and its bench of locally resident magistrates. It was presided over by a single, non-resident district justice. Between late 1918 and April 1926, no fishery prosecutions were reported in the press. When they began again, it was clear that a new regime, new outlook, and new form of coercion had begun (Case 12.6).

Case 12.6: Two Fishery Prosecutions in the District Court, 1926

John and Christopher O'Neill, Mill Street, were charged with 'unlawfully beating the water' to drive fish to the bank so that they could be 'gaffed.' The O'Neills had no solicitor. John Cotteral, water bailiff, said that he was lying in ambush and watched the defendants for about three-quarters of an hour. He saw them coming down the river in a cot and beating the river with a paddle and pole. He saw John search under the bank. Christopher then came in onto the bank where Cotteral was. Cottteral charged him with the offence. They both then went to where John was searching under the bank. Both defendants denied the offence, saying they 'were gathering timber.'

'John O'Neill (to Cotteral): Have you ever known me to break the fishery laws?

'Cotteral: I am sure you often did but I suppose you were not caught (laughter).' Cotteral admitted that he did not see any fish or a gaff. 'But when he went down to the bank, John O'Neill drove the cot out 10 or 12 yards. There could have been a gaff in the cot without his knowledge.' Both men denied this on oath. Christopher O'Neill, in cross-examination, said that there were a number of woods around Thomastown, but they went down the river to pass the day for pleasure. They also were paddling 'a bit rough to put up muscle' because they were training for the regatta. The prosecution solicitor countered: 'And I suppose you also wanted to put up fish (laughter).' The 'District Judge said he had a prejudice against defendants in fishery prosecutions. He thought it a pity that

Cotteral had not examined the cot ... He believed the defendants were guilty.' He fined them each 10s. and costs.

At the same court, four Bennettsbridge fishers (Thomas Kelly, Patrick Kelly, Thomas Power, and Thomas Jackman) were charged with using a net within 200 yards of a mill weir. Again the fishers had no solicitor. Samuel Ireland, inspector of fisheries, said that he saw the men fishing and that they were not disguised. 'When challenged by him, the defendants said they did not think there were any weir there at all. But any person could plainly see the weir.' Ireland's father, ex-Inspector W.C. Ireland, deposed that he had brought several similar cases, although it was about ten years since any one had been fined. One of the fishers swore that John Dunphy, now a conservator, had told him that the weir was not a Queen's share and they could fish there without committing an offence. The District Court Justice 'said that judging by the defences made in fishery prosecutions, it must have gone out that he knew nothing about fishing. He convicted the four men.' *He ordered a fine of £2 and 5s. costs, the nets forfeited.*[21]

Decisions in local fishing cases had been removed from the jurisdiction of local agents and given to outsiders. The pre-1920 magistrates, with their locally sited relations and knowledge of people and the past, were replaced by bureaucrats. In the Free State, the 'benefit of the doubt' was to be given to those who represented its authority rather than those who challenged its legitimacy

Partly because of this, a novel respectability began to accrue to inland fishing. Thomastown's annual regatta, with its renowned cot races among the main fisher families, was revived. An aspect of cot fishing was thus converted into sport and put alongside angling as public recreation. Also, water bailiff Sam Ireland, in true artisanal fashion, had learned and inherited his father's job. As McCalmont's fisherman, John Dunphy was elected to the board of conservators. The reputations of conservators as self-serving prevaricators was altering. In the 1926 obituary of Martin Cantwell, 'a highly respected' Mill Street publican, it was duly noted that he 'was a member of the Waterford Board of Fishery Conservators' as well as 'a prominent member of the Thomastown Cricket Club and Musical Society.'[22]

However, as bourgeois respectability grabbed hold of, and transformed, state organs, labouring people such as John Dunphy were not made part of it; they also were put into potentially conflicting situations. As McCalmont's fisherman and representative on the board, John Dunphy was expected to represent his employer's angling interests. But, as a cotman, he was concerned with the viability of the netting interest.

Agents of Hegemony

In the mid-1920s, out of the political economy and relations of class that accompanied the growth of the new state, the contours of agency could be seen. They came from new links among institutions, symbols, and memories. For example, local Catholic clergymen began to move into the political spaces created by the events of the previous fifteen years. Their agency in farmers' causes in the late nineteenth and early twentieth centuries had secured two major successes: the destruction of the landlord class and the concomitant creation of a freeholding farming class, and the achievement of a new Gaelic and Catholic state. Clergy now had the time, energy, and inclination to address, in a more formal and deliberate way, the morals, interests, and politics of working people. The entry into recreation in 1925, via the CYMS, was just the start.

Such intrusion immediately became linked to the symbolic and spatial dimensions of class. This was dramatically illustrated by the new cemetery. The planning was done during 1925 by a committee of local Catholic clergy, retailers, and farmers.[23] With the first burials, it emerged that the cemetery had three sections, according to price. Retailers and farmers were to be buried near the front, labourers at the back. Workers faced this situation without the help of many of their former patrons and the jobs they had provided. The Troubles had caused many resident gentry to leave. They would not be replaced. The Boer War and Great War had killed most of their sons and land reform had destroyed their material base. Labouring relations with them had, in any case, become somewhat equivocal with the decline of the Irish Party after 1916. Stories emerged, told by labouring people, that reflected this ambivalence. Ned Maher, Labour League secretary, had a small newsagency. After the Sinn Fein electoral victory in 1918, he put up a tri-colour flag. Mrs Solly-Flood (née Connellan) strode inside to express her disgust. Maher's wife retorted 'that she hoped to see the day when the tri-colour flew over the Connellan House.' Yet, in clear and unequivocal contrast, Walter Lindsay was vividly recalled as a 'great man for the labouring people.' Thus were positive recollections of the gentry brought forward to colour the present.

Without the actual gentry present, labourers had to deal directly with the agency of retailers and farmers, materially and symbolically. In early 1925, some labourers living in Ladywell retained a solicitor to proceed against the rural district council for the damage that their houses had sustained because the council had failed to clean a sewer. The residents also applied for coal to dry their houses. The councillors flatly refused to help.[24] They also quickly appropriated both the moral and military credit for the new Irish state. Heroic and dramatic stories of the Troubled Times that farmers told in the 1980s never included labourers. Labourers were excluded as well from the financial recompense that the new state gave its veterans. The IRA pension was the oft-cited example; so, too was access to work. A widespread perception among labourers in the 1980s was that 'no working man ever got an IRA pension.' Specific examples could be given. Councillor James O'Neill, 'despite his time in jail, was told by farmer Forristal and the surveyor that he was not entitled to a pension. All he ever got was a medal.' Faced with thousands of claims, state agents decided who would receive pensions, and Thomastown's labourers saw themselves as utterly discriminated against in this process. Equally, they often saw the claims of others as false. In 1983 a carpenter told how his father, a postman, was robbed by the IRA. The farmers who had allegedly held him up later contacted him to find out what had happened so that they could claim a pension.

Labour was also excluded by the Gaelicization of the bureaucracy in the new state. As early as 1921, the Local Government Department of the Dáil Éireann advertised for a doctor, matron, and porter in the workhouse: 'a knowledge of Irish is essential.'[25] In a locale where no Irish was spoken except by a few who had joined the Gaelic League, the bureaucracy of the new state, and its white-collar jobs, became inaccessible to Thomastown's working people.

Conclusion

National political histories have placed an inordinate emphasis on the precarious nature of the new state, torn apart as it immediately was by partition and a civil war. Indeed, the fight over the legitimacy of the new state continued, in both constitutional and extralegal ways, for many years after 1923 as republican factions continued to assert their claims. Yet, from a local and labouring perspective, it is the continuities through time that are so striking. The immediate routinization of the revolution, as the new Free State appropriated the bureaucratic apparatus of the colonial state, provided an underlying coherence. At the same time, the revolutionaries had made many promises to diverse allies about numerous issues: agricultural policies, Gaelic culture, Catholic values, and, of course, jobs, wages, and housing. Local farmers and retailers, who had already achieved most of what they had aspired to in material, political, and symbolic ways, now saw the Irish nation and culture as central. In contrast, the nationalist sentiments of many workers during the Troubled Times had been aimed at controlling future conditions rather than simply cleaning up past injustices. For them, whether Free Staters or republicans, the central issue was the state and its management of inter-class relations. How should property and governance be constructed? How could labour be an active agent? How should labouring combinations be structured? The contradiction between class and nation, which had been so obscured, slowly came to the fore both during and after the Troubled Times, as most labourers looked for the material improvements, personal dignity, and political equity which they had been promised. In such a context, leaders of national labour organizations made choices which, as labour historians have long noted, marginalized them and their followers. Indeed, the failure of this leadership has long formed the framework for labour histories. Yet it was at the local level that material and ideological life was lived. What was that life like?

13. Labouring Viewpoints and Lives: The *Metissage* of Experience and Identities, 1914–30

Peter Brophy wrote to the guardians: 'I have been in Thomastown hospital. I am a wounded soldier, discharged from the Army, and my pension is only for 12 months. The master wants to stop 1s. a day from me, and I am satisfied to pay 6d.' A farmer guardian said: 'Why doesn't the state look after the wounded? Is this the beginning of the disabled, decrepit soldiers who are going to be returned to us?'

– Kilkenny Moderator, 29 January 1916

Oral and written materials such as life histories, employment narratives, eulogies, memoirs, and stories are all means for seeing how individuals shaped their lives and were, in turn, shaped by social conventions, beliefs, and experiences. At the same time, because these materials always emerge out of particular contexts, they also provide insight into socio-cultural worlds. In this chapter, through portraits of individuals and situations, I try to highlight processes of socio-cultural reproduction and some of the threads that formed the *metissage* of working-class awareness and experience in the early twentieth century.

Being a Labourer: Three Constructions

When Thomastown people constructed images of workers and their lives, they used various styles. At one extreme was an archetypical mode, in which an ideal personal and social standard was purveyed. This image, particularly compelling when constructed as a eulogy just after a death, set up a timeless model to emulate as well as memorializing a par-

ticular life. In the early 1980s, a son of James Beck had carefully preserved a newspaper clipping relating his death. It had no date or source,
but the family knew that James Beck had died in 1930. According to
parish records, he had been born in 1871 and had married in 1893
(Case 13.1).

Case 13.1: Constructing a Labouring Life – Eulogizing James Beck, 1930
'Sad death of a Thomastown Man. On Wednesday afternoon last ... Mr James
Beck, Ladywell Street ... a respected employee of Messrs Pilsworth, Grennan Mills,
died suddenly while engaged in his work at the mill. The deceased, who was about
60 years, was apparently in his usual health during the day, and at 2 o'clock, his
son Thomas, who is also employed at Grennan Mills, made the tragic discovery
when he went to relieve him for dinner. The body was then warm, but apparently
lifeless. Rev. E. Doody was quickly on the scene, and Dr. P.J. Murphy, who on
arrival, pronounced life extinct.

'... The late Mr Beck has been a trusted employee of Messrs Pilsworth since his
boyhood, and was held in the highest esteem by his employers. He was an intelligent and well-read man, and a very interesting conversationalist. He was
extremely popular with his fellow workers, who deeply regret the unexpected death
of a loyal colleague. The sad news created a painful sensation in ... the district
where the deceased was rightly regarded as a quiet, inoffensive and respectful man
and a good Catholic. Much sympathy is felt for his widow and sons and daughters in the very sad bereavement they have sustained by the loss of a good husband
and father.'

This report cum eulogy created an archetype of the respectable,
indeed essential, working man. His relations with his family, employers,
and fellow workers were exemplary. He was self-improved and engaging
but not arrogant or obtrusive. He was intelligent but not brash. He was a
private man, yet well known in the locality. His son had followed in his
footsteps and he was, appropriately, attended on by both doctor (body)
and priest (soul).

Of course, such an ideal could not be attained by most labouring people: neither the economy nor personal resources allowed it. Yet it was a
publicly sanctioned model and, thus, subscribed to by both working
people and those from other status-classes. It represented one end of a
continuum of forms. At the other extreme was the construction of a
labouring life that sought validation by emulating the stature and pres-

tige that was thought by some to accrue to other, higher status-classes. In the early 1980s, Dolly Doyle was an elderly, alert, and extremely competent woman. Born in 1904, the daughter of a millwright, she had never married. Instead, she had worked all her life, for fifty years, as a shop assistant for one of the larger retailers in the town. In chatting about the shop and the now-deceased retailing family, Miss Doyle described her own background and connections (Case 13.2).

Case 13.2: Constructing a Labouring Life – Dolly Doyle's Farming Connections, 1983

Miss Doyle's description. (1) The Doyle side of the family. Dolly's grandfather, Patrick Doyle (her father's father), was evicted from a farm in south Kilkenny. He then worked at Mount Juliet and had a small farm in Ballydonnell townland, near the town. All his brothers emigrated. He married a local labourer's daughter. This grandmother, according to Dolly, reared a hundred turkeys a year, and pigs, for sale. Their children all emigrated except for Dolly's father who left Ballydonnell to live in Mill Street. He married Bridget Ryan [see (2) below]. His first job was as second whip to the hunt. In his second job, he sold beer for a Waterford brewery in the Thomastown area. The farming Fitzgeralds of Ballydonell were related to the Doyles 'because they were all buried together.' They were related through a Fitzgerald mother and, importantly, this Ellen Fitzgerald was 'a Healy of Sm...n,' that is, the daughter of a very large-scale farmer in a nearby townland. (2) The Ryan side of the family. Dolly's grandfather, John Ryan (her mother's father), was born on a farm in south Kilkenny. He apprenticed as a miller in Belfast, worked in Dublin, and married a woman from County Laois. He came to Grennan Mills to help install the new steel rollers. He stayed on in the mill. He died aged thirty-seven. Dolly's mother, the daughter of John Ryan, had a sister who became a nurse in Dublin and a brother who became a millworker and cot fisher.

Parochial and Land Records. *Archival materials highlight the nuances that Dolly put on her connections. Patrick Doyle, her grandfather, was indeed born in 1846 in south Kilkenny. He said that he was a farmer's son when he married in 1869. At that time, he gave his own status as 'farm servant' and his new wife's as 'farm servant/labourer's daughter.' Their son Robert married a domestic servant/labourer's daughter from the south. Dolly was born in 1904. Taking the 1846 birth as a final link with the farm, the Doyles were three generations removed from the farm.*

There was no record of a Doyle marrying the daughter of farmer Fitzgerald. However, labourer Joe Healy, the son of an artisan-miller (not a farmer), did indeed marry Ellen Fitzgerald in 1913. Ellen, born in 1880, was the daughter of a Ballydonnell labourer. In 1845, however, two Fitzgeralds in Ballydonnell had eight acres each. At the time of the next survey in 1857, and until 1861, they held ninety-five acres which they sub-let, as middlemen, to others. By 1861 and until 1911, however, the Fitzgeralds were reduced to eleven acres. In other words, the Healy-Fitzgerald marriage was not with the farmer Healys while, apart from fifteen years or so (1845–61), the Fitzgeralds were, by Thomastown standards, not farmers. They did not have land at the time of the Healy marriage. Moreover, Patrick Doyle, Dolly's grandfather who lived in Ballydonnell, was not a farmer. He had only a house and garden.

How Dolly Doyle traced her kinship connections fits with the records in a particular way. Her construction was a pastiche that highlighted her links with farmers and de-emphasized those with labourers. Moreover, that Dolly had been a shop assistant provided some provenance for her farming connections. At the time, only daughters/sons of farmers and retailers were taken on as assistants, usually as an apprenticeship until the assistant used his/her 'fortune' to buy a shop. That Dolly was a shop assistant was proof of her good connections. That she never acquired the capital to become a retailer in her own right was equally proof of her labouring ties.

However, the respectability that both biographies emphasized, albeit in almost opposite ways, still had to be maintained through interaction with other people as well as by way of retrospective, public presentations. Other people, in other words, had to collude with such representations. This sometimes led to questions and conflicts about reputations, status-class boundaries, and identities. An example was when a draper charged her domestic servant, Maria Jackson, with theft. The report of the court case named the Healys of Sm ... n as Jackson's kin.[1] Another court case ensued over who precisely these kin were (Case 13.3).

Case 13.3: 'Accusations about Relations': The Healys of Sm...n, 1928
Farmer Joe Healy, from Sm...n townland, summoned labourer Joe Healy [sic], a farm labourer also of Sm...n, for assault with a stick. Farmer Joe Healy (complainant) said he had gone to labourer Joe Healy to complain about a trespassing goat. Labourer Healy started a row. Farmer Healy's sister came out of the house with a stick; labourer Healy grabbed it and beat him. Farmer Healy denied he had threatened labourer Healy's wife. He also denied telling labourer Healy's

wife 'that if her husband's hands had been greased with 30 shillings the [Jackson] case would not appear on the papers.'

'Solicitor Crotty [defence]: Is [labourer Healy's wife] any relation of yours? – None whatever.

'Crotty: ... I think it was the Jackson case working in your brain when you went to the defendant's house and not the goat? – It was not ...'

Julia Healy [sister of farmer Healy] *said that the defendant/labourer Healy 'came to the door, asking for her brother who went out with him. She heard ... noise, ran out, and got between them ...*

'Crotty: What relation are you to the Jacksons? – None.'

Farmer O'Neill, *a neighbour, corroborated Julia Healy's version of events.*

Labourer/defendant Healy's wife, Ellen, *said that [farmer] Healy came to 'her house to complain about the goat ... He said that if his (defendant's) hands were greased with 30s., the Jackson case would never appear on the papers ...*

'Solicitor Nolan [for complainant]: Why would he be interested in the Jackson case? – They are related.'

Defendant/labourer Healy *said that he 'heard ... the remarks made to his wife, and he went to the plaintiff and asked him to explain. He asked [farmer] Healy did he realize the seriousness of his statement about the Jackson case. The plaintiff said "yes" and that it was true. Witness/labourer Healy then asked what he [farmer Healy] meant by stating that he (witness) was not a farmer or a farmer's son. And farmer Healy replied that one would think he was by the high head he carried. Witness/labourer Healy retorted that he would not feel a bit honoured by being a farmer or a farmer's son. Farmer Healy then hit him with a walking stick. Julia Healy then came and tried to hold him for [farmer] Healy to strike him. He shoved her and she fell. She had a stick also ... [Farming neighbour] O'Neill ... then came along. [Witness/labourer] Healy, who had his bicycle, did not wait for him.'*

Nolan: 'You know there is no relationship between ... [Jackson] and [farmer] Healy?'

Defendant/labourer Healy: 'There is a relationship.'

Justice McCabe: 'I don't think there is any necessity in going into these ridiculous accusations about relations.'

Nolan [to witness/labourer Healy]: 'Didn't you strike him? – I just shoved him ... He is biassed against me over the getting of a labourer's cottage ... *When [farmer] Mr William Regan, Healy's first cousin, voted for me for this cottage, O'Neill abused him and told him that he should stick his head in the ditch and allow everybody passing to have a kick at him. Mr Regan is in court and would prove that ...*

'Justice: Why did you go up to him? – I wanted to prevent him from circulating the matter further.

'The Justice said that … [farmer] Healy was an ill-tempered man with an enmity against the defendant … The defendant should have had more sense [but] … he did not think he seriously assaulted Healy.' He fined the defendant 10s. and dismissed the cross-summons.[2]

Because of identical names and addresses, the accounts of Jackson's theft raised questions about status-class boundaries, respectability, and reputation. Who were Jackson's kin? The farmer, the labourer, or, even more troublesome, both? For then the two Healy families were themselves kin. Each, however, denied kinship to Jackson and each attributed such a connection to the other. Farmer Healy went further, clearly agitated at the imputed link to a proven thief, a servant, and one whose odd surname suggested questionable origins.[3] He thus accused labourer Healy of trying to extort 30s. to keep the story out of the press. He also accused him of having notions above his station. Labourer Healy affirmed his contentment with his labouring status and, also, his contempt for some farmers, particularly those such as Healy and O'Neill who begrudged him the cottage that farmer Healy's cousin had helped him obtain. Such contempt was mutual. Said farmer Julia Healy at one point: 'I wouldn't mix with him.'

The detailed newspaper coverage of the Healy dispute highlights what reporters defined as being of interest to the reading public: status-class boundaries, identities, and the interpersonal conflict that might derive from them. However, permeating all the above three constructions were clear ideas about respectable people and appropriate behaviour. These constructions, created at least in part by working people themselves, also referred to the material resources important in labouring lives: work, housing, kin, and ties to other people.

Life in the Working Class: Three Views

The constructions of labouring lives by the writer of James Beck's obituary, by Dolly Doyle in an interview, and by the report of the Healys' interactions all highlighted that status-class identities and reputation were not simply ideas but also the grist of everyday life, as lived encounters as well as representations of selves and as materially propelled as well as performance. Other constructions by local people pointed to this more directly. In 1983 I asked Katie Drennan (born 1912), whom I had known for several years, why she had never married. In telling me why, she explained much about labouring women's lives in the first half of the twentieth century (Case 13.4).

Case 13.4: A Story of the Drennans, 1989

Born in 1879 to a carpenter who had a cottage and three acres and who worked steadily for a local retailer, Nora Drennan was one of four children. She had three brothers: Jack, Willie, and Pat. Nora began working part-time at age thirteen for the wife of the Protestant rector. At nineteen, she took a job as a domestic for Mrs Nolan, a draper's wife in Market Street. She then worked in a gentry house, as a house-maid and, then, as a general maid for seven years until 1912 when her daughter Katie was born. Nora was thirty-three at the time and unmarried. She never worked again. Her father was in his nineties and her mother was seventy. So she stayed at home to look after them. Her father died soon after, and her mother died in 1917. Nora then looked after her brother Jack who was still at home. Jack Drennan once told Katie that it 'took three women's lives to look after him.' And 'this didn't bother him at all,' said Katie.

Nora's brother Willie emigrated in 1914. After their mother's death in 1917, the plan was for Nora to join her brother Willie in the United States. Katie would be sent to her uncle Pat, Nora's other brother who had moved to Callan, until Nora could send for her. The idea was that Jack would marry and stay in the home place. But Jack did not marry. So Nora stayed to look after him.

Nora had been fond of Tom Dwyer, a railway worker. But the Drennans wouldn't allow a marriage because Dwyer had tuberculosis. Katie assumed for years that Dwyer was her father. But one night in around 1940, after Katie had returned from five years in England because her mother Nora was ill, Jack Drennan 'had a few jars' and told that her father was the son of a local farmer. Although the farmer would never have married Nora, Katie knew that her mother would not have married him. This was because Dwyer had died shortly before Josie was conceived, 'and the spirit went out of my mother.' Her brother Willie supported her and was kind to her after she became pregnant, but he left for the United States when Katie was two. In contrast, Nora's brother Jack was condemning. Katie thinks that her mother spent the rest of her life doing penance by taking care of the unforgiving Jack Drennan. For 'the pregnancy was a terrible blow to the family, especially to proud Jack Drennan. It was a horrible disgrace.' Canon Doyle, for example, never spoke to Nora the whole time he was parish priest. Nora did not leave the house for two years after Katie's birth. Finally, Mrs Nolan, Katie's godmother, would take her out – to Mass, for a walk. 'But she spent her life doing penance.' Katie, however, went off to England in the mid-1930s and worked as a maid in a big house. She returned when her mother became ill in 1940 and, after her mother died in 1943, she stayed on. Katie 'felt grateful' to Jack for giving her a home and for taking her in instead of throwing her and her mother out. Jack also told Katie that he would leave her the house and acre. So Katie stayed. She was grateful to him, for he made her independent and free from financial worry. But Katie also felt as if life had passed her by. She did not think that Jack would have objected to her marrying. He more or less expected Katie to find a husband and bring the husband in. But Katie could not imagine all three living together. So that was part of the reason for not marrying. Now, however, having taken care of her mother and uncle, there was no one to take care of her.

Out of this story comes the notion of stigma as it operated in daily life. In this case, it was the stigma of illegitimacy which, once assigned, could become the dominant force in a woman's life, affecting not only the trajectory of her own life but that of her child. The complicity of priest and brother in the stigmatizing process is, of course, striking, as is the terrible fear of public shame. Such a blow to the family's respectability could be tempered only by someone from a higher status-class (the draper's wife) who became a personal patron to the stigmatized labourer. It was not, in other words, another labourer who insisted that Nora come out in public. Likely they were avoiding her, as Nora was them.

The obverse of a woman's capacity to bring shame on a family through illicit sexual behaviour also emerges from this story, namely, her role as natural caregiver for the elderly, ill, and demanding. Women were thus the 'carriers' of both respectability and care. They also might be carriers of property when men were unavailable. Indeed, the story shows how property had a key place in the lives of working people. Arranging access to it, and heirs for it, could become the dominant motifs of a person's life. In this world, men had complementary obligations. For, if women were the 'carriers,' men were the 'providers' – of everyday goods and property and, through these, of respectability. Such expectations formed a context within which labouring men plotted their lives. The story of Johnny Egan, born in 1910, is an example (Case 13.5). It was elicited in 1980 during ongoing talks with Johnny about many and wide-ranging Thomastown issues.

Case 13.5: A Life Story of Johnny Egan, 1980

Johnny's father had learned gardening on a gentry estate a few miles from Tho-mastown. He then held various gardening jobs elsewhere but returned to Thomas-town to be near his aging parents. In 1908 his father became gardener to mill owner Pilsworth at 18s. a week. As gardener, he was given a house in the Mall, coal, milk, and vegetables. At the time, the going wage for labourers was 14s. So the gardener's job was considered a good one. Old William Pilsworth was a 'good man' who wanted an up-to-date garden. He had daily consultations with Johnny's father.

Johnny's own first job was with a Thomastown baker-retailer. But around 1920, his father became ill and was unable to work. Johnny took over his job with Pilsworth. Soon after, his father died. Four years later, Johnny 'was sacked.' He was found hurling when he should have been at work. The firing was considered by his mother and neighbours to have been a great calamity. Johnny had lost a well-paid, regular job. The family had to leave the house on the Mall because Pilsworth wanted it for his new gardener. According to Johnny, William Pilsworth's son was less interested in the garden than his father had been and had given Johnny little help or advice. So, Johnny, his mother, and sister went to lodge in Market Street, with Simon Murphy, cooper. Johnny continued to do odd jobs for Pilsworth's brother who lived nearby, but he had no permanent work. The family suffered a great deal of distress. The children, including Johnny, got jobs here and there and, luckily, when Johnny was out of work, another brother would be in work, usually at 15s. a week. That, according to Johnny, was enough for food. But still there was little food, and money for clothes was scarce. In 1926 Johnny got temporary work with a retailer, cleaning and sorting eggs for export to England. A tiny cabin owned by the retailer fell vacant and the family moved in. The rent was 2s. a week.

In 1927 Johnny began as a road worker for the county council. He earned 28s. a week. He worked from 8 A.M. to 6 P.M. (2:30 P.M. on Saturday) with one hour for dinner. In the beginning, Johnny walked to Stonyford, which took one and three-quarter hours each way. He was away from home from 6:15 in the morning to 7:45 at night. Later, he bought a bicycle and cut the travelling time consider-ably. He took a lunch to work with him, but sometimes he was so hungry that he ate it all when he arrived and then had nothing all day. At that time, the county council took on workers for a few months – breaking stones, laying road surfaces, ditching, and so on. Most workers were then let go and a new set employed in the next year. Only a few labourers were kept on full time. Johnny was lucky. He was kept on. In 1929 his wages went up to 30s. a week. Two years later, however, the county council ran out of money and Johnny was laid off. He worked for the For-

estry Department for three months; then he went back to the county council. In 1932 he began earning an extra 6s. for time-keeping (that is, supervisory) work. At first, this was intermittent, but after a year or two he became a regular ganger (foreman). In 1937 he earned 42s. a week. This was the rate for a semi-skilled worker. In 1942 he and his mother moved into a new labourers' house built by the county council. In 1945 he earned 50s. a week as a workman and 12s. a week as a ganger.

In 1954 Johnny became supervisor for a large district around Thomastown, responsible for all council work (roads, houses, and the like). He married in 1955, after his mother died. Seven years later, his wife died, leaving two small children. As a supervisor, he was able to arrange his work so that he could look after them. He was helped by his brother-in-law's family which gave midday dinner to his small daughter. Generally, he thought that his living standard was adequate for the time. They ate meat only on Sundays, with perhaps some left over for Monday. There was rabbit on Wednesday and some left over for Thursday. Meat was never eaten on Friday. Barmbrack (sweet currant bread) was eaten only at Christmas. There was no baking at other times. Johnny tasted cake for the first time at age nineteen.

Johnny said that he had always been a Labour Party supporter and trade-union member. He always voted Labour in elections. But he always gave his second preference to Fine Gael because he once received help from the local Fine Gael representative in the Dáil [TD]. In 1954, when the post of county council supervisor came vacant, Johnny applied. His application was rejected because he was too old. In fact, as a long-term employee, the rule about the age limit did not apply to him. So he went to the TD who got him back on the list of applicants. He was given the post. During the interview for the job, Johnny was asked if he would sack a worker who did not work properly. Johnny said that he would not but that he would report the man to his own [non-unionized] boss and leave him to deal with it.

Johnny Egan spent his life providing for women (mother, wife, and daughter). He portrayed his life as a series of wage levels and work promotions. Yet his life also had general trajectories: from poverty to some security to relative comfort; from homelessness to poor accommodation to council house; and from occasional worker to full-time labourer to foreman. His assessment of each stage was always relative, in terms of what a working man might aim for and expect. His dependence on others was highly limited. His brother-in-law, married to his wife's sister, became a widower at about the same time as he did. Together, the two did the best they could, without assistance from other kin and/or neighbours. It was the link between the two wives that created the closeness. Politically, too, Johnny did what was right. He was a union man throughout and a Labour voter. However, the Irish multi-seat constituency system allowed him to vote for another party as well, in return for a personal favour sought and received. Johnny was never active in either the union or the party. Johnny's life story also showed the patrilineal inheritance of skills (gardening); the patronage that was given in exchange for loyalty in enterprises such as the mill; the vagaries of waged work and the value of permanent work; and the occasional importance of kinship, especially through female ties. How did this compare with a farm worker's life? (Case 13.6)?

Case 13.6: Recollections of a Farm Worker, 1983

Ned Forristal was born in 1909 on a small and poor thirty-acre farm. His father worked for a neighbouring farmer and rented out the thirty acres. Ned's elder brother also was a labourer. As soon as he finished school at fourteen, Ned, without any skills, also began as a farm worker. At his second job, he learned to plough and this meant a bit more money. Over subsequent years, Ned worked for a series of farmers in the vicinity. He could list all these jobs and his wages. He began at 1s. a day and, over the next nine years, he worked for six different farmers. His wages rose to 8s. per week and then to ten. They dropped to 1s. a day in 1930. In 1932 Ned worked for the county council concreting the town streets and on drainage works. In 1936–7 he returned to farm labour at 8s. a week. He then went home. He and his brother bought in sheep, took extra land on conacre and tried to make a living from farming. However, his brother married soon after and brought his wife home. Ned sold his sheep and returned to labouring. He brought his father with him. 'By then, wages had risen and labouring was more profitable. The farm didn't have enough in it for both brothers.' Ned worked for the same farmer for seven years, living with his father in a tied cottage and earning £6 a week at the end of it. During this time, Ned managed to save £100 and take his father on a pilgrimage to Rome. The return fare was £49 each, including food. His father had not wanted to go 'because he could not understand spending money like that.' Soon after, his father became ill, entered the 'county home' (workhouse), and died. Ned left his job and tied cottage and worked for another farmer at £5–6 per week. In 1969 he contracted bronchitis and was unable to work any more. He was given a disability pension for fourteen years and, then, the old age pension.

During those latter years, Ned found the time to help out and do chores for an *elderly women who had two acres of land and a small house a few miles away. When she died in 1982, she willed her property to Ned. He 'did not know until six months before that she would leave him the house, even though I had been helping her for years.' Indeed, just before she died, he had wanted to buttress the walls of one of the outbuildings but 'couldn't do it because she'd think I was putting in for the place.' He did it only after the place was his. But why had she not told him until near the end? Because 'she didn't want me to know and she wasn't sure. But the older she got, the more the farmers around began pushing her to sell and give them the land. The more they did this, the more she turned to me. She didn't want them to have it. Not after the way they treated her father and stole his land.'*

As a farm labourer, Ned worked six full days a week plus Sunday morning, feeding livestock and milking cows. The normal day was from 7:45 A.M. to 6 P.M., even in winter. He was expected to turn out at night if an animal was ill. He slept in the hayloft. He was given three meals a day which he sometimes ate with the farmer's family and sometimes separately. 'Breakfast, dinner and supper: a lot of bacon, cabbage, potatoes and milk.' He could not spend the evenings with the farm family: 'You couldn't be so bold and they wouldn't want you.' Because he had only the hayloft, he would go off somewhere at night. He would roam around with other labourers, hurl, visit other houses. But Ned had his brother's home to go to if the farm on which he worked was not too far away. Many labourers had no such refuge. The winter nights were long and empty. Some labourers took to drinking. One Saturday night, Ned drank the whole of his week's wages. After that, he took the pledge and stuck with it. Ned said that unmarried farm labourers were pitied. He recalled, as a boy, seeing workers who were drunk, sleeping at the side of the road: 'They had no home life.'

Farm workers were not unionized. Ned's life was one of drudgery and loneliness, although he did not complain. It was simply how it had worked out and how, as he saw it, most farm workers lived. Indeed, he saw himself as lucky. He had his brother and nephews, and his work, nearby. He was a devout Catholic and an abstainer. He had been to Rome; he had taken care of his father. As he saw it, he had controlled his life and had fulfilled his obligations. He saw not the constraints that held him but the possibilities that had opened up. This was especially so with the house and its two acres. It was the only property he ever owned. He regarded it as his home place, even though he only 'fell into' it when he was elderly and even though he still lived part-time at his brother's house. For Ned, his own property was his greatest pride. He had been careful not 'to put in for it,' for that would have been unseemly. Indeed, it was also Katie Drennan's wish (Case 13.4), that someone would care for her and become her heir. Yet, for both her and Ned, circumspection in discussing or disposing of property was the ideal. So, too, was owning it. At the same time, however, work was central. Johnny and Ned could list their jobs and wages and Katie would often talk with pride about her years in a big house in England.

Being a Labourer: Life in the Working Class
Out of the many constructions and representations of labourers' lives emerge some integral socio-cultural features of working class life and experience by the early twentieth century.

Poverty
The notion of the 'poorer classes' in the early nineteenth century had given way to a more rigorous term, that of 'labourer.' Yet the new term contained elements of the former and, indeed, the two were often combined, as in 'poor labourer' ('poor angler'). As such, the term referred to an objective economic condition. For, although poverty, or the idea of the 'poor labourer,' might imply a debased moral state, it also connoted a morally neutral condition when it was caused by economic downturn and high unemployment, the life cycle (a large family, old age), or bad luck (premature death of a male household head, disability). In other words, people saw that the categories of 'well-off' worker and 'poor labourer' as two ends of a continuum. They saw that any labouring family could, through no fault of its own, be or become impoverished.

At its extreme, poverty meant the workhouse. 'Some fine, decent people had in the past through necessity to go there,' said a Kilkenny city councillor in 1919. 'It was just the ups and downs of life.' Yet this same councillor insisted that workhouse children be boarded out in order to 'remove the brand of pauperism.'[4] The stigma of the workhouse was thus palpable, and the fear of ending there was both a nightmare and a possibility. Women on their own, with children, were especially vulnerable. In 1916 Ellen Campion, employed at Ballylinch, was reported by the head constable to be unable to supervise her four children properly. They were committed to an industrial school in Kilkenny and Campion made to contribute towards their support.[5] In another case, an inspector for the Society for the Prevention of Cruelty to Children asked Thomastown's magistrates to have two children (aged eleven and five) committed because they 'had no guardianship.' Their father had joined the army but the mother had not received any money from him. The magistrates took the youngest away but had to adjourn the application on the eldest because she had not appeared in court. 'She was evidently stowed [hidden] away by some of her friends – by her aunt, the Inspector believed.'[6]

Such vulnerability, even if protested, was actualized by current or anticipated poverty. It induced emigration and enlistment in the army. Most elderly, labouring people in Thomastown in 1981 had uncles, aunts, and siblings who had emigrated in their youth. Many had never been heard from again. Most had kin who had joined the British forces; many had been killed.

Respectability and Reputation

Poverty could afflict any labouring household. It took on a moral tone only if people were seen as causing their own misfortune: alcoholism, a man 'not fond of work,' a slovenly homemaker, illegitimacy and a female-headed household, working children who did not contribute, and the like. Through such actions or inactions, the idea of poverty became implicated in a central code of local life, that of respectability.

Respectability was a quality to which people of all classes aspired and which they assigned to others. It was not, however, defined in the same way for all status-classes; nor did it mean that individuals within classes behaved or thought alike. For labouring people, faced with real economic vagaries, respectability was not based on achieving high points on an immutable scale of expectations. Rather, it had to be, and was, a flexible attribute assigned or assumed through numerous criteria, not all of which had to be satisfied all or even part of the time. As an overall assessment, it was best reflected in the attribution: 'S/he is a decent person.'

The various criteria for assigning respectability among Thomastown's labouring people were based both on people's relationships to material goods and on their appropriate behaviour. Respectable 'goods' referred to their owning, or properly caring for, personal and private property. Respectable 'behaviour' was located in five domains: language, alcohol use, religion, work, and sexuality. A respectable working-class person did not have to excel or even achieve adequacy in all these areas. As well, within each area was a great deal of leeway.

Respectability in relation to goods generally meant, by the 1920s, living in a good house, one that was 'fit for human habitation.' The 1883 Labourers Act had thus established one of the diacritical features of a quintessential respectable worker. However, not all workers could get a labourer's cottage. Keeping rental accommodation in good repair, having a productive garden where possible, and paying the rent promptly were all acceptable substitutes. Conversely, a poorly maintained cottage or an untilled garden elicited comment. In a similar way, respectable behaviour in the five areas was flexible, not only because assessments were subjective but also because moderation was crucial. Swearing was permissible but the language could not be 'abusive.' A few 'jars' were acceptable but drunkenness was not. Religious observance was important but over-zealousness ('eating the altar') raised grave suspicion, in part because it was farmers' sons who became priests and they looked down on working people. A desire to work was important even when unemployment was the reality. Indeed, in the 1980s, people seldom commented on how often a person worked because that was seen, usually, as outside a worker's control. To say, however, that someone 'was not fond of work' was a major moral statement. Finally, sexuality was private. The stigma of illegitimacy, like pauperism, was virtually ineradicable.

The behaviour of women, therefore, and their labour, was thus central for maintaining the respectability of both household and kin. However, it is important to recognize that respectability was, in its essential character, the attribute of an individual. An exemplary wife married to a n'er-do-well husband was a respectable woman. She could be pitied, for her lot was hard; but she was not to be avoided. Similarly, a decent man married to a promiscuous or alcoholic wife was to be sympathized with but also accorded respect. Even the behaviour of both spouses did not determine the reputation of their children, or vice versa. However, if too many members of a household, family, or kin net behaved badly, then suspicion began to attach to all members because it was thought that inherited attributes which 'ran in the blood' might be taking over. Even then, with proper behaviour and property, an individual could be respectable, despite his or her kin.

The problem of asserting respectability in the face of poverty, old age, or infirmity formed the plot of many local stories. A young widow on Mill Street was said to fry onions every Sunday, even though there was nothing to eat with them, so that the neighbours would think she had meat for dinner. An elderly couple in Ladywell Street left the door open while they ate so that people could see that they had two eggcups with eggs in them. In fact, the so-called eggs were only empty shells turned upside down. Such stories point to a central feature of respectability: its public presentation was key, even in the face of realities that were known to everyone.

In addition to respectability, working people had varying reputations or prestige. The cynical expression of a 'penny looking down on a ha'penny' summarized the fact of a pecking order, as did the over-zealous efforts of some working people to improve their reputations. In all this, however, the criteria for deciding who was where in the minutely graded, ever-changing hierarchy of relative prestige could never really be established. How lush did the flower garden have to be before it was too showy ('Sure, wouldn't she be better tending her children'); how white the whitewash on the house ('Only for the money sent her by her sister, they'd have nothing'); or how often was drunkenness allowed and why ('He was an awful man for drink but, sure, didn't he have cause')? All criteria were flexible. Nor was there anyone to pronounce, or any mechanism to establish, a final assessment. In any case, there was no point at which a reputation might be firmly or irrevocably fixed. Thus, claims to reputation might be made but not accepted; they might be accepted by some but not by others; or they might be differently made at different times. In other words, the politics of reputation were essential and never-ending.

Working Women

Crucial for avoiding poverty and maintaining respectability was the work of women, both waged and unwaged. Invariably unrecorded, its extent emerged only in talking with elderly women about what life was like in the past. Often, the women did not see what they had done as 'real work'; it was simply what women did. The employment history of Aggie Donovan, born in 1896, is an example (Case 13.7).[7]

Case 13.7: Aggie Donovan's Employment History

Aggie's mother died when she was eleven and her father, an alcoholic, was often unemployed. She moved in with her grandparents. She immediately began casual work for farmers. She also worked in the market garden that her grandfather kept on the one acre which was attached to his labourer's cottage. They grew cabbages and berries for sale and kept small livestock (pigs, turkeys, ducks, and chickens), also for sale. She took care of her grandparents as they aged, and she managed the money that was provided by an emigrant aunt and uncle. Aggie married a local farm labourer in 1916. Throughout the marriage, while rearing five children, she did part-time work with farmers: weeding and picking turnips; binding corn sheaves during cutting; opening sheaves for the thrashers; rubbing long grass to get the yellow seeds ('troneens'). When her last child was in school, she began part-time work as a domestic for a nearby farmer. As the children left home and/or married, they began to send money. 'It's as if they weren't married. I reared them good.' She continued to work part-time, as a domestic for local farmers and, later, in the kitchen of a pub. In 1972, at the age of seventy-six, she 'retired.'

In her own view, Aggie had never really worked except in the latter years in the pub. Yet her husband's wages, as an agricultural labourer, had been poor, and her 'non-work' had been essential in maintaining the household, economically and socially. Her case was not untypical.

Charity

To be a worker was to be exposed to the economic downturns and personal accidents that could impoverish, even if only temporarily. As the nineteenth century progressed, ad hoc relief and charitable societies, tied securely to lessons of deference, were slowly displaced by governmental institutions intended to relieve distress for particular individuals and/or in times of dearth. Ideas about 'the deserving poor,' the dangers of idleness, and the notion of poverty as a moral and punishable failing were built into these institutions and became part of their daily practice. Yet, alongside, working people had their own views on how poverty might come about. So, too, did those from the better-off classes who, in the context of the locality, continued to underwrite personal, charitable largesse. Paternalism and deference, as reciprocity, hierarchy, and exploitation, thus remained part of the working class experience in Thomastown. By the early twentieth century, such charity might be generalized from an individual to a broad category of recipients; it might be particularized between, for example, an employer and his workers; or it might be personalized between two individuals (Case 13.8)

Case 13.8: Three Cases of Charity

Generalized *charity. A large-scale farmer, William Walpole, 'placed his two woods ... at the disposal of the poor people of the parish to provide them with firewood for the coming winter.' The only condition was that none of the standing trees was to be cut down.*[8]

Particularized *charity. On St Patrick's Day was 'one of the happiest fancy dress dances ever held' at Mount Juliet 'for the servants and staff ... The servants' hall was tastefully decorated and Major and Lady Helen McCalmont showed their usual keen interest in the welfare of their employees by becoming interested spectators.'*[9]

Personalized *charity.* William Pilsworth, as churchwarden, summoned Anne Kavanagh for allowing her fowl to trespass on the graveyard and damage graves. Kavanagh was fined 2d. A month later, she was again summoned and fined a ha'penny for each fowl. She told the court that 'she was a poor lone widow and could not afford to pay the fine. On the last occasion, Mr. Pilsworth paid it, and she hoped he would again.'[10]

Housing

The importance of property and of obtaining a cottage took on an added dimension by the early 1920s. Could a labourer transmit his or her cottage to an heir? (Case 13.9).

Case 13.9: 'Inheriting' a Labourer's Cottage, 1919

Sergeant James Whelan, Royal Irish Regiment, fell out with the rural district council when he learned that, after his father had died, the council had given away 'the house occupied by himself and his parents for 26 years.' The chair maintained that his father 'had no proprietorial' or 'inheritable rights' in the cottage and that 'no relative could succeed him in the tenancy without being ... appointed by the council.' Pat Ryan, Labour councillor, supported Whelan: 'It would be a cruel hardship to deprive him of the cottage.' No one on council seconded Ryan's motion that Whelan keep the cottage. Instead, the council's solicitor was instructed 'to recover possession.' Two months later, Whelan informed the council that the new tenant, Edward Sheehan, 'had given up all claims to it.' He said that he had now been demobilized and asked to be appointed tenant. He assured 'council that practically every ratepayer in the district was in his favour.' The council also had a letter from Sheehan surrendering possession. The chair retorted that 'some undercurrent [was] working in the case' but did not elaborate. Whelan was appointed. Said the clerk: 'He had a very decent father. He was one of the best tenants we had.'[11]

In this dispute was encapsulated the basic material and symbolic divide between farmers and labourers: the ownership of fixed property. By 1919, most councillors owned their houses and lands as a result of various land acts. To gain these, they had been most vocal in denouncing English landlordism. Clearly, their rights were not to be extended to labour. However, labourers themselves had ensured the Whelan 'inheritance.' Expectations about property and kin rights were thus growing up alongside a worker's right to decent housing, provided by the state.

Poaching and Gleaning

It was not only salmon that labourers caught illegally, but also rabbits and pheasants. As Johnny Egan's story showed (Case 13.5), such game was an important part of people's diets. As in salmon-fishing cases, poaching cases provided the petty sessions with entertainment and a forum for negotiating relationships (Case 13.10).

Case 13.10: A Case of Poaching Pheasants, 1914

William Swanick, McCalmont's gamekeeper, prosecuted Patrick Gardiner for 'trespass in pursuit of game.' Swanick said that he heard a shot and saw Gardiner beating the fields. He waded across the river and saw Gardiner 'rise' a hen pheasant with his dog. Gardiner fired and 'she fell up the field.' Swanick came up to him and asked what he was doing. Gardiner said that 'he came there to train a young dog.' Chairman Connellan retorted: 'It was a very practical way of training him (laughter).' A witness, labourer Edward Gibney, swore that he asked Gardiner 'to go there to shoot an old dog for him.' Gardiner corroborated this. Chair: 'Did he ask you up to shoot a pheasant? (laughter).' Gibney said no. Chair: 'Well, that's what he did shoot (laughter).' Because Gardiner had 'never given trouble before,' he 'was fined £2 and costs, one-third of the penalty to go to the complainant.'[12]

Gleaning and gathering were also important. Berries and wild mushrooms were used as food and sometimes were sold to retailers. Firewood was important and Dangan Wood was a major source for many people who could not afford to buy fuel (Case 13.8). Because it was private property, however, altercations could occur over who could take what (Case 13.11)

Case 13.11: Gathering Firewood in Dangan Wood, 1919

The paid caretaker of the wood, Patrick Keefe, prosecuted Sarah Cox for threatening him. He said that he had found Cox and her mother with an ass and cart in the wood and, about five feet away, three bundles of newly cut, green timber. The women denied cutting the wood but, according to their testimony, Keefe put his hand on the bundle and threatened: 'Whoever cut this, it was a damn shame for them.' Cox, according to Keefe, however, had shoved him and' swore ... she would take my life.' Cox, in turn, said that she had two 'gresnas' of rotten timber and that Keefe had tried 'to tear them asunder.' Keefe interjected: 'That is a lie.' Cox did admit, however, that she 'gave Keefe a little shove.' She agreed not to threaten him again and the case was dismissed.[13]

Interpersonal Conflict and Avoidance

The altercation between Keefe and Cox points to the kind of interaction or behaviour that might emerge among labouring people. Assault, abusive language, public drunkenness, disorderly conduct, and fighting, however, were all under a person's control and they were, therefore, actions that decent, respectable working people avoided. But what if someone were continually accosted by another person to have another drink, to fight? The solution, for respectable working people, was to avoid not only the action but also the person. In part, this was the outcome of petty-sessions practices when magistrates placed people under their own recognizances to see 'how they would get on.' It was a practice adopted in the district court after 1923. It meant that some people never went to a particular pub or that they took the long route home or shopped in a different grocery. Avoidance became a central component of the working-class repertoire and of respectability.

Conclusion: Constraint, Choice, and Socio-cultural Reproduction

In the face of the odds, working people constructed both their lives and representations of their lives. Examples of how they did so highlight the flexibility and leeway of practice and belief in a context of immense constraint. Examples also show the importance of individual choice. Through these cases, then, can be seen the threads that formed the *metissage* of working-class awareness and experience in the early twentieth century and the processes of socio-cultural reproduction which underlay them.

14. The Uneven Economy and the Moral Economy, 1926–50

The population decline that began in the 1830s and accelerated thereafter resulted from persistent emigration impelled by what was an underdeveloped economy. The pulse of this economy, especially its local employment levels, engaged people of all classes in Thomastown. Depression affected not only the quality of life among workers but also their buying power in shops. Conversely, a labour scarcity meant higher wages and better work conditions which would have an impact on farmers, retailers, industrialists, and professionals. In other words, people of all classes had a direct interest in the local economy and in the condition of labour.

Such interest was heightened because labourers continued to form such a large proportion of the population. In the 1901 census (Table IV.1), 1,086 parish people gave an occupation.[1] Of these, 149 were artisans and 586 were labourers (farm, non-farm, domestic). In the context of Thomastown as an underdeveloped economy, these 735 indeed comprised a superabundance. The situation, of course, had been eased over the years by extensive emigration (Table 14.1). In 1901 the parish population was less than 40 per cent of what it had been sixty years before. Nevertheless, a reserve army of labour remained: underemployed, casual, and poorly paid. It was continually being reproduced. In 1901, 29 per cent of the people in the parish was under sixteen years of age.

Several sources give insight into the condition of the local economy and of labour and into the views of these that people had at the time. The sources include retrospective narratives, such as by Johnny Egan (Case 13.5) and Ned Forristal (Case 13.6), job histories that were collected in 1981, and the two county newspapers which published a weekly

Table 14.1: The population of Thomastown parish and town, 1841–1956

Census Year	Parish (includes the town)	% of 1841 population	Town only*	% of 1841 population
1841	7,410	–	2,335	–
1871	3,840	52%	1,202	52%
1901	2,840	38%	909	42%
1936	2,840	38%	769	33%
1951	2,620	35%	–	–
1956	–	–	1,208	52%

*It has always been difficult to ascertain where the town ends/begins vis-à-vis the countryside since there has always been fairly dense housing extending out along the various approach roads to the sixteen-acre townland of Thomastown. Census-takers therefore changed the boundary of the so-called town at various times, often without specifying precisely how. The town population is thus only an approximation.

column on Thomastown happenings and news items which might appeal to a county readership.

The Pulse of the Economy: Employment Histories

In 1981 Philip Gulliver and I collected job histories for all adults in 504 households. Among them were thirty-four men of labouring status born between 1894 and 1913. All began working between 1918 and 1927. A large number began as farm labourers (n = 14). Of these, ten later did other work, either in the primary sector, as gardener, forestry worker or groom (n = 5), or in road works (n = 5). There were four who moved up within their occupations: from tailor's assistant to tailor, millworker to roller miller, gardener to head gardener, and railway worker to station-master. Two became drivers (cab, truck) after being a garage attendant or delivery boy. Of the thirty-four, eight never changed occupations: seven were in the primary sector (farm, stables, gardens, forestry); one was a creamery worker. Four of the thirty-four had highly varied careers as caretaker, farm labourer, 'odd jobs,' lorry driver, 'timberman,' and, in two cases, the Irish army. The average number of jobs held by the thirty-four men was 3.7, but this hid immense variation: from the farm worker who put in fifty-two years in Mount Juliet to a farm labourer who held eleven jobs. Employers of these thirty-four men were not numerous: farmers, retailers, Grennan Mills, and Mount Juliet. A few unskilled jobs had also been available in the workhouse, convent, bank, and gentry houses. State employers included the county council, the electricity supply board, and the railway. Importantly, several men had worked away from Thomastown, as far as England. They did the same kind of work there as they had at home.

On the one hand, the survey suggests a complex picture from the perspective of how individuals put together their working careers. On the other hand, it suggests a simple and highly constrained picture in terms of job opportunities, choices, and possibilities for improvement.

The Pulse of the Economy: Two Retrospective Accounts

In many contexts, during my visiting, chatting, and interviewing, Thomastown people spoke about their pasts. Occasionally, they wrote something down. Two recollections are given below. The first is from Jim Doyle, born in Maudlin Street in 1916. The son of a labourer who worked in the convent laundry, he told me about the mid-1930s when he began cot fishing to fill in the time and 'earn a few bob' (Case 14.1).

Case 14.1: Jim Doyle's Recollections of the Mid-1930s, Part I
'We were unemployed. We joined the [Irish] Volunteers and did weekends without pay in Kilkenny barracks. We only received 13s. 2d. for a week of training once a year. It was simply accepted that there was no work. To get a permanent job at that age was unheard of. The county council ran a pre-Christmas scheme to give a few weeks' work.' Occasionally, Jim also broke stones for roads. This was casual work, 'until the county council ran out of money. You got a half-crown a box. Breaking stones was really a full-time job for council men; they were quicker at it. You had to learn to find the vein. You ended with blistered, bleeding hands. Extra work at the mill went to the locals. Comerfords [bakery] had no extra work, although there was a turnaround on bread boys.'

A similar pattern of casual and seasonal work, occupational multiplicity, boredom, and struggle typified not only young men but also those who had young families to support. William Pinchin, born in England, had married an emigrant daughter of a Jerpoint labourer. They came 'home' in 1926. A former British soldier, Pinchin was allocated a 'soldier's cottage' in Jerpoint, built by the Irish Soldiers' and Sailors' Trust for rental to ex-service men. Ten years later, the Pinchins left and never returned. In the 1980s, William's son, Harry, wrote about his Thomastown childhood, filtered through nostalgic hindsight, an adult lifetime in England, and the deep-seated deference that often accompanied life in the working class (Case 14.2).

Case 14.2: Selections from Harry Pinchin's Memoirs, 1926–36

'Times were tough on some families ... Money was scarce, especially for those families whose ... breadwinner ... [was] unable to acquire ... permanent employment. Therefore those families ... were always more than grateful to accept any ... employment ... regardless of how arduous the job or season or ... wages. My own dad was one of those ... Here ... are a few examples of temporary work he accepted and was grateful to do ... [He painted] the pylons of the new Shannon scheme electricity supply.' Then, 'when the road between Thomastown and Jerpoint required resurfacing, lorry loads of large flint rocks were transported from a quarry and ... distributed at equal distances all along the road ... These rocks had then to be broken down into a small suitable size ... to resurface the road. Later to be steamrolled. The method of getting these stones broken ... was ... by employing unemployed men who, by sitting down beside the road on a sack of straw and ... using a small half pound metal hammer ... would toil away breaking up these flint rocks ... This was very hard work. Fingers cut to the bone by the flint stone. And not for a very well paid wage. The arrangement for ... payment was by the amount ... broken down to the size required ... The stones broken were measured into boxes by another individual to see no dishonesty ... took place. To break one box measure of stones took quite some considerable time ... This was very hard earned money. My dad ... was very grateful ... for the wages ...

'During those years another temporary job my Dad was pleased to accept was ... when the streets of Thomastown became so ... broken up that the council decided to relay the whole area with concrete. [This] took some considerable time ... First, the wonderful old big tree was pulled out by its roots. Then all the old street surface had to be broken up and taken away ... The sides of the stream had to be reinforced ... When Market street was completed ... the Council realized that the new concrete area ... was ... far too smooth and slippery ... Horses with their carts were sliding all over the street. To overcome [this], the Council recalled the workmen: this time to sit down in the street and with hammer and cold chisel cut alternate grooves on the slant to the depth ... of 3/4 inch ... This ... seemed to suffice. But it was a long and laborious job. However, the workmen ... did not seem to mind. It was money earned.

'Dad was temporary [sic] employed by Mr Hoyne [retailer] to ... wrap [and] pack turkeys ... for [export at] Christmas. He was [also] self-employed ... to collect holly, moss, ivy and various ferns, bring them home, pack them within hesson sacks, label them, transport them by rail to the various florists within the capital *to be used in the manufacture of holly wreaths ... Moneywize this project was far from successful. On another occasion Dad was delighted to redecorate the complete interior of the Mall [doctor's] House, a very ... large house with the most beautiful orchard ... And what an experience to have seen that wonderful ... kitchen ... with its very old black ranges for cooking, all heated by coal.*

'... The Lawn Tennis Club ... had two courts. For a considerable ... time, my Dad was the caretaker. During the winter, he would repair any broken windows [and] seats, paint the pavilion and all that was required ... Due to a change in circumstances, my Dad was unable to spend sufficient time to keep the courts in the peak condition required. I was then approached by the ... club and asked if I thought I could take over the job. I was delighted to accept: ... to cut the grass, roll it, and mark the white lines. The ... people then using the courts were the bank clerks and shop proprietors ... [At] the home matches, ... I was always ... invited to help the local ladies at the pavilion to prepare the tea by keeping kettles boiling.'

The Pinchins had great difficulty surviving economically. In 1929 William Pinchin was summoned for rent arrears. The court gave an eviction order.[2] The image of the times is equally bleak: either back-breaking labour, the wages for which a son recalls with gratitude, or small, unremunerative enterprises. Equally clear is kindness from some people of other status-classes: the tennis club members who hired the son part-time when his father was no longer able to do all the work. This, of course, was part of a more general pattern whereby labourers' sons, in the mill or creamery, for example, joined their fathers at the behest of labourers themselves and with the collusion of employers. It meant that the permanently employed were seen to have a complete monopoly on the best jobs. Still, there were never enough jobs to go around. Even constant workers saw most of their children struggling to earn a living or emigrating.

The Pulse of the Economy: *Thomastown Notes* through Time

Ned Maher, son of a car driver, was born in 1885. He began working at age fourteen as a farm servant. When he married Labour councillor Pat Ryan's sister in 1913, he was already a local journalist. He was a member of the Trade and Labour League and he joined the IT&GWU. In his weekly newspaper column, *Thomastown Notes*, Maher gave local news (deaths, sports, events) and reviews of the local economy, as well as information on employment or lack thereof and working conditions.

Maher thus expressed how labouring people, like himself, saw their condition. Equally, of course, the column expressed how Thomastown people were being told to see by journalist Maher.

From both perspectives, an analysis of Maher's column over time shows the gradual rise of a common-sense idea that the Irish state should provide, and could be induced to provide, sufficient public projects to furnish jobs for underemployed local men and, thus, to alleviate unemployment. Insofar as such public works improved local amenities for people of all classes, broad support for these works emerged. In turn, arguments about the broad-based advantages of particular amenities became a useful discursive tactic for procuring the works from government in the first instance. In all, it was a conjuncture in which labouring experiences of underemployment came to underwrite a general, local notion that public works and employment were interdependent ideals. This view linked people from all classes in a common concern that found expression in a slowly deepening sense of localism. As part of this, local people also developed the idea that private employers should be encouraged to maintain their enterprises in the locality and, thus, the workers whom they employed. In other words, in a labour-surplus economy, notions of local employment and public works together became a central material and discursive motif. In tracing its growth after 1927 through Maher's column, one can also draw a picture of the evolving local economy, socio-economic conditions, and values and morality.

A Model of Employment, Amenities, and State: Structuring Common Sense
In early 1927 Maher wrote an article entitled 'Relieving Unemployment.' He said that 'practically all the unemployed in the district who are willing to work have been provided with employment' on the Shannon electricity project. This had been accomplished 'through the agency of ... the painstaking manager of the local unemployment office.' As a result, 'up to 50 men have been taken on.' Wages were 8½d. per hour and daily work hours averaged from 11 to 12. 'Therefore, workers will not receive less than £2 weekly.' A month later, Maher reported that the scheme was employing over eighty men from Thomastown, Ballyhale, and Graigue.[3] Clearly, in Maher's view, access to jobs on non-local, government schemes was through the actions of relevant agents. It also was important that these jobs provide what he saw as acceptable wages and working conditions.

Later in 1927, Maher highlighted another dimension when he reported that the tarring of Thomastown's streets was in progress. Not only were 'about a dozen men ... employed' but the 'work was badly needed as ... it was difficult to keep the streets clean.' Maher thus linked the provision of jobs to the simultaneous need for public amenities. In contrast, when he reported that 2,500 Christmas turkeys had been packaged at a local retailer's for export to England, he made no mention of wages, working conditions, or public benefits.[4] A different morality obtained when it came to temporary and seasonal work for the private sector.

Then, in early 1928, twenty-six farmers asked for a drainage scheme to alleviate periodic flooding in the northern part of the parish, adjacent to Tullaherin. A deputation to the county council was led by Tullaherin's parish priest, Father Drennan. He asked that their request be forwarded to the commissioner for public works. He also said that rates were already high and the farmers did not want a council loan which would have to be repaid. Instead, he asked the council to recommend that the monies be allocated from the central government's Unemployment Relief Fund. A councillor asked if it could be proved that there was unemployment in the district. Drennan replied that 'we can get sufficient proof of that to get a grant.' Councillor O'Gorman observed that, the previous year, 'a good many people in the Thomastown area were working on the roads, and the Shannon scheme.' However, in the current year, 'there was a great many unemployed, and he would ask the council to especially recommend that a portion of the £150,000 for the relief of unemployment be spent on this scheme.' It did so.[5] Thus was reflected the dependence of labour on the agency of people from other status-classes for external funding for public works and, hence, jobs. Certainly such people did not themselves want to pay for easing unemployment. Reflected too, of course, was labour's failure to frame local projects for itself.

In such a context, works of all kinds could be suggested, small as well as large. In early 1928, it was the town's underground stream that received attention. A deputation to the county council from the town's retailers asked that the stream be cleaned. Paved twenty-eight years before, it had begun to overflow and flood the streets, 'damaging property and shops and making the atmosphere unhealthy.' The county council agreed to spend £300. Three years before, labourers in Ladywell had failed in a similar request to the rural district council.[6] Now, however, with the county council as the local authority, Maher tried to emulate the strategy being developed by farmers and retailers. In late 1928, he began to harp on a housing shortage and the 'many complaints' being made. He reminded readers that over £3000 was left from the rural district council for building labourers' cottages. Ten houses, he wrote, could be built for that sum 'if proper representations' were made to the County Board of Health (that is, the housing authority). Unfortunately, said Maher, Thomastown had only one representative on the board and this would affect the outcome. Nothing in fact came from Maher's agitation.[7]

Two observations can be drawn from Maher's efforts and the different outcomes of the various attempts to alleviate flooding in 1925 and 1928. The abolition of the rural district council by the centralizing Free State had altered the meaning of 'local' decision making. Farmers and retailers, as well as labourers, now had to access a distant council. Yet nuances remained. Parish priests who led deputations for farmers and retailers never did so for labourers' housing.

Alongside such developments, Maher's review of local economic conditions continued. In late 1928 he noted 'considerable unemployment in Thomastown. Large numbers of ... workers are on the dole. The advertisement for re-building the courthouse and the acceptance of the contract is being anxiously looked forward to by the unemployed workers.' Three weeks later, he reported that the county council had accepted a tender for the work.[8] In the autumn of the next year, he again referred to high unemployment and the fact that 'prospects for the unemployed and their families look gloomy for the winter.' Few labourers were employed on the roads while other works that had provided jobs for the previous six months (courthouse, Mount Juliet housing) had been completed. Yet, as he pointed out, 'well over 100 men and women are in constant employment on the Mount Juliet estate.' In the town, Grennan Mills and the Ryan tannery were also large employers, 'but it must be admitted that traders in general employ as many hands as they reasonably can afford or have work for.'[9]

Nine months later, Maher was able to report that the work of cleaning the sewer which had caused flooding and 'much inconvenience to shopkeepers' would begin two days later, using direct labour supervized by the council's overseer. He added that there was 'very little unemployment in Thomastown district at present.' Indeed, at that time, in July 1930, Maher cheerfully bragged about the buoyant local economy and the reasons for it (Case 14.3).

Case 14.3: The Buoyant Local Economy, July 1930 to Mid-1931

'Few towns in this or any other county can boast of the unique distinction of having no unemployment in their midst ... [It] is due to the scheme of road improvement, building ... at Mount Juliet, cleaning the main sewer in the town, and other minor works [for example, hay making] which have absorbed all the unemployed workers. Such a happy state of affairs has not existed ... for many years ... It is a great boon to the workers and their families as well as to the local merchants.' Maher's lively discourse was induced, too, by the 'prosperous conditions' at Grennan Mills. The mill used its own lorries and the latest machinery, bought grain from local farmers who were thus provided with 'a ready market,' and employed 'a large number of contented hands' who were paid the 'recognized trade union wage for mill workers' and who had 'a week's holidays each year with full wages.' The owners 'are deservedly popular and have always been ... generous supporters of all classes of sport in the county.'

In early 1931 Maher happily reported that the roads department had granted £5,500 to the county council for concreting the town streets and steamrolling the main road to Kilkenny city. 'It is to be hoped,' he wrote, 'that all the unemployed workers in the district will be employed at the work before those from other districts are brought in, as unfortunately has too often been the case.' Two months later, it was disclosed that the drainage scheme near Tullaherin would be built. Maher wrote that the news had come via the Dáil representative, Tom Derrig, who in turn had been informed by the public works' commissioner. Within six weeks, work had begun using direct labour. It was 'expected to last six months and absorb all unemployed workers in Thomastown and surrounding district. Wages are ... 27s. per week.' A week later, Maher jingoistically noted again that 'Thomastown is one of the few towns in the Free State which can boast of having no unemployment problem.' The above schemes had 'absorbed the unemployed workers within a radius of 6 miles. A number of men ... unemployed since last summer, are glad to cycle 20 miles a day, to and from work. Few county councils in the Free State have done more to cope with the unemployment problem than Kilkenny.'[10]

In depicting a buoyant, local economy and an effective local government, Maher located the cause in extensive state intervention and large private enterprises which provided employment. Alongside, small enterprises hired as much labour as they could. It was a view that was parochial, however: only local workers should be employed.

How had booming economic conditions come to Thomastown? The answer was via successful agency in the public sector. Public works using external funding created employment but it had to be 'looked for.' It had to be extracted by making 'proper representations.' This meant that local opinion had to be fomented and the county bureaucracy leaned on through connections in both the county council and the Dáil. All this brought public monies and employment. It also brought direct labour schemes and decent wages.

These were the viewpoints that Maher had fully espoused by 1931 and that he propounded in his weekly column. It was a perspective that came to have wide currency and that became deeply enmeshed in common sense.

Making Common Sense Work: Morality and Economy

Six weeks after the drainage scheme began, its thirty workers were on strike. They had demanded a 3s. increase on their weekly wage of 27s. It was refused. The men maintained that, because they were not paid for wet days when they could not work, the weekly wage was only about 22s.6d. The engineer from the Board of Works countered that the men were doing agricultural work and, outside Dublin County, the highest wage was 27s. A meeting ensued among Father Drennan, local farmers, the engineer, and a workers' spokesman. It was agreed that the men would return to work at the same wage but that the drainage committee, made up of priest and farmers, would apply 'to the proper quarter for a reasonable increase in wages.'[11] In fact, Johnny Egan recalled that the strikers had wanted the same 30s. per week pay as council workers. The strikers were not, however, members of a union and, as 'poor' casuals, they had little withholding power. Nothing was achieved.

The strike signalled that international depression was reaching the locality. Falling farm prices, as Maher reported in late 1931, meant that 'some farmers in south Kilkenny find themselves reluctantly obliged to reduce the number of their employees.' He noted the seriousness of this, 'especially [for] married men with families, who have poor prospects of obtaining employment during the winter.' Appealing to moral sensibilities, he said: 'It is hoped that employers ... will not inflict undue hardship if they possibly can avoid it by dispensing with the services of married employees at this season of the year.' He noted, however, that 'unfortunately, we find employers ... who have reduced their staffs, advertising their example to other employers, regardless of the hardship and misery that may be caused to helpless families.'[12]

In Maher's view, employment was a moral affiliation as well as an economic one. It should be rooted in principled behaviour which insulated the vulnerable from all but the most severe economic exigencies. However, as Maher was soon to report, the putative moral bases of contractual relationships were also affected by politics. In March 1932 the Fianna Fáil party came to power. Its aim was to develop national self-sufficiency. It introduced protective tariffs on industry and withheld land annuity monies owed to Britain.[13] The result was the Economic War between the two countries – a war of countervailing tariffs and import quotas. The effect in Ireland was to depress agriculture and to cut severely into farm incomes which, in turn, dampened consumption and the local market for Irish goods.[14] From Thomastown's perspective, the Economic War brought the world's great depression to the locality. In mid-1932, Maher responded to lay-offs on Mount Juliet estate, as did the editor of the Kilkenny *People* (Case 14.4).

Case 14.4: Firing Mount Juliet Workers – Two Views in 1932

Ned Maher: 'A sensation was caused ... when it became known that Major McCalmont ... had dispensed with 19 employees and reduced the wages of the remaining 200 by 15 per cent. Four of the dismissed employees will receive a pension of 12s.6d weekly. On the eve of the introduction of the Free State budget, Major McCalmont [said] ... that, in the event of an increase in income tax ... he would reluctantly be obliged to make drastic economies, and reduce the wages of the entire staff, as well as their number. On the following day, Major and Lady Helen McCalmont left on a Mediterranean cruise ... The reduction in numbers and wages means a loss in trade of close on £100 a week to the merchants of Thomastown among whom the greater portion of the wages of the Mount Juliet staff is spent.'

The editor of the People: 'It is certain that nobody regrets the necessity of [lay-offs] more than Major McCalmont who, it will be universally admitted, has been extremely generous in the employment he afforded and in his benefactions and patronage in various directions. It is, we are sure, with the greatest reluctance that he has taken this step and ... only because of the circumstances of the times.'[15]

The views of both writers were similar: times were bad but local, private employers were good. Maher, however, added local knowledge and gave his report a critical, political slant. He imputed some hard-nosed planning by the major and downplayed his moral past. He then blithely noted that while local workers and retailers were suffering the 'economies,' McCalmont was on a cruise. In contrast, the discourse of the *People* editor was distant and ritualized, focused solely on the *noblesse oblige* that unfortunately could not be maintained at the time.

However, there still was the state. At the time of the Mount Juliet lay-offs, Maher reported on several small-scale public works which were providing 'much needed employment' for 'a large number of workers and carters.' Concreting two town streets and a new bridge on the town's outskirts led him to 'hope' that work would ' be found for those who have registered at the local unemployment office.' Then, too, there was Grennan Mills. The tariff on foreign flour and the inelastic demand for bread had caused a boom in milling. The mill began three shifts, twenty-four hours a day. Four motor lorries, a number of horses and carts, and, occasionally, hired motor lorries were working continually. Extra workers were hired and Maher thought more might be taken on. He also noted that the average weekly wage was up to 42s.6d. plus overtime, with one week's holiday on full pay each year. Maher added that local retailers were 'highly gratified.'[16]

It is highly unlikely that Maher's enthusiastic assessment of the mill's impact on the local economy and on unemployment was entirely shared. Labourers were aware that, while millworkers were paid more than 42s. a week, county council workers received 30s., drainage workers 23s. to 27s. depending on the weather, pensioned Mount Juliet employees 12s.6d. and old age pensioners, dependent on the non-contributory state pension, 10s. This awareness of 'local conditions,' as juxtaposed with the varying material circumstances of individual labourers, was an important consideration throughout the period.

The Pulse of the Economy in the Early 1930s: Amenities and Jobs

By the early 1930s, people of all classes had come to see certain amenities as desirable: sanitary sewage disposal, a dump site, potable water, decent housing, and electric lighting. Many of these desires had been generated over the previous half century by growing state intervention in public health and housing. The Shannon electricity project, built by the state, had also brought electricity to some parts of the country. Other parts, like Thomastown, wanted the same. Meanwhile, rising living standards after the 1860s or so had led to rising expectations. When such desires were linked to a continuing need to generate employment in the locality, these amenities became the crux upon which local parochialism crystallized (Case 14.5).

Case 14.5: Seeking Amenities for Thomastown, 1932–4
A fresh water supply *was discussed in early 1933, when the doctor, mill owner Pilsworth, and several retailers and notables attended a CYMS meeting. Water was coming from private wells, natural springs, or public pumps built by the rural district council during the previous half century in various locales in town and countryside. A committee was now appointed 'to progress forward.' Because two representatives were taken from each town street, baker-artisan Jim Cahill and retired postman James Lee were on the committee. At a subsequent meeting of the County Board of Health, a member plumped for Thomastown. The county engineer was asked to prepare a plan; nineteen months later, the commissioner for public health had the engineer's report. It still had to be approved by the department.*
Housing. *A public meeting presided over by the curate was attended by Pilsworth and several retailers and notables where it was said that, in some cases, two or three families were living in the same house. They appointed a deputation to the Board of Health. It included millworker James O'Neill.*
Dumping site. *At the same meeting, Pilsworth suggested that the deputation for housing also 'raise the need for a rubbish dump outside the town.'*
Electric lighting. *A retailer wrote to the Kilkenny Board of Health that the 'traders and users of electric light' had decided to send a memorial to the Electricity Supply Board (ESB) to get the Shannon project extended to Thomastown.*[17]

Maher also played his role by mobilizing opinion in the locality through the use of dramatic and provocative rhetoric. He called for local patriotism and for people of all classes to combine (Case 14.6).

Case 14.6: The Discourse of Development in Thomastown, 1934
'No town in County Kilkenny ... [is] so badly in need of a pure water supply as Thomastown. There are but two public pumps in the vicinity of the town, and one is frequently out of order. A public sewer runs by the side of the pump in Logan Street and the water has long ... been regarded as a menace to health ... The people ... are practically depending on the courtesy of owners of private pumps ... A gravitation supply for ... Graigue is about to be provided at a cost of £3,600 towards which the ratepayers of Thomastown will be obliged to contribute. In Thomastown ... waste ground cannot be provided for ... refuse, while a ... field has been obtained for the same purpose ... [in] Tullaroan. At present, the side of the road leading to the railway station is utilized as a dumping ground ... with the result that it is infested with rats ... The merchants and principal ratepayers are

not entirely free from responsibility for [this] ... They are content to pay for water and sewerage schemes for other towns while [their own] town ... is sadly neglected. A few months ago, a move was made to have a pure water and sewerage scheme as well as a refuse ground provided, but because Thomastown had no local representative on the Kilkenny Board of Health, the scheme fell through. Is it too much to hope that the merchants and ratepayers of the town will ... now ... appoint a deputation to wait on Commissioner Meghen?[18]

Maher called for a combination to put Thomastown's case to the authorities, to use an argument about the relative rights of a particular locality, and to demand the town's due. Because local ratepayers contributed to the general purse, they were entitled to whatever any other locality was given. For this purpose, Maher appealed to the leadership of the 'merchants and principal ratepayers.' He did so because of the desperate need for jobs. Indeed, his agitation at the time was propelled by the most serious unemployment to date. He noted, for example, that many road workers 'had not worked one week during the present year, and with winter approaching, the prospects are very gloomy for themselves and their families.' As depression deepened, at least eight Thomastown labourers between the ages of seventeen and thirty-six joined the Irish Volunteer (Reserve) Force, stationed in Kilkenny. It was a stopgap. Said Jim Doyle in hindsight: 'There was nothing else to do.' A few months later, Maher reported that fifty labourers had five weeks' work on an afforestation project at Inistioge. He again wrote about the unusually high unemployment and pointed out that it would likely continue because the previous ten years had seen virtually all the main roads tarred and steamrolled. Maher, however, moved on: 'The public are at a loss to know the reasons for the delay in starting the [town's] housing scheme as well as the cottage scheme in the rural districts.' He said that 'the Dáil representatives for the constituency, irrespective of party, ought to be asked to push forward both schemes. If a start was made, much needed employment would be provided.' Indeed, despite the hardship, Maher carefully pointed out that the council's rent collector had collected 'the *total* rents and rates amounting to £225.12.6 due on labourers' cottages for that quarter.'[19] In other words, labourers were holding up their part of a contractual relation despite severe economic hardship. The state, therefore, should hold up its part by providing more houses and jobs.

In such ways was the contractual and moral tie between workers and employers extended to the relation between workers and the state. It was replicated, too, in the relation between labourers and their political representatives who were expected to mediate so as to expedite both amenities for the locality and jobs for the labourers. What was muted, so far, was the issue as to who, precisely, would provide this mediation. Moreover, insofar as combination from 'merchants and principal rate-payers' was touted as most efficacious, another issue was how much labourers should depend on their efforts. Most generally, however, it was clear to everyone that they had become increasingly dependent on state intervention for satisfying local needs and wants. Local patriotism and local disempowerment were mutually constitutive processes.

The Pulse of the Economy, 1936–50: Processes of Reproduction

The 'feast and famine' of local economic life continued. However, by the mid-1930s, the worst was over. In early 1936 Maher reported that local trade before Christmas had been much better than in the previous three years.[20] The kinds of work that contributed to this, and the economic events that he saw as ensuing, are described in Case 14.7.

Case 14.7: The Local Economy through Thomastown Notes,
June 1936–Autumn 1938

1936. June. *New machinery was installed in Grennan Mills. It was now 'one of the best equipped in the Free State.' Extensive repairs to the parish church led to 'a good deal of local labour' being hired by the Waterford contractor.* August. *'Few were unemployed' because of work on the church, roads, new cottages, and harvest.'* November. *Twenty-five labourers were building fences and gates on a Jerpoint estate which was being divided by the Land Commission for allocation in ten-acre plots to local farm labourers.* December. *Men were employed to 'groove' the concreted streets of the town. Farm prices improved and 'large numbers of fat pigs' were 'being conveyed ... each week [to] the railway station.' This gave work to carters and higher profits for the labouring households which reared pigs. Thomastown electoral division received an £800 grant and Maher reported that 'there has seldom been so little unemployment in the town at this season of the year.'*

1937. January. *Three motor cars and a motor lorry had been bought by local residents and two cars and a delivery van were on order. 'Notwithstanding the economic war,' said Maher, 'Thomastown is certainly holding its own, if not progressing.' Thirteen cottages in Newtown and Grennan were completed and handed over to labouring tenants.* February. *The Thomastown creamery purchased a new lorry to pick up farmers' milk. The permanent workforce was expanded to include a lorry driver and helper. The so-called 'good news,' as Maher called it, continued.* Autumn. *Thirty men were hired to erect poles for bringing ESB lighting from Jerpoint to the town of Graigue. Contractors were completing the £2,000 sewerage scheme which had given work to twenty men during the previous three months.*

1938. June. *Under a Shops Act, the town's retailers arranged a forty-eight-hour week for assistants.* Summer. *'A number of Thomastown folk have left on their annual holidays ... Some years ago, holidays were unknown, except to public officials and those ... with plenty of the world's goods. Nowadays, all classes, with the exception of farmers and agricultural labourers, enjoy at least a week's annual holiday.'* Autumn. *A slight downturn. The ESB and road workers were discharged. Maher reported 'much unemployment' with prospects gloomy for winter. However, a few weeks later, Thomastown division received £500 under a Part-time Employment Scheme. Unemployed road workers were given three days' work weekly. 'The amount the workers will receive ... will be only a bare existence, but "half a loaf is better than no bread."'*

1939. January. *The Board of Health disclosed that a Carrick-on-Suir contractor was to start forty-four cottages the following month. Maher warned that 'there ought to be no importation of tradesmen or labourers into Thomastown' and that men who intended to work on the scheme should learn about 'wage rates and conditions of employment before starting ... so as to obviate the possibility of strikes.' It was to be, in other words, a local project and a unionized site.*[21]

The portrait of the local economy was of improving material conditions. Technological progress was visible in new mill machinery and motorized transport. A finer church interior, fewer working hours for retail employees, and summer vacations for many 'folk' signalled better living standards. So, too, did, the few new permanent jobs for drivers, higher pig prices, and more work for carters. Yet the local economy remained rooted in its older production forms: mill, farm, and public works. Carters were threatened by new transport technology and local entrepreneurship was stifled as the contractors for government schemes came entirely from outside the locality. In such a context, casual workers lurched from one job to the next and from one job to the dole, depending on government works, relief schemes, and seasonal farm work. Labourers, however, were able to control many of the work sites to ensure that most workers were locals. Some sites, too, were unionized.

'The Emergency' and After

With the Second World War, three new buyers emerged for men's labour power: the British war economy, the Irish national army, and the British army. Maher began to comment on the 'deplorable' situation for young men who, unable to find work locally, were 'obliged to seek employment in what used to be known as "the enemy country."' These 'self-respecting young men,' he said, 'have refused to draw the miserable 6s. per week dole or become a burden on their parents.' He reported on recruiting agents from English construction firms who set up in Waterford, hiring 'married as well as single men.' As the war years progressed, Maher continually related how 'still they go' – to England and to 'guaranteed employment.' However, he also told of those who enlisted in the Irish army and the Local Defence Force. He provided the prices for rabbits and news of relief schemes which provided part-time work, the progress of the forty-four-houses, and the number of men working on the roads.[22] After the Emergency, these themes and this discourse continued to frame and express local views in *Thomastown Notes* (Case 14.8).

Case 14.8: Themes and Discourses after the Emergency, 1945–50

Turkeys were still dispatched to England and the prices for rabbits listed. In mid-1946, Maher informed people that there was little unemployment because of several temporary projects (tree felling, painting the railway bridge, renovating two big houses). A new Thomastown Flood Committee, made up of miller Pilsworth and retailers, had obtained £1,000 to repair the bridge and clean the river near the town after a disastrous flood in 1947. These works, it was carefully noted, were done by 'the employees of the county council' (that is, not casual labour). The county council gave Thomastown a fire engine and established a brigade, thus providing part-time work for five labourers. Grennan Wood was reforested, employing a 'big staff of workmen.' A scheme of twenty-four houses was begun, using direct labour. A contract for a new boy's primary school was given to a Galway contractor and a dozen men had work for six months. The county council planned a new water scheme. Yet, noted Maher, 'still, they emigrated.'[23]

In 1950, alongside the amenities and services that had come out of the previous twenty-five years, the rising expectations, and the quickened pace of government intervention, continuity was clear. It could be seen in the division between the permanent and casual workers, the use of direct as opposed to contract labour on government projects, and the impulsion for the young to emigrate. It could also be found in the motifs and issues that Maher had long addressed and that had become a way for local people to envision their locality, define issues, and approach solutions. Importantly, too, Ned Maher's labouring world was a world of men (Case 14.9).

Case 14.9: Maher's World of Men in 1950

A local road was repaired (cost: £492) but, the following month, twelve permanent forestry workers were fired because no land remained to be planted. Some had been employed almost fifteen years. However, fifteen men were taken on by the ESB to erect poles for the rural-electrification scheme with more to be employed later. In July, Maher wrote that there was now 'no unemployment ... Electrification, forestry, housing, road improvements and ... drainage schemes have absorbed all unemployed workers in the area.' Major McCalmont increased the wages of over 100 employees by 6s. per week. Later that year, Maher wrote that labourers Danny Lennon, Donal Hennessy, and Ollie Langfry had emigrated.[24]

The Quality of Life in the Mid-1930s

The state of the economy and the aggregate description of local conditions did not necessarily capture the life of the individual. Jim Doyle (Case 14.1) and his wife, Chris, provided insight into some of these (Case 14.10).

Case 14.10: Jim Doyle's Recollections of the Mid-1930s, Part II

'It was a parochial life. We were so cut off from the world. There was no radio and only a few newspapers. There was very low political consciousness. And the church preached its view. You took being poor for granted. There was no sense of being hard done by; that's just how it was. I would have liked to go to St. Kieran's [college], but it was 11 miles away and there was no money. There was no sense of radicalism at being deprived ... Education belonged to people who could afford it. And that's how it was. There was so much poverty and so little to be had. One was grateful for a job with a wage at a subsistence level. It was extraordinary. There was no class resentment at being deprived.'

But there was fear. Jim and a friend once went to a fair in Kilkenny and stopped in for tea and a bun. The charge, 10d., was more money than they had. They had not expected it to be so much. The publican threatened to call the guards, and they were terrified of the police. So they gave the publican what they had and went hungry for the rest of the day. They did not blame the publican.

Jim: He was just getting as much as he could out of a fair day. But we were frightened of the police.

Chris [Jim's wife]: 'Life was drab. Clothes were dull, so as "not to show dirt." Women looked old. Houses were dark – without electricity, only candles. There were small windows and deep sills. The food was monotonous. Breakfast was yellow meal (oatmeal, later on), sugar and occasionally an egg. Hoyne's shop sold cracked eggs very cheaply. They were no good for export. Tea. Dinner was potatoes, cabbage or turnips. Carrots were uncommon; there were no beans or peas and no tins.

'[Q]: Meat? – [Chris]: Sausages. Stews were common. You were never hungry but there was never any variety. Tea [supper] was an egg, home-made jam and bread.

'[Q]: What about recreation? – [Jim]: There was handball, and hurling on the fair green or in a field where you'd be hunted out. There was cards in houses in winter. For a penny or ha'penny you could spend an evening at it. And there was rabbit hunting. Everyone did that using snares, traps and terriers. Farmers were happy to let you on their land, as long as you didn't tear up walls to get at the rabbits. There was fishing for fluke or eel. No skill was needed; just a hook and stick. And there was orchard robbing ...

'[Q]: Did every one go to Mass in the 1930s? – [Jim]: They might stay outside the door, but they came. You'd be stigmatized if you didn't. It wasn't a horrible existence. You didn't know anything else or what happened anywhere else, in Waterford for example.

'[Q]: Were there strangers in town? – [Jim]: New guards, nuns, priests. Otherwise it was static. But Mount Juliet was different; workers came from Scotland. Otherwise, there was little movement; and the scandals weren't that numerous. But if an unfortunate girl got pregnant, Canon Doyle would announce from the altar: "Another bastard coming into our community."And everyone knew who it was.'

Conclusion: A Story of the Tannery and the Image of the Labourer

Dynamics of underdevelopment, an uneven economy, and experiences of underemployment gave rise to understandings as to how the Free

State worked, how public amenities and local jobs were connected, how proper representations were made, and how morality and economic ties were linked. This common sense became shared by people of all classes as it found expression in a deepening sense of localism. The idea of 'Thomastown' that journalist Maher both presented and represented between 1930 and 1950 was of an unbounded district comprised of people who, for various reasons, were concerned with amenities and jobs and of people who were competing with other localities for the patronage of the state. Dependency, localism, and empowerment became mutually complementary. Yet it was the workers in the locality who struggled with the poor job market, limited choices, and meagre possibilities for advancement. Although material conditions improved somewhat after 1936, it was the result of the old economy being reproduced, along with its uneven distribution of benefits. The differences between permanent and casual workers remained palpable. The future for the young was bleak. Emigration flourished.

In such a context, local people came to hold different opinions about who or what was the best way to obtain state largesse. This was highlighted in the 1980s by a story told by several elderly people as to why the tannery closed. In 1932 it was doing poorly. Fianna Fáil had formed the government and owner Michael Ryan was approached with a view to it being nationalized. Ryan was offered the manager's position. He sought advice from the parish priest. Both were pro-Treaty, supporters of the opposition party (Cumann na nGaedheal). Ryan was urged by Father Doyle not to acquiesce to the government. To thwart it further, Ryan bought the adjacent currier's tannery to prevent it getting a foothold there. Thomastown's tannery closed soon after while the government developed a tannery in Portlaw which employed four hundred workers. It was all because the priest feared nationalization and an influx of labourers into Thomastown.

In fact, the tannery's closing was a harbinger of the future. For that future, Maher had (re)presented an image not only of the locality but also of its labourers. Maher never suggested that workers form a contracting cooperative or become contractors themselves. He never suggested that labourers frame public projects which could be sought from the state. Instead, both he and his labouring colleagues, from an industrial-union position, saw themselves strictly as wage earners. As a reflection of this, workers could look back from the 1980s and see their lives at the time as filled with drab poverty, struggle, and fear which were not resented but simply accepted.

15. The Quality of Charity, Values, and Entitlements, 1908–50

'No one wants to rock the boat except against a working man.'
– Ned Ryan, cot fisher/labourer

The ways in which Thomastown's labourers viewed both themselves and people of other classes and status-classes hinged on at least three features. First, it rested on a worker's personal ties to individuals from other classes. Second, it depended on the ways in which people of other classes viewed labourers as a group and concerned themselves with their condition. Third, it evolved out of how labouring people assessed their own economic and social place in the locality and their perceptions of their rights as citizens. What were these viewpoints, in what ways did they change, and what were the implications for ideas about locality and class?

Changing Viewpoints, Persisting Structures

During the first half of the twentieth century, as at other times, some people from non-labouring classes concerned themselves with the welfare of workers. Through time, these agents changed. So, too, did ideas about how the archetype of 'labourer' was to be defined and by whom. The process can be illustrated through the issue of public health.

The men elected to the Thomastown Board of Guardians prior to its dissolution in 1926 believed that they were the legitimate caretakers of the public weal. They took this view because of the authority that the board had as an administrative agent of the state, their perceived obligations to those who had elected them, and their self-perception of being, for the most part, strong farmers and ratepayers whose opinions on public issues were knowledgeable and apposite. The resident gentry of the district were also concerned with public health. Partly this fell under the rubric of caring for the poor and providing charity for the deserving, behaviour that had a long history in the locality. Partly it was because they were interested in the health of their employees. Not only did healthy labourers work better, but a good employer was impelled to help pay the costs of illness. For various reasons, then, people of various status-classes saw themselves as responsible for public health and, hence, for labouring people as a group and for labouring individuals. In the early twentieth century, competing jurisdictional claims over public health led to conflict (Case 15.1).

Case 15.1: The Contest over Public Health, 1908

In 1908 an advertisement was placed in the Moderator, *signed by the parish priest and curate, doctor, and all the wives of the resident gentry and notables. It asked for applications for the position of district nurse, to be paid £100 per year from a voluntary subscription fund. The nurse was to work 'all over the country' and teach 'the poor ... proper sanitation procedures.' She would 'work under ... a medical practitioner' and was 'not allowed to interfere with the religious opinions of patients or their families.' Her patients, 'when able, are encouraged to make some contribution to the funds of the organisation.' The response of the guardians was to pass a resolution, put by R.J. Ryan (Sinn Fein), which 'condemned the proposed hiring ... considering it an insult to the guardians and ratepayers since four nurses were already employed by the guardians to serve the district.'*

In fact, the four nurses worked in the fever hospital/workhouse and did not visit homes. Three weeks later, councillor Lindsay came to discuss the matter. He said that he had spoken with Ryan who had not changed his opinion. Lindsay said that 'a nurse would be a good thing for the poor. As well as tending sickness she could teach them how to cook and how to keep their places clean. The people were willing to subscribe and he thought it a pity that there should be dissension on the matter.' He explained that the nurse would be Catholic and this was 'fair as the majority of the people were Catholic.' He said that Father Bowe had approved when that guarantee was given. Bowe came in. He 'did not see why [the guardians] should interfere in this matter when the guarantee was given that it would be a Catholic nurse for a Catholic institution. After some discussion, Ryan said that he had changed his mind and proposed they withdraw their previous resolution. This was unanimously passed.'[1]

From the efforts of the Catholic clergy and Protestant gentry, the Thomastown District Nursing Association came into being. Every year thereafter, the wives of the council clerk, mill bookkeeper, millwright, and numerous gentlemen collected small sums in their neighbourhoods to pay some of the costs. However, over 90 per cent of the volunteered funds came from the gentry. During 1911, the nurse made 2,502 visits. The households that she visited were headed by bakers, blacksmiths, charwomen, labourers, farmers, tailors, millers, grooms, shoemakers, fishers, postmen, and constables. Clearly, the association was for working people, organized by the gentry with the endorsement of the parish priest and, in part, funded by labourers themselves. However, the contest over public health had not ended. Although the parish priest had forced the farmers on council to withdraw their opposition, this did not mean that they had to cooperate (Case 15.2)

Case 15.2: The Contest over Public Health, 1913
Colonel F. Shore (later Lord Teignmouth), an executive member of the Nursing Association, wrote to the rural district council to correct a recently published statement made by the guardians that the district nurse 'was simply a midwife' and that she was paid for by the Women's National Health Association. He reiterated what the guardians already knew: her salary and expenses were 'defrayed by the residents of Thomastown and the vicinity.' He added that her services were 'appreciated by the poor of the neighbourhood,' as evidenced in the number of visits which she paid. However, the colonel and the association were also wanting help with the costs. Shore noted that the county council had 'the power of appointing nurses for domiciliary visits ... under the Insurance Act' and that perhaps the district nurse might be given this appointment. This had 'financial merits and would also prevent the overlapping of the duties of the two nurses should another one be appointed under the Insurance Act.' The council's clerk was instructed to respond that it was the county council which made the appointment and that, in any case, the district council had already hired their medical officer and nurse.[2]

After the Great War, several prominent gentry families, such as the Lindsays, did not return. Others left during the Troubled Times; still others had lost their male heirs in the war. In any case, their tenanted, agricultural lands had been expropriated and many faced stringent financial circumstances as a result. Only the newly arrived McCalmonts maintained an aristocratic lifestyle. In the face of this economic and physical decline, gentry charity altered. Indeed, 1919 saw the last 'traditional' gentry effort to organize and educate labourers as a group, inculcate values, and improve their condition (Case 15.3).

Case 15.3: Comrades of the Great War, 1919
Founded in 1919 by Lord Teignmouth and Major R.B. Seigne, son of a former land agent with several generations of residence in the locality, the Thomastown chapter of this London-based association was for former British soldiers. It aimed 'to promote the interests of the discharged men' by affording 'members the means of social intercourse, mutual helpfulness, mental and moral improvement and rational recreation.' The subscription was 3d. a week. Club premises, and a bar, were set up in Market Street, open five evenings a week and all day Sunday, Thursday, and holidays. Dubbed 'The Legs and Arms' by local labouring humorists, the club was a recreational facility for several years after.[3]

In place of educative and ameliorative causes such as those of the Comrades, gentry largesse, insofar as it continued, turned towards patronizing individuals rather than organizing broad-based charitable projects. This was exemplified at a 1931 meeting of the County Board of Health as it grappled with allocating a vacant labourer's cottage to the most worthy candidate (Case 15.4).

Case 15.4: Five Applications for a New Cottage in Oldtown Townland, 1931
There were five applicants to the County Board of Health: James Kavanagh (Oldtown), John Roche (Grove), John Costigan (Jerpoint), Philip Dunne (Jerpoint), and James Spellane (Annamult).
To support his application, Kavanagh submitted recommendation letters from the parish priest (Msgr Doyle), Major McCalmont (Mount Juliet), a large-scale farmer and county councillor (William Deady), the Dáil member for the constituency (Richard Holehan), an ex-county councillor and ex-chair of the Thomastown Rural District Council (E. O'Gorman), and two Protestant rectors. He also submitted a letter signed by forty-four ratepayers in Thomastown district including Father Doyle and the curate. McCalmont's letter stated: 'James Kavanagh, who has been employed on the estate for many years – and is still employed here – informs me that he is applying for possession of the new labourer's cottage which has just been built close to the kennel here. I am writing to say that I consider him in every way to be a most suitable person to occupy this house. He is strictly honest

and a highly respectable member of society. Owing to the close proximity of this cot-
tage to my estate, I am sure the Board will realize the importance of the house
being occupied by a man of exceptional character and that one employed on this
estate should, as far as possible, be given preference.'

Msgr Doyle recommended John Costigan, as did farmer William Drea (on
whose land the cottage was built), four farmers, and water bailiff Cotterell. In his
turn, Philip Dunne sent in testimonials from the same William Deady as had
Kavanagh and, also, from a large-scale farmer/his employer (William Forristal).
Roche sent in a large number of recommendations from ratepayers in five town-
lands as well as from two parish priests, William Drea (site owner), the above-
mentioned William Deady, retailer William Hoyne, and the manager of a cream-
ery. Finally, it was reported that 'a number of ratepayers from [the locality] ...
recommended Thomas Fitzgerald for the vacancy.'

County councillor (Labour) Pat Ryan began discussion. 'As the board is
aware, the cottage was built for Kavanagh.' Twelve years before, when Richard
Holehan was chair and he himself was a member, the rural district council had
given the plot of ground to Kavanagh 'from amongst seven applicants. And when
the council gave him the plot it was their intention to build a cottage for him ...
He is a man of excellent character as long as I know him and that is a long time.
He was employed as a farm labourer in the district before he went to Major
McCalmont.

Mr Brophy [member]: I understood he was not an agricultural labourer at all.
– Ryan: I worked with him myself.

Mr Brophy: Some people said he was a tailor. – Ryan: He is over 37 years in
the district.

Mr Brophy: How long was he in it when you gave him the house? – Ryan: A
long time.

Mr Brophy: Is it true that this house was built for Kavanagh? – Ryan: I may
say it was the rural district council's intention.

Mr Brophy: ... If Kavanagh got the plot it doesn't follow that he should get the
house ... I think it is a wrong statement to make that the cottage was built for
Kavanagh.

Ryan: This plot of ground was first owned by a man named Phelan. He joined
up in the war and when he returned ... he got a soldier's cottage. Then Kavanagh
came before the rural district council and got the plot. I may say that there was
no man more anxious that Kavanagh get the plot than the owner, the late
Mr William Drea. He applied for the plot in 1916 and we considered him a good
tenant ...

Mr O'Meara [clerk of works]: He has put up a fence there.

Mr Gibbons [member]: Does he intend to continue working with Major McCal-

mont? – Ryan: He has no guarantee of continued employment, no more than any other man.

Mr Magennis [member]: How many of the other applicants are employed by Major McCalmont? – Ryan: They are all employed except one. There is not a tenant of a labourer's cottage within a radius of 3 miles but is employed on the McCalmont estate ... There is not an hour's work in the district – there is no place for the men to get employment – were it not for the work they get at Mount Juliet.

Mr Brophy: The original owner of the plot and Mr Drea came before us in Thomastown and pressed us very hard to give the house to a different man. Is that true? – Chair: It is true.

Mr Ryan: ... No man is more anxious to give the plot to Kavanagh than Mr Drea's father.

Mr Murphy (Chair) said they should give some consideration to Major McCalmont's letter.

Mr Magennis: He is an asset to Thomastown. – Mr Murphy: And to the county as well.

Kavanagh was elected by five votes to one.'[4]

The number of testimonials provided by each applicant was staggering. It showed the intense competition that surrounded the allocation of housing. In such a context, it was McCalmont's preference that secured the cottage for Kavanagh, even in the face of opposition from several board members. This reflected, of course, the influence that job-givers had in the locality and, as a result, the continuing need for labourers to maintain good relations with such people. However, the competition had forced Pat Ryan, and McCalmont as well, to support one labourer over others. Their patronage had also become a scarce, sought-after resource.

The episode also illustrates the growing alienation of the Free State bureaucracy, in this case, the County Board of Health, from locals of all status-classes and, therefore, the need for locally based relations and combinations, across class and denominational lines, in order to access and/or confront it. This added to the importance of patronage ties, as did the allocation process itself which ignored such historical associations as the wishes of the farmer who sold the plot to the council in the first instance. Ultimately, however, such a system was made even more potent because housing was one way by which farm labourers might be anchored to a locality. Of the four applicants who were resident in Thomastown parish and for whom parochial data was therefore available, none of them, or their wives, had kin relations traceable to an earlier generation. Their lack of roots made contemporary relations all the more important.

This change from gentry charity in aid of good causes and of inculcating values to personal patronage from employers soon had another permutation. Since 1880, the provision of labourers' housing had rested with the local authority. So, too, had the local debt burden which accompanied these works. After 1932, to encourage public housing, the state began to contribute from one-third to two-thirds of the cost. Associated with this was a local government act in 1925 which allowed the minister to dissolve any local authority council if it was 'in the public interest' to do so and to appoint commissioners to run local affairs. By the early 1930s, several councils began to function in association with civil service commissioners. Kilkenny was one of them. As of 1934, its Board of Health, as the housing authority, had a professional civil servant in charge. Thus, three years after the Oltown house was allocated to labourer Kavanagh amidst a good deal of local jockeying, thirteen new cottages in two rural townlands were straightforwardly 'handed over ... to labouring tenants.'[5] Recipients had been selected by need, according to the reported opinions of the county medical officer and the commissioner of health.

What this did, of course, was remove decisions from farmers cum councillors and from the influence of local patrons and put them into the hands of bureaucrats who were ostensibly concerned with the objective needs of particular labouring applicants rather than with the desires of local farmers or patrons. Yet common sense dictated that influence would surely be helpful. How could it be exerted? Clearly, it had to be through those closest to the bureaucrats, namely the politicians – county councillors and members of the Dáil. There thus was reproduced the notion that access to cottages still required 'strings.' It was a view encouraged by the politicians: they used it as a way of appearing indispensable to constituents who, in exchange, would proffer their votes. In the 1980s, although the county housing officer insisted that council houses were allocated according to medical and economic criteria, not a single person in Thomastown thought this, not even the councillors who believed that their interventions had secured houses for their political clients.

The Construction of Entitlements

These changes meant that, from the early 1930s in sites wider than a particular farm, business, or demesne, labourers were removed from dependence on the patronage of individual farmers, retailers, or gentle-men. Instead, they were given over to the influence of politicians and state bureaucrats. This did not, however, simply replicate the earlier pattern. Politicians were not, like gentry or farmers, relatively free agents in how they treated their workers. If labourers perceived themselves as dependent on the interventions of politicians, politicians knew that they depended on labourers for votes. From this came a change in the views that labourers held of their rights. It was exemplified in a column written by Maher in the midst of economic depression after the law on unemployment benefits had been changed (Case 15.5).

Case 15.5: The Rights of the Unemployed, 1934

'During previous winters, when work was slack,' building labourers, road workers, and casual labourers 'had the unemployment benefit to fall back on ... so long as they had unemployment stamps to their credit. This ... will not be the case ... [this] winter ... Instead, unemployed workers are to be given a weekly allowance under the new ... Act.' Not only is this 'a tawdry sum,' but 'the worst system of red tape ... invoked ... under the British regime pales into insignificance in comparison ... There can be no blame attached to the Gardaí [police] on whom the duty devolves of making inquiries from the applicants regarding their means ... But can anyone say that it is just – that in the case of an unemployed father, a portion of the earnings of his son shall be regarded as an income and the amount of unemployment assistance to which the father is entitled, calculated accordingly?' Or, if a son is unemployed, he 'may be entitled to 6d. or 1s. a week ... How any self-respecting young man should be obliged to report to an unemployment office daily and then receive [that] magnificent sum ... is degrading, to say the least. ... But the worst case which occurred in Thomastown is of a widow with one dependant who applied ... more than 3 months ago and after frequent visits to the local unemployment office received notice that her application had been refused on the following grounds: "the applicant is not genuinely seeking and unable to obtain suitable employment." It is not known how she is to prove [this] to officials. Is she expected to insert an advertisement in the "situations wanted" column of the local press, to ... canvass ... the different employers ... accompanied ... by a member of the local Gardaí? Of one thing the writer is convinced, and that is ... that the unfortunate widow ... [was] obliged to degrade herself by seeking such assistance and then after ... 3 months ... to be insulted.' This 'decision ... will not be allowed to go unquestioned. The deputies for the constituency will have a say in this matter.'[6]

These discursive categories of 'degradation,' 'insult,' and 'self-respect' were recent. They signalled new ideas about personal and political entitlements which were actualized not via good behaviour and generosity but through Free State citizenship. Specifically, the educative projects of the gentry and the coercive designs of the Poor Law and its farmer agents had been displaced. Gentry and employer patronage had become private concerns. Meanwhile, elected politicians had become the main mediating agents between bureaucrats and voters. As the purveyors of relief and influence changed, so too did ideas regarding the rights and obligations of the recipients, the political objects. By 1934, housing allocations no longer depended on moral integrity but on need, the view that ratepayers had authority simply because of their monetary role was challenged, and the right of the unemployed to decent support was being demanded.

These new emphases on objective criteria and citizenship rights muted the moral tone underlying relations between people of different classes. The deference cum paternalism that had linked receivers and givers began to fade, leaving more naked the exploitation that linked the various classes in the locality. Yet, in a small locale, antagonisms were heavily masked by emotional sentiments which inhered in many personal relationships. They also were veiled by an ideology of localism, the deep-seated legitimacy of hierarchy and status-class, the code of respectability, and the various hegemonic beliefs and practices that state agents might perpetrate at particular times. All this was, in turn, connected to events and ideologies in other political domains, especially the salmon fisheries (see below) and the politics of unionization (chapter 18).

The Inland Fisheries: Changing Entitlements and Persisting Sentiments

In Thomastown, ideas about entitlements were directly implicated with the inland salmon fishery. Here, a conjuncture was formed as the accumulations of the past met the agency of fishery owners, the law and its courts, and the bureaucrats of the Free State. Through this conjuncture, the sympathies, views, and values of Thomastown people from other classes were, yet again, made to conform in large measure with those of the fishers and, hence, of labour.

During the Troubled Times, 'the task of administering the fishery laws ... was ... impossible ... Private rights were ... invaded ... and the weekly close season was ignored.' In some districts, 'bailiffs were overawed by armed bandits.' To gain control over its fisheries, the new state increased penalties for offences and limited the government's right to mitigate fines. An advisory committee was then established and its recommendations incorporated into a 1925 act. Licence duties were increased to give conservators more funds, the Fishery Board was given the right to collect rates on fisheries for fifteen years, and the Fisheries Department was to audit conservators' accounts. The advisory report also had noted that angling associations had been growing up and suggested that they be encouraged and, perhaps, funded by the state. This recommendation tied explicitly into a general policy which favoured sport fishing/angling as well as commercial sea fishing. Indeed, the Fisheries Department quickly published an *Anglers Guide to the Irish Free State* to encourage tourism. The 1926 Statistics Act provided for the systematic collection of fishing catches.[7]

What all this meant was that the *geist* propelling the actions of the civil service in the Free State was a direct continuance of British policies. The rights of private and commercial fisheries were paramount and citizens, formerly 'peasants,' were to be coerced into complying with both the laws and the various bureaucratic regulations that were produced. These policies were continued by the recommendations of yet another Fisheries Commission in 1935.

In this context, conflict emerged among cotmen and former landlords. In Bennettsbridge, Lord Bellew no longer held tenanted lands but had retained the fishing rights for his lifetime. In a case brought in 1927, local cot fishers maintained that they had received permission to net from the farmer on the opposite bank. They were found guilty.[8] Two years later, two similar cases were heard at the Thomastown district court before Justice F.W. McCabe (Case 15.6).

Case 15.6: Lord Bellew's Fishery Prosecutions, 1929

Solicitor Crotty, for the defence of the cotmen, asked water bailiff Ireland if he ever saw anglers within Lord Bellew's private fishery. Ireland said that he often did. Crotty retorted that 'he had not seen evidence of Lord Bellew authorising this angling.' Moreover, 'Lord Bellew had not fished in the place for the last 20 or 30 years. It seemed to him that the conservators were trying to take shelter under Lord Bellew's title ... Rod fishermen were allowed to go there but poor cot fishermen were prosecuted ... These men, although they were poor, were entitled to protection, and why should the conservators single them out and let the rod fishermen go free?

'*Justice McCabe: Your clients are guilty … unless they produce Lord Bellew's [written permission].*

'*Crotty: As far as I can see, any interest Lord Bellew had in the place has lapsed …*'

Healy, solicitor for the conservators, proved that he had received the authority of Lord Bellew for the proceedings. Crotty then queried 'the conservators' right to bring the prosecution … The cotmen should have the same right as the rodmen.'

Justice McCabe, in summing up this case and a similar one that followed, said: 'There is the idea that these proceedings were brought without Lord Bellew's sanction … that the conservators were doing a thing they had no right to do. The sooner this [idea] is removed the sooner these [cot]men will know they are not entitled to fish there.' He 'suggested … that they … get permission from Lord Bellew, and then they need not care about conservators or anybody else.' Healy said that 'he never liked to press a case and therefore refrained from mentioning that these men defied the bailiffs over and over again.' The justice added: 'I have dealt with you extremely leniently … owing to the peculiar circumstances of the case and the very bad season. But if there is a prosecution against you again, and if Mr Healy comes forward to say that you have treated the authorities with disrespect, you will certainly be dealt with seriously.'[9]

Private property was inviolate but, from the cotmen's perspective, this was so only in relation to them. Two years later, another two cases were brought against cot crews for the same offence. In the first case, water bailiff Ireland explained how Lord Bellew's fishing had been let to the Kilkenny [city] Anglers' Association. Although some of their members were on the board of conservators, Ireland maintained that he 'did not look after their interests' nor had he received any payment from them. The cotmen again said that they had been netting with permission on the other side of the river and had pulled into Bellew's side owing to rough water. Ireland denied the truth of these statements. McCabe said that, because the plaintiff had not proved the case, he would dismiss it. However, he warned 'that the penalty for such an offence was very severe and that in future he would not recommend any reduction in fines imposed by him.'[10] Two months later, another cot crew was charged with the same offence. Bailiff Ireland told what had occurred: the cotmen were on Bellew's preserve which was rented to the Kilkenny Anglers and that the fishers admitted to the offence at the time. The cotmen denied it all. McCabe concluded: 'I think the defendants are a pack of liars. It is obvious that after the last court day when a similar case could not be proved here the defendants ... to-day thought they had the same defence. They got it into their heads that it was the same type of offence, and they are determined to come here and swear lies and per-jure themselves. Those people think that perjury doesn't matter. If people come here and swear lies to the court again the penalty will be increased.'[11]

What these cases show is that evidentiary procedures had changed. What the cotmen said to the bailiffs at the time of their confrontation on the river was now taken in evidence. In turn, bailiffs were now obliged to call out the cotmen's names at the time and state the charge. This, of course, simply expanded the possibilities for conflicting stories in court. Equally important was that locally resident gentry no longer sat on the bench. Local knowledge and 'the benefit of the doubt' were displaced. Moreover, the only way fishers and gentry now met each other was as adversaries. Lord Bellew's charges were an example. Major McCalmont and Lord Teignmouth were the other two gentlemen who determined to keep cotmen out of their fisheries.

Between 1933 and 1935, a government commission took evidence on the inland fisheries. In anticipation of this, Lord Teignmouth called a meeting of Nore anglers and cotmen so that he could 'collect representative evidence to present.' All the views that he elicited denounced the destruction of spawning fish and the voracity of the big net at Inistioge. The meeting then passed motions calling for the abolition of the big net, replacing water bailiffs with gardaí, reducing the price of licences, and extending the daily open hours for cotmen. It also was decided to form a Fishermen's Federation of anglers and cotmen. Teignmouth was elected president and cotmen John Kelly and James O'Neill were put on the committee. Teignmouth then gave his evidence to the commission. It was never published, although journalists provided the gist (Case 15.7).

Case 15.7: Lord Teignmouth's Evidence to the Inland Fisheries Commission, 1934

The fisheries 'would deteriorate unless steps were taken to control ... the river Nore ... No limit was placed on the number of cot licences' and, as a result, 'the river was continually fished night and day for a length of 30 miles. The watching staff was ... inadequate to deal with such conditions.' Teignmouth suggested that all cots 'be padlocked to numbered posts during illegal hours' and that 'no cot netting ... be allowed by owners of fishery rights unless these rights extended to both banks. At present, few rod licences were ... taken out because the cost was too high and,

because, with the extensive netting, the chances of catching a salmon were very
small ... Anglers should be encouraged as much as possible. They did no damage
to the supply of fish' while extracting 'a considerable amount of money ... from
abroad.' He also considered it 'most inadvisable' to hand over fishery rights to
purchasers of land under the land acts.[12]

The evidence, directly contrary to what the Thomastown meeting had
decided, was almost identical to what owners of private fisheries had
been saying for over seventy-five years. Teignmouth added the view that
farmers, that is, the new owners of inland fisheries, could not be trusted
to manage either their fisheries or the cotmen. The 1935 report
reflected this outlook (Case 15.8).

Case 15.8: The 1935 Report of the Inland Fisheries Commission
The commissioners noted that salmon had been common in the Irish diet a cen-
tury before but, since the railways, almost all the catch had been exported. How-
ever, because 'a salmon harvest, fluctuating though ... in quantity ... is always
there,' the commissioners recommended that 'the industry be expanded.' Their
data showed that each rod caught 76 pounds of salmon per season; each draft net
caught 1,620; each snap net caught 941; and each fixed engine/weir caught
4,249 pounds. From this, the commissioners deduced that rods contributed the
most to protection in terms of licence fees but caught the smallest amount. Indeed,
they were 'deeply impressed by the evidence ... showing the value of the angling
industry to the community at large' through licence fees, hotels, employment of
boatmen, motor cars, and so on. Therefore, 'sporting salmon caught on rod and
line is perhaps 10 times as valuable as a salmon taken by a net or weir.' Angling
thus had 'vast' potential.

The commissioners went on to point out that 'netting in fresh water is held by
many authorities to be a big factor in the decline of our salmon fisheries.' They
cited the 1901 Irish Inland Commission, which reported that netting 'counter-
acted the benefits accruing from the abolition of fixed engines in tidal waters.' In
any case, they wrote, inland netting was 'not based on any long continued use'
and a 1912 report had recommended its abolition. Therefore, 'we also recommend
that it be abolished with compensation on the basis of proof of loss.'

Having constructed a history and ethnography of the inland fisheries,
the commissioners cited 'anglers, such as Lord Teignmouth,' who

'deplored the dearth of fish for angling' given that angling had 'vast' potential. With this view, the commission put forward proposals for a national policy on the inland fisheries. Netting was to be abolished while the 'owners of angling stretches [were to] ... be left in undisturbed possession' so that they could retain 'an active interest in protection.' The commission thus quashed the idea of nationalizing the inland fisheries.

How, though, should these private fisheries be managed? It was recommended that the boards of conservators be abolished and their powers given to a central board and superintendent. Local committees, made up of fishery owners, would then manage the members' fisheries.[13] What this model did, given that most inland fishery owners were disinterested farmers, was to hand over the inland fisheries to men such as Teignmouth and urban, middle-class anglers. It was a model founded on the sanctity of private property and safeguarded by the civil service and bourgeois volunteers. In this model, citizens such as cotmen were excluded. Local fishers tried to manouevre. In fact, prior to the report, they had taken action. The Thomastown branch of the Irish Labour Party in 1935 decided to send representatives to the national convention to put motions calling for the abolition of fixed engines (that is, the big net) and for the nationalization of the fisheries. Their resolution was passed by the national Labour convention.[14] Cotmen were on the offensive.

Then the report came out. The fishers approached local agents of Fianna Fáil, the political party in power. The local branch, aware of the votes of local fishers and labourers, passed a motion in May 1936 'urging the government' not to put into effect the commission's proposal to abolish inland netting on the rivers Nore and Barrow.[15] A year later, in the context of a general election, the cotmen sent a circular to all Dáil candidates, signed by thirty-eight snap-net fishers, to canvas their opinions on the commission report. The fishers said that much of the evidence 'heard by the commission was biassed because financial and other considerations often ... prevented the net fishermen from presenting their point of view.' They pointed out, too, that such legislation would be a 'great injustice.' Their tactics had no effect. A new fisheries act became law on 14 July 1939. Sections 35 and 36 abolished netting on fresh inland waters, specified the compensation that would be paid to those affected, and made it unlawful even to have a net 'in or near fresh water.' However, these sections were not to take effect until the government set a 'commencement order.'[16]

Fifty years later, Thomastown men who were interested in fishing, as anglers, net men, or observers, had a singular version of what had occurred. Said a cotman's son who was an angler: 'The Kilkenny Anglers pushed the cots off the river. They pressured the powers that be. They were solicitors and doctors; and they were Lord Teignmouth's friends ... It was string-pulling, because it wasn't government policy to remove the snap nets; they were doing the least damage of all the nets. It was political pressure to get the cots off in order to have the fishing for themselves.' According to a former cotman, Lord Teignmouth and the Kilkenny Anglers' Association pressured the Fianna Fáil government – even though, he said ironically, 'the party was "the friend of the working man." But it wanted the middle-class votes and sold out the fishermen. The Anglers put pressure on the Fisheries Board and on places we wouldn't have a clue about.'

The perceived duplicity of Teignmouth was aggravated by stories about the so-called Brownsbarn fishery. Years before, Teignmouth had, depending on the version, 'tricked,' 'browbeaten,' or 'hoodwinked' several farmers' widows into selling him their fishing rights. The next generation harboured great resentment. They 'would accuse Teignmouth of trespass if he stepped on the wrong blade of grass along the right of way. They resented him doing their mothers and aunts out of the fishing.' Said a former cotman: 'They not only had the fishing, but they would never let anyone else fish. Not Teignmouth, not McCalmont, not Solly-Flood' (née Connellan). Another said that 'Lord Teignmouth and Justice McCabe were shooting buddies.'

Through all this, and along with their changing agency in the political economy of the locality, the gentry as a status-class lost much of its lustre for working people. Their charity was now was seen simply as the moral component of the employer-employee tie while their actions in the fishery were seen as reprehensible. Out of this came a renewed sense of locality which joined people together from other status-classes in common sentiment. For the cot fishers were still supported by local people – particularly in the face of what was seen as persecution from a district justice who had friends among non-local, wealthy anglers. In 1930 councillor John O'Neill and three cotmen faced Justice McCabe, charged with netting in the weekly closed time. The men maintained that they were not the fishers whom the two guards had seen. A report of McCabe's judgment said that 'he believed the defendants had perjured themselves. He was often criticised for what he said on the bench, but he could not allow perjury to pass. He would fine the defendants £5 each and allow £1 costs against each. If a petition was sent to the Minister he would go against, and he sincerely hoped the defendants would get gaol. He would not give them time to pay the fines. "I am never lenient with liars," added Mr. McCabe, "and the defence, in this case is a tissue of falsehoods."' In fact, O'Neill had leapt into, and swam across, an icy river in February to escape. Both his heroism and the judge's comments caused forty-nine local people, including miller Pilsworth, tanner Ryan, fifteen retailers, six farmers, the creamery manager, mill bookkeeper, postmaster, mill workers, and other labourers to contribute £5.15s to pay his fine.[17] The support continued (Case 15.9).

Case 15.9: The Persecution of Cotmen, 1936, 1943

In 1936 cotman Ned Ryan and two others were found guilty of netting too close to a weir. They were convicted on the evidence of two bailiffs who identified them from thirty yards away according to the clothes which the fishers wore. The cotmen said that the bailiffs had the wrong crew. Justice McCabe 'rejected completely the evidence of the defendants ... as a pack of lies.' Ryan, fined £3 plus one guinea costs, did not pay. Six months later he was arrested and conveyed to Mountjoy jail to serve a two-month term. A day later, his employer, retailer John Crennan, paid the fine and Ryan was released.

In 1943 a local committee organized a dance to raise money to pay fishing fines for Pat and James Kelly (two labourers 'with families') who had been sent to Mountjoy. The men had pleaded guilty to charges of night fishing and fishing too close to a weir. Their solicitor said that they had no previous convictions and had been unemployed. He therefore asked 'his worship to deal ... leniently ... with them.' McCabe fined each man £10 and forfeited their nets.[18]

In addition to the biases of the justice and the impossibly high fines and jail, the petitions by the convicted poachers to have their fines remitted, as had happened up until the late 1920s, were being refused. They were instead given more time to pay before they were sent to jail. People of other classes invariably became involved (Case 15.10).

Case 15.10: The 1939 Act and the Sale of Unlawfully Captured Salmon, 1945

The conservators charged Ned and James Ryan with selling nine salmon caught with an illegal drum (cudhail). Bailiff Purcell said that he and bailiff Ireland had gone to the fish merchant, Kehoe, in Carlow town, and found a case of nine fish consigned from Thomastown retailer Jack Crennan. Kehoe opened the case and found that eight of the fish were very badly marked: the 'scales were abrasioned' and the skin was, in one case, 'gone off, and the tails and fins were slit.' They also smelled strongly; 'they appeared not really fresh.' If the eight had been caught legally, in a snap-net, said Purcell, they would not have been marked in this way. Defence solicitor O'Hanrahan produced a letter from Messrs Kehoe saying that the fish were fresh.

Retailer Crennan then gave evidence. Ned Ryan had come into his shop, which was licensed to purchase salmon, to say that he had salmon for sale. Crennan told him to bring them down. They were brought in by Ryan's brother, James. Three of the fish were a bit stale; their tails and fins were split but that happens to all the fish. He did not notice any abrasions. He paid Ryan £7.11.10. He said that the fish were reasonably fresh and he often bought fish marked similar to these. When buying them, he believed that they were caught in a snap-net. 'At this time of year the scales were nearly all washed off salmon.'

Ned Ryan stated that he had caught these fish with a licensed snap net. A fish weighing fifteen pounds would be marked on the scales. 'Mr Crennan said the fish were perfect. On Friday evening, they got three, five on Monday, and one mid-day on Monday.

Frizelle [for the conservators] asked Ryan: I suppose fish caught in a cudhail would be more marked than those caught in a snap net? – I have no idea.

Justice McCabe: You never heard of that kind of net at all? – Yes.'

Labourers Patrick O'Neill and John Gorey then stated that they had been with the defendant when the fish were caught. They corroborated when and how. The justice then said that 'if the case was heard under the ordinary rule of law, the prosecution would have to prove their case. But under the section under which the prosecution was brought, the onus lay with the defendants. He didn't believe the defendants' evidence or the witness ... and therefore he would convict them.' He fined Ned Ryan £10 or six weeks imprisonment. He added: 'It is customary ... that persons lodge petitions with the minister for a reduction of fines and these petitions come back to me ... Unless some [new] fact is brought ... as far as my recommendation goes, it will only be a waste of time ... These are most serious offences and will be put down by heavy penalties.'[19]

It is not known if someone informed on Ryan or if the guards, knowing that he sold salmon to Crennan, were simply checking up. We also do not know how the fish were actually caught. Clearly, Justice McCabe 'knew.' However, what is striking is McCabe's implicit indictment of retailer Crennan. At the time, Crennan was the most extensive, respectable, and well-liked retailer in the town. His custom was largely based on providing fine foods and wines to Mount Juliet house. The outcome of the case severely offended local, respectable sentiment. It resonated back to the comments and attitudes of men like Major Hayes almost sixty years before.[20] It was now exacerbated by the burden of proof requirements under the 1939 act. Cot fishers were being victimized and local people impugned while Kilkenny city anglers and the big net took all the fish.

Conclusion

As part of a changing political economy, the competition and jurisdictional disputes between the agents of charity and those of local government were displaced by the emergence of individual patronage, a growing scarcity of patrons, the more distant bureaucracy of the Free State, and the perceived functions of local combinations and elected politicians. Out of this, in turn, came new ideas about entitlements, as notions of citizenship and personal dignity became part of the labourers' repertoire in their dealings with both state and patrons. Ultimately, events and agency in the salmon fishery brought many local people of other classes into some degree of sympathy and conformity with labourers' new viewpoints and values.

16. Redundancy and Status-Class: Purveying Values through Recreation and Education, 1929–50

'Few parishes in the Free State can boast of being so well catered for in the matter of sport as Thomastown. In it ... are a football club, five hurling clubs, three cricket clubs, a handball, golf, lawn tennis, badminton and dramatic club, as well as a Catholic Young Men's Society Hall, a Labour Hall and a Concert Hall.'

– Thomastown Notes, Kilkenny *People*, 16 August 1930

The changing definition of entitlements and of the importance of the state, its bureaucracy, and politician-brokers created both dependency and opportunity. However, the state and its civil servants were not simply neutral referees in competitions for scarce resources. Rather, the anti-treaty Fianna Fáil party which formed the government of the Free State after 1932 had a definite and explicit view of how Irish society should look: economically self-sufficient, Gaelic, and Catholic. On the one hand, self-sufficiency from a Thomastown perspective had come to mean that the state should be the main purveyor of the amenities and jobs that citizens required to remain at home. Moreover, as far as labouring people were concerned, the state had been successful in appropriating the role of purveyor even if it was far less able actually to deliver the requisite resources. On the other hand was a cultural agenda: to revive the Irish language and 'traditions' and to secure a central role for Catholicism. This meant that a framework and facilities had to be organized to encourage Irish culture and, also, that a space had to be kept for the spokesmen of the Catholic hierarchy. In this context and through these policies, Thomastown people of all classes were brought into interaction with each other and with the agents of state and church. Importantly, however, all this was filtered through pre-existing notions about status-class and class, through common-sense ideas about how the locality was constructed, and through patterns of social interaction which had long typified the locality.

Vignettes of Status-Class: Redundancy, Boundaries, and Difference

During field research in the 1980s, when local people looked back to earlier decades of the century, they often related brief stories to illustrate to an outsider what life was like, how local society worked, and how people interacted. Such vignettes, despite different tellers, usually centred on class. This did not mean that the stories focused on conflict. On the contrary, they often highlighted commensality or, at the very least, mitigating circumstances. The vignettes were of three types: those that included the teller as a participant, those that told about other people, and those that were general morality tales. Much depended on the teller's own purpose and predisposition in telling the story and on the structure of the general conversation within which the story was told (Case 16.1).

Case 16.1: Tales of Boundaries and Difference – Labourers,
Farmers, and Retailers

On farmers and labourers. *Frank Neill was 'doing a strong line' with a shop assistant. 'But his mother didn't think she was good enough because she wasn't a farmer's daughter. So it fizzled out. He never took any interest in anyone else'* (said a farm labourer). *Will Millea, a small-scale farmer, 'was disinherited in 1937 for marrying a labourer's daughter'* (several labourers). *His brother who inherited the farm 'also disapproved of the marriage. So the two are not on speaking terms. Farmers are like that. People with property get snobbish'* (retailer). *'My sister wasn't given a dowry when she married. It would have been different if she'd married a farmer'* (farmer Millea). *'The Doyles were farmers about thirty years back. They had no children. Their only close relation was their niece who looked after them. But they threw her out when she married a farm labourer. They gave the farm to a distant relation'* (labourer). *'It's well known that at thrashings, farmers' sons were fed in the dining room and labourers were fed in the kitchen'* (farmer's daughter). *'A farm servant, if it was a small farm, would eat with the family. The farmer and his family would be given meat; the servant would be given an egg'* (farm labourer). *'There was a former British soldier who was badly shell-shocked and who lived with the [farmer] Healys of Sm...n. I don't know how he lived with them. He was probably not related to them because boys from industrial schools at age fourteen would be sent out on their own, and farmers often used them as slave labour'* (homemaker). *'There's a tradition that certain people could get on the GAA hurling team. If you're a farmer, or a shopkeeper, you get on, [even] when others are far better hurlers. My uncle [fisher/millworker] was turned off the county team by [publican] Traynor who put a farmer's son on instead. He stayed away from hurling for years; and when he came back he played for another parish, never Thomastown'* (teacher). *'Creamery workers should be farmers' sons. You couldn't trust a labourer. All that feed and fertilizer lying around would disappear'* (farmer).

On retailers and labourers. *'The Traders' Development Association was for shopkeepers. It fell by the wayside in the 1950s. Then, the new generation came up with another association but, by the 1970s, I dropped out because I saw little cliques forming. So, too, did two other labourers who had been invited to join. Shopkeepers were the clique. They would go out for a drink after meetings and not ask us'* (mill worker). *'I grew up on Mill Street' in the 1930s. I 'didn't know any of the [labouring] people but the daughter of the mill's bookkeeper and the labourers who actually worked for my father. My father had lorry drivers. He was strongly anti-union but he always took care of his workers and paid them a fair wage. When he sold the lorries, he tried to find other jobs for his drivers'* (retailer's daughter). *'When my uncle was ... retiring, he was worried about how we would manage. That year, when I went to collect the con acre money from C.J. [retailer], because his field was next to ours and he took ours each year, I found that he had a list of 10s. here and there that my uncle had drawn out from him. He had used it for drink. All that was left of the £24 for the year was £4. I went down and told him they weren't to advance my uncle any more money. They were after our land [three acres]. Then C.J. hired my uncle at 30s. a week. That was a great help. After a few months, C.J. came to the house and said that he wanted to add a quarter acre from my holding to his. But my uncle in America had made us promise never to the sell the land; he never sent a letter that didn't have money in it. So I couldn't say yes. Two weeks later, my uncle was fired. C.J. did that to get back at me. I never liked him after that. Never'* (homemaker). *When retailer M.D. 'bought the field near his shop, he built a wall to stop the lads from hurling. M.D. was boycotted by customers but it blew over. No idea why he done it. We used to hurl in the field and he put a pump in the field to obstruct us'* (labourer). *'The shopkeepers didn't want to pay the wages. If shopgirls were paid a half crown a week, they were paid only once a month, twelve times a year — so the shopkeeper got four weeks off them for free'* (labourer). *'Farmers would approach my husband to get their daughters employed. May Connors was taken in. She was only a labourer's daughter and a local nun commented disapprovingly; but he kept her on anyway'* (retailer's widow). *'My first job on leaving school, age thirteen and a half, was at Thomastown Hotel. My wages were ... three shillings a week [for] a seven-day week. The hotel was mostly for the bank clerks ... and for the occasional visitor to town. There was plenty of work ... Each morning I had to polish fifteen pairs of shoes, chop ... firewood for ... the rooms ... One murderous job ... gave me blisters.'* I had to *'pump water up to the top of the hotel to a tank ... to supply baths, wash basins, toilets ... It would take me two hours ... to refill the tank. Then it was always run here, run there for the clerks. My parents decided that I should leave that job as far too much was expected of me. There was no such thing as a regular time for me to finish in the evenings'* (Harry Pinchin).

Both men and women from all status-classes, aged thirty-five to eighty-five in 1981, told these kinds of stories, although labourers certainly related far more of them. Some tales were told by numerous people, such as the one of the threshings and of the farm labourer's egg. Yet, regardless of teller or style, all the vignettes were seen by the tellers as timeless. Thus, the norms, experiences, and lessons were relevant to the present. Moreover, although the stories presented images of extreme inequality and discord, and although they were often told with deep resentment, their starkness was sometimes alleviated by ambivalent emotions or mitigating conditions. These sometimes came from the teller's knowledge of other, less dramatic cases or, most often, from the teller's personal experiences which eased and blunted somewhat the intensity of the anger. For example, a farm worker recalled how the labourers who worked for a particular family of 'strong farmers' were called 'galley slaves' because of how hard they were worked and how much they resented their employers. However, the teller was also extremely concerned that this story not be passed on because the farmer's 'children were very kind to me as a child when my family was poor.' Or, a creamery worker, who had two acres of land on which he kept cattle, spoke of his neighbour, a large-scale farmer. 'I would borrow his mare and cart whenever I wanted to spread dung. In fact, I didn't even have to ask. I just caught and used her.' Another labourer was willing to say that 'some farmers were better than others' before he added that 'still they exploited the workers.' Similar ambivalence was apparent in how workers saw their relations with retailers (Case 16.2).

Case 16.2: Choosing a Shop and Retailer – Two Versions

(1) *Mick, born 1916, was a mill worker. His family shopped at Power's. 'We had nothing in common with Willie Power, yet we had a great loyalty to his shop. When the [urban landlord] Clifford was selling out, Power was buying up the property and asked our permission to buy our house. We couldn't afford to buy it ourselves.' This was taken by the family as an example of Power's courtesy and led to their 'tremendous loyalty until the cooperative opened. Even then we still gave him some custom because some things were not available at the co-op. The choice of shop in the old days was based on family tradition.' Yet Mick had some doubt. On the one hand, retailers were anti-union and helped destroy the co-op in the 1940s. On the other hand, 'retailers carried farmers during the lean years.'*

'[Q]: But Power was known as "the grabber?" – A: He got that from the Murphy situation. Murphy had a farm. When he died, his widow couldn't manage. Power bought the farm. Murphy's sons were sent to orphanages, the family was scattered and put out of the house. Except for that, he was alright.'

(2) *Pat, builder's labourer, was born in 1911: He recalled that 'Murphy died. He was a drinker and not a worker; the farm was in debt. It was put up for auction by the bank and Willie Power grabbed it. What happened was that somebody was bidding for the children but the auctioneer was being given a few quid.' Pat 'never heard tell of shopkeepers coming down on you. They might prosecute and get an order to pay so much a week, but they never took your property. Perhaps they did long ago, but not in my lifetime or in my parents' time. Power grabbed the Murphy farm, but not for debt.' His grandson 'is no good. He hires travelling lads because you get them cheaper.'*

Both Mick and Pat saw mitigating circumstances that allayed any absolute judgment which they made, or might be made by others, of 'Willie the grabber.' These circumstances related both to their personal experiences and to historical knowledge. In any case, Murphy was a farmer, not a labourer. All this left space for moderated judgments.

There is, in other words, a redundancy in social relations in localities where people have numerous ties to each other and knowledge about each other from multiple sources. This means that information and ideas about others can always be avoided, allayed, or rationalized. So, at the same time that people's stories were both starkly retrospective of the past and clearly educative of the present, they also left space for individual assessment and choice. From a political perspective, of course, this could complicate local allegiances. Moreover, such tales could become self-fulfilling prophecies. Katie Drennan described 'old man Shea,' a farmer who 'was a hard taskmaster.' However, 'he did have long-time workers ... but *possibly* they were long-time because they had tied cottages. Shea also brought in a lot of strange workers, *probably* because locals wouldn't work for him if they could help it' (my emphasis). In other words, just as the tales structured people's perceptions about the status-class structure and life in the locality, so, too, did the perceptions structure the tales. Within such a frame came individual flexibility, in action and thought, wrought by the redundancy of local social life.

Irish Language and Culture: Education and Recreation in the Free State

In the last census prior to the Great War, only 18 per cent of the Irish population spoke Irish.[1] In the Thomastown area, the language had not been in use since at least the mid-nineteenth century. This was related to the locality's position in international trade networks along which English had long been the lingua franca. It was a product, too, of the National Schools after the late 1830s in which English was the language of instruction. After 1898, however, the use of Irish had been promoted by the Gaelic League which had an intermittent branch, and language classes, in Thomastown. Attended by some of the teachers, retailers, and notables, the language became a point at which class and nationalism met. This was because, as workers pointed out, labourers were hardly going to join, or be welcomed into, a League dominated by 'local nobs.'

With the founding of the Free State, Irish language instruction became compulsory in primary schools. The aim was to create an Irish-speaking nation in the next generation.[2] For Thomastown's working men who went to primary school in the 1920s and 1930s, learning Irish had virtually no place in their recollections. What did have an impact, however, was contained in two common memories. First, they remembered how teachers were biased against working people's children and how labouring children had little chance of obtaining more than a primary education. For teachers, like priests, were the sons of farmers and were prejudiced against workers. Second, they vividly recalled a particular teacher, Peadar Laffan (a farmer's son), who was appointed to the boys' school in the mid-1930s. On the one hand, he exacted such perfection from the better students that some labouring boys, for the first time, received scholarships to secondary schools. On the other hand, he was recollected as a bully who terrorized the less able. 'He was mad for scholarships,' said several working men. His impact on those individuals who succeeded, and then usually emigrated, was profound. For the less able, his impact was limited. They left school, age fourteen, retaining nothing of the Irish language. For some, the Irish emphasis was just another example of how labourers were always being 'codded.' Yet, for a tiny number, the experience had instilled a deep love for Irish language and literature.

One aspect of Gaelic culture did, however, penetrate deeply into working-class life via the school system. This was Gaelic sport. Played by school children both during and after school and then into adulthood, these games came to link Catholics of all status-classes. Handball, hurling, camogie (women's hurling), and Gaelic football were initially promoted by the Gaelic Athletic Association which formed its Thomastown branch in 1901. Their immediate popularity was reflected in *Thomastown Notes* which always contained the latest results and which, in notices of emigration or death, always gave the sporting provenance of the subject. Gaelic games, in short, provided an entry and focus for a kind of cultural nationalism in Thomastown even as alternate institutions failed to revive other aspects of Irish culture.

The workings of the GAA also had unintended results. Because leagues were based on parish, county, and province boundaries, local loyalties were given an additional focus. This was enhanced because schools were also parish-based; and they became the key site for learning and playing Gaelic sports. School, GAA, and spatial loyalties thus became mutually reinforcing. In the 1980s for example, every twelve-year-old boy in the parish knew that Thomastown had won the senior county hurling championship in 1946. Wearing the blue and white colours of Thomastown parish, the team was a mixed status-class group of retailers', farmers,' and labourers' sons.[3]

This spatiality had other aspects. Thomastown parish for a time had two hurling teams and two GAA clubs. The Mung GAA hurling team was founded in 1913; the Thomastown hurling team was founded in 1918. The two clubs represented and created a split between town and country and between farmers and farm labourers on the one hand and, on the other, retailers and labourers. The GAA also legislated that those who played non-Irish (that is, English) games such as cricket, soccer, and field hockey were banned from Gaelic League sports. However, many workers had learned these other games, particularly if their employers were Protestant. Most prominent of the games was cricket, and the best-known team was from Mount Juliet. It included labourers (estate, millworkers) and gentlemen. Like GAA teams, it thus cut across class boundaries, albeit different ones. Like the GAA, the Cricket Club held annual dances to raise money.[4] Also like the GAA, it was run by men from the 'better' classes. The former was headed by farmers and retailers; the latter by gentlemen. The two associations thus mirrored each other in terms of the position of labourers. Moreover, because the two clubs/sports were mutually exclusive owing to the GAA ban, labourers were cut off from each other and from common experience. They also had different encounters with ethnicity. The GAA was Catholic, the banned games were Anglo-Irish.

Most people also knew, certainly labourers did, that the GAA was involved in politics, often to the detriment of the very sports it was promoting. A former millworker told how a TD, Richard Holehan, was chairman of the southern County Kilkenny GAA in the early 1930s. When Éamon de Valera formed the government, 'word came out that Fianna Fáil would take over the GAA.' At the following year's annual general meeting, a Fianna Fáil candidate was put forward to oppose Holehan and won. At the time, 'Knocktopher had one of the finest GAA pitches in the county, and it happened to belong to Holehan. So he threw the GAA out of the pitch.' In such a way, conflicting loyalties and sentiments were engendered: how to separate Gaelic sport from the organization which promoted it and the political party which appropriated it. For most workers, this was impossible.

The GAA, then, in espousing a unifying ideology and cultural nationalism through sport, in fact fractured labouring-class experience by creating spatial loyalties, by banning those who played English sports as a result of their ties to particular employers, and by becoming implicated in party politics which themselves were divisive of working-class sentiment. At the same time that it caused these divisions, the GAA also encouraged the idea that Irish nationalism was associated with leisure, free time, and fun. Indeed, into the recreational cum Irish cultural spaces left by the GAA came other associations which promulgated nationalistic, Fianna Fáil policies during the 1930s. Irish language, music, dancing, and drama all came under their purview (Case 16.3).

Case 16.3: The Gaelic Revival in Thomastown during the 1930s
The Gaelic League resurfaced in Thomastown in 1933, led by a Kilkenny city teacher. His Irish class presented an Irish drama, and the daughters of retailers

and farmers followed with Irish dancing. A postman's son played the violin. By 1931, Thomastown had a state-sponsored Feis Commitee. *It awarded two-week summer scholarships for students to study Irish in an Irish-speaking area and recipients, in fact, included labourers' children. It also organized an annual festival. In 1932 the feis committee was made up of the curate, retailers, teachers, notables, and a single labourer, Gerard Doyle. The feis was reportedly attended by more than 3,000 people. Language and violin competitions were held, as was an Irish industrial exhibit of flour, meal, leather, woodwork, tweeds, blankets, and boots. Mill owner Pilsworth, tanner Ryan, and tailor Woods all had stalls. Six years later, the annual Feis was still 'a great success.' The parish priest thanked teacher Peadar Laffan who was the secretary and retailer Michael Ryan, 'assisted by [labourer] John Voss,' the dance teacher. Held in farmer Deady's field, there were hurling matches and competitions for schoolchildren in Irish culture (language, storytelling, history, singing, dancing, violin). The 'newly organized* Thomastown Pipers' Band *played.' On the platform for the opening ceremony were priests, teachers, and retailers – not, however, John Voss. In his address, Father Doyle said: 'Holding a feis ... reminds us of our duties to our native language ... to preserve it and hand it down as a spoken language.'*[5]

The stimulus from the state encouraged more local efforts. *In 1933 Maher reported that the Shamrock Dramatic Class had been organized by blacksmith Larry Ryan. It gave a concert in aid of the newly formed Pipers' Band. Ryan and a rural postman sang. John Voss's pupils performed Irish dances and a comedy was presented by the labourers' sons. According to Harry Pinchin's memoirs, 'Larry Ryan ... had fantastic knowledge of the theatre, books ... and was very musical. Nothing gave [him] greater pleasure than to organize all the local boys and girls to form a concert or ... a play ... When Larry had his play organized ... he would ... hire the Concert Hall where he was always assured of a full house.' The Thomastown Dramatic Class also emerged. It presented an Irish drama in 1932 with a cast of labouring men and women, varying in age from their twenties to their forties, married and unmarried.*[6]

This flurry of cultural activity in the 1930s, and the national sentiment created by it, was also a spurt of local, parochial activity. Unsurprisingly, then, participation was heavily influenced by status-class ascription. On the one hand, labourers participated on all occasions. On the other hand, when they themselves organized these local events, people from other status-classes were not involved. Moreover, when the activities crossed status-class lines, labourers had no visible or important role in their organization and management. Nor was this flurry of activity, this commitment to Irish language and culture, universally and unequivocally supported. In 1937 a new constitution promulgated by the Fianna Fáil regime stated Irish to be 'the national language' and 'the first official language.' English was 'recognised' as '*a* second language.'[7] Eight years later, the issue came to a Kilkenny County Council meeting (Case 16.4).

Case 16.4: Divergent Views at a Kilkenny County Council Meeting, 1945
The Westmeath County Council asked for support of its motion to raise the school-leaving age to sixteen and to have children taught in Irish for the first five years of school. Discussion ensued among the councillors:
  '*Walsh:* ... *If Irish was going to become the spoken language* ... *it was in the first five years that* ...
  '*Mahoney [interrupting]: How many farm labourers with 4 or 5 children are satisfied to keep their children going to school until they are 16? We have too much damn education in this country and the more education we have the less work we have* ...
  '*Pattison [Labour, Kilkenny]:* ... *I am sure people who sit here are not going to rear their children in ignorance. I suggest the matter be left to the Commission on Youth Education.*
  '*O'Neill [Labour, Thomastown]: There is not a trader in Thomastown who does not wait until a child leaves school to employ him and when he reaches sixteen he is let go and another child taken on.*
  '*Mahony: That is not the case in the rural districts.*
  '*O'Neill: I have proof of it in my own town* ...
  '*Walsh: I do not hold with Mr O'Neill about people looking for cheap labour* ... *We have too many unskilled workers in this country and we should extend vocational* ... *education.*
  '*Hayes: It is deplorable to see the number of children in the country suffering from malnutrition. It is* ... *wrong to suggest that any man, especially* ... *with a large family, should be expected to keep his sons at school until they were sixteen* ... *We find that the people dictating these measure are all in good jobs* ...
  '*Burke: I do not favour compulsion of any kind except where there is food to be provided for the people. I would not force any man to keep his children at school if he is not in a position to provide for them* ... *If we educate the children in Irish a considerable percentage of them will have to leave this country and they will be little better than illiterate when they get out of it.*
  '*The [Westmeath] resolution was marked "read."*[8] *That is, it was ignored.*

When the issues of Irish education and school-leaving age were raised together, it was the latter, as well as related issues, that caught the councillors' interest. For Labour councillor O'Neill, it was the exploitation of teenage labour: how fourteen-year-olds were hired and, when it was time for employers to pay higher wages and into the unemployment scheme, they were fired. For Labour councillor and TD, James Pattison, a professional politician, the entire discussion was irrelevant, and thus to be sidelined using appropriate platitudes. In other words, the views of the Labour men were pragmatic and materialist, located inside a frame that highlighted immediate conditions and entitlements rather than hypothetical possibilities. The views of the other councillors were also rooted in their experiences as farmers who recoiled at the idea of labourers, and themselves, having to maintain children until age sixteen. Significantly, the issue of compulsory Irish education was ignored except for the point that it was the last thing an Irish emigrant needed. Thus, in a county with virtually no 'native speakers,' issues linked to cultural nationalism rated a poor second to questions of jobs, work conditions, and household economics. This was especially true for O'Neill who had joined the anti-Treaty, republican IRA and who had, at the time, changed his name from 'James' to 'Seamus.' Cultural nationalism had become, at best, something to which a labourer might subscribe in a general, abstract way or for sport. Otherwise, it was immaterial to everyday concerns.

Purveyors of Values and the Role of Capital: Paternalism and Deference

The last efforts of resident gentry to organize and educate local people were contained in the District Nursing Association (Case 15.1) and the Comrades of the Great War (Case 15.3). Such projects were replaced by individualized patronage and, alongside, the institutions and agents of the Free State. This meant that the stories that labourers told in the 1980s about the gentry were differently coloured than the ones that they told about retailers and farmers. Whereas the latter contained clear lessons and norms for use in the present, the former were about a time, a morality, and a world that had passed and, indeed, was in the process of disappearing even as the episodes being related had occurred. As a result, stories about the gentry, whether complimentary or critical, evoked nostalgia – for the safety net of paternalism, the moral relations between classes, and the mutual respect that might obtain between people of different classes. Workers were saying that these values continued to be important to them even though the gentry had ceased to be the purveyors of values in the locality. Most importantly, the belief that the landlords and their world were gone formed part of an ideology which masked the immense role that capital continued to play in the locality and in labourers' lives. In other words, as embodiments of values and of power, the gentry remained pertinent to life in the Free State. An example is from 1943, when labourer Gerard Doyle described the Power family (Case 16.5).

Case 16.5: A Tale of/from the Past, 1943

'The present owner of Kilfane is May, the daughter of Vera Power and Colonel Evans-Johnson. Unmarried, she presides over an almost empty house with a decorum and dignity that are strangely out of place. At Christmas she makes a feeble attempt to emulate the charitable practices of her mother, but her gifts are regarded as a bit of a joke ... She is odd, somewhat eccentric and intensely proud of the family name. She likes to be known as "Miss Power"; the use of her Christian name, on envelopes, she regards as a levelling practice not to be encouraged. Today Kilfane is practically derelict. The ... staff do not exceed half a dozen. The land is let [on conacre] and the wood is being cut down. Still the house and the grounds are kept in fairly good condition and preserve much of the old world charm which so impressed nineteenth century-visitors. Even the peacocks still remain. But in common with many other "big houses" ... its decline has been rapid and continuous. The hospitality of former days, the constant stream of distinguished visitors, the hunters, hounds and kennels – all these are rapidly fading memories.'

This view of the gentry as past, through a nostalgic image of life on a large landed estate, was complemented by stories from the 1980s through which local people recalled experiences of, or gossip about, the locally resident gentry and their relations with labourers (Case 16.6).

Case 16.6: Tales of the Past – Labourers and Gentry

'My grandmother remembered buying part of a Concert Hall share [a Lindsay project] for 2s.6d. in around 1910. People regarded it as a donation to the Hall' (told by a labourer). 'The Major [McCalmont] always lent his agricultural machinery. That's how workers got their own gardens tilled' (labourer). 'A Mount Juliet worker lost an eye while at work and they allowed him to come

back and work as he pleased. He got his wages regardless' (common story).
'A worker's child needed expensive surgery in London and the McCalmonts took him there and paid (common story). *'Lady Helen [McCalmont] was very well liked, especially by workers who she didn't hesitate to help in times of trouble'* (millworker). *'The gentry around here were good people. The Lindsays were great people for the poor. The Pilsworths were terribly generous. Every house would have a half-ton of coal and a half-ton of sticks at Christmas. In times of sickness, they'd send over pies and puddings. They were very charitable. They'll never be in it again, the likes of them. The D-Hs weren't liked though. They were close to the British soldiers [during the War of Independence]. Officers would dine there and possibly they passed on information to the soldiers'* (millworker/cotman). *The Hunts [Jerpoint] were good people; they brought out biscuits at Christmas for the workers, not like the B...s [local Catholic farmers] who were awful mean'* (labourer).

After the Land Acts expropriated landlords, and in the Free State after 1922, the gentry were no longer seen as the dominant purveyors of values. Some of their good works persisted, inscribed in physical space, such as the Concert Hall, or in services, such as the Nursing Association, which continued not only through the exertions of those gentry who remained or had moved in but also through the efforts of the town's more eminent retailers and notables who raised the funds and became officers. Indeed, in each year until at least 1950, an annual report of expenses, receipts, and number of nurse's visits was published in the newspaper, thus reminding local people that good works were still being done, however modestly. As well, the deaths of various gentry personages became occasions to recall past values, indulge in nostalgia, and engage in rituals which had long formed part of local society (Case 16.7).

Case 16.7: Representations of the Gentry, 1935 and 1939
When Isabel Butler died, in 1935, aged seventy-eight, her obituary read: *'The Butler family has been resident at Kilmurry for generations and were always popular with all classes and creeds. [Her brother] ... was a liberal landlord who took a very sympathetic interest in the welfare of his tenants and the employees of this estate. Miss Butler was prominently identified with the Thomastown District Nurses' Association ... [She] was most charitable and a generous benefactor to the poor, who have lost a good friend by her death.'* When William Pilsworth died

in 1939, the report noted: '*The family are large and generous employers of labour and the most cordial relations have always existed ... Indeed, it may be truly stated that the staff takes the greatest possible interest and pleasure at the continued progress and expansion of the trade at Grennan Mills, and almost regard themselves as partners in the firm. It would be difficult to conceive a more contented body of workers, thanks to the courtesy and kindness of every member of the Pilsworth family. When a member of the staff retires owing to ill health or old age, he is given a weekly pension by the firm.' Mr Pilsworth himself 'was a sportsman, concerned with shooting and golf ... He never took part in politics or public life, but he displayed an abiding interest in the welfare ... of his native town and was a generous contributor to every worthy object. The poor, and those stricken with illness, always enlisted his practical sympathy and have lost in him a never failing friend.*'[9]

The list of mourners at the Butler funeral included employees: four indoor servants and ten outdoor workers. The kinship connections among them were striking: two sets of brothers, two brothers-in-law, and two cousins. Several of these were sons and grandsons of former employees. It raised the question, which several labourers asked in relation to the mill, tannery, and creamery, as to who was really doing the hiring: the owners or the workers. In 1981 I showed the Butler obituary to one of the former maids who was listed as a mourner in 1935. It elicited the memory of how Colonel Butler, when walking through the garden, would always whistle as he came around a corner so that the workers would know he was there. Obituaries, in other words, evoked and provoked values that people regarded as important. So, too, were such values evoked when 'the bells of both the Protestant and Catholic churches tolled in turn' at the funeral of William Pilsworth.[10] The fact was remembered by everyone a half-century later.

The kinds of life, person, and position attributed to Butler and Pilsworth were, of course, highly emotional and rhetorical because of the occasion (death), medium (newspaper), authors (local), and convention (obituary). Yet the representations both embodied and created a standard against which not simply gentry, but all who purported to purvey values, had to measure up. For workers, it was the epitome of the moral economy and a way in which an ideal world might be constructed: hierarchical yet humanitarian. Thus, although the stories about landlords and gentry were about a world that had passed, and although the obituaries were idealized and nostalgic, this did not mean

that the views and values embodied in them did not continue to reso-
nate for labourers. For although the gentry no longer purveyed values,
images of what they had purveyed, and how, remained as standards.
That some landlords were arrogant or ungenerous was not in question.
The issue after 1922 was not the historical veracity of particular tales or
memories but the meanings and values of compassionate inequality
which they furnished.

How did actual experiences with the gentry in the Free State measure
up to these ideal and nostalgic standards? Mount Juliet estate, where the
cultural forms of high patronage had been adopted, provides an example (Case 16.8).

Case 16:8: Cultural and Material Patronage at Mount Juliet, 1933–50
The housing, perks, and charitable acts towards employees were augmented by
annual rituals, *such as the puppy show for young hunting dogs and the Christ-*
mas distribution of sweets, children's toys, and meat (1,700 pounds in 1933).
They were augmented by occasional rituals *which marked fortuitous happenings,*
as when a dance and supper were held for five-hundred guests, including two-hun-
dred employees and wives, to celebrate the victory of Lady Helen's horse in the Irish
Grand National. Rites of passage *for the McCalmont family also became public*
occasions. When a son, away with his regiment, came of age in 1940, 'all the
employees assembled at the estate office' and his father 'personally gave a cash
payment to each of his 250 employees.' A dance was later given in the servants'
hall. Family deaths were also marked. Lengthy eulogies in 1938 followed the pass-
ing of Lady Helen, whose 'death will be regretted ... by the numerous employees ...
who ... always ... [spoke] very highly of her charity and of the deep interest she
evinced in their welfare. Many touching stories are told of her wonderful kindness
of heart and of the countless good deeds.' Finally, reports of *exemplary working*
conditions *and wages surfaced. In 1950 it was reported that the major had*
'increased the wages of over 100 employees on his estate by 6s. a week.' Ten years
earlier, the major had granted a weekly half-holiday to all employees.[11]

The 1950 report of a wage increase noted that the major's weekly
wage bill was a generous £450 per week.[12] Thus was highlighted the capital that underlay the lifestyle, high patronage, and public posturing
which typified the estate. However, its coercive nature was made abun-
dantly clear in 1936 when two of the major's foxhounds were found poisoned and, as a result of what the editor of the Kilkenny *People* called

'this wanton act ... of gross barbarism,' the major threatened to 'close up Mount Juliet and leave the country' (Case 16.9).

Case 16.9: The Mount Juliet Crisis, 1936

A letter from the major was published. 'My main reason for living here,' he wrote, is because 'of the hunting. I have been [Hunt] Master for 15 years and during this time the upkeep of the hunting establishment has cost me between £8,000 and £9,000 per annum. This is spent ... on wages, foodstuffs, repairs ... and is over and above anything spent on the stud farm or gardens. [It] does not include the money spent by the Hunt Club in ... claims for damages.' During this time, 'I have lived on terms of the greatest cordiality with the farmers and landowners ... and have done my best to support ... sport[s] in the neighbourhood. Now by this act of blackguardism the situation ... has undergone a complete change.'

Three pages of editorial comment followed: how the family had 'carried on during the Troubled Times' and had been rightly 'left unscathed.' The editor focused on the jobs that would be lost if the major left and on the fact that, 'at the outset of the economic war, every inducement was held forth to Major McCalmont to translate his stud farm to England.' He stayed. 'If he does not so continue, the fault will not be his.' At Sunday Mass, Father Doyle condemned the outrage and outlined what workers and local retailers gained from having the Kilkenny Hunt in the vicinity. That week, retailers met 'to convey' to the major 'the people's strong condemnation of such a foul act.' They also called a public meeting to confirm the resolution. Parish priests, retailers, farmers, and workers from a broad area attended. Letters were read from Richard Holohan, TD, councillor William Deady, and William Pilsworth. Three full columns of speeches were published. Over two hundred estate workers then held a meeting to discuss 'what action' to take 'considering that the livelihood of the employees and their families was at stake.' They confined themselves to 'a resolution of protest ... and of sympathy ... determining to leave nothing undone to trace the culprit.' They also said 'that in the event of a repetition they would ... take drastic steps regardless of the consequences. It was only as the result of strong appeals from influential quarters that they refrained from now doing so.' The Thomastown branch of the Irish Labour Party and of the IT&GWU called special meetings to pass resolutions condemning the outrage. McCalmont stayed.[13]

Unmentioned in all these entreaties was that Mount Juliet had survived the Economic War partly by firing workers and lowering wages and that the employers were viciously anti-union. Instead, it was dire economic dependency that was loudly expressed by people of all religions and classes, including McCalmont himself. What the crisis thus highlighted was the immense power and privilege of contemporary capital and the extent to which all local people relied on it, regardless of ideological or political sentiment. Thus, the patronal values of 'humanitarian hierarchy' or 'compassionate inequality' which enterprises such as Mount Juliet, Grennan Mills, or Kilmurry estate purveyed were not the result of 'tradition' or the survival of nineteenth-century 'customs,' even though people then, and later, described them as such. Rather, the cultural forms and the values that they purveyed were rooted in contemporary material exigencies.

At the same time, Irish people in Thomastown and elsewhere had been told, and had come to believe, that the land acts and the Free State had ended the agency of landlords and/or gentry in local life. Their roles, as intentional purveyors of values, had been declared over, replaced by an economically independent, Gaelic, and Catholic state. Yet the Free State was itself dependent on private capital. This inevitably reproduced the structures of exploitation for most labourers, masked, however, by the trappings of political independence and the Irish cultural revival.

Thus, through nostalgic memory, extensive obituaries, and workplace practices, the values of compassionate inequality and humanitarian hierarchy continued to permeate local life. They did so because, in evoking deep-rooted sentiments, they successfully rationalized and masked the real power that capital still commanded. Labourers, perhaps, should have seen that capital had power, regardless of whether it was tied up in land, machinery, or foxhounds and that, as people without capital, their relation to landlords, capitalists, or rentier capitalists was the same – that they had only their labour power to sell to whichever gentleman was buying. The mask, however, was oftentimes dazzling, both materially and ideologically.

Purveying Values through Thrift and Leisure

In the 1930s, some national organizations aimed to improve people's material rather than cultural condition. The Savings Committee, founded in 1930, was one. Both the Catholic and Protestant bishops became patrons of a local branch chaired by the parish priest and run by a committee intended to represent all classes and provide a clear aura of respectability. The committee was made up of two curates and a

Protestant rector, mill owner Pilsworth, a bakery-owner, a postmistress, a stationmaster, a former tannery owner/now retailer Ryan, seven retailers, two teachers, county councillor Pat Ryan (Labour), journalist Ned Maher, and three labourers.[14] What caused the inclusion of the three? Each worked in a different sector (mill, farm, construction) and came from a different part of the town. None was a fisher; all were members of the Labour Party. The image of the respectable worker at the time, then, was of a permanently employed, organizational man. Three workers, too, were seen as representing all labouring people, and three were all that were required.

The interdenominational and interclass effort of the Savings Committee, and the idea that labourers could be represented by a profile of three men, can be compared to another association which aimed to educate, the Catholic Young Men's Society (CYMS). It was founded by retailers in 1925 with 'up to date' facilities in Market Street, the same year that labourers were evicted from their League Rooms. Although workers founded another facility (Labour Hall) in Maudlin Street, it never had the same amenities as the CYMS. A worker recalled this in 1981 (Case 16.10).

Case 16.10: A Labourer's Recollections of the CYMS

Dick, a millworker, explained how 'labourers resented the CYMS because it was formed largely by shopkeepers, and they wouldn't dream of coming into the Labour Rooms. So the workers wouldn't want to go into the CYMS, although W.B. [shoemaker] was actively involved in the CYMS ... It was a penny looking down on a ha'penny. K.P. [retailer], for example, shouted at his workers. You had to bow and scrape to get a job from them.' There was also indebtedness. Mick's mother was indebted £30 to retailer Willie Power in the 1930s. 'She paid it back, and no interest was charged and the prices weren't raised. There was honour among them. But shopkeepers exploited workers because of low wages and unemployment.' The 'gentry treated their labourers better. [Retailer] S.J. was an exception. My brother worked for him. He gave the brother Christmas presents and the brother was happy there, bottling stout, delivering groceries.' But millworker/councillor James O'Neill would never have gone into the CYMS. [His brother] did because he was a billiards player.'

In these comments were encapsulated so many of the contradictions and ambivalences of everyday life for labour as a class and for labourers as individuals. First, the shoemaker who became involved in the CYMS was not untypical of many labourers, such as Dolly Doyle (Case 13.2), who saw themselves as having more in common with people of other status-classes and who thus aspired to respectability by emulation. Other labourers saw this, with some irony, as 'a penny looking down on a ha'penny.' Second, the facilities that the more monied retailers were able to provide, through a bank loan, were far better than those in Labour Hall. Even politically astute workers, who frequented Labour Hall, also went to the CYMS because they 'were daft about billiards and that way they could get two games in the same evening.' Third, generation differences meant that sons did not particularly want to frequent places where their fathers were. So the 'Labour Hall didn't have the support from the younger people. They joined the CYMS,' said a builder's labourer. 'Older workers, though, held out to the end.'

Fourth, in their relations with retailers outside the CYMS/Labour Hall, labourers were simultaneously consumers and workers. Even as their labour was exploited by retailers, their relations with them as consumers might be adjudged fair and affable. And even as one retailer exploited their labour, another might mask the relationship with decent working conditions and a generous Christmas basket. Finally, even if all the retailers were not exploitative all the time in all contexts, there were those from other status-classes, such as the gentry (or farmers), against whom the retailers might be compared and found wanting. Then again, not all gentry were 'good.' And so on.

We are thus led back to the redundancy and complexity of social life in a local place and, therefore, to the difficulty that labourers had in making absolute moral judgments, clear ideological commitments, and firm material interpretations. In other words, the interplay between personal and class experience rendered a consistent, radical critique ('good sense,' in Gramsci's terms) difficult. In such a context, the impact of the CYMS was important, the more so because recreation was a vital facet of labouring life. What values was the CYMS purveying? And how did it do so?

First, the CYMS was intended not simply as a recreational endeavour but as a Catholic one. The curate therefore held an official position as spiritual director. Second, it was mainly an association for retailers and notables. All executive members and/or delegates to national conventions were retailers, teachers, or gardaí sergeants. At the same time, labourers were encouraged to use the premises. Their presence might be occasionally noted, publicly, when they were on a subcommittee for the billiard or card room or in a billiards tournament. Otherwise, they were invisible and, like the Savings Committee, in their place. Third, in the mid-1930s, the CYMS expanded its educational activities by opening a branch of the Carnegie Library on its premises.[15] Among its activities was to encourage members to take part in essay-writing competitions directed by the national CYMS. In 1933 third place was won by the son of a retailer. The subject of the essay was: 'Why a Catholic cannot be a Communist.'[16]

Conclusion

Throughout Labour Hall's existence, the Labour Party and the IT&GWU never met in the CYMS rooms. If necessary, they used the Concert Hall, built by the efforts of the gentry in 1911. In fact, Labour Hall was seen by many elderly workers in the 1980s as explicitly 'in opposition' to the CYMS even though some went to the latter place for billiards. More generally, however, it was through the vehicles of recreation, education, and public ritual that the agents of capitalism, Catholicism, cultural nationalism, and the Free State found key nodes for articulating with working-class life. At the same time, local narratives and knowledge about status-class boundaries and differences structured responses to such agency, just as the outcomes of such agency, in turn, were made to fit the status-class structure. However, there also were other agents active at the time. They were impelled by more radical socialist ideas, by a counter-ideology of anti-communism and by tenets of pragmatic accommodation. I turn now to these, bearing in mind that such agency was also affected by the redundancy and complexity of local life such that the profound ambivalences were invariably (re)created between lived experience and political ideas and between class experience and personal understandings.

17. 'And the Church Preached Its View'

'The wife of a handyman died in the late 1920s. Soon after, the widower met a poor woman who was on her way to the County Home; he invited her to stay with him. Father Drea paid him a visit. 'I believe you are living with a woman,' said Fr Drea. 'I wouldn't put it that way, Father. She's my housekeeper, just like you have one. And, anyhow, if [retailer] Power is allowed to have a housekeeper, why amn't I?'

– Mrs Stasia Byrne, 1985, aged seventy-two

The nature of individual experience in a rural locale, which created complex and often contradictory images, possibilities, and conclusions, could of course be mediated and organized by formal associations and/ or coherent ideological interpretations. However, not only were such associations and ideas often in competition, but some had strategical and perhaps compromising alliances with other groups. Sometimes, these coalitions also had the backing of the state. In this kaleidoscope of ideas and structures, the Catholic Church had immense influence – spiritually, organizationally, and ideologically.

In the Thomastown area, the few non-Catholic, labouring families worked on Mount Juliet estate. Two farmers, several notables, and residents of big houses comprised the remainder of local Protestants. In writing the constitution for the Free State, efforts had been made to recognize the presence of such minorities and to retain some semblance of religious pluralism. By the late 1920s however, conservative forces, particularly the Catholic hierarchy, had begun to undermine these intentions.[1] Three aspects of this became particularly implicated in class awareness, experience, and consciousness among Thomastown's labouring people. First was the way in which religious practice, belief, agency, and morality contributed to the reproduction of status-class in the locality. Second was the depth of piety which typified individual consciousness and which was reinforced through a devotional swell in the 1930s. Third was the way in which the Catholic Church entered political society through its defence of the faith and of morals.

'... And the Only Difference Was Status'

The boundaries between status-classes, which infused life in Thomastown, also permeated formal Catholic practices. In 1943 Gerard Doyle, clerk, recorded his observations (Case 17.1).

Case 17.1: Mass and Status-Class, 1943

'Let us look at ... the segregation of classes in the church. The "elite," consisting of ... shopkeepers and the richer farmers, go right up to the top, generally occupying the first 6 or 7 seats on the left-hand side of the nave. The rest of this left-hand side is occupied by the better-off classes. Of late however, there has been some infiltration of workers ... particularly since (some 12 or 14 years ago), the railings separating the nave and the aisles were removed. [But,] ... generally workers are not to be found between the pulpit and the altar ... The end of the left-hand side ... exhibits a more democratic character ... undoubtedly because men can enter that section almost unnoticed. Here there is a fair proportion of wage-earners. [But] there is a disinclination to enter this section of the church; and when entry is made it is usually done surreptitiously and with an air of apology. For a worker to walk up the middle passage and to take a seat in one of the top rows is almost unheard of ... The left-hand side of the nave is occupied by both men and women. As a rule, women take their seats there if accompanied by their husbands; but they often enter this section, even if alone, and a great many girls of the "better class" also sit there. The right-hand aisle is occupied entirely by women: poor, elderly women are in the vast majority. The left-hand aisle is the preserve of men of all ages but all of working class. Then there are those who kneel round the doors, some of whom do not go past the porch. Workers predominate but there is also a fair number of farmers. These generally arrive late and depart early.'

Doyle concluded that 'this segregation of the people at Mass did not result from any action by the priests. It is spontaneous in the sense that people go to the place where they consider they should be. It reflects the generally accepted class divisions of everyday life.' In the 1980s, older working people had numerous, similar tales: of their experiences as labourers cum Catholics and of the visible and taken-for-granted practices of exclusion (Case 17.2).

Case 17.2: Vignettes of Status-Class and Religious Practice
'Religious processions and church collections are examples of what may justly be called class discrimination ... I have never known a single instance of a working man acting as canopy bearer in a procession or as a collector at the Christmas, Easter, or November Offering. Funerals are another example. When a local "notability" is being buried, it is nothing unusual to see three or more priests attending the funeral. Very seldom indeed is more than one present at the funeral of a working man' (Gerard Doyle, 1943; and others, 1981). *'The Dublin road cemetery opened in 1928. Father Doyle had three prices for graves. The most expensive was at the back, near to the cross; the medium-priced ones were behind the most expensive; and the ones that cost the least, for the poor, were near the entry gate and road. And the only difference was status'* (mill worker, 1983). *'High Mass was said for the wealthy but only an ordinary Mass for other people'* (carpenter, 1981).

This association of religious practice with status-class in routinized and public ways was accompanied by a deep-seated piety which, in contrast, was very private. In the 1980s, no one spoke or told stories about religious beliefs, just as Gerard Doyle in his 1943 essay never mentioned the tenets of Catholicism. In June, one might be told about the annual 'pattern' to St Columkille's well and how people used to believe that the well cured warts. Or someone might mention a purported historical happening, such as the friary which gave its name to a place called Friars' Hill or the rural crossroads where three monks were murdered by Cromwell's forces in the mid-seventh century. But key theological doctrine, such as the Trinity, the Virgin, and so on, were so fundamentally part of common sense that no one ever spoke of them. Nor did we ask many questions. For what could we ask? Questions such as 'do you believe?' directed at those who, in the early 1980s were somewhat lax observers of the formalities, elicited a response of 'who knows?' and a shrug of the shoulders. Similar responses came from those who would have supported firmly the Marxist dictum that religion is the opiate of the masses. Religious belief, in other words, was not something that people spoke about. It had no historical or political dimension; it simply

was. Formal instruction began in primary school as children were prepared for first communion (age six) and later for confirmation (age
twelve). Thus, just as Doyle noted how 'people go to the place where
they consider they should be,' so too did they come to believe what they
knew they should. Belief was essentialized, naturalized, and timeless. In
being so ingrained in the very bedrock of common sense, such belief
was, of course, potentially powerful.

Belief, however, was also enmeshed in observances and duties.
Although the shape of such actions cannot measure belief, their sheer
repetition inevitably became implicated with it. Doyle's 1943 essay, however, also noted the role of sanctions (Case 17.3).

Case 17.3: Religious Duties and Observances – Doyle's View, 1943

'The great majority of people attend their religious duties fairly regularly. The
number who miss Sunday Mass is very small ... An insignificant number ...
habitually ... stay away and ... a somewhat greater number ... still insignificant,
miss Mass occasionally, generally on some pretext ... which, theologically speaking
would be regarded as insufficient ... They always ... say ... they have a reason for
absenting themselves. The fact, however, that [they] always have an excuse is ...
significant. It ... clearly implies that those people feel that they should attend ...
The same attitude is noticeable in the case of those who scarcely ever miss Mass.
They attend because of ... public opinion ... The habitual or even occasional
"mass-misser" is commented on unfavourably by neighbours. Consequently, a certain number, quite impossible to determine accurately, are exact in their observance because failure to do so would result in their being ostracised to a certain
extent. That this is the case is clearly proved by the attitude of these people when
they migrate to England. These emigrants are, for the most part, of the working
class and it is well-known that some of them at least are not exemplary Catholics
when they go to live in England ...

'... On the whole, attendance at the Sacraments is fairly good. Even those who
go only at intervals of 6 or 12 months cannot be regarded as lax Catholics. In
their view, regularity is not a necessary hallmark of a "good" Catholic. [In any
case] there is a tendency, particularly among the older people, to regard with suspicion the too frequent reception of the Sacraments. This is looked on as only
proper for priests and nuns and something out of place or too ambitious for ordinary people. In fact, too-frequent attendance at church is regarded as a sign
of hypocrisy. Constant church-goers are referred to as "craw-Thumpers" or "voteens;" and one who goes frequently to Communion, particularly if his motives
are suspect, is said to be "eating the altar.".'

The import of public opinion and of an audience to observe the observances were central for people of all status-classes in Thomastown. It was a severe and highly critical public. Said Jim Doyle in 1995: 'Everyone went to Mass. They might stay outside the door, but they came. You'd be stigmatized if you didn't.' Another worker said in 1983: 'Michael Tierney was a communist, yet he went to Mass. He said: "If I didn't go, I'd be victimized economically and socially." Anyone who didn't go to Mass would be hounded down.' That the observances or liturgy may not have been entirely understood or engaged in attentively detracted neither from the need to be seen as present nor, for many, from the religious solemnity of the occasion, even while they were chatting at the church door. Nor did it detract from the fact that belief had long been firmly embedded in individual consciousness. Even Thomastown's socialists, said a labourer, were eventually 'brought back to the fold.'

Yet some labouring people at certain times of their lives, or in certain places such as England, contested such regular, public religious observance. On the one hand, they saw the personal failings of 'voteens' and 'altar-eaters' who had succumbed to blandishments of doctrine, respectability, and/or clergy. On the other hand, they saw the failings of a church that not only differentiated and segregated people but that also discriminated against some of them. The perpetrators of this were the agents of the church – priests and nuns. However, the deficiencies of these agents were seen in relation to religious practice rather than belief. That priests mediated between human beings and God was not in question. Rather, the problem for most Thomastown labourers was that they did not do so impartially (Case 17.4).

Case 17.4: The 'Attitude' of Labourers towards the Clergy, 1943
Wrote Gerard Doyle: *'There is a tendency to represent priests and people as being closely bound together – the former acting as guides and mentors who ... have the spiritual and temporal welfare of their flocks at heart. This is a sweeping generalisation [and] I can speak with reasonable authority only for the working classes ... Priests are always treated with respect. But the important thing is not how people act, particularly when those acts are conventional, but what they think. What is the attitude of the ... working man towards the priest? There is a ... deep-seated conviction that many, if not most, of the priests incline unduly towards the wealthier sections of the community. And I do not think that this opinion is far wrong. The ordinary, secular clergy are drawn almost exclusively*

from the merchant and farming classes; and, generally, they tend to form their friendships with members of these classes. It would ... be unfair to suggest that priests should not ... pick their own friends. That is not the point. The complaints of the working man are that he and his class are ignored by the priests. It is a rare occurrence to see a priest visiting a working class house or to be seen speaking to a working man in public, except, of course, in discharge of his priestly duties. There is also the belief, sometimes erroneous, that the mere possession of wealth entitles one to violate the moral law with impunity. Still, it is incontestable that the wealthy wrong-doer is generally let off lightly as compared with his poorer brother.'

The favouritism and discriminatory practices were intensified by the power that priests were believed to have. 'People were terrified of the priest,' said a labourer. 'Old people believed that he could damn them to hell.' In the light of this bias cum power, priests were often criticized by working people for extending their authority beyond what was appropriate or, alternatively, for failing to extend it in fitting directions. Several workers told the story of the handyman and his housekeeper or how Father Doyle caused the tannery to close despite the economic hardships of the 1930s. Conversely, priests did not intrude where, in moral terms, they should have. Between 1910 and 1950, the convent had a laundry which was intended to turn a profit. A common story was that poor, labouring girls and orphans provided unpaid labour under the guise that this was a school of domestic economy. Many also told of how unwed mothers were treated in the workhouse. A labourer saw them 'being made to scrub the flagstones so hard that their hands were bleeding. They got not a penny; only a little food. They were put there by their parents as punishment. It was deliberate. These people were imbued with Catholic faith – maybe that's why. But it was sheer cruelty. You wouldn't treat your dog like that.'

In relating these stories, people were highlighting the immorality of situations in which deliberate punishment/cruelty rather than charity was meted out by those professing the faith. This was particularly obnoxious in the case of unwed mothers because, as labourers put it, it was 'well known' that 'farmers' sons often used female farm servants' and that was why they were in the workhouse in the first place. Where was the priest when that was taking place?

It has often been noted that 'devotion to the faith in Ireland was often accompanied by an outspoken anti-clericalism.'[2] However, what was happening in Thomastown was more complex than a distinction between belief and practice/agency. Rather, numerous facets comprised the religious domain, each made up of belief, practice, and agency. These were Mass, sacraments, doctrine, priests, and morality. Although all were interconnected, some labouring people distinguished each facet from the others, separated out belief, practice, and agency, and then were able to see consistencies and contradictions. At the same time, all working people took it for granted that, whatever the contradictions, religion itself was simply one more aspect of the status-class and material structure of local life.

'... And the Church Preached Its View'

Formal religion in Thomastown was subsumed under the diocesan structure of the Roman Catholic Church in Ireland. There were twenty-four dioceses, each headed by a bishop. These combined to form four archdioceses, each led by an archbishop. These agents, who represented priests, parishes, and people, comprised the so-called hierarchy. Local labouring people, however, had no personal stories about this structure or its agents. The odd bit of gossip emerged, for example, that a large-scale farmer was 'close' to the bishop or that, when a Catholic man married a wealthy Protestant, he received dispensation without difficulty from the bishop. Overall, the bishop was far away and became visible only through the actions of wealthy or important locals.

Yet the hierarchy had a good deal of agency vis-à-vis local people. Weekly sermons and face-to-face admonitions from the parish priest or curates transmitted the hierarchy's orthodoxy and behavioural rules. These were also conveyed by pastoral letters several times a year, prepared by the bishop, read at Mass, and sometimes published in newspapers. Doctrine and values were also promulgated through local, religious organizations attached to church and hierarchy. From the perspective of local labouring people, three associations were relevant: sodalities for men and women; a secret organization known as the Knights of Columbanus; and informal cliques of select parishioners who regularly reported on the behaviour of their fellows to the parish priest.

The Pastorals: Belief, Practice, Agency, and Morality, 1913–50
The pastoral letters aimed to educate people about belief, values, conduct, and authority.[3] Via such religious assertions, however, many pastorals impinged on politics or addressed the structure of political society.

Indeed, through time in the context of the Free State, the hierarchy managed to expand its influence and jurisdiction in both civil and political society. What were these pastorals? In 1914 as an example, a letter addressed the 1913 general strike/lockout in Dublin (Case 17.5).

Case 17.5: A Pastoral Address – The 1913 Labour Dispute

'Out of the average ... business, the workman may ... claim in return for his honest day's work what will at least procure ... maintenance for himself and his little family.' In contrast, socialist proposals are 'so clearly futile ... that if they were carried out, the working man himself would be ... the first to suffer. Moreover, they are ... unjust, because they would rob the lawful possessor, bring the State into a sphere that is not its own, and cause complete confusion in the community.' For it is an erroneous idea that 'rich and poor are intended ... to live at war with one another ... [Rather,] each requires the other; capital cannot do without labour, nor labour without capital.' Syndicalism, too, is to 'be condemned as a system' under which 'the employer is ... to disappear and ... workers are ... to ... manage everything in an industrial federation away from State control.' In contrast, 'through Trade Unions, with all their shortcomings ... the working classes secured something corresponding with the protection which ... the Church promoted in former times. Their organisation is most desirable.'

In this nineteenth-century view, a worker should be maintained by his wage but did not have the right to accumulate. Such maintenance was also necessary for quieting dissent and ensuring that private property, the state, and the 'community' were preserved. Then, when all people were appropriately treated and in their proper places, capital and labour could co-exist peacefully under a system of private ownership. In the context of the Free State, the Catholic hierarchy retained this common sense. It expanded it to include a place for trade unions to help ensure the balance, but not ones that had syndicalist or socialist philosophies that might challenge the dominant outlook. This amplified viewpoint, stemming in part from a papal encyclical entitled *Rerum Novarum* in 1903, was fleshed out by ideas about the religious duties which owners had towards their workers. In a 1927 pastoral letter, the bishop of Ossory diocese, in which Thomastown was located, wrote how it was incumbent on the employer, with the help of the church, to provide religious and moral leadership for the poorer classes. In a similar vein, the 1929 Lenten pastoral was entitled *How Ireland Stands*. Playing on the lyrics of a nationalist song about the 1798 rebellion,[4] this was a clear effort to appropriate such sentiment to the church while alerting people to dangers emanating from working people's behaviour (Case 17.6).

Case 17.6: Pastoral Letters from the Bishop of Ossory, 1929 and 1930
1929. **How Ireland Stands.** '*... We have no ... reason for alarm or pessimism ... with crowded churches ... overcrowded confessionals, crowded altar-rails, flourishing Confraternities ... We can say ... that all is fairly well. Still, things could be better ... The break-up of home life and the passing of parental authority, deplored by the Pope as one of the evils of today, has been very marked in Ireland ... The humbler classes ... seem to have less regard for purity and morality than in the past, and I make an earnest appeal to employers ... to the clergy, to keep a more stringent control over these poor people.*'
1930. **Sodalities and the Working Class.** '*... The humbler classes ... have ... been noted for their religious spirit [but] ... I am not sure that masters and mistresses in Catholic houses realize their responsibilities for the souls of their servants ... But for all such, our Sodalities offer a safe home ... and ... I appeal to ... employers, not only to afford facilities, but also to make it a matter of conscience that their employees shall join and attend these sodalities. I appeal to all priests to make this deserving class the special object of their zeal and charity ... Employers should inform the Clergy of changes in their staffs.*'

As in the nineteenth century, it was the labourers, the so-called humbler classes, who were dangerous to public order and morality. Equally, it was incumbent on those from the better classes, including the clergy, to lead them to Mass and into sodalities. Thomastown had two sodalities, one for men and one for women. They met on Sunday evening, once a month, for prayer and the rosary. As the pastoral noted, the aim was to promote religious observance and deepen belief through practice. This was deemed essential because 'grave' dangers were lurking, according to a 1931 pastoral. Read at all Masses in Ireland on the third Sunday in October, this pastoral was prepared by the archbishops. It was also published by the Kilkenny *People*. An introduction by the editor noted the 'grave anxiety' with which the hierarchy 'view the progress made by anti-social and anti-Christian organisations' and the 'call for a great crusade of prayer to stay the peril which is threatening the land' (Case 17.7).

Case 17.7: The 1931 October Pastoral from the Hierarchy

'... We cannot remain silent in face of the growing evidence of a campaign of revolution and Communism, which, if allowed to run its course ... must end in the ruin of Ireland, both soul and body ... It is to be clearly understood that this statement ... has reference only to the religious and moral aspect of affairs, and involves no judgement ... on ... public policy, so far as it is purely political.

'... The existing government ... is composed of our own countrymen and ... entrusted with office by the votes of the people ... No individuals or combination ... are free to resist its decrees or its officials by armed force, violence or intimidation ... A new organisation entitled Saor Éire ... is ... Communistic in its aims. [Its] ... programme ... is to mobilise workers and working farmers ... behind a revolutionary movement to set up a Communistic State. That is, to impose upon the Catholic soil of Ireland the same materialistic regime, with its fanatical hatred of God, as now dominates Russia and threatens to dominate Spain ... This organisation ... proposes to attain its object by starting ... "cells" ... to serve as revolutionary units to infect their disciples with the virus of communism, and create social disruption by organised opposition to the Law of the Land ... If their efforts are successful, [we will see] the ruin of all that is dear to us ... For ... Communism ... means a blasphemous denial of God, and the overthrow of Christian civilisation. It means ... class warfare, the abolition of private property and the destruction of family life ... To obtain those ends, Communists shrink from nothing and fear nothing; and ... it is unbelievable ... how cruel and inhuman they [are] ... while their antagonism to Holy Church and to God Himself are, alas ... well known ... It is our duty to tell our people plainly that the Organisations to which we have referred, whether separate or in alliance, are sinful and irreligious, and that no Catholic can lawfully be a member of them ... We appeal ... to all our people, and especially the young, ... to abandon them at once ... You cannot be a Catholic and a Communist. One stands for Christ, the other for anti-Christ. Neither can you, and for the same reason, be an auxiliary of communism ... With anxious hearts we turn to God ... to open all eyes to the danger ... and to strengthen all hearts to resist the forces of evil with unflinching faith.'

Saor Éire, meaning 'Free Ireland,' had been formed in 1931 as an offshoot of the IRA to create an independent, revolutionary leadership for 'the working class and working farmers' in order to overthrow both British imperialism and its associate, Irish capitalism. It aimed to unite republicans and socialists. Its national leadership included Peadar O'Donnell and Frank Ryan. On 17 October 1931, in the midst of IRA drilling, intimidations, and shootings, the Free State government, headed by W.T. Cosgrave and his Cumann na nGaedheal party, proscribed twelve radical organizations. The above pastoral was issued the following day, condemning not only Saor Éire but all secret and/or left-wing organizations.[5]

From the perspective of historians and political scientists, such events were related to problems of state formation after the Troubled Times: to the slow emergence of political parties and the even slower disarming of disaffected republican and socialist agents. For labour historians, such events were related to the splintering of republican-left organizations and the complex factions and alliances that ensued. Specifically, the 1922 Treaty had alienated republicans and led to continuing violence amidst claims by republicans that they were the legitimate government while the 'pro-Treaty majority in the Dáil were usurpers.' In 1924 an army mutiny was staged by republicans who had fought in the war of independence, who had followed Michael Collins into the pro-Treaty camp, and who had fought in the civil war for the Free State, all on the premise that Collins would deliver the republic which, now, seemed not to interest the Cosgrave government.[6] This crisis was immediately followed by the Boundary Commission's failure to repatriate the Catholic parts of Ulster to the Free State in 1925, and by the split between de Valera and the IRA/extreme republicans, with the latter increasingly committed to ending partition by force, especially in the face of de Valera allowing his Fianna Fáil party finally to enter the Dáil. IRA violence again emerged in 1926 and a Public Safety Act was imposed.[7] Events throughout these years were also attended by the formation of various left-wing organizations dedicated, in varying combinations, to trade unionism, socialism, communism, and republicanism. All this was accompanied by the failure of the Labour Party to provide any alternative but an alliance with Fianna Fáil's now diluted republicanism and economic protectionism.[8]

In 1928, after the repeal of the last Public Safety Act, violence and illegal drilling resurfaced. In October 1931 a 'ferocious' constitutional amendment concerning public safety was passed which set up a military tribunal and the death penalty to deal with political crime and which gave the Executive Council the right to proscribe any association by simple order.[9] In this context of uncertainty with regard to the stability of the state and to the activities of left-wing and/or republican alternatives, the hierarchy of the Catholic Church acted. However, it also acted in terms of its own particular history. For it was also 'a time when the

Papacy was attempting to posit Catholic social action as a political creed.'[10]

Although historians have seen all this from the perspectives of state formation and of factionalism within the Irish left, Thomastown's workers recalled different understandings. What elderly labourers remembered was the heavy-handedness of the hierarchy, the heroism of radical leaders on the national scene, and pieces of ideology. People also recalled that 'the church didn't let up,' that 'the propaganda was incessant.' In fact, by 1933, the hierarchy's campaign was still heating up. In a pastoral read on two consecutive Sundays at Mass, the bishop of Ossory noted that the spread of communism was facilitated by 'economic depression, unemployment and poverty, and labour and political unrest.' Although there was, as yet, 'no reason for alarm or panic ... as there are no great dangers so far,' there also was 'no doubt but that we have the symptoms of the Communistic disease' in County Kilkenny (Case 17.8).

Case17.8: A Pastoral Letter on the Dangers of Communism in Kilkenny, 1933
'... We in Kilkenny ... have the only coal-mining area in the country, employing hundreds of workers. Such a centre is always the hope of the Communist agitator. A few weeks ago our city and the industrial area of the county shared in the communistic "push" organized in practically every country. It was on a small scale, but it was real, and had the marks of "the Beast." We had the secret inspiration from headquarters, the paid agitator, the preaching of labour unrest, the veiled incitement to looting and rioting. We also had the irreligious part of the Communist programme which denied the Divinity of Christ, the Church, Private Property. We have the machinery of Communism here in the Soviet cell, union, "contact" and [in] the active support ... by the Communistic Party proper.'

The bishop went on to define communism and its methods, focusing on its desire 'above all to pervert youth, abusing their simplicity and ignorance.'

'Poisoned lies ... are whispered into the ears of workers; class hatred is engendered. Their object is [to] ... disrupt the lawful trade unions ... and throw Labour back 100 years ... These Communist agents even assume the role of Religion, the better to deceive the decent Catholic working man. They make it a point to be seen at Church, at Mass ... and even at the Sacraments ... They say to the worker: I am a

Communist, but I am also a Catholic ... [But] I ... say: No Catholic can be a communist. No communist can be a Catholic.' Therefore, 'it is my duty to tell my people plainly that the revolutionary Workers' Group ... every local union, cell or "contact"' which is Communistic in aim ... has come under the ban and censure of the Church. NO Catholic can be ... a member of such unions, no matter what name they ... adopt. No Catholic can buy, sell, read or support any Communistic literature, journal or paper, such as "The Workers' Voice."... It must be ... understood that my ... condemnation has no reference whatever to the main body of Labour in ... the ... Diocese who are united in the ordinary ... Trade and Labour Unions ...'

The *Notes for Priests* attached to the pastoral said that sermons on the next three Sundays should explain the Catholic doctrine of private property, expose false systems (communism, socialism), and exhort workers to abandon condemned unions and join lawful ones. Moreover, 'as Communism is likely to be a troublesome evil for some time,' priests were to form study circles. Priests were also warned to moderate their 'language and exposition ... Do not alarm, or over-paint the picture.' For 'in the rural areas, Communism is practically unknown, and is only dangerous in the city, towns and industrial areas. But ... the greatest necessity is vigilance.'

With the premises that society was a religious edifice and that the state was Catholic, the hierarchy's doctrine and practices were invariably extended into domestic and personal relations. In the midst of its anti-communist crusade, the 1934 Lenten pastoral was devoted to *The Catholic Home* (Case 17.9): how to govern labour, preserve the family, and maintain women's sanctity. Through this hegemonic thrust into civil and political society could be seen a conflating of the private and the public, the household and the state, the person and the organizational affiliation.

Case 17.9: Pastoral Letter on 'The Catholic Home,' 1934

(1) People were enjoined, 'before God,' to 'supervise the lives and conduct of their servants and the working class' who 'should be given every opportunity for their Religious duties.' (2) The 'break up of the home' was the result of 'secularism.' However, in Ireland, because of 'religious influence in schools' and measures in the constitution (for example, the ban on divorce), 'the Catholic Home is free to flourish under the fostering care of a very sympathetic State.' The greatest dangers were from the foreign press, cinema, theatre, and dance hall. However, 'our Irish

press is not included in any ... criticisms made.' (3) Women were central to this stability. 'It is the mother [whom] the children copy, [whose] ... example goes deepest ... The Home is the mother's special work. The father provides; the mother trains and educates.' When things go wrong, 'the woman is most to blame ... The sin of these deliberate sinners who use scientific ... means to escape the results of sin [birth control] is more terrible still.' In the 'ideal Catholic Home ... we see the prudent ... watchful mother, the Angel of the house, a tower of strength in anxiety and sorrow, who knows that sacrifice is gain and selfishness is loss ...'

What is striking about this material is the hierarchy's assumption of almost complete and uncontested hegemony over state, schools, media, and domestic relations. In part to achieve this, church leaders appropriated early-nineteenth-century images of a naturalized hierarchy and the dangerous, labouring classes. They then placed this into the fertile ground of a modern, centralized state. This permitted an appeal to deep-seated common sense and stereotypes even as it was a contemporary response to current labour unrest and ideologies. It was then taken further. This common sense allowed, indeed required, a dialectical expression of concerned paternalism for workers and, thus, an approval of certain unions in order to undermine the more radical ones. It ensured, too, that capital/employers, notables, and retailers would collude as agents for the hierarchy and help to civilize labourers, both spiritually and materially. At the same time, however, such a hegemonic intent conflicted with notions of self-determination and entitlement which workers had acquired because of their role in the achievement of the Free State and their activism in unions. Moreover, the hegemonic ideas themselves provided points of entry. For example, how many shillings in fact constituted the living wage to which the hierarchy said that workers were entitled? Inevitably, such inconsistencies, both potential and actual, added to the redundancy of cultural meanings and social relations in the locality.

The Organizational Impetus: Belief, Practice, Agency, and Morality, 1914–50
The pastorals periodically referred to local sodalities and their role in ensuring piety, integrating workers, and securing peaceful relations among classes. Other organizations were also fostered. A 1935 pastoral endorsed the Catholic Truth Society, encouraging people to join and to read its publications which were 'sadly needed to counteract the poison of the Radio, Press and Platform of false political and economic sys-

tems.' The 1939 Lenten pastoral referred to the association for the Propagation of the Faith; all parishes were asked to lend it financial support, and 'no head of a Home or Family should be missing' from its membership list. A special appeal was made to youth to contribute the 'small sum of 2s.2d. a year for God.' For 'our young people are not prominent ... in their ... support of the Church. They are too fond of themselves, and forget God.' In 1940 the pastoral of 1930 was repeated, enjoining people to enlist in sodalities. In 1944 the Pontifical Association of the Holy Childhood was founded to appeal to youth and to complement the Association for the Propagation of the Faith. In 1946 yet another sodality emerged, the Confraternity of Christian Doctrine, aimed at both adolescents and adults.

Out of all this organizational fervour, no records remain and few memories. Older people did recall that everyone in the 1930s and 1940s belonged to sodalities and went for prayers on Sunday evening. Of the other associations, nothing was recollected. However, one association that was not mentioned in the pastorals was one that many labouring people did remember. It, too, left no records. This is because it was a secret society in which membership was by invitation only (Case 17.10).

Case 17.10: Recollections of the Knights of Columbanus

'They were strong in Thomastown. They held secret meetings. Members included a garage owner and Herbert Devoy [a leader of the Labour Party in Thomastown]' (Mason). *'The Knights were very much against trade unions. It was a secret organization which was encouraged before the Emergency. Devoy was a member, along with National Labour people like him, and shopkeepers. The secretary was a teacher from Inistioge. Tailor X was another member. The Knights kept tabs on people and their private lives. They brought in speakers. A Father Dudley once gave a vociferous anti-labour and anti-communist talk. The Knights created and exploited a lot of anti-labour sentiment'* (millworker). *'The Knights kept tabs on the simplest things: unmarried girls who were pregnant and men who had communist leanings. The members were mostly shopkeepers' (Labourer). 'Devoy was a member; he was "in with the clergy." The Knights met in the convent, with the parish priest. They were underground spies. They spied on anyone out of order, irregularities with women, or if a girl got into trouble. They told the priest what was going on in the parish. Carpenter X was another member, as was Tailor X. It was hard to know who belonged because it was highly secret. They "were dangerous, to be shunned by any decent person. You didn't know who they were. They were initiated with hoods on"'* (labourer).

Actual knowledge about the Knights was in fact extremely limited, in direct contrast to the anger expressed against them by some workers in the 1980s. No other person, organization, or event in the locality elicited such response. The reputed activities and actions of the Knights were seen as concealed, hostile, and malevolent. They became a way of summarizing the repugnance that many labourers felt towards those times, especially the snobbery and the role of the hierarchy. Imputed membership in the Knights became a way of condemning both a labourer and his/her class disloyalties while, in turn, the condemnation of a labourer assigned him/her membership in the Knights. Ultimately, as the hierarchy divided workers against each other, the Knights of Columbanus became the metaphor for disunity, animosity, and evil.

The Devotional Swell

The intensity of religious activity at the time was reflected in *Thomastown Notes*, as Ned Maher gave long descriptions of the processions, masses, and choirs which celebrated Corpus Christi, the Quarant Ore, and the Devotion of the 40 Hours Adoration.[11] Religious observance also became implicated in personal identities, particularly among retailers and farmers. Maher's obituaries at the time reflected this change (Case 17.11).

Case 17.11: Obituaries, Religious Observance, and Respectability
When the elderly Stasia Murphy (farmer) died, Maher listed the five priests at the funeral and the mourners. Little was said about the deceased except that she had been in poor heath and that 'she was a most devout Catholic who put her religion before every other consideration.' When a victualler and 'extensive farmer' died, Maher listed the twelve priests who attended the High Mass. It was also noted that he was 'a generous supporter of the Kilkenny Hunt' and a 'most charitable and a generous contributor to church funds.' When the owner of Ballyduff Mill died in 1937, he was said to be 'noted for his industry and integrity.' He 'was a member of Thomastown Parochial Committee and of the Committee for the Co-operative Creamery. He held a high place in the opinions of the priests of Thomastown parish ... He was an ardent and most devout Catholic and a weekly Communicant, and he leaves behind him ... an unsullied name and noble example. He reared a large and most respectable family ... The parish ... has lost one its most respected members who during his long and useful life was never known to be absent from the monthly meeting of the Confraternity of the Sacred Heart.'[12]

Public adherence to formal religious practices had become implicated in attributions and definitions of respectability. Devout Catholicism had come to define public worth, and public worth required clear
and public expressions of piety. This devotional swell, however, seemed
not to require any mention of generous acts or help for the poor, only
contributions to parish funds. Clearly, as farmers and retailers displaced
the gentry as the dominant classes, agency in religion rather than in
charity became the dominant motif. In this intensely Catholic world
devoid of charity, the *Note* marking the 1937 death of labourer Ellen
Dermody was short. No priests were listed; nor was there a reference to
a High Mass. Her remains were simply received at the church by 'the
priests of the parish.'

'... The Church Had a Terrible Hold'

The devotional swell, and the hierarchy's persistent campaign, was crucial for labourers who had radical political beliefs. It meant humiliation,
discrimination, ostracism, and, in some cases, threats to their livelihoods
and homes. Michael Tierney, born in 1888, married in 1922. He was a
full-time millworker. Like many labourers, he also had other means for
earning cash. In hay-making season, he worked for a farmer; with his
pony and cart, he collected and sold timber; he bred ponies; he tilled an
unused section of a nearby field as well as the acre adjoining his cottage;
and his wife, Kate, reared fowl and pigs for sale. According to Kate, the
family was never hungry 'though food might be a bit scarce on a Thursday.' Tierney never drank. In 1981, Mrs Tierney, now widowed, and one
of their sons, Dick, spoke about Michael Tierney and their lives (Case
17.12).

---

*Case 17.12: 'That Was the Power of the Church' – Recollections of
Michael Tierney*

Mrs Tierney: *'Michael was a strong nationalist but not a republican. He was
anti-British. He voted for de Valera in the 1926 election.'* Tierney went to the
Labour Hall but never to the CYMS, even though a lot of labour people went into
the CYMS. He got along with Father Drea because *'Michael was anti-church but
not anti-churchman. He once challenged Father Drea to a debate, but was
refused.'* Canon Drennan of Tullaherin, in contrast to Drea, was *'an intellectual.'* Around 1940, he invited Gerard Doyle and Tierney, as labour men, to
debate/talk with him.

Dick: 'When I was a child, my father would seat all the children around the kitchen table and lecture then on Lenin and Marx. Then, as we later ran off to bed, my mother would sprinkle us all with holy water.' Mrs Tierney (laughing): 'Why not be sure.'

Dick: 'My father received a newspaper called The Workers' Voice. This paper was not lent to other workers. We children knew it as "Daddy's paper" and never mentioned it to anyone. It was a secret. [But] ... the workers in the post office used to open my father's mail and tell the priests. The church had a terrible hold on people ... In the late 1940s, I was working with the county council on the roads. It was Friday. The men stopped for lunch and I pulled out a tin of corned beef. All the other workers looked at me and moved away. One of them called me "godless." Nine years later, after things had loosened up a bit, I was again working on the roads. One of the men came up to me and said: "I remember you. You ate corned beef on a Friday." I had not seen him for almost a decade and he remembered me just from the beef incident. That was the power of the church.

'The left wing people in Thomastown were discriminated against. My mother was often heckled a bit and called a communist. As a child, I wasn't allowed to compete in a Feis. It was a punishment for my father's politics. There was no danger in my father losing his job because Pilsworth, although he was right wing, was Protestant and anti-Catholic. But there was discrimination against a leftist teacher in Waterford in the 1930s. He was fired because the clergy intervened. The teacher's son, living in Callan, later put an announcement in the newspaper disassociating himself from socialism and communism. This was a story which my father often told ... I never got into any fights as a youth because people in Thomastown don't speak their own minds. People seem to feel they have to do and say the right thing.'

In 1932 Michael Tierney wrote a letter to the secretary of the Communist Party of Ireland. It, too, highlights life at the time (Case 17.13).

Case 17.13: Letter from Michael Tierney, 1932

'Dear Comrade. I wish to congratulate the editor of the Workers' Voice on his spirited ... reply to the Standard ... Of course its [sic] the same old game all along the line. If the workers showed sufficient courage and determination these attacks would be bound to fail. Things are beginning to get a bit lively around here ... I am writing you a few particulars as a means of pushing the sale of the Workers' Voice. I hand your weekly Poster to the bill poster who I have to tip now and again. He places it at the foot of the wall ... where the workers going to the two *masses could see same. Your poster for a Communist Party offended some of the members of the [CYMS] here [so] ... that one of them, a gentleman named McKenna a son of an R.I.C. man and a licenced vintner, when going to first mass on Sunday mornings he turns the poster wrong side out, and then made inquiries from the bill poster to know who was giving them [to him]. Of course he told him. The result was [that] I had to watch the poster; of course he took good care not to stir it while I was looking. His brother-in-law also approached the [secretary] of the I.T.G.W.U warning him to be very careful as to the conduct of the Branch. A rancher ... named Forristall has done the same. This gentleman I might state has a brother who is a priest; also an uncle and first cousin. Just imagine the irony of this. I got this indirect as this secretary is hostile as well. The latest is that the nuns of the Convent ... sent for my wife and appealed to her to use her influence with me. They also told her it would injure me in my employment and also in my home. As you may know I am a married man with eight children. Three or four workers who used to take the paper also has got the wind up.'*

Another of Michael Tierney's sons wrote a comment on his father's letter and recollected something of the times (Case 17.14).

Case 17.14: Letter from Bob Tierney, Son of Michael and Kate Tierney, 1995
"'Things are beginning to get a bit lively around here," says [my father's] letter at one point; and that must have been an understatement. It also mentions pressure on my mother by the nuns, and their suggestion that his "activities" could "injure" him in his home and employment. Fortunately for him he worked in the local flour mill, which was owned by Protestants (who would have been more or less out ... of sympathy with Catholic concerns). The "home" business is more subtle, I think. It may been a veiled reference to the possibility of eviction, because the house was County Council property. However, they paid their rent so the Council never had a reason to move against them. I remember the same nuns giving us 8-year-olds cogent advice about the dangers of Communism and how we shouldn't buy sweets in a Communist shop, for instance. Where the f... you'd find a Commie sweetshop in Thomastown was irrelevant to the principle, I suppose. They used to put the heat on my sisters about attendance at mass, etc. At that time I think my father was not practising and "encouraged" the kids not to attend either, but they did so anyway: forbidden fruit, I suppose, and in any case our generation was one of religious nerds, at least in youth. I myself (b.1938) recall no such restrictions, but had terrible qualms of conscience about the fact of Communism, which seemed to me, as a result of the nuns' warnings to be a monstrous thing:

and my daddy it! I was far too young to understand the controversy at its worst (which was before my time anyway), but my older siblings say it was quite bitter. The priest would spew from the pulpit of "a paid agent of Communism," or warn the congregation that "There is a viper in your midst." It's a wonder the viper wasn't killed! And would you believe he became reconciled to the Church – though without losing the True Faith – in his old age? He died in 1970.'

Kate Tierney said that her husband was not 'anti-churchman' but that he was 'anti-Church.' In contrast, most of Thomastown's labourers who were critical of the church during those times had an opposite view: that it was the priests who acted with prejudice. Thus, in this religious world of beliefs, practices, and agency – of Mass, sacraments, doctrine, priests, and morality – local workers had different understandings of the politico-religious problems which they were experiencing and which they confronted as individuals and as a group. For the vast majority, it was because agency subverted essential moral elements. For a very few, however, the entire edifice had to be torn down. The problem in both views was the bedrock tenacity of belief.

Conclusion: 'The Church Ruined the Country'

The Catholic agenda of the Free State, like its Gaelic agenda, became implicated with local ideas about class, common-sense ideas about how the locality was constructed, and notions of respectability and avoidance as these were enmeshed in the redundancy of local life. In such a context, the hierarchy's hegemonic offensive created ambivalent sentiments for many labourers who tried to reconcile their religious beliefs with what they knew from their own material experiences and what they hoped for as workers. Catholicism thus came to be highly divisive: 'the church ruined the country' said a labourer in 1983. Indeed, the actions and views of the hierarchy, parish priests, and nuns divided families even as they proclaimed the sanctity of domesticity. They exacerbated class divisions even as they preached the unity of society. They divided individual psyches as labouring people had to reconcile their material experiences with their religious obligations. Finally, they divided workers as a class by fomenting and formalizing a contradiction between labour activism and godlessness. For it was a world in which numerous allegiances and nuances were possible: anti-British, nationalist, republican, anti/pro-Treaty, socialist, communist, Labour Party, trade unionist. The

hierarchy essentialized such nuance and turned all dissenters into 'aux-
illiaries of communism.'

Labourers thus had to reconcile what they knew to be the shortcomings of both church and state with their own deep-seated Catholic
beliefs. They had to develop a radical critique in the face of the hegemonic efforts of church and state and in the context of redundant local
life and meanings. In attempting to do so, workers invariably became
implicated in the available organizational possibilities. One of these was
the IT&GWU.

18. 'We Had a Live Union Then'

'In the 1920s, labourers worked 5½ days a week, from 8 in the morning to 6 at night without a break except a half hour for dinner. And there was always some-one to take your place if you didn't like it.'

– Builder's labourer, 1983

Individual experiences, and the redundancy of social relations in a rural locale, created diverse and often contradictory images and possibilities which might be clarified or made coherent by formal associations and/or by the dissemination of ideological formulations. Catholic beliefs and practices, as mediated by the hierarchy and as supported by those who framed the policies of the Free State, were one such example (chapter 17). Another included ideologies of a Gaelic past and future, as mediated through the educational system and recreation (chapter 16). Yet others were the values of a benevolent capitalism, a moral economy, and a hierarchical yet humanitarian inequality, located in private property and the rights of shared citizenship and dedicated to the simultaneous betterment of public amenities and underemployment through state interventions (chapters 14, 15). Alongside these were the activities and interests of yet other agents and organizations. One of these was the Irish Transport and General Workers' Union.

A branch had been founded in Thomastown in 1913. Many local men had therefore been members of an organization that had long affiliated and linked workers from diverse economic sectors, both permanent and casual. With the branch's 'Minute Books' that survived from mid-1935 as a means to stimulate recall, older workers in the 1980s remembered much of those earlier times. The occasional newspaper report helped. Out of these a picture of the pre-1950 period emerged.[1] It was of a union that, through its structure and modus operandi, constrained ideology and agency in particular directions. In so doing, the IT&GWU was a central focus and force for working people.

Association and Ideology: The Erratic Process of Unionizing Labour

The IT&GWU had a hierarchical structure. A Dublin Head Office (HO) oversaw its many local branches and managed external affairs with other labour organizations, such as the Irish Labour Party (ILP) and Trades Union Congress (TUC). Inside this structure, the Thomastown branch contained different sections. At various times there were sections for millworkers, council workers, casual/road workers, building labourers, forestry workers, and creamery workers. Of these, millworkers formed the backbone. From that position, they guarded their borders, work conditions, and wages, and they formed a core and elite which others envied, sought to emulate, or avoided.

Grennan Mills was the first unionized site in the locality. For its workers, the union was a source of great pride, material success, and radical ideology about the nature of capital and labour. Yet, from this centre, the IT&GWU had only limited success in expanding. This reflected at least five related features: anti-union sentiment or apathy among many non-millworkers; the diverse character of the labour process in different sectors of the local economy; the tactical power of particular employers; the limited concern of millworkers to recruit locals who worked in other sectors; and the narrow ideological focus and limited practical support that HO offered to the local branch. The case of lorry drivers illustrates this. It was here that the greatest tactical control could be exercised by members of the local IT&GWU, but only so far (Case 18.1).

Case 18.1: Unionizing Lorry Drivers at Bookle's Transport
In 1935 a local transport firm owned by retailer Bookle was targeted by the executive of the local IT&GWU. 'Bookle got a lot of work hauling to and from Grennan Mills, even though the mill had its own lorries. And the millworkers didn't want him using non-union, cheap labour.' Bookle himself 'was a republican, but not necessarily anti-union. It was his drivers who didn't want to join the union.' Two of the four lived outside the parish. One was a farmer. The fourth, a brother of a local union activist, 'used to beer a lot, and even though his brother was

political, John was an outcast.' Bookle's men were finally forced into the union because the millworkers refused to let his lorries into the mill premises. The drivers had to pay all back dues. 'If they hadn't, the stoppage would have continued.'

This success with lorry drivers resulted partly from the actions of local workers. It also was because Irish ports were unionized. 'The union had great muscle because the dockers were in the union and could stop imported wheat going to any mill if there were local difficulties. And local men knew that.' This meant that in 1935, when Thomastown Creamery bought lorries, the IT&GWU could unionize there.[2] It was 'because the creamery lorries also did contract work for the mill.' Similarly, in 1937, when Grennan Mills bought Callan Stores, an old mill to be used as a grain store in the town of Callan, its workers, and the lorry drivers who now made regular trips to Grennan Mills, were brought into the union.

This strategy, however, had two problems. First, it focused on a particular occupation and/or a worker's relation to Grennan Mills. The focus was not on unionizing work sites per se. So when Bookle added a threshing machine to his enterprise, 'he used only casual labourers, and these were never unionized.' Then, in 1936, his lorries were nationalized and integrated into the Great Southern Railway company. A driver from Waterford was soon after appointed to its third Thomastown lorry. The local IT&GWU wrote to the company in Dublin 'asking for an explanation [given] that the position was promised to Martin Byrne, a member of Thomastown IT&GWU.' HO was also informed. What had occurred was that 'the railway company, in taking over transport, appointed their own people. They would be union, but not local. And local was important. Jobs were scarce.' Trade unionism could reproduce parochialism.

This focus on occupations, mill links, and localism had particular outcomes within Grennan Mills itself, particularly in the efforts of its workers to maintain a closed shop. They did this even though the mill occasionally hired outside tradesmen, such as painters and masons, on contract or as casuals. The permanently employed saw these hirings as threats (Case 18.2).

Case 18.2: Casual Tradesmen in Grennan Mills
Denis Roche was born in a rural townland but lived in the town. In 1935 he was hired as a 'handyman' for the mill. Before this, 'only tradesmen were employed'

and 'the lads didn't like Roche doing all kinds of work. The Kellys [permanently-employed carpenters] were very against this.' In fact, 'they didn't want Roche at all because he wasn't a tradesman, he had never served his time. But he lived near the mill and the workers didn't want to be too hard on him; so they let him join the union. But they insisted that he do only masonry work' for which there was an opening at the time. A similar situation occurred when Peter Reddy was hired as a mason. He had been working in Mosse's Bennettsbridge mill but lived in an outlying parish townland. 'His brother was a small farmer and Peter was well-known around the town. He did odd jobs and was liked. He was in the parish, so he wasn't an outsider. We did not resent these scutchgrass farmers. Denis Roche also came from that stock. On the other hand, they weren't numerous. If they had been, there would have been conflict.' But before Roche could come into the mill, the branch members wrote to Mosse's to find out his union status there. They also passed a motion that, in future, all casual workers like Roche had to pay a new entry fee or their back dues.

The premise was that 'head office would get concerned if this Roche pattern was the start of a trend,' so all casuals were made to join the union or have their memberships up-to-date. Thomastown's millworkers, however, added other criteria. The worker had to be local and he had to be part of the labouring class. Thus, boundaries were marked around Grennan Mills, aided by an employer whose management style accommodated his unionized shop.

However, there was virtually no success otherwise. This led unionized mill workers to have contradictory sentiments towards other labourers. On the one hand, they were profoundly cynical of their motives and values. On the other hand, they recognized how difficult life was for most workers. In early 1936 'the local was trying to get Thomastown shop boys [porters and workers] to join.' They 'failed because of pressure from shopkeepers and labourers themselves who shied away even though working conditions could be improved because emigration was rampant.' So shopworkers were not organized. 'It's like Mount Juliet. The ordinary worker would think it safer to play up to the boss than to join the union. And the boss would play on this.' Yet a millworker added, that if shop boys joined a union, 'they may not be fired, but they might be asked to leave.' However, shop assistants, usually the sons of farmers, would never join because they had 'got this respectability.' Assistant 'Dan Fitzgerald was called "Mr" by [retailer] Tom Kelly.' So 'they preferred favours from shopkeepers instead of support from fellow workers.' Anyway, 'the church was against unionization. Canon Doyle was reactionary. He brought a London speaker to lecture against communism in the Hall. The meeting was chaired by [a retailer]. Rumour has it that Canon Doyle wouldn't let a vocational school into Thomastown because ordinary children would be going.'

Contradictory sentiments were also felt about labourers at Deady's Mill, a small corn mill and farm outside the town owned by a former county councillor. In 1937 'some workers like Joe Wemyss joined but it fizzled out ... Joe couldn't get the rest of them into it. They were "shoneens" and "yes-men," afraid to be sacked. But one week without wages and people were hungry; so the union failed. The wages at Deady's were lower than average; but you wouldn't know for sure because a man would hide his wages and negotiate directly with the boss for the extra shilling.' Similarly with farm labourers: 'Farmers were bad. If you looked for good wages, you were out. And you lost your house also.' At Mount Juliet, a unionizing effort in the 1920s apparently ended when 'the workers were told they'd be fired.'

Other ambiences, however, seemed to provide greater potential. In 1938 Thomastown's branch 'decided to accept 32 road workers and casuals.' Their entry had been preceded by a good deal of publicity about working conditions on a site at Jerpoint where the Land Commission had bought up the former Hunt estate. It hired men from the local pool of casuals to drain and fence before giving the land, in ten-acre plots, to labourers. Part of de Valera's effort to create an independent, Irish-speaking peasantry, the allotments were seen by most people in the 1980s as a reward to Fianna Fáil's labouring supporters. In the event, Patrick Doolan (alias TUSA, poet), who was working on the site, and millworker James O'Neill (secretary, local Irish Labour Party) began to complain about working conditions. It was 1937. A new constitution was being promulgated as the regime moved the Free State from dominion to republic status (Case 18.3).

Case 18.3: 'Employment Conditions at Jerpoint' – TUSA's Letter

'With all the rumours of dawning freedom and prosperity ... one looks ... about one's district for the ... signs ... Old people often refer to [the 1845–9 famine] ... as "the time of public works," when ... our ancestors imbibed ... yellow meal ... from the ... skillet on the roadside. The skillet has disappeared but the hardship and the intolerable conditions ... are present ... at Jerpoint today. Stunned with misery, the victims so far have remained silent. On the few occasions when driven *beyond endurance, he has revolted, the ganger in charge has not hesitated to use the state machine ... [to] ... bring him to heel: men who refuse to accept the coolie conditions [are] ... debarred from all state benefit or employment.*[3]

'*... The greatest of Catholic writers ... C.K. Chesterton, wrote ... [that] "Any law that sends a man back to work when he wants to leave it is ... a fugitive slave law." And Pope Leo XIII was, in ... the* Rerum Novarum, *very definite: ... "If through necessity or fear ... the workman accepts hard conditions because an employer ... will afford him no better, he is ... the victim of force or injustice." We find then ... something amiss with a government which [claims to be] ... Christian [and tries] ... to explain away the huge unemployed army ... If conditions ... in Jerpoint obtain to any great extent throughout the country, it is small wonder that the cross channel boats are filled with Irishmen [going] to the land ... they have been taught to hate ... in search of work which ... [has] conditions fit for human beings and not for brute beasts. I will quote two instances ... At noon on the 8th of December, the ... two men detailed to light a fire and boil water [for lunch] found it impossible to do so as the firewood was damp and the time ... insufficient ... Upon the expiration of the allotted ... half hour, no man had had his lunch ... The ganger's whistle blew for resumption ... Few responded. He rushed up to know why ... and on being informed ... [ordered them] to start work immediately or get out. One man who remonstrated with him was dismissed on the spot. All hands struck work and he was reinstated. The ganger then shouted ... about cutting everyone a quarter. Again the men struck and once more he capitulated. Truly a splendid type. The other incident occurred the following Saturday [with] an attempt to make the men work after the official hour of 1 P.M. Various watches amongst the men had passed this hour, and upon this being brought to his notice, the ganger shouted that ... work in hand [had] to be completed before cessation. An argument developed with one of the men and he was dismissed. Threatened strike action induced the ganger to reverse his decision.*

'*There are many more incidents, but these will suffice ... Are these conditions a forerunner of the ... freedom we are to enjoy under the new Constitution? Was it for this that Patrick Pearse faced the British firing squad, and James Connolly, broken ... but still defiant, was dragged to his equally splendid death? Was it for [this] ... that our own local men [paid] the supreme penalty? Fianna Fáil, deeming itself omnipotent ... will be relegated to permanent obscurity on Ireland's national scrapheap.*'[4]

TUSA was a poet. Through dramatic imagery, he connected the Jerpoint workers with two key events in the Irish historical pantheon, the Great Famine (1845–9) and the Easter Rising (1916). For the latter, he highlighted Pearse and Connolly, the socialists among the heroes. He also appealed to Catholic values, citing an essayist, a pope's encyclical, and the idea of Christian government.[5] At the same time, the 'state machine' and 'unemployed army' hearkened to Marx. TUSA's essay was thus an eclectic amalgamation of themes from history, political economy, the New Testament, and Catholic ethics. It was intended also to critique the Fianna Fáil government.

A few days later, James O'Neill, as secretary of the Thomastown Labour Party, followed with his own letter. After a brief nod to 'Christian standards,' he gave examples of exploitation on the site, pointing out that the 'personal conditions' being experienced by labourers should lead them to recognize their political affinity with the Labour Party (Case 18.4).

Case 18.4: 'Employment Conditions at Jerpoint' – The Workers' 'Friends'
Mr Doolan's [TUSA] ... letter will go a long way towards enlightening the workers as to their friends. Any Government which professes Christian principles must be judged by Christian standards, and ... at Jerpoint ... there are ... glaring discrepancies. The men ... are paid 26s. per week, but owing to ... bad weather, the average weekly wage has very seldom exceeded 19s ... It would ... require a[n] ingenious apologist to explain how anyone could support himself and his family [on this]. Again, contrary to universal practice, [the workers] ... are only allowed a half hour for dinner. Can it be seriously suggested that this is an adequate rest period? As to the erection of ditches, each man is expected to complete 5½ yards per day. Those who fail to maintain that pace have been dismissed. For similar work, cottage contractors get ... double the Land Commission rates. It would appear therefore that ... this State department has been influenced more by David Ricardo than by Leo XIII. The workers on this scheme may be unorganised and defenceless, still they cannot be exploited with impunity. Personal experience is often more convincing than argument ... and we confidently predict that these workers will not be influenced in the future by either political catch-cries or demagogic oratory.'[6]

Both letters, with an erudite framing of material conditions with moral arguments, ethical principles, and appeals to higher authorities, aimed to raise the consciousness of workers. What they failed to do, however, was to offer solutions. At a time when everyone knew that a Dáil election was in the offing, they simply asked workers to cease supporting Fianna Fáil, the party that formed the government. Despite their familiarity with Marx and Connolly, both O'Neill and TUSA seized only the electoral route. The secretary of the local IT&GWU, Herbert Devoy, offered even less. In a brief note to the press, he 'protest[ed] ... the wages and conditions ... which seem ... very near ... to forced labour.' He protested the way that 'the men formerly employed there' were 'being treated by the Labour Exchange authorities. We consider,' he concluded, 'that these matters call for a strict inquiry.'[7]

In the 1980s, men recalled that there had been 'a bit of bother' at the Jerpoint site but, despite the lofty discourse at the time, they could not remember any details. The Jerpoint site was never unionized. Instead, the casual workers who had laboured there, and road workers, joined the union the following year. They were 'put in a section of their own, with a committee and collector.' Their key issue was immediately addressed by the wider Thomastown branch when it decided to bring a resolution to the annual IT&GWU conference, asking the National Executive to press for a single wage (36s. a week) for all road/casual workers in rural areas. The aim was to ensure that all workers would get the same wage, regardless of project scheme and/or contractor.

However, the section was quickly in difficulty, as evidenced in a mounting backlog of uncollected dues. In March 1939 the Thomastown branch secretary, Devoy, was instructed 'to get the Section together to face up to their position' and 'decide whether [it] is to continue.' A meeting was held. Branch members 'pointed out the serious position ... in regard to arrears so bad that in effect the section was almost lapsed.' Section members said they would try to clear them, keep the section going and get some non-unionized men working on a local housing scheme to join. A week later, Devoy reported failure. The branch 'instructed [him] to drop the section if things do not improve within a couple of weeks and to notify Head Office.'

The reasons for failure were clear to local men in the 1980s. 'Those workers were isolated, scattered all over where they lived and worked.' In contrast, 'millworkers lived and worked close together. Some road workers in the same union may not even have known each other.' In any case, millworkers felt no political affinity to these workers. 'We didn't know them and left it to others to do the donkey work of organizing them. But we would support them if they ever went on strike.' Clearly, then, the labour process militated against broad-based sentiment by dispersing the men or, alternatively, bringing together those who were unconnected by kinship or common residence. Shared work experience was seemingly less important than the ties generated by social and physical proximity. This was exacerbated by the millworkers' unwillingness to spend time educating and organizing and, in turn, by the subordinate position that the casuals/road workers were given inside the branch. Yet millworkers felt that, as long-time union members, they had the knowledge to negotiate for the casuals/road workers. In any case, 'we weren't going to hand authority over to men who knew nothing about unions.'

Another factor also was clear. In organizing a casuals/road workers' section, the branch focused on the category of worker rather than on the work site. This made sense given that sites closed after schemes were completed, whereas the workers, as casuals, would persist. Yet this strategy exacerbated the atomization of these workers vis-à-vis each other while, alongside, the union failed to alter individual consciousness amongst these least skilled and most vulnerable of workers. For there were some casuals who, despite shifting from site to site, kept up their union membership throughout the 1930s. Several were building labourers, one of whom said that he and several of his fellow-workers 'would always be hired whenever a building site was in progress,' despite their union affiliation, because 'we were *skilled* building labourers. We were drain diggers, and able to help plasterers and carpenters.' Indeed, in 1939, as the casual section struggled, the IT&GWU's efforts with local building labourers were fairly successful. In fact, as well as several committed union men among them, local construction workers had a longer-term, albeit erratic, involvement with the Thomastown IT&GWU. It was a political experience that involved both (re)constitution and dissolution, strikes and negotiation (Case 18.5).

Case 18.5: The Builders' Labourers and the Thomastown IT&GWU,
1928–46

In 1928, when Thomastown's barracks were rebuilt, the building workers were unionized by Michael Kelly, then secretary of the local IT&GWU. Membership then lapsed until the next major project, rebuilding the courthouse in 1934. A one-day strike, organized by Kelly, took place when the contractor made the men work from 8 A.M. to after 6 P.M. The strike gained them a 6 P.M. closing time as well as 6d. an hour. Then, in 1936, the county council built cottages in Jerpoint West townland. Michael Tierney and the local branch tried unsuccessfully to unionize that site (Case 20.9).

In early 1939 the local IT&GWU sent a deputation to contractor Edward Fitz-

patrick from Carrick-on-Suir, who was to build a new council project of forty-four houses. The deputation, led by James O'Neill, discussed wages and the new Housing Act which required government contractors to pay trade-union rates. Fitzpatrick agreed to pay 36s. for a forty-eight-hour week, with carters receiving 10s. per day. The delegation also demanded only local labour and, as far as possible, Irish materials. Fitzpatrick agreed 'to employ local labour as far as possible.' Ned Maher, in Thomastown Notes, *warned labourers about undercutting these efforts at combination (Case 14.7). Within four months, Fitzpatrick was bankrupt and the project halted. Five months later, the commissioner of health ordered it completed using direct labour under the supervision of the clerk of works. In January 1940 work began and, in March, the building labourers on the site joined the Thomastown IT&GWU. Reportedly 'very enthusiastic, they were enrolled as a separate section.' Seven of the initiating eight members came from various locales in and near the town; 'they all knew each other.' Three of the eight were cotmen. Their initial political action was to demand a wage increase, based on Kilkenny city rates (42s. a week). 'They knew what was going on; they had their contacts.' In April 1940 they asked Head Office and James Pattison, secretary of the Kilkenny IT&GWU, to press for the increase. Three weeks later, however, after two carpenters and two labourers were dismissed, 'over 40 tradesmen and labourers' went on an 'unofficial' strike. The county engineer had refused the wage increase: current rates were the 'prevailing' ones and, as the project was being completed with Fitzpatrick's sureties paying, 'difficulties would arise.' Pattison mediated. The strikers agreed to resume work, and the dismissals would be investigated later. The day after, the clerk of works 'handed ... them a list of the labourers whom he proposed to employ, which meant the unemployment of an additional 6.' The workers 'refused to resume work ... and the deadlock continues.' The town's retailers, via their Traders' Development Association (TDA), passed a motion 'regretting' the stoppage, adding that a deputation of workers had 'conveyed' to them that 'there is an atmosphere of victimisation.' In the 'interests of the town,' the TDA asked the commissioner of health, responsible for housing schemes, to intervene. Soon after, secretary Devoy told a section meeting that 'the Commissioner had admitted victimization' and had ordered 'all the men' back to work. A month later, the labourers received a wage increase of 6s. a week. The scheme was finally completed and several of the labourers on the site were allocated houses. For the next five years, no reports on the section appeared anywhere or in men's recollections. It simply faded away. It was reconstituted in 1946 when a new project was in the offing.*[8]

The revival of the building labourers' section in 1946 was followed in later years by the formation of sections for forestry workers, County

Home employees, and so on. In other words, the unionization process in the locality after 1913 was very much impelled/constrained by local economic conditions, the union's internal structuring, and the varying kinds of consciousness among labourers and enterprises. The process was erratic and incomplete, favouring certain workers, abandoning others. Local intellectuals had also absorbed a plethora of learned, but often contradictory, ideas. All this was implicated with other trajectories: how unionization contributed to local differentiation (see below), how local agitation empowered the already powerful outside the locality (chapter 19), and how internal differentiation and external empowerment reflected back onto the locality (chapter 20).

The Unionization Process and the Economy: Patterns of Differentiation and Discrimination

The uneven economy and the varying labour processes on different work sites, when linked to an erratic unionization process, created distinctions, diversity, and disparities among local workers. Between enterprises were inequalities in wages, work conditions, job security, and perks, and in how these were negotiated. Between full-time workers and the casually employed was a wide gap in living standards. These material differences were reproduced and elaborated in at least five ways: by stereotyping among workers; by the role of kinship ties in labour recruitment; by residential segregation; by the way work was organized on-site; and by age-grading in the labour process.

In 1983 a former millworker spoke about IT&GWU's casual/road workers' section. 'When they asked to join the union in 1939' he said, 'they ... took the initiative. They were poorly paid.' It was the branch of mainly millworkers that 'decided to put them into a separate unit because they knew there would be drop-offs because of the casual nature of the work. Mill/ union people didn't want to give an impression of fluctuating membership.' Casuals 'also had less status. There were three kinds: those who wouldn't work, those delicate ones who couldn't, and those who couldn't get permanent work ... Often, those who wouldn't work preferred to be on the river.' Similarly, several labourers said to me in conversation that farm labourers were 'ill-educated' and 'shopboys played up to the boss.' Mount Juliet workers were 'like slaves and kowtowed to petty bosses' while creamery workers were 'a crowd of unreliable yahoos.' Said another worker on an another occasion, 'Buckley and Ryan were not real fishermen. The only fishermen were from the town.'

And, from the 1983 perspective of a former casual worker: 'it was impossible ... to get a job in the mill. During harvest, when extra workers were taken on, they did all the dirty work while the regulars grabbed the better-paid, overtime work. The regulars also encouraged Pilsworth to let the temporaries go ... You couldn't be happy working there. There was no comradeship. Not like other jobs I been in.'

Such stereotypes were, of course, situational, enunciated in particular contexts when a particular point was being made. Yet, in pointing to views that were 'true' at least some of the time, they informed or rationalized behaviour. Equally 'true' were the beliefs enmeshed in such common expressions as 'Dunphy's river and Synnott's mill,' or, 'only a Challoner could get a job in the Creamery.' These expressions vocalized a taken-for-granted belief that certain labouring families controlled jobs in particular enterprises. Certainly some of the facts bear this out. The already-noted kin and affinal links among workers on the Butler (Kilmurry) estate in 1939 was an example. At Mount Juliet, the major had an explicit policy of 'trying to hire sons when possible.' At Grennan Mills, sons often joined or followed their fathers (Cases 13.1, 13.5), and Pilsworth saw himself as hiring 'families' (Case 8.8). Finally, in the Creamery in the 1930s were several brother, son, and nephew dyads. Adding to certainties as to the efficacy of kin ties was that skills were handed down patrilineally and certain patronyms were associated, in belief and in fact, with particular trades. For all these reasons, kinship recruitment to an enterprise could be perceived if people had a predilection to see it that way. And they did.[9]

Some workers also presumed that another recruitment mechanism operated, namely, a personal tie to the owner. One of the two Pilsworth brothers was reputed to have been 'like one of the lads' and a frequenter of local pubs. It was said that a job might be secured through him if a vacancy existed and that, for example, he was responsible for the Roche hiring (Case 18.2). Or, the McCalmonts liked to hire ex-soldiers. On the other hand, it was also said that 'the closer you were to the McCalmonts, the closer you were to the gate.' Thus, garage and house employees turned over rapidly. At Grennan Mills, a worker emigrated in 1930. He reputedly said on leaving that 'the grass would soon be growing in the mill yard.' The Pilsworths heard about this and, when the labourer returned a year later, refused to hire him back. Eventually he was taken on 'because of herself [his wife] and the children. He also had a brother in the mill. But he was only hired as packerman for the night shift.'

Given, then, the sometimes fragile nature of ties to employers, given that kinship and affinity provided not only access but security in a world of scarce jobs and labour surplus, and given patrilineal skills transmission, kinship was both a discursive idiom and, often, a material means for getting jobs and holding on to them. This meant that non-kin, from their own perspective and that of other people, were discriminated against by other workers.

Both the material disparities and feelings of difference and inequality, expressed through stereotypes and engendered in part through kinship, were reinforced by residence patterns. The River Nore was key. 'Mill Street people' were seen as separate and different from 'townies.' They drank in different pubs and shared different gossip. 'Being on that side,' said a labourer, 'I didn't know what was happening in other places. I have no contacts over there. I have no friends there.' They also tended to work in different places: 'Millworkers lived in Mill Street' and 'the real fishermen were from Mill Street.' The people from the two sides of the river were also reputed to have different attitudes. 'On Mill Street, people would walk into anyone's house and borrow a frying pan without asking. On Ladywell, you had to knock formally on the door and be let in.' Finally, a good deal of men's leisure consisted of walking out with friends. Townies gathered by the church gate, at the head of Market Street, chatting. Mill Street men congregated at 'the stones,' across the river. Said a townie: 'It was us at the church and them at the stones.' Johnny Egan said that he changed from the stones to the church gate after he moved from the Mall across the river to Ladywell.

Ultimately, unionization itself structured disparities, even within work sites. Grennan Mills, for example, had finely drawn distinctions which affected wages and working conditions. These included distinctions between permanent workers and casuals, mill versus grain-store workers, and mill/store workers versus Pilsworth's farm workers. The last 'could never work in the mill because they weren't unionized and they didn't have the skills. They would be lost in the mill.' However, 'in later years, the millworkers would be sent to threshings. They really enjoyed it. The beer flowed and the food was great. It was a day in the country.' (See cover photo.) This country/farm versus town/mill distinction was augmented by others. In the mill, packermen and screensmen (who looked after the machinery) counterposed ordinary day workers. The 'former were paid a few shillings more because of their skill and because they did night work. They couldn't be replaced by casual workers in an emergency.' Men also distinguished tradesmen (carpenters) from others. The 'carpenters stayed in the shop and did nothing else in the mill.' Finally, there were distinctions based on age. Until age sixteen, employers were not required to pay into benefit programs for workers. This was James O'Neill's complaint when he said that young workers were often fired when they reached age sixteen (Case 16.4). However, further age-grading occurred, rooted in perceptions of what constituted men's work, in union contracts, in labour law, and in the fact that young men in their early twenties could perform heavy labour but, as 'chaps, they received lower wages' (Case 18.6).

Case 18.6: Men's Work and Boys' Wages in Grennan Mills
In 1935 the local IT&GWU wrote HO to request that 'chaps' Christie Beck and William O'Brien be reclassified and paid as adults. Beck was twenty-one and had worked in the mill for six years; O'Brien was twenty-three. The two occasionally did adult work as well as a lot of overtime. They earned only 6d. an hour as compared with an adult's wage of 1s.6d. Six months later, the Joint Industrial Council (JIC) of the IT&GWU, 'made up of union people in Dublin,' had investigated the local branch's request. They sent the 'famous' Cathal O'Shannon to Thomastown. 'We had a live union then!' He met with Pilsworth, who agreed to raise the wages for every year after age twenty-two until an adult wage was reached or a vacancy occurred. Six months later, in late 1937, the local again discussed 'chaps' who now included John Burris, Kieran Neary, and Jim Power. The secretary was instructed to ask HO to intervene. When HO did not reply, the local asked for help from James Pattison (Dáil deputy for Labour) and secretary of the Kilkenny IT&GWU). The local also decided that, if they had no response within a fortnight, then Tom Beck, James O'Neill, and the secretary would themselves approach Pilsworth.

Said Christie Beck in 1983: 'The Pilsworths really had enough men. They only hired me because of my father. At the time, the mill was the job to get. Wages were higher than anywhere else and there were never any firings. So plenty of lads were looking for work there.' As for the other lads, 'Power's father was on the Pilsworth farm and he was entitled to a job. The O'Briens were all in the mill; so was Burris's father.' In the case of Neary, 'rumour had it that Pilsworth had gotten his sister into trouble.' Beck further explained that 'we in Thomastown were only a small unit, and Head Office and Pattison were probably too busy to answer our letters. So the local was willing to fight it out locally.' However, 'Head Office had the contacts and the strike pay; so we had to tread carefully. The mill lads, though, being in a union, stood up to be counted. You have to give them credit; they were the black sheep of the community. It was a penny looking down on a ha'penny.'

The material differentiation of local workers, according to wages and living standards as a result of varying work processes and enterprises, was reproduced through erratic unionization and elaborated through stereotypes, kinship ties, residential segregation, work organization, and age-grading. In this context, paternalism and deference between employer and worker remained important: a worker should not be heard to say that the grass would grow in the yard. In turn, the owners of Grennan Mills had an undemanding management style. 'They were not anti-labour and they weren't difficult to negotiate with.' Grennan Mills thus stood in stark contrast to all other enterprises and work sites in the locality, just as it had in the 1890s. A strong union and paternal management produced a work ambience and living standard envied by other workers.

At the same time, the activities of the IT&GWU did foment broad-based, common sentiment by linking workers from different locales. Long-time secretary Michael Kelly worked at Deady's; member James Whelan was at Mount Juliet. Although neither their work sites nor occupational category nor most of their fellow workers were unionized, the presence of a few men who, as individuals, had joined the union, created a network which linked enterprises, sites, and kinds of workers into common concern and organization. Moreover, as Case 18.6 shows, the local branch and, thus, the network, were also enmeshed in nation-wide structures. Not only was Head Office informed of local issues but men such as Cathal O'Shannon, a radical unionist, often came to Thomastown to deal with local problems or attend branch meetings.

The Practice of Difference: The Clash of Individuals

The privileged position of millworkers in both the locality and the union was reflected in the fabric of the branch. In the late 1930s, as the union was expanding, local members changed its structure. First, they tightened the boundaries of locality when they legislated that executive committee members had to come from the Thomastown area. Second, only the chair and vice chair were thenceforth to be elected at the annual general meeting. Instead, the other four members of the branch's executive were to be elected from sections (three from the road workers/casuals and one from flour milling). The changes were because 'the casuals wanted representation.' However, the millworkers also 'wanted to retain control of the executive because the new workers were an unknown quantity.' Within a month, at the 1939 annual general meeting, the number of trustees on the executive committee was increased. These additional four were millworkers.

The influence of new members was accompanied by another change. During 1935 and 1936, secretary Michael Kelly kept saying that 'he was getting on in age' and wanted to resign. The members wouldn't let him go. However, by the 1937 annual meeting, a replacement had come forward. This was millworker Herbert Devoy. He

> was nominated ... only out of necessity. Most men lacked the education ... Herbert had self-confidence and, anyway, no one wanted the job. Before his election, he may have attended some meetings, but he and his father were not great union-men. They didn't pay their dues and only pressure prevented the father, Joe, being thrown out. Joe looked down on the others. He played golf and didn't want to be associated with the union. Herbert was not aggressive, not like James O'Neill. Herbert didn't want to rock the boat. He wanted to improve conditions, but diplomatically. 'He was a man of peace,' according to the parish priest's eulogy for him. I think though, personally, he wanted status and importance.

When Devoy replaced Michael Kelly, he created and embodied ambivalences which Kelly had not. Devoy was needed by all but disliked by many. The events in Case 18.7 brought this out in sharp relief while firmly establishing Devoy's position in the branch.

Case 18.7: The Ascent of the New Secretary of the Thomastown Branch, 1938
In April 1938 Devoy arranged with the Moonrue/Kilkenny branch that it would send delegates to the annual union congress in Dublin that year and Thomastown branch would go the following year. The action caused a 'heated discussion' at the next branch meeting when Devoy proposed that no delegates be nominated from Thomastown. This was not seconded. Michael Tierney then moved, seconded by Pat Dunphy, that James O'Neill be nominated. This was passed with only Devoy dissenting. Devoy then tendered his resignation 'as he considered that the vote was a censure on his actions.' Two weeks later, at the branch's annual general meeting, eighteen members were present (forty-four were absent). A long discussion took place on 'the resignation. It was then proposed by M. Synnott and

*seconded by Ed Dunphy that the nomination of James O'Neill ... be withdrawn in
favour of Moonrue. J. O'Neill assented ... An amendment was proposed by
Michael Tierney and seconded by Christie Beck that the nomination not be withdrawn.' For the amendment were two votes; for the resolution were twelve. O'Neill
and Devoy did not vote. Devoy then 'withdrew his resignation at the request of the
branch.' Michael Tierney offered his resignation from the executive committee. It
was accepted. He left the meeting. Peter Walsh was then nominated for the committee in place of Tierney. This was 'passed without dissent.'*

Devoy had clearly exceeded his authority. 'He did it on his own, and
that wouldn't go down well in the local branch. But there was always friction with Devoy. For example, Devoy was more lenient toward the
church. He joined the Knights of Columbanus' (Case 17.10). Other
members 'didn't want the church near politics.' This 'shows how weak
Devoy really was. The others wouldn't dream of associating with shopkeepers, at the CYMS for example ... O'Neill only agreed to the Moonrue decision because he didn't want dissension and he didn't want to
lose the secretary.' In contrast, 'Tierney and Beck wanted the principle
established that Thomastown was an old branch and should have been
in Dublin, and that Devoy was acting outside his authority.' But, after
that event, 'everyone recognized that there were serious differences.' In
fact, 'we appealed to Tierney to stay on. It wasn't as simple as in the minutes.' Peter Walsh 'was a blacksmith's son. He was very reserved and
never very active. Everyone regretted the Tierney case; but he did come
back to fight a council election.'

Tierney was abandoned for several reasons. On the one hand, Devoy
was indispensable because he wanted to be secretary. On the other, Tierney was 'difficult. He could not be a friend, he was too aggressive.' He
was also a communist, anti-church, anti-Franco, intense, and well read.
'He was a man of principle.' Interestingly, Devoy's resignation was
widely accepted at first. The later about-face suggests sober second
thinking about the practicalities and the personalities as well as, equally
likely, the preferences of the parish priest. Devoy was entrenched as secretary for the next three decades. For some, he was a slippery diplomat,
'a twister'; for others, he was an unaggressive 'man of peace.' Importantly, however, his advent corresponded with a narrow volunteerism
within the branch itself. Of sixty-two members between 1936 and 1945,
only sixteen served in an executive position. Fifteen of these did so

more than once and ten did so three times or more (Table 18.1). By the late 1930s, these ten formed an activist core. Nine were millworkers. They were usually elected by acclamation. From an outsider's perspective, it might indeed look as if a mill clique, of the best-paid and most secure workers, was running the union.

However, that clique was committed to equity. In 1945, for example, the flour packers asked Pilsworth to rotate shifts because the night shift earned more. Or, as another example, there was the so-called confusion about the labour process in the mill in 1939. At that time, no work was done on church holidays. However, workers preferred to work rather than lose a day's pay. Moreover, casuals worked some holidays while regular workers were not being asked in, or the mill worked with only some of the regulars. 'The branch and the workers wanted the system regularized. They wanted it the same for all workers. The fear was that favoured men would always get extra.' The executive approached Pilsworth: either the church holidays would be worked in full as an ordinary day or no mill work would be allowed. Pilsworth agreed.

Undercutting favouritism, however, was not simply about equity but also about preventing petty bosses among the workers themselves. This often occurred at Mount Juliet, with its larger workforce, a management style that kept the owners at a great distance, a formal hierarchy of workers, and no union. From the perspective of casual workers, however, efforts by unionized workers to avert boss-ism in the mill made it more difficult for them to get work there. It added to the view of the millworkers as an elite. From the perspective of some millworkers, equity kept them from getting ahead. For occupational multiplicity was common. Michael Tierney did much on the side: harvest work, selling timber, and so on. Another millworker took care of a retailer's garden in his off-hours. However, in 1940, it was reported that a member, a postman, was doing post work while on holiday. The chair and secretary warned him that drastic action would be taken if he continued. 'He was getting paid twice. If he persisted, he would have been expelled from the union and lost his job. He probably got the fright of his life. He probably only did it for few bob without thinking!' In other words, it was accepted that men who worked shifts might do other part-time work and that skilled workers might get a lot of overtime. However, it was still the notion of 'one man, one job.' A millworker once was sent to decorate Pilsworth's house. He was approached by someone else to do her own house after. He refused. 'I am a trade unionist. I am doing this work during the reg-

Table 18.1: Thomastown IT&GWU executive, 1935–45

Positions: Chair [c] or Committee/Trustee [x]:	1935	1936	1938	1939	1940	1941	1942	1943	1944	1945	1946
M. Walsh*	x	x									
Robt Wemyss#		x					x				
Wm O'Brien*		x									x
Wm O'Neill+	x	x									
Michael Tierney*		x	x								
Michael Synnott*	x	x	x	x	x	x	x	x	cx	cx	c
Tom Beck*	c	x	x	x	c	c	c	c	x	x	
Pat Dunphy*+=	x	x	x	x	x	x	x	x	x	x	x
James O'Neill*=		c	c	c				x			
Pat Kelly*			x	x	x	x					
Michael O'Neill*				x	x	x	x	x	x	x	x
Peter Walsh*	x			x	x	x	x	x	x	x	x
Ed Dunphy*=				x			x	x			
Christie Beck*					x	x	x	x	x		
James Power@					x	x	x	x			
Denis Landy#=									x	x	
J. Gardiner*										x	
John Challoner*											x
John Burris*											x
William Phelan											x
Herbert Devoy	x										

Key: c = Chair; x = Committee member or trustee
Occupations: *millworker; + Bookle employee (non-local); # railway man; = cotman; @ postman

ular mill day. I didn't consider the other job for a moment. No trade unionist would. I would never do two jobs. It would have been very much frowned upon.' That same worker, however, dealt in cattle on the side, renting fields for their keep, and trading for a decided profit. Similarly, other workers fished, trapped, and shot game. What they did not do, however, was hold down two unionized/well-paid jobs. Yet, from the perspective of the casual labourer, or the man with less initiative or ability, or the man with no capital, it did seem as if these well-paid millworkers might be taking too great a share of the total economic pie.

Clearly, then, equity was flexible when enmeshed in a labour-surplus economy; nor did it preclude differences. At the same time, the IT&GWU clique tried to educate. It was an enormous task. In 1942 a fine was to be imposed on any member 'who ... denied to [his] employers ... [any] previous statements [he] made to union officers re any disputes in negotiation.' The branch, in other words, had 'men who ran with the hares and hunted with the hounds.' In the mill, 'every worker believed that if one man had a grievance, all were involved.' In other work sites, however, isolated workers 'might blame the union for their own personal agitation when face to face with the boss. They'd knuckle under and blame outsiders and the union. That had to be stopped.'

In all, the Thomastown branch of the IT&GWU, run largely by Grennan Mills workers, had firm boundaries, a clique of committed leaders, members who enjoyed superior wages, and several organic leaders able to enunciate complex ideological positions and rationales. Some of these were committed to political education and some had a deep sense of their own abilities. At the same time, as Case 18.6 showed, Head Office was ubiquitous. Its representatives attended every local annual general meeting. In 1940 Cathal O'Shannon and James Pattison came. It was a ritual occasion, intended to express the unity of the local and the national, town and country, IT&GWU and Labour Party.

Conclusion: 'We Had a Live Union Then'

The interplay and contradictions between individual experience and class experience seemed to render impossible a consistent and general, radical critique among all workers in the locality. Indeed, the redundancy of local relations, the variations in living standards and work processes, and the intricacies of belief, affiliation, and allegiances all militated against uniform understandings and practices.[10] Yet formal associations and their intellectuals claimed to simplify these complexities as they organized people into new structures, with new interpretations and loyalties. Thomastown's IT&GWU certainly made such a claim and such an effort. Central for the outcome of its agency, however, and for its local workers and intellectuals, was that its dynamism was framed by hierarchy and the state. These are the subjects of the next two chapters.

19. 'Much Wants More:'
Framing the Politics of Labour

'... I have nothing but praise ... for the action of Labour ... in ... the Diocese, who have passed resolutions to condemn Communism, disassociate their Unions from the great apostasy, and pledge support to the Church, their Bishop and priests.'
— Bishop Patrick Collier, Lenten pastoral, 1933

The IT&GWU, as an organization and way of thinking, helped to clarify for many the often-contradictory images and potentialities that underpinned local life. Like other beliefs and practices, ideologies, and organizations, such as the Catholic hierarchy and the state, the local IT&GWU was immersed in relations and ideas which circulated from outside the locality. For example, local IT&GWU members, sympathizers, and detractors were linked to other labourers via the union's Head Office and/or the Irish Labour Party. Both union and party, in turn, existed in a wider world of competing agents, organizations, ideologies, and institutions, such as, for example, the Kilkenny Trades Council (KTC). It was through all these that the politics of labour were framed and refracted. It was also through them that the locality empowered those outside in ways that had implications both for Thomastown's workers and for the locality.

The Ties Between: Head Office, Kilkenny Trades Council (KTC), and the Local

Communication between the local IT&GWU branch and HO in Dublin waxed and waned depending on context, time, and issue. The situation was summed up by a former member in 1983: 'The local union had a lot of freedom; HO would support local actions. On the other hand, if a local decision was taken, you had to check to see if you had their support.' This meant that the Thomastown branch could happily use the precedents and gains obtained by national agents for its own local members. In 1935, for example, screensmen and packermen received a raise because rates were found to be higher in mills elsewhere.[1] However, the interests of those outside might differ. In 1935 government and HO were negotiating the building of a flour mill in Waterford. Thomastown workers, and other inland labourers, became concerned. Located in a port, close to supplies of imported durum wheat, the new mill would be too competitive, drive other mills out of business, and destroy inland jobs. The mill was built in 1938. 'HO saw the new jobs. The locals saw the loss of theirs.' Demands from the local to HO in 1935 to explain what was going on in the negotiations, and to respond to the local's resolutions opposing the mill, went unheeded.

Alongside such examples showing the dependence of the local branch on HO and on other local branches are those that show the opposite. Since the IT&GWU's inception, contract negotiations for all millworkers had been centralized, taking place between HO and an Irish mill owners' consortium. Said a former mill worker: 'HO would take into account the local position, but negotiations were fought from a national point of view.' In 1938 these negotiations reached a critical stage and the dependence of HO on the branches became clear (Case 19.1).

Case 19.1: The 1938 Contract Negotiations in the Mill

A circular, sent to all branches, said that the millers had refused workers' demands. This elicited a unanimous motion from Thomastown that 'the full demand be proceeded with up to and including a strike.' A month later, a new contract was negotiated and a vote was taken. Branch members voted thirty-one against the new contract, thirty for. As local branches pushed HO closer to a strike, Pilsworth asked the branch to leave three men on the job to handle incoming Irish wheat. It agreed. The branch was then informed that the millers had proposed arbitration. The branch met and approved this step, as did the general membership. Thomastown branch was then asked for information and arguments which could be used at arbitration. The branch wanted a 10 per cent wage increase, shorter hours, paid days and travelling expenses for ill-health, a pension scheme (of 30s. per week, given the 'heavy incapacity in the industry' and the number of redundancies), and an agreement that government exclude mill pensions from their means test for state-based, old age pensions.

Thomastown's members were seeking to force HO to make radical demands. The branch also demanded representation at the national conference which would make decisions about the union's position. HO was to pay the expenses of one delegate from the area and it was the turn of Bennettsbridge branch to send a representative. Thomastown paid the expenses for Devoy: 'We were important enough to have our own delegate there.' Why, however, did local millworkers make such extensive demands? Said a former activist: 'Much wants more. And Thomastown was no more militant than other local branches.'

At the same time that it demanded more, the Thomastown branch had informal deals with its main employer. The decision to carry out essential work in the mill should a strike ensue in 1938 was an example. That same year, three lorry drivers came to Pilsworth with a grievance. They wanted 'adults to carry the sacks of wheat and meal which they delivered and picked up. The young "chaps" who went with the lorries wouldn't do this because they were too small and weren't being paid for the work. The sacks weighed 10 and 20 stones; and it was the drivers who were carrying them.' Pilsworth gave the 'chaps' a two-year contract to help carry the sacks. At the same time, Pilsworth was also using hired lorries. 'One of these carters was from Inistioge. A helper always came with him and that helper was not unionized. The mill workers didn't push this.'

Such reciprocity was also symbolic. Anticipating the 1940 annual conference, the branch proposed that delegates 'vote for strike action failing receiving a 6s. increase.' An amendment by Tierney, seconded by Tom Beck, said that 'delegates be instructed to accept 6s., same to come from millers' profits.' Only Tierney and Beck supported the amendment. For the others, it was acceptable and necessary to make radical material demands in national sites without raising ideological issues in local ones. At the same time, symbolic combinations linked the local branch to others. A 1941 strike at Athlone Woollen Mills elicited a Thomastown motion that each member pay a shilling into their strike fund. A motion during a 1943 strike in Castlecomer obliged each Thomastown member to contribute 2s.6d. Yet such inter-local activity was constrained in certain directions. This emerged in the branch's links to the Kilkenny Trades Council (KTC) (Case 19.2).

Case 19.2: Thomastown IT&GWU and the Kilkenny Trades Council
In 1937 the KTC, having virtually disappeared, was reorganizing itself. Located in Kilkenny city, it was trying to bring together unionized city workers, IT&GWU

members from rural towns, and the state's railway and transport workers. Devoy and O'Neill attended the first meeting. 'Devoy was interested in this career-wise,' said a former member, but in 1939 he was told by the Thomastown executive to write the KTC to say 'that attending Council would serve no useful purpose' and that, instead, 'what is favoured here is a District Council of IT&GWU Union branches.' The latter never materialized. Said a former member in 1983, 'there was little or no contact between Kilkenny city and Thomastown from a union point of view.' The KTC 'could offer nothing to Thomastown that local members couldn't do for themselves.' The KTC was also concerned with Kilkenny city matters and 'their brewery workers, for example, would care nothing for Thomastown's millworkers, especially if they belonged to different unions. So the idea was to have a District Council – a rural council – which would incorporate men who had common interests.'

Such relations and viewpoints reflected the fragmentation and factionalism so often cited by Irish labour historians and usually attributed to the machinations of national leaders. Clearly, however, these processes were locally driven. Different industries, material interests, and local histories, as well as a rural-urban divide, infused grass-roots experience and sentiment. These were also rooted in a common sense which privileged internal vertical ties, in this case, to HO and within the IT&GWU, rather than horizontal ties to other unions, workers, and locales. It was equally rooted in a common sense which directed activism towards material rather than ideological ends and towards gains for insiders rather than education for outsiders.

Certainly these features were part of the defeat of the above Tierney-Beck amendment. They also permeated the branch's everyday practices. The minutes are clear in this respect. Most meeting time was spent discussing proposals on wages, bonuses, benefits, and working conditions which branch delegates would bring to annual conferences. Always, too, these demands were lavish and passed unanimously or by a huge majority. A pension scheme for millworkers was an example. As of 1940, no such scheme existed. Owners did not want to finance it and workers did not want to increase their own dues to pay for it. Such a stalemate showed, of course, the intrinsic conflict with capital. However, why did workers not want to pay for themselves? Said a former member in 1983: the 'men didn't want dues increased because they didn't want the benefits for Dublin workers to become top-heavy and supported by the rest of the country.' Such comment summarizes the failure of HO, and/or local branches, to build broad material cum ideological combinations which overrode local and begrudging self-interest.

Thus, the extensive time that local millworkers spent in framing proposals for national conferences, and their withdrawal from the KTC, had several outcomes. On the one hand, it brought national issues into the locality and empowered local members through their belief that they could affect their own material well-being and influence national decision making. They were part of a wider world and their local activists had a role there. On the other hand, it encouraged a rural-urban divide, truncated links to other unions and workers, and deepened parochial sensibilities.

Such double-edged consciousness was impelled not only by the branch's external relations but also by the nature of local society. Two strikes in 1936 illustrate this (Case 19.3).

Case 19.3: Two Strikes in 1936

A railway strike took place in Waterford. By that time, government had bought up local lorries around the country and created a national transport firm (CIE). In Thomastown, heavy goods came to the railway station, where CIE had a large store, and were then distributed around the locality by carters, retailers who owned transport, and Mount Juliet's steam engine. Local IT&GWU workers tried to convince them not to deliver during the strike. They had limited success with the retailers and none with Mount Juliet. That same year, they 'again took on the retailers' during a strike at Waterford's meat factory. 'Farmers tried to break the strike,' said an elderly worker, and [retailer] 'Crennan tried to recruit local labourers to go into Waterford factory to work. Signs were put around the town, organized by James O'Neill, saying, "Boycott Crennan." This embarrassed him even if he didn't lose custom. Crennan was anti-union and a customer of the factory.'

In the 1930s, then, through industrial action, much about local life was reproduced as local life framed the politics of labour. The beliefs that farmers and retailers were anti-union and acted in concert against labour were reinforced, and carters were still shown to occupy a contradictory class position. The industrial action also disclosed that attacks on respectability could be a potent weapon. In all this, local sentiment was reproduced while a wider view was encouraged, one which held that the state did not protect labour but that the IT&GWU and HO did.

The union and its HO thus encouraged both parochialism and wider horizons through local political action. It also did so though national contract negotiations. On the one hand, HO could negotiate for 'much and more' only if local members supported it. On the other hand, by directing local radicalism into demands for 'more,' HO defused this radicalism, channelled it into a formal framework, and helped turn mill-workers into a local labour elite. Simultaneously, the radicalism fuelled and channelled by the negotiating process was in part deflected by informal transactions which linked labour and capital in small localities. All this, in turn, limited the formation of ties between the local branch and other unions, workers and locales, thus intensifying yet again paro-chial sentiments. Importantly, through all this, the material rather than ideological components of labour activism were privileged.

The Labour Party: A National View

The fragmentation that historians have noted was apparent in the many organizations that claimed to represent workers and in the splits that typified their histories.[2] The Irish Trade Union Congress (ITUC), founded in 1895, brought together 93 unions with a total membership of 17,476.[3] Between 1912 and 1914, it formed a political party which was to be so closely associated with Congress that 'the latter was renamed the Irish Trades Union Congress and Labour Party.' Throughout the 1920s however, Congress/Party was bedevilled by 'bitter rivalries' within its trade unions, especially the IT&GWU, and between Larkin's view that an OBU should overthrow capitalism as against William O'Brien's position that a union was a means for bettering workers' condition.[4] After Larkin left for the United States, in 1914, O'Brien transformed the IT&GWU. On Larkin's return in 1923, the IT&GWU was financially sol-vent, with 100,000 members, and ideologically conservative. The rivalry initiated by Larkin's return led to his expulsion in 1924 and his forming an alternative union. This occurred while employers were attacking wages and when a general election was in the offing. The ITUC&LP polled poorly, owing to limited funding, poor organizing, and public factionalism. For Larkin's expulsion signalled that reformism had won and, as radicals formed splinter-groups which were socialist or republi-can, no labour group was able 'to offer a credible alternative to the con-servative regime' of Cosgrave. Then, when de Valera and his Fianna Fáil party finally entered the Dáil after the 1927 election, the ITUC&LP lost its role as opposition. De Valera's entry also revived the ideological conflict over the 1922 Treaty and republicanism. This 'succeeded only too well after 1932 in deafening the ears of the electorate to social and economic abuses that clamoured in vain for redress.'[5]

Between 1924 and 1932, Congress membership declined as an 'expression of disunity and depression.' In 1930 the ITUC&LP split into an Irish Trades Union Congress and an Irish Labour Party (ILP). It was an effort to widen the appeal of the party among the 'rural and small-town proletariat.' However, it found it difficult to compete 'either with the extremism of the IRA or the reformism of Fianna Fáil.' Moreover, after the latter came to power in 1932, its appeal to the labouring voter increased.[6] For it legislated some small social reforms, succeeding thereby in retaining labourers' votes and responding to pressure from the Labour Party whose support Fianna Fáil needed in the Dáil.

The general consensus among historians is that labourers were either foiled or fooled into supporting Fianna Fáil during all those years before and after 1932. They were foiled by the Labour Party's lack of radicalism and its focus on reformism and fooled by Fianna Fáil's seeming republicanism and its ability to maintain an illusion of progressiveness by nationalizing a few industries and encouraging indigenous capitalism. Labourers were also deceived by the close ties that grew up between Fianna Fáil and Labour in the Dáil. This created the myth that Fianna Fáil was 'mildly socialist.' The myth was maintained during the 1930s because 'the perspectives of the leaders of organized labour came to coincide with Fianna Fáil on a variety of issues.' These issues included the perceived rise of a fascist threat in the form of the Blueshirts from within the ranks of Cosgrave's pro-Treaty party (Cumann na nGaedheal); the perceived growth of communism and the espousal by both Fianna Fáil and Labour of a devout and militant Catholicism in response; the acceptance by both parties of anti-communist sentiment during the Spanish Civil War; and the divisions that emerged among Labour, fanned by Fianna Fáil policies, over banning married women from paid employment and over the move, supported by the IT&GWU, to ban British-based unions. Many unionized Irish workers belonged to the latter, including those in Thomastown.[7]

Overall, historians present a picture of Labour's failure on the national level: of false consciousness and reformism, of nationalist and republican sentiments trouncing socialist ones, of Catholicism, of factionalism among leaders, and of pragmatic but foolish alliances. It is a portrait of a virtually complete hegemonic construction: Roman Catholic Church, de Valera, and Labour, if not in complete ideological accord

Table 19.1: Occupations of 33 Labour Party members,
Thomastown, 1926

Occupation	Number
Grennan Mills worker	9
self-employed (carter, carpenter, barber)	4
postman	4
teacher	3
railway worker	3
Mount Juliet estate	3
tannery	2
builder's labourer	1
fisher (full-time)	1
water bailiff	1
retired British soldier	1
Deady mill	1

then in an alliance based on a sufficiently shared view of the world to
nullify other possibilities. It is an image of labour struggling against
itself rather than against capital. It is a picture of an historical bloc
wrought by workers' failure to understand their historical role. Yet questions remain: 'How exactly does hegemony function as a set of concrete
linkages between the political and cultural sphere?'[8] What was the material structure of ideology during that time and what was the *metissage* of
class experience which underlay this historical outcome?

The Irish Labour Party: The Local View

The Thomastown branch of the Irish Labour Party was formed in 1926.[9]
The thirty-three men who attended the founding meeting illustrate its
broad-based support. The men came from all parts of the parish – rural
and urban, both sides of the river. They had varying ideological views
(social democrat, republican, socialist, communist) and, sometimes, as
in the case of a water bailiff and cotmen, they had opposed material
interests (Table 19.1). They earned different wages and had different
roles in the labour process: full-time/casual, waged/self-employed, general worker/artisan, white collar/blue collar, agricultural/non-agricul-
tural. However, it was the unionized, full-time, non-agricultural workers
who formed the majority.

Importantly, this Thomastown branch was founded in a locality that had a history of electoral support for labour. From its founding in 1898 until its dissolution in 1926, the rural district council always had at least one labour representative from the area.[10] After 1926, when local government was centralized at the county council level, several local men were elected as Labour: Pat Ryan (1928–34), James O'Neill (1942–50), and Herbert Devoy (1950 and later). Only while the county council was suspended (1934–42) was there no labour representation. However, the way in which such representation came about was complex. Early on, it came to include parochial views as well as labouring ones. The 1928 county council election illustrates this (Case 19.4).

Case 19.4: The 1928 County Council Election

Twelve candidates ran for eight seats in the constituency in which Thomastown was located. Three of the twelve were locals: mill owner/large-scale farmer William Deady (Farmers' Union/Party); mill owner W.J Pilsworth (Independent); and carter Pat Ryan (Labour).

Of the 2,542 ballots cast, the local men received 584 first-preference votes (23 per cent). Of these, Deady received 235 (40 per cent), Ryan 214 (35 per cent), and Pilsworth 135 (23 per cent). The quota for election was 283. Pilsworth was eliminated after the sixth count as the candidate with the least votes (166). In contrast, Deady was elected after that sixth count with a total of 285 votes, having picked up transfer votes from two other Farmers' Union candidates, one of whom was eliminated and one of whom was elected. Ryan was elected after the seventh count with 313 votes. Ryan had finished the earlier sixth count with 278 votes and it was the distribution of Pilsworth's surplus that pushed Ryan over the top. Clearly, Pilsworth had little support beyond his first-preference supporters, who likely were from the locality. After five transfers he had increased his vote only marginally from what he had obtained in the first round. In contrast, Ryan's first count of 214 was increased to 253 on the second count after the other Labour candidate, from Goresbridge, had been eliminated. He then had a slow increase until Pilsworth's surplus votes elected him.[11]

The farmers voted clearly along status-class lines whereas labourer Ryan was elected by Labour votes only when combined with local ones. This actualization of local sentiment cum party interests was reproduced through time. The 1942 elections provide an example (Case 19.5).

Case 19.5: The 1942 County Council Election

The constituency in which Thomastown was located had six seats and fourteen candidates. The quota for election was 599. Labour ran four candidates. Two were from Thomastown (James O'Neill, Michael Tierney). They split local Labour's first-preference votes: O'Neill received 277; Tierney received 184. Tierney was then eliminated after the fourth count. His surplus elected the Labour candidate Richard Cass from Kells, who already had 563 first-preference votes. He was the second candidate to be elected (the first was from Fianna Fáil). James O'Neill was the third elected, but only after a tenth count as he slowly accumulated transfer votes from both the Thomastown locality and labourers elsewhere. Few of Cass's transfers had come his way or he would have been elected earlier.

The Thomastown labour vote elected a labourer from Kells while transfers from both the locality and labourers elsewhere (but not from Kells) elected a Thomastown worker. In that election, 4,188 first-preference votes were cast. Fine Gael received 11 per cent, the Farmers' Party 25 per cent, Fianna Fáil 29 per cent, and Labour 35 per cent. Labour topped the poll.[12]

Thomastown branch was also sited in a Dáil constituency which consistently elected a Labour candidate (Table 19.2). This multi-seat constituency was either 'Carlow-Kilkenny' (1925–33 and 1943 and later), with five seats and a total electorate of about 60,000, or it was 'Kilkenny' (1937–8), with three seats and an electorate of 40,000. Labour support was reflected in the successful outcomes of elections (Table 19.2). Only in 1932, in a disastrous election for Labour generally, was the party shut out from a Dáil seat in the constituency.[13]

Clearly, the political party that claimed to represent labour nationally had a long and fairly secure presence in the locality. Even more deep-rooted, and certainly going back to the founding of the rural district council in 1898, was that most labourers believed that they should elect workers to represent their interests. Equally crucial was that this party and belief, as well as the local branch of an associated union, were inside hierarchical structures which transcended the locality. These organizations thus linked Thomastown's labourers to those in adjacent local places or branches. This created parochialism at the same time that it created a national outlook. It was this double-edged consciousness, this dual view, that framed the politics of labour in the locality.

Table 19.2: Party distributions in the Dáil, 1922–43: Thomastown and Labour

Year§	Number of seats	Pro-Treaty; Cumann na nGaedheal; Fine Gael	Anti-Treaty; Republican; Fianna Fáil	Farmers' Party; Centre Party‡	Labour
1922	4	W.T. Cosgrave + 1		1*	Pat Gaffney
1925	5	W.T. Cosgrave + 1	1	D.J. Gorey	Ed. Doyle
1927(June)	5	W.T. Cosgrave D.J. Gorey	Tom Derrig	R. Holehan	Ed. Doyle
1927(Sept)	5	W.T. Cosgrave	Tom Derrig	R. Holehan	Ed. Doyle
1932**	5	D.J. Gorey Des Fitzgerald	Tom Derrig Sean Gibbon + 1	***	***
1933	5	Des Fitzgerald	Tom Derrig Sean Gibbons	R. Holehan	J. Pattison
1937	3	D.J. Gorey	Tom Derrig	‡	J. Pattison
1938	3	D.J. Gorey	Tom Derrig		J. Pattison
1943	5	D.J. Gorey + 1	Tom Derrig +1		J. Pattison

§By-elections in 1925 and 1927 are omitted: Labour was not involved.

‡In September 1934 the Farmers' Party/National Centre Party joined with Cumann na nGaedheal to form Fine Gael.

*This candidate ran as both Pro-Treaty and Farmers' Party.

**This was the first election in which de Valera and Fianna Fáil stated that they would take their seats in the Dáil if elected.

***Both Holehan and Doyle ran but were defeated. Also running for Labour was James Pattison.

The Politics of Labour: Competing Ideologies and Organizations

Agents from the Labour Party and IT&GWU were not the only competitors for the material and ideological support of Thomastown's labourers. Indeed, the early 1930s were about not only economic depression and hard times but also, as in the early part of the century, heightened organizational and discursive activity. This, too, framed the politics of labour in the locality. For example, in 1931, Tom Derrig, T.D. (Fianna Fáil), outlined his party's platform to Thomastown's electorate. What local workers heard in this lengthy oration was not unacceptable. Derrig promised local industry, jobs, and housing (Case 19.6).

Case 19.6: Fianna Fáil Policy in Thomastown, 1931 – Extracts from Derrig's Speech

'... Last year the country imported 60 million pounds worth of stuff. If we were to put our own people to produce all that ... there would be nobody unemployed ... People should give Fianna Fáil their votes. It was the only possibility for change.' The Farmers' Party voted with Fianna Fáil anyway while Labour would not put up enough candidates to form a government. In any case, 'since Fianna Fáil had entered the Dáil, they had done their best for labour. They had ... a housing programme and a programme [to] protect home industries ... to solv[e] the problem of unemployment ... They stood for de-rating; farmers at the present [could] not ... employ labour because many ... [could] not ... make ends meet and it was Fianna Fáil policy to subsidize tillage ... It would take a long time to absorb all the unemployed unless they could give employment on the land also ... The question of housing generally and of labourers' cottages was one that was receiving careful consideration by the party; they were in favour of a 10-year programme of house-building which would give employment ... and more houses at reasonable rents.'[14]

Jobs and housing were what labourers heard, along with decent wages. Yet workers also knew that farmers paid low wages, tried to dispense with hired labour, and were committed to livestock, not labour-intensive tillage. Supports for agriculture would not help most workers while, in any case, de Valera and Fianna Fáil had deserted the republican ideal. And where, in all this, was the martyred Connolly's idea of a workers' republic? Thus, alongside Fianna Fáil's voice after 1931 were other voices which appealed to old allegiances and new material concerns.

First, there was the church in the guise of the parish priest, the hierarchy, and the 'never-ending' crusade against communism. Second, after the Labour Party was trounced in the 1932 Dáil election, a defeated James Pattison said that it was because 'they were passing through a time ... when the workers' party had to bear the brunt of both sides of the big parties.'[15] In fact, in the 1980s, local labourers said that civil war politics had again come to overshadow all other issues. Thus, the profound pro-Treaty and intense anti-de Valera sentiments of many workers translated into votes for Cosgrave and Cumann na nGaedheal. Third was the republican/united Ireland sentiment which was fanned by IRA activities, such as the parades commemorating the Easter Rising. In April 1932 the 'celebration' in Thomastown was addressed by the well-known, locally-born nationalist Sean O'Mahoney, who, although no longer resident in the town, came back for this annual ritual. The press gave a three-column description of a march through the town by five IRA companies, an audience of 4,000, and three bands. The 1916 proclamation of the republic was read and a decade of the rosary said for the three local men who had been killed. Among the parade marshals were well-known nationalist farming and retailing families and, also, Herbert Devoy.[16]

Fianna Fáil, the church hierarchy, Cumann na nGaedheal, and the IRA, as organizations, shared two important features. They were not class-based and their programs explicitly aimed to mask class conflict and create cross-class alliances. Thus, in responding to these voices, ideologies, and causes, local labourers became associated with the people and interests of other classes. This occurred in the context of everyday life and experience which had, for generations, reproduced a deep awareness of hierarchy and status-class. In contrast, Labour and the IT&GWU were explicitly class-based. So, too, was another segment of local society, namely, its reserve army of labour. At this time, leaders had emerged and were trying to organize and insert this army into the political process. As they did so, others worked to appropriate it.

In October 1932 a meeting was held to bring 'the unemployed together,' to have 'them become members of the IT&GWU and to form a branch of the Unemployed Able-bodied Men's Association' (UAMA). Michael Kelly, IT&GWU secretary, presided and Patrick Walsh, Kilkenny chairman of the UAMA and 'a real lefty,' according to a labourer in the 1980s, attended. Casual worker Tom Walsh spoke. He criticized the use of non-local labour on local council projects 'while local men were idle.' He protested unskilled labourers doing skilled work, farmers carting for road works and not hiring labour, and youths being assigned adult work. He condemned employers who refused to pay a living wage and the bureaucrats who made men form 'unseemly' queues outside the employment office 'as if they were beggars.' He said that the men should join the IT&GWU so as 'to enjoy a wage which would ... support them and their families in a manner befitting Christians and human beings.'[17]

Clearly, the disaffection was profound; the issues, however, were familiar. The leadership kept up the pressure. In late 1932, UAMA marched in Kilkenny city and sent a deputation to 'wait on' the Kilkenny Board of Health. The deputation included chair Patrick Walsh, two Thomastown men (Tom Walsh and building labourer Mick Lonergan), and workers from four other rural towns in different parts of the county. The board allotted them twenty minutes. The men demanded work and the same make-work scheme as was being used in Clonmel, County Tipperary (Case 19.7).

Case 19.7: 'I Am Not a Robber or an Extremist' – 'Waiting on' the Board of Health, 1932

'Chair: Officially we know nothing about the Clonmel scheme ... We are governed by ... regulations, and if we go outside that we are liable to surcharge ...

'Tom Walsh: There are at least 250 unregistered unemployed. The position is ... appalling ... I appeal to the Board to put some scheme into operation immediately.' The district of Thomastown is large. 'If you organize a scheme here, men will come from other places ... This is very unfair [because] Thomastown is a very good rate-paying town ... I suggest that there should be special schemes [for each place] ...

'Chair: ... Something must be done and that something must be done by Government; the Government of the day must realize the importance of dealing with ... unemployment ... We have brought the matter under the notice of the Government on every occasion we could, and it will not be our fault if anyone suffers hardship and misery during the coming winter. We have taken every step we can to alleviate distress.'

Deputation member: 'We have decided that if we did not get an honest answer ... we would go into the County Home [workhouse] ...

'Secretary: ... The very name of your organization would prevent you from being legally admitted. The County Home is for the aged and infirm, chronic invalids and unmarried mothers.

'Patrick Walsh: ... [You] could ring up the Tipperary Board and ask ... how *their scheme is getting on ... Perhaps [it] could be put into operation here and now. We have 400 unemployed [outside] and with ... about 4 in each family, it brings the number up to ... 1600 absolutely destitute. They cannot go into the County Home; they cannot draw benefit. There is nothing left only to go to gaol. There is no reason why we should be starving ...; you had an abundant harvest. Something must be done here and now ...*

'Tom Walsh: I stand here as a representative of a family of nine ... I left home with one meal this morning and a damn bad one at that. I came here to fight for my rights and the rights of my children and my wife. I am not a robber or an extremist ...'

Councillors suggested that the men renew their claims at the Unemployment Exchange, that the Board instruct the relieving officers 'to see that no person within our jurisdiction would suffer for want of food,' and that they get information from Clonmel. Councillor Magennis added: 'It is impossible for this Board to deal with the demands of the men. We have no resources ... We are only ... administrators as far as grants from the Government are concerned. I have done my best ... for the relief of unemployment. But ... we must face facts and see where we are. I know that a good deal of these people are suffering ... ' After some discussion, the board decided to ask 'the Local Government department to amend the regulations governing admission to the County Home to enable the destitute able-bodied ... to enter, the Government to bear the expense, pending the provision of relief schemes by the Government.'[18]

Clearly, local councils were constrained, and allowed themselves to be, by government grants and schemes and by the personal interests of rate-paying members. Even the final decision to allow the destitute, able-bodied into the workhouse was premised on the government paying.

Such agitation, however, was disquieting to some, and it elicited a backlash of anti-labour and anti-union sentiment from a combination that contained other labourers. A week after the UAMA march, some council workers met in Thomastown. Retailer John Kelly presided and Larry Ryan, blacksmith cum Gaelic nationalist, addressed them. They wanted to oppose new legislation which would require unionized labour on building sites and to build opposition to the local IT&GWU's efforts to organize council workers and the unemployed. The key ideological phrase for this opposition was the 'right to earn an honest living.' Said Ryan: 'A gang of usurpers' have 'attempted to form a union behind our backs to oust us from our jobs, placing us in the light of scabs.' The meeting passed a vote of confidence in the county surveyor who, as retailer Kelly noted, made great 'efforts to ... provide work for the men of the district. They also appreciated the ... overseers who had always behaved in a gentlemanly way towards the workers.'[19]

Two nights before, an IT&GWU meeting in the Concert Hall had been chaired by Michael Kelly. He 'reviewed the events of the past three weeks and appealed to workers to sink their differences and unite under the banner of the IT&GWU.' Cathal O'Shannon from HO spoke, raising and praising the history, heroes, and hopes of Irish trade unionists (Case 19.8).

Case 19.8: Cathal O'Shannon and Thomastown Labour, 1932

O'Shannon said that 'it gave him great pleasure to ... meet some of the veterans in the Labour movement whom he had met in 1917 and 1918. He reviewed the history of the IT&GWU ... since its inception, and the many benefits the workers of Ireland had derived from its membership. He paid ... tribute to the memory of ... James Connolly and ... to all Connolly had done for the ... movement up to Easter 1916, when he was led to his doom before a British firing squad ... [He] pointed to the flour mill workers as an example of what organized labour could achieve ... [They] were the best paid workers in any town or district ... It was only where the workers were not organized that the wages were low. [He] explained that the ban on foreign flour would be increased every month and it was expected that ... every mill ... would [soon] be working at full power. He referred to the government's Housing Bill ... that only union labour would be employed. [This] would show how essential it was that all labourers and tradesmen ... be organized.'[20]

As part of this flurry of organizational and ideological fervour, non-labouring interests were also organizing, often through local branches of national associations. Thomastown's farmers and retailers founded a branch of the National Farmers' and Ratepayers' Association in 1932. Miller/farmer William Deady was elected chair.[21] That Deady was also a county councillor at the time highlights the fact that the organizational impetus was part of an increasing agency among elected politicians. It was alongside this that ideologies were being honed – to voice, clarify, and disseminate views. However, no singular or static structure emerged. Rather, the organizational and ideological frameworks were continually being dialectically (re)made. As UAMA marched in Kilkenny city, causing disquiet over its meaning and intent, it collided not only with the minimally organized sentiments of Larry Ryan but also with the church hierarchy. Both the local IT&GWU and Labour Party therefore had to engage in a public ritual of reconciliation. In January 1933 the leaders repudiated communism in the press and promised a public meeting to reiterate this declaration (Case 19.9).

Case 19.9: 'Communism Repudiated by Workers' – A Letter to the Press, 1933
'At a meeting of members ... the following resolution, proposed by M. Kelly, secretary IT&GWU, and seconded by Thomas Walsh, secretary I.L.P. was passed: "We, the members of the IT&GWU and the ILP, strongly protest against the innuendo that we ... are connected with the Communist movement. Therefore, we declare to the public that we have no connection with the Communist party; neither do we believe in their policy. We recognize no organization outside the IT&GWU and the I.L.P. On account of those statements being made, we shall hold a public meeting in Thomastown in the market square on Sunday, January 8, immediately after second mass, and declare our views to the public. Should the day ... be inclement, the meeting will be held in the Concert Hall." Signed: M. Kelly, sec. IT&GWU; Thomas Beck, Pres, do; Patrick Dunphy, do; Thomas Walsh, sec. ILP; James Walsh, president, do.'[22]

The public meeting was held and described by the press as a 'protest against communism.' Tom Walsh presided. Both he and Michael Kelly 'disassociated the workers of the parish from Communistic teaching and practice. The meeting pledged unswerving support to [the] ... Bishop of Ossory and the clergy in crushing any attempt to undermine the Catholic Faith.' Earlier, the parish priest 'at first mass ... [had] expressed his gratitude ... to the deputation of workers who waited on him and assured him of their hostility to the policy of Communism.'[23]

On the one hand, local labour had capitulated and been humiliated. On the other, public obeisance meant that the hierarchy would support its agitations and recruiting efforts. Three weeks later, a Dáil election was held; James Pattison won a seat. At a Thomastown labour meeting soon after, Pattison 'made an earnest appeal to all the workers in the area to organize under the banner of the IT&GWU which had the approval of the present bishop (Applause).'[24]

The pragmatics of electoral politics thus intruded on the organizational flurry and framed the politics of labour. It was partly because politicians saw the potential for advancement and partly because politics was seen as the route to administration. If the county health board could not help the men of UAMA because board members were only helpless administrators (Case 19.7), then a clear deduction was that more sympathetic interests ought to control that board. This was Maher's view: 'There is a very strong feeling' that whoever is elected to the county council 'should also be a member of the Board of Health. Thomastown has no representative on the Board since it was established, and the local ratepayers have had no one to air their grievances.'[25] Two responses ensued. The flurry among purely local interest groups intensified as people tried to secure local amenities and jobs (Cases 14.5, 14.6). Second, immense concern with elections emerged. Indeed, two Dáil elections, twelve months apart in 1932 and 1933, contributed to the frenetic quality of organizational and ideological life at the time. Fianna Fáil's local drive to raise funds counterposed Labour's 'enthusiastic meetings' in more than a half-dozen towns in south Kilkenny, addressed by Michael Kelly, Tom Walsh, and James O'Neill.[26]

County council elections, as well as Dáil ones, created organizational bustle. A council election had been held in 1928. The next one had been postponed but was anticipated at any time. This, of course, provided ongoing organizational incentive. However, instead of an election, the minister, using the 1925 Local Government Act, ordered an inquiry into the affairs of the Kilkenny County Council. It found that over 52 per cent of the rates were unpaid. In June 1934 he dissolved the council and appointed a commissioner to take charge of county administration.[27]

This direct rule was in part stimulated by the ascendancy of the Blueshirts, a fascist faction within Cosgrave's Cumann na nGaedheal party. Stimulated by depression, economic war, and admiration for anti-communist/fascist parties on the continent, the Blueshirts appealed to farmers and retailers who were being hurt by Fianna Fáil's economic policies and, also, to labourers who had been pro-Treaty in 1922 and hated de Valera. Out of this, Cumann na nGaedheal and two small right-wing parties together formed the Fine Gael party in September 1933. One of the small parties was the National Centre Party (formerly the National Farmers' and Ratepayers' Association), a branch of which had been founded in Thomastown in 1932 with county councillor Deady as chair. With its anti-communist, pro-Catholic, and fascist rhetoric, and with charismatic leader Eoin O'Duffy, both Fianna Fáil and the Trade Union Congress were, together, concerned with the seeming threat to the state. One of O'Duffy's close lieutenants was D.J. Gorey, a T.D. for Kilkenny-Carlow. Both Gorey and Deady were standing for election to the county council in 1933–4. A meeting in Kilkenny city in October

1933, with O'Duffy, Cosgrave, and Deady on the platform, ended up in a scuffle between Blueshirts and Fianna Fáil men.[28] In August 1934 a Blueshirt rally in Thomastown led to what the *Journal* called 'exciting scenes' (Case 19.10).

Case 19.10: The Blueshirt Rally in Thomastown, August 1934
The 'exciting scenes' took place as 500 Blueshirts marched to the Concert Hall and as a crowd began to gather, crying 'up Dev' [de Valera]. A 'fracas' took place near the Mall when a flag taken from the Blueshirts was dragged in the mud. The men who did this were beaten up. After the rally, a crowd tried to prevent Commandant Cronin, head of Fine Gael's youth wing, from leaving. The guardaí had to intervene. The press reported 'an air of tension in the town, throughout that evening, which increased as fresh parties of Blueshirts arrived for a dance. Skirmishes [took place] once or twice during the night' and, on one occasion, the guards had to protect a dozen young men who were surrounded by a large number of Blueshirts who asserted that they had been insulted. After the dance, as Cronin was leaving, eight revolver shots rang out. The matter was raised a week later in the Dáil. Cronin insisted that the guards had fired at him. The superintendent of police refused to examine the guns to ascertain this.[29]

Local people in the 1980s said the shots were fired in the direction of the Concert Hall where the dance was in progress rather than at any particular target. As well, the local altercations were between Fianna Fáil followers and Blueshirts. A few local labourers who 'ought to have known better' were reportedly seen among the Blueshirts. More of them, however, were in the Fianna Fáil crowds.

The threat was soon over because the Blueshirt base was never sufficiently extensive to effect a *coup d'état*.[30] O'Duffy, forced by Fine Gael to resign in late 1934, led his Blueshirts to fight for Franco in 1936 and was joined by a farmer and a retailer from Thomastown. Fine Gael continued as an anti–de Valera party, opposed to the republicanism of Fianna Fáil which was regarded, in turn, by many republicans as a chimera. Some local labourers, whose inclinations were both socialist and republican, had supported such splinter groups as Saor Éire. By the end of 1935, these had largely disappeared. For these workers, the Labour Party and the IT&GWU were the only organizational options.[31]

Through all this, Thomastown's labourers were drawn in several ideological and associational directions. Workers in the 1980s were clear about how the Blueshirt-Fianna Fáil riots had polarized local labourers along the old pro and anti-Treaty lines and how the local Labour Party was caught in the middle, trying to carve out a space for itself. To an extent, this effort was made easier by multi-member constituencies for both the Dáil and county council. With transfer voting, a labourer could, in almost good conscience, give the Labour Party candidate his/her first vote and give his/her second choice to another party, or vice versa (Case 13.5). The electoral system thus allowed and even fostered multiple and sometimes conflicting sentiments and organizational affiliations. At the same time, elections were increasing in importance, fostered both by agents and by the associational flurry.

20. Inside the Frame: The Politics of Mediation

'The essential purpose of the Labour Party is to challenge and change the whole structure of society ... It is no longer possible to argue that the interests of the people are best served by a system of production based on minority ownership and control.'

– James O'Neill, Thomastown ILP Kilkenny *Journal*, 26 February 1938

The Labour Party has 'been repeatedly assured [by the Fianna Fáil government] that a social order was being created on ... Christian lines.'

– James Pattison, T.D. Kilkenny *Journal*, 26 February 1938

During the 1930s, experiences of underemployment conjoined with a belief that public amenities and jobs were interdependent goals, obtainable through state intervention (chapter 14). This common sense, shared by people of all classes, merged with and reproduced sentiments of localism. Yet locals did not agree on the precise means or agency for achieving these goals while, at the same time, competing ideologies, organizations, and agents had proliferated, fracturing loyalties and viewpoints (chapter 19). In addition, a political economy that implicated paternalism and 'compassionate inequality' (chapter 16) became meshed with ideas about Christian morality and personal entitlements (chapter 15). In the framework provided by the conjuncture of all these processes, the stage was set for material, ideological, and discursive conflict.

The Politics of Labour: Creating the Mediation Process

From a labouring perspective, at least four relations were vital. First was the tie between employees and employers with regard to wages and work. Second was the relation between, on the one hand, workers' obligations vis-à-vis the state and its bureaucratic agents (for example, to pay cottage rents, eschew violence) and, on the other, the state's obligation to provide amenities and jobs. Third, there was the relation between workers as voters and those political agents who professed to represent their interests. Fourth was the link between workers and a church hierarchy that claimed to know God's will. In all these relations, underpinned as they were by a particular morality, disputes might arise, non-compliance could occur or be perceived to occur, one party might introduce change, or other relations or interests could impinge. As a result, mediators were often required and/or emerged to settle disputes, gain compliance, intercede during change, and/or insulate the relationship to protect its vitality. At different times in Thomastown's past, various people or organizations took on such mediating roles. In the twentieth century, employer-worker grievances were often mediated by the Trade and Labour League or an IT&GWU official in a unionized shop or in the context of a unionization drive (chapters 18, 19). Or ad hoc mediators were available from among those with influence: Lindsay (Cases 10.6, 15.1), Pilsworth, priest, or retailers (via their Association). However, with a common-sense view that the state was to alleviate unemployment and provide amenities, and with a new Irish state that had appropriated colonial administrative structures and reproduced the relation between capital and labour, the salience of mediation increased.

Making 'Proper Representations': The Nature of Mediation
In Thomastown, when self-appointed mediators stepped in, additional disputes sometimes arose over the utility of mediation and/or the quality of the mediator. An example of the former was when conditions at Jerpoint induced IT&GWU/Labour Party agents to insert themselves, despite local dissent (Cases 18.3, 18.4). An example of the latter was Lindsay's effort to mediate the 1913 tannery strike over the objections of nationalists (Case 10.6). The Jerpoint situation, however, did highlight three aims which local labouring activists had at the time: to move beyond representation on formal bodies into mediating conflicts which derived from their relations with employers, bureaucrats, politicians,

and church hierarchy; to monopolize links between local agents and others; and to depict both the conflicts and links through a discourse of class and class conflict. These efforts were opposed by those who had different political outlooks, who wished to dominate mediation themselves, and/or who wanted to check the audacity of, and threat from, labour and labourers. In other words, securing state funding for the locality raised questions of how and who: of means, of mechanisms and agency, and of mediators and mediation. The different answers that various people arrived at reflected status-class differences and class tensions, ideological dissension, and ethical ambiguities. They also reflected the material interests, resources, and moral concerns of agents, organizations, and institutions outside the locality which had goals that touched upon and articulated with those being pursued by Thomastown people.

Discursively, the mediation process was what Thomastown people called 'making proper representations.' It had several stages. Locals had to combine to frame project proposals, plan deputations and arguments, and exert influence. In all stages, three tactics were key: discourse, agitation, and agency. So, too, were there various sites: bureaucratic, legislative, and organizational. These stages, tactics, and sites might occur on any relevant level: local, district, county, region, constituency, nation. With all these stages, arenas, and levels, the number of strategical options was immense. In the early years of the Free State, many of these were tried. Within two decades, only a few had proved effective. The honing of these had particular implications for local labour.

Making 'Proper Representations': Changing the Political Mode

Thomastown Notes provided information, gossip, and rumour about people, politics, and the economy against which locals could compare their own experiences and make assessments about themselves, other people, and formal organizations (chapter 14). Such information, however, was neither complete nor neutral. Gossip moved along networks structured by class/status-class, residence, and gender. As journalist Maher picked it up, assessed it, and wrote about it, he was in fact conveying views about what and who were important for the locality. Indeed, his complaints were really an effort to agitate: to mobilize public opinion around certain issues, people, and institutions. His column, then, along with other press reports, minutes, and interviews, can shed light on labour politics and the changing mediation process as these were enmeshed in com-

mon sense and moral ideas which local people held about labour, public amenities, and the state.

It had long been accepted that people might petition or send deputations to government agents. It also was accepted that personal favours
and/or individual generosity were essential in easing the condition of
working people. In the late 1920s, several such examples were recorded.
Combinations of local people waited on government in 1928 to obtain
drainage, sewerage, and housing schemes (chapter 14) and, in 1929, to
object to the closing of the old burial ground. Numerous employers,
priests, councillors, and farmers wrote references when labourers tried
to obtain the Oldtown cottage in 1931 (Case 15.4) while, in 1930,
farmer Walpole allowed locals to glean timber from his lands in Dargan
Wood (Case 13.11). Mediators and patrons in these cases included
priests, gentlemen, farmers, or council/board representatives. Importantly, no formal organizations were identified as being connected with
the combinations or largesse.

Changes, however, were in train. After the 1927 election, Fianna Fáil
terminated its boycott of the Dáil. This ended the Labour Party's role as
the opposition to Cummann na nGaedheal and as the sole exponent of
social reform. Competition for electoral support intensified. It was at
this time, too, that Maher began providing his detailed news of individual workers and their life passages. In 1931, for example, the retirement
of two rural postmen, 'on pension after 40 years service,' was reported.
So, too, was the 'very pretty wedding' between a mechanic and the
daughter of a shoemaker. The long list of gift-givers that Maher furnished was a clear emulation of reports of weddings among people of
higher status-classes. Or, the note about James O'Neill's departure for
America told about his work (Grennan Mills), formal positions (rural
district councillor), republican credentials ('he served ... 3 months in
Waterford gaol'), and labouring commitments ('an active trade unionist').[1] Socially, then, labourers had become a fair and respectable focus
for the public spotlight, just like gentry and retailers, with their charities, rites of passage, and organizations. Politically, too, labourers were
insisting that local works projects use local labour. Both these facets
articulated with the normative approval of deputations, petitions, and
patronage and with the recent, intensified competition for the Dáil. In
tandem, the material and discursive character of petitions, deputations,
and patronal largesse began to change.

It could be seen in mid-1931 when the Tullaherin farmers and priest
secured their drainage scheme and Maher wrote: 'The Commissioner of

Public Works has informed Mr. T. Derrig, T.D., that the Minister for
Finance has confirmed the ... scheme' (Case 14.3). The message was
clear: it was all attributable to Derrig's effective mediation among locality, government (party), and bureaucracy. However, what about future
projects? Which politician/mediator and party would be most efficacious? Intense rivalries emerged among self-appointed, hopeful organizations and individuals as they competed to control the stages, tactics,
and sites that together comprised the 'proper representations' which
brought jobs and amenities to the locality. What was labour's approach
to these contests? How did it affect mediation and class awareness and
experience?

The Politics of Mediation

Thomastown's workers entered the political fray of 'proper representations' by emulating known stages, tactics, and sites. In 1934 *Thomastown
Notes* disclosed that 'J.P. Pattison, T.D., has arranged with Mr P.J.
Meghen, Commissioner administering ... the Kilkenny Board of Health,
to receive a deputation from the Thomastown Branch of the Irish
Labour Party.' Maher listed the projects that the deputation would seek.
He concluded that 'members of the Thomastown branch of the ILP are
to be congratulated on making a genuine move to have the schemes ...
provided.'[2] What happened to the deputation was described the following week (Case 20.1).

---

*Case 20.1: A Deputation from the Thomastown Labour Party
to the Commissioner, 1934*

*'J.P. Pattison introduced the deputation: ... Mr Patrick O'Reilly [postman],
chairman, Thomastown Labour Party; Mr Daniel Dilworth [waged mechanic],
secretary; Mr James O'Neill [millworker], treasurer, Labour [Party] executive.
Mr O'Reilly read a document setting out the pressing need for ... housing: ... 54
families were involved – 37 ... residing in insanitary houses and 17 ... in rooms.
Taking five as the average ... in each family ... 270 people or [about] 37 per cent
of the ... population ... [were] living under conditions which must adversely
affect their health. [In] Mill street ... all the homes on one side were built under
an overhanging rock. As a result they were badly lighted and ventilated and
almost continuously damp. The only remedy was to demolish them ... Mr O'Reilly
[then] read a report from Dr D.J. Moloney ... that there was great need for proper
housing for the working classes ... Mr O'Reilly said that the local Labour Party*

[thought] that first preference should be given to families residing in rooms ... The statement went on to deal with the necessity for a pure water supply.' It was backed up by letters from the county engineer, a solicitor and Dr Moloney. 'The statement also pointed out the ... need for a public lavatory and a ... dumping site ... Flooding in the town was [also] referred to: ... this could be lessened by removing obstructions ... and ... refuse ... [from] the river.

'... The statement said there was much unemployment in the town' and suggested 'immediate schemes': closing dangerous entrances to the river, improving the workhouse sewerage and entrance, fixing several local roads, removing scattered refuse, and providing more street lamps. 'The statement asked that maximum [monies] be expended on wages ... Schemes involving the purchase of large quantities of material would be opposed; ... also ... workers should be drawn from the area where the work was being carried out. Attention was directed to the practice of cutting men for a half-day when they [had] to discontinue work on account of bad weather. This caused ... hardship and discontent among the road workers. The men should be paid for the full half-day.

'The Commissioner said that with regard to the housing problem, the government were taking up the case of small towns and ... were awaiting a report. – [J.P.] Pattison: It is expected that a special scheme will be available for small towns ...

'Commissioner: Yes. [But] we cannot say [anything] until we get the report. – [J.P.] Pattison: The accommodation in some of the new houses was just as bad as in the old ones, as they had only two or three rooms, and families of six or seven boys and girls were not properly provided for.

'Commissioner: The standard ... at present is a four-roomed house. [This] should be suitable for Thomastown ... He would go into [their] statement and get in touch with the secretary of the Labour branch in Thomastown after ... discuss[ing it] with the county surveyor and clerk of works. Some of the matters would be seen to immediately but some ... would have to wait ... With reference to ... lighting ... the streets, he was already in communication with the E.S.B. ... and would try to have it settled ... The clerk of works was ordered to prepare reports [for] a ... dump ... and [one of] the roads. The Commissioner said that improvements to the County Home entrance and sewerage ... were [already] sanctioned ... and would be proceeded with in the near future. He would go carefully into all the matters in the statement ... and ... let them know how things were going. The Labour Party had gone to a great deal of trouble to put the problems of Thomastown before him and the people there should be very grateful to them ... Pattison, on behalf of the deputation, thanked the Commissioner for the patient hearing ... and said he felt assured that the Commissioner would do all in his power to help them.'

In fact, most of the requests had already been brought to the commissioner by other interested local agents (Case 14.5). However, the above meeting did not end there. The formal routine and the smooth bureaucratic assurances rankled. So, too, did Pattison's obeisance, as he quickly conceded over the one explicit point of contention, the size of houses. Thus, at the end of the meeting, as Pattison ceremonially thanked the commissioner and as he, in turn, gave ritual responses, mechanic Dilworth raised another matter (Case 20.2) .

Case 20.2: The Mechanic and the Commissioner, 1934

'Mr Dilworth asked the Commissioner if he had received [his] letter ... and if he could state what ... wages a man should have that would prevent him from obtaining the services of the dispensary doctor or midwife. In Thomastown ... the doctor took ... the tradesmen as men with sufficient wages to prevent them getting free medical attention for their wives.

'Commissioner: You cannot lay down regulations or rules on that question.

'Mr Dilworth: I would like to know if there is any ruling on the point. My wife got a ticket from the relieving officer but the doctor would not attend her and said that I was a tradesman. I wrote to him explaining what my wages were and ... my expenses but he never answered my letter and did not attend my wife for a fortnight.

'Commissioner: I imagine he has a grievance about the issue of tickets to people who are, in his opinion, able to pay. I think he should report the facts to this board.

'Mr Dilworth: He absolutely ignored my request to have an answer ... I offered ... to publish the full contents of [my] letter and then he came to my wife. That is only my own case, but there are others also.

'Secretary (Mr Treacy): Did you serve a ticket on the doctor?

'Mr Dilworth: Yes, my wife brought it over from the relieving officer who, in my opinion, was the best judge as to whether I was entitled to it or not. I think the doctor should first of all attend the patient and make his complaint afterwards.

'Secretary: That is the usual practice ...

'Mr Dilworth: The relieving officer said he had been ordered by the doctor not to issue any more tickets to my wife ... The Commissioner said he had received Mr Dilworth's letter and the reason he did not take up the matter officially was because he understood that the doctor had ... been there ...

'[J.P.] Pattison: I understand this ... is ... new; the workers ... were never asked before to pay. I hope the Commissioner will go fully into the matter and give a ruling in such cases.

428 An Irish Working Class

> '*Commissioner: There is no question of a ruling ... If a relieving officer ... gives a ticket it is the doctor's place to attend ... If he considers ... the ... officer ... is giving tickets to people who are able to pay he should report the matter here.*
>
> '*Mr Dilworth said that ... he asked the doctor to accompany him to his employer [to] ... prove ... his wages were only £2 a week. "If," said Mr Dilworth, "I have to pay the nurse, an extra woman, and the doctor as well as ... other expenses, I would want to be a Vanderbilt, especially as the family is increasing from year to year" (laughter).*
>
> '*Commissioner: I will look into the matter if you will leave it to me.*
>
> '*Another member of the deputation, Mr O'Neill, said that he was a warden who issued tickets and he would also like to have a ruling on the question ... The midwife is threatening ... during the past year to take no tickets from the mill workers ... Twelve months ago I issued a ticket to ... a blacksmith that I would not have issued ten years ago because his trade was since a dead one.*
>
> '*Commissioner: I will write to the doctor ... and if there is a continuance of this trouble ... the only way ... will be to ... have the matter inquired into.*
>
> '*Mr O'Neill: I am so "fed up" that I don't think I'll issue any more tickets at all.*
>
> '*The matter dropped.*'[3]

The newspaper report of this discussion created difficulties. It suggested that workers could not maintain a respectable decorum, the everyday indignities of labouring life had been exposed, and Dr. Moloney had been maligned. A week later, Thomastown's deputation/executive members wrote to the Kilkenny *People* to say that the 'question of the duties of the dispensary doctor ... was entirely unauthorized.' They apologized to the doctor who had always been most 'conscientious' and whose 'services are highly valued by the poor of the district.' He also 'has ... a keen ... interest in ... housing, water and sewerage, and we feel deeply indebted to him for the help he has rendered us.' Several of the executive signed their names in Irish, as a sign of independence and intellectual acumen in what was an embarrassing situation.[4]

However, the altercation had highlighted an inherent tension: workers had to comply with highly formal conventions when using such mediation sites and tactics while simultaneously being agents in the conflicts that required the mediation. On this occasion, Dilworth succumbed and O'Neill leapt into the fray. That it all was made public, and that both men had to recant, detracted from labourers' credibility with both the commissioner and those labourers whose concern with respectability was greater than their care for jobs and amenities. In contrast, Pattison was deferential, yet concerned. He knew the rules of such formal deputations and stuck to them. He raised issues that, when brushed aside by the commissioner, he did not publicly pursue. He was unwilling to engage in a public mêlée. He was also a key agent: Labour TD (Carlow-Kilkenny constituency) after 1933; head of the Kilkenny IT&GWU; alderman, Kilkenny city corporation; and member of the county council. Through such posts, he monopolized all the Labour lines that local workers might wish to accesss: to union and party (Case 18.5), county council and Dáil, county and state bureaucracies. At the same time, Pattison was conservative in his views about unions, the Labour Party, and the church hierarchy (Case 20.3).

Case 20.3: Two Speeches at a Labour Party Meeting in Thomastown, 1933
James Pattison. *It was just after his election to the Dáil. Pattison 'thanked people' and said that 'he would always do what he could to forward their interests in the Dáil.' He criticized a Fianna Fáil minister who, in a Dáil speech, 'tried to justify ... wages of 24s. weekly for road workers. If that starvation wage [was] the policy of the Fianna Fáil government, it would meet with unrelenting opposition from the Labour Party ... The working classes would never allow themselves to be humiliated ... by accepting such an ... un-Christian wage.' He asked workers to put forward candidates for the upcoming county council elections. 'Let them select men [like] the late, lamented Pat Ryan who would look after their interests.' He appealed to 'all the workers in the area to organize under the banner of the IT&GWU which had the approval of the present bishop ... (applause).'*

Michael Kelly, *secretary of the local IT&GWU, spoke. He 'referred to a recent meeting of the Farmers and Ratepayers Association where a member ... proposed that they sack all their workers and ... within a fortnight they would be starving ... and would come begging for board alone ... These are the type of men ... who are trying to make communists of the decent Catholic, God-fearing men of County Kilkenny, but they would never succeed. (applause) He appeal[ed] to ... employers ... to ... study ... the ... encyclical of ... Pope Leo XIII: "To defraud anyone of wages ... is a crime which cries to the avenging anger of heaven ... The rich must religiously refrain from cutting down the workman's earnings whether by force, fraud or usurious dealings ... because the labouring man is ... weak and unprotected, and because his slender means should ... be accounted sacred." Were these precepts carefully obeyed ... would they not be sufficient ... to [halt] all strife and all its causes? (applause).'* [5]

The emotional fervour of Kelly's speech contrasted with Pattison's pragmatic one. Yet both had appealed to Christian ideals: Kelly cited an encyclical on labourers' rights whereas Pattison cited the bishop's approval. Pattison told workers what the next practical step should be (council elections) whereas Kelly tried to incite political zeal. However, it was Pattison who held the formal positions and who had honed the tactics that made him a consummate mediator: he tried to fix problems, guard his credibility, and never rock the boat. As a TD cum mediator, Pattison had counterparts in the other two, main political parties. Lines of influence reputedly went from the local branch of Fianna Fáil and of Fine Gael to their TDs. This, not surprisingly, led to competition among local branches as each plumped for its own party, TD, and, by implication, mediator. The contest was waged in both public and private sites. In the former, politician-mediators aimed to obtain publicity in the press and in local gossip (Case 20.4).

Case 20.4: The Tactics of Political Mediation in the Public Domain
[1] Local branches of parties often took on popular causes to garner votes while also giving the impression, sometimes correct, that the branch was using its lines to its TD to get the problem fixed via his influence. In so doing, however, branches were constrained by their support base and their pasts. In 1935 the Inland Fisheries Commission was about to ban inland netting. The Fianna Fáil branch, to show support for fishers but also to maintain its cross-class support and republican face, condemned the conservators for appointing a British policeman as a water bailiff.[6] This contrasted with the Labour Party branch which sent secretary Michael Kelly to the annual national convention to put a motion to nationalize fishing rights and abolish stationary engines. [2] On various public occasions, a mediator often came forward so as to ensure that his own personal affiliation would be publicized. This occurred after McCalmont's two hounds were poisoned in 1936 (Case 16.9) and the branches of the Labour Party and IT&GWU held meetings and passed motions. Pattison attended, announcing that 'he wished to associate himself with the resolution.' [3] Such exposure might also be chosen because it could be linked to particular ideological positions which illustrated that general, moral concerns underlay specific political interests. At the 1936 Fine Gael convention, where farmer/miller William Deady was elected to the county executive and, hence, to a position of potential, albeit lower-level mediation, a resolution congratulated Fine Gael members of the Kilkenny city corporation for 'the manner in which they were exposing communism.' [4] Recreational events also provided a commonly used venue for a mediator to receive publicity, advertize

affiliations, and even do business. A Thomastown Labour Party dance brought in local, labouring people and J.P. Pattison from Kilkenny city.[7]

Through the formalities of associational life and the actions of local branches of the main political parties, mediators highlighted their particular ideological wares and advertised their efficacy and agency. In fact, however, local party branches were active mainly before elections as they raised funds, arranged public meetings, canvassed voters, and tried to be publicly visible. What the branches mainly did at other times was to provide private sites in which politicians cum mediators could meet with potential clients, listen to their problems, and offer solutions. In 1935 Sean Gibbons, Fianna Fáil TD (Kilkenny-Carlow), attended a 'clinic' in the Concert Hall. 'The proceedings, which were private, occupied three hours.' However, a Bennettsbridge delegation was reported on. It was led by James Lawlor, chair of the Labour Party branch, and was concerned with house sales in the locality. 'Mr Gibbons assured the deputation of his sympathy and support.'[8] In crossing party lines, Lawlor was saying that Labour on its own was unable to deliver on the request. The 1935 clinic thus highlighted the problem that Labour had in carving out its own patronage structure without controlling the Dáil. Yet Lawlor's attendance also showed that local agents would cross if there was some hope of delivering what local voters wanted. This not only added to the personal credibility of the mediator but, if Lawlor's request was seen to bring results, local votes would flow to him and thus to Labour. In such a way were local sentiment and political sentiment inextricably combined through the mediation process.

Lawlor's attendance also shows that a great deal of faith was put into the efficacy of such private occasions. However, the 1935 clinic was unusual in that any business was reported on at all. Usually, it was only announced that a clinic would be held. There, individuals, using a personal introduction from branch activists, spoke with the TD-mediator who, it was hoped, would exert influence in bureaucratic, legislative, or organizational sites. In Thomastown, apart from the Labour Party, such activists were retailers or large-scale farmers who had partisan loyalties to Fianna Fáil or Fine Gael. Sometimes these loyalties emanated from deep political sentiment; sometimes they had been purchased. A common story was of a publican who was a staunch Fine Gael supporter until he failed to get appointed as court clerk. He then changed to Fianna

Fáil. He was popularly regarded as a link to its TDs and his pub was used for their clinics.

More, however, was expected of local agents. Their role also required them to become active in local organizations and causes. Retailers on the CYMS executive in the late 1920s began to address 'town concerns and problems' which went well beyond the management of their recreational-religious organization. They formed savings (1930), flood (1932), *feis* (1932), and ad hoc committees (1933, Case 14.5). In 1936 they formalized themselves into a Thomastown Traders Development Association (TTDA) which, over the next few years, 'concerned itself with a number of local issues and sought, by petitions and deputations, to press the relevant authorities – county council officers and councillors, state officials, TDs, and cabinet ministers – to act'[9] (Cases 14.5, 14.6). In this evolution from CYMS to TTDA, retailers entered sites that were of great concern to local labourers and to Labour/union activists. Competition thus emerged between the two groups, via their respective political organizations, as each claimed to represent the interests, voice, and needs of the locality (Case 20.5).

Case 20.5: Party Politics and Local Amenities after 1936

In early 1936 the Labour Party (ILP) branch secretary reported on 'the work accomplished during the year.' He referred to the establishment of the Savings Society and how he was 'instructed to make further representations to [J.P.] Pattison in connection with an application for a grant to clean Thomastown bridge.' Later in the year, an invitation from the TTDA to cooperate with regard to housing was not accepted. Instead, Labour entered the contest on its own. James O'Neill, secretary, wrote the Board of Health asking when the new housing project would begin: 'They were needed before winter, as people living in condemned houses in some cases could not possibly remain in them during the bad weather.' The commissioner referred the matter to the county engineer for a report.

In September 1937 the local ILP picked up an issue which had been concerning the TTDA: the water supply. An ILP committee meeting discussed the 'unwarranted delay' and 'decided to request J.P. Pattison, TD, to question the minister for local government when the Dáil reassembles next month.'

Three months later, the TTDA had found a dumping site, owing to 'the generosity' of a large-scale, local farmer who was willing to sell a site. A week later, Tom Derrig, TD and now a minister, was in Thomastown for a Fianna Fáil meeting. He received a deputation from the TTDA which raised several topics: the delay   in the water supply, the need for a sewerage scheme, and how to expedite the housing project. 'The Minister said he would take up the matter with the various authorities.'[10]

This competition for amenities put the local Labour Party in the same position as that of all other local agents: trying to access government largesse while using such efforts as political capital. As the requests dragged out, however, competition escalated. For Labour, the contest itself raised questions as to what precisely the party ought to be doing. This was highlighted in a report prepared by James O'Neill for the branch's annual general meeting in February 1938. He noted that more people had begun working with the Labour Party and that these extra canvassers had helped secure Pattison's re-election. He said that this showed 'a growing realization on the part of those who formerly were apathetic that the only hope of social and economic advancement lies in implementing the Labour Party programme.' What did he mean by this (Case 20.6)?

Case 20.6: James O'Neill's Report to the Thomastown Labour Party, 1938
It is not 'necessary for me to review ... the work of the branch during the past year. Repeated representations on the housing and water questions have not, I regret to say, met with any great success. Deputy Pattison raised a question of the water scheme in the Dáil but the reply ... by ... the Minister ... could not be regarded as ... encouraging. However, it is his intention to have the matter raised again in the near future ... During the year, the [party] secretary dealt with numerous claims for widows and orphans, pensions [and] unemployment assistance ... and in certain cases has succeeded in having those dealt with more speedily than would otherwise have been the case. Considerable success also attended the efforts of the committee to have conditions improved on the ... relief scheme. Deputy Pattison has rendered invaluable assistance in this respect and has placed all casual workers under a deep debt of gratitude.

'It cannot be too strongly stressed, however, that the Labour party is not concerned primarily with work of this kind. Its ultimate aim is more far reaching and fundamental ... Its essential purpose is to challenge and change the whole structure of society in which unemployment and destitution are accepted as permanent and inescapable necessities. Can anyone seriously deny that the present system, based ... on private enterprise has ... failed to deliver the goods? It is no longer possible to argue that the interests of the people are best served by a system of production based on minority ownership and control ... The Labour Party does not

exist primarily for dealing with 'hard cases.' Its main purpose is to transform and revolutionize. Its immediate aim may be to effect an improvement in social and economic conditions. But its ultimate object is to place workers in such a position that they can decide for themselves what those conditions shall be. Up to the present, we have tended to concern ourselves exclusively with political freedom. It is now time that we gave our attention to the ... more ... important question of economic freedom. This can only be achieved when the workers ... organize themselves into a body that will work for ... this object with vigour and determination. In the Labour Party you have such a body, and for that reason, it claims the allegiance and enthusiastic support of all members of our class.'[11]

The idea of the Irish Labour Party as a revolutionary vanguard was certainly not shared by J.P. Pattison whose speech on the same occasion focused on Dáil politics and the failure of the Fianna Fáil government to provide a 'Christian social order' (Case 20.7).

Case 20.7: J.P. Pattison's Speech to the Thomastown Labour Party, 1938
Pattison spoke of the gains made by the Labour Party in the Dáil, such as its 'strenuous fight against the scandalous low rate of wages which were being paid under [government] relief schemes.' He referred to a recent speech by Tom Derrig, minister for education, in which Derrig 'described as blatherumskite ... the claim of the Labour Party to have improved the social legislation of Fianna Fáil ...' Such a 'pompous statement,' said Pattison, 'was a reckless disregard for facts ... In the case of the Widows' and Orphans' Pension, the Labour Party [did] pioneer work [and] ... energetically engaged in rousing public opinion to the necessity of the measure.' When in opposition, Fianna Fáil 'incessantly' claimed that it had a plan to deal with unemployment. 'The plan was now in operation over 6 years, yet there were today over 100,000 unemployed and a still greater number in casual and lowly-paid work. During the same period, over 100,000 people had been compelled to emigrate to the land of the traditional and hereditary enemy.' Labour has 'been repeatedly assured during the past few years that a social order was being created on essentially Christian lines.' Yet the weekly dole for a married man was 'a miserly 8 shillings: Fianna Fáil had enthusiastically accepted the capitalist ideal.'

O'Neill and Pattision occupied a common continuum. At one end was the party's concern to ensure that 'hard cases' received the benefits to which they were legally entitled. At the other extreme was the party's commitment to abolish private property by, for example, nationalizing the fisheries (Case 20.4[1]). In between was the reformist position: to squeeze local amenities and national welfare programs out of the Fianna Fáil government in order to improve the condition of working people. This reformist middle ground also required labour to compete for votes and, hence, greater leverage in the Dáil. The revolutionary position required control of the Dáil. Handling the hard cases was one means of garnering the votes.

In the context of this common continuum, O'Neill and Pattison clearly occupied different positions. For O'Neill, as a dependent agent in the lower tier, the revolutionary aims of the party were key. For Pattison, with a parliamentary career, reformist goals were sufficient. Only once in his speech did Pattison depart from the minutiae of practical politics: 'Reasonable economic security for workers ... and real social and economic progress [were] not possible until all economic activities were socially controlled.' This ideological comment was unconnected to anything else that he had said and was inserted at the end of his speech. It clearly aimed to assuage those supporters who awaited such comment. He then turned the meeting away from ideas and back to hard cases and reformism by starting to discuss 'various matters of concern to the members.' He asked 'that any grievance ... members [had] ... be reported to the secretary who would transmit the report to him. He assured them he would have the matters brought under the notice of the proper quarters.'

Pattison and O'Neill both wanted a strong Labour Party for different reasons. Yet, because it was commonly assumed that all goals could be achieved through the electoral system, they shared a concern with hard cases and the middle ground. For both, helping hard cases, securing local amenities, ensuring ameliorative welfare practices, and obtaining social legislation translated into the votes that, in turn, gave the political leverage necessary to obtain these goals. The activities and interests of Pattison and O'Neill thus dovetailed. At the same time, O'Neill's other options were highly constrained. Private property and capital underlay and infused national policies and politics, the goals of interest groups and parties, and the consciousness of individuals. They were promulgated by the church hierarchy which, on that and other related issues, infiltrated the common sense of labouring people (chapter 17). Finally, local labouring organizations, such as union and party, were vertically structured with few lateral or horizontal formal ties to other localities or interest groups. O'Neill was structurally isolated. He was also constrained because his immediate superior, Pattison, was concerned with his own career and with regional and national politics. O'Neill, in contrast, combined a highly parochial view alongside an international socialist one. Indeed, his wider horizons were not focused on the middle ground at all. His goal was to help the Labour Party actualize a more radical ideology.

Yet, because Pattison and O'Neill had certain common interests and activities, they cooperated. Indeed, as their agency brought the local Labour Party into contention with the local branches of other political parties and as it brought O'Neill and Pattison into competition with other mediators, their cooperation intensified. With a Dáil election in April 1938, both the TTDA and the Labour Party published competing claims of equally dubious accomplishments (Case 20.8).

Case 20.8: The Claims of Local Agents, April 1938

The Labour Party branch announced that the 'secretary of the Kilkenny Board of Health, has informed Mr. O'Neill, secretary ... that plans have recently been sent to the Local Government Department for sanction of the erection of 68 houses at Thomastown.' With regard to a water supply, a solicitor and the county engineer 'had the matter ... in hand and ... the documents will be forwarded to the Local Government Department in due course.' Two weeks later, the TTDA's annual report gave 'a list of improvements effected by the Committee.' Among them were 'a site for a dumping ground, a definite promise of a water and sewerage scheme and a definite promise of a housing scheme.'[12]

Clearly, little had been achieved. Both the ILP and the TTDA were making the best of it and hoping voters would not notice. For it was important for people to believe that mediation was both effective and in train (Case 20.4).

Accumulating Animosities: The Political Dynamics of the Local Labour Party, 1936–8

Cooperation always contains the potential for dispute and, given the divergent ideas of Michael Kelly (Case 20.3), James O'Neill (Case 20.6), and J.P. Pattison (Case 20.7), conflict was not slow in emerging. A telling example was the local ILP's efforts to ameliorate working conditions on a building site in 1936 and, at the same time, to turn this action into a cause célèbre and thus organize the workers. They counted on Pattison to use his influence to support them. The extent to which Pattison did so is unclear. What is clear is that local agents felt he let them down badly, and in public (Case 20.9).

Case 20.9: Mediating Conditions on the Cottage Scheme Site, 1936

After it was announced that cottages would be built in Jerpoint West townland, the local ILP wrote contractor Edward Fitzpatrick that 'Trade Union wages and conditions would have to be observed on the job.' Two weeks later, the branch decided that Gerard Doyle and James O'Neill should interview Fitzpatrick 'and inform him that if the wages and conditions for builders' labourers in the district were not observed, then the matter would be taken up with the proper authorities.' Fitzpatrick did not comply, and, a fortnight later, the Kilkenny Board of Health had a letter from O'Neill. 'I am directed by my committee to inform you that Mr Fitzpatrick ... is not paying trade union ... wages, nor observing trade union conditions as regards hours ... Mr Fitzpatrick is paying 30s. per week, whereas the rate of wages prevalent in this district for such work is 36s. Further, the men are compelled to work until 4 P.M. on Saturdays, contrary to the invariable practice of terminating ... at 1 P.M. I am to ask you to bring this matter before the next meeting of the Kilkenny Board of Health with a view to compelling the contractor ... to comply with ... statutory requirements ... and to inform him that failure on his part to do so will result in the cancellation of the contract.' The board had also received a letter from Pattison, stating these complaints and adding that local Labour representatives had approached Fitzpatrick who told them that he would not pay more. The board referred the matter to the county engineer, T. Kelly. He reported that, according to the 1932 Housing Act, the wages for Thomastown, a rural district, should be '30 shillings and work to cease at 1:30 on Saturdays.' The commissioner 'instruct[ed] the contractor accordingly.'

The Thomastown ILP again wrote to the Board of Health to say that 36s. was the normal wage in the locality. Pattison, in his turn, wrote the branch: 'The Commissioner has promised him to review the position ... if evidence could be submitted to prove that contractors had paid 36s. to builders' labourers' in the past. The ILP decided to ask a Waterford contractor and a local carpenter to certify this and to obtain statements from workmen who had built the courthouse in the early 1920s. It also decided that a meeting of the building workers would be called to discuss 'the possibility of presenting a demand for increased wages to the Contractor' and that the secretary would issue a statement to the press pointing out that engineer Kelly was incorrect when he reported that 30s. was the norm. A letter was also to be sent to the commissioner to 'take exception to certain [of his] remarks.' This letter, read at the next Board of Health meeting, restated that the recognized minimum wage in rural areas was 36s. as 'proved by the fact that ... Cork Board of Health [will] insert a clause in all future cottage contracts that 35s. shall be paid by contractors.' The letter went on to say that the ILP had received complaints that Fitzpatrick had 'refused to employ men ... who are members of a trade union or of the labour party. This ... is tantamount to the denial of the legal rights of workers to associate for mutual protection and advancement. It is all the more serious since the scheme is sponsored by a local authority ... The attitude of the contractor should convince you that he is not a proper person to be entrusted with such work.' The commissioner responded to this letter by supporting Kelly's position on wages, adding that 'the matter of membership of a trade union is not a matter for our consideration.'

A week later, O'Neill wrote to the Kilkenny People *stating that Kelly's position was 'definitely incorrect' and offering 'conclusive proof that the recognized minimum wage is 36s. ... If Mr Kelly had taken the trouble to institute serious inquiries he would have discovered that the staple industry of this town, flour milling, pays a minimum wage of 43 shillings ... and that on several building schemes in recent years, unskilled builder's labourers were paid a weekly wage of 42 shillings.' O'Neill went on to address the board's position on the contractor's refusal to hire trade union/ILP members: the board 'cannot quite so easily divest itself of all responsibility; nor can it save its face by advertising an attitude of specious neutrality. If at the present juncture, when the right to associate is being challenged, the Board of Health decided to remain inactive, then such inactivity must be interpreted as implying approval of this iniquitous campaign.'*

A day later, the ILP received a letter from the Waterford contractor that in 1923 and 1925 'he had paid 10d. per hour. It was decided to give Pattison this information along with a signed statement from the men employed by Mr P. Stapleton that they had been paid 36s.' It was also decided to call a special meeting of the branch after the Board of Health considered the new evidence. However, at that special meeting, the secretary said that, 'according to press reports of the meeting of the Board of Health, the evidence in connection with wages ... had not been submitted by Mr Pattison.' The meeting then 'expressed disapproval of the manner in which Mr Pattison had acted in this matter' although 'no definite action was decided on.' No meetings of the local ILP were recorded for two months. At a meeting at the end of May 1936, the secretary read a letter from Pattison stating 'that this matter was still occupying his attention.' Pattison also enclosed 'a copy of a letter which the commissioner had sent to the Department of Local Government in which he expressed the view that 30s. was a reasonable wage. It was decided to request Mr Pattison to make any further representations which he considered necessary in connection with this matter.'[13]

Nothing else was recorded about the site, wages, political agitation, or anti-union sentiment. Indeed, between May and November 1936, only one ILP branch meeting took place. In the latter month, the branch was reported to be in financial difficulty and Gerard Doyle resigned as chair.[14] After that meeting, Minute Book entries ceased. Clearly, the failure at the cottage site, associated with Pattison's inability or lack of desire to deliver, caused a crisis for the local party branch. It precipitated the withdrawal of Labour's intellectual chair and it left a deep resentment against Pattison and, as it turned out, against all who were seen as aligned with him. Most important, the local events of 1936 put any and all future Labour Party activism into the hands of Pattison, a fact confirmed by the Dáil election in July 1937. In the new Kilkenny constituency which had three seats, Pattison was the second to be elected, after the fourth count. He came in ahead of Fianna Fáil incumbent Tom Derrig. Labour had never done so well. Why?

The crisis in the Thomastown Labour Party branch, which marginalized the activities of its radical intellecutals and virtually caused it to fold as a result, effectively transformed Pattison, as the sitting TD, into the only potentially effective Labour mediator in town. In January 1937, too, the secretary of the IT&GWU branch, Michael Kelly, resigned just as the same Labour Party activists relocated their efforts to, and tried to revitalize, the union branch through their agitation on the Jerpoint site (Cases 18.3, 18.4). At that moment, radical UAMA and IT&GWU activist Tom Walsh died.[15] It was a few months later that Pattison won easy re-election. Partly this was because all labourers could find, in the political events of the previous eighteen months, reasons to vote for him. From the perspective of conservative workers, an elderly worker in the 1980s said: 'You have to remember how the church had everyone terrified. It was the time of the Spanish Civil War and the local lads were tainted as Red. But Pattison was always careful to denounce communism and to keep his nose clean.' Conversely, from the perspective of radical labourers, 'How else could they vote?'

Many, of course, supported Fine Gael or Fianna Fáil. Still others looked for a republican alternative. After de Valera and Fianna Fáil came into the Dáil in 1927, thus abandoning armed struggle, and after the Blueshirt threat was averted in the early 1930s, IRA violence erupted in the Free State. In 1936 de Valera declared the IRA illegal. In the two years before, however, the IRA upsurge seemed to provide an option for many workers. In 1934, at a republican dance in Thomastown, the masters of ceremonies were Daniel Challoner (creamery worker) and Herbert Devoy, both of whom were on the organizing committee. Mrs Devoy was on the catering committee. Many local retailers and farmers, well known as republicans in their earlier support for de Valera, attended, along with workers from various sectors and locales: fishers, millworkers, farm workers, building labourers, creamery workers. The following Easter, a commemoration was held for 'those who in each generation have died that Ireland might be free and undivided from shore to shore.' Eight hundred people reportedly marched through the town along with a pipers' band, relatives of those killed in 1919–22, and representatives from the North and South Kilkenny IRA and the Kilkenny Cumann na nBan. On the platform were Herbert Devoy (secretary of the commemoration committee) and Tom Beck (IT&GWU). Representatives came from Kilkenny city corporation and the GAA. At the end of the report, the editor noted that, because of government censorship, the message from the IRA council could not be included. Several months later, a Thomastown Association of Old IRA Comrades was formed. The chair was a farmer; the secretary was James O'Neill and the treasurer was his brother, Michael, also a millworker.[16] In part, the organization aimed to distinguish the violence of the 1922 civil war ('Old IRA') from that of the mid-1930s. In part, the association aimed to help these Old IRA combatants get their pensions under the 1934 Military Pensions Act.[17]

In the event, the new IRA was banned in 1936. From an organizational perspective, labourers cum republicans again had little choice apart from the Labour Party or Fianna Fáil. As to the Old IRA, labourers obtained little but an abiding and deep-seated sense of grievance. After thousands of pension applications were reviewed, many of them suspect, all of Thomastown's labourers concluded that 'no labouring man ever got his IRA pension.'[18] In the early 1980s, this commonly asserted invocation summarized the profound resentment that workers held of the status-class structure and of the everyday discriminations endured by labourers. The widow of James O'Neill added: 'When the Gunner [James O'Neill] died, some IRA pensioners, mostly farmers and shopkeepers, turned up at our house the morning of the funeral with the tricolour for his coffin. We sent them away. And you know, those men just could not understand why. But we knew. So did every other labourer.'

Inside the Frame: Locality, Association, and the Mediation Process

In 1933 it was unclear precisely which means, agents, and mechanisms were to be most efficacious in providing the material and ideological resources with which to revive the moral economy and bring jobs and amenities to the locality. Class antagonisms and local loyalties, associations and redundancy, intense divisions over the 1922 Treaty, and a devotional swell, abetted by the church's blatant entry into political society, all impinged on political choices and combinations. So, too, did the claims of political parties and politicians as they came to compete in elections and the mediation process. These processes of petition, deputation, and representation had their roots in the locality since at least the early nineteenth century. After 1926, however, when rural councils were abolished and more direct rule instituted, and after the entry of Fianna Fáil into constitutional politics, access to largesse and bureaucratic interventions became directly sited in Dáil representatives via the agency of the county council and local branches of political parties. In turn, 'making proper representations' was a mediating form that masked ideological and material differences and animosities. It either forced mediating agents into cooperative endeavours or subordinated ideologies to material self-interest. Often, of course, it did both. Said a worker in the 1980s: 'It was one way those old-style TDs maintained their feudal power.' More generally, it was a way in which local people and class segments gained access to resources while simultaneously disempowering themselves.

21. Organizing Labour in the 1940s: The Politics of Combination

'Thomastown Concert Hall has been converted to a cinema ... Renovated and fitted with tip-up chairs, it is the last word in comfort. The latest and cleanest pictures will be shown ... The entire hall will be centrally heated.'
– Kilkenny Journal, 5 August 1939

'Not alone would I sacrifice my seat in the Dáil but my life; but I wouldn't be associated with the Labour Party anymore because it is reeking of communism.'
– A statement attributed to J.P. Pattison (1944) by a labourer in 1983

The forces that had channelled politics after 1926 derived in large part from prior agency, ideologies, and organizations. So, too, was this the case during the Emergency. It began in late 1939 and lasted until 1945. It was a time of Irish neutrality and when an Allied or German occupation seemed possible. The physical isolation of the state exacerbated the material problems that working people had long faced: high commodity prices relative to wage and relief rates. Shortages of fuel, clothes, and the basic foodstuffs of the underemployed (bread, tea, butter, and sugar) caused living standards to fall.[1] As part of this, the Fianna Fáil government tried to devolve some of its economic responsibilities onto local units while retaining centralized fiscal and political structures. Overall, it was a variation of oft-experienced state intervention: anti-labour and pro–church-hierarchy policies and sentiments, along with local class difference. This time, however, it provided a space for a different kind of labouring combination.

National Necessities and Local Organizations:
Labour as Political Object

To mask discontent and relieve itself of responsibility, the Fianna Fáil government tried to establish parish councils. As described by Tom Derrig, TD, at a 1941 Thomastown meeting, they were to be headed by 'men of initiative.' They were to 'help people ... with food and fuel and other essentials,' 'relieve ... people who are thrown suddenly out of employment,' and set up 'relief schemes for the unemployed.' There was 'no use just sending resolutions asking the Government to do this and that,' said Derrig. Rather, 'the idea of Parish Councils was to get things done voluntarily, by local effort and ... by the people feeling they were with one another.' So, although they 'had no statutory power,' they could 'collect money and finance schemes for food production and the supply of fuel ... or buy essential supplies in case of need.' Moreover, 'if war occurred in the country ... each small unit would have to ... carry on for itself, and now is the time for people to get into the habit of doing that.' As for the fuel shortage, 'you will have to try to make the best arrangements you can, or ... go ... to the local merchants and solicit ... their aid.'[2]

This entire policy, of course, ignored the historical dependence of localities on the state; it disregarded the lack of collective or financial resources at the parish level; it overlooked the way in which merchandizing worked in small towns; and it played shamelessly to the deep-seated cleavages that typified such localities by suggesting that 'men of initiative,' or a 'few active men,' provide the impetus. Not surprisingly, the council that emerged in Thomastown looked exactly like every other cross-class association: curate, notables, several large-scale farmers and retailers, and two token labourers, including Herbert Devoy. The council also had no real tasks or authority. All it could do was recommend to local householders that they lay in stocks of salt, bread soda, and candles, have a bucket of sand handy for fighting house fires, and provide themselves with air-raid shelters. Such recommendations, however, masked genuine coercion from the state in relation to attaining national self-sufficiency in food production. Farmers were compelled to till their grasslands and labourers to till the plots attached to their council cottages. The rent collector inspected all council plots, compiling a list of defaulters against whom the commissioner could take 'drastic action.' Farmers were told 'to be generous ... and help till the plots of cottiers.'[3] That the request had to be made several times suggests that such aid was not always forthcoming. An allotment system was also set up by the county council, administered by parish councils. In early 1943, one-eighth acre plots near the town were allocated. 'Invariably,' said a labourer in 1985, 'one or two families always managed to get their hands on two plots.'

Another problem masked by the use of parish councils was a severe fuel shortage. Complaints to Derrig escalated and he, of course, promised to help. However, with a drastic shortage looming in 1941, the parish council organized an expedition to turf bogs five miles from the town. The bogs were to be 'invaded by farmers, traders and labourers of the parish' as a 'first start' in setting up 'large supplies of turf to have in reserve in the coming winter.' The press eagerly reported that 'all classes are co-operating wholeheartedly ... Close on 200 workers will assemble on the bogs to do their bit.' In the event, one retailer lent his lorry to convey workers from the town; other employers sent their workers. The ladies of the Red Cross provided dinner and tea.[4] The expedition was not repeated. Partly it was because the turf was very poor quality, which was why the bog was not normally used. Partly, employers did not want to subsidize fuel supplies by paying their labourers to do the work; nor did retailers want to undercut their own sales. Turf-cutting did not become a manifestation of collective sentiment.

Labouring women in the 1980s recalled that they were aware that something was going on but that they simply carried on. They especially remembered the rationing of tea and sugar and the fact that 'some shopkeepers helped out' their regular customers with extra portions. Labourers were not among these. Workers also 'did not have access to the black market' through which 'shopkeepers favoured their friends.' Men, in turn, recalled military exercises as members of the volunteer, military-like Local Defence Force (LDF), made up of younger men, and of the less militaristic Local Security Force (LSF). They received 'instruction in musketry' and had weekly parades, drills, and lectures. Both forces also held annual dances. Retailers were the officers; labourers were the soldiers.[5] Complementing men's military preparations was a Red Cross branch organized by the wives and daughters of gentry and notables. The parish priest was president and the Protestant rector was vice-president. Sessions were held for making bandages and knitting, with fifty local women reportedly taking part. Dr Moloney gave first-aid lectures. The branch established first-aid field stations around the parish and supplied the LSF with first-aid kits. At the same time, a dozen Thomastown men joined the British armed forces. Many more joined the Irish National Army. Patriotism aside, it was a pensionable job. As of June 1940, 'close on 100 young men from Thomastown, Ballyhale and Stonyford ha[d] ... enlisted,' including a dozen from Mount Juliet. A week later, 'all the indoor male staff ' at Mount Juliet joined. The next week, thirty men enlisted and Mrs Solly-Flood (*née* Connellan) 'presented cigarettes to the recruits.'[6] Other labourers emigrated to England, to well-paid jobs in factories and construction.

Overall, the state-sponsored associations and the experiences of labour as political objects had a déjà vu quality: rooted in class categories, propelled mainly by outside interests, fragmented and mundane. The parish council, for example, like so many others of its kind before, was formed explicitly by reference to the status-class and class categories of its members. The one attempt at collective effort, turf-cutting, was organized by local businessmen; the notability and remnant gentry organized the Red Cross; and farmers had to be entreated to cooperate with labourers. Projects requiring capital expenditures still needed state intervention and the superabundance of local labour was yet again alleviated by emigration or military service. Indeed, very early on, by the end of 1941, any of the collective sentiment that the parish was to have created had been precluded when the council was absorbed by the national association of Muintir na Tire. As was the case with most nation-wide organizations built from parish branches, its leaders talked about inclusiveness. It was to be for 'rural people': for 'farmers, farm labourers, organized labour, the unemployed, professional and business people.' It was to emphasize 'unity, and cooperation' based on 'self-reliance;' and it was 'never mixed up with politics.' However, in its policies, for example, to encourage young farmers to build new houses so as to marry young and fight depopulation, it is hardly surprising that this organization had little appeal for labourers. Indeed, none was ever reported as joining. All members were farmers and retailers.[7]

Labour Organizing Labour: Labourers as Subject

In this context, labourers had begun, yet again, to organize their own combinations, with the same ideas of self-reliance, unity, and cooperation. For them, the wartime economy threatened to create a shortage of cash as well as of commodities. The former was because of government policy. It was presented to local people in early 1940 by the Fianna Fáil TD: 'It is well known that in the last great war when increases in wages were granted they were quickly nullified by further increases in the cost of living, so that ... the worker suffered. The ... purchasing power of his wages ... could not keep pace with the rising prices ... After the war, the great slump occurred. Prices fell catastrophically; wages did not come down ... Necessary adjustments were only effected after a series of economic crises [and] serious losses to the community through depression, strikes and unemployment. We must guard against allowing a "spiral" of this kind ... The workers would not benefit in the long run.'[8]

Such economic history, of course, had a political intent. To prevent inflation and the inevitable lowering of wages after prices fell in the longer term, current wages had to be kept low, prices had to find their own levels, and labour unrest had to be quashed. The ensuing Dáil politics, the trajectory of industrial relations, and the machinations among the national leadership of Fianna Fáil, the Irish Labour Party, and the IT&GWU have often formed the analytical foci for labour historians. In Thomastown, however, local experiences mediated and mitigated the politics of national sites and agents as these, in turn, became part of the ongoing *metissage*.

Thomastown Labour Party Branch
In 1936 a crisis ensued after the aborted effort to organize the building site in Jerpoint West. The chair, Gerard Doyle, had resigned, and James Pattison, blamed by members for having let down the branch, in turn blamed the branch for its suspect, left-wing agitation (Case 20.9). In mid-1941, however, a meeting of workers, presided over by Michael Tierney, reorganized the branch. Long-time activist Tom Beck (millworker) was elected treasurer and his brother, also a millworker, became secretary. Former activists, who also were the core of the local IT&GWU, made up the committee: fisher Paddy Dunphy and Herbert Devoy (millworkers), fisher Denis Landy (railway worker), James Kelly (Mount Juliet), and John Ryan (Kilfane).[9] Within two months, they had formed a retailing cooperative.

Thomastown Co-operative Society
According to the surviving Minute Book, the organizing meeting, in mid-November 1941, was attended by seventeen men. Gerard Doyle, in the chair, talked about 'the Co-operative Movement ... He pointed out what had been achieved in other places and stressed the urgent necessity for the formation of a local cooperative society.' A motion to this effect was passed, and the seventeen men joined. Each was to subscribe £1 share capital within three months and a 2s.6d. entry fee. Doyle was

elected chair; Daniel Challoner and Herbert Devoy were elected trustees; J.J. Maher, son of the journalist, was elected secretary. Over the next four months, several meetings were held, collectors were appointed, and a subcommittee was set up to vet anyone who might be asked to join and to meet monthly 'to review the position.' The secretary prepared a subscription list and receipt forms, and he wrote to a Cork TD 'for names and addresses of wholesalers from whom supplies might be obtained and other information re cooperative societies.' During all that time, new names were submitted and new members enrolled. All this was done secretly (Case 21.1).

Case 21.1: A Secret Meeting of the Thomastown Co-operative Society, March 1942

Doyle (chair) 'congratulated ... members on the enthusiastic manner in which the first share had been subscribed.' This, he said, 'was the best ... proof of their sensibility of the need for such a Society. Because of the abnormal conditions prevailing in practically every sphere, the sub-Committee did not consider it advisable to ... start a business with the small capital at their disposal, and for that reason, [it was proposed] "that each member subscribe at least one further share of £1 not later than the 30th of September 1942." By that date, the chairman said, the sub-Committee will have formulated a scheme [to submit] to the general meeting for approval. He ... ask[ed] everybody ... in a position to do so to subscribe more than one share. [He] again stressed the absolute necessity for maintaining the strictest secrecy and ... appealed to members not to discuss the existence of the Society with anybody – not even in their own homes.' Christie Beck then proposed that 'to obviate the necessity for calling general meetings, which he thought would likely attract a certain amount of attention, a committee be formed ... of the chairman, secretary and two trustees, and a further three members ..., who would manage the ordinary business of the Society, make ... arrangements as to meeting, and do all ... matters ... they might deem requisite for furthering the objects of the Society.' The motion passed. The committee arranged the second-share offering and bought a site on Maudlin Street for a co-op shop.

By the autumn of 1942, according to the Minute Book, the co-op shop was open and was selling staples. There was discussion about adding milk and fresh vegetables and also about starting a sawmill. Indeed, the secretary inserted an advertisement in the press to investigate obtaining an electric motor. Soon after, a meat section was added. Said Doyle at a meeting: 'Co-operation was an excellent [antidote] to the individualist spirit which capitalism engendered. He pointed out the achievement of co-operation in many parts of this country, particularly in Belfast, where ... membership was over 56,000, share capital £1,250,000 and annual trade almost 2½ millions. The immense possibilities ... therefore ... demand our ... careful study, as by it people could progress step by step to control the whole scheme of production and distribution.' Who were the Thomastown members? (Case 21.2).

Case 21.2: The Seventeen Original Co-op Members and the Ten Later Applicants

Of the seventeen subscribers, eight were millworkers, supporters of the Labour Party, and living on Mill Street. Another four also worked for the mill and were Labour Party supportees, but lived in Jerpoint (n = 1) or across the river (n = 3). Another member was a Pilsworth farm worker – also a Labour man, living just beyond Mill Street. Two of the other four were Gerard Doyle (clerk, Labour, 'townie') and J.J. Maher (journalist, Labour, 'townie'). The final two were Fianna Fáil supporters: one worked in the creamery, the other for the railway. All but two of the seventeen members (the farm labourer and Maher), were unionized; thirteen of the seventeen were married. They ranged in age from twenty-seven to fifty-four years. The average age was thirty-six years; the median age was forty. In all, it was a fairly homogeneous group – in politics, occupation, and life-cycle stage.

Of the ten men who later applied to join, this was not so. Only one was a Labour supporter. The rest were either Fianna Fáil or reputedly 'had no politics.' Only two were millworkers. Three of the ten never joined. In one case, it was because he was a Mount Juliet worker and 'was afraid for his job.' The seven who did join had varying occupations. They also lived in dispersed parts of the locality. Only the two millworkers were unionized. These later ten members were also younger. Their average age was twenty-eight years; the median age was twenty-five. Only two of the seven were married at the time.

Former members in the 1980s had few ideas about the co-op's ideological or sociological underpinnings. They did not point to the social relations of production in the mill or residential contiguity which had created common experience. They did not cite past involvements in labour organizations and, as a result, a propensity for social action. Instead, they recalled only that they had tried to do something different because all was not right with things as they were. They also recalled, very clearly, Gerard Doyle's leadership (Case 21.3).

Case 21.3: Memories of the Co-op from the 1980s

'*Secrecy was kept early on, to keep the shopkeepers from organizing against us. They could also have interfered with us getting supplies and renting shop premises.*'

– '*The ambition behind the co-op was so that people could better themselves. There was also the view that because shopkeepers have money they must be making excess profits. And there was resentment against their clannishness. It was Gerard Doyle who was behind it all. As a bookkeeper [in a Kilkenny city shop], he had a notion of shopkeepers' profits and how large they were.*'

– '*The idea for the co-op came out of the local Labour Party branch, though Gerry Doyle was the initiator. It was partly involved with Labour men and socialist thinking.*'

– '*The co-op was located opposite the Labour club in Maudlin street. Michael Tierney did volunteer work for the co-op. So did other men.*'

Given the co-op's immediate success in collecting entry fees (2s.6d.) and the first share capital (£1 per member), and given the need for more capital, the executive had asked for another share contribution of £1 (Case 20.1). Six months later, in May 1942, the minutes reported that the majority of members had not subscribed. This continued into November when the payment deadline was again extended. However, the Society had already collected enough capital to begin the shop. What was clearly missing at this early stage, however, was the personal and political commitment that would come from members buying shares which, in turn, would bring greater involvement. This experiential process never materialized (Case 21.4).

Case 21.4: The Latter Years of the Thomastown Co-operative Society

In April 1943 according to the minutes, *the trustees again reported that a number of members had still not subscribed to the share. Devoy then proposed that* '*each member ... contribute at least £3 before 31st December 1943.*' *Challoner seconded.*' *Other ways of rasing money were discussed, for example, a '*sweep' *run under the auspices of the Labour Hall; but the executive decided to put Devoy's motion to a general meeting in May 1943. It was passed unanimously. Problems* of collecting soon ensued, and another tack was tried. In February 1944 the executive 'decided that members be asked to subscribe at least 1s. per week.' A general meeting passed the idea but not enough men had attended. It was decided to hold another meeting. During the spring and summer of 1944, small amounts dribbled in. The total amount subscribed by March was £52.3.0; by June it was £56.0.0 and by September, £59.15.11.

At the September meeting, 'several members expressed dissatisfaction with the financial position. The chairman pointed out that the average amount per member since the Society's inception was only £3.' In fact, 'the position was ... worse ... for the majority ... had subscribed only 2 shares, while a number who would appear to be in a position to do so, had submitted less than 2 shares and had made no effort since. It was ... obvious that those members had ceased to take any interest in the Society and the Committee would soon have to decide what action to take.' The secretary then read a subcommittee report on the proposed butcher's stall. It recommended where the stall and slaughter house should be located, their sizes, and an estimate of costs. It concluded that £80 had to be subscribed to set it up. However, 'the figure may be higher as ... the paid up shares of [some] members, amounting to about £10 or £15, will have to be refunded, since they have ceased to take an active interest in the ... Society.'

In October 1944 a general meeting decided that each member subscribe £7 within twelve months. However, by the next general meeting in February 1945, 'dissatisfaction with the financial position of the Society' was again the main agenda item. It was proposed by Doyle and seconded by Tierney 'that each member pay 10s. per month ... and that any member who fails to pay ... will automatically cease to be a member.' Two members were excepted from this rule, and Herbert Devoy was given extra time to pay. The secretary, J.J. Maher, disagreed. He proposed that 'any member who had subscribed less than £3.10.0 should automatically cease to be a member.' There was no seconder and Doyle's motion was carried. J.J. Maher resigned as secretary. No one else would agree to take on the job. It was 'decided to defer the appointment to the next Committee meeting in March.' No one had volunteered by that time. At the general meeting in June 1945, 'a lengthy discussion' took place on 'the present financial position and future objects of the Society.' Devoy proposed that the Society be dissolved and the capital refunded to members; and that the houses and yards in Maudlin Street, the property of the Society, be sold to Gerard Doyle for £20. This was seconded by Christie Beck and passed unanimously.

Why had the co-op failed? In contrast with the meagre memories that former members had about why the co-op was formed, they were quite definite as to what had gone wrong. They blamed local retailers and each other (Case 21.5).

Case 21.5: Why the Co-op Failed – Memories from the 1980s

'The shopkeepers cut their prices and undercut the Co-op. They were against us and they were vicious.'

– 'The men in the Co-op had little experience in business and the Co-op was poorly managed. For example, the meat business was pretty poor. With little experience of cattle buying, we couldn't compete with someone like [butcher-retailer] David Murphy.'

– 'The Co-op didn't have a policy of soliciting customers, though some people shopped there out of sympathy for the enterprise.'

– 'One cause of failure was a lack of experience. There was also the "dread of being involved." People were very poor and fear was an important component in their lives. They sacrificed principle for survival, and they were terrified of the priests.'

'People liked to play up to the shopkeepers instead of coming to the co-op. Shopkeepers could have an influence on their getting a job. For example, Costello might have pulled for D.J. for a mill job. Costello had been buying flour from Pilsworth; and Bob Pilsworth squandered a lot. Costello possibly put pressure on him. Doolan shouldn't have got a job. He wasn't a millworker; he didn't come from mill stock. But both were strong Fine Gael supporters.'

– 'There were lots of reasons why men pulled out of the co-op. Michael Synnott was just married and had a new house. Landy was unemployed and probably couldn't afford it. Spellane had no interest. Doolan had only been following along. He wasn't true labour. Walsh was quiet and reserved, and never went to meetings.'

– 'The co-op failed because they disagreed among themselves. They fell out over the spoils. Some stole [the butcher's] cow in the middle of the night. There was awful bitterness over it. But it wouldn't have succeeded anyway. People wouldn't support it because they were labouring men. They also began in poor times; now it might succeed, but not then. They also lacked experience and the business instinct. Shopkeepers also lowered prices.'

– 'The co-op was affected by political disputes among members.'

– 'Shopkeepers were against it – particularly Costello. When the Co-op secured a batch of seed potatoes which were sold more cheaply than anywhere else in Thomastown, Costello reported this to the guards who issued a summons for the sale of non-certified seed. [Butcher-retailer] Davey Murphy lowered his meat prices when the co-op began a butchery.'

The recollections of failure highlighted the personal inadequacies of labouring people, the political deficiencies of their class, and the antagonistic reactions of retailers. Yet problems were apparent from very early on when the leadership could not induce members to commit more share capital to the endeavour. This highlights, generally of course, the difficulty of educating people at the time to the kinds of political understandings which a few local labourers, such as Doyle, O'Neill, and Tierney, had developed. It also highlights the problems encountered at the time by combinations which were financially and politically isolated or unconnected to other organizations or localities. Problems of capital formation were likely exacerbated, too, by the emigration of some men who would have joined. A few workers recalled that several sympathizers had gone to England and that one of them became a co-op member when he returned two years later. Yet none of the elderly workers in the 1980s attributed failure to a capital shortage. Nor did they find the leadership faulty or feel that the idea had been a bad one. Instead, failure came out of personal antagonisms, the way labouring people begrudged each other and, thus, their incapacity to act collectively, and the antagonistic actions of people from other status-classes. Indeed, while trying to recall the co-op and its failure, most men in the 1980s immediately began to talk about other animosities and breaches which occurred around the same time and which involved the same people. As they spoke about 'political disputes,' 'poor times,' and 'influence,' they were voicing profound disillusionment. 'It was very bitter,' said a former millworker, 'very bitter.' From where else did such deep sentiment come?

Party and Union

As Gerard Doyle said, the co-op was located in 'conditions prevailing' in the wider economy. So, too, were its politics. In 1940 the Fianna Fáil government passed the County Management Act. Thenceforth, every county was to have an appointed manager as well as an elected council.[10] In August 1942 the first county council elections since 1928 were held. The year before, the Thomastown branch of the Labour Party had been reconstituted. In the race for the six seats that the district had on the county council, four of the fourteen candidates were Labour. Two were from Thomastown: James O'Neill and Michael Tierney. Tierney polled 184 first-preference votes and was eliminated after the fourth count. O'Neill polled 277 first-preference votes and was elected after the tenth count (Case 19.5). The election, however, had bitter repercussions, a feature reflected in very divergent memories (Case 21.6).

Case 21.6: Divergent Recollections of the 1942 County Council Election, 1983
– '*Only O'Neill was elected. Tierney almost made it. He was very disappointed. There was no friction at the time, but Tierney took it personally. He felt let down by the people who might have given him a vote. He got a fairly substantial vote. He settled down after, but he went into a shell and never came out. It was the only time he ran for office*' (*Christie Beck, former millworker*).
– '*It shows how strong Labour was at the time that they would field two candidates from the local area*' (*James O'Neill's son*).
– '*Michael entered the race and, almost immediately, O'Neill entered. O'Neill liked the limelight, so he stepped in and won. Michael ran for the council only that once; he never ran again*' (*Mrs Tierney*).
– '*My parents were very bitter about this. It was unfair for O'Neill to run, to be a second Labour candidate and to split the labour vote*' (*Joe Tierney*).

The Beck-O'Neill view, that Tierney and O'Neill were not running against each other but that both were running for Labour, was not without basis. The Labour Party was popular at the time and some local agents saw the possibility of electing two local cum Labour men. This was not how the Tierneys saw it, however; and this was important. For both Tierney and O'Neill were united in their radical politics and anti–church-hierarchy views, certainly as compared with two other key locals, Michael Synott and Herbert Devoy (Table 18.1). In fact, Tierney, O'Neill, and others had fallen out with Devoy in 1938 in the context of the IT&GWU (Case 18.7). What the 1942 council election did was create personal animosities among this anti-Devoy cum radical segment.

A Dáil election took place in June 1943. At the time, labour was under attack from the government, disputes had arisen over the Labour Party's relation to Fianna Fáil, and factionalism among the Labour Party's national leadership was again prevalent (Case 21.7).

Case 21.7: The National Context of Labour – Union and Party
A Trade Union Bill brought in by Fiánna Fáil in May 1941 contained two awkward provisions: unions had to pay a large sum to obtain a negotiating licence and a tribunal would decide which union in any particular sector/industry would have the sole right to organize. At the same time, a wage freeze, via Emergency Powers Order #83, was promulgated. Labour's response from around the country was far more intense than such leaders as William O'Brien (IT&GWU)

*had predicted to the Fianna Fáil government in their prior secret and suspect dis-
cussions. Indeed, demonstrations led by the Dublin Trades Council and James
Larkin ensued, along with 'opposition to the leadership's collusion with Fianna
Fáil ... However, at no stage was the campaign ... able to produce ... industrial
action.' Instead Emergency Power Order #166 allowed the wages' tribunals to
award cost-of-living bonuses. A compromise was thus effected and the bills were
passed. The IT&GWU leaders, including William O'Brien, had supported the
Trade Union Act put by Fianna Fáil. The Labour Party and the Trade Union
Congress were against it. Larkin's union, the Workers' Union of Ireland (WUI),
had been accepted as a member of the TUC and Larkin was now a member of the
Labour Party. Indeed, the bill to license only one union per industry was
intended to eliminate Larkin's union.*[11]

The Thomastown IT&GWU supported Larkin and the dissidents. As
soon as the intent of the Trade Union Bill and of Order 83 were known,
a Kilkenny area conference was called to protest. It was attended by
Labour Party branches from the city and county, the Kilkenny Trade
Council, and various IT&GWU branches, as well as by the entire committee of the Thomastown branch who were instructed 'to give full support, [and] if necessary, the withdrawal of labour' in order to have the
bill and order rescinded. The Kilkenny conference called on the
Labour Party to move a writ for a by-election to fill a Dáil vacancy and to
make the Trade Union Bill and the wages order the key issues in that by-
election. The conference then brought this proposal to the annual
Labour Party Convention. However, the party's administrative council
and its Dáil members decided that the proposal was not practicable
'since neither Fianna Fáil nor Fine Gael ... favour[ed] a by-election' and
'there was no way a campaign could be confined' to those issues. A Dublin representative objected to this, and IT&GWU secretary William
O'Brien told him that the Kilkenny conference had not been confined
to Labour Party members. Moreover, 'all the advice they got from the
Kilkenny Labour Party was against the resolution.' In any case, he
added, 'Kilkenny was not the best constituency for a test of the Trade
Union Bill and Emergency Power Order 83.'[12] The protest and challenge had been quashed.

The Thomastown IT&GWU continued to agitate. At its annual general
meeting in early 1942, it passed unanimous resolutions protesting Order
83 and the Trade Union Bill 'which was ... in complete conflict with all ...
accepted principles of democracy. Complete withdrawal of the Bill was

demanded.' Union members, however, were vulnerable on two fronts. First, the Fianna Fáil government, in imposing wage restraints, had not imposed price controls. In July 1942 flour-mill workers in Limerick circulated a letter asking for support in demanding a bonus under Order 166. A long discussion ensued at a Thomastown's branch meeting, and the letter was rejected (thirteen votes to eleven). Instead, a motion was passed for submission to HO (fourteen votes to three): 'That the flour millworkers demand a full 15 per cent [wage] increase and that steps be taken to implement same in spite of Emergency Reg. 83.' This radical position, however, was not sustained. A few months later, an executive meeting unanimously 'moved that the bonus obtainable under Order 166 be pressed for.' When the motion was brought to a general meeting three weeks later, twenty-four members voted to seek the bonus, four voted against, and four abstained. Further collusion followed. In May 1943, two months after another Emergency Power Order (260) allowed for 'a further relaxation of pay restraint,' the local branch agreed to apply for a bonus without any discussion. It was, however, also agreed to see if casual workers qualified under the order.[13]

The second weak front was the nationalist sentiment which Fianna Fáil was now exploiting through the Trade Union Bill. A long-simmering tension among Irish labourers revolved around the link, opposed by many nationalists, which many Irish unions had to their British counterparts. Under the tribunal's rules set up by the bill to decide which union would represent a sector, British-based unions were excluded. In 1942 the Thomastown branch took the anti-British bait and refused to send representatives to the Irish Trades Union Congress since it was affiliated to the British TUC. In 1945, when the Council of Irish Trade Unions (CoIU) engineered a break with the TUC and, by implication, with international labour, with Larkin's radical outlook, and with the potential for developing an 'organic politics,' members of the Thomastown branch acquiesced to the nationalist argument without a murmur: 'All members present ... considered it essential that Irish unions should be in a position to run their own affairs without crossblamed [sic] interference and that a break with the TUC seemed the only way.'[14]

In the interim, Labour polled well in the 1943 Dáil elections, both in Kilkenny-Carlow and in the country as a whole. Pattison, elected again, called it an 'outstanding triumph.' However, the enmity among national agents – William O'Brien (secretary, IT&GWU) and Jim Larkin, now back in the Labour Party through pressure wielded by Dublin branches – continued. Larkin was elected to the Dáil in 1943 and, after

another failed effort to expel him, five of the eight Labour TDs sponsored by the IT&GWU broke away from the Irish Labour Party (ILP) to
establish the National Labour Party.[15] Among the five was J.P. Pattison.
The response of the Thomastown branch was recorded in the minutes
of their subsequent meetings (Case 21.8). It condemned Pattison's
actions and supported the Irish Labour Party and Jim Larkin.

Case 21.8: Irish Labour Party versus IT&GWU/National Labour – Local Responses, 1944

*16 January 1944 (IT&GWU branch). At its annual general meeting, a long
discussion took place 'on the recent break of the Union with the Irish Labour
party.' County councillor James O'Neill proposed and C. Beck seconded 'that this
branch strongly condemns the action of the National Executive Committee [NEC]
of the ... [IT&GWU] in disaffiliating from the Irish Labour Party and that at
any future election, it will support only the official Irish Labour Party candidates. Further, that members of this branch will refuse to pay the political levy to
the IT&GWU.' Secretary Devoy said that the last part of the motion was out of
order because 'the political levy is voluntary.' The movers agreed to the change.
Devoy then moved an amendment: 'That this branch calls on NEC to send down a
representative, to make a full statement re the recent break ... Further, that a full
conference of branch delegates be called as soon as possible to discuss the problem.'
Seconded by Peter Walsh. The vote was eleven for the Devoy/Walsh amendment,
six for the O'Neill/Beck resolution.*

*10 January (IT&GWU branch). 'The secretary [Devoy] read a report issued by
our NEC [re] the union break with the Irish Labour Party.' The minutes noted:
'No comments.'*

*22 January (Labour Party branch). 'The committee ... at a special meeting
passed a resolution disassociating themselves from the action of Mr J.P. Pattison
TD in seceding from the Labour Party.'*

*29 January (IT&GWU branch). At the annual general meeting, elections
were held as usual and the usual clique took the executive positions (Table 18.1):
Michael Synnott (chair), Herbert Devoy (secretary), Peter Walsh, Michael
O'Neill, Tom Beck, John Challoner, James O'Neill, Denis Landy, and Paddy
Dunphy (trustees and committee).*

*30 January (IT&GWU branch). 'A letter from J.P. Pattison invited the branch
to send delegates to a county meeting to discuss ... the dispute ... After a long discussion, Devoy was instructed, on the proposal of Tom Beck, seconded by Michael
Synnott, to write to Pattison that 'we would not send delegates as we considered
that no useful purpose could now be served.'*

23 February (IT&GWU branch). An invitation was received from the National Labour Party to send delegates to the Kilkenny Conference. After discussion, Devoy proposed and Synnott seconded that no delegate attend or action be taken.[16]

The Thomastown branch remained firm in its support of the Irish Labour Party and Larkin and united in its condemnation of Pattision. Then, the communist card was played. Among the few papers left by Devoy in 1981, but kept by him for thirty-seven years, were two 'official statements.' One was from the Irish Labour Party and the other, in response, was from the IT&GWU. Each explained why the IT&GWU had disaffiliated from the Labour Party (Case 21.9).

Case 21.9: 'The Party Is Communist-Dominated' – Two Documents from 1944
The Labour Party document referred to certain IT&GWU members in Dublin, 'only a handful of whom support the Labour Party' but who 'appear to hold the view that the size of the Union's industrial membership should secure for it a decisive voice in directing the policy of the Party.' As result, tensions emerged, exacerbated by the Trade Union Bill early in 1941. Larkin's 'move to the Labour Party deepened divisions' and because 'of the disaffiliation of the IT&GWU in January 1944, five Deputies, members of the [IT&GWU] ... seceded from the ... Labour Party.' These deputies 'issued a joint statement on 26 January 1944 enquiring what action "has been taken to remove the Communists and Communist influence from the Party?"' Yet, 'during the time they were in the Party, none of them made a complaint regarding Communist influence ... It is necessary to say that until they wrote us ... we never received from these Deputies a word of complaint.' Referring to a circular sent by the IT&GWU leadership to its branches on 15 January, which 'for the most part ... is concerned with the age-old feud between James Larkin and themselves,' the Labour Party statement took issue with the IT&GWU 'innuendo that persons associated with the Communist Party are members of the Labour Party. The officers of the IT&GWU are aware that the Constitution of the Labour Party was framed to exclude the possibility of Communists or members of similar organizations becoming members.'
The response of the breakaway TDs and the IT&GWU leadership was that Labour's statement 'failed to refute the charge that the Party is Communist dominated.' They claimed that Larkin was destroying the union: 'he had then as he has now, the active and sinister backing of the Communist Party.' They gave several examples of Communist congresses that Larkin had attended.

With this kind of ideological tension, and their own interpersonal difficulties and ambitions, the Thomastown branch fractured. Devoy and Synnott came out in support of Pattison. The invective from elderly union members in the 1980s about what had become known as 'The Split' was bitter and personal. 'The branch favoured Larkin,' said a former millworker in 1983, 'but Devoy wanted to get ahead. He was the first one into the church on a Sunday.' Said another: 'Devoy was in the Knights of Columbanus ... He was a churchman.' Synnott, too, was 'very church-oriented and good friends with Devoy.' As to Pattison, a labourer said: 'He was following the vote and following the money.' Said another: 'Devoy and Pattison were "yes-men" and "shoneens" [would-be gentlemen]. Devoy's choice was based on what the clergy wanted.'

Throughout numerous conversations in the early 1980s about the split, the only reasons given for the actions of Devoy and Synnot were the influence of the church and the ambitions of individuals. However, the bitterness that their actions elicited was about far more than the disaffection of two men. What former Labour Party activists failed or refused to see about the split was the way in which Synnot and Pattison, and particularly Devoy, had come to embody an evolved ideal of the labouring man and, as such, how Devoy had slowly appropriated popular political support in the locality.

By the mid-1940s, Devoy presented an image of the archetypal, respectable labourer: competent in his permanent, pensionable job; pious and dutiful in his relations to God and clergy; and active in approved political associations, whether labouring combinations or such cross-class associations as the parish council. Also, as a member of the Old IRA, he was a respectable nationalist. In this persona, Devoy never fomented political action nor did he ever denounce capitalism and exploitation. Instead, like Pattison, he called for inquiries and bureaucratic rulings. Unlike the radical activists, he was never tainted and never labelled. He was the consummate, new labouring man – the product of several generations of evolution. He was never, however, referred to by other workers as 'a decent man.'

The first casualty of the split, therefore, was the image of the heroic labourer: the hard-drinking cotman from Mill Street who challenged magistrates and swam icy rivers to escape persecution. This change had a spatial manifestation. In 1942 forty-four new and modern council houses were completed on the northern side of the town. Most of the Mill Street and Mall houses were emptied of their labouring people, who now moved across the river, next to the townies and away from their stones, pubs, and river.

The second casualty, just after Devoy and Synnot defected and the anti-communist fervour intensified, was Labour Hall on Maudlin Street. At the end of 1944, its furniture was sold and the building emptied. The better facilities of the CYMS, with its table tennis and billiards tables, its retailers, and its spiritual adviser, had slowly supplanted the Labour Hall. Said a labouring member of both: 'Clubs were important then. People only drank on Saturdays. There was a stigma to being seen going into a pub and the cost was prohibitive. Shopkeepers never came into the Labour Hall, but everyone went to the CYMS. The CYMS broke barriers. It provided a social outing. Cards and billiards were mixed, class-wise. Wages were improving and labouring men were dressing better. But Michael Tierney never joined the CYMS. Nor did James O'Neill or Gerry Doyle. On purpose. It was for them a political position. "It's them and us." They felt that they would be joining the oppressors.' Labour Hall, with its working-class atmosphere and radical newspapers, had been fading. The split finally, in souring personal relations, killed it off. This, in turn, contributed to a third casualty in June 1945, namely, the Co-operative Society. Its minutes attributed the Society's collapse to a failure to raise sufficient capital. Its former members, in 1983, saw it as a victim of inexperience, personal animosities, and the antagonism of retailers and clergy. The pressure and motion to dissolve the co-op came from Devoy, who had himself not paid up all his shares (Case 21.4).

The fourth casualty was the radical, local leadership of the IT&GWU. During 1945, after the split, 'a substantial increase in membership' was reported. At the next annual general meeting, Synnott was elected chair, Devoy secretary, and four new members were elected to the executive (Table 18.1). Former IT&GWU stalwarts, such as James O'Neill and Beck, were gone. Several, however, did make the transition: Pat Dunphy, Michael O'Neill, and Peter Walsh. Two weeks later, the minutes noted that Michael Tierney's dues were in arrears. He was also said to be refusing 'to abide by branch rules' and as engaging in 'threatening and abusive behaviour.' It was proposed by Synnott, and seconded by O'Brien, 'that the rules on arrears be strictly enforced' in relation to Tierney. All agreed.' It was then reported by Devoy that 'Tierney refused to have the fine for his arrears inserted on his [union] card.' When Devoy insisted that the fine had to be paid, Tierney 'went so far as to take off his hat and coat and challenge the secretary to a fight.' Two new members proposed that Tierney be asked to apologize and fined 5s. All agreed. Tierney 'then came into the meeting and made a half-hearted apology for losing his temper, but denied the charges as made by the secretary and generally was very ugly about the Union.' He was ordered out of the meeting, which then 'agreed to enforce the above rulings.'[17]

The final casualty of the split remained to be played out. It was related not simply to labouring organizations, Catholic sentiment, the image of respectability, or activists' political careers and ideals. It related more fundamentally to the structure of power in the locality.

22. Reproducing the Political Regime and Regimen, 1940–50

'The millworkers were more radical and more independent. It was because they had a Church of Ireland boss, not a Catholic. If the millowner had been Catholic, these people would have been fired.'

– Mrs James O'Neill, 1983

In the May 1944 Dáil election, J.P. Pattison ran as a National Labour candidate for one of the three seats in Kilkenny constituency. No one ran for the Irish Labour Party. Pattison held onto the third seat, although with a much reduced vote.[1] The result, however, pointed to the solid bedrock of labour sentiment in the locality which, despite the factionalism, did not defect to Fianna Fáil and continued to choose a labouring option. Equally, it pointed to the personal quality of political loyalties resulting from the agency of mediation. Indeed, the interplay of these features formed the dénouement of the drama.

Mediating Local Amenities: Taking Care of 'The Poor'

In 1940, when deputy Tom Derrig explained to a Fianna Fáil meeting in Thomastown why wages would be held down, he was brought up short by retailer and supporter John Woods, who relayed his concerns about everyday, local problems (Case 22.1).

Case 22.1: The Fianna Fáil Retailer and the TD, 1940–1
'Referring to flooding at Thomastown on Saturday,' Woods said that 'it was ...

outrageous the way ... unfortunate people were situated in the town – for the sake of spending a miserable couple of hundred pounds ... and the flood 3 or 4 feet deep around them.' He then asked *'if the Commissioner could give relief in that respect since they had a large number of men drawing the dole.'* He *'did not know how they were living on the miserable sum they received [and] thought that work could be found for them in a relief scheme which cleaned up the river.'* Derrig said that a drainage commission would report soon. *'It naturally took time,'* he said, *'for a very large scheme, including drainage, was wanted.'*

Woods: *'A small sum could be granted for the time being.'*

Derrig: *'There is no point to that.'*

Woods: *'It would give a lot of relief in the meantime.'*

Derrig: Relief-scheme monies were allocated *'on the basis of unemployment in each district ... The county surveyor would not [approve your idea given] that it would be unnecessary when a large scheme would be coming forward.'*

Woods: *'Some years ago,'* the commissioner agreed that something ought to be done. He wrote to the county surveyor and *'they got something done and that cost only £25.'* Derrig said that he would put the matter *'before the ... Secretary to the Board of Works, but I feel not much can be done until the drainage report comes along.'*

Woods: *'Can we not do it ourselves in some manner?'*

Derrig: The county council was *'the proper authority 'but he would assist in any way. 'He was ... sorry the old drainage scheme fell through'* but he had hopes for the new one.

'It was decided to leave the matter in Mr Derrig's hands.'

A year later, the town's water-supply scheme was being *'blocked because certain landowners and others thought it would interfere with their own supply.'* The outlook was thus *'very gloomy.'* Said Derrig: *'The only thing to do is to keep up the pressure with the commissioner.'* He asked if retailer Woods had spoken with the county surveyor. *'We went through that formality,'* said Woods. *'Can there be a little urging done from your place? ... Yes, there can,'* said Derrig.[2]

Derrig's indifference did not deter retailer Woods and the Fianna Fáil branch from still handing him local problems. The mediation process, firmly established, thus continued through the Emergency, reinforced by food rationing and low wages. Labour activists, having also accepted the mediation as a common-sense strategy, continued to try and keep a foothold in the process. However, labouring agents also began appealing to a new constituency. As wartime conditions and Fianna Fáil's control of government blocked Labour's agency in relation to extensive public amenities, the sufferings of 'the poor' were being exacerbated (Case 22.2).

Case 22.2: Milk for the 'Deserving Poor,' 1943–6

In mid-1943 the county manager accepted a tender from a Thomastown retailer to reinstate the Free Milk Scheme. It had been in abeyance for two years and, according to Ned Maher, was to be revived because county councillor James O'Neill 'press[ed] on the proper authorities the advantages to the poor and delicate children.' Three years later, the scheme was again halted. O'Neill informed the county manager that the supplier had said that he 'could not be troubled giving these people pints and half pints.' The manager asked O'Neill to try again: Thomastown was 'the only district in the county where a contractor cannot be got ... and the result is that the children of the deserving poor must suffer.' Six months later, a supplier had still not been found. The Free Milk Scheme in Thomastown ended.[3]

That O'Neill could not procure a local farmer or retailer to provide milk suggests that members of both status-classes were doing sufficiently well without such a contract. It also points to O'Neill's limited leverage outside the labouring class and the fact that neither of the other two main political parties saw the issue as providing sufficient political capital to bother. The deserving and labouring poor thus became part of the natural and uncontested constituency of the two competing Labour parties (Case 22.3).

Case 22.3: Conditions in the County Home, 1944

Irish Labour Party councillor James O'Neill was on the visiting committee to the County Home/workhouse. He reportedly made a fuss about how the weekly pensions of the elderly (10s.) were being entirely appropriated by the matron for their keep and how the meat had maggots because it had been so cheaply bought. The other visiting committee members disagreed. The food, they said, was 'fresh and of good quality.' O'Neill countered by saying that 'we got complaints from every department in the hospital ... The inmates stated that the meat could walk to the table' by itself.[4]

As they espoused the cause of the poor, labouring agents began to leave deputy Derrig, Fianna Fáil, and the retailers in the Thomastown

Development Association to agitate for the major schemes (water, sewerage). However, this division of labour was soon overtaken by general afflictions. Extensive flooding took place in late 1944. Because coal and firewood were scarce, the dampness threatened 'to remain during the winter and spring ... as a ... danger to the health of the people affected.' Maher added: 'It is time the ... public ... demand[ed] the government have the Nore drained' and obstacles removed.[5] Nothing was done. Fourteen months later, as the fuel shortage continued, O'Neill and Pattison together engaged with a local retailer at a county council meeting over equity in the sale of rationed fuel (Case 22.4).

Case 22.4: The 'Desperate' Fuel Situation in Thomastown, 1946

O'Neill announced that the fuel situation was 'acute,' especially with the advent of winter. In fact, no fuel whatsoever was available. The county manager said that the 'council has no function in that matter.' Councillor/National Labour Party deputy Pattison said that he had complained to the department about the tops of trees being burned when people 'would be more than glad to buy them. This was a ... crime.' He also said that a Thomastown retailer would supply only six-ton lots or more. 'If people were licensed as fuel merchants,' said Pattison, the minister ought to 'make it obligatory on them to supply the needs of the community ... One of the fundamentals of fuel rationing was fair distribution.' Two weeks later, Pattison answered a letter from a retailer who had taken exception to his comments: 'Fuel rationing – just the same as the rationing of any other commodity – is designed to secure equal treatment for all citizens, both the rich and the poor, but from the information furnished to me it would appear that it was only those members of the community who could afford to purchase their fuel in large quantities ... [who] were supplied by you.' Pattison concluded: 'I should like to ... dispel from your mind that I have ... allowed anybody to use me ... in this ... matter, and in particular that such a party would be one "motivated only by malice." I wish to state that ... you in common with the people of Thomastown could not but attribute only the highest motives to my informant who has a life-long reputation for honesty and courage.'[6]

Clearly O'Neill, the 'informant,' had fallen out with the retailer. Pattison, however, backed him. A month later, the shortage was raised by the Fine Gael TD for the constituency, E.J. Coogan. He asked a question of Sean Lemass, minister for industry and commerce. In so doing, he appropriated both the poor and the issue of equity in a major mediation site (Case 22.5).

Case 22.5: Fine Gael and the Poor, 1946

'Mr Coogan asked ... if the Minister is aware that there is no fuel depot in Thomastown; that the nearest fuel depot is about one mile ... from the town; if he will ... have a depot established; also if he is aware that deliveries of turf to Thomastown are most irregular ...

'Mr Lemass [minister]: ... From inquiries I have made, I am satisfied that the ... distribution of turf in the Thomastown area is adequate ...

'Mr Coogan: Is the Minister not aware that the only supplier of turf fuel ... is the creamery which is ... a mile ... from the town? I am informed that the supplies from there are most irregular and that at times the poor of Thomastown are unable to procure any fuel.

'Mr Lemass: The [Creamery] ... say they have no difficulty in meeting local demands ...

'Mr Coogan asked the Minister ... if he is aware of the grave shortage ... of timber fuel ... and of the fact that local fuel merchants do not sell timber fuel in small quantities, with consequent hardship upon poor people ... and if he will take steps to ... order ... fuel merchants to sell in small quantities to the poor of Thomastown.

'Mr Lemass: There is no order in force relating to the distribution of timber fuel. [My] inquiries ... do not indicate that the firewood position in Thomastown is one of peculiar gravity ...

'Mr Coogan: Is the Minister not aware that there was considerable controversy in the local press ... that ... poor people in Thomastown cannot get timber in quantities of less than a ton. Would the Minister consider ... bringing in some order to compel the fuel merchants to sell in reasonably small quantities to poor persons – quantities which their purse will reach?

'Mr Lemass: Since [then] ... felling has been resumed in the ... forestry at Grenan, about a mile from Thomastown, and the officer in charge has been instructed by the Department of Lands to dispose locally of firewood blocks and light brushwood.

'Mr Coogan: Is the Minister not aware that felling was suspended during harvest?

'Mr Lemass: On October 21st, the Department of Lands had several hundred tons of timber for sale in the area.'[7]

The situation continued to deteriorate and, in early 1947, local agents again mobilized themselves. The TDA passed a motion protesting that timber from Grennan Wood was sent to Waterford while Thomastown 'residents [could] ... obtain only meagre supplies. The poor ... unable to purchase one-ton lots, are left without.' The resolution was forwarded to Lemass and to the TDs of all parties. It was also brought by representatives of both Labour parties to the county council (Case 22.6).

Case 22.6: The Fuel Shortage and the County Council, 1947

James O'Neill told a council meeting that Grennan timber had been sent to Waterford, that the TDA had passed a protest resolution, and that 'it was pitiable to see unfortunate people in the locality having to bring small quantities of fuel in truck cars and on their backs from the forestry department's woods at Grenan and being only allowed into the wood one day each week ... The council should call on the department to ease the situation ... No turf was available and the timber ... negligible. He passed through a big demesne outside the town and there was no end to the timber that was in it. He failed to see why this timber – in such trying times – was not allocated to the needs of the people ...

'Mr T. Walsh [Fianna Fáil]: Would that be commercial timber?

'Mr O'Neill: Yes, but what would not be commercial timber should be used for firewood. I know people who went to their beds for the simple reason that they had no fires to sit at.

'Mr Pattison: The fuel position was very serious all over the county ... There appeared ... complete lack of control in the matter of rationing fuel. They all knew that people with money and cheque books could not only get enough fuel for the current year but in some cases had next year's supply already in stock.' He moved that the council endorse the TDA resolution. O'Neill seconded. The Fianna Fáil chair said that the county council 'had no jurisdiction over the distribution of fuel ... They had their elected representatives to look after the needs of the people, and a question like that had no use coming before them ... These resolutions are snowball resolutions.

'Mr O'Neill: It is not a snowball resolution.

'Chairman: Coming from county or urban councils, resolutions like this are of no use; it is for our representatives to make representations in the proper places and at the proper time ... County Councils count for nothing.

'Mr Cleere [Independent]: What are we here for if we cannot compel anybody to do anything; who are in higher office than ourselves? Are we here only as a waste of time?

'Chairman: Absolutely, if you like. Why shouldn't the representatives of this county be asked to come down and see the people ... and have the timber made available?

'Mr Grace: Who do you want to come down?

'Chairman: Whoever they are.

'Mr Aylward [Fianna Fáil]: Mr Derrig and Mr Coogan.
'Deputy Pattison said that ... the greatest support the parliamentary represen-
tatives in any democratic country could get was the wholehearted backing of their
local authorities. In Britain and elsewhere it was the local government force
behind these ... representatives that got things done.
'Deputy Pattison's resolution was unanimously adopted. [8]

The council motion sent the issue back to the Dáil via Coogan, who
used the information about Grennan timber being sent to Waterford to
ask why. Lemass answered: 'substantial quantities' were available for
local sale. 'When did that become available?' asked Coogan. 'It is available now,' said Lemass.[9] Thus had proper representations finally yielded
results, but only after much pressure and agitation from a series of
agents from varying classes and parties and in a number of sites. Agents
from different parties, however, had different tactics. Pattison, supporting O'Neill, used the county council to pass resolutions while trying to
influence the government through private lines. Fianna Fáil deputy
Tom Derrig was publicly silent, a minister in the government that had
caused the problem in the first instance. Fine Gael took the issue into
the Dáil and thus appropriated the discourse of 'the poor' and the constituency which the Labour representatives had been courting to offset
Fianna Fáil influence. Fine Gael, however, was also cultivating those who
usually engaged the market without difficulty in normal times. These
were the respectable workers, and the 'natural' constituency of both
Labour parties.

The fuel crisis was overshadowed a week after the Dáil encounter by
'the worst flood experienced in the memory of the oldest inhabitant.'
The water in the town's main streets rose to seven feet, one hundred
houses were flooded, foundations were undermined, and shops were
damaged. To a public meeting a few days afterwards came clergy, doctor, and deputies Derrig and Coogan (Case 22.7).

Case 22.7: The Public Meeting after the Flood, 1947
Derrig promised to have lost ration cards replaced and 'stocks of tea, sugar, flour,
etc. ... replenished immediately ... He would do everything possible to have fuel
made available.' He also promised a general flood-control scheme but pointed out
the difficulties of obtaining the necessary machinery from abroad. He suggested
that local charities, such as the Red Cross and the Society of St Vincent de Paul

'minimize the hardships of the victims.' Fine Gael deputy Coogan then spoke of his unceasing efforts 'since his entry into the Dáil ... to ... pressure ... the government regarding the drainage of the Nore ... Only a week ago he had raised the question of fuel supplies in Thomastown and had been told by the minister that there was plenty of timber and turf. "Have you firewood?" asked Mr Coogan, to which there were loud cries of "no." "Have you turf?" he asked, and again there were shouts of "no." Turning to Mr Derrig, Mr Coogan said, "I can only say that the replies the Minister gave me were inaccurate."'

Retailer/baker Joseph Comerford 'said they would take no more nonsense from the government ... The people of Thomastown had suffered enough. They now demanded action.' Publican P.F. Walsh then spoke of how 'he and his family had been marooned in an upstairs apartment of his premises for the past week ... They had been told that it would be from 3 to 5 years before the draining of the Nore would begin ... Inspectors and engineers on the Nore are as numerous as ... flies. The people of Thomastown would not stand idly by while their homes were being washed away and the health of their children endangered. They demanded immediate action from the government.'

A general discussion ensued. It was decided that the local branch of the Society of St Vincent de Paul 'would hold a meeting immediately, co-opt a number of traders and victims of the flooding and furnish full particulars of the losses to Messrs Derrig and Coogan.'[10]

While Fianna Fáil threw the initiative back onto the locality yet again without providing any resources, the Irish Labour Party and the National Labour Party (and IT&GWU) – their agents, activists, and representatives – were invisible. They were also unmentioned as part of local initiatives to deal with the flood's impact. Rather, it was the county council that began to repair footpaths and roads, the McCalmonts and the convent that distributed hot meals daily, and a newly constituted Relief Committee that supplied fuel, tea, and sugar. The funds were raised by public donation, as they had been one hundred and fifty years before. It was also left to the Fine Gael's deputy Coogan to bring the issue to the Dáil (Case 22.8).

Case 22.8: The Thomastown Flood and the Deputies in the Dáil

Lemass said that the 'government did not propose to establish the precedent of asking the general community to meet the losses incurred by flooding in Kilkenny and Thomastown.' Instead, 'the efforts being made locally would enable many of the greater hardships to be relieved.' Coogan replied that the situation 'was too severe and vast for people to rehabilitate themselves without assistance from the State.' The distress was 'too large for the local authority to handle.' Pattison then gave a long speech on the fuel situation as well as the flood, and the way in which the rich were getting fuel but not the poor. He commented also on low wages, especially of road workers who had a lot of 'broken time' in their workday/work week owing to rain, and on the 'terrible tragedy of emigration.'[11]

Both O'Neill (ILP) and Pattison (NLP) were completely out of step with the sentiments of the town's retailers. A public meeting in late May set up a new local committee to deal with the flooding. Pilsworth presided. 'Sympathy is very nice indeed,' said retailer John Woods, 'but we want something practical done.' Devoy and O'Neill also spoke. Echoing Pattison in the Dáil, they said that the new committee should also deal with amenities (housing, sewerage), unemployment, and emigration as well as with flooding. Devoy and O'Neill were overruled by the retailers and notables for whom the flood was the single, immediate concern.[12]

On the one hand, Pattison, O'Neill, and Devoy saw the flood as mainly a problem for retailers whose shop premises and stocks had been badly damaged and who had lost custom for weeks. They also knew that working people needed more general ameliorative action. On the other hand, these agents were still busy with the ramifications of the 1944 split between the IT&GWU and the Irish Labour Party, with Pattison supported by Devoy against O'Neill. Thus, while retailers and notables organized a Flood Committee, and Fine Gael made discursive inroads into Labour's support base via the flood, Devoy published an angry letter in the local press accusing O'Neill and 'his group' of agitating among the electorate and of having 'an axe to grind.'[13]

Yet, if ever a single event induced a sense of locality and collective consciousness, devoid of political partisanship and experienced by people of all classes, it was this 1947 flood. It evoked from elderly labourers the most graphic of all their memories. They recalled cotmen rescuing people from upper stories of houses, they remembered kegs of ale floating out of pubs and down the river, they spoke of a publican's cache of banknotes, kept in a tin box, being carried away by the flood waters and washing up for people to gather. Some told of the terror of being stranded by rising water, not knowing when the high-water mark would be reached. They recalled the damp, the homelessness. The flood reminded older workers of the disingenuousness of politicians and the fickleness of the state. It taught a new generation that necessities such as fuel, and luxuries such as children's milk and decent food in the county home, were still, at times, beyond their own reach and, always, beyond the reach of those among them who were poor. The flood intensified localism as it engendered a new sense of pragmatism. Ultimately, such sentiments enabled a newly formed political party to harvest local discontent. In the process, old party loyalties, which the flood and the resultant localism had softened, were revived and aggravated.

The 1948 Dáil Election: The Clann and Labour

In 1946 Sean MacBride, son of an insurgent executed after the 1916 Rising and an anti-Treatyite barrister and republican, formed the core of a new political party from the remnants of the defunct Saor Éire and from disenchanted nationalists who had once belonged to Fianna Fáil. The new party, Clann na Poblachta ('Republican Family'), had two main aims: to establish an Irish republic and to end partition. The party also seemed to have a social radicalism which appealed to many on the left. A branch was founded in Thomastown in January 1948.[14] This was six months after the local Flood Committee received £1,000 from the county council to repair the bridge and clean the river without waiting for a major scheme (Case 22.1). It was four months after the work was carried out and a week after the Nore again flooded several of the town's streets, damaged winter wheat, and made country roads impassable.[15]

The executive of the local Clann was a study in contrasts, populism and the cross-class appeal of republicanism. The chair was Mrs Pilsworth, the vice-chair was a local gentleman, the secretary was a farmer, and the treasurers were carpenter Podge Dack and retailer Peter Lennon.[16] All were active in the run-up to a Dáil election in February 1948 which, in Thomastown, became a face-off between Fianna Fáil and Clann na Poblachta (Case 22.9).

Case 22.9: 'Pandemonium' in Thomastown – The 1948 Election Campaign
Charges were brought against Patrick Heafey for damaging a motor lorry belonging to retailer Joseph Comerford. Six other men were charged with 'malicious damage to an electric line' with 'the intent to cut off ... the supply of electricity to the town.' All were labouring men. All pleaded guilty and chose to be dealt with summarily by District Judge McCabe, who observed that their offences 'made for pandemonium and breach all rules.'

Heafey's case. *Comerford's lorry was to be used as a platform for Sean McBride's speech but Heafey pulled out a wire to disable it. He told the court that 'he did it on the spur of the moment and was sorry.' When imposing a £1.8s. fine, McCabe said that 'it was a small amount of damage and the defendant seemed ... a decent sort of man. [But] it was the purpose for which he did it that made the matter serious. At election times parties were entitled to be listened to ... It was a rotten thing to do.' Prosecuting solicitor Crotty pointed out that Comerford loaned his lorry to all parties.*

The 6 young men. *The incident occurred on the night following Heafey's action. At a Fianna Fáil meeting, when Tom Derrig was speaking, the men threw a wire across an electric cable and blacked out the entire district, as far as eight miles away. Defence solicitor Hoyne said that the act 'was committed in the heat of the atmosphere' and would never have happened if Heafey had not disabled the lorry at the Clann meeting. The defendants agreed to pay for the damage. 'They were all working men and two of them were married,' said Hoyne. He asked that they be given four months to pay. Adjourning the case to the May court, McCabe said that they had to have at least half the damage paid by the time the claim came to the circuit court for criminal injury. 'It is a serious crime.'*[17]

The defendants included a nephew of IT&GWU activist Tom Beck. Pat Heafey's family were long-time Fianna Fáil supporters. Heafey had interfered with the Clann meeting so, in turn, Clann supporters retaliated at the Fianna Fáil meeting. All this signified the intensity of the Fianna Fáil-Clann contest. The result was that young labouring men were had up in court while the labour interest, in its turn, continued its internal, public squabbles under the guidance of the church hierarchy. At a National Labour meeting in Thomastown, presided over by Devoy a week before the election, Pattison spoke of how he left the Irish Labour Party 'as a protest against the failure of its leadership to prevent Communists from using that party for their own ends.' He said this 'issue was again in this election. In the 1944 election, the Labour Party failed to find dupes to oppose him, but they had succeeded in getting a pair for this election.'[18] Workers, in their turn, however, were simply searching out those who could best further both their ideals and their interests; and, of course, such agents were equally seeking labourers' votes. At a Fianna Fáil clinic, after the private proceedings, John Woods introduced a deputation of cotmen who explained that the section of the 1939 Fisheries Act which banned inland netting was being proclaimed. When the Clann na Poblachta candidate visited Thomastown, he, too, was sent a cotmen's combination from Thomastown, Bennettsbridge, and Inistioge. He 'assured [them] that, if elected to the Dáil, he would leave nothing undone to have the Act repealed.'[19]

For this 1948 Dáil election, Kilkenny-Carlow was again a five-member constituency. Fourteen candidates ran. The results confirmed the status quo ante as incumbents Derrig (Fianna Fáil), Coogan (Fine Gael), and Pattison (National Labour) were re-elected. The other two seats were won by Fianna Fáil and Fine Gael. The Irish Labour Party, and the Clann, were shut out. Of the first-preference votes, National Labour received 11.5 per cent (5,234 votes), Clann na Poblachta 10.5 per cent (4,792), and Irish Labour 7.7 per cent (3,528). This contrasted with the national results in which both the Clann and Irish Labour polled higher (13.2 and 8.7 per cent respectively) and in which National Labour polled much lower (2.6 per cent).[20] Clearly, local events, personalities, and perceptions profoundly affected voting while Pattison's anti-communism and connections were seen by a sufficient number of labourers as legitimate and efficacious. Thus, Pattison held on to enough lower preferences to be elected after the eleventh count. Derrig, whom Pattison had topped in 1942, was elected on the first count.

Just as working people's 'natural' Dáil seat was controlled by Pattison, regardless of his formal party affiliation, the local IT&GWU was similarly in the hands of Devoy and Pattison as a result of both new and revisionist old members (chapter 18). However, most of the new IT&GWU members did not vote Labour, whether Irish Labour or National Labour. They voted Fianna Fáil or, at this time, Clann. In this ironic way, the purge of radical activists from the IT&GWU had indeed disaffiliated and distanced the union from any party dedicated solely to labourers.

Organizing Labour: Reproducing the State

The reconstituted IT&GWU branch was shaped by the politics of Pattison and Devoy: ameliorative, non-confrontational, and narrow in ideological reach (Case 22.10)

Case 22.10: The View from the Local IT&GWU, 1949

At the annual general meeting, Devoy's report reviewed the branch's activities during the year and 'the improved conditions obtained by members.' It was unanimously adopted. Complaints were made about the price of coal and discussion ensued on the deteriorated position of farm workers whose recent wage increase was obviated by the fact that they were now employed by the hour, treated as casual, and deprived of previous perks. Pattison then spoke. He 'congratulated the members on the very ... satisfactory position of the branch' and 'assured them that ... the loyalty of the members was very much appreciated by the Head Office.' He then 'referred to a rumour ... that he was seeking a more lucrative post and was about to desert the cause of labour. He entirely repudiated the unfounded allegations. He had given his life in the cause of labour in Kilkenny city and county and he hoped to die in the cause which was so near and dear to his heart.' There was then a vote of thanks to Pattison 'for attending the meeting and presiding, and for the great interest he had always manifested in the welfare of workers.'[21]

James O'Neill was still a county councillor and still representing Thomastown district. Tellingly, his grander ideological statements disappeared as he adapted to the new political status quo. He continued to deal with individual hard cases and had begun to carve out a constituency of 'the poor' (Cases 22.2, 22.3). As Fine Gael moved into this latter area, he turned back to town amenities more generally. Here, however, he was forced into narrow goals. In mid-1948, even as Ned Maher gave him credit for a new water pump built by the council, O'Neill was in fact cut off from the vertical relations and political hierarchy which most people believed were responsible for delivering the important amenities and work schemes. Thus, at a conference in Kilkenny city in mid-1948 to discuss a greater Nore drainage scheme under the Arterial Drainage Act, it was Pattison and Deady who spoke. Although O'Neill attended, he was reported only as making a point about a local weir which was hardly relevant to this wider audience.[22] O'Neill also had to compete with the retailers' Development Association. For example, as rural electrification came into the area, it was the TDA and farmers who reportedly 'received encouragement' from the Electricity Supply Board, organized a public meeting, and selected canvassers to sign up subscribers.[23] Thus, as both O'Neill and the TDA claimed to represent the locality, both in public and to the authorities, they came to focus on different issues. O'Neill picked up on labourers' issues, such as housing, while the TDA took up general amenities, such as electrification, the idea of a secondary school, and the overall economic development of the town.[24]

Despite this renewed division of labour and the discursive posturings, the effectiveness of all agents – the TDA, O'Neill, and even the TDs – was highly circumscribed by the state bureaucracy (Case 22.11).

Case 22.11: The Posturing of Politicians, 1948

A report in late 1948, in obfuscating the lines of agency, highlighted the central role of bureaucrats. 'Mr Seamus O'Neill, Co.C., has received a communication from the secretary about his question at yesterday's meeting regarding the present position of the Thomastown water supply.' The letter explained a communiqué from the Department of Local Government which stated that the 'matter is now being referred to the county surveyor directing him to have the necessary instruction given to the consulting engineer,' and so on.

Similarly, at a council meeting in late 1948 to review the rural housing program, O'Neill said that an area in Thomastown where a site had been acquired for twenty-four houses had remained empty for years. Yet 'in his area, there was an overwhelming demand for houses and they were living on top of one another in rooms.' Not to be outdone, Pattison added that 'marriages in many cases were being delayed owing to the hopeless position, insofar as houses were concerned.' As it turned out, none of the new sites that the council acquired were in the Thomastown area. O'Neill, however, did derive some political credit through the report that, when 'replying to Mr. O'Neill, the chairman said there were forty-four new houses going to be built in Thomastown. That would be twenty-four in the town and twenty in the district.'[25]

The civil service was in complete charge. All that politicians could do was make public pronouncements about their constituency, poke holes in technicians' plans, complain if their area was not being properly treated, and take credit for any amenities that were forthcoming. It was the outcome of a long process of state formation which had been impelled by centralization during the Emergency and by the County Management Act (1940) which, as well as centralizing decision making, furthered the pretence of local agency through county councils and the defunct parish councils. Indeed, the above important meeting on housing policy (Case 22.11) ended with Pattison and the Fianna Fáil deputy complaining about individual hard cases and their disputes with cottage rent collectors. Ultimately, in this narrow-minded concern with votes and voters, it was in fact the politicians who left the space for the civil servants to take over. It simply remained for politicians to keep individual constituents content with minor help, where possible, and the public content with loudly voiced representations of successful mediation.

The 1950 County Council Election: Reuniting Labour

In 1950 a county council election was held. By that time, the joint participation of both National Labour and the Irish Labour Party in the inter-party government after the 1948 Dáil election had been leading to a rapprochement and an eventual union which was very much the result of the fact that the Labour Party proved to be 'as deferential to the bishops as any other party.'[26] By then, arch-rivals Jim Larkin was dead (1947) and William O'Brien retired (1946). The Thomastown branch of the National Labour Party was integrated into this process, largely through the exclusive agency of Pattison.

In 1947 local delegates (Devoy, Synnott, Challoner) were sent to the 1947 National Labour conference 'to support Pattison as a candidate for the forthcoming [Dáil] election.' Local members, including several mill-workers, also became election agents to canvas for votes, post bills, write slogans on walls, and plan a victory dance. After the 1948 election, Pattison came to the branch to explain why National Labour would participate in an inter-party government. A motion of approval was passed: 'our ... representatives are fully entitled to partake or govern in the best interests of our country.' Local activists from National Labour then began to compete for political capital by contacting Pattison about amenities. Most importantly, Thomastown's National Labour Party had become virtually indistinguishable from the IT&GWU branch. Devoy was secretary, and Pattison key agent, of both. In May 1949, for example, when the party held a meeting of forestry workers and Pattison addressed it, the topics were union matters: wages, holiday work, and unemployment insurance. Indeed, in August 1950, a party meeting was combined with an IT&GWU branch committee meeting. That branch had been virtually expunged of former activists.[27] It also had fully embraced the reformist position which had been Pattison's all along: seeking incremental, ameliorative policies in relation to wages and living costs.

For the 1950 county council election, Pattison told the branch to 'select men with the proper outlook from a worker's point of view, men who would see justice done to their fellow workers.'[28] With this search for candidates with a 'proper outlook,' Devoy spoke of the pressure being place on him to stand. He asked a branch meeting of the Labour Party if it approved, and the executive 'guaranteed full support.' There was, however, the fact of O'Neill's incumbency. In August 1950, at a joint Labour and IT&GWU meeting, Devoy was nominated for the Thomastown area 'in the Labour interest.' A motion was also passed that, if James O'Neill were 'nominated on the same ticket at the convention, our delegate would demand a vote of Thomastown Electoral Division delegates to decide which should be nominated and that only one be nominated.'[29] Clearly, one aim of the local branch was to get rid of O'Neill.

The county council election was held in September 1950. There were six seats for the Thomastown division and sixteen candidates. James O'Neill was not nominated by the convention and ran as 'Independent Labour.' Devoy and two others, from Graigue (Reeves) and Callan (Rochford), were the officially sanctioned Labour Party candidates. Table 22.1 shows the outcome of the twelve counts and the transfer votes for Labour and local candidates.[30]

O'Neill polled more first-preference votes than did Devoy or any of the other Labour candidates. It reflected his solid, Thomastown support. He held this lead by picking up small numbers of votes, like the other candidates, until virtually after the fifth count. Reeves (Labour, Graigue) was then eliminated. Clearly, Reeves's transfers stayed within the Labour Party for virtually none went to O'Neill. Instead they went almost equally to Devoy and Rochford (Labour, Callan). Interestingly, Graigue was far closer geographically to Thomastown than was Callan. Normally, the Thomastown candidate within a party would pick up the Graigue transfers. Graigue was also well known as a radical, working-class place, with a good deal of labour unrest. A not uncommon sentiment in Thomastown was that 'they'd go on strike for anything.' Devoy appealed to only about half their voters. More damaging, however, was that O'Neill picked up none of the transfers from Graigue.

Local Thomastown candidate William Deady (Farmers' Party) was himself eliminated after the sixth count. His papers then went largely to another Farmers' Party candidate ($n = 104$) and to two Fine Gael candidates ($n = 35$; $n = 22$). Only a few went to Labour, and those went mainly to Devoy, most likely as another Thomastown candidate. It was these transfers to Rochford and Devoy, from labourers within the Labour Party and from farmers within the locality respectively, that put O'Neill hopelessly behind. He held on for two more counts which saw one Fine Gael candidate elected and another eliminated. Then he, too, was eliminated. Ironically, virtually all his transfers went to Devoy. This put Devoy ahead of Rochford, whose elimination, after the tenth count, gave Devoy enough votes to be declared elected after the twelfth count but without having reached the quota.

Table 22.1: The results of the 1950 county council election

Candidate:	Count											
	1	2	3	4	5	6	7	8	9	10	11	12
Pilsworth (C)	79	82x										
Deady (F)	216	225	231	234	242	244x						
Reeves (L)	180	200	202	203	203x							
O'Neill (IL)	302	310	325	328	333	340	350	351	364x			
Rochford (L)	278	280	285	333	334	379	381	381	392	409x		
Devoy (L)	262	264	273	274	282	334	368	368	380	538	620	629*

Key: x connotes eliminated; *connotes elected. The quota for election was 720 votes. C = Clann na Poblachta; F = Farmers' Party;
L = Labour Party; IL = Independent Labour

O'Neill was defeated. This was clearly because Labour Party transfers from other localities went only to other, formal Labour Party candidates. Interestingly, it was O'Neill's supporters who elected Devoy by keeping their transfers both within the locality and within the so-called labour interest. The first-preference votes though suggest that, despite his defeat, O'Neill was a far more popular man in Thomastown.

The outcome of the 1950 county council election was recalled by every former Labour Party and/or IT&GWU member who had witnessed the so-called split. It was cited, over and over again, as the end of an era. Indeed, neither the failure of the cooperative nor the closing of Labour Hall marked for local working people what O'Neill's defeat signified: that the split engineered by the church, and the likes of Pattison and Devoy, took all the life out of the local men. Said Joe Tierney: 'Devoy went on to improve his vote with each passing election. But that was only because the other side no longer contested.' Gerard Doyle's son commented: 'By the time I was born in 1953, my father's politics were in his past.' James O'Neill's son commented in 1983 that 'after my father lost to Devoy, he did nothing but work in the mill until it closed ... He never ran for the county council again. He was uninvolved in politics.' Said Ned Maher's daughter in 1985: 'The Pattison defection to National Labour was the end of their political lives.'

Reproduction and Turning Points

The year 1950 marked the end of a radical critique and viewpoint of society from a generation of activists whose ideologies were rooted in the late nineteenth century and whose political and economic antecedents emanated from even earlier labouring experiences. The year coincided with the ban on inland netting. In 1948 the 1939 Fisheries Act was promulgated and the cot fishers were evicted from the river. They were given compensation payments of £200 each for their customary right. In 1949 a Thomastown Angling Club was formed. It was made up of former cotmen and a mixed-class group of rodmen (gentlemen, retailers, and labourers) anxious to preserve the river bank from the encroachment of the Kilkenny Anglers Association, which was taking leases from farmers for exclusive rights to angle. Some cotmen, as was their custom, continued to poach. The sense of loss, however, both for the nets and for the possibility of a new order, was captured by local poet TUSA, who found reason to blame an anonymous 'them' whose actions were worse than those of Cromwell himself.

Maybe 'tis sinful, perhaps it is not
(Didn't God put the fish in the sea for the lot.) ...
The net was abolished, the rod was the thing,
The cotman was broken, the tourist was king ...
Black Cromwell an' all he did, never did what
They've done to me river, me net and me cot.[31]

The elimination of any semblance of customary right on the river was accompanied by other tentative steps to modernity. In 1947 the county council installed a fire engine, and a fire brigade, comprised of labourers, was established in the town. In 1950 the convent 'laundry and school of domestic economy,' founded in 1910, was closed, thus ending an extreme form of labour exploitation and stigma.[32]

Yet, after 1950, the bedrock of labour support cum local sentiment remained, to be tapped for elections by labouring agents. Also replicated was an image of society as comprised of networks for mediation by which jobs and amenities could be accessed. Thus, political representatives continued to plump for housing and a water supply scheme for the locality: there were numerous reports of Devoy, and occasionally Pattison, agitating at county council meetings and accessing seemingly relevant bureaucrats. Also in 1950, the CYMS was reported as flourishing, with an increase of 57 new members, bringing the total to 114. It had moved into 'commodious, new premises' which had a second billiards table, a radio, darts, library, and card room. As usual, all the officers were retailers while the billiards tournament was won by four labourers. At the same time, CYMS's religious observances were increased via a weekly study circle and a Daily Mass Crusade. Certainly, the relations among recreation, religious devotion, and politics were being reproduced. However, the harbinger of an impending confrontation between devotion and economic relations was contained in a December 1950 issue of *Thomastown Notes*. It reported 'an abuse which has, we regret to say, become rather prevalent in this district of late. The people of Thomastown were shocked ... as the congregation were returning from last Mass to see three lorry loads of gravel being driven through the town' on a Sunday.[33]

PART V

Conclusions: Political Economy and Culture, 1800–1950

23. Theory, Concept, and Text: A Holistic Approach to the Politics of Class

Among the topics essential for understanding the processes of capitalism, colonialism, and state formation are the political economy and culture of people who have contributed their labour. In this present incursion into the social history of a working class in southeastern Ireland, I have tried to construct both an analytical and historical ethnography of class awareness and class experience as these comprised part of more general hegemonic and political-economic processes over a period of one hundred and fifty years. My aim has been to explore the historical dynamics of inequality as actualized through the economy and the state. To do this, I examined socio-political relations and cultural codes as these intersected with the materiality of working-class lives. I also focused on the accumulating layers or strands of experience through time: the *metissage* or braiding of ideas and practices which created particular outcomes cum potentialities along the way.

Some Theoretical Basics

The construction of such an ethnography necessitated an engagement with certain theoretical and sometimes contentious issues. I refer, particularly, to the nature of the state and capitalism; the concept of culture and its relation to material and social life; and notions of hegemony and power. A recent discussion by Joseph and Nugent started from the view that the state is an idea or mask which hides 'real history' and 'relations of subjection.' Following Corrigan and Sayer, the triumph of capitalism was therefore implicated not simply in relations of production and exchange, but in the ways in which the idea of the state, and the associated 'activities and cultural forms,' were formed and sustained. Inevitably, such a view leads to an analysis of popular culture which, in its nuanced form, is defined as embodying and elaborating dominant symbols, categories, meanings, and identities while simultaneously challenging, revaluing, and presenting alternatives to them. In other words, 'popular and dominant culture are imbricated in one another.'[1]

On the one hand, and in general terms, there is little to disagree with here. On the other hand, certain dangers inhere in how such a conceptualization is concretized and used for detailing empirical cases. Among these are a risk of conflating the state, as an idea, with 'dominant culture' and, second, of homogenizing both this culture and the so-called popular one. Moreover, those who exert a successful claim to run the state also claim a spatial jurisdiction and, within that space, subjects or citizens and foreigners, however defined, are physically dispersed. Among these people will be those who own the means of production, those with critical skills, those who control mercantile wealth, and those who have labour power to sell. Also among them will be agents whose activities and convictions comprise the administrative apparatus required to keep the idea and practices of the state alive. Overall, one is confronted by a physical, material, and organizational complexity which comprises a labyrinth of diverse yet interconnected socio-cultural forms and meanings. Such complexity is made even more confounding when one moves from focusing on a particular conjuncture, such as a revolt, to exploring an epoch or the *longue durée*. Then, to add to the complexity, there is the concept of 'power.' If popular culture is about 'power – a problem of politics,' the question is immediately raised as to how each can be defined in terms of their relation to the other. The view that power should be observed through its organization, and that one form for regulating power is the state,[2] leads only to teleology.

In the present volume, then, as in any work, certain foci had to be selected as vehicles for representing and constructing general processes. The foci that I chose for exploring capitalism and state formation were local-level political economy and the culture of class. To do this, I took concepts from three key sites (as explained in chapter 1): anthropological approaches to local-level politics; elaborations on Gramsci's idea of hegemony; and notions of class awareness and experience as used by some social historians. Together, these seemed to offer a coherent way of approaching the political and culture history of a localized segment of a working class during the nineteenth and first half of the twentieth centuries.

The Sites: Local-Level Politics, Hegemony, and Experience

In chapter 1, as I located my historical ethnography in these three sites, I discussed the directions that they provided and the issues that they addressed. I then used these to orient my presentation of the data. In highlighting here what I tried to do, I offer some suggestions as to how a new and holistic political anthropology might be constructed.

The concept of hegemony, although fraught with contested interpretations, provided a political approach to culture at the same time that it constituted an approach to class relations and to economic and material conditions. However, as I used the concept here, I tried to avoid some of the more common ways in which the idea has entered anthropology. For example, in the present ethnography, hegemony is *not* about structured outcomes nor is it the opposite of class consciousness; it is *not* about cultural impositions/domination and resistance; it is *not* focused on culture contact and acculturation nor constructed around protagonists defined in binary terms ('oppressors-oppressed'; 'dominant-subordinate'); and it is *not* about consent divorced from coercion and culture unfettered by material relations. Instead, I have aimed for a more holistic approach to the politics of class. I thus began with the Gramscian idea that, because hegemony is the *process* of gaining consent in civil society, we must explore the so-called material structure of ideology: the nature of exploitation, and the experiences, institutions, intellectuals, and organizations which, together though time, create 'common sense' ideologies, sentiments, or understandings of the world. Simultaneously, we are led to explore how, in dialectical fashion, counter-ideologies ('good sense') are formulated by 'organic intellectuals' and leaders and, also, how such critical reasoning may be appropriated by 'traditional' intellectuals to thwart its growth, subvert organic intellectuals, or divide people by formulating new identities. In the Gramscian sense, then, ideology is, simultaneously a world-view, an instrument of domination, and an instrument of liberation. Ideology itself, however, is composed of many interwoven strands. These may be contradictory, unclear, contested, or generally accepted. Ideological formulations are therefore heterogeneous, creating the probability of complex 'contradictory consciousness.'

The historical dynamics of consciousness are actualized through politics. Politics are the means by which leaders are linked to the led and, therefore, the means through which hegemony operates.[3] Indeed, 'it is within the framework of concrete political activity that ideology constitutes an instrument of domination.'[4] Thus, in relation to ideology, consciousness, and leadership, Gramsci discussed the role of political action and political alliance ('historical blocs'). The question that he left behind, however, is an empirical as well as theoretical one: how 'does hegemony function as a set of concrete linkages between the political and cultural spheres?'[5]

To explore this, I have used ideas from an older paradigm in political anthropology. In this transactional approach, entrepreneurial leaders formulate political strategies as well as ideologies. They recruit factions, supporters, and followers; they form political cliques and groups which compete for economic resources, political capital, and legitimacy; they form strategic alliances with other leaders and groups; they become links in chains of mediation which both bridge and separate localities, organizations, institutions, and societal levels. Such political entrepreneurs are always implicated with processes of class formation and class politics, whether overtly or implicitly, intentionally, or unintentionally.[6] Looking at their activities and agency allows, too, for nuanced uses of the concept of power: as personal, tactical, organizational, or structural,[7] rather than as undifferentiated and totalizing. Such entrepreneurs may be the organic and/or traditional leaders whom Gramsci saw as central to hegemonic processes. Most generally, they are the localized agents and agency through whom hegemonic processes are at least in part actualized.

From the perspective of social history, such agents are 'activists.' They operate within particular empirical contexts, channelling class awareness and experience into political action by elaborating ideologies, symbols and programs. Thus does the social historians' use of 'awareness' and 'experience' extend the canvas on which an holistic ethnography of class politics can be drawn. For not only do these two notions fit Gramsci's idea of common sense but they allow a good deal of nuance to be introduced. 'Awareness,' particularly class awareness, allows for the inclusion in the ethnography of those commonplace, routine, and mundane beliefs and practices that people uncritically espouse. Awareness, in other words, is part of common sense: habitual, unquestioned, normal. Experience, however, as partaking directly in production, exchange, gossip, rituals, and so on, reinforces awareness while simultaneously providing the potential space for discordant notes to be elaborated and awareness to be made manifest. In Thomastown, since at least 1800, the status-class hierarchy formed the bedrock of common sense. That people actually experienced this hierarchy, through their work, talk, expectations, and so on, not only reinforced this knowledge but also, occasionally, raised their hackles sufficiently to question its naturalized and, even perhaps, its exploitative qualities.

Choosing Themes

The three sites, taken from Gramsci, transactional politics, and social history, provided the anchoring from which I explored capitalism and state formation in this historical ethnography. In their turn, however, the ideas from these sites had to be concretized and elaborated. I therefore chose five central themes. First, the idea of *cultural codes* has long had a place in socio-cultural anthropology, along with debates about their deterministic versus derivative role.[8] In this ethnography, I have equated codes with Gramsci's notion of common sense. Neither common sense nor codes determine behaviour; nor are they the mere by-product of material action. Rather, they are everyday ways of seeing and interpreting the world. They are accretions and secretions of both the historical past and the experiential present. They accumulate, they change, they get lost, they are reproduced. In the present ethnography, I argue that three key codes have been pertinent, in different ways and at different times, to everyday life and experience: status-class, respectability, and locality. How and why this was so are intrinsic parts of the historical ethnography.

Second, I have focused on labour processes and the nature of *exploitation*. This was such an elemental facet of Thomastown life, both past and present, that I cannot envision the so-called dialectics of cultural struggle without reference to the material bases of socio-economic life which were associated with common sense, beliefs, symbols, and meanings. This, in turn, related to a third theme: the fact that *domination* or physical *coercion* were intrinsic to political society, either as a threat or an actuality wielded by those who governed. Aspects of this were explicitly addressed in chapter 6, in a discussion of the law, petty sessions, and respectability in the nineteenth century. More generally, however, a backdrop of violence from state agents, claimants, and dissenters framed the past: the death penalty for labouring combinations in 1800, military incursions in the 1830s, the actions and counter-actions of fishers and bailiffs, the general strike of 1913, the war of independence and the civil war, the executions of republicans in the 1920s, the damning of souls in the 1930s, the Spanish Civil War, and so on. To view all these simply from the perspective of negotiated cultural forms is inadequate.

Instead, both material exploitation and coercion were essential aspects: experienced, conceptualized and integrated into common sense and other ideologies and, sometimes, translated into political cum organizational tactics.

This, in turn, points to the final two themes: the *organizational dimension* and *agency.* A focus on organizations and institutions as they become relevant to the research aim and narrative does not have to create a narrow and formalistic approach to working-class consciousness, about which there have been ample criticisms. Similarly, a focus on decision making or action, and the nature of agency, does not have to imply unconstrained and de-cultured actors. Rather, when Corrigan stated that the key question 'is NOT *who* rules but *how* rule is accomplished,'[9] he was, in effect, creating a false separation. For 'who' and 'how' are the same, connected via agency and the use of particular and variable associational forms.

Elaborating Conceptual Ideas

In creating an historical ethnography of Thomastown's labouring class, I have been concerned with what Gramsci called 'the material structure of ideology,' with the *metissage* of experience as it stretched through time. In orienting this via the above themes, other refinements were made. I review some of these below, assessing both their uses and their ambiguities.

Languages of Class
Field work in Thomastown during 1980–1 brought out clearly the vitality and immediacy in everyday life of class identities, categories, and differences. Ongoing field work since then has further provided opportunities to explore how class was conceptualized and talked about and how people self-categorized themselves or were assigned a station by others. Archival materials, too, fleshed out the emic presence, since at least the late eighteenth century, of what I have called the status-class hierarchy. Also present at times, but not coterminous with status-class, was a Marxist conceptualization. It entered the local lexicon in 1898 but was, by 1950, swamped by the language of status-class. Occupational categories, too, containing notions of hierarchy and worth, were also ubiquitous. Especially pertinent to Thomastown were such categories as cotman, tradesman, shopkeeper, farmer, and millworker. Class-like categories also emerged from competitions over reputations and the face of

respectability: 'strong farmer,' 'respectable labourer,' 'young men in good employment,' 'decent woman.' Equally, other categories, such as 'shoneen,' 'perjurer,' and 'informer' were ways of specifying the state of coercion and socio-political relations as well as the cultural sentiments that particular actions elicited and certain people embodied. How these emerged and why, and the changing contexts in which they were embedded, provided insight into processes of reproduction. Importantly, too, discursive changes highlighted relational changes and key moments, such as that from 'landless peasant' to 'wage labourer' or the resurfacing of the idea of 'poor labourers' at particular times.

At the same time that the languages of class provide insights, I also think it is essential for an ethnographer to anchor them in analytical, etic categories. For these situate emic discourse, prevent the ethnography from becoming a cacophony of the loudest voices, and deter undefined and homogenized usages (for example, 'subalterns,' 'dominant class'). Most crucially, analytical categories of class create a framework for siting labour processes and exploitation through time. They give a materiality to cultural codes and a base from which to view coercion, agency, and organizations.

In this volume, I have conceptualized such analytical categories as dyads, focusing on those that were directly relevant to the story: landlord-labourer/artisan; manufacturer/capitalist-labourer/artisan; and tenant farmer-labourer/artisan. In addition, Thomastown had those who occupied contradictory locations (for example, artisans who hired labour) and anomalous positions, such as retailers and notables (for example, professionals, clergy). These, with the dyads, provided a framework which, very importantly, standardized class concepts for the entire one-hundred-and-fifty-year period and thus allowed me to specify and compare political combinations in terms of their 'class composition.'[10]

Paternalism, Deference, and Dearth

The seeming tenacity of paternalism and its permutations through time was striking. Its roots could be located in a world that pre-dated this study and its branches could be followed, through such traces as relief and charitable works and state interventions, for the next one hundred and fifty years. In saying this, however, I want to highlight the danger of turning 'paternalism' into a static cultural thing and of insulating it from the historical dynamics of hierarchy, domination, and exploitation. Thus, throughout this ethnography, I have tried to situate paternalism in the materiality of social life, such as the varying nature of dearth, and to see it always in relation to the changing character of its corollary, deference. My aim was to analyse reproduction rather than to assume crude cultural persistence. This also allowed insight into the variable educational goals that were aimed at working people at different times. Between 1800, when the Earl of Ormond donated blankets, and 1947, when Major McCalmont provided hot meals, lay a myriad of experiential and organizational layers which points to a similarity of cultural form, a variation in meaning, a difference in function, and a dramatic dissimilarity of context. Clearly, all these aspects, and how they accreted, are equally relevant. The focus, then, must be on processes of reproduction, not persistence.

The Political Domain and the Politics of Combination: Labour as Subject, Labour as Object

As subjects, Thomastown's workers formed various kinds of combinations at different times. These could be put along a continuum in terms of spatial distribution, degree of centralized coordination, and claims and actions in relation to property and/or persons. On one extreme was insurrection; on the other were breaches of public demeanour. In between were riots, mobs, crowds, strikes, petitions/delegations, and interpersonal disturbances. Each of these forms or manifestations might, of course, be differently labelled either by different contemporaries or by later historians. Much depended on what actions were discerned by or reported to commentators, who was seen as forming the combination (for example, kinds of workers; locals or strangers) and the economic and political context out of which the combination arose. This means that collective action is best understood when the details and subtleties of the socio-economic context are known and when designations or labels are used only in a comparative or relative way.

Such a comparative focus, however, has sometimes been pushed too far by historians or sociologists who put types of collective action and/or social movements along temporal and modernizing continua: from disorganized (riot) to organized (unions, strikes) forms; from violent action (insurrection) to non-violent activities (petitions, delegations); and, most generally, from small local combinations to mass constitutional politics. Such evolutionary progressions not only impose an historical outcome beforehand, they also ignore the particular historical and structural contexts, and the emic meanings, of each manifestation. In any case, the aim of an historical cum political domain is not to build typologies or to see the evolution of one form into another. It is to see how combinations form part of hegemonic processes and become implicated in that process, as ongoing strands in the *metissage* of common sense and experience, as leaders emerge and as ideologies and counter-ideologies are formed. In other words, the focus for an holistic approach to the politics of class is not collective action, but hegemony.

An aspect of this hegemonic political process was rooted in the fact that labourers did not only combine but were often constituted as a political category or group by agents from other classes. As these agents engaged in political argument, competed over scarce resources, or actualized their responsibilities as patrons, labourers were used as discursive or rhetorical devices, physical resources, or educational projects. Such objectification, of course, invariably connected to labourers' actions as subjects, forming thereby a dialectic of political action

Politics and the Relations of Production, Exchange, and Consumption

In this book, I have given a lot of space to the changing 'condition' of labour. This concept of condition was a nineteenth-century one, reflecting a concern that some people had with the economic and moral circumstances of others. At particular times, such concerns might broaden or narrow to include or focus on political combinations, education, public health, and so on. The expression of such concern, in relation to labourers, was usually initiated by bureaucrats who perceived a problem or who were convinced by other agents that a problem existed: for example, the fisheries were in decline, the poor were too numerous and unruly, the county council had failed to collect rates, and so on. The investigations that ensued provided a wealth of documentary data on material circumstances and on perceptions. Similarly, as magistrates at the petty and quarter sessions sifted through the ins and outs of local relations, events, and knowledge contained in the evidence before them, a good deal of insight could be gleaned from the press summaries about local society and the meanings which people said they espoused. When these materials were placed alongside field data (interviews), primary materials (for example, censuses, deeds-registry materials, valuation records), and published secondary sources, it became possible to depict the forces and relations enmeshed in production, exchange, and consumption. I then tried to weave these portraits into my understandings of the hegemonic process, as changes in both actual and perceived conditions became intrinsic parts of cultural codes, political awareness, experience, and consciousness; and, also, as they became implicated in combinations, organizations, and the actions of leaders. In other words, I have made the economy an intrinsic part of the political-cultural analysis.

The Politics of Mediation

Physical, social, and cultural spaces inevitably separate some individuals, groups, and classes. So, too, can a gap be conceptualized between political and civil society. Some way of seeing connections and/or disjunctions among these is therefore necessary. In political anthropology, the idea of intermediary roles and/or mediation has long served as a way of doing this. Mediation also has been used by those studying disputing processes, social control, and political competition. In all cases, the concept has provided a way of seeing how, at different times, and in different situations, societal and cultural disjunctions were bridged, or kept discrete, and how the political economy and state were implicated and affected.

In this vein, mediation was relevant to three empirical situations in the early nineteenth century (chapter 2). First, some artisans, in serving as witnesses and agents in the conveyancing of small-scale property, provided a bridge among people of different status-classes. Second, mediation was an aspect of the agency of patrons who linked dearth and deference via their charitable and relief works. Finally, mediation became important as some gentry reorganized the relations of capitalist production by instituting Owenite models. Mediation during this period thus occurred in dispersed sites and via the activities of various middlemen who straddled different kinds of interstitial spaces, linking resources, people, and meanings. This variability, and the links between civil and political society which were implied, contrast with the post-1927 period when Fianna Fáil entered the Dáil. Then, a form of mediation matured which tied people, institutions, and localities to the interests and agents of the state via the actions of politicians and new ideas about entitlements. The contrast between the two moments supports the oft-cited point that mediation varies in form, function, and criticality,[11] as well as in terms of stages, tactics, and sites (chapter 20). It is therefore essential, when using the idea of mediation, to specify the particular historical and political economic context and, importantly, to define its agency in relation to the state.

At the same time, it seems plausible to suggest that there might be a direct connection between the mediation of the above two historical moments, and between the artisans/gentlemen on the one hand and the post-independence politicians on the other. Indeed, given that intermediaries also emerged in the interim period, when landlords mediated class relations via the petty sessions while farmer-guardians mediated bureaucratic directives, it even seems plausible to posit a continuity over the entire 150-year period in which early mediators (landlords, artisans) were slowly displaced by part-time, citizen functionaries (guardians) who in turn were displaced by professional politicians and bureaucrats in the post-independence period. Such seeming persistence might even imply that mediation was a cultural code. However, I do not see it as such largely because some form of mediation inevitably forms part of all complex social formations everywhere. As well, it was only after 1930 and the emergence of the idea of 'making proper representations' that local people had an explicit discursive expression for the mediating role and process. Even then, it referred to only one particular political form. In contrast, other cultural codes (for example, status-class, local parochialism, and respectability) were sited in everyday, explicit language and were broadly used and understood. Mediation is thus used as an etic concept in this ethnography.

This decision, that mere persistence of a structural form does not necessarily imply a cultural schema, is abetted by the view that a far more interesting issue than mere persistence is how continuity was actualized. For this leads into reproduction – into analyses of the material contexts and conditions which enabled ideas and roles to be replicated through time. Simply put, in Thomastown, the political economy of dearth, in its various forms, continually accompanied the reproduction of mediation over the long term. So, too, did the ubiquity of class awareness and the escalating jurisdictional claims of state agents, their bureaucracy, and their allies, such as the Catholic hierarchy. As the state, whether colonial or Irish, centralized and as dearth was reproduced alongside capitalist relations of production and ideas about a moral economy, so too did the domains covered by mediation. By 1950, people and middlemen believed that nothing was possible without mediation. Hence the frantic competition over who should have the role.

Mediation has thus been a focal albeit etic concept. It provided a way of exploring the relations between political and civil society and, thus, of looking at state formation and capitalism. This was partly because the concept allowed a focus on local productive relations while providing a way of linking these to the state. The concept of mediation then led, neatly, into the politics of class and class struggle and into the formation of awareness and experience.

The Idea of Redundancy

As mooted by Frankenberg,[12] redundancy is a way of depicting the structural density of local social relations, the overlapping of multiple local meanings, and, thus, the potential ambiguities and conflicts that inhere in local life. The idea obviates any need to apply such essentializing terms as, for example, community or subalterns, which impute a priori characteristics and homogeneity. Instead, redundancy posits problematic ties and sentiments which accrue to local places, groups, or classes, leaving relatively open-ended and indeterminate the outcome of choices and interactions. As a result, the accumulating and changing content and parameters of sentiment and common sense, the ups and downs of parochialism, and the permutations of understandings can be specified only in particular empirical contexts and moments, as products of both past and current experience. In this ethnography, the concept of redundancy fits well with the notion of contradictory consciousness, providing a means for explaining the heterogeneity of political ideologies held by people, the multiplicity of their political loyalties, and the fracturing of common political experience and consciousness.

Law as Complex and Coercive cum Educative

The law, whether legislative or administrative, and various legal agents have been ubiquitous threads throughout this ethnography. They surfaced not simply in visible ways, as in the petty sessions with its aim of educating people of all classes, but they also were central to the hegemonic process in other direct ways. The law in the inland fishery comes immediately to mind. Here, both legislative and case law were relevant; and how they became implicated in local life depended on political pressure (mediation), the decisions and sentiments of bureaucrats, and the interests of people from numerous classes. In contrast, the laws that, for example, altered franchise rights, revised local government structures, and banned inland netting were starkly experienced. Although political pressure, bureaucratic intervention, and private interests certainly helped to frame those laws and, then, came to accompany their outcomes, their initial impact was experienced as absolute and coercive. Yet, in all cases, people were educated. They learned how to use their votes, to make proper representations, and to angle as well as poach. Overall, then, the so-called law was not a singular structure or experience – features often lost in anthropological approaches that emphasize 'the imposition of the law' or 'social control.' However, it is precisely because of this complexity, indeterminacy, and location in wider political processes that the law can both educate and coerce at the same time; that it is part of both political and civil society.[13]

Constructing the Ethnography: Textual and Conceptual Strategies

The Notion of Locality

As should be clear, this ethnography is *not* a 'community study'; it is not even a study of a locality. Rather, it is an historical analysis of political processes as these were viewed from the perspective of local, everyday life. In this approach, locality, depending on the political context, was a state of mind or a sentiment, a part of common sense, a variable administrative unit for agents of state or church, a discursive device, a site, an object of agency. It was not, ever, a fixed, bounded unit with any kind of coherent culture or social matrix. What was important about locality for my purposes, then, was that it formed a point of reference from which to address the nature of political meanings and ideologies as these were grounded in social relations and material life. All this formed a single and mutually constitutive process which comprised an historical moment in European and Irish history. What was that moment?

The 1800–1950 Period

That moment, as I defined it, was a one-hundred-and-fifty-year period in the British Isles which saw, depending on one's theoretical outlook, the formation of the Victorian state, the growth of modernity, the consolidation of industrial capitalism, a stage in the world capitalist system, and, *inter alia*, the constitution of an Irish state after centuries of colonialism. Such macro-models, as per the critiques made of them, thus provide grand narratives. However, the aims of this study are far more modest: to explore the relations and ideas of the people whose actions and beliefs underlie these macro-formulations in the first instance. To do this, I viewed the 1800–1950 period in terms of the changes that occurred within persisting macro-structures comprised of capitalist relations of production and the idea of the state. The issue was how working-class life was experienced as an intrinsic and active part of the processes of reproduction.[14]

The Shifting Documentation

The 1800-1950 period certainly did see shifts in the foci and content of the documentation. Indeed, the influence of this on both macro-models and micro-ethnography should not be underestimated. In terms of the present study, early-nineteenth-century records focused on landlords and gentry – their social and political (but not economic) lives and, occasionally, the activities of others that impinged on these. Subsistence crises were therefore reported, as were outrages and combinations, but not the details of endemic poverty or everyday politics. One partial but major exception, at least as far as economic data were concerned, was Tighe's survey, published in 1802. Partly because of it, I began this study using 1800 as the base point and, apart from Tighe's material, I focused on the main and virtually only feature of labouring experience visible in the early documents, namely, paternalism and deference. By the 1830s, the records increased in number, as did their topics. Many of these, such as parliamentary papers, reports of local market prices, and valuation records, were themselves manifestations of such macro-process as the expansion of political society and, alongside, the entrenchment of private property. As a result, these records, in terms of their relevance for working people, were slanted in particular ways. Thus, as property relations and rights were extensively covered, so too were efforts to educate the propertyless to the legitimacy of such rights. Hence came coverage of the salmon fisheries, agrarian combinations, petty and quarter sessions, and relief efforts. By the late nineteenth and early twentieth centuries, ideological and electoral challenges against those who claimed such rights were being made by numerous agents and formalized into vertically integrated associations. The activities of these came to concern the record makers. After independence, the idea of the Irish state – politically, economically, and culturally – became the focus.

From a certain perspective, then, historical trajectories are simply the paths left by the documentation and, as well, by the happenstance of which records survived. Certainly in locality-based ethnography, seren-·dipity is an important consideration and every surviving scrap is a gift. For some analysts, however, both chance and the biasses of the record makers invalidate or at least taint the resulting narrative. But another view is possible. That the past enters the present is a truism for anyone with any historical sensibility. That the past – through the vagaries of surviving documents and our interpretations of it – continually guides current (re)constructions, is also inevitable. Assuming that the ethnographer, like the historian, 'interrogates the sources,' 'reads against the grain,' and contextualizes the documents, then it seems to me that it is not a bad thing that the past continues to speak in the present. Is that not our anthropological aim: to silence neither the emic nor the etic, but to represent both?

The Issue of Gender

Nevertheless, the biases in the records do leave some disturbing lacunae. In the present ethnography, women's lives and recollections were used to build up the layers in the *metissage* of daily labouring experience. In addition, women could often be seen as political objects. Their imputed character and needs were often used as discursive devices by men of all classes, including labourers, and as the targets for educational projects by agents from other classes. At the same time, the absence of women's political agency, as subjects, is most striking. In large measure, this reflects the so-called place of women in the political domain, at least after the 1880s, with the formalization of much political dissent and the introduction of universal male suffrage. It was exemplified most dramatically by the Co-operative Society in the 1940s. That a consumers' co-op was founded without the apparent involvement of women was striking indeed. It may, of course, have signalled the highly politicized nature of the endeavour; equally, it likely reflected the deep division between women's and men's worlds.

The processes of production partly militated against women's involvement in political activity or combination. They worked as casual labour during certain times of the agricultural cycle and/or as domestic labour on large farms and in the houses of gentry and large retailers. Sometimes, women carved out small entrepreneurial niches, such as taking in laundry, sewing, laying out the dead, renting a room to a lodger, making blood puddings for sale to neighbours, or, if in the peri-urban areas, raising hens or buying small items (matches, cigarettes, tea) for re-sale to people around.[15] In all these cases, the work process separated labouring women from each other either in time (seasonal work) and/or space (domestic work; home-based work).

Women were also peripheralized by expectation. The striking gender divide that has been noted for working-class England was certainly central in Thomastown. Labouring men and women simply did different things at different times: work, leisure, and gossip were rooted in single-sex peer and kin groups. They sat in different places at Mass (Case 17.1) and, until the early 1950s, women did not go into pubs. Part of this division was that men were involved in politics, women were not. Ultimately, stereotypes of labouring women in the latter nineteenth century and after, as prone to gossip and troublesome quarrels with neighbours, suggest that ideals of respectable female comportment precluded any public, political role.

Prior to 1870, I am less sure. The mention of women and children in the various agrarian combinations in mid-century is provocative. Their disappearance from the petty sessions, a likely sign of growing respectability, suggests a more prominent public and political role prior to the 1860s. This is somewhat substantiated by the fact that fisher wives and mothers remained publicly and politically visible until somewhat later. To some extent, this was associated with the intensity of the conflict in the fisheries, but it also was linked to the downward mobility of cot fishing as an occupation as the encroachment process cut into the profits to be made and the propensity of men to net. By the turn of the twentieth century, as only women of low reputation came to the petty sessions, so too had any trace of labouring women disappeared from the political domain. The extent of this invisibility is apparent from the fact that, in the early 1980s, former millworkers did not know whether the two 'bag women,' who sewed the flour bags in Grennan Mills, were members of the union. Such recollections, and the silence of the recorded material for Thomastown, suggest that any historical ethnography of women, in both the private and the public spheres, requires a different spatial sweep than that covered by this study.

Memory and Historical Construction: Accessing the Hegemonic Process
Yet locality-based research provides the potential for in-depth and highly contextualized research. It can unearth very local documentation, such as minute books from local organizations. These can then be used as triggers for peoples' memories. Such memories, of course, are not neutral. They are selective, formed by storytelling conventions, self-interest, the audience, and so on. Still, such memories, if cross-checked, can flesh out the historical documents. As well, ways of remembering can become, in themselves, data that can be used to understand the past.

In Thomastown, a good deal of political knowledge was created and stored through informal transmission and public labelling. In the early 1980s, when I asked elderly workers to look back to the politics of the 1930s, they easily recalled those who had been locally active or, even, those who had occasionally attended local meetings. Their occupations, kin, and residences were recalled, as were anecdotes about them. However, instead of saying that a person belonged to a particular organization or had particular ideas, they described him by using stereotypical labels: 'old IRA,' 'republican,' 'nationalist,' 'trade unionist,' 'lefty,' 'socialist,' 'communist.' Or it might be said that 'he was a de Valera supporter.' In addition, political agents might be assigned different labels by the same informant, depending on the context in which the names were raised. Then, if I asked what a particular label meant, informants never described ideas or viewpoints. Instead, they simply referred me to other well-known agents who fit that label. Most often, they selected those who had been active nationally and who somehow figured in Thomastown life. Oft-cited examples were James Pattison, Cathal O'Shannon, Sean O'Mahoney, and republican novelist Peadar O'Donnell. When I then pressed for information on what these men believed or spoke about, former millworkers, for example, recalled that O'Shannon, Pattison, and the parish priest had often lectured them but they could not recall the content except for the fact that the priest 'spewed anti-communist propaganda.' Finally, the great icons of the Irish left, James Connolly and Jim Larkin, were occasionally named to illustrate a label although, again, little was known about their ideas or their activities. All this meant that local men's knowledge of their labouring, political pasts varied significantly from the past as constructed by labour historians. Their memories did not include the formal organizations of the period, the factionalism within the Irish left, or the ideological differences that informed so many of the splits and labels.

We have argued elsewhere that, in Thomastown, people remembered other people and/or physical objects rather than events or ideas.[16] We argued that this was largely because nationalist agents had so completely appropriated the past and disseminated their version in schools, pulpit, and media. As a result, local history and knowledge, except for people and places actually known to informants, were overwhelmed by these national and nationalist constructions. Moreover, labour and the left were seldom included in these constructions and the narratives written by labour historians were never incorporated. The fact that Irish history and Irish labour history constitute distinct genres speaks to this separation and to the latter's isolation from the mainstream. Exceptions to this were the martyred Connolly and the flamboyant Larkin who could not be excluded from the nationalist story. They, therefore, became known to local labourers, albeit as icons rather than as intellectuals. Meanwhile, local political memories, in normal fashion, centred on people who were personally known even as the details of their ideas, affiliations, and activities were lost and their ideological views encapsulated in popular labels.

This remembering process was enhanced by the informal aspects of local life. In the summer of 1936, Gerard Doyle was twenty-four years old, with a permanent job as a clerk in a large shop in Kilkenny city to which he cycled every day. For three months that summer, he kept a diary in which he entered a few lines, in Irish, about each day. The Irish reflected his interest in Gaelic culture while the simple entries reflected much about the daily round of men's lives (Case 23.1).

Case 23.1: The Circuit of Daily Life: Learning to Label, 1936

After a line about the weather, Doyle always wrote a line or two about a bike ride or walk with a male friend or friends around the town or countryside. The friends tended to be his own age, living in the same street (Ladywell) or an adjacent one. One Sunday each month, he went to a sodality meeting. Occasionally, he and a friend visited a pub, sat in a friend's house and perhaps listened to the radio, went to a dance, or went fishing, swimming, or shooting. However, for a few hours on most evenings, especially when the days were long and the weather good, Doyle and his friends 'did the circuit': they walked along the four streets that formed a square in the town's centre. Its was a well-known, working man's pastime. Doyle often met others, such as Johnny Egan, who joined in the walk. Doyle occasionally wrote that he went to the 'church gate' for 'a sort of meeting' with Ned Maher and others who had gathered there: Tom Beck, James O'Neill, Paddy Dunphy. Thus, 'spending some time talking' and/or 'walking about the town' were daily activities for Doyle and most labouring men. That summer, too, Doyle read Peadar O'Donnell's latest novel and went to Dublin with four friends by hire car for the all-Ireland hurling final. He bought a watch and he 'stood for' (became godfather to) his neighbour's son. Gerard Doyle did not record what was discussed on the circuit or the church gate, but men in the 1980s recalled that it was local gossip, sports, and political news gleaned both from local networks and from the daily or weekly paper which many homes took in the 1930s. While the men did this daily circuit, women gathered in neighbours' kitchens for long talks and cups of tea. Through such informal interactions, working people came to know each other's news and views on a range of topics. What they also experienced through the gossip, and what they learned about others, were 'labels.' Said Mrs James O'Neill in 1981: 'My husband, Michael Tierney, and Tom Beck were labelled "communists" because of their politics. People would talk behind their backs and even be rude.' Said a labourer in 1983: 'We had a piper's band in 1933. We were asked to play at a rally in Waterford. We went and found it was for a candidate ... who was against the bishop. After that, people branded us communist and put up notices on Chapel Lane saying "down with the band." The priest mentioned it. We got no more work, and the band broke up.'

Labelling or branding was used to simplify the complex *metissage* and the redundancy of local life. In fitting also the informal quality of local learning and the casual rhythm of daily life outside the workplace, it also could be turned back on itself and used to ostracize. Both the acronymic quality and the emotional content of the labels are what enabled remembrances a half-century later. Thus, like the labels 'informer' and 'perjurer' which local people had long used as both designators and epithets, the political labels were widely disseminated, they rationalized material discriminations, and they were deeply felt by those who were so branded. What local people did not learn in all this, and therefore could not recall, were systematic interpretations and coherent political narratives of local events, ideologies, and organizations.

At the same time, written traces from the past point to the ideological sophistication of a series of local, organic intellectuals: from the Thomastown shoemaker in 1892 who urged workers to overthrow capital to, after 1922, the reported comments made by Pat Ryan and Tom Walsh, speeches given by Michael Kelly and James O'Neill, articles written by Paddy Doolan, essays composed by Gerard Doyle, and reading done by Michael Tierney. None of these men was alive at the time of field work. Those who had known them remembered them vividly as persons, but not their ideas or organizing activities. In other words, three aspects of politics and ideologies were important in Thomastown: the heroic, radical leadership of several key agents on the national political scene; local activists, because of their compelling presence; and the political sentiments that became encapsulated in commonly shared labels. This was the process, then, by which ideological domination by nationalist and theocratic agents worked itself into the redundancy and informality of local life. It was a key aspect of the hegemonic process and of the process of Irish state formation.

Chronology, Theme, and Theory

The available pieces of data, however sparse, rich or skewed, had to be connected and moulded into a coherent story and presentation in order to write this book. Choices had to be made. One was central: whether to construct the narrative as a chronology or to focus on themes. The problem, of course, was that the two were not discrete. A thematic presentation had to chronicle movement through time while a chronology, to be more than a depiction of 'one damn thing after another,' had to be built around themes that could be threaded through one hundred and fifty years. My decision was to periodize the one hundred and fifty years and to pursue, in each of the three periods, both micro-chronologies and key themes: cultural codes, exploitation and domination, labour processes, organizational dimensions, and agency. In addition, at certain points, particular empirical events became important, and some of these led into particular theoretical explorations: the nature of political action (chapters 4, 5), law (chapter 6), class formation (chapters 3, 9), redundancy (chapter 16), religion (chapter 17), and mediation (chapter 20). In all, the manuscript aims to mesh chronology, theme, and theory. Throughout, however, the tension of how best to construct an historical ethnography is apparent.[17]

Whose Voices?

A tension also was created by the need to include multiple voices, my own as well as those from Thomastown's past (through archival materials) and present (through interviews). The issue here is how historical ethnography, with its theory, themes, chronologies, and multiple voices, can be made into a text that is not rendered unreadable by dense detail; not made parochial by its failure to theorize or conceptualize; and not cast as colonial by its omission of local viewpoints. My solution was to create discrete 'cases' which contained, mainly, the voices of Thomastown people or indigenous observers. These cases thus separated much of the empirical data from the theory and segregated the native voices from much of the etic interpretations. In all, my aim was to achieve a balance: to let people talk while not allowing myself, as an anthropologist, to be overwhelmed by local interpretations. Importantly, too, I think that any analytical ethnography creates data for future writers to measure and reinterpret. Thus, to my mind, theoretical treatises have a limited shelf life in an academic world which rewards innovation, often for its own sake. At the same time, the publication of unedited data, conversations, and/or documentary evidence not only obscures the extent to which the interlocutor's presence and choices have structured the text but it also turns anthropology into local history and/or narrow ethnology which is of interest only to a very limited audience. My aim in this book, therefore, was balance. Just as I used documentary evidence to elicit conversations in the field and interviews to expand on the documents, so too in this text did I aim for an interplay of different voices and of conceptual levels.

Tensions and Questions

Other tensions that arose when constructing the present text deserve a brief mention. Should dramatic case studies be emphasized or the mundane rhythms? Which audience should the ethnography address: the local or the academic? In Thomastown, local people had clear preferences. They wanted to read about other local people and local happenings, written in plain language. They were unconcerned with theory, concepts, and discussions of how the world should be viewed. For whom should the anthropologist write?

How can different versions of the past, such as national histories and local histories, be tied together? One answer is to study the 'anthropology of history.' However, what if one is concerned with historical ethnography and not simply in 'the past as ideology'?[18] It is interesting to note, however, as anthropologists in recent years have discovered history and the past, that most of their empirical research focuses on how people in the present construct, portray, and use their past. In other words, even as we have discovered history, we turn away from historical ethnography and focus, still, on the present.

How tight should local boundaries be drawn? If materials are available from another adjacent or distant place and are, therefore by definition, not contextualized, should they be brought into the local story? In the present work, for the early decades of the nineteenth century, the dearth of data on Thomastown led me to look to the better documentation for Kilkenny city on the premise that conditions there were generally analogous. Was it correct to do so?

The Siting of 'Culture'

According to Gramsci, culture is political. The opposite, however, is not the case. Politics are not simply about culture contact or cultural contests, conflicts over words and meanings, or cultural impositions and negotiations. This point was made in my discussion of the law (chapter 6) and it bears repeating here. Thus, in lieu both of a culture-centred approach and of a mechanistic view of structure and superstructure, I have been arguing, through this ethnography, for an expanded approach to political economy in which meanings, ideologies, and beliefs, alongside material conditions, form interconnected and integral parts of awareness and experience and, hence, of political consciousness and agency. I have also argued that this political economy must place analytical categories of class and class identities at centre stage and locate them inside the structures of domination perpetrated by the state, capitalism and colonialism. In such ways, I believe that a critical and reinvigorated political anthropology can emerge.

General Processes through Time

If viewed in terms of traditional labour or Irish history, what happened in Thomastown as well as in Ireland was a defeat: the inadequacy of labour leaders in promulgating a new ideology and historical bloc, and the failure of labourers to sustain a revolutionary or radical momentum. Much of labour history in Western Europe focuses on these issues and asks 'why.' Alternatively, some labour historians focus on specifying 'labouring culture' as if, in failing to seize the state, at least workers were sufficiently innovative to create culture even though, for some, this culture contributed to failure. In the present ethnography, I have tried hard to steer away from these issues and, to do so, I have avoided two concepts common in labour history and sociology: 'labour movement' and 'collective action.' This is because these notions assume an evolutionary trajectory and impute a homogeneous coherence to the political actions of workers. Hence, the issue of failure and a focus on large groups become central. The ways in which I have tried to depict Thomastown's past are rather different. Because the so-called collective is complex and the so-called movement is heterogeneous, I have fixed on other features, namely, the resilience of capital, hierarchy, and the idea of the state; the *metissage* of common sense and the complexity of ideologies and consciousness; and the obvious conclusion that political-economic processes have no outcomes, only ongoing trajectories that can be observed and analytically constructed for particular periods of time. These processes were the subjects of this volume and Thomastown's working people were its agents.

Notes

1. Political Economy, Class, and Locality

1 Our field work began during a sabbatical in 1980–1 and has continued intermittently thereafter. Overall, we have spent a total of about four years in the
field, variously funded by the Social Science and Humanities Research Council (SSHRC), the Wenner-Gren Foundation, and York University.. The nature
of the research process is described in Silverman and Gulliver (1992);
Gulliver (1989).

2 Graham 1977:33, 38–9. Customs receipts between 1276 and 1333 show that
these two ports handled over 50 per cent of Irish external trade (Orpen
1920, iv: 276–7; Graham 1977: 40–2).

3 Tighe 1802:465.

4 Cullen 1972:100–1.

5 This period and outcome is discussed in detail in Gulliver and Silverman
(1995, chapter 4).

6 Extracted from the *Thomastown Corporation Book*, National Archives, Dublin.

7 Bric (1985:151–2); Burtchaell and Dowling (1990:268). Tithes were paid
only on tillage.

8 Thompson 1974: 395; 403 (italics mine).

9 'Emic' refers to the local, native, or indigenous view or model; 'etic' refers to
the anthropological or outsider's model.

10 Stedman-Jones 1983:7. In the present volume, I am careful to retain consistent vocabulary. For example, I use 'shopkeeper' only in an emic sense and
'retailer' in an etic one. The use of the term 'gentry' is discussed in chapter
2, n.45.

11 Iberian ethnographers, as suggested by Lipuma and Meltzoff (1989), see this

complexity as resulting from a great diversity of local emic class systems. This was not the case in Ireland.

12 Grubgeld 1993.

13 For example, recent studies of hegemony retain their 'community study' focus: hegemonic struggles are linked to faction formation within particular villages (Brow 1988; Woost 1993); 'the class-stratified community' is the object of study (Lipuma and Melztoff 1989); and the analysis of regional cultures is built out of the culture of a 'localised class' (Lomnitz-Adler 1991).

14 This argument is presented at greater length in Silverman and Gulliver (1992a).

15 A recent critique is Spencer (1997).

16 Adamson 1980:206; 10.

17 This point was noted by Lears (1985:572).

18 Hall 1986:48; 27.

19 Lears 1985:574.

20 Augelli and Murphy 1988:24.

21 Gramsci 1971:333.

22 Lears 1985:576. The appropriation and reinterpretation of cultural meanings/symbols has become a major anthropological approach to hegemony, for example, Lagos (1993); Seligmann (1993).

23 Adamson 1980:150–5; 139; 142–3.

24 For example, see Brow (1988), Comaroff (1992:29), and Woost (1993).

25 Cultural approaches to hegemony have been tellingly critiqued by Kurtz (1996). This is discussed further in Part IV, the Conclusions.

26 Adamson 1980:245.

27 Sewell 1990:52–4.

28 McClelland 1990:3.

29 Thompson 1978:150.

30 McLelland 1990; Eley 1990; Sewell 1990:57, 73.

31 Epstein 1986:202.

32 Hobsbawm 1984:191; 204–7; 27.

33 Sewell 1990:55; 59.

34 Marwick 1983:220; 221; 224.

35 Oestreicher 1988:1269–70; 1286.

36 Stedman-Jones 1983:19.

37 McLelland 1990; Sewell 1990:66.

38 For example, Kirk (1991:211).

39 Kirk 1987:47; 38–40.

40 Kirk 1987:42.

41 Kirk 1991:221. Much research focused on that key working-class organiza-

tion, the British Labour Party, and on particular localities to show why 'apparently similar communities, with similar economies, produced such very different forms of working class political action' (Lancaster 1987:xix). Such studies, however, usually saw working-class culture as bounded and internally consistent, with disagreement centring on whether this culture was class-conscious and cooperative (Hobsbawm 1984), conservative and defensive (Stedman-Jones 1983), or personalized and competitive (Johnson 1983; Kirk 1991). At the same time, the 'working class' became coterminous with the 'labour movement.' This came out of 'E.P. Thompson's conception of class in which overt manifestations of class conflict or class conscious rhetoric reflect[ed] the underlying experience inherent in class relations' (Oestreicher 1988:1266).

42 Recent examples include Allen (1997), D'Arcy and Hannigan (1988), Merrigan (1989), Nevin (1994), and O'Connor (1993). The dominance of such foci has currently given rise to a debate as to what should constitute 'Irish labour history' (Devine and O'Connor 1997).

43 In some localities, this may have been the case. Fitzpatrick (1977) found that, in western county Clare, the overlapping of 'small farmer' and 'labourer' meant that working-class identity was undeveloped. This was certainly not the case in the highly commercialized southeast.

44 Gulliver and I also began to explore empirically the seemingly silent role of labour in Irish great events in Silverman and Gulliver (1986:162–94). We also discussed it in a more theoretical way in Silverman and Gulliver (1992a).

2. Relations of Class and Thomastown's 'Lower Order' in 1800

1 Thompson 1974:403, 395.

2 This description is from Pilsworth n.d., citing Rawson's *Statistical Survey of County Kildare*.

3 Ideas of who and what was a 'farmer' varied in different parts of Ireland (for example, Birdwell-Pheasant 1992:215; n.45). Thus, classifications in particular contexts are extremely pertinent.

4 Corporate boroughs ('corporations') were towns that had received royal charters which gave them certain rights: to charge tolls, hold a court, elect members (freemen, burgesses), and send representatives to the Irish parliament. Thomastown's corporate status, dating from the thirteenth century, applied to the sixteen acres that comprised the 'townland' of Thomastown (see n.31 below). With the union of Ireland and Great Britain in 1800, its parliamentary seat was lost. In the 1830s, the corporation was reported as

barely functioning (H.C 1835, xxviii:573). The status was revoked in 1841 (see Gulliver and Silverman 1995, and Silverman 1995).

5 One pound (£) = 20s. (shillings). One shilling = 12d. (pence). One guinea = 21 shillings.

6 See Tighe 1802:475; *Finn's Leinster Journal*, 27–31 March 1802.

7 J. Robertson in Tighe 1802:474.

8 Tighe 1802:473, 475–6, 481, 482, 485, 486, 491.

9 Tighe 1802:475; and Tighe citing R. St. George (1802:487).

10 Two gentlemen observers were cited by Tighe (1802:473, 477–8, 487, 490–1).

11 R. St. George, cited by Tighe (1802:489).

12 Tighe 1802:507.

13 Tighe 1802:497.

14 The Irish Parliament, in turn, passed acts to regulate working conditions and wages and to impose 'increasingly stiff penalties' for combination (Boyle 1988:8–9).

15 *Finn's Leinster Journal*, 14–18 February 1801; 24–7 March 1802.

16 *Finn's Leinster Journal*, 31 March–3 April 1802.

17 Boyle 1988:10.

18 Pilsworth 1948:31.

19 R. St. George, cited by Tighe (1802:491).

20 Tighe 1802:516.

21 My emphasis. Tighe 1802:475, 516–37.

22 Tighe 1802:533; *Finn's Leinster Journal*, 11–14, 14–18, and 18–21 February 1801.

23 My emphasis. *Finn's Leinster Journal*, 30 September–3 October, 17–21 October 1801.

24 Tighe 1802:535.

25 *Finn's Leinster Journal*, 28–31 January, 11–14 February 1801, 21–5 August 1802.

26 Tighe 1802:532.

27 The reasons were not given (Tighe 1802:537).

28 There also were agricultural tradesmen: three gardeners, three sportsmen, a land steward, and a forester.

29 Tighe 1802:464, 456–61. 'Civil [Protestant church] parishes' were the units used at the time. The civil parishes that incorporated a large part of Thomastown Catholic parish and that contained the town as well as some hinterland were 'Thomastown' (urban), 'Columkille' (peri-urban) and 'Jerpoint Church' (rural).

30 All babies were baptized. It is fair to assume that the baptism and birth rates were the same.

31 'Townlands' were and are the basic spatial units which cover the entire island. Their origins are unknown but their boundaries are clear. They can range from a few to several thousand acres. They were/are used as a discursive, administrative, and legal means of locating people in space.

32 Tighe 1802:561.

33 Pilsworth n.d, citing Atkinson, *Irish Tourist*, 1815.

34 Some of these, cited in Curtis (1932–43, vols. 3, 4), date back to the early sixteenth century.

35 Pilsworth 1953:12.

36 A cot was a small, narrow, flat-bottomed boat made locally by carpenters. It held two men. A salmon-fishing crew comprised two cots and four men. In each cot was a paddler and a netman. The two cots travelled in tandem, with the snap net suspended between them, sweeping the river bottom. When a salmon hit the net, it was pulled in. Only one salmon was caught at a time.

37 Clarke noted that, in the seventeenth century, fishing, 'as an export activity ... was largely centred on the ports of the south coast, to such an extent ... that these were exit ports for Derry salmon' (1976:177–81).

38 Tighe 1802:150–1.

39 HC 1836, xxxi:71.

40 Tighe 1802:151, 152. Tighe complained that millers 'abuse[d] the indulgence ... of being permitted to convert the public stream to their private use.'

41 Tighe 1802:152. The closed season act was 31 George II, c.13.

42 *Index to the Statutes in Force in Ireland, 1310–1838*, 2nd ed.

43 Tighe 1802:152–3.

44 An 1806 association was called the Association for the Protection of the River Nore (*Finn's Leinster Journal*, 15–18 October 1806). Another, in 1820, according to its name, aimed to be broader-based. It was the Association for Protecting the Fishery of the Rivers of the County of Kilkenny (Kilkenny *Moderator*, 8 April 1820).

45 Historians have used the term 'gentry' in varying and often confusing ways (Gulliver and Silverman 1995:348–55). I use it here in the same way that it was used *in situ* – that is, as an emic term that included those from varying classes (for example, landlords, capitalists, professionals) who considered themselves to be, and were accepted as, 'gentlemen.' This again points to the presence of various 'languages of class' (chapters 1, 23).

Part II: Labouring Experience in the Nineteenth Century

1 John Power married the daughter of Henry Amyas Bushe and received a

baronetcy in 1836. His residence was at Kilfane, the former Bushe estate, a few miles north of Thomastown. Charles Kendal Bushe had been born in Kilmurry, the adjacent estate.

2 Brunswick clubs were local and ultra-Tory. There were nearly two hundred of them in Ireland by 1828. They were evangelical, anti-Catholic, and aristocratic in leadership but dominated by lawyers and clergy (Foster 1989:304).

3 The Insurrection Act allowed a barony to be proclaimed as disturbed and for extraordinary policing measures to be applied (for example, dusk-to-dawn curfews, punishment for oath taking, the extension of summary trial without jury, and so on).

4 Hay and Snyder 1989:12.

5 Aspects of this process are described in Gulliver and Silverman (1995) and Silverman and Gulliver (1997).

6 Doyle 1997.

3. Realizing the Working Class: Political Economy and Culture

1 The witnesses included several resident landlords and land agents, retailers, large-scale farmers, one cottier, and two local labourers. They appeared together in front of the commissioners, giving their observations in conversational format, occasionally interrupted by commissioners who wanted specific topics covered. All this was published in H.C. 1836, Appendices D, E, and F and Supplements to Appendices D, E, and F. All materials in this section are taken from these.

2 Silverman 1992.

3 This is discussed in Gulliver and Silverman (1995). See also Cullen (1972) and Halpin (1989).

4 See chapter 2, n.6.

5 Most townspeople took one or two roods/rods of conacre (4 rods = 1 acre). The rent was £6 to £8 per acre, depending on the quality of the land and whether it had been manured by the farmer.

6 Farm servants earned between £3 and £5 per year with lodging and diet. 'Most farmers keep one or two such workmen.' Their diet was milk and potatoes, twice a day.

7 At the petty sessions in 1837, forty-one labourers and artisans were fined for having a pig on the street (Kilkenny *Journal*, 10 July 1837).

8 H.C. 1836, Appendix D:21 and E:11–2.

9 Kilkenny *Journal*, 1, 8 January; 1, 12 February; 23, 27, 30 May; 1 July; 1, 22 August 1840.

10 See chapter 2, n.31.

11 It is unknown when the houses in the core streets were built. Pilsworth suggested that a lot of construction occurred about 1790 (1953:26). This corresponded with an economic boom in the town, as in Ireland generally. Pilsworth also cited 'Atkinson, writing in 1815,' who described the town as having 'for the most part ... tolerably good slated houses' (1953:28). This likely referred to the core streets. It means that most buildings there were extant by at least the late eighteenth century.

12 This was published as Griffith's *Primary Valuation*, 1849.

13 H.C. 1836, Appendix E:45.

14 These houses were not separately valued but were added in with the values of out-offices and factories. Ryan's tenement was valued at £22.5.10, Bull's at £134.0.0, and Nugent's at £52.10.0.

15 In later years, Griffith's values became a means of assessing what was a 'fair rent.'

16 H.C. 1836, Appendix E:46. The conditions in Inistioge would have been attributed to the stewardship of 'improving landlords,' the Tighe family.

17 H.C. 1836, Appendix E:46. Also H.C. 1836, Supplement to Appendix E:73,76.

18 These tenements were eighteen houses, four quarries, and two plots of land of nine and nineteen valued acres.

19 The parish population was 7,410 in 1841, 4,340 in 1861, and 3,440 in 1881. The town's population was 2,335 in 1841 and 1,202 by 1871.

20 I used eight townlands (c. 3,000 acres) which together comprise the 'civil parishes' or census units of Ballylinch, Jerpointabbey, and Pleberstown. They do not abut the town. In 1861 they had 532 people, or 56 per cent of their 1841 number. It was a decline greater than in the town.

21 The difference was removed by 1911 when over 70 per cent of housing in both town and country was of second-class quality. See also Gulliver and Silverman (1995:178).

22 Lewis 1837. A Thomastown informant, whose great-grandfather attended one of the private schools, stated that these schools persisted only until the late 1840s.

23 H.C. 1862 lx. Data were not given for units smaller than counties.

24 Grennan Mill Books, 1873–86. Private collection, Thomastown.

25 The Thomastown Poor Law Union was the reporting unit for all censuses (population, agriculture) after 1850.

26 Agricultural Censuses 1852, 1874. Publication of these data began in 1847. The year 1874 was the last in which livestock cum size of holding was published.

27 Thomastown Union Admission Books, Kilkenny County Library.

28 In 1868, for example, the guardians substituted skim milk and cocoa for the evening soup. The Local Government Board inspector forbade this (Silverman and Gulliver 1986:235).

29 In 1873 the soup was made from two ox-heads per 100 inmates, plus turnips or split peas. The inspector called for improvements and onions were added (Silverman and Gulliver 1986: 235).

30 The proportion of pasture was likely higher: the 1884 census put 'meadow and clover' under 'crops.' Of the cattle in Thomastown Union in 1854, 45 per cent were dairy, 55 per cent were beef. By 1884, herd sizes had increased but dairy cattle were only 28 per cent of the total. Sheep numbers doubled between 1850 and 1854 and remained high (Agricultural Censuses 1850, 1851, 1854, 1884).

31 Cullen 1972:143; Kilkenny *Moderator*, 10 May 1848.

32 H.C. 1836, Appendix E:46.

33 H.C. 1836, Appendix D:21–2.

34 The availability of household returns for the 1901 census permit detailed observations. In that year, 60 per cent of parish rural dwellers had agricultural pursuits; in the town, less than 5 per cent per cent.

35 Silverman 1990:92–3; Silverman and Gulliver 1986:60

36 DEDs were purely administrative units created by aggregating a group of townlands. The DED was the area of charge for levying local rates; voters from each DED elected two representatives to the Board of Guardians, and groups of DEDs were combined to create Thomastown Union and parliamentary constituencies. Thomastown and Jerpoint DEDs contained the town and twenty-six townlands (*c.* 9,500 acres). The 1901 census was the first, after 1861, to give house types for small units. It is therefore used here.

37 For comparable studies of local kinship in rural Ireland, see Smyth (1983) and Vincent (1984).

38 This was not simply an aberration of the period. Similar patterns were apparent one hundred years later. See Silverman and Gulliver (1990).

39 In the controversy over the relevance of Malthusian analyses to Ireland, Mokyr argued that the Irish did not marry young, as compared with people elsewhere in Europe. He dismissed contemporary accounts as 'based more on myth and prejudice than on facts' (1983:36–7). Yet these accounts are important: they formed part of common sense which, in turn, affected how people acted in numerous contexts.

40 H.C. 1836, Appendix F:47.

41 Ibid., 10.

42 Ibid., 10, 11. Said by Father Doyle and farmer O'Keefe.

43 The 1845–9 famine in Thomastown is described in Silverman and Gulliver (1997).

44 H.C. 1836, Appendix D:22.

45 H.C. 1845, xxi.

46 H.C. 1836 Appendix D:22; F:46.

47 H.C. 1836, Appendix F:47–8; D:22.

48 Kilkenny *Moderator*, 28 March 1868.

49 Ibid., 30 May, 7 July, 20 October 1866; 19 October 1867; 29 May, 15 December 1869; 15 June 1871; 15 June 1872; 2 December 1874; 27 February, 16 June 1875; 21 July, 1 August 1877. Kilkenny *Journal*, 8 August 1846, June 1866, 30 May 1877, 21 July 1877, 23 February 1884.

50 Kilkenny *Moderator*, 22 November 1856.

51 Ibid., 9 March 1861.

52 Ibid., 8 January, 1868.

53 Kilkenny *Journal*, 31 December 1879.

4. Political Domains and Working Combinations after 1815

1 Migliaro and Misuraca 1982:74.

2 This summary is taken from Boyle 1988:1–36.

3 H.C. 1836, Supplement to Appendix E:73, 76.

4 See n.2 above.

5 Kilkenny *Moderator*, 3, 10 May 1828.

6 Ibid., 9 October 1833, citing the Clonmel Advertiser. See Boyle 1988:36–7. In the early 1830s, Daniel O'Connell linked his Repeal movement to trade unionism in an effort to gain mass support. By 1837, he had recanted and refused to ally with English Chartists (1838). In major Irish cities, however, trades societies continued agitating (Boyle 1988:41–4, 54).

7 Kilkenny *Journal*, 12 April 1834, 15 November 1837 (from the Waterford *Chronicle*).

8 Ibid., 12 April 1834.

9 H.C. 1825[20] vii; H.C. 1825 [200] vii. Baronies were territorial, administrative, and policing units which came into common usage after 1649. Baronies were comprised of townlands; several baronies comprised a county. See Map 1.

10 H.C. 1825 [200] vii:148, 103, 108.

11 Kilkenny *Moderator*, 26 January 1833, 2 February 1833.

12 Ibid., 8, 11, 15, 18 August 1832. Italics mine. The 'Tithe War' was a time of violent and non-violent protest by tillage farmers against paying tithes to the Protestant church, with the focus of anger being tithe-process servers, large-

scale farmers, and middlemen. The war lasted until 1838 although, in the Thomastown area, action had abated by early 1834.

13 Ibid., 14 August 1858.

14 Ibid., 11 August 1858. Italics mine.

15 The resident magistrate (RM) was usually a solicitor appointed by the state to advise local magistrates (landlords) at the petty and quarter Sessions. His interests were presumed to be professional and legal, not local and landed.

16 Kilkenny *Moderator,* 11, 14 August, 15 September 1858.

17 Italics mine. The Kilkenny *Journal* agreed that the 'natives must have mustered also with considerable strength' (14 August 1858).

18 Kilkenny *Moderator,* from the *Dublin Evening Mail,* 21 August 1858.

19 Ibid., 14, 25 August 1858.

20 Kilkenny *Journal,* 14 August 1858.

21 Kilkenny *Moderator,* citing the Dublin *Evening Post,* 18 August 1858.

22 Kilkenny *Journal,* 14, 18, 28 August 1858.

23 Letter to ibid., 18 August 1858, from the Reverend C.B. Stevenson, rector, Callan.

24 Hoppen 1984:399–400.

25 Hoppen argued that this was the result of sectarianism and rural unrest (1983:388–99, 420).

26 Lord James Butler (Tory) received 500 votes. The Hon. Agar Ellis (Whig), polled 350. Shee received 2,622 and Greene 2,537 (Kilkenny *Moderator,* 28 July 1852). Shee supported 'a Tenants' Rights Bill, religious education, [the contradictory position of] low food prices cum tariffs on foreign corn, and an extended franchise.' Greene supported universal suffrage. Tenant farmers who had the vote supported an Irish party with its promise to work on tenants' rights (Kilkenny *Journal,* 7 April 1852; Kilkenny *Moderator,* 28 July 1852).

27 Kilkenny *Moderator,* 28, 31 July, 4 August 1852. Italics mine.

28 Kilkenny *Journal,* 14 August 1852.

29 Kilkenny *Moderator,* 3, 21 September 1870, 15 October 1870; Kilkenny *Journal,* 15 October 1870. Two of the twelve defendants could not be traced in local records. Italics mine.

30 Kilkenny *Moderator,* 30 September 1865; Kilkenny *Journal,* 30 September, 28 October 1865, 3 February 1866.

31 Kilkenny *Journal,* 28 May, 1853.

32 Kilkenny *Moderator,* 3 April 1867.

33 Ibid., 19 November 1853.

34 Ibid., 6 February, 1869.

35 Ibid., 5 November 1873.

36 Ibid., 28 May 1858; 5 December 1863; 22 May 1869.
37 Kilkenny *Journal*, 6 January 1864.
38 Ibid., 3 February 1881.
39 Kilkenny *Moderator*, 11 June 1862.
40 Kilkenny *Journal*, 15 July 1853.
41 Ibid., 5 August 1863.
42 Ibid., 18 September 1867.
43 Wolf 1982:360.
44 Kilkenny *Moderator* and Kilkenny *Journal*, 30 June, 3 July 1830.
45 Ibid., 6 August 1851.
46 Ibid., 18 August 1832.

5. The Political Domain: Labour as Device, Resource, and Project

 1 Kilkenny *Moderator*, 19 March 1816; Kilkenny *Journal*, 19 November 1831 (citing the Waterford *Chronicle*); Kilkenny *Journal*, 23 May 1838, 10 August 1839; Kilkenny *Moderator*, 25 November 1840.
 2 It was also argued that the able-bodied should work and that local gentry were able to deal with local poverty (Kilkenny *Moderator*, 11 February 1843). See also Vincent (1992).
 3 Kilkenny *Journal*, 17 February, 10 March 1841. This is discussed in more detail in Silverman (1992b; 1995). The case also forms part of disputed fishing rights discussed here and in chapter 7.
 4 Kilkenny *Journal*, 26 March 1846.
 5 Ibid., 21 November 1857. The writer and locale were not given.
 6 Kilkenny *Moderator*, 20 October 1869.
 7 Kilkenny *Journal*, 1, 5 January 1831.
 8 Ibid., 26 July 1882.
 9 Kilkenny *Moderator*, 12 August 1854.
10 Kilkenny *Journal*, 13 October 1866.
11 Ibid., 24 December 1859; 5 May 1860.
12 Ibid., 30 August 1882.
13 Kilkenny *Moderator*, 12 September 1860; Kilkenny *Journal*, 12 February 1859.
14 Ibid., August 18, 1841.
15 Ibid., 20 July 1870.
16 Ibid., 5 September 1849; 20 October 1866.
17 Kilkenny *Journal*, 9 September 1837.
18 Kilkenny *Moderator*, 30 October 1830 and 11 June 1831.
19 Kilkenny *Journal*, 25 October 1837.
20 Ibid., 6 May 1846. Letter dated 16 June 1846, Famine Papers, State Paper

Office. Sir John donated £28; other landlords gave £10–20, and clergy £10–15. Mill owners donated £10; other notables subscribed £5 and retailers £1. The local branches of the Turnpike Trust, the Loan Fund, and the Tipperary Bank gave £50, £12 and £10 respectively.

21 Letter, 7 December 1846; deposition from John Hutchinson, 24 December 1846; memorial to the lord lieutenant, 1 January 1848. Outrage Papers, State Paper Office, Dublin.
22 Kilkenny *Moderator*, 12 May 1847, 30 June 1849. See also Silverman and Gulliver (1997).
23 Kilkenny *Journal*, 11 February, 1880.
24 Ibid., 3 March 1880.
25 Ibid., 9 January 1864, Kilkenny *Moderator*, 30 January 1867, 2 August 1880.
26 Kilkenny *Moderator*, 28 November 1868.
27 Kilkenny *Journal*, 16 January 1867; *Kilkenny Moderator*, 6 November 1872. See also Gulliver and Silverman (1995).
28 Kilkenny *Journal*, 4 January 1862; *Kilkenny Moderator*, 8 January 1879, 13 March 1880.
29 Evidence from Simon Blackmore (land agent), Sydenham Davis (landlord), Father Cody (parish priest), and Father Ryan (Catholic curate) (H.C. 1836, Appendix D:22, 86, 98).
30 Kilkenny *Moderator*, 30 November 1839.
31 IUP 1843, xxviii:29. No report was issued from Thomastown.
32 Kilkenny *Moderator*, 26 August 1865.
33 Ibid., 10 February 1875; 6 January 1876.
34 Kilkenny *Journal*, 2 January 1864.
35 Kilkenny *Moderator*, 24 February, 31 March, 28 April 1883.
36 Ibid., 18 September 1876.
37 Ibid., 17 March 1838.

6. Custom and Respectability: The Petty Sessions

1 Emphasis mine. H.C 1836, Appendix F:47.
2 Cain 1983:101.
3 Gramsci argued that the overlap of the civil and political was contextual. 'Institutions which supported the state's claim to monopolize the means of violence' formed part of political society. Those which 'organized consent through some combination of cultural, spiritual and intellectual means' formed part of civil society. Church, media, or political parties could be part of either, depending on time and place (Adamson 1980:219–20).
4 Gramsci 1971:246–7; emphasis mine.

5 Conversely, the role of the law is often omitted from studies of hegemony, reflecting either a Marxist assumption that the law, as part of the coercive apparatus of the state, requires no exploration (Vincent 1990:423) or a cultural approach that marginalizes material relations.

6 Hirsch and Lazarus-Black 1994:10–11; Lazarus-Black 1989:11; Merry 1994:36, 53; Hirsch 1994:208.

7 Yngvesson 1993:6; 1994:148; Merry 1994:54.

8 Hirsch and Lazarus-Black 1994:9,13; Yngvesson 1993.

9 Vincent has noted that when manufacturing consent is presumed to be the main activity of the state, the concept of power is so deconstructed as to make 'domination by coercion and legitimized force virtually disappear from the hegemonic equation' (1994:120). This cultural approach has also been critiqued for conflating the law with the capitalist state and ignoring different kinds of law (statutory law, administrative directives, codes of practices) (Vincent 1994: 120). Moreover, it totalizes the law by treating it as 'a single, coherent ... interpretative perspective' when, in fact, diverse ideological views are enmeshed in law (Philips 1994:61).

10 Philips 1994:65.

11 My aim is also to refute the idea that law is an 'imposition' which engenders 'resistance' because this cannot capture the complexity of hegemonic processes. See critiques by Comaroff and Comaroff (1992:260), Hall (1981), and Smith (1991). The idea that the law and courts are mechanisms of 'social control' is also fraught with difficulty. Conflict theorists have argued that this masks why compliance occurs (utilitarian, coercive, normative reasons) and the role of differential power, manipulation, and negotiation (Comaroff and Roberts 1981; Coser 1982). Others have argued that social control implies an ideal order which is incompatible with the fact of endemic class conflict (Stedman-Jones 1983). For a general critique in British social history, see Thompson (1981).

12 Cain 1983:101. Gramsci's view of the law was developed as part of his analysis of revolution. Cain argued that 'presumably the same analysis could be applied to law in the bourgeois state.'

13 Nun and Walsh 1844:45, 1–3.

14 Palmer 1988:106–16.

15 A series of Insurrection Acts were passed between 1796 and 1835 to deal with perceived law-and-order problems in Ireland (Connolly 1989). These acts allowed, *inter alia*, a greater use of summary trial without jury, curfews, and more severe penalties (Hay and Snyder 1989:12).

16 Hay and Snyder 1989:12–13.

17 Palmer 1988:245–6.

18 Nun and Walsh 1844:77–8, 81, 83. Although magistrates could still act privately if they were investigating complaints rather than acting judicially, even this was no longer encouraged.

19 Indictable complaints (homicide, fraud, serious assault, or larceny) were sent for jury trial to the quarter sessions in Thomastown or to the assizes in Kilkenny city.

20 Official court records have not survived. My use of the newspaper accounts is thus an example of 'opportunistic sampling' (Honigman 1982:83) in the archives. Such problems in 'doing history' are discussed in Silverman and Gulliver (1992a) and Gulliver (1989).

21 Two complaints against labourers were also brought by the railway company and two by professionals. Farmers comprised 17 per cent (43 cases) of the defendants in the 253 cases and 7 per cent of the complainants (17 cases). The lack of landlord complaints against farmers is because 'ejectment notices' for non-payment of rents, a key issue, were taken to the quarter sessions. Apart from plainting against each other, farmers mainly complained about labourers (eight cases) for deserting service, cutting furze, stealing turnips. Retailers defended in twenty-one cases, a result mainly of complaints from the inspectors of weights and measures (twelve cases). Only three reports saw retailers bringing complaints: two of these were against labourers.

22 Because artisans increasingly moved into the labouring class during the nineteenth century (see chapter 3), I use the term 'labourer' to cover both status-classes.

23 Complaints against farmers were for assault (n = 15), wages (n = 3), collision with a cart (n = 1), poisoning a dog (n = 1), and breaking windows (n = 1). The other seven of the twenty-two cases brought by workers against those in other classes were: one versus a landlord (obstructing fishing), one versus a constable (assault), two versus water bailiffs (presenting a revolver), and three versus retailers (abusive language, manipulating a shop account, theft). The last two against retailers are described below.

24 I take the notion of theatre from Thompson (1974:396; 1978:145) et al. (e.g., Hay 1975). Legal anthropologists have also used the term as well as 'forum' (e.g., Hirsch 1994:208) and 'arena' (e.g., Grossberg 1994:153). However, the terms have not been used in analytical ways.

25 This concept is from Goffman (1962).

26 Kilkenny *Journal,* 3 June 1863. Both the board's minutes and the newspapers reported on workhouse incidents, but only the latter described the petty sessions cases which ensued.

27 The board brought complaints against defaulting ratepayers and against

contractors who failed to deliver goods or services. These incidents were very seldom described as being of public interest.

28 Kilkenny *Moderator*, 10 May, 10 June 1865.

29 Ibid., 7 November 1863.

30 Ibid., 15 June 1859, 7 March 1877, 9 April 1881.

31 Other cases brought by landlords/gentry were against fishers for 'threatening and abusive language' and for trespass. Two of the landlord cases are described as Case 6.2.

32 Kilkenny *Moderator*, 17 March 1849, 15 July 1863.

33 Ibid., 11 February 1865.

34 Ibid., 6 October 1876; 20 October 1877.

35 In only six of the eighty-five cases were workers charged with assaulting/intimidating non-labourers.

36 Kilkenny *Moderator*, 10 October 1863.

37 Ibid., 10 February 1866, 9 June 1877, 7 March 1883.

38 Ibid., 1, 8 September, 6 October 1866.

39 Doran was fined 2s.6d. and costs or a week in jail (Kilkenny *Moderator*, 6 November 1858).

40 The court found against Costigan. She had to find £10 bail and two £5 sureties or serve 14 days in jail (Kilkenny *Moderator*, 5 August 1882).

41 In only one reported case did affines (sisters-in-law) charge each other.

42 Kilkenny *Moderator*, 20 January 1866, 11 November 1876, 9 June 1877, Kilkenny *Journal*, 2 May 1883.

43 Emphasis mine. Kilkenny *Moderator*, 10 April 1869.

44 Ibid., 15 July 1863.

45 Ibid., 18 January 1873.

46 Ibid., 8 June 1878.

47 Ibid., 16 August 1851.

48 Kilkenny *Journal*, 7 April 1880, Kilkenny *Moderator*, 7 November 1883.

7. Privatizing the River: Politicizing Labouring Fishers

1 Tighe 1802:149–50.

2 Acts protected salmon fry (17 and 18 George III.c.19; 10 Charles I.sess.3, c.14; 12 George I.c.7) and defined a closed time. Under 28 Henry VIII.c.22, the sheriff could level weirs which impeded navigation while 5 Geo II.c.11 prevented their reconstruction (Tighe 1802:152–3).

3 IUP 1849 [536] xiii:555–6; IUP 1837 [82] xxii:558.

4 Kilkenny *Moderator*, 31 May 1828; 6, 13 September 1828; 27 June 1829; 31 July 1830; 19 January 1831.

5 Kilkenny *Moderator*, 8 October 1828; 14 March, 27 June 1829; 16 October 1830.

6 IUP 1849 [536] xiii:553, 555, 578; IUP 1837 [82] xxii:548, 558.

7 Kilkenny *Moderator*, 6 September 1837. The *Moderator* reported similar actions on 14 June 1837 and 20 July 1839. The *Journal* (25 June 1834) reported that 3,000 people levelled all the Scotch weirs between New Ross and Carrick-on-Suir on the rivers Nore and Suir.

8 Kilkenny *Journal*, 19 March, 12 July 1834. IUP 1837 [82] xxii:555.

9 Kilkenny *Moderator*, 25 February 1835; Kilkenny *Journal*, 28 February 1835. Those charged were the Earl of Carrick, Sydenham Davis, Edward Hunt, Anthony Nugent, and William F. Tighe. A weir could violate the law in several ways. Its charter could be doubtful; its gap for allowing salmon to pass could be too small, blocked, or badly placed; it could extend too far into the river; and /or abutments could be built on for attaching illegal nets.

10 Kilkenny *Journal*, 9 September 1838; Kilkenny *Moderator*, 18 January, 29 April 1840; 4 August 1841; 26 March, 1842; 13 April 1842.

11 IUP 1849 [536] xiii:549.

12 IUP 1837 [82] xxii:548.

13 IUP 1837 [82] xxii:490. Tidal catches were larger, the fisheries were closer to English markets, and salt-water salmon, seen as of superior quality, fetched a higher price.

14 4 Bur 2162. Cited in *Murphy* v. *Ryan*, *The Irish Reports (Common Law Series)* 1867.

15 IUP 1843 [224] xxviii: 21.

16 Kilkenny *Moderator*, 15, 26 October 1842; IUP 1843 [224] xxviii:21.

17 IUP 1837 [82] xii: 561; 1849 [536] xiii:271–2, 547; 1844 [502] xxx:37.

18 IUP 1843 [224] xxviii:21; 1844 [502] xxx:36, 37–8; 1845 [320] xxvi:217, 219; 1849 [536] xiii:177–9.

19 IUP 1844 [502] xxx:36; 1846 [713] xxii:255–7.

20 IUP 1846 [713] xxii:244–5.

21 IUP 1845 [320] xxvi:211–13; 1846 [713] xxii: 186.

22 IUP 1847–8 [983] xxxvii:240, 243; 1849 [1098] xxiii:494. In Thomastown between 1846 and 1851, only one charge was reported as laid (Kilkenny *Moderator*, 30 September 1846).

23 IUP 1846 [713] xxii:199; 1849 [1098] xxiii:493, 485, 496–7, 713.

24 IUP 1851 [1414] xxv:71, 239, 240, 72; 1854 [1819] xx:179, 167.

25 IUP 1856 [2021] xix:39; Kilkenny *Moderator*, 10 February 1849, 13 February 1850.

26 Kilkenny *Moderator*, 20 April 1853.

27 IUP 1857 [2272, sess. 2] xviii:28; 1860 [2727] xxxiv:671.

28 IUP 1861 [2862] xxiii:31, 34.
29 IUP 1864 [3256] xxxi:33–4, 45. All legal fixed nets and inland weirs had their dimensions recorded. They could not be altered nor new ones built (IUP 1865 [3420] xxviii:433–6).
30 Kilkenny *Moderator*, 9 February 1861.
31 In 1857 four cases were reported in the Thomastown area. In each of 1858 and 1859, two were reported. In 1860 there were none; in 1861, one; and in 1862, none.
32 IUP 1866 [3608] xxviii:370–1.
33 Kilkenny *Moderator*, 7 April 1855, 14 May 1856.
34 Ibid., 8 March 1845, 15 November 1856, 15 July 1863.
35 Ibid., 24 April 1844, 14 February 1857.
36 Such detailed analysis results from collating numerous local archival sources.
37 Kilkenny *Moderator*, 10 September 1859, 8 December 1860, 6 April, 1861.
38 Ibid., 9 May 1863.
39 IUP 1854 [1819] xx:193; 1866 [3608] xxviii: 392.
40 Salmon hide from daylight in deep, inaccessible pools. They also can see and avoid a net.
41 Kilkenny *Moderator*, 24, 28 October 1863.
42 Ibid., 5 March 1864.
43 Ibid., 6 April 1864, 6 May 1865, 12 August 1865, 19 July 1865. Kilkenny *Journal*, 11 August 1866.
44 IUP 1866 [3608] xxvii:394; 1867 [3826] xviii:33; 1867–8 [4056] xix:653; Kilkenny *Moderator*, 24 March 1866.
45 Court of Common Pleas, *The Irish Reports (Common Law Series)* 1867:143–55.
46 Kilkenny *Moderator*, 11 April, 6 June, 21 October 1868, 7 July, 6 August 1870; Kilkenny *Journal*, 8 February 1868, 30 June 1869, 8 October 1870.
47 Kilkenny *Journal*, 14 January 1871.
48 Kilkenny *Moderator*, 10 April 1869.
49 Ibid., 11 March 1871, 15 May 1872.
50 Ibid., 11 March 1871.
51 Ibid., 27 October 1869.
52 Ibid., 9 May, 6 June 1868; 5 October 1872; 18 January 1873; 8, 26 March 1873; Kilkenny *Journal*, 8 June, 7 December 1872.
53 Kilkenny *Moderator*, 28 February, 25 March 1874. Salmon fetched about 1s. a pound.
54 Ibid., 12 March 1875; IUP 1873 [c.758] xix:644; 1874 [c.980] xii:601; 1876 [c.1467] xvi:582; 1877 [c.1703] xxiv:391.
55 IUP 1870 [c.225] xiv; Kilkenny *Moderator*, 27 October 1869.

56 IUP 1866 [3608] xxvii:374–5; IUP 1867 [3826] xviii:41.
57 Kilkenny *Moderator,* 21 April, 15 May 1875.
58 Ibid., 17, 31 March, 21, 28 April, 19 May, 9 June, 21, 28 July, 11, 18 August 1875.
59 Ibid., 13 July 1876.
60 Ibid., 22 July, 22 November 1876; 7 March, 21 April 1877.
61 Ibid., 9 June 1877.
62 Ibid., 10 November 1877.
63 Ibid., 8 June, 17 July 1878; 10 May 1879; 6 September 1879; Kilkenny *Journal,* 3 July 1878; 12 July, 6 September, 8 October 1879; 7 April 1880.
64 Kilkenny *Moderator,* 6 March 1880.
65 Ibid., 6 March, 1 December 1880; Kilkenny *Journal,* 11 February, 29 May 1880.
66 IUP 1881 [c.2871] xxiii:431.
67 For example, in one appeal, cotmen argued that the penalty should not have included the forfeiture of fishing gear. The conviction was quashed (Kilkenny *Journal,* 25 June 1881).
68 Kilkenny *Moderator,* 5 September 1883, 3 May 1882, 10 May 1884.
69 *Reg.* [*Morrissey*] v. *Justices of Kilkenny, Law Reports (Ireland),* vol.14, 1884:349–52.
70 Kilkenny *Moderator,* 10 May 1884.

8. Political Sentiment and the Inland Fisheries

1 IUP 1887 [c.5035] xxi:165; 1886 [c.4809] xv:113.
2 IUP 1884–5 [271] xi:107–9, 99, 56, 137.
3 See chapter 7, p.159.
4 IUP 1884–5 [271] xi:69, 84, 115, 133, 71.
5 IUP 1884–5 [271] xi:53, 103, 51, 88, 89, 90.
6 IUP 1887 [c.5035] xxi:165; 1897 [c.8628] xviii:299.
7 IUP 1894 [c.7404] xxii:265.
8 IUP 1884 [c.4109] xviii:505.
9 IUP 1895 [c.7793] xx:269; 1896 [c.8250] xx:309.
10 Kilkenny *Journal,* 3 November 1888.
11 IUP 1892 [236 Sess. 1] xvii:1, paragraphs 1062, 1142–4, 1392–7, 1399, 1405, 1412, 1415, 1480–1, 7048–61, 7214, 7344–53, 7360.
12 Kilkenny *Journal,* 18 October 1894; Kilkenny *Moderator,* 13 January 1894.
13 Emphasis mine. Kilkenny *Journal,* 18 October 1893.
14 Ibid., 9 March 1895, 8 August 1896; Kilkenny *Moderator,* 12 September 1891, 9 March 1895.

15 Kilkenny *Journal*, 6 August 1898.

16 Kilkenny *Moderator*, 8 June 1895.

17 Ibid., 8 June, 10 August 1895.

18 At the head of the tidal waters in Inistioge, the Tighe estate worked a large, legal draft net.

19 Pender, a cotman from the Barrow, also netted on the Nore (IUP 1901 [Cd.450] xii.539: paragraphs 9084–91; 9106–17; 2185; 9134–59).

20 Kilkenny *Journal*, 6 August 1898.

21 Kilkenny *Moderator*, 5 June 1897.

22 Kilkenny *Journal*, 11 June 1898.

23 IUP 1901 [Cd.450] xii: paragraphs 2188–91, 5702–7. Pilsworth family letters, 1899–1900.

24 A commission of inquiry into the salmon fishery was held in 1891 because of 'an extensively signed memorial presented to the Irish Fisheries Board, Dublin Castle, by a number of persons living in the county and by the members of the Upper and Lower Nore Angling Club' (Kilkenny *Journal*, 29 July 1891). The outcome was minimal. The Waterford board ignored complaints about the 'big net' and the need to protect spawning grounds. It did pass a by-law prohibiting inland cot fishers from keeping nets in their cots during the nightly and weekly closed time (IUP 1892 [c.6682] xxi:307).

9. Social Organization and the Politics of Labour

1 There were no Clooneys, Culletons, or Currans in the wage books for the 1873–86 period.

2 These cotmen are known from the petty sessions, parochial records, and / or 1901 census.

3 This is discussed in greater detail in Gulliver and Silverman (1990).

4 Parish records are the sole source of systematic genealogical data prior to the introduction of the civil register in 1864. In these, however, only the bride's address was given. It is only after 1864, with the addresses of both partners recorded, that it is possible to trace the spatial patterns of marriage choices. One problem remains. Sometimes one or both of the marrying pair gave an address simply as 'Thomastown.' This could mean 'town' or parish. Such cases were eliminated and, in part, this accounts for the fairly small number of cases even after 1864.

5 For example, Hoppen (1984) and Mitchell (1974).

6 Kilkenny *Moderator*, 28 February, 28, 31 October 1885.

7 'If some labourers and semiskilled unions antedated 1889 ... the agitation of

that year helped to throw up a number of others between 1889 and 1891'
(Boyle 1988:105).

8 Boyle 1983:326.

9 Kilkenny *Journal*, 28 February 1891; Kilkenny *Moderator*, 7 March 1891. The
Thomastown Band had been a working men's organization and a way of
expressing nationalist sentiment (Silverman and Gulliver 1986:159–62).

10 Boyle 1988:107.

11 Kilkenny *Journal*, 4 June, 14 December 1890. Mitchell (1977) and Boyle
(1988) discuss why labour did not form a party in these early years. They also
describe some of the various political ideas and organizations which were
current at the time.

12 Boyle 1988:125. In Thomastown, the next report of a formal labour organization was in 1908.

13 Kilkenny *Journal*, 31 March 1897.

14 Chubb 1970:276. This was the Local Government (Ireland) Act, 1898 (61
and 62 Vict. c.37).

15 Boyle 1988:164,165; Mitchell 1974:19.

16 Ryan, the son of a local currier, was apprenticed to a victualler in England
but returned to open a shop in Market Street. Ryan, like Pender, spoke in
favour of the cotmen's association (Case 8.7) at the 1899 inquiry (IUP 1901
[Cd.450], xii). Ryan later became a Sinn Fein stalwart.

17 Kilkenny *Moderator*, 8 April 1899.

18 Pilsworth was elected with forty votes, Connellan received six.

19 Kilkenny *Moderator*, 19 April 1899.

20 H.C. 1887, lxviii, v.202; H.C. 1888, cxxxiii, v.83.; H.C. 1903, lvii, v.198.

21 Kilkenny *Moderator*, 27 October 1883.

22 Ibid., 23 November 1887.

23 Ibid., 6 March 1884.

24 Ibid., 7 November 1885.

25 Ibid., 3 September 1884, 3 December 1887, 30 March 1895.

26 Ibid., 17 December 1887.

27 Ibid., 21 August 1895.

10. The Organizational Impetus: Class and Nationalism before the War, 1906–14

1 Kilkenny *Journal*, 22 February, 14, 19 and 21 March 1908; Minutes, Thomastown Rural District Council, 19 March 1908.

2 See Gulliver and Silverman (1995:309–11); Kilkenny *Journal*, 13 May, 23 September 1911.

3 Kilkenny *Moderator*,1 May 1907. O'Mahoney (1872–1934) did not remain in

Thomastown. He became a Sinn Fein activist and was elected MP for South Fermanagh in 1918. See Doyle (1996).

4 O'Mara won the seat (Kilkenny *Journal,* 24 November 1906, 5 January 1907; Kilkenny *Moderator,* 15 December 1906; 2 February, 24 August, 28 September 1907; Kilkenny *People,* 5 January 1907.

5 O'Connor 1992:34.

6 Other officers were John Murphy and J. Whelan (tannery workers) and J. Kelly (carpenter). (Kilkenny *Moderator,* 22 February 1908, *Kilkenny People,* 7 March 1908.)

7 Kilkenny *Journal,* 18 March, 23 May 1908.

8 Kilkenny *Moderator,* 9 January 1909.

9 Ibid., 12 June 1909.

10 Ibid., 22 October 1909; Kilkenny *Journal,* 23 October 1909, 2 April 1910.

11 Kilkenny *Journal,* 2 April 1910.

12 Kilkenny *Moderator* 17 June 1911.

13 Kilkenny *Journal,* 14 June 1911.

14 Kilkenny *Moderator,* 29 April 1911; Kilkenny *Journal,* 13, 20, 27 May, 3 June 1911. Elderly people said that Ryan was the first retailer to have his name in Gaelic above his shop and the only person to hang out a black flag when the Princess of Wales visited in 1910.

15 Kilkenny *Journal,* 14 June 1911.

16 Ibid., 12 August 1911.

17 Kilkenny *People,* 12 August, 9 September 1911.

18 The 1910 auditor's report showed £73 in the bank; the 1914 report showed £99. Kilkenny *Journal,* 2 April 1910; Kilkenny *Moderator,* 14 March 1914.

19 The benefit scheme paid burial costs for a member and his spouse (Kilkenny *Moderator,* 16 October 1909).

20 Kilkenny *Journal,* 13 September 1913. The paper's owner was chair of the tram company.

21 Kilkenny *People,* 3 April 1909; Kilkenny *Moderator,* 20 February 1909.

22 Kilkenny *Moderator,* 11 July 1908, 28 April 1909; Kilkenny *Journal,* 28 April, 12 June 1909.

23 Kilkenny *Journal,* 9 February 1910.

24 Lindsay received 428 votes to his opponent's 264 (Kilkenny *People,* 2 May, 13 June 1914; Kilkenny *Journal,* 13 June 1914).

25 Kilkenny *Moderator,* 13 June 1914, Kilkenny *People,* 4, 11,14 July 1914; 21 November 1914; Kilkenny *Journal,* 31 January, 27 June, 11 July 1914.

26 Kilkenny *Journal,* 26 September 1914.

27 The contrast with mining towns in Wales, for example, is called to mind here.

28 Kilkenny *People*, 31 January 1914.

11. From Class to Nation: National Chronology and Local Experience, 1914–23

1 Kilkenny *Journal*, 19 September, 31 October 1914; Kilkenny *Moderator*, 28 November 1914.
2 Kilkenny *Journal*, 13 March 1915.
3 Kilkenny *People*, 15 November 1915.
4 Report of the Irish Rebellion Commission, Kilkenny *Moderator*, 3 June 1916.
5 Lyons 1973:375–7, 380.
6 Kilkenny *Journal*, 15 August 1914; Kilkenny *Moderator*, 17 June 1916.
7 A sweepstake to raise funds was held in 1916. After this, only annual general meetings were reported. In 1918, eighteen new members joined and the League affiliated with the Kilkenny County and City Labour Union. The only news about this liaison was that a League delegate went to its meetings. In 1918 the League had £55 in the bank, certainly less than in pre-war years (Kilkenny *Moderator*, 3 June 1916; Kilkenny *People*, 8 December 1917; Kilkenny *Journal*, 30 March 1918).
8 Kilkenny *Journal*, 28 July 1917, 16 February 1918.
9 Lyons 1973:399.
10 Farrell 1994:42–7.
11 O'Connor 1992: 91; 1994:54.
12 O'Connor 1994:55, 56–8.
13 O'Connor 1992:99; 1994:60.
14 Lyons 1973:392–4; O'Connor 1992:98; IT&GWU archives, MS no.7282.
15 IT&GWU, Annual Report 1918; Kilkenny *People*, 14 September 1918; Kilkenny *Moderator*, 17 August 1918; O'Connor 1992:99–100.
16 IT&GWU, Annual Report 1918; Kilkenny *People*, 22 February 1919.
17 Kilkenny *Moderator*, 23 March 1918; Kilkenny *People*, 23 March, 27 April, 4 May, 6 July, 30 November, 7 December 1918.
18 Lyons 1973:398.
19 Kilkenny *People*, 7, 14, 21 December 1918; 4 January 1919.
20 Lyons 1973:399.
21 Kilkenny *Journal*, 1 April 1916.
22 This description has been abstracted from Lyons 1973:400–20.
23 See O'Malley's (1933) disparaging view of insurrection and events in County Kilkenny.
24 Kilkenny *People*, 31 May, 14 June, 5 July 1919; 3, 10 April, 12 June, 24 July, 28 August, 4, 11, 18, 25 September, 9, 23 October, 6 November, 4, 18 December

1920; 29 January, 5, 12 March, 30 April, 14 May, 4, 25 June, 9, 16, 24 July; 17 December 1921; 28 January, 18 February 1922.
25 Kilkenny *People*, 17 April 1920; O'Connor 1994:62.
26 Emphasis mine. Kilkenny *People*, 10 April 1920.
27 Ibid., 12 June, 17 July 1920. Only one report of this court in Thomastown was found. County councillors acted as magistrates and cases typical of the former petty sessions were heard (Kilkenny *People*, 1 October 1921).
28 Ibid., 24 July 1920.
29 Ibid., 9 December 1922, 17 March 1923.
30 Ibid., 1 April, 27 May, 10 June, 22, 29 July, 19 August, 2, 9, 30 September, 7, 14, 18 October, 11, 2, 23 December 1922; 24, 31 March, 7, 28 April, 30 June, 3, 24 November, 24 December 1923; 22 December 1924. Kilkenny *Journal*, 29 April, 25 November 1922; 17 March, 7 April, 26 May 1923.
31 Those listed were one gentleman, one family of retailers, twenty-two farmers or their wives and/or children, and twenty labourers and/or their wives and/or children.

12. From Nation to Class in the New State: Replicating Capital and Labour, 1920–6

1 Kilkenny *People*, 2 October 1920.
2 Ibid., 2 January 1921.
3 Kilkenny *Journal*, 3 May 1924.
4 O'Connor 1992:108–13; 1994:63–5.
5 Kilkenny *People*, 28 August 1926.
6 Kilkenny *Journal*, 6 November 1926.
7 Kilkenny *People*, 11 April 1953.
8 Ibid., 25 February 1922, 23 January 1926; Kilkenny *Journal*, 3 January 1925.
9 Kilkenny *People*, 24 January 1925.
10 O'Connor 1992:118.
11 Kilkenny *Journal*, 24 November 1923; Nevin 1994:90.
12 Nevin 1994:88; O'Connor 1992:120, 124.
13 Kilkenny *People*, 19 December 1925.
14 Ibid., 10 July 1926.
15 At the first elections for the Thomastown Union's board of guardians held in 1850, with landlords already appointed, a limited franchise, and only local notables running (for example, brewer Nugent, large-scale farmer Cantwell). The nominators and seconders all tended to come from the same or a nearby DED as their candidates.
16 Kilkenny *Journal*, 31 May 1924.

17 Emphasis mine. Kilkenny *People*, 2 February 1925, 20 March 1926.
18 Kilkenny *People*, 28 March 1925.
19 Ibid., 23 January 1926.
20 Ibid., 30 January 1926.
21 Ibid., 10 July 1926.
22 Ibid., 28 August 1926.
23 Ibid., 24 January 1925.
24 Ibid.
25 Ibid., 4 December 1921.

13. Labouring Viewpoints and Lives: The *Metissage* of Experience and Identities, 1914–30

 1 Kilkenny *Journal*, 4 February 1928.
 2 Ibid., 14 April 1928.
 3 At one point, Crotty (for the defence) asked farmer Healy if he knew any-thing about the defendant/labourer Healy 'making inquiries to know what "blue school" the child was in.'
 4 Kilkenny *People*, 9 August 1919.
 5 Ibid., 29 April 1916.
 6 Kilkenny *Moderator*, 9 August 1919.
 7 A fuller description of Aggie's life, and how she constructed her own respect-ability, is given in Silverman (1989).
 8 Kilkenny *People*, 19 September 1925.
 9 Ibid., 24 March 1923.
10 Kilkenny *Moderator*, 9 August, 6 September 1913.
11 Ibid., 25 January, 5 April, 10 May 1919.
12 Kilkenny *Journal*, 7 November 1914.
13 Kilkenny *Moderator*, 11 January 1919.

14. The Uneven Economy and the Moral Economy, 1926–50

 1 This included farmers (n = 193), farm workers (n = 244), non-farm labour-ers (n = 491), and commerce/professionals (n = 158).
 2 Kilkenny *Journal*, 14 September 1929.
 3 Kilkenny *People*, 19 February 1927; Kilkenny *Journal*, 19 March 1927. The Shannon Scheme was a large-scale project for producing electricity. It was located in County Limerick.
 4 Kilkenny *Journal*, 22 October, 31 December 1927.
 5 Ibid., 4 February 1928.

6 Kilkenny *People*, 24 January 1925; Kilkenny *Journal*, 4 February 1928.

7 Kilkenny *People*, 10 October 1928; Kilkenny *Journal*, 27 October 1928. The Board of Health notified the county council that the monies had been spent (Kilkenny *Journal*, 5 April 1930).

8 Kilkenny *People*, 1, 22 December 1928. The amount of the tender was £1,830.9.2.

9 Ibid., 26 October 1929; Kilkenny *Journal*, 26 October 1929.

10 Kilkenny *People*, 12, 19 July, 30 August 1930; 28 February 1931; Kilkenny *Journal*, 12 July, 30 August 1830; 30 May, 11, 18 July 1931.

11 Kilkenny *People*, 15 August 1931.

12 Kilkenny *Journal*, 7 November 1931.

13 These annuities were mainly monies being paid by Irish farmers, formerly tenants, to buy their land from landlords, via the Land Commission, under the various Irish Land Acts.

14 Lyons 1973:610–13.

15 Kilkenny *People*, 2 July 1932; Kilkenny *Journal*, 2 July 1932.

16 Kilkenny *People*, 20 August 1932.

17 Kilkenny *Journal*, 10 December 1932; 18 March, 22 April, 20 May 1933; Kilkenny *People*, 9 December 1933, 10 November 1934. The estimated cost for a sewerage scheme was £4,183. As of 1924, townspeople had electric home and street lighting supplied privately by a small generator owned by tanner Ryan.

18 Kilkenny *People*, 11 August 1934; Kilkenny *Journal*, 11 August 1934.

19 Kilkenny *Journal*, 18 August, 1 December 1934; Kilkenny *People*, 13 April, 18 May 1935. My emphasis.

20 Kilkenny *People*, 4 January 1936.

21 Ibid., 25 July, 29 August, 28 November, 5, 12, 19 December 1936; 16, 23 January, 20 February, 18 September 1937; 23 July, 29 October, 5 November 1938; 7, 14 January 1939; Kilkenny *Journal*, 20 June, 29 August, 19 December 1936; 23 January, 18 September 1937; 4 June, 29 October, 5 November 1938. The work on the forty-four cottages did not start for three months; the contractor then went bankrupt. The scheme was begun again in January 1940 using direct labour. Workers were paid 36s. for a forty-eight-hour week and carters were paid 10s. a day.

22 Kilkenny *Journal*, 4 March, 9 December 1939, 20 January, 22 June 1940; 26 July, 8 November 1941; 2 February 1942; 1 April 1944; Kilkenny *People*, 4 March, 21 October 1939; 13 January, 29 June, 21 December 1940; 12 April, 23 August, 11 October, 8 November 1941; 23 May, 21 November 1942; 23 December 1944; 3 February, 2 December 1945.

23 Kilkenny *People*, 2 December 1945; 1 June, 6 December 1946; 22 February,

5 July, 2, 16 August, 5 November 1947; 16 October, 18 December 1948; 2 January, 10 April, 9, 10 July, 26 November, 24 December 1949; Kilkenny *Journal*, 1 June 1946; 2 August 1947; 13 March, 4 December 1948; 10 April, 9 July, 24 December 1949.
24 Kilkenny *Journal*, 4 March, 13 May, 22 July, 21 October 1950.

15. The Quality of Charity, Values, and Entitlements, 1908–50

1 Kilkenny *Moderator*, 10 June, 7, 21 November 1908.
2 Ibid., 12 January 1910, 8 February 1911, 18 January 1913.
3 Kilkenny *People*, 6 August 1949.
4 Kilkenny *Journal*, 9 May 1931.
5 Lyons 1973:615, 483–4; Kilkenny *People*, 11 August 1934, 16 January 1937.
6 Emphasis mine. Kilkenny *Journal*, 18 August 1934.
7 *Report of the Sea and Inland Fisheries*, 1923–5:36,40 and 1934.
8 Kilkenny *Journal*, 9 April 1927.
9 Kilkenny *People*, 15 June 1929; Kilkenny *Journal*, 5 June 1929.
10 Kilkenny *People*, 9 May 1931.
11 Ibid., 4 July 1931. The cotmen were fined £2 each and £1 costs.
12 Kilkenny *Journal*, 28 April, 12 May 1934.
13 *Commission on Inland Fisheries, 1933–1935*, para. 10, 12, 33, 34, pgs. 12, 13, 18, 28, 29, 37, 47, 49, 108, 109.
14 *Minutes, Thomastown Branch of the Irish Labour Party*, 7 September, 17 December 1935; 16 February 1936.
15 Kilkenny *People*, 30 May 1936.
16 Ibid., 26 June 1937; *Report of the Sea and Inland Fisheries*, 1946.
17 Kilkenny *People*, 9, 16 August 1930.
18 Ibid., 4 July, 21 November 1936; 2 July, 1942; Kilkenny *Journal*, 3, 24 July 1943.
19 Kilkenny *Journal*, 15 September 1945; *Minutes, Board of Conservators*, 21 September 1945.
20 Kilkenny *Moderator*, 12 March 1875.

16. Redundancy and Status Class: Purveying Values through Recreation and Education, 1929–50

1 Lyons 1973:635.
2 Lyons 1973:635–40.
3 Kilkenny *People*, 15 November 1946.
4 Ibid., 12 April 1941.

5 Ibid., 25 March 1933; 15 April, 18 June 1932; 8 July 1933; 18 June 1938; Kilkenny *Journal*, 6 July 1929, 4 July 1931, 24 June 1933.
6 Kilkenny *People*, 2 April 1932, 17 December 1932, 21 October 1933.
7 Lyons 1973:539.
8 Kilkenny *People*, 10 February 1945.
9 Ibid., 6 April 1935; Kilkenny *Journal*, 6 May 1939.
10 Kilkenny *People* 13 May 1939; Kilkenny *Journal*, 13 May 1939.
11 Kilkenny *Journal*, 7 May 1932; 6 May 1933; 22 July 1950; Kilkenny *People*, 30 December 1933, 31 December 1938, 20 April 1940.
12 Kilkenny *Journal*, 9 March 1940.
13 Kilkenny *People*, 22, 29 February 1936.
14 Ibid., 15 November 1930; Kilkenny *Journal*, 6 December 1930.
15 Kilkenny *Journal*, 24 January 1931, 8 October 1938; Kilkenny *People*, 2 July 1932, 10 March 1934, 14 November 1936, 19 March 1949.
16 Kilkenny *People*, 10 June 1933.

17. 'And the Church Preached Its View'

1 Keogh 1986:160.
2 Lyons 1972:688.
3 These pastorals are in the Diocesan Library, Kilkenny.
4 The chorus is: 'I met with Napper Tandy and he took me by the hand. / Said he *"how is old Ireland and how does she stand?"* / "She's the most distressful country that ever could be seen, / For they're hanging men and women for the wearing of the green"' [Emphasis mine].
5 O'Connor 1992:126.
6 Lyons 1973:488–90.
7 Lyons 1973:486; 492–8.
8 O'Connor 1992:124–6.
9 Lyons 1973:502–4.
10 O'Connor 1992:126. See also Keogh (1986).
11 Kilkenny *People*, 26 June 1937.
12 Ibid., 23 July, 1949; 16 October 1937.

18. 'We Had a Live Union Then'

1 The numerous quotes in the text come from interviews and conversations with labouring people in Thomastown during field work in 1980–1, 1983, and 1987. Materials in the Cases are also extracted from the Minute Books of the local IT&GWU.

2 Until then, milk had been brought in by farmers or by small carters working on contract.

3 This referred to the difficulties labourers were having in securing unemployment benefits. See Case 15.5.

4 Kilkenny *Journal*, 6 February 1937.

5 These views were available from various Catholic tracts. A volume known to local organic intellectuals was entitled *The Church and Labour* (McKenna n.d.). It covered such topics as: 'The Church and Trades Unions,' 'The Church and Social Work,' the *Rerum Novarum* encyclical (1891), the idea of 'a family wage,' and why socialism was to be condemned. It offered 'a Christian view of labour' which many agents cited at this time for particular and, very often, conflicting purposes.

6 Kilkenny *People*, 13 February 1937; Kilkenny *Journal*, 9 February 1937.

7 Kilkenny *People*, 13 February 1937.

8 Kilkenny *Journal*, 2 February 1935; 7 January, 25 March, 23 December 1939; 18, 25 May 1940, 6 July 1941; Kilkenny *People*, 14 January 1939; 13 January, 11, 18, 25 May 1940.

9 At the same time that kinship was so important, no Thomastown enterprise had a majority of workers linked into a single kinship net.

10 Such fragmentation is discussed in Silverman and Gulliver (1990).

19. 'Much Wants More': Framing the Politics of Labour

1 *Minutes of the Thomastown Branch of the IT&GWU*, 26 August 1935. All materials on the local branch, unless otherwise specified, are taken from this *Minute Book* of eighty-eight handwritten pages which spans the period August 1935 to January 1947.

2 Aspects of this are discussed in chapter 11.

3 Beresford-Ellis 1972:177.

4 Lyons 1973:281, 524, 676.

5 Lyons 1973:674–6.

6 Lyons 1973:676–7.

7 Allen 1997:38–9, 51–60. The 1934 annual general meeting of the Thomastown IT&GWU passed a motion supporting the National Executive in its aim to convince 'Irish workers that an Irish union should be their aim' (Kilkenny *People*, 10 March 1934; Kilkenny *Journal*, 1 March 1934).

8 Adamson 1980:245.

9 Kilkenny *People*, December 1926.

10 These were millworkers John Magee (1899–1907), Pat Magee (1907–10), and James O'Neill (1920–6); baker Jim Cahill (1902–11); carpenter James

Walsh (1916); fisher John Dunphy (1911–20); and carter Pat Ryan (1911–26).

11 Kilkenny *Journal*, 3 July 1928.

12 Ibid., 8 August, 19 August 1942.

13 Lyons attributed this to factionalism within; the resurgence of the Treaty versus anti-Treaty division after de Valera's ascendancy; the sidelining of social issues; the small size of the urban proletariat; and the lack of coherent ideology (1973:524–5). Why, however, did Labour re-emerge after?

14 Kilkenny *People*, 1 August 1931.

15 Ibid., 13 February 1932.

16 Ibid., 2 and 27 April 1932.

17 Ibid., 20 October 1932.

18 Ibid., 5 November 1932. Delegates came from Castlecomer, Ballyraggett, Callan, Urlingford and Thomastown.

19 Kilkenny *Journal*, 12 November 1932.

20 Kilkenny *People*, 12 November 1932; Kilkenny *Journal* 12 November 1932.

21 Kilkenny *People*, 26 November 1932.

22 Ibid., 7 January 1933.

23 Ibid., 14 January 1933.

24 Kilkenny *Journal*, 18 March 1933.

25 Kilkenny *People*, 15 April 1933.

26 Kilkenny *Journal*, 21 January 1933.

27 *Post*, 25 April, 6 June 1934.

28 Allen 1997:53; Kilkenny *Journal*, 14, 28 October, 16 December 1933.

29 Kilkenny *Journal*,11, 18 August 1934.

30 Allen 1997:54–5. Neither the urban middle classes nor rural labourers had been mobilized.

31 Lyons 1973:532–3.

20. Inside the Frame: The Politics of Mediation

1 Kilkenny *Journal*, 28 March 1931; Kilkenny *People*, 2 August 1930, 3 December 1932.

2 Kilkenny *People* and Kilkenny *Journal*, 8 September 1934.

3 Kilkenny *People*, 22 September 1934; Kilkenny *Journal*, 22 September 1934.

4 Kilkenny *People*, 29 September 1934.

5 Kilkenny *Journal*, 18 March 1933.

6 Ibid., 12 January 1935. The Fianna Fáil branch passed a stronger motion only after the report called for abolition (cf. chapter 15; Kilkenny *People*, 30 May 1936).

7 Kilkenny *People*, 10 March 1934; Kilkenny *Journal*, 9 June 1934; 16 May, 22 February 1936.

8 Kilkenny *People*, 2 November 1935.

9 Gulliver and Silverman 1995:326–7.

10 *Minutes of the Thomastown Branch of the Irish Labour Party*, 1 March, 1 November 1936;. Kilkenny *People*, 25 September 1937, 12 February 1938; Kilkenny *Journal*, 21 August 1937, 5 February 1938.

11 Kilkenny *Journal*, 26 February 1938.

12 Kilkenny *People*, 2 April 1938.

13 *Minutes of the Thomastown Branch of the Irish Labour Party*, 19 February, 1, 21, 28 March, 5, 9 April, 31 May 1936; Kilkenny *Journal*, 14, 28 March 1936; Kilkenny *People*, 4 April 1936.

14 *Minutes of the Thomastown Branch of the Irish Labour Party*, 1 November 1936.

15 He was aged sixty (Kilkenny *People*, 13 February 1937).

16 Kilkenny *People*, 27 April 1935; Kilkenny *Journal*, 10 November 1934, 14 April, 5 October 1935.

17 Lyons 1973:532.

18 See also chapter 12, p.279.

21. Organizing Labour in the 1940s: The Politics of Combination

1 Lyons 1973:557–8.

2 Kilkenny *People*, 12 April 1941.

3 Ibid., 16 November 1940, 22 February 1941; Kilkenny *Journal*, 15 February 1941.

4 Kilkenny *People*, 12 April, 17 May 1941; Kilkenny *Journal*, 17, 24 May 1941.

5 Kilkenny *Journal*, 20 July 1940; Kilkenny *People*, 11 October, 8 November 1941.

6 Kilkenny *Journal*, 25 May, 22 June, 20 July, 7 September 1940; Kilkenny *People*, 27, 29 June, 7 September 1940.

7 Kilkenny *Journal*, 29 November, 6 December 1941. Kilkenny *People*, 6 December, 1941.

8 Kilkenny *People*, 24 February 1940.

9 Kilkenny *Journal*, 30 August 1941.

10 Lyons 1973:484.

11 Allen 1997:73, 74–5; O'Connor 1992:138–50; Beresford-Ellis 1972:289.

12 *Minutes of the Thomastown Branch of the IT&GWU*, 14, 28 June 1941; Irish Labour Party, *11th Annual Administrative Council Report*, 1941:99–100.

13 Kilkenny *Journal*, 31 January 1942; *Minutes of the Thomastown Branch of the IT&GWU*, 13 July, 5, 26 September 1942; 29 May 1943; O'Connor 1994:149.

14 Allen 1997:73, 74; O'Connor 1994:154; *Minutes of the Thomastown Branch of the IT&GWU*, 10 May 1942, 25 April 1945.

15 Kilkenny *People*, 26 June 1943; Allen 1997:78–9.

16 *Minutes of the Thomastown Branch of the IT&GWU; Kilkenny Journal*, 22, 29 January 1944.

17 *Minutes of the Thomastown Branch of the IT&GWU*, 21, 27 January 1945; 31 March, 14 April, 12 May 1946; Kilkenny *People*, 6 April 1946; Kilkenny *Journal*, 6 April 1946.

22. Reproducing the Political Regime and Regimen, 1940–50

1 Pattison had been the first elected in 1943, with almost as many first-preference votes (6,417) as Fianna Fail's Tom Derrig (6,852) (Kilkenny *People*, 26 June 1943).

2 Kilkenny *People*, 24 February 1940, 12 April 1941.

3 Ibid., 21 August 1943, 13 April 1946; Kilkenny *Journal*, 6, 13 April, 28 September 1946.

4 Kilkenny *People*, 11 November 1944.

5 Ibid., 23 December, 1944.

6 Ibid., 21 September, 5 October 1946.

7 Ibid., 16 November 1946.

8 Ibid., 22 February 1947; Kilkenny *Journal*, 22 February 1947.

9 Kilkenny *People*, 15 March 1947.

10 Kilkenny *Journal*, 22, 29 March 1947.

11 Ibid., 29 March, 3 May 1947; Kilkenny *People*, 29 March, 10 May 1947.

12 Kilkenny *People*, 31 May 1947; Kilkenny *Journal*, 31 May 1947.

13 Kilkenny *People*, 5 April 1947. Nothing further was recalled or reported on this incident.

14 Lyons 1973:560; Kilkenny *People*, 17 January 1948.

15 Kilkenny *People*, 5 July, 16 August 1947; Kilkenny *Journal*, 10 January 1948.

16 Kilkenny *People*, 17 January 1948.

17 Kilkenny *Journal*, 6 March 1948.

18 Kilkenny *People*, 7 February 1948. ILP candidates were from Kilmacow and County Carlow.

19 Kilkenny *People*, 10, 24 January 1948; Kilkenny *Journal*, 24 January 1948.

20 O'Connor 1992:164; Kilkenny *Journal*, 14 February 1948. Fianna Fáil and Fine Gael polled 41.7 and 28.6 per cent respectively in Kilkenny-Carlow constituency.

21 Kilkenny *Journal*, 5 February 1949.

22 Kilkenny *People*, 15 May, 5 June 1948.

23 Kilkenny *Journal*, 24 July, 21 August 1948; Kilkenny *People*, 8 January 1949.
24 Kilkenny *People* and Kilkenny *Journal*, 19 January, 6 August, 24 December 1949. For example, O'Neill complained about the condition of the town's footpaths, adding: 'The people living in the flooded areas were clamouring for houses and it was 12 months since development work was carried out on the site ... He would like an explanation.'
25 Kilkenny *People*, 2 October, 6 November 1948.
26 Allen 1997:99.
27 *Minutes of the Thomastown Branch of the National Labour Party*, 5 December 1947; 10 January, 7, 10, 29 February, 30 April 1948; 22 May 1949; 3 August 1950.
28 Kilkenny *Journal*, 4 March 1950.
29 *Minutes of the Thomastown Branch of the National Labour Party*, 14 January, 3 August 1950.
30 Kilkenny *Journal*, 17 June, 26 August, 22 September, 30 September 1950.
31 Extract, *The Cotman's Lament*, by TUSA, a.k.a. Paddy Doolan, Thomastown labourer.
32 Kilkenny *People*, 2 August 1947, 18 February 1950; Kilkenny *Journal*, 2 August 1947, 18 February 1950.
33 Kilkenny *People*, 17 May, 4 November, 6 December 1950.

23. Theory, Concept, and Text: A Holistic Approach to the Politics of Class

1 Joseph and Nugent 1994:22.
2 Joseph and Nugent 1994:15, 19.
3 Kurtz 1996.
4 Augelli and Murphy 1988:24.
5 Adamson 1980:245.
6 Silverman 1979.
7 Wolf 1990.
8 For example, see Casson (1983); Shore (1996).
9 Corrigan 1994:xviii.
10 The problems of loose usage and slippage, and of comparability over a long period, were discussed in Gulliver and Silverman (1995:348–53). See also chapter 2, n.45.
11 For example, see Blok (1969), Gulliver (1980), Silverman (1965).
12 Frankenberg 1966.
13 This is further discussed in Silverman (2000).
14 Why stop in 1950? Some reasons were practical. The volume's length was a consideration; so, too, was my wish leave the more recent past to a different

venue. As well, 1950 provided a kind of end – of a generation and a kind of political combination.

15 See Gulliver (1993) on 'huckster shops.'
16 Silverman and Gulliver 1992a; 1996; 1997.
17 This is discussed in Silverman and Gulliver (1992a).
18 This distinction was explored in Silverman and Gulliver (1992a; 1996). Work in the anthropology of history is in Silverman and Gulliver (1997).

Bibliography

PRIMARY SOURCES

British Parliamentary Papers

Second Report of Commissioners under Act 59 Geo III for the Year 1820. IUP 1821 [646] xi:13.

Appendix to the Report of the Select Committee on the Salmon Fisheries in the United Kingdom. IUP 1824 [427] viii:1.

Minutes of Evidence Taken before the Select Committee Appointed to Inquire into the Disturbances in Ireland, in the Last Session of Parliament, 13 May to 24 June 1824. H.C. 1825 [20] vii:1.

Minutes of Evidence Taken before the Select Committee of the House of Lords Appointed to Examine into the Nature and Extent of the Disturbances Which Have Prevailed in Those Districts of Ireland Which Are Now Subject to the Provisions of the Insurrection Act and to Report to the House. 18 May–23 June 1824. H.C. 1825 [200] vii:501.

Report of Evidence from the Select Committee Appointed to Take into Consideration the State of the Salmon Fisheries of Scotland, and of the United Kingdom and the Laws Affecting Same. IUP 1825 [173] v:283.

Report from the Select Committee on the State of Ireland ... with the Report of Minutes of Evidence. H.C. 1825 [129] vii:1.

Minutes of Evidence before the Select Committee on Salmon Fisheries of the United Kingdom. H.C. 1825 [393] v:315.

Reports from Commissioners on Municipal Corporations in Ireland. H.C. 1835, xxviii:573.

First Report of Commissioners for Inquiring into the Condition of the Poorer Classes in Ireland. H.C. 1836, xxxi, xxxii, xxxiii.

Second Report of the Commissioners of Inquiry Respecting the Present State of the Irish Fisheries, the Laws Affecting, and the Means and Expediency of Extending and Improving Them. IUP 1837 [82] xxii, 489.

Fifth Annual Report of the Commissioners of the Loan Fund Board of Ireland, Pursuant to the Act 1 & 2 Vict., c. 78. IUP 1843 [224] xxviii:29.

Annual Report of the Commissioners of Fisheries, Ireland: IUP 1844 [502],31; IUP 1845 [320] xxvi, 211; IUP 1846 [713] xxii, 175.

Report of the Board of Public Works in Ireland in Regard to Fisheries in that Country. IUP 1847–8 [983] xxxvii, 213.

Report from the Select Committee on Fisheries (Ireland); together with the Proceedings of the Committee, Minutes of Evidence and Appendix. IUP 1849 [536] xiii:1.

Returns and Statements Respecting Fisheries in Ireland. IUP 1849 [1098] xxiii, 433.

Reports and Statements Respecting the Fisheries in Ireland. IUP 1851 [1414] xxv, 1.

Reports of the Commissioners of Fisheries, Ireland, to His Excellency the Lord Lieutenant. IUP 1854 [1819] xx, 163; IUP 1856 [2021] xix, 31; IUP 1860 [2727] xxxiv, 663; IUP 1861 [2862] xxiii, 27.

Return of the Average Rate of Weekly Earnings of Agricultural Labourers for Ireland for the Last Six Months Previous to January 1, 1861. H.C. 1862 lx.

Report of the Special Commissioners for Irish Fisheries. IUP 1864 [3256] xxxi, 27; IUP 1865 [3420] xxviii, 431; IUP 1866 [3608] xxviii, 355; IUP 1867 [3826] xviii, 33; IUP 1867–8 [4056] xix, 653.

Reports of the Inspectors of Irish Fisheries, on the Coast, Deep Sea and Inland Fisheries. IUP 1870 [c.225] xiv, 193; IUP 1873 [c.758] xix, 607; IUP 1874 [c.980] xii, 591; IUP 1876 [c.1467] xvi, 555; IUP 1877 [c.1703] xxiv, 351.

Annual Report of the Local Government Board for Ireland, under the Local Government Board Act (Ireland), 35 & 36 Vic.c.69. Reports from Inspectors on the State of the Potato Crop, the General Harvest, and Condition of the Poorer Classes. Report from Mr. W.J. Hamilton, District Comprising the County of Kilkenny, and Portion of the Counties of Carlow, Limerick, Tipperary, Waterford, and Wexford. HC 1881 xlvii.

Report[s] of the Inspectors on the Sea and Inland Fisheries of Ireland. IUP 1881 [c.2871] xxiii, 401; 1882 [c.3248] xvii.557; 1884 [c.4109] xviii.505; 1884–5 [c.4545] xvi.121; 1886 [c.4809] xv.113; 1887 [c.5035] xxi.165; 1888 [c.5388] xxviii.237; 1889 [c.5777] xxii.313; 1890 [c.6508] xxi.241; 1892 [c.6682] xxi.307; 1893–4 [c.7048] xvii.265; 1894 [c.7404] xxii.265; 1895 [c.7793] xx.269; 1896 [c.8250] xx.309; 1897 [c.8628] xviii.299; 1898 [c.8932] xv.303.

Report from the Select Committee on Salmon Fisheries (Ireland) together with the Proceedings of the Committee, Minutes of Evidence and Appendix, July 1885. IUP 1884–5 (271) xi:29.

Return Showing the Working of the Labourers' Act (Ireland), the Number of Cottages Erected and the Expenses Connected Therewith to 31ˢᵗ March 1887. H.C. 1887, lxviii, v.202.

Return Showing the Working of the Labourers' Act (Ireland), the Number of Cottages Erected and the Expenses Connected Therewith to 31ˢᵗ March 1888. H.C. 1888, cxxxiii, v.83.

Report from the Select Committee on the Salmon Fisheries (Ireland) Acts Amendment Bill, together with the Proceedings of the Committee, Minutes of Evidence, Appendix and Index. IUP 1892 [236 – session 1] xvii.1.

Irish Inland Fisheries Commission. *Report of the Commissioners, Appendix and Minutes of Evidence.* H.C. 1901 [448], [450] and [451].

Return Showing the Working of the Labourers' Act (Ireland), the Number of Cottages Erected and the Expenses Connected Therewith to 31ˢᵗ March 1903. H.C. 1903, lvii, v.198.

Saorstat Eireann Papers

Report of the Sea and Inland Fisheries, 1923 and passim to 1946. Dublin.
Commission on Inland Fisheries, 1933–5. Dublin.

Newspapers

Finn's Leinster Journal
Irish Independent
Kilkenny *Journal*
Kilkenny *Moderator*
Kilkenny *People*

Government Offices

Civil Registry of Births and Marriages, Kilkenny
Deeds Registry, Charlotte Street, Dublin
Land Registry, Henrietta Street, Dublin
Public Record Office, Dublin
    (Encumbered Estate Court Papers; Griffith's House Books, November 1845; Censuses of Ireland, 1831 and passim; Probate Court Papers).
State Paper Office, Dublin
    (Outrage Papers, Famine Papers)
Valuation Office, Ely Street, Dublin

Published Primary Sources

Agricultural Censuses, 1847 and passim.
Agricultural Statistics for the Year (1890)
Annual Report of the Irish Labour Party, 1934/5
Censuses, 1841 and passim.
Griffith's *Primary Valuation*, 1845
Index to the Statutes in Force in Ireland, 1310–1838, 2nd ed.
Irish Labour Party, 11th Annual Administrative Council Report, 1941.
IT&GWU Annual Reports. Archives of the IT&GWU, Dublin.

Local Records

Diocesan Library, Sion House, Kilkenny
Doyle Family Papers, Thomastown
Minutes and Letter Books of the Thomastown Board of Guardians; Workhouse
   Admissions Records. Central County Library, Kilkenny
Minutes of the Thomastown Rural District, 1899–1926. Central County
   Library, Kilkenny
National School Records, 1873–1981. Thomastown Boys' School
Parochial Records, 1798+, Parochial House, Thomastown.
Minutes of the Thomastown Branch of the IT&GWU, Thomastown, 1935–47.
Minutes of the Thomastown Branch of the Irish Labour Party, Thomastown,
   1935–6.
Minutes of the Thomastown Branch of the National Labour Party, Thomastown,
   1948–50.
Pilsworth Family Papers, Thomastown
Wage Book, Grennan Mills, Thomastown
Wage Books, Ryan Tannery, Thomatown

SECONDARY SOURCES

Adamson, Walter L. 1980. *Hegemony and Revolution: A Study of Antonio Gramsci's
   Political and Cultural Theory.* Berkeley: University of California Press.
Allen, Kieran. 1997. *Fianna Fáil and Irish Labour: 1926 to the Present.* London:
   Pluto.
Augelli, Enrico, and Craig Murphy. 1988. Gramsci's Understanding of Ideology
   (chapter 1). *America's Quest for Supremacy and the Third World: A Gramscian Anal-
   ysis.* London: Pinter Publications.

Beresford-Ellis, P. 1972. *A History of the Irish Working Class.* New York: George Braziller.

Birdwell-Pheasant, Donna. 1992. 'The Early Twentieth Century Irish Stem Family: A Case Study from County Kerry.' In Marilyn Silverman and P.H. Gulliver eds., *Approaching the Past: Historical Anthropology through Irish Case Studies.* New York: Columbia University Press.

Blok, A. 1969. 'Variations in Patronage.' *Sociologische Gids* 16 (6):365–78.

Boyle, John W. 1988. *The Irish Labor Movement in the Nineteenth Century.* Washington D.C.: Catholic University of America Press.

Bric, Maurice J. 1985. 'The Whiteboy Movement, 1760–1780.' In William Nolan, ed., *Tipperary: History and Society – Interdisciplinary Essays on the History of an Irish County.* Dublin: Geography Publications.

Brow, James. 1988. 'In Pursuit of Hegemony: Representations of Authority and Justice in a Sri Lankan Village.' *American Ethnologist* 15 (2):311–27.

Burtchaell, Jack, and Daniel Dowling. 1990. 'Social and Economic Conflict in County Kilkenny 1600–1800.' In William Nolan and Kevin Whelan, eds., *Kilkenny: History and Society.* Dublin: Geography Publications.

Cain, Maureen. 1983. 'Gramsci, the State and the Place of Law.' In David Sugarman, ed., *Legality, Ideology and the State.* London: Academic Press.

Casson, Ronald W. 1983. 'Schemata in Cultural Anthropology.' *Annual Review of Anthropology* 12:429–62.

Chubb, Basil. 1970. *The Government and Politics of Ireland.* Oxford, U.K.: Oxford University Press.

Clark, Samuel, and James S. Donnelly, Jr, eds. 1983. *Irish Peasants: Violence and Political Unrest, 1780–1914.* Madison: University of Wisconsin Press.

Clarke, Aidan. 1976. 'The Irish Economy, 1600–1660.' In T.W. Moody, F.X. Martin and F.J. Byrne, eds., *A New History of Ireland* (vol. 3): *Early Modern Ireland, 1534–1691.* Oxford, U.K.: Clarendon Press.

Comaroff, John, and Jean Comaroff. 1992. 'The Colonization of Consciousness.' In *Ethnography and the Historical Imagination.* Boulder, Colo.: Westview.

Comaroff, John, and S. Roberts. 1981. *Rules and Processes.* Chicago: University of Chicago Press.

Connolly, S.J. 1989. 'Union Government, 1812–23.' In W.E. Vaughan, ed., *A New History of Ireland: Ireland under the Union, 1801–70* (vol. 5). Oxford, U.K.: Clarendon Press.

Corrigan, Philip. 1994. 'State Formation.' In Gilbert M. Joseph and Daniel Nugent, eds., *Everyday Forms of State Formation: Revolution and the Negotiation of Rule in Modern Mexico.* Durham, N.C.: Duke University Press.

Coser, Lewis A. 1982. 'The Notion of Control in Social Theory.' In Jack Gibbs, ed., *Social Control.* Beverly Hills, Calif.: Sage.

Cullen, L.M. 1972. *An Economic History of Ireland since 1660.* London: B.T. Basford.

Curtin, Chris, Hastings Donnan, and Thomas Wilson, eds. 1993. *Irish Urban Cultures.* Belfast: Queen's University of Belfast.

Curtis, Edmund, ed. 1932–43. *Calendar of Ormond Deeds, 1172–1350*, vols. 3 and 4. Dublin.

D'Arcy, Fergus A., and Ken Hannigan, eds. 1988. *Workers in Unions: Documents and Commentaries on the History of Irish Labour.* Dublin: National Archives, Stationery Office.

Devine, Francis, and Emmet O'Connor, 1997. 'Editorial: Labour History and the Future.' *Saothoar 22: Journal of the Irish Labour History Society*: 3–5.

Donnan, Hastings, and Graham McFarlane. 1989. *Social Anthropology and Public Policy in Northern Ireland.* Aldershot, U.K.: Gower.

Doyle, Joseph. 1997. 'An Experiment in Co-operation: National School Management in County Kilkenny, 1831–1870.' MEd thesis, National University of Ireland, Maynooth.

Eley, Geoff. 1990. 'Edward Thompson, Social History and Political Culture: The Making of a Working-Class Public, 1780–1850.' In Harvey J. Kaye and Keith McClelland, eds., *E.P. Thompson: Critical Persepctives.* Philadelphia: Temple University Press.

Epstein, James. 1986. 'Rethinking the Categories of Working-Class History.' *Labour/Le Travail* 18 (Fall):195–208.

Farrell, Brian. 1994. 'Labour and the Political Revolution.' In Donal Nevin, ed., *Trade Union Century.* Dublin: Mercier.

Fitzpatrick, David. 1977. *Politics and Irish Life, 1913–21: Provincial Experience of War and Revolution.* Dublin: Gill and Macmillan.

Foster, R.F. 1988. *Modern Ireland, 1600–1972.* London: Penguin.

Frankenberg, Ronald. 1966. *Communities in Britain: Social Life in Town and County.* Hammondsworth, U.K.: Penguin.

Goffman, Erving. 1962. *Asylums: Essays on the Social Situation of Mental Patients and Other Inmates.* Chicago: Aldine.

Graham, B.J. 1977. 'The Towns of Medieval Ireland.' In R.A. Butlin, ed., *The Development of the Irish Town.* London: Croom Helm.

Gramsci, Antonio. 1971. *Selections from the Prison Notebooks.* Edited by Quintin Hoare and Geoffrey Nowell Smith. New York: International.

Grossberg, Michael. 1994. 'Battling over Motherhood in Philadelphia: A Study of Antebellum American Trial Courts as Arenas of Conflict.' In Susan F. Hirsch and Mindie Lazarus-Black, eds., *Contested States: Law, Hegemony, and Resistance.* New York: Routledge.

Grubgeld, Elizabeth. 1993. 'The Hyphen as Intermediate Territory.' A Review of

Heather Bryant Jordan, *How Will the Heart Endure: Elizabeth Bowen and the Landscape of War* (1992). *Irish Literary Supplement* (Fall):9.

Gulliver, P.H. 1980. *Disputes and Negotiations: A Cross-Cultural Perspective.* New York: Academic Press.

– 1989. 'Doing Anthropological Research in Rural Ireland: Methods and Sources for Linking the Past and the Present.' In Chris Curtin and Thomas Wilson, eds., *Ireland from Below: Social Change and Local Communities.* Galway, Ireland: Galway University Press.

– 1993. 'Hucksters and Petty Retailers in Thomastown.' *Old Kilkenny Review* 4 (5):1094–9.

Gulliver, P.H., and Marilyn Silverman. 1995. *Merchants and Shopkeepers: A Historical Anthropology of an Irish Market Town, 1200–1991.* Toronto: University of Toronto Press.

Hall, Stuart. 1981. 'Notes on Deconstructing "The Popular."' In Raphael Samuel, ed., *People's History and Socialist Theory.* London: Routledge and Kegan Paul.

– 1986. Popular Culture and the State. In Tony Bennett, Colin Mercer, and Janet Woollacott, eds., *Popular Culture and Social Relations.* Milton Keynes, U.K.: Open University Press.

Halpin, T.B. 1989. 'A Brief History of the Brewing Industry in Kilkenny.' *Old Kilkenny Review* 4 (1):583–91.

Hay, Douglas, and Francis Snyder. 1989. 'Using the Criminal Law, 1750–1850: Policing, Private Prosecution, and the State.' In Douglas Hay and Francis Snyder, eds., *Policing and Prosecution in Britain, 1750–1850.* Oxford, U.K.: Clarendon Press.

Hay, Douglas, Peter Linebaugh, John G. Rule, E.P. Thompson, and Cal Winslow. 1975. *Albion's Fatal Tree: Crime and Society in Eighteenth Century England.* New York: Pantheon.

Hirsch, Susan F. 1994. 'Kadhi's Courts as Complex Sites of Resistance: The State, Islam, and Gender in Postcolonial Kenya.' In Susan F. Hirsch and Mindie Lazarus-Black, eds. *Contested States: Law, Hegemony, and Resistance.* New York: Routledge.

Hirsch, Susan F., and Mindie Lazarus-Black, eds., 1994. *Contested States: Law, Hegemony, and Resistance.* New York: Routledge.

Hobsbawm, Eric. 1984. *Workers: Worlds of Labor.* New York: Pantheon Books.

Honigman, John J. 1982. 'Sampling in Ethnographic Field Work.' In Robert G. Burgess, ed., *Field Research: A Sourcebook and Field Manual.* London: George Allen and Unwin.

Hoppen, K. Theodore. 1984. *Elections, Politics, and Society in Ireland, 1832–1885.* Oxford: Clarendon Press.

Johnson, Paul. 1983. 'Credit and Thrift and the British Working Class, 1870–1939.' In Jay Winter, ed., *The Working Class in Modern British History,* 147–70. Cambridge, U.K.: Cambridge University Press.

Joseph, Gilbert M., & Daniel Nugent. 1994. 'Popular Culture and State Formation in Revolutionary Mexico.' In Gilbert M. Joseph and Daniel Nugent, eds., *Everyday Forms of State Formation: Revolution and the Negotiation of Rule in Modern Mexico.* Durham, N.C.: Duke University Press.

Keogh, Dermot. 1986. *The Vatican, Bishops and Irish Politics, 1919–1939.* Cambridge, U.K.: Cambridge University Press.

Kirk, Neville. 1987. 'In Defence of Class: A Critique of Recent Revisionist Writing upon the Nineteenth-Century English Working Class.' *International Review of Social History* 32:2–47.

– 1991. '"Traditional" Working-Class Culture and "the rise of Labour": Some Preliminary Questions and Observations.' *Social History* 16 (2):203–16.

Kurtz, Donald V. 1996. Hegemony and Anthropology: Gramsci, Exegesis, Reinterpretations. *Critique of Anthropology* 16 (2):103–35.

Lagos, Maria L. 1993. '"We Have to learn to Ask": Hegemony, Diverse Experiences, and Antagonistic Meanings in Bolivia.' *American Ethnologist* 20 (1):52–71.

Lancaster, Bill. 1987. *Radicalism, Co-operation and Socialism: Leicester Working-Class Politics, 1860–1906.* Leicester, U.K.: Leicester University Press.

Lasswell, Harold D. 1950. *Who Gets What, When, and How.* New York: P. Smith.

Lazarus-Black, Mindie. 1989. Review of *History and Power in the Study of Law. APLA Newsletter* 12 (2):8–12.

Lears, T.J. Jackson. 1985. 'The Concept of Cultural Hegemony: Problems and Possibilities.' *American Historical Review* 90 (3):567–93.

Lewis, Samuel. 1837. *Topographical Dictionary of Ireland.* London.

Lipuma, Edward, and Sarah Keene Meltzoff. 1989. 'Toward a Theory of Culture and Class: An Iberian Example.' *American Ethnologist* 16 (2):313–34.

Lomnitz-Adler, Claudio 'Concepts for the Study of Regional Culture.' *American Ethnologist* 18 (2):195–214.

Lucas. 1788. *Directory.*

Lyons, F.S.L. 1973. *Ireland since the Famine.* London: Fontana.

Marwick, Arthur. 1983. 'Images of the Working Class since 1950.' In Jay Winter, ed., *The Working Class in Modern British History.* Cambridge, U.K.: Cambridge University Press.

McCarthy, Charles. 1977. *Trade Unions in Ireland, 1894–1960.* Dublin: Institute of Public Administration.

McKenna, Rev. L. n.d.. *The Church and Labour: A Series of Six Tracts.* Dublin: Office of 'The Irish Messenger.'

McLelland, Keith. 1990. Introduction. In Harvey J. Kaye and Keith McClelland, eds., *E.P. Thompson: Critical Perspectives*. Philadelphia: Temple University Press.

Merrigan, Matt. 1989. *Eagle or Cuckoo? The Story of the ATGWU in Ireland*. Dublin: Matmer Publications.

Merry, Sally Engle. 1994. 'Courts as Performances: Domestic Violence Hearings in a Hawai'i Family Court. In Susan F. Hirsch and Mindie Lazarus-Black, eds., *Contested States: Law, Hegemony, and Resistance*. New York: Routledge.

Migliaro, Luis Razeto, and Pasquale Misuraca. 1982. 'The Theory of Modern Bureaucracy.' In Anne Showstack, ed., *Approaches to Gramsci: A New Science of Politics*. London: Writers and Readers Publishing Co-operative Society.

Mitchell, Arthur. 1974. *Labour in Irish Politics, 1890–1930*. Dublin: Irish University Press.

Mokyr, Joel. 1983. *Why Ireland Starved: A Quantitative and Analytical History of the Irish Economy, 1800–1850*. London: Allen and Unwin.

Murtagh, Ben. 1982. 'The Fortified Town Houses of the English Pale in the Later Middle Ages.' MA Thesis, Department of Archaeology, University College, Dublin.

Nevin, Donal, ed. 1994. *Trade Union Century*. Cork: Mercier.

Nun, Richard, and John Edward Walsh. 1844. *The Powers and Duties of Justices of the Peace in Ireland, and of Constables as Connected Therewith*. 2 vols. Dublin: Hodges and Smith.

O'Connor, Emmet. 1992. *A Labour History of Ireland, 1924–1960*. Dublin: Gill and Macmillan.

– 1994. War and Syndicalism 1914–1923. In Donal Nevin, ed., *Trade Union Century*. Cork: Mercier.

O'Malley, Ernie O. 1933. *On Another Man's Wound*. London: Rich and Cowan.

Oestreicher, Richard. 1988. 'Working-Class Political Behavior and Theories of American Politics.' *Journal of American History* 74 (4):1257–86.

Orpen, Goddard Henry. 1920. *Ireland under the Normans, 1216–1333* (vols. 3 and 4). Oxford, U.K.: Clarendon.

Otway-Ruthven, A.J. 1968. *A History of Medieval Ireland*. London: Ernest Benn.

Palmer, Stanley H. 1988. *Politics and Protest in England and Ireland, 1780–1850*. Cambridge, U.K.: Cambridge University Press.

Philips, Susan U. 1994. 'Local Legal Hegemony in the Tongan Magistrate's Court: How Sisters Fare Better Than Wives.' In Susan F. Hirsch and Mindie Lazarus-Black, eds., *Contested States: Law, Hegemony, and Resistance*. New York: Routledge.

Pilsworth, W.J. n.d. Unpublished notebooks. Private archives. Thomastown, County Kilkenny.

– 1948. The Merino Factory: Old Kilkenny Industry. *Old Kilkenny Review*: 26–31.

– 1953. *History of Thomastown and District*, 1st ed. Kilkenny: Kilkenny Archaeological Society.

Proudfoot, L.J. 1993. 'Regionalism and Localism: Religious Change and Social Protest, c.1700 to c.1900.' In B.J. Graham and L.J. Proudfoot, eds. *An Historical Geography of Ireland*. London: Academic Press.

Seligmann, Linda J. 1993. The Burden of Visions amid Reform: Peasant Relations to Law in the Peruvian Andes.' *American Ethnologist* 20 (1):25–51.

Sewell, William H., Jr. 1990. 'How Classes Are Made: Critical Reflections on E.P. Thompson's Theory of Working Class Formation.' In Harvey J. Kaye and Keith McClelland, eds., *E.P. Thompson: Critical Perspectives*. Philadelphia: Temple University Press.

Shore, Bradd. 1996. *Culture in Mind: Cognition, Culture and the Problem of Meaning*. New York: Oxford University Press.

Silverman, Marilyn. 1979. 'Dependency, Mediation and Class Formation in Rural Guyana.' *American Ethnologist* 6:3.

– 1989. 'A "Labouring Man's Daughter": Constructing "Respectability" in South Kilkenny.' In Chris Curtin and Thomas Wilson, eds., *Ireland from Below: Social Change and Local Communities*. Galway, Ireland: Galway University Press.

– 1990. 'The Non-Agricultural Working Class in 19th Century Thomastown.' In William Murphy (ed.), *In the Shadow of the Steeple*, vol. 2. Duchas, Ireland: Tullaherin Heritage Society.

– 1992a. 'From Kilkenny to the Sea: By River, Canal, Tram or Rail? The Politics of Transport in the Early Nineteenth Century.' *Old Kilkenny Review* 4 (4):988–1011.

– 1992b. 'From Fisher to Poacher: Public Right and Private Property in the Salmon Fisheries of the River Nore in the Nineteenth Century.' In Marilyn Silverman and P.H. Gulliver, eds., *Approaching the Past: Historical Anthropology through Irish Case Studies*. New York: Columbia University Press.

– 1995. 'The "Inhabitants" vs. The "Sovereign": A Historical Ethnography of the Making of the "Middle Class" in an Irish Corporate Borough, 1840–1.' In Pat Caplan, ed., *Understanding Disputes: The Politics of Argument*. Oxford, U.K.: Berg.

– 2000. 'Custom, Courts and Class Formation: Constructing the Hegemonic Process through the Petty Session of a Southeastern Irish Parish, 1828–1884.' *American Ethnologist* 27(2):400–30.

Silverman, Marilyn, and P.H. Gulliver. 1986. *In the Valley of the Nore: A Social History of Thomastown, County Kilkenny 1840–1983*. Dublin: Geography Publications.

– 1990. 'Social Life and Local Meaning: "Thomastown," County Kilkenny.' In William Nolan and Kevin Whelan, eds., *Kilkenny: History and Society: Inter-*

disciplinary Essays on the History of an Irish County. Dublin: Geography Publications.

- 1992a. 'Historical Anthropology and the Ethnographic Tradition: A Personal, Historical, and Intellectual Account.' In Marilyn Silverman and P.H. Gulliver, eds., *Approaching the Past: Historical Anthropology through Irish Case Studies.* New York: Columbia University Press.

- 1992b. Eds. *Approaching the Past: Historical Anthropology through Irish Case Studies.* New York: Columbia University Press.

- 1996. 'Inside Historical Anthropology: Scale Reduction and Context.' *FOCAAL: Journal for Anthropology* 26/27. Special Issue on *Historical Anthropology: The Unwaged Debate.*

- 1997. 'Historical Verities and Verifiable History: Locality-Based Ethnography and the Great Famine in Southeastern Ireland.' *Europaea* 3 (2):141–70.

Silverman, Sydel. 1965. 'Patronage and Community-Nation Relationships in Central Italy.' *Ethnology* 4 (April):172–189.

Smith, Gavin. 1991. 'The Production of Culture in Local Rebellion.' In Jay O'Brien and William Roseberry, eds., *Golden Ages, Dark Ages: Imagining the Past in Anthropology and History.* Berkeley: University of California Press.

Smyth, W.J. 1983. Landholding Changes, Kinship Networks and Class Transformation in Rural Ireland: A Case Study from County Tipperary.' *Irish Geography* 16.

Spencer, Jonathan. 1997. 'Post-colonialism and the Political Imagination.' *JRAI* (incorporating *MAN*) 3 (1):1–20.

Stedman Jones, Gareth. 1983. *Languages of Class: Studies in English Working Class History, 1832–1982.* Cambridge, U.K.: Cambridge University Press.

Tighe, William F. 1802. *Statistical Observations Relative to the County of Kilkenny Made in the Years 1800 & 1801.* Dublin: J. Archer.

Thompson, E.P. 1974. 'Patrician Society, Plebian Culture.' *Journal of Social History* (Summer):383–405.

- 1978. 'Eighteenth-Century English Society: Class Struggle Without Class?' *Social History* 3 (2):133–65.

Thompson, F.M.L. 1981. 'Social Control in Victorian Britain.' *Economic History Review,* 2nd Series, 34 (2):189–208.

TUSA (a.k.a. Patrick J. Doolan). n.d. Poems by TUSA. Thomastown: Muintir na Tire.

Vincent, Joan. 1984. 'Marriage, Religion and Class in South Fermanagh.' In O.M. Lynch, ed., *Culture and Community in Europe.* New Jersey: Humanities Press.

- 1990. *Anthropology and Politics: Visions, Traditions and Trends.* Tucson: University of Arizona Press.

– 1992. 'A Political Orchestration of the Irish Famine: County Fermanagh, May 1847.' In Marilyn Silverman and P.H. Gulliver, eds., *Approaching the Past: Historical Anthropology through Irish Case Studies*. New York: Columbia University Press.

– 1994. 'On Law and Hegemonic Moments: Looking behind the Law in Early Modern Uganda.' In Susan F. Hirsch and Mindie Lazarus-Black, eds., *Contested States: Law, Hegemony, and Resistance*. New York: Routledge.

Wolf, Eric R. 1982. *Europe and the People without History*. Berkeley: University of California Press.

– 1990. 'Distinguished Lecture: Facing Power – Old Insights, New Questions.' *American Anthropologist* 92 (3):586–96.

Woost, Michael D. 1993. 'Nationalizing the Local Past in Sri Lanka: Histories of Nation and Development in a Sinhalese Village.' *American Ethnologist* 20 (3): 502–21.

Yngvesson, Barbara. 1993. *Virtuous Citizens, Disruptive Subjects: Order and Complaint in a New England Court*. New York: Routledge.

– 1994. '"Kidstuff" and Complaint: Interpreting Resistance in a New England Court.' In Susan F. Hirsch and Mindie Lazarus-Black, eds., *Contested States: Law, Hegemony, and Resistance*. New York: Routledge.

Index

ANTHROPOLOGICAL HORIZONS

Editor: Michael Lambek, University of Toronto

This series, begun in 1991, focuses on theoretically ethnographic works addressing issues of mind and body, knowledge and power, equality and inequality, the
individual and the collective. Interdisciplinary in its perspective, the series
makes a unique contribution in several other academic disciplines: women's
studies, history, philosophy, psychology, political science, and sociology.

Published to date: